AF291777

REVIEWS OF THE SERIES'
FIRST TWO BOOKS

How Maritime Trade and the Indian Subcontinent Shaped the World
Ice Age to Mid-8th Century

Shortlisted for Mountbatten Maritime History Award 2022

'Remarkable and fascinating…History with a capital H…the author's capacity to make effective use of archaeological and scientific data, alongside the economic, cultural and linguistic is impressive… The emphasis on the importance of maritime trade as a fundamental driver of human development…is very well made…a remarkable achievement well worth investigating…this reviewer will be looking forward to the appearance of the next two volumes…definitely recommended.'

Professor Geoffrey Till, The Naval Review

'I am utterly astonished by it…clearly a most important work…the control of detail is remarkable…most enlightening.'

Dr Ronald Hyam

'This book deserves to be widely read…fascinating and convincing…written with skill and enthusiasm…makes rather complex topics both interesting and coherent…both remarkable and more importantly enjoyable.'

Emeritus Professor Malcolm Falkus

'Well written, informative and engaging. I regard it as essential reading on ancient Indian history.'

Professor DAP Sharma

An epic tome that sets out to put merchant history at the centre of world history…an interesting work, ambitious in scale but accessibly written and divided into manageable chunks…and will surely encourage readers to read…his upcoming books covering later periods…Nautilus Book of the Month for September 2022.'

Nautilus International

'Well written…very readable…the author has done a good job in tackling such a large subject, breaking it down into the relevant parts…vast amounts of information…the author is to be congratulated.'

ARRSE Review

'A broadly-based and exciting account…for general readers, specialists and practitioners…with an attractive writing style and full of fascinating sidelights illuminating the historical narrative [from]…an author with life-long experience in international shipping.'

SAFETY4SEA

'Well written and informative…While I can single out many other issues and topics the thing that impressed me the most was [the] attempt to put India on the map of world history.'

Alfons van der Kraan

The Millennium Maritime Trade Revolution 700-1700.
How Asia Lost Maritime Supremacy

Nominated for Maritime Foundation Award for Best Book of 2024

Ambitious and strikingly well informed…based on an impressive range of scholarship. It makes connections across fields of enquiry that are rarely, if ever, linked…it is also a timely text, coming as it does when Asia has recovered the dominion it once exercises over global maritime trade.'

Professor Andrew Lambert

'An original incursion into and explanation of a topic that warrants examination…broad and ambitious and…compares very well and strongly with other recent popularized publications in the field.'

Professor George Bryan Souza

'Why maritime history is everyone's history…Collins uses meticulous research and engaging storytelling to highlight the pivotal role of maritime history in shaping world events [and] employs a diverse collection of sources to provide a comprehensive understanding of this transformative period.'

Nautilus International

'Fascinating fact-lets jump out at you from every page…This is someone clearly familiar with today's trading system, who really, really knows his stuff…The author's sheer enthusiasm for this vast subject is truly inspiring-in the sense of making the reader want to know more. And that's not something reviewers often say about other peoples' books.'

Professor Geoffrey Till, The Naval Review

Refreshingly, this is a global history that does not centre around European successes and failures but provides a primary viewpoint from Asia looking towards Europe…the text provides an exceptionally rich array of case studies with many fascinating details of what was traded and how merchants and commodities operated across time…this is an engaging, well-written story of the supremacy of maritime trade in shaping world history.

Marion Uckelmann, New Book Chronicle.
Cambridge University Press 29/10/24

The Ascent of
Maritime Trade
1700-2025

The Ascent of
Maritime Trade
1700–2025

Enlightening the World

Nick Collins

Pen & Sword
MARITIME

First published in Great Britain in 2026 by
Pen & Sword Maritime
An imprint of Pen & Sword Books Limited
Yorkshire – Philadelphia

ISBN 978 1 03613 889 9

A CIP catalogue record for this book is
available from the British Library.

Typeset by Mac Style
Printed in the UK by CPI Group (UK) Ltd, Croydon, CR0 4YY.

The Publisher's authorised representative in the EU for product
safety is Authorised Rep Compliance Ltd., Ground Floor,
71 Lower Baggot Street, Dublin D02 P593, Ireland.
www.arccompliance.com

For a complete list of Pen & Sword titles please contact

PEN & SWORD BOOKS LIMITED
47 Church Street, Barnsley, South Yorkshire, S70 2AS, England
E-mail: enquiries@pen-and-sword.co.uk
Website: www.pen-and-sword.co.uk
or
PEN AND SWORD BOOKS
1950 Lawrence Road, Havertown, PA 19083, USA
E-mail: uspen-and-sword@casematepublishers.com
Website: www.penandswordbooks.com

Contents

Acknowledgements

Many specialist historians have enabled me to step back and tell a broader story, the valuable perspective Prof. Malcolm Falkus thought worthwhile on first hearing of my three-volume project. I thank my Bolton School mentors Richard Wilkinson and Alan Benson and Magdalene College Cambridge's Ralph Bennet and Ronald Hyam. Ronald was supportive of this series, one of his last acts of mentoring, urging me to pursue the line of argument in the last chapter, providing me with a comprehensive reading list up to the early 20th century to support it.

My outlook has been shaped by many in the shipping industry with whom I have worked as colleagues, clients and friends, who I thank collectively. MOL London's Richard Evans generously invited me to spend some days with his drybulk team in 2023 bringing me up to date with developments since my 2014 retirement and offered photo options for the book's jacket, which Lindsay Howard gave her time to get permission from various departments. Thanks to them and MOL. The IMO's Marine Environment Director Heike Deggim helpfully fact-checked Chapter 45 in 2024. When she retired in 2025 and the Net-Zero Agenda was postponed, Natasha Brown kept me updated of IMO events and developments. The maps are by Stafford Douglas. Thanks to my sons' encouragement. Any mistakes are mine.

Introduction

'The sea was the gateway to wealth.'

Fernand Braudel[1]

While this book may be read as a stand-alone volume, to give greater context it will be better appreciated after reading the two previous volumes, *How Maritime Trade and the Indian Subcontinent Shaped the World, Ice Age to Mid-8th Century* and *The Millennium Maritime Trade Revolution 700–1700, How Asia Lost Maritime Supremacy*. The latter ends as northern Europeans vigorously penetrated voluminous intra-Asian trades, still mainly Asian-controlled, dominated Asian, North American and Caribbean imports, stimulating manufacturing at home and agriculture in the Americas. This book continues the story.

The themes and philosophy outlined in the first book's Chapter 1 and briefly in the second's Introduction continue; maritime trade as a driver of world history, the cultural difference between maritime-influenced societies, cosmopolitan, inclusive, tolerant, innovative, wealth-creating and continental regions, conservative, autocratic, hierarchical and agricultural, with consequential tendencies for rulers to impose uniformity. Twentieth-century Germany, Japan, Russia and Turkey imposed ethnic and linguistic homogeneity just as continental countries earlier strove for religious uniformity. Maritime trade by contrast is cosmopolitan, promotes economic development, wealth-creation, toleration, creative, intellectual and practical progress.

Ancient king lists perpetuated a sense of continuity, legitimacy of rights to rule. European aristocracies emphasised their genealogy, many forged, to show ancestry from Charlemagne, even Trojans. In contrast, Thomas Paine's 1789 *Rights of Man* stated, 'It is the living, not the dead that are to be accommodated.'[2] Despite maritime trade's importance, most historical writing is political and land-based. Furthermore, historians are often reluctant to abandon old historical constructs, even when modern research contradicts it; that Mesopotamia is the cradle of civilisation, Aryans invaded India, a Mediterranean Bronze Age chronology necessitating insertion of a non-existent Dark Age, that Anglo-Saxons 'invaded' England, that Anglo-Saxon spawned English, and Latin, Romance languages.[3] In this period, another continental distortion deflects from maritime trade's importance; a French-driven Enlightenment. But enlightened inventiveness, intellectual and practical progress were always features of maritime societies, which France wasn't. Ancient examples include northwest India where the *Vedas* and their voluminous offspring were the greatest body of ancient knowledge-collection at the time of maximum maritime endeavour, continuing in the Mediterranean, especially Greece, continued by Rome until the mid-2nd century, when it declined. In Europe's 6th–7th-century Dark Age, maritime trade virtually ceased, revived by medieval north Italian ports, all oligarchies. Venice's was broadly-based, its Great Council often over 2,000. Democratic principals were observed, power entrusted through councils and committees. Their stringent electoral rules and changing memberships frustrated individual power grabs by collective responsibility.[4] Northwest European ports followed. Hansa protectionism against non-Hansa merchants and north Europe's denial of English finished and dyed cloth exports were eventually overcome. Late-15th century Mediterranean trade declined because religiously fanatical Ottomans and Hapsburgs damaged wealth-creation and livelihoods.

Trade necessitates tolerating different races, languages, culture, beliefs and outlook. A Madras lawyer in 1728 asked about admitting non-Christian testimony in court, explained 'the great extent of our commerce…[caused] the Courts of Justice to admit [them]…who in elder times would not be admitted,' trade specifically the reason for secularisation and toleration.[5] Maritime trade creates wealth. An 1804 agricultural survey of Hampshire noted Portsmouth the richest and healthiest because of the port and shipyard. Three-quarters of its and Portsea's population were employed in the docks. Sailors spent money. Chandlers, rope-makers, sailmakers, caulkers, traders, etc. provided employment.

North European merchants, freed from Catholic influence increasingly dominated maritime trade in the Mediterranean, Atlantic and grew in Asia. Despite Peter the Great's establishment of a Baltic presence, Russia's repressive serfdom was incompatible with maritime values. Repression remained and remains. Ottoman and Spanish indifference to the maritime world led to ossification. Only France, on Colbert's model, tried copying maritime societies' trade, but its hierarchical society and exclusion of non-Catholics made it unachievable. Eighteenth-century France imported and re-exported huge quantities of Caribbean sugar but did not change French merchants' or society's character.

In this period, rapidly accelerating problem-solving, inventive application of science, law and the growth of humanitarianism occurred in the fastest-growing maritime nation, Britain, parts of maritime North America, with outposts in Sweden, Denmark and Hamburg. Britain, unlike France, avoided revolution, caused by *ancien regime* intractability and flawed *philosophe* ideas, the reason for its failure. After 1945 maritime trade became more diversified, less nationalistic. Volumes accelerated, ships reached hitherto undreamed-of sizes, enabling specialisation, economies of scale and efficiencies. Japan, Korea, Taiwan, Singapore and China used shipbuilding, demolition, shipowning, trade and finance to kick-start their economies, with huge global impact. Britain's major 1700–1960s role faded. It shunned policies which had encouraged success, much like 18th-century Dutch, and thus declined. How and why will be examined. Inward-looking continentalism dominated Russia, China and EU.

Maritime trade is uniquely important. Technical and commercial challenges encourage inventiveness in shipbuilding, cartography, sail, ropemaking, means of propulsion and in the 18th century, watchmaking to accurately measure longitude at sea. Adaptive innovations and technical ability were needed in commerce, industry and transport. Merchants had to understand currencies, legal codes, different languages, cultures, prices, weights, measures, laws and customs. Only in shipping and maritime trade were there so many financial, commercial, technical, geographical, logistical, cultural and intellectual challenges to overcome in fiercely competitive environments. Imports needed processing, encouraging experimentation, inventiveness, adaptability, calculation of risk, costs and quality assessment, creating a virtuous circle of improvements and efficiency. This maritime commercial revolution was the necessary foundation of accelerating financial, scientific, intellectual, agricultural, industrial and communication improvements and increasing long-haul volumes. According to 1724's *The Plain Dealer* 'a complete trader…should be…proficient in languages, history, geography and mathematics.'

Free thinking and interaction with different cultures bred philosophical and scientific thinking as with ancient Greeks. Sixteenth-century Ragusa banned slavery and Venice refused to man its galleys with slaves. Late-16th and early-17th-century English governments and traders were uneasy about slave trading and American colonists' treatment of natives. They were unable to influence the latter, but growing sugar imports seemed to make slavery and slave trading a necessary evil. British public opposition erupted from the mid-18th century.

No continental country however, promoted abolition. A few French *philosophes*, impressed with freedoms in merchant-driven, maritime England, opposed it in theory, but condoned it as necessary. They wrote about reason and liberty but did not understand how liberty worked, ideas alien to France. By contrast, the concept of liberty was engrained in English political and economic thought. How it evolved from not being slaves of Spain, France or royal absolutism to freedom for slaves was complex, but the essential elements were freedom of thought and religious toleration, features of maritime societies. Those not displaying these traits withered, hence the demise of Venice and Lubeck, replaced by tolerant Livorno and Hamburg. Dutch and English dissenting sects, especially Quakers, some of whom emigrated to North America, were crucial vectors popularising humanitarianism. Blackstone's English law's codification was also essential, more influential in spreading real enlightenment into the 19th century. Apart from some in North American colonies, it was alone!

The author's aim is an accessible narrative. For readers unfamiliar with shipping terms, the Glossary is for clarification, probably best perused in advance.

Part One

Sugar, Slaves and Wars

Chapter 1

Setting the Scene in the Atlantic

'The whole creation is one vast Exchange.'
Edward Young (1683–1765)[1]

Portuguese, Dutch and English expanded worldwide in the 16th-17th centuries, specifically for trade. Portugal pioneered Asian trade but lost many bases to the Dutch after 1580. They retained Brazil, upon which Portugal's two million people economically depended as the world's leading sugar producer until late-17th-century Caribbean competition. It also exported hides, whale-oil, brazilwood, cotton and tobacco. Portuguese Angola was Brazil's main slave-source and it kept Mozambique. Portugal, seemingly near collapse in 1691, revived by increased European demand for sugar. By the early-1700s, it had 528 sugar estates, many large.[2] William Dampier, visiting Bahia (Salvador) in 1699 noted its 'great trade' with 32 large ships in port, two slave ships from Angola and much coastal shipping.[3] The 1690s discovery of gold and 1720s of diamonds revived its economy spectacularly. In 1703, Portugal got more gold than it ever had from Africa, or Spain from 16th-century America, enabling it to settle unfavourable European trade balances, enriching Crown and Church. But divine right monarchy and lack of an educated middle class or strong merchant ethos hindered economic development. First-half 18th-century Anglo-Portuguese trade was based on Brazil's demand for light woollens for gold, sent to England in weekly packets from Lisbon from 1706.[4] Preferential duties from 1690 gave Portugal's fortified wine, port, its 18-century fashionable status in England. The 1703 Anglo-Portuguese Methuen Treaty fixed Portuguese wine import duties 30% less than French, extended to the Dutch in 1705. Portugal's salt was still sold Europe-wide especially for Dutch herrings and it imported Baltic grain in Dutch ships.

By contrast, Spain hijacked Inca and Aztec people, agriculture, gold and silver, settling temperate inland highlands. After 17th-century silver production decline, 1690's levels again matched the 1580s and grew. Its priority was its safe carriage from Puerto Bello to Seville by monopoly groups with no interest in expanding trade, returning with mainly expensive French manufactured goods. Havana's and San Juan's fortifications were sited to ensure its safe passage, not develop commercial opportunities. Huge smuggling resulted. Official fleets shrank, costs mounted and less silver and taxes were remitted to Spain. Seville declined. By 1700 its American trade was mainly controlled by foreign Cadiz-based merchants.[5] There was almost no inter-colonial trade, banned to support Spanish exports. Dependence on the bullion fleet meant that when it was lost, as in 1715, it was disastrous, deepening depression.

Asian products transplanted to the Americas were sugar, indigo, ginger and coffee. Plantation-grown, they were shipped to Europe quicker. California and River Plate settlements produced hides for Europe's growing leather market. But there was no large Spanish seafaring population. No Spaniard could have adapted Lord Halifax's 1694 words; 'The first article of an Englishman's political creed must be that he believeth in the sea.' Colonists were banned from trading with foreigners, except the *asiento de negros*, shipping African slaves by Genoese, then Portuguese, Dutch and French companies. Reliance on foreigners demonstrated inability to mobilise skills, capital and enterprise.

Castile was moribund, economically retarded. Foreigners contrasted the 'vitality and populousness of…peripheral regions' with Castile's 'emptiness and misery.'[6] After losing the Spanish Netherlands and Italian lands in 1713, battling 1687–1714 Catalan revolts, it could have reformed, but Spain's Bourbons doubled down, imposing Castilian law and language throughout Spain, especially on wealthier maritime Catalonia. For 200 years commercial forces were neutered. J.H.Elliot describes a time of 'maximum political and intellectual stagnation especially in inward-looking Castile,' distrusting foreigners, despising trade, especially with heretics.

1700 is as good a watershed as any, but Europe's maritime trade's growth trajectory really starts on foundations laid by 16th-17th-century Dutch merchants who supplanted Spanish and Portuguese, achieving commercial hegemony by the 1650s. Thereafter, their relative not absolute decline was mainly due to damaging, expensive, defensive wars against France. Commercially still strong, they had insufficient Caribbean colonies. Nevertheless, a 1701 French guide referred to Amsterdam's 8,000 ships 'whose masts and rigging form…a forest so dense…the sun could hardly penetrate.' Whatever the number, it elicited many similar comments on exceptional volumes. Daniel Defoe described Amsterdam's people as 'middle persons in trade, the factors and brokers of Europe.'[7] Its monopoly West Indies Co. (WIC) was however, much less effective than England's many competing companies. Surinam and Curacao, with Willemstad's excellent port an important slave gateway to Spanish America, hosted displaced Dutch from Brazil, including Jews. By 1700, it traded cocoa, tobacco, indigo, sugar, coffee and hides, was a ship repair and financial centre, but small when England dominated North American and Caribbean trade, which in 1700 provided 21% of English imports, 33% by 1750.[8] In 1700, American trade and settlement trends were clear; Dutch influence was declining, Portugal only had Brazil, Spain was on the defensive, France's Canadian colony lacked people. England's colonies' lacked unity but their populations increased impressively and local representative institutions were strong.

Andrew Lambert stresses that dynamic economies need regular supplies of new merchants, which occurred in English ports after the 1651 Navigation Act and subsequent refinements, requiring English ships to carry its American and Caribbean imports and exports, triggering merchant shipping companies' formation. By 1680 London's Port Book recorded about 1,500, including Jews, officially readmitted by Oliver Cromwell. Shipping became England's fastest-growing industry. After the 1688 Glorious Revolution the royal prerogative was subordinated to Parliament where merchants' interests were championed. It was understood that maritime trade was England's future. By contrast Dutch merchants after the 1670s-1680s, switched investment to land, bonds and country houses.[9] Comparison with Venice's commercial families from the 1500s, eschewing maritime risk to become landlords and bondholders is irresistible.[10] Herring fishing was still strong in 1728 when an English resident estimated 800 herring busses employed; less than a century earlier, but each nearly twice as large, declining thereafter.[11] Cod and whale fishing declined due to competition. Portuguese and French salt imports and cask-making thus also declined. Leiden's cloth industry's 1671 production, 139,000 pieces, fell to 85,000 in 1700, 54,000 in 1750.[12] The Anglo-Dutch scientific revolution also stopped in Holland in the 1670s. Furthermore, Jan Pietersen Coen's 17th-century call for Dutch emigration to Java's fertile soil went unheeded, massively outweighed by English North American settlement, creating a growing market. England thus gradually overtook Dutch economic dominance by about 1720.

In absolutist, agrarian-dominated France, Colbert's commercial policies backed by a huge naval fleet in the 1660s-70s, tried copying and competing, but in Court-dominated monopoly companies, merchants were not represented. Its colonies were ruled by military governors, unlike merchant-driven English colonies' representative assemblies. Most settlers were from Gascony, Normandy, Provence and Dunkirk, maritime provinces of a continental-influenced country. Louis XIV's Catholic obsession, epitomised by his 1685 Revocation of the Edict of Nantes, triggered the exodus of 175–200,000 Huguenot artisans and entrepreneurs in wool, linen, silk, velvet, watch and clock makers, printers, papermakers, navigators and shipbuilders, over-contributors to France's economy, settling in the United Provinces, Switzerland, England and Ireland, invigorating their economies. French Baltic trade was conducted by Dutch merchants, which Louis kept attacking.

France and England accelerated in different directions. War after 1688 was the prelude to another Hundred Years War, fought worldwide, funded by over-taxed, subsistence peasants against a stronger Britain, due to trade-created wealth. Resource-rich France had four-times more people. Its ability to rebuild, to attack English trade and possibly invade to install an intolerant, Catholic, absolutist, Stuart king were religious, political and commercial threats.

As Louis sold offices and titles with tax-free salaries, to clear indebtedness, many French merchants abandoned trade for judicial and administrative sectors, buying offices to lose the stigma of being 'in trade'. As Defoe said, 'an estate's a pond, trade's a spring.'[13] The idea that the nobility's job was to fight and die for France, this their tax-free pay-off, was outdated with maritime trade's wealth-creation clearly demonstrated for over a century. Heavier tax on merchants, industry and agriculture discouraged investment in wealth-making sectors nurtured by Colbert. Because England's and Holland's wealth derived from maritime trade, France tried destroying it. Strategy shifted to privateers funded by investors throughout France. Dunkirk's and Ostend's claimed thousands of ships and cargoes, especially returning Mediterranean and Caribbean convoys.[14] Charles Davenant's 1696 *An Essay on East India Trade* asked what supported 'this expensive war so long,' the answer 'the great wealth which for 30 years has been flowing into us from Our Commerce Abroad;' cloth and coal exports,

Norwegian and Baltic timber imports, trans-Atlantic tobacco and sugar imports and re-exports, increasingly significant to England's economy. The ascent of maritime trade had begun.

Because the ton-mile ratio involved in long-haul volumes far exceeded European trade, more ships were needed to carry the same tonnage. As Josiah Child said, 'No trade deserves so much…as those that employ most shipping…they are…the most profitable…ships and seamen…[are] the strength and safety of England. As England's fastest-growing industry, perhaps 25% of the population depended on shipping, more than any other sector except cloth-making and building.[15] Its 115,000 tons in 1629 increased to 340,000 in 1686, but due to war losses 323,000 in 1702. Maritime trade value in 1700 was five-times higher than 1600,[16] 20% of it trans-Atlantic, from almost nothing in 1650.[17] Dependence on unfinished woollen cloth exports to Europe ended. Finished, bleached, dressed, dyed, expensive cloth where profit margins were greater was exported further and wider with diversification into cottons, silks, shoes, hats, glass and ironmongery for captive North American markets. Thus, cloths' value rose, but fell from 75% of all exports in 1660 to 50% in 1700. As volumes increased, economies of scale reduced costs.

With France hostile, Royal Naval protection was needed where merchant interests were threatened, its manpower, 22,000 in 1689 rose to 48,500 in 1695. The 1696 Plymouth naval dockyard commanding the Channel approaches reflected trans-Atlantic and Mediterranean trades' recent growth. Some specialist dockyard facilities like rope, sail and block and tackle-making were among the earliest factories, blocks perhaps the first mass-produced products using machine tools. The 1697 Treaty of Ryswick made Louis restore all territory taken, renounce Spanish Netherlands' claims, recognise William and his heirs, allow United Provinces' border fortresses and cancel Dutch import duties.

France could not match English borrowing or interest rates after the 1694 Bank of England's establishment. English debt was national, not royal and personal, a monarch's promise inadequate against a funded National Debt, loans guaranteed by Parliament and extraordinary expenditure spread over longer terms. Money voted for the navy was double France's. The 1696 Board of Trade and Plantations liaised between traders and Admiralty on convoy protection. The Royal Society promoted inventive culture. With rational Newtonian thought, ideas of improvement accelerated in a widening, trading world. England's financial, economic, intellectual and political infrastructure, necessary for a dynamic trading nation, was established just before 1700. Royal Navy ships defending Caribbean trade enabled increased sugar exports, slave imports and provisioning by New England, New York, Rhode Island, Pennsylvania and the Carolinas; fish, cattle, horses, pigs, grain and timber, ideally inter-dependent not only to British islands but French, Spanish and Dutch, contravening the Navigation Acts, but unenforceable.

London's 1660–1700 trade tripled. In the early-1720s it handled 80% of imports, 67% of exports and 87% of re-exports.[18] Increasing volumes encouraged lower insurance rates, faster loading and discharging in larger ships and faster financial and business information. Thousands of jobs depended on London's port, from dockers to insurance, banking and service industries. London's 2,000 coffee houses in 1700 were information exchanges, diffusing knowledge. In 1702, 140,000 tons of shipping was London-owned. No other port owned more than 20,000 tons. Trading companies consolidated. For example, in 1676, 573 firms handled 11,000 lbs of tobacco, by 1719, 117 handled 22,000.[19] London dominated 'sack trading', from *vino de sacca*, Iberian wine to England, stores and people to Newfoundland and fish back to the Mediterranean, for which local and Norwegian supplies were inadequate. Vibrant London merchants, continually re-invigorated by Dutch, Jews, Huguenots and Germans, accessing credit without government hindrance, dominated growing trans-Atlantic trade, although in the 1720s, Europe still provided 55% of Britain's imports, 77% of its exports and 72.6% of its re-exports. London manufactured ship's instruments, telescopes, clocks and navigation tools. By 1700 it was Europe's leading instrument maker, many exported. Other industries were created; clay pipes for imported tobacco, earthenware cups for imported tea and coffee, leading to specialised pottery manufacture. Thus, increasing maritime trade led directly to new industries, wealth-creation and employment. For all except the very poor, life improved.

There were vast differences in individual merchant fortunes; spectacular failures to impressive successes, some in the same lifetime. War made and broke fortunes. Detailed evidence is sparse for middling English merchants. Most progressed through enterprise and hard work. Gilbert Heathcote (1652–1733), apprenticed to an Eastland merchant in 1667, spent time in the Baltic, returned to the City, built a business network in the Baltic, Africa, Spain, Newfoundland, New York where he had a brother and Jamaica where he had three more, shipping slaves to Spanish colonies. In the 1690s he imported sugar, ginger and indigo from Jamaica, his commodity and shipowning business worth twice his original Baltic base. A Glorious Revolution supporter, he was one of many who loaned William money in 1689 for war with France and more thereafter, was a member of the Eastland Company, the Vintners Company, the Honourable Artillery Company, eventually becoming an MP. Active in the formation of the new East India Company (see Chapter 3), he gave evidence against the Royal Africa Company (RAC) when its monopoly was up for renewal and played a leading role in forming the Bank of England. He combined many ingredients of successful merchants; apprenticeship, education, a period overseas to accumulate start-up capital and an extensive kin network.[20]

Shipping was serviced competitively in English-built ships, huge capital investment drawn from London's commercial community with new docks, shipyards, wharves and warehouses. Caribbean sugar and American tobacco became so cheap, prices rock-bottom by about 1685, that demand soared. English 1650–1700 per capita sugar consumption quintupled. Imports of 23,000 tons in the 1690s encouraged sugar refining in London, Bristol, Glasgow and Liverpool, supporting re-exports, shipping and shipbuilding. Bristol had 25 refineries by 1750. Consumption continued increasing as sugar-infused cocoa, jam, chocolate, confectionary and rum punches became popular. Over 200,000 North American and 30,000 Caribbean settlers' considerable purchasing power bought British manufactured goods. In 1708 Bridgetown Barbados had 1,200 stone houses with glass windows on wide streets, rents equivalent to Cheapside's houses.[21]

In 1700 Chesapeake Bay sent 38,000 lbs of tobacco to England, 80% of Europe's tobacco, the rest from Brazil for Iberia. Over 200 snuff-types were mixed with sugar, orange blossom, jasmine and bergamot. British manufactured porcelain, gold and ivory snuff boxes became status symbols. In 1700 London was the main tobacco processor and sugar refiner. Britain's 1729–1770 tobacco imports tripled with 85% re-exported. For strategic reasons, early English settlers took hemp seed, a vital Baltic import to plant, becoming important in New England's, Virginia's and Maryland's economy, producing cordage, cloth, canvas, sacks and paper. England soon re-exported its surplus hemp, tar and turpentine imports.

Indian, American and Caribbean re-imports rose from almost nothing in 1640 to nearly £2 million in 1700, tobacco and sugar 40% of England's re-exports, prices competitive with Spanish and Portuguese.[22] Trans-Atlantic trade, of greatest commercial value to England/Britain, rose nine-fold from 1700 to 1774, but all non-European trade grew. By 1700, 30% of imports and 15% of exports by value were Indian and American,[23] Britain increasingly the world's trading hub. Indian textiles clothed Caribbean and American freemen and slaves. In 1700 England's colonies provided about 39% of its imports and 18% of its exports. By the 1730s that became 48% and 24% of an ever-growing volume. Although 70% of colonial goods entered through London, 55% went beyond, encouraging improved roads, canal and river navigation, bringing some of England's most fertile and productive regions within affordable reach of London and Bristol. By 1695, the Ouse was navigable to Bedford. All sucked wealth inland, exactly as maritime trade had stimulated medieval northern Italy, Flanders and Brabant.

In 1701 when England's deposed James II died in France, Louis recognised his son, further breaking the Ryswick treaty, having already cancelled Dutch import duty reductions. War resumed in 1702, the War of Spanish Succession, sparked by Louis' grandson's inheritance of Spain's throne which, with Naples and Sicily, threatened English Mediterranean trade. Furthermore, their American and Caribbean colonies would encircle English colonies from Quebec to South America. Defoe outlined the issues. 'What is England without trade? Without her colonial trade, her trade in Turkey and Spain? What will become of her when a French garrison is installed in Cuba, when a French fleet returns with Havana's silver? What would be the value of… Virginia were the French to trade from Quebec to Mexico?'[24] The 1700–01 French Council of Trade identified French weakness compared to Dutch and English, not in merchant capability, but overcomplex regulations, control and restraint.[25]

In 1702, France and Spain excluded Dutch and English merchants from their ports. The valuable *asiento de negros*, the slave supply contract to Spanish American colonies, earlier held by a Portuguese company with WIC links, was granted to France's Guinea Company. French troops marched into the Spanish Netherlands, forcing Dutch withdrawal from frontier fortresses, threatening Amsterdam with abolition of Scheldt restrictions, so Antwerp could compete. England and Holland could not let the Spanish Netherlands fall to France. It drew Austria's Emperor, whose son was a

Spanish claimant and Brandenburg-Prussia's Frederick into alliance. The underlying cause however was the same; Louis' drive for European hegemony and Anglo-Dutch resistance to Catholic absolute monarchy. William instructed John Churchill, Earl of Marlborough, while negotiating alliance to especially attend 'to the security and improvements of the trade of our kingdoms.'[26] England's merchants enthusiastically backed war, the strategy blockading Spain and France. In 1704, England's fleet seized Gibraltar, too small for overwintering, so in 1708 Minorca was taken. After the 1707 Toulon raid resulted in scuttling France's fleet, its strategy reverted to privateering.[27] Lisbon became England's Mediterranean fleet's winter base and Gibraltar's supply base. French privateers took nearly 700 Mediterranean ships during the war but Gibraltar and Lisbon impeded French ships to and from the Caribbean. Marlborough's victories from Blenheim to the Spanish Netherlands secured the Dutch frontier, preventing invasion.

Privateers attacked English and Dutch merchant ships in the Channel and Atlantic approaches, taking 4,500 prizes and 2,000 ransoms, escalating marine insurance and reducing trade volumes. The 1708 Cruisers and Convoys Act allocated 43 ships to home stations and relinquished Crown rights to captured ships and cargoes, distributed to capturing ships' crews from captain to ratings, incentivising naval officers, increasing social mobility. Losses were contained and trade volumes rose again. Dutch trade was hit harder as it depended on France, Spain and Spanish America. St. Malo gradually abandoned privateering for more profitable, safer trade with Spanish America's west coast. In 1705, three ships returning from Peru declared cargoes over half the value of all privateers between 1702 and 1713. In 1709, seven returned with Spanish silver.[28]

By 1708 French industry was decimated, its shipping reduced and cut-off from the Levant. Louis, dependent on unreformed, inefficient tax farmers' advances, increased excise duties and forced loans, further depressing trade. Currency manipulation meant capital fled. Borrowing at punitive interest rates ruined trade and industry, whereas England, Britain after 1707's Act of Union with Scotland, financed war by higher taxes on every class and voluntary loans, no sales of tax-exempt offices and no reneging on interest payments. The union, triggered by a doomed Scottish colony in Panama, was built on hopes of participating in English and American markets. Scotland, of no economic importance to England, benefited disproportionately. Taxes grew from 3–4% of national income in the 1680s to 9% in 1710.[29] Britain was the most heavily taxed European country, levied by professionals, not farmed-out, nor resented because war was fought for national interests, not dynastic glory. Its permanent debt, over £40 million by 1713, cost 50–60% of normal state revenues to service, but long-term borrowing was developed.[30] The war damaged English trade less than French, certainly after 1707, although the Bahamas in 1705, St. Kitts and Nevis in 1706 and 1712 suffered and Montserrat was laid waste, slaves and booty worth £80,000 taken.[31] Antigua's 1689–1713 sugar production doubled to 10,000 tons and survived attack. Port Royal in Acadia (Nova Scotia), France's privateering base to attack New England and Newfoundland, was taken in 1710.

Royal Naval protection kept trade flowing. By 1709 France's Flanders army was destroyed. France faced famine, banditry, civil and religious disorder, Louis's reign an abject failure except for small territorial border gains. The 1713 Treaty of Utrecht gave the Bourbons the Spanish throne. The Spanish Netherlands were ceded to Austria. The Scheldt remained closed. Britain gained France's part of St. Kitts, Newfoundland, Nova Scotia, the Hudson Bay area, Minorca and Spain's *asiento*. Portugal's alliance was reaffirmed. Spain ceded Gibraltar to Britain 'for ever', but intolerantly asked that Jews and Moors not live there, although Jews had already moved from Morocco. British warships used Minorca's Port Mahon as a revictualling, repair and refitting base. It introduced better quality livestock, drained marshes which became orchards and new dockyards were built. Protestant, Jewish, Genoese and Greek merchants settled hoping it would become a commercial hub like Livorno, Britain's Mediterranean base. After English 17th-century success, French merchants increased Levant trade with lighter, brighter cloth exports, better-suited to Turkish taste and climate. British merchants concentrated more on long-haul American, Asian and African trade. European anti-Semitism continued retarding economic development. Sicily for example, Castilian since 1492 when Jews were expelled, was already condemned to backwardness. Rescinded in early-17th-century Messina, they were discriminated against, mistreated and expelled again in 1740.

Having lost Port Royal, France built Louisburg on Cape Breton, retaining a right to cure Grand Banks' fish. Louis agreed to destroy Dunkirk's privateer base and returned Ypres, Menin and Tournai fortresses. The pretender was banished from France and Hanoverian succession recognised. Dutch national debt absorbed 70% of tax revenue. With security guarantees, its army and navy had to be shrunk, needing decades of peace to rebuild finances, but retained many merchant ships. Amsterdam was still Europe's main financial hub but declined. Its industries contracted as British trade grew. France was bankrupt, its revenue spent on interest payments, two years in arrears, large sections of industry ruined. Its population declined by over two million. Roads and waterways fell into disrepair. Britain's navy was stronger than France's, Spain's and Dutch combined, her trade increasing especially with and between her North American and Caribbean colonies.

Boston, Massachusetts, depended on whaling, cod and trade. In 1716, New England processed 6.5 million fish, by 1765, 19 million,[32] sent to Bilbao and the Caribbean for fruit, wine, molasses, spices, coffee, flour, beef, pork, salt and indigo. Its waterfront of rope-makers, joiners, riggers, molasses' refineries, rum distilleries, flour mills, tanners and taverns hosted innumerable ships. Cotton Mather in 1702 described it as 'the metropolis of the whole English America' ruled by the 'codfish aristocracy'. Imported English furniture, ironmongery, ceramics and tea bound it to Britain with streets named Orange, Marlborough and Hanover and 26 annual patriotic events.[33]

After 1688, England's trade revenues enabled her to break French and remaining Spanish power, despite their richer natural resources, more people and favourable geographical position on Atlantic and Mediterranean trade routes, because of detrimental hierarchical, authoritarian, absolutist insistence on religious uniformity. Britain's 1713 'great power' status was transformed from 1649, when maritime trade was deliberately promoted as the national goal, despite Charles II's intervening weakness when Dutch warships towed away England's capital ship from the Thames. Post-1713 policy changed with different administrations but was not diverted by absolutist whims.

The 1688 settlement created stability, consensus, political and commercial direction. Political disagreements, institutionalised by Parliamentary parties, ensured political stability. Growing British trade required an enlarged, efficient bureaucracy. Customs service employees between 1690 and 1716 increased 30%. The excise service almost doubled. Dockyard workers tripled.[34] With justification, this period has been called 'a commercial revolution.'[35] Joseph Addison in 1711 wrote 'Trade without enlarging British territories has given us a kind of additional empire.'

The other early-18th century war concerned Baltic ports, caused by changing trade patterns. With Dutch drainage engineers transforming English wetlands into grain-growing lands, English exports replaced some southern Baltic grain, while surging trans-Atlantic trade and naval growth meant stronger northern Baltic and Norwegian timber, tar, hemp and iron bar demand from Swedish Livonia. Riga overtook Danzig as its largest port. Sweden, at the height of its territorial power, controlled many Baltic exports. Narva's hemp and timber exports grew. Russian-controlled from 1558 to 1581, Czar Peter wanted it back! Sweden controlled Pomeranian ports. Brandenburg-Prussia and Hanover wanted them back! Denmark wanted Scania and Schleswig-Holstein back! Poland coveted Livonia. These trade issues caused the 1700–1721 Great Northern War. In 1703–1704 English tar prices rose from £16.15s to £36. Baltic dependency as merchant and naval fleets grew was a major British concern, encouraging American masts, hemp, pitch and tar imports. The Bounty Act subsidised New England producers, further increasing trans-Atlantic shipping, helping stabilise Swedish prices. Peter started building St. Petersburg, his 'window in the west' in 1703, the war far from over. Sweden's population was insufficient to win. The 1721 Treaty of Nystad gave southern Pomerania including Stettin and the Oder to Brandenburg-Prussia, Bremen and Verden to Hanover and Livonia to Russia, including Viborg, Novgorod, Reval, Narva and Riga. St. Petersburg, not Narva, was developed and made Russia's capital. Its navy, swelled by British purchases after 1713, dominated the Baltic.

Thus, Europe's 18th-century opened with two wars dominated by maritime trade issues. Britain controlled the Sound, Channel and Gibraltar choke points. Its home fleet depended on Baltic supplies, a British fleet sent nine-times between 1715 and 1727.[36] St. Petersburg became the centre of British Baltic trade, a city of canals and shipyards. Peter imposed protective 37.5% tariffs on imports competing with Russian goods. Non-local essentials were tariff-free. But maritime curiosity and an open economy were impossible in authoritarian Russia. People and property had no security. Peter would not share power with anyone, let alone merchants, so maritime trade was insufficient to generate commercial wealth.[37] After Peter's death, his navy disintegrated. National objectives returned to territorial expansion. The 1734 Anglo-Russian Treaty provided Britain with much timber, hemp, flax, pitch, tar and pig iron, mainly in British ships, in return for luxuries and colonial goods.[38]

One more war opened the 18th century; Continental Christian Europe's 1684–1718 Holy League against Turkey, starting the process whereby it lost chunks of territory, not maritime driven, although leading to 19th-century maritime trade issues. Smyrna was Turkey's main port, its 1739 cosmopolitan population an estimated 84,000 Turks, 8,000 Greeks, 6,000 Jews, 2,000 Armenians and several hundred western Europeans.

Maritime trade stimulated Britain's domestic economy. However, apart from usual maritime risks, the early decades presented extra difficulties; the Baltic's 1710–22 closure, Caribbean pirates until the Royal Navy eliminated them in the 1720s, French privateers and Barbary pirates. Capital was tied-up for months on long-haul trade, years for Asian trade. Merchants were therefore the largest occupational group among English bankrupts; 13% between 1700 and 1730. Gregory King thought there were 2,000 maritime merchant and trader families, many dissenters who could not hold office.[39] As Voltaire remarked of Quakers, 'they are reduced to the necessity of earning money through commerce'; interesting word choices, 'reduced', 'necessity', implying that while admiring English freedoms, he did not connect it with maritime trade, thinking it demeaning: typical French elite ideas.

With Voltaire, the narrative arrives at the artificial construct historians call the Enlightenment, (See Chapter 8) which most describe as French *philosophe* advice to absolute rulers of exploitative continental peasant-serf societies where enlightened ideas did not penetrate. Real enlightenment continued 17th-century Anglo-Dutch maritime-inspired improvements and inventions. Tutored by Locke, influential British philosopher Anthony Ashley Cooper, Earl of Shaftesbury (1671–1713), wrote in 1706's *Thoughts Concerning Education* of 'a mighty light which spreads itself over the world, especially in those two free nations on whom the affairs of Europe now turn.' The Dutch contribution faded after 1672's 'Disaster Year', French invasion and economic meltdown. After Anglo-Scottish union, Scotland's enlightenment developed with Edinburgh's medical school, Europe's leading scientific institution. Thomas Savary (1650–1715), whose forebearers were Devon merchants, in 1698 patented a steam engine, demonstrating it to the Royal Society in 1699. Thomas Newcomen (1664–1729) also from a Devon merchant family, together improved it, the design spreading throughout Britain and Europe. New iron casting techniques developed by the Coalbrookdale Company in the 1720s led to larger cylinders. Political, intellectual, technical and scientific freedom to think, still went hand-in-hand with maritime trade: maritime enlightenment.

Chapter 2

The Baltic's Interaction with the Atlantic Market

'Trade is the Wealth of the World…Trade nourishes Industry, Industry begets Trade; Trade dispenses the national wealth of the world.'

Daniel Defoe 1728[1]

After the 1721 Treaty of Nystadt ending the Great Northern War, Baltic trade benefitted British, Swedish, Danish and German shipping. Previous Dutch dominance suffered with declining Polish grain exports. In 1700 England took 44%, Scotland 5%, the Dutch under 25% of Baltic-Norwegian timber and Swedish iron exports, still exported by Stockholm's Dutch-origin De Geers, who initiated the industry in the 1620s. Ambrose Crowley in the late-1680s became England's largest metal producer, making nails, fittings, fixtures, anchors and edge tools. Before his 1713 death, his three large factories in northeast England, Greenwich depot and Midlands' warehouses supplied the Navy with anchors, nails, chains, etc. Crowley's largest market was the Caribbean and North America for tools, pots and nails, using Swedish *Oreground* bar iron, over 300 tons annually in the 1720s-1730s.[2] By the 1720s, British annual imports were 15,000 tons. Rising demand meant merchants also imported Russian iron from St. Petersburg.[3] The Caribbean and North America were pivotal for Crowley.

After its 1670 charter, the Carolinas were settled mainly from the Caribbean, Charles Town (Charleston) by Barbados planters. Native Americans sold deerskins to settlers for Europe's leather industry and raided other tribes for slaves, triggering Indian wars, which with European diseases, depleted coastal areas. Between 1699 and 1715 the Carolinas sent England about 53,000 deerskins worth £30,000 annually.[4] Unable to compete with Chesapeake tobacco or Caribbean sugar it produced logwood, brazilwood and cochineal. Rice, planted in South Carolina in the 1690s was its economic base by 1710, a European market developing during the Great Northern War when Baltic closure stopped Polish grain exports. Cultivation was labour intensive. Marshes were laboriously converted into rice fields, planted, harvested and processed, facilitated by slaves, first from the Caribbean and from 1714, direct from West Africa. In 1700, African slaves constituted 43% of its population, 70% by 1720. Rice exports were 1.5 million lbs in 1710, six million in 1720, nearly 20 million in 1730.[5]

This slave-based agricultural revolution used hoes, mattocks and axes made from *Oreground* bar iron. Crowley, pre-eminent in the trade, exported them to Charleston on his ships, the *Crowley* and *Ambrose*. An inventory after his 1728 death listed eight types of 'Barbados hoes', eight 'Carolina hoes', 'Carolina axes' and padlocks 'for negro necks.' Over 80 file-types and 154 nail-types were manufactured at his Tyneside factories.[6] Iron exports were the basis of Sweden's renewal after Great Northern War defeat. Producers visited British customers regularly, especially Crowley's factories. Baltic-Caribbean-Carolina interdependence hinged on British ironware manufacturing.

Parliament identified South Carolina as also having tar and pitch potential. Charleston's exports of rice, deerskins, pitch and tar reached 44,000 barrels in 1717,[7] many on Crowley's ships with back-haul hoes, axes, spades, machetes and mattocks. A typical Bristol-bound cargo in 1723 had 222 barrels of rice, 457 of pitch, 267 of tar and five chests of deerskins.[8] Indigo and logwood were often included. Baltic timber however remained two-thirds cheaper, so only large masts justified long-haul higher freight rates. In 1715 America satisfied half England's pitch and tar demands. France relied solely on Baltic imports.

Bristol's leading iron merchant, Quaker Graffin Prankard, friend of Abraham Darby, who pioneered coke instead of charcoal for smelting in 1709, although not widely used until mid-century, partnered his Coalbrookdale works. Specialising in cast iron pots for export, he also made brass plates, iron hoops, rods and nails. His main business, shipping ironmongery to America, expanded in the 1720s. He imported Swedish bar iron, timber and hemp through Stockholm's leading export agent, Francis Jennings who pioneered and dominated western Britain's iron markets. Prankard imported four tons of bar iron in 1721, 198 tons in 1723, 395 tons in 1726, 933 tons in 1728 and 2,000 tons in 1738, dominating Bristol's Baltic trade with 54% of Sweden's iron in 1730, as Bristol overtook London as Britain's main Baltic counterpart.[9] His 100-ton *Parham Pink* carried nails, pots, chains, hoes, steel and gunpowder to South Carolina, returning with rice, naval stores and logwood for Hamburg, a short ballast to Stockholm to load bar iron and timber for Bristol; efficient shipping, minimising ballasting.[10] Ironmongery was Britain's star 18th-century export; nails, firearms, buckets, coaches, clocks, saddles etc. Exports to Europe doubled but grew faster to America and Africa. In 1700 Europe was Britain's biggest market. By 1775 long-haul exports were three-times as important.

Britain also imported smaller quantities of iron from Bilbao and Rotterdam, but De Geer's Leufsta forges were especially valued for cutting-edged tools. In 1730, 94% of bar iron exports to Britain were organised by ten Stockholm merchants, six originally British.[11] Prankard tried dominating English imports, but competition was fierce. Stockholm agent Henry Norris acted for Abraham Spooner, Midland ironmonger, rival of John Kettle, Prankard's main customer,[12] whose two steel furnaces, like Crowleys', were established in the 1690s. In 1732 Prankard bought the Bristol-registered 226-ton *Baltick Merchant* to carry growing volumes. After Sheffield's Samuel Shore partnered him, they bought the whole 1734 production, 1,470 tons, 270 more than envisaged, so sales had to be carefully managed.[13] Bar iron varieties encouraged experimentation by saw-makers and clockmakers in London, Lancashire, Sheffield and Birmingham in forging, temperature regulation, crucible construction and coal quality to make steel varieties with consistent qualities needed for edged tools, clock springs or polished items, for example. Maritime trade's encouragement of innovation contrasts with

Spain and its colonies; a monopoly inadequately supplying them, iron demand left unfulfilled, private trade deterred and inter-colony trade banned.

Charleston, South Carolina's commercial hub, America's fifth-largest city, had 4,500 people, behind Boston's 13,000, Philadelphia's 11,500, New York and Newport, Rhode Island about 8,600.[14] In 1737 the *Carolina Merchant* discharged Charleston's rice in Bremen, ballasted to Stockholm, loaded 163 tons of bar iron and 2,280 timber deals for Prankard, one of about 350 iron-laden ships leaving Stockholm annually, 50 monthly from May to September.[15] Francis Jennings in 1737 shipped 12,993 tons; 1,100 to Bristol, 825 to Ireland, 404 to Liverpool, 419 to London and 100 to Scotland while Prankard sailed his two ships to St. Petersburg and chartered six for Stockholm for iron and deals.[16] Slave rebellion in Stono near Charleston in 1739 disrupted Atlantic trade, especially with the Carolinas, whose assembly suddenly realised the racial imbalance was potentially dangerous and that slaves born into slavery were more malleable. Its 1740 Negro Duty Bill taxed slave imports highly, which reduced from 22,215 in the 1730s to just 2,841 in the 1740s.[17] Anglo-Spanish war, also from 1739, hit Prankard hard. In 1740, the *Baltick Merchant* sailed from Charleston with her usual rice and logwood cargo but was captured by a Spanish privateer. Almost simultaneously, a Prankard-chartered ship was wrecked in the Baltic. Saved from bankruptcy by his wealthy son-in-law, he lost status. War made and lost fortunes.

Russian iron competed with Swedish from 1721, when Czar Peter allowed merchants to buy serfs, formerly an aristocratic privilege. Serf labour in 54 Ural foundries in 1745 made this lower-quality iron competitive for making nails, exported to America in their millions. Swedish iron was best for anchors. Dependence on Baltic iron encouraged American furnaces. There were 28 furnaces and 46 forges by 1750, worked by felons and indentured servants provided by Bristol's Stevenson, Randolph and Cheston. Pig iron was sent to Britain as ballast in tobacco ships.[18] In the late-1730s, 25–30% of Prankard's imports were Russian.[19] St. Petersburg's 1740 population of 75,000 surpassed Stockholm's and outperformed Riga and Reval. With Livonian access, St. Petersburg also exported grain, timber, canvas, flax, tar and hemp.

Previous Dutch control of Baltic trade declined to 42% of the total in the first half, 28% in the second half of the century, hit by declining Polish grain exports and increasing iron and naval stores to Britain. Hamburg and Copenhagen supplanted Amsterdam as entrepots for sugar, rice, coffee, tea and tobacco. Gradually Carolina's rice-growing concentrated on coastal lands using tidal flooding to nourish rice plants, lessening demand for hoes, mattocks etc. But British iron demand continued rising, shipped to London, Bristol, Plymouth, Hull and Newcastle, used for ironmongery expors increasing to North America and West Africa.

Chapter 3

Setting the Scene in Asia

'And seas but join the regions they divide.'
From Alexander Pope's *Windsor Forest* (1712)

India had always traded its precious stones, ivory, pearls, textiles, teak, spices, dyes and peacocks for gold. A Russian visitor in 1470 described a 20-year-old ruler leading a million men on a gold saddle with diamond- and sapphire-embroidered clothes, sapphire-inlaid gold armour, his brother and chief minister carried on gold beds.[1] Such wealth never enriched its people, except in its maritime parts. Muslim Mughal Emperor Akbar (r. 1556–1605) pursued toleration, although the Mughals' Eurasian origin made them uninterested in maritime trade's potential benefits. Francis Bernier, Louis XIV's agent, reported Indian peasants living in 'a debasing state of slavery;' considering French peasants' wretchedness, quite a statement. 'As the ground is seldom tilled, otherwise than by compulsion…[no one is] willing and able to repair the ditches and canals…the whole country is badly cultivated and a great part rendered unproductive for want of irrigation.' Under Mughals, an estimated 26 million depended on the military machine, 25% of the population, all revenue going to the Court.[2] Bernier doubted 'whether any other monarch possesses more…wealth…the enormous consumption of fine cloths of gold and brocades, silks, embroideries, pearls, musk, amber and sweet essences is greater than can be conceived,' but employed unproductively.[3] The 1660s-1670s Maratha revolt was led by Sivaji at whose coronation, in Hindu tradition, he was weighed in gold.[4] Rivalry and rebellion were endemic. Every succession after Akbar was contested, involving murder, blinding, alliances with rebels and general slaughter.

The early-17th-century English East India Company (EIC), which hardly registered on Mughal radar, boldly decided to market Indian cotton cloth in Europe. It gained traction in the second half, becoming its most valuable commodity, increasingly popular due to its washability and fast, vibrant colours, when printed known as *chintz*. Indigo, saltpetre and pepper were also important, paid for with American silver bullion from selling English goods in Spain. The EIC grew impressively after Cromwell's 1657 charter renewal. Imports increased 14.4% annually due to comparative stability in Emperor Aurangzeb's (r. 1658–1707) early years and Bengal's importance with Calcutta, largely EIC-built from the 1690s. Dutch East India Company (VOC) and Armenian merchants also relocated there as Calcutta became key to the Ganges, India's richest region.

With EIC trade value almost half of England's total, Whigs, hating monopolies, encouraged English interlopers. In 1693 the EIC offered Parliament £700,000 for continued exclusivity. Rival merchants bid two million and a new company was formed. The EIC became its largest shareholder. Lacking forts, factories, supplier networks, agents and financiers, a merger suggested in 1700 was consummated in 1702, the mechanisms fully agreed by 1708; Britain's biggest business used the world's largest merchant ships, imported about 750,000 pieces of Indian calicoes and muslins, Persian, Indian and Chinese raw silk, about 1.5 million bolts annually. In 1700 cloth constituted 83% of EIC import value,[5] 30% re-exported, mainly to the Americas and West Africa; high fashion and cheap, mass-consumption cloth, 68% of 18th-century exports to Africa,[6] traded for slaves. The united EIC increased trade, warehouses and ships, its 8% dividends twice the bond debt rate,[7] despite expensive ships' 12-month round-voyages. Its transactions and commercial activity were as important as the Bank of England.[8] Fifteen 300-tonners went to Asia in 1710, about twenty 490-tonners by 1740. Annual sales fluctuated between £1.25 and £2 million.[9] About 80% of outbound cargo was bullion, 20% woollen cloth and metals.

Aurangzeb, an aggressive Muslim bigot, tortured to death Sikh and Maratha leaders, crushed his son's 1680 rebellion, subjugated Bijapur in 1686, Golconda in 1687, but could not control Marathas in the northwest who sacked Surat, west coast India's greatest port, in 1664. Aurangzeb's last decades cost about 100,000 lives annually, wasting huge gold reserves, taxing peasants and neutering economic opportunities. His 500,000 camp followers stripped the Deccan of wealth and grain. Two million died in famine and plague following the 1702–13 Deccan War which broke Mughal power and unity. The Marathas became dominant in north and central India, the Mughals confined to Delhi. Mughal governors acted independently, calling themselves Nizams of Hyderabad, Sultans of Mysore, Nawabs of Oudh and Bengal. The new Emperor, like Aurangzeb, fought his brothers for the title, costing 10,000 lives in battle, imposing Islamic law, ordering temple destruction, reimposing tax on non-Muslims.

Traveller-writer John Henry Grose (1732–1774) explained Surat's late-16th-century rise as 'one of the greatest instances…of the power of trade to…[quickly encourage] wealth, arts and population.'[10] Sivaji's 1664 raid on it was soon forgotten, stability quickly restored, but as merchants became prey to robbers and Mughal officials, stability eroded. Large shipments, credit payments, advance orders and foreign agents were compromised. Thus, some Surat- and Cambay-based merchants left, for Gujarat's Mandvi, Oman's Muscat, East Africa's Zanzibar and British Bombay, despite its less attractive hinterland often partnering each other in an interconnected western Indian Ocean.[11] Surat was still a great port, home to over 100 ships, mainly 200–300-tonners. Indian shipowners dominated its 16-million-rupee trade, of which only 1.5 million was European.[12] Early-18th-century Mulla Abdul Ghafur had 17 ships. His will left property worth 8.5 million rupees, ships and land around Surat.[13] In 1725, Surat's leading merchant Nagarseth Kulsanchandi agreed with besieging Marathas not to plunder it. The Mughal navy raided it instead, capturing Red Sea-bound ships because the emperor had not paid them, stealing merchant ships they supposedly protected.[14] This instability allowed Bombay's rise.

In Bengal by contrast, Mughal governor Murshid Quli Khan ruled independently, built a new capital, Murshidabad and annexed Bihar and Orissa. Despite the emperor's

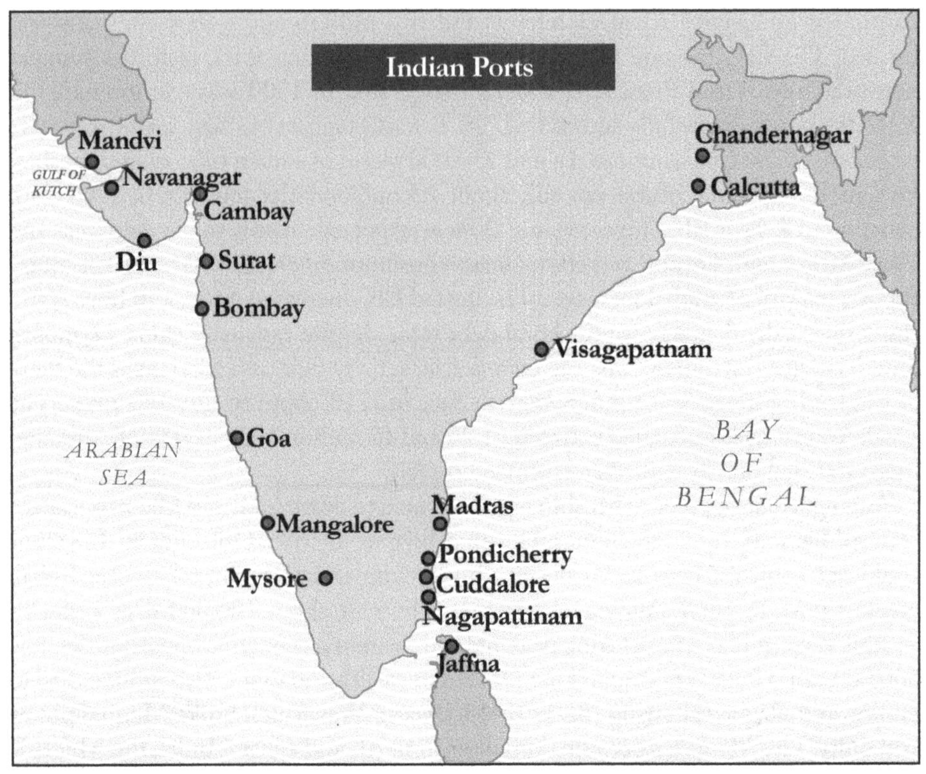

1717 free trade and coinage grant to the EIC, they had to deal with Murshid's banker, Fatehchand, known as *Jaged Sheth*, World Merchant. The EIC pragmatically worked with him, increasing their trade, whose value equalled all other foreign trading companies. By 1720 half EIC imports came from Bengal, a third from Madras, a tenth from Bombay, mainly cottons, silks, spices and indigo.

But they became a political issue. Unlike sugar and tobacco, which stimulated industry and employment, cotton imports competed with woollen cloth manufacturers. Despite reducing costs by cheaper Irish wool imports, depression and discontent led to late-1690s petitions to Parliament for relief. France banned calico imports in 1686, Spain and Prussia in 1713. The House of Commons twice voted to ban cotton cloth imports but the EIC's Josiah Child in the Lords killed them, until the 1699 Calico Act banned imported painted, printed or dyed calicoes. Silks and unpainted fabrics carried 15% duty, resulting in English cotton printers working on plain Indian cloth. Silk weavers repeatedly attacked printing works and shops selling calicoes until in 1721 Parliament also banned plain Indian cloth, protecting small industries near Bristol, Glasgow and Liverpool, only Indian thread imports allowed. Innovators tried improving spinning and weaving processes, brought to fruition by John Kay's 1733 flying shuttle, doubling production, increasing thread imports and cloth exports, especially to Europe, North American and West Africa. The Dutch never banned their import, actively re-selling them in Europe.

Despite cloth import restrictions, EIC 1717–1727 Bengal trade more than doubled, growing 70% in the 1730s.[15] 1724–1742 inter-regional private trade value also doubled, in mainly Indian, Armenian and Burmese ships,[16] more valuable than British-bound EIC cloth shipments. Growing Chinese tea and porcelain from Guangzhou (Canton) started contributing to British re-exports. By contrast, the VOC ossified. At its 17th-century height, it had sold Sumatran gold and tin, Chinese silk and Caribbean sugar in Nagasaki for copper, sold to India for Bengal cloth, sold to Southeast Asia where Sumatra's pepper and Timor's sandalwood was sold at Macao. Centred on Batavia (Jakarta), its commercial empire turned territorial from the 1670s. Realising the futility of attempting trade monopoly after their 1641 Malacca conquest, when many merchants left for competing ports, they continued it anyway. The VOC, unlike the EIC, forbade its employees to trade, who did so secretly in Asian merchants' names. VOC books were 'cooked' by entering goods at higher prices, stolen or damaged goods overvalued, materials and wages entered at higher rates than actually paid. Profits were remitted to Amsterdam banks on EIC bills of exchange.[17] Officials, loading and discharging supervisors and Governor-Generals bribed and were bribed. The VOC built, owned and operated their ships, but with fluctuating trade volumes, the EIC who chartered ships could adjust quicker.

Andrew Lambert thinks its post-1713 Asian empire 'existed on the sufferance of more powerful states…unable to compete at sea, no longer controlling a staple trade. Corruption, incompetence and the growing costs of running a distant territorial empire combined with a weak financial base, reliant on loans to cover operating costs meant…disaster was inevitable.'[18] The governing council, the Heren XVII, gentrified, excluding rich merchants from the Amsterdam Chamber after 1690, becoming a hereditary elite divorced from trade. Their debates focussed on territorial expansion as British merchants took Asian markets. In 1618, 10% of Amsterdam's elite had country houses, by 1748, 81%.[19] The EIC by contrast became more dynamic, concentrating on shipping Asian products to Britain, while its employees partnered local merchants in intra-Asian trades without EIC interference, spreading British commercial influence.

Territorial administration, defence and interventions in local wars increased VOC expenses, costs running three-times that of revenues. After 1688 it consistently lost money and borrowed to pay dividends. Its 2,500 employees in Asia in 1625 became 13,000 in 1799 and 20,000 by 1750.[20] Dutch residents were at each Asian Court. Java's largest polity, Mataram was plagued by succession wars. The VOC controlled nutmeg, mace and clove production and export, had a virtual pepper-buying monopoly in Cochin and a near-monopoly of Ceylon's cinnamon. Barely profitable, feuds with the King of Kandy interrupted cinnamon and areca nut collection as new vegetables varied Europe's diet, lessening spice imports. Spices and pepper, 75% of Dutch returns in 1620, were 23% in 1700. New fashions, cotton, coffee, sugar, cacao, tea and tobacco, required more bulk shipping, partly replacing them, which apart from coffee and cotton, the Dutch lacked. VOC Nagapattinam, Bengal and Bihar factories shipped cotton cloth to Batavia, but former Javanese merchants, prevented by the VOC from trading, became pirates. A consequently poorer Java demanded less Coromandel textiles and European goods. Indian cloth was the largest VOC export to the Netherlands after the 1680s, still 55% by 1700, but the EIC shipped much more. VOC rigidity and Batavia concentration made it miss Indian and Chinese opportunities. Profitability of their exclusive Japan market declined after 1680 when silver exports were banned. Except for Javanese coffee production, 2,000 lbs in 1715, six million by 1735, the VOC's 18th-century story was one of gradual decline.[21]

Opportunities to re-establish Chinese trade links after the Manchu conquered Taiwan were squandered, tea's importance underappreciated, while English and Dutch demand, like tobacco, sugar, cocoa and coffee, boomed. Chinese junks took tea to Batavia, mainly for the 10,000-strong Chinese community, some re-exported to Amsterdam. They did not send ships to China for it or grow it in Java, handing the EIC advantages. Amsterdam complained of Batavia's high prices and poor quality, urging them to go direct. Not being proactive was bad enough, but in 1718 Batavia's Governor-General arrogantly demanded lower prices. The Chinese refused to come until 1723. The EIC imported it from Canton directly, 43 ships from 1698 to 1715, compared to the French Compagnie des Indes' 23, but none for five years thereafter. EIC tea imports, about 100,000 lbs in 1700, accelerated after 1717,[22] rising to a million and after mid-century, rarely less than three million.[23] a trade revolution Batavia did not understand, as corruption and luxurious living replaced commercial instincts. The EIC paid increasingly in Indian cloth.

France's Compagnie, encouraged by Aurangzeb at Pondicherry outperformed the VOC, joining Indians, Armenians and Jews trading pearls, coral, ivory, gems, cloth, saltpetre, camphor and spices, bringing wine, clocks, hats and luxury goods, trading reasonably profitably. They needed Indian merchants with capital, credit, local knowledge and networks like Nainiyappa Pillai, a Hindu, Madras-based merchant, *dubash* or translator (1708–1716). However, Jesuits got Governor Herbert who appointed him, recalled. In 1711 the Royal Council resolved that the post of *mudaliar, chef de courtier* or chief merchant and *dubash* after Thanappa Mudaliar, the first (1674–1691), controlling all Compagnie business with Indians, should only be given to Indian Christians. New Governor Dulivier refused to dismiss him as it risked undermining Pondicherry's trade. Many merchants and artisans left in 1714 because of Jesuit intolerance and he had to ask Pillai to persuade them to return, but Jesuits eventually forced him out and many left.[24]

* * *

The Manchu regarded trade as a privilege bestowed on foreigners, imports as tribute to a superior country and culture. In 1710 they regulated it, permitting the EIC to enter Canton, through licensed associations of Chinese merchants, *hongs*, who fixed prices and collected duties. Two monopolies, *hongs* and EIC, worked together. Merchants lived in a separate Canton quarter, left for Macao in summer and were not permitted inside China to assess or access the domestic market. Much South American silver ended-up in China, payment for tea, porcelain and silk. Tea exports, just five chests in 1684, grew to 400,000 lbs by 1720 with porcelain vessels to drink from. By the 1720s,

10% of EIC imports were Chinese, paid for mainly with bullion, its import value, not volume, similar to the Americas.

China's coastal population expanded rapidly. In 1727 Fujian's Governor-General reported rice production insufficient to meet demand and recommended imports. 'The lifting of the ban on overseas trade would…greatly benefit the people of the coastal areas.' He succeeded, then due to 'inconsistencies' in adjacent Kiangsu and Chekiang, suggested their merchants 'should also be permitted,' and were. A 1749 wreck carried rice, silver, canvas, ox hides, tobacco, betel nuts, dried meat, sesame, sappanwood and coconut meat from the Philippines.[25] Manila's Hokkien Chinese merchants enabled vast amounts of silver, potatoes, maize, groundnuts and tobacco to be shipped to China, transforming Fujian and bolstering China's economy, but unacknowledged and unappreciated by its government. Macao also facilitated Portuguese Brazilian tobacco and Timor's sandalwood imports.

Fujian and adjacent provinces' traders had no official support, legal or political protection. They lived by their wits, trading in Japan, which with Korea had withdrawn from international trade, except with them and the VOC. From 1688, Chinese merchants were enclosed and guarded in Nagasaki's Chinatown, administered in 1708, by 96 Japanese and 250 foreign staff, including 167 interpreters for Chinese dialects, 101 for Quanzhou (Hokkien and Xiamen), while 134 plus 138 foreign staff administered Deshima's tiny Dutch enclave.[26]

*   *   *

With growing European penetration, Muslim trade networks lost market share to British and Dutch, increasingly British, as they pushed into production centres, eliminating middlemen. Late-17th century Ottoman, Safavid and Mughal empires and economies weakened and reached their geographical limits. Asia's powers continued looking inward. Ottomans ignored the Indian Ocean, concentrating on taking taxable land and people in Europe. Tartars raided Ukraine and Polish provinces, seizing cattle and people. Russia advanced south to the Dneiper, in stalemate with Ottomans. Safavid successors to Shah Abbas mismanaged revenues, failed to invest in roads and irrigation, falling in 1722 to Afghan invasion. As British Indian Ocean power expanded, Surat's Parsi merchants increasingly moved to Bombay.

Armenian merchant networks tied by religious, linguistic and kin bonds were embedded in large European, Middle East and Asian ports. Those at Isfahan sold an impressive range of English cloths, bought in east Mediterranean ports. They were in all major Indian textile weaving towns and ports, active in indigo production and were the only non-Catholic merchants with Philippines access.[27] The most well-known, because of his 1682–1693 journal, Havannes Joughayetsi, travelled to Banda Abbas, Surat, Agra, Tibet and Bengal, for a large merchant from New Julfa, Isfahan's Armenian suburb, where the Safavids had moved them in the late-16th century to increase Persia's silk exports. An Armenian merchant manual gave instructions for places visited. Joughayetsi depended on fellow Armenians for hospitality, contacts and translations. They were classic commercial intermediaries operating in the Muslim world despite being Christian. There were several large, kin-based merchant New Julfa-based companies sending hundreds of agents around the Indian Ocean.[28] By 1700 Armenians were important in Amsterdam and London, were major EIC freighters and traded as far as Sweden. An English tea buyer at Canton in 1724 found all Chinese traders had already pledged their credit to Armenians.[29] Overall, European involvement in expanding Asian trade became deeper and more interconnected.

Chapter 4

After Utrecht

In 1716, the Deputies of Trade blamed France's sorry state on the Revocation of the Edict of Nantes, exodus of artisans and navigators and the 1702–1713 Spanish Succession war, ended with the Treaty of Utrecht. But lessons were not learnt. Huguenot communities continued to be harassed. In 1724, Catholic baptism was made compulsory within 24 hours, Huguenot marriages declared illegal and Protestant preachers executed. Nobles could trade wholesale, but not retail, much scandal caused in 1721 when the Duc de La Force set-up a soap and perfumery business. Reprimanded by the Paris parlement, tradesmen associated with him were fined. France's misgovernment continued, a chaos of independent and semi-independent cities, internal customs barriers, different administrations and unreformed tax. The infamous *gabelle*, the salt tax, bore down heavily in some areas, light or exempt in others, smuggling between adjacent areas routine. Such was the *ancien regime*.

After Utrecht, peacetime governments tried reducing debt. Britain converted short-term debt into long-term securities, enabling Walpole to reduce land tax 75% and reduced or removed taxes on exports and imports not competing with domestic products. As tariffs reduced, volumes increased, revenue unharmed. France by contrast, did not reform, but did not follow Spain into decline and foreign dependence for shipping and trade due to three factors.

First, French and Spanish Bourbons cooperated. Spain and its colonies became France's main market for linens, lace, hats and luxuries, which revived, helping it regain Levant and Italian markets shipped through Marseilles, still closed to foreigners and non-Catholics. Secondly, Walpole (1721–42) and Fleury (1726–43) wanted peace and prosperity. France took advantage in the Indian Ocean too, developing Mauritius, renamed Isle de France after Dutch abandonment, with sugar plantations worked by slaves from Oman's East African ports, Reunion in 1721 and occupied the Seychelles and Rodriguez Island. Thirdly and most importantly, the economy's most dynamic sector, Caribbean sugar exports and slave imports, saw dramatic volume increases, especially St. Domingue. Ceded to France in 1697, St. Croix planters were transferred, quickly increasing production. In 1714, despite war, it produced almost 7,000 tons of sugar, 10,000 in 1720. Its 3,400 slaves in 1686 rose to 47,000 in 1720. It became France's most important colony, vital for sustaining an otherwise inefficient, unreformed regime, competing with smaller, over-cropped British islands. Thus, soon after Utrecht,[1] French sugar replaced British re-exports to Europe. Between 1715 and 1740 French trade grew six-fold, mainly due to larger plantations and cheaper production. British sugar imports grew slower; 25,000 tons in 1710 to 97,000 by 1775. By mid-century St. Domingue's population was 172,000, mainly slaves, by 1789 a huge 513,000.

Martinique's 45,000 and Guadeloupe's 22,000 population in 1720 rose to 102,000 and 117,000 in 1789.[2] Refining on Martinique and Guadeloupe moved to France in 1695, further assisting French industry. Caribbean sugar was probably responsible for postponing bankruptcy and revolution.

*   *   *

In India, in the 1720s the Ostend Company, mainly competing British traders, built a fortified factory at Bankibazar, 15 miles up-river from Calcutta. Never threatening, it lingered until 1744. The Swedish India Company, Madagascan ex-privateers, also tried from 1732. But it was France's Compagnie that closed the gap with the EIC in the 1730s. Reorganised in 1723, with vigorous state-backing, it built a fleet to develop Indian trade in enclaves close to British ports. In the 1720s its volume was about half the EIC's. Pondicherry and Chandernagore, founded by France in 1674 and 1688 increased trade ten-fold between 1728 and 1740.[3] The Compagnie was also a political instrument, assisting legacy Mughal polities against the EIC. Francois Dupleix, head of Chandernagore's factory (1731–1741), participated in 91 voyages: 16 to Surat, 14 to Basra, some to the Maldives, Mozambique, Malabar, Mocha, Jeddah, Bandar Abbas, Aceh, Pegu, Malacca, Manila and Canton.[4] In 1726 Nantes attempted to bribe the French Court to withdraw exclusivity from the Compagnie, in favour of free trade.[5] But it survived, as in Britain, despite the 1701 *Considerations upon the East India Trade*, suggesting free trade with government-owned factories financed by customs dues. Before 1740, pepper, spices, cotton and silk cloth were 75% of Asia's exports to Europe. Thereafter, tea and coffee became more important.

European companies could not trade, develop contacts or take loans without Indian entrepreneur involvement. Overcoming Jesuit-created problems, French merchants shipped cloth, opium, saltpetre and firearms to Manila, Aceh and Pegu, for pepper, teak, eaglewood, rubies and rice. Anand Ranga Pillai (1709–61) who inherited a Pondicherry business in 1726, was the governor's chief *dubash*, from 1747 to 1756, exporting cloth to Mocha, Mauritius, Ceylon and France. French officials trading privately needed his loans, credit and his storage for Ceylonese areca nuts imported in his ship.[6] Kedah sent tin to Porto Novo (Parangipattai) nearby, its hinterland's blue cloth exported. The Compagnie saw commercial toeholds as trojan horses for territorial influence. London-based EIC directors failed to appreciate this threat.

Coromandel and especially Bengal cloth exports through Madras and Calcutta boomed due to European, American and West African demand. EIC merchants also shipped them to Southeast Asia. Apart from Chinese tea, its porcelain, silks, lacquerware, Japanese copper, Indian saltpetre, Yemeni coffee, Bengal opium, Maldivian cowrie shells, pepper and spices were shipped to Europe and increasingly throughout Asia. Madras was also a diamond trading centre for Golconda's mines, diamonds outside EIC monopoly, freely imported into Britain for a 4% fee. London diamond merchants appointed Indian-based commissioners to procure them for 7% commission. Individual merchants sometimes joined 'joint stocks', which bought shares in ships. Sunku Rama, Madras' chief EIC merchant's private trades with Manila and Macao often involved

Armenian, Spanish and Portuguese intermediaries. From there, secondary investments and voyages were arranged to Trengganu, Siam, Aceh, Banjarmasin and Java.[7]

Madras' so-called Golden Age was mainly created by Governor Thomas 'Diamond' Pitt, Pitt the Elder's grandfather, who founded the family fortune. New Shah Alam asked for his help to capture a rival brother. In return, between 1713 and 1716, Pitt humbly asked for islands off India's west coast, a general grant of privileges, a Calcutta mint and easier customs officials. In 1715, nearing agreement, he gave 40 tons of valuable presents, a successful prescription for the ill young emperor and a veiled threat to leave Surat, which might have affected bullion supply on which Mughal fortunes had become dependent.[8] More bribery encouraged the 1716 imperial *farman*, confirming EIC commercial and territorial privileges, constitutionally elevating it to equality with Nawabs, the most extensive privileges granted a foreign power, giving it competitive advantage.

In Siam's Ayutthhaya, an important east-west meeting point, Indian, Siamese and Chinese ships traded. In 1718 Pitt established privileges there for Madras' ships. During the 1720s-1730s, six to twelve mainly Indian ships annually left Madras for Pegu for gold, timber and rice. By 1739 that increased to 21. Chinese ships regularly called at Aceh, making it another source for camphor, benzoin, wax, pepper, Chinese silk, porcelain and tea, exchanged for Coromandel cloth, rice, slaves and opium although 1717–1730s trade was interrupted by Aceh's seizure of gold from a Madras ship and a retaliatory seizure of the Sultan's ship at Madras. On Sumatra's west coast, the EIC had a small factory at Bencoolen. Its main traders were Malays, Javanese Bugis and Chinese, outnumbering Europeans 100:1.

Between 1715 and 1732 the EIC imported 1,499,145 lbs of pepper but the VOC still dominated with 5,996,573 in 1745.[9] Clove, nutmeg and mace imports declined. Coffee imports, gaining traction from the 1690s, were 21% of EIC import value. In 1721, 90% of Europe's coffee imports came from Mocha, 10% from Dutch plantations on Java. By 1726 this ratio reversed. Introduced to the Caribbean in the 1730s,[10] by the 1770s it produced 20-times as much as Asia. VOC tea imports in the 1720s averaged 234,776 lbs, the EIC's 793,491 lbs, growing to 913,700 in the 1740s and 1,688,200 in the 1750s.[11] Because woollen cloth was still the main British export, with linens becoming important, dye was increasingly imported, its value rising from £226,000 about 1700 to over £500,000 in 1773.[12]

A 1728 letter to Bombay's Governor Robert Cowan still thought Surat 'a very convenient port.' A 1729 Calcutta to Surat ship carried a typical cargo of cotton, cotton-silk, sugar, raw silk, sugar and untypically, iron from Orissa's furnaces. The same year, Cowan sent 500 bags of Bengal sugar to Cambay with instructions to sell quickly, as hearing reports of other ships *en route*, he thought prices would drop.[13] From 1720 to 1729 about 50 ships called at Surat, 33 of them Indian, but its 1734–1738 trade halved because success encouraged endemic Indian Ocean piracy. Fast Maratha ships from an island 16 miles from Bombay demanded tolls on passing Mughal and European ships, prompting the EIC to form the Bombay Marine and increase troops. Indiamen were well-armed and factories well-fortified. In 1713 the Marathas agreed not to attack British ships, the basis of a non-aggression pact, but continued raiding damaged Bombay's trade until the 1730s when Bombay Marine convoys countered the threat.

As Bombay grew at Surat's expense, EIC Indian agents persuaded weavers to produce Europe's latest fashions. Ghafur's grandson Muhammad Ali inherited his Surat-based trade empire. Due to Maratha insecurity, he built an adjacent fortified port, angering the Mughal commander who imprisoned him, where he died in 1733.[14] In 1736 the EIC established a Bombay shipyard, built by originally Surat-based Parsi master-builder Lovji Nusserwanjee Wadia. Teak ships lasted 40 years, had lower building and repair costs, which gave higher investment returns. The Wadias built dozens over the next century, including Indiamen and warships, considered one of the world's best shipyards. In 1744, Surat's Mughal governor required neutrality in Anglo-French war but on his 1747 death, his troops assaulted EIC factory members, further encouraging merchant relocation to Bombay. Meanwhile, the Mughal empire continued unravelling. Kabul was lost in 1739, Sind and Gujarat in 1750, Oudh and the Punjab in 1754. Growing militarisation encouraged Middle East horse imports by Gujarati merchants, while VOC Gujarati factories in Mandvi and Navanagar trading cotton textiles and pearls were expelled in 1758.

*   *   *

Surinam was Spanish America's Dutch entrepot. Most of its first-half 18th-century sugar and cacao plantations were Jewish-owned. In the 1730s its wealth surpassed Philadelphia, Boston and New York. Its annual 1700–1748 sugar production doubled to 20 million lbs. Amsterdam refineries increased from 20 to 95.[15] But Martinique's, Guadeloupe's and St. Domingue's production grew faster. British tobacco re-exports rose from 64% of imports in 1711 to 84% in 1754. Over half British mid-century maritime trade depended on Asia or America,[16] but from 1720 to the 1780s, French overseas trade increased five-fold, British trade 2.5-fold.

Portugal's main problem, like France and Spain, was its rigid military, ecclesiastical and noble hierarchy. Disdain for traders was deeply-rooted, despite its pioneering Asian role. Lisbon mercers addressed the Crown in 1689, 'Without trade, there is not a kingdom which is not poor,' but in Lisbon 'merchants are so little favoured and commerce despised to such a degree…men [are] discouraged from becoming traders [which is]…why so many foreigners swarm here…the bloodsuckers of all your Majesty's money.'[17] Regular complaints continued but the Crown continued selling monopolies in spices, tobacco, slaves, sugar, salt, whaling, dyes, logging, even river crossings, took 20% of gold's import value and sold offices. Religious orders held large landholdings, Jesuits 17 sugar plantations, seven ranches with over 100,000 cattle each and 186 buildings in Salvador. Discrimination led to further Jewish emigration to Amsterdam, Livorno and especially London. Lord Tyrawley in 1732 claimed 'the greatest dealers of Portugal in our woollen goods are the Jews of London,' refugees from Portugal's Inquisition, trading with Lisbon under assumed names.[18] In 1759 a French traveller thought Portugal 'an English colony' because an English company bought port wholesale from vineyard-owners, prices fixed by it.[19] Two or three ships annually still left Lisbon for Goa, Macao and Timor and until 1739, from Bassein to Diu, when conquered by Marathas. Portuguese was still the *lingua franca* of Asian maritime trade. Every factory had a Portuguese translator,[20] but Portugal's greatest asset was Brazil: gold, sugar, cotton, tobacco, hides, brazilwood, diamonds and Peruvian silver. A chronicler in 1724 described 100 ships annually, with 24,000 chests of sugar, 18,000 rolls of tobacco, many hides, timber and 'millions of…gold dust, ingots and specie.'[21] Declining gold production after 1760 meant exports slumped.

Eighteenth-century North American colonies thrived, everything England had hoped for as a new market. Less indentured and more skilled labour plus unemployed Scots and Irish migrated for higher wages, while Huguenots and Germans went to tolerant Pennsylvania. Annual port populations increased quickly. In 1742 Boston had 16,000, Philadelphia 13,000, New York 11,000, Charleston 7,000, playing catch-up with Mexico City's 112,000, Lima's 52,000 and Havana's 36,000,[22] none of which however were maritime orientated. Rhode Island built hundreds of ships. New England, especially Boston, sent about 300 annually to the Caribbean with cod, timber and flour[23] and to West Africa with rum made from Caribbean molasses, for slaves; 80 gallons per slave. French molasses was cheaper than British, shipped into quiet North American bays, avoiding naval patrols or bribing officials, evading Navigation Act provisions, for mutual prosperity. British islands also prospered due to Britain's increasing sugar demand in the 1730s-1740s. Responsible for nearly half Britain's mid-century sugar, Jamaica's 400 sugar mills in 1740 increased to over 1,000 in 1786, its average Caucasian far richer than England's or New England's.

Spanish America officially had to buy expensive Spanish and French imports. But French, Dutch and English traders illicitly sold necessities Spain could not provide, exchanged for silver. A self-defeating, failed 16–17th-century model continued into the 18th. At Utrecht, Britain acquired the *asiento* for 30 years to ship 4,800 slaves to Spanish colonies with a Buenos Aires base, not an important slave market, more an excuse for illicit trade with Chile and Peru. Britain also got the right to annually send a 500-tonner to Puerto Bello in Panama, with two auxiliary ships for factors' provisions, cover for multiple re-loads from Jamaica. But only eight voyages occurred from 1717 to 1733 in rancour and suspicion, both with financial claims, while British loggers in Belize and Honduras, supported from Jamaica, sold logwood used for dyes. In 1728 the Bilbao-based monopoly, Royal Guipuzcoa Co. was formed for Venezuelan trade through Caracas to benefit ports other than Seville and Cadiz, but Castile's Mexico-Peru monopoly remained.[24] Venezuelan cacao prices collapsed in the 1730s-40s, because it used monopoly to force export prices down and European prices up. Campillo in the 1740s noted that high duties 'shut the door of the Indies upon manufacturers of Spain and invited all other nations to supply those goods.'[25] Suspended in 1749, restored in 1751, then restrained, Spain still ignored monopolies' deficiencies. Its empire was maritime only because communication between it and colonies was by sea. France's Compagnie de la Mer du Sud traded with Chile and Peru, 62 ships visiting between 1713 and 1724.[26] Two Spanish officers, ordered in 1735 to gather information on Pacific coast colonies, reported in 1747 of administrative corruption, native mistreatment but many mining centres and high-grade ores.

* * *

Scores of London coffee houses catered for shipping and trading professionals and political, scientific, literary and artistic clientele in a spirit of free enquiry. The first monthly journal was founded in the Hague in 1686, the first English daily newspaper published in 1702, followed by over 50 others in the next 25 years, rapid diffusion following looser control after 1695, Locke arguing strongly for a free press. By contrast, there was no daily French paper before 1777. *The Spectator* from 1711 aimed at news, comment and discussion about national, international, scientific and philosophical subjects. Literacy was higher in towns and a French visitor noted how London's 'workmen habitually begin the day [in]…coffee rooms…to read the latest news.'[27] Foreigners were struck by the poor's ability to afford shoes and white bread. Early industrialists like Watt, Boulton, Wedgwood, Arkwright, Fielden, Peel, Wilkinson and others emerged from educated lower-middle classes, which with a growing labour force, capital and expanding markets were prerequisites for industrialisation, impossible elsewhere.

Montesquieu and Voltaire, in 1726–1729 exile, escaping French arbitrary imprisonment and torture, were among notable Frenchmen surprised at English freedoms. French royal and religious censorship neutered free expression or individual rights. But in England many religious sects flourished, while clerics and nobles paid taxes. Montesquieu thought it, 'the freest country in the world…because the sovereign… controlled and limited, is unable to inflict any imaginable harm on anyone.' Voltaire noted London's Stock Exchange on which Jews, Muslims and Christians dealt with each other, 'for the utility of mankind' describing England as 'the land of liberty' with 'a wise system of government in which the prince…has his hands tied for doing evil…[while] aristocrats are great without arrogance and…the people share in the government without confusion.'[28]

Dutch agricultural innovations were introduced to Britain, marling, liming, clover, rye grass and sainfoin; nitrogen-fixing fodder crops, enhancing soil fertility. Turnips, winter feed for cattle, were common when Thomas 'Turnip' Townsend (1674–1738) tried claiming credit. Improving agricultural changes were largely driven by incentivised tenant farmers, unlike Europe's peasant farmers. Selective breeding produced better sheep and cattle, most famously by Robert Bakewell (1725–95) to maximise wool and meat. Shrewd landlords and tenant farmers profited from efficient four-course crop rotations of wheat, turnips, barley and clover producing more grazing, fodder and manure, fast-evolving agricultural improvements, a product of the maritime-inspired concept of improvement, rational ideas, conquering nature, reflected in landscape gardening. Consequentially, 1700–1750 output grew faster than demand, prices fell and grain exports peaked in 1751.

In 1688 Gregory King estimated 2.8 million out of the 5.5 million population did not earn enough to sustain themselves, including many paupers and cottagers. By 1750 anecdotal evidence suggests the rising population and trickle-down effect of London's and other ports' huge growth had beneficial effects. Poor relief principles remained. Acts of 1597 and 1601 provided the old, handicapped and orphaned were entitled to relief, those who could work should and pauper children should be apprenticed in trades provided by propertied classes. No continental country had organised relief. Defoe's *A Tour Through the Whole Island of Great Britain* thought its wealth due to the cloth industry and London's influence, most counties contributing to its market, Britain 'the most flourishing and opulent country in the world.'[29]

Newton died in 1727 aged 84 after witnessing a social and political transformation, due to concentration on the national interest, maritime trade, making his work on gravity, the solar system, optics and calculus possible. Wood's 1718 *A Survey of Trade* noted 'our foreign trade is now…the strength and riches of our kingdom.'[30] Defoe wrote in 1726, 'Our merchants are princes, greater and richer and more powerful than some sovereign princes.' Freedom of speech, worship and press were celebrated. Social mobility was normal. The century after Francis Bacon's 1626 death demonstrated an intellectual revolution with practical experiments he had encouraged. It continued evolving and developing because maritime trade remained at the heart of Britain's cultural dynamic and vision.

Although shipping costs fell in preceding centuries with more accurate navigation, bigger ships and better rigging, one problem was inability to accurately calculate longitude. Following Sir Cloudesley Shovel's returning Mediterranean fleet's 1707 wreck in exceptional storms when 10,000 seamen and almost 100 merchantmen were lost, in 1714, Parliament offered £20,000 for discovering a reliable way of doing so. Without it, voyages were made longer, less efficient, less reliable, less profitable. Huygens's 1658 *Horologium* thought clocks could establish it. His *Kort Onderwys* explained directions for their use,[31] but rolling seas upset the pendulum swing and changing temperatures made its metal parts and lubricating oil expand and contract and was thus inaccurate. Huygens and Hooke, apparently independently, developed the spiral balance swing as an alternative in the 1670s, but discovering longitude became a synonym for attempting the impossible.[32] Parliament's Board of Longitude met in 1737 to inspect John Harrison's clock, now called H1 after a successful voyage to Lisbon. Hogarth, originally a watch engraver, described it as 'one of the most exquisite movements ever made.'[33] It and H2, presented in 1741, despite being praised, were not good enough for the perfectionist Harrison. Other scientists tackled the problem by closer observation of stars and in 1731 John Hadley in England and Thomas Godfrey in Philadelphia created a quadrant with paired mirrors, a big improvement on the astrolabe. It developed into the sextant, incorporating a telescope and a wider measuring arc, assisted by John Flamsteed's star catalogue. Halley predicted the return of the eponymous comet and Bradley calculated the speed of light, Jupiter's diameter and variations of the earth's axis's tilt. Tobias Mayer's lunar tables allowed calculation of longitude by lunar movements, sent to the Admiralty in 1757 and was used by mariners.

Harrison completed H3 in 1757 and H4 in 1759. His son took it on a sea trial to Jamaica in 1761, losing only five seconds in the 81-day outward trip via the Azores to Port Royal. Captain James Cook in 1770 praised the timekeeper method. After Harrisons' death, various horologists tried improvements including miniaturising, until John Arnold created the pocket chronometer in 1779, accurate to under three seconds a day, opening a factory for mass production. Thomas Earnshaw enabled price reductions to affordable levels. By the 1780s ships' logbooks showed daily references to longitude, its credibility growing over astronomical observations, dependent on good weather. By 1800 Portsmouth's naval yard had a chronometer stock. When *HMS Beagle* set-out in 1831 to fix foreign longitudes, it carried 22.[34] These progressive developments flowed directly from maritime trade.

* * *

Every study on merchant correspondence after the Geniza letters[35] stress their uniqueness and reflect different societies, trades and cultures. There are however, compelling themes and similarities. One was what Britons called private credit, merchant reputation, from Latin *credere*, to believe, meaning trust in performance of obligations. An English trader summed-up in 1717, 'To support and maintain a man's private credit 'tis absolutely necessary [to]…have a fixed opinion of the honesty and integrity as well as the ability of the person.'[36] Prominent 18th-century Surat banker, Atmaram Bhukan's credit was said to be so great that even if his *hundis* (credit notes) were tied to tree branches they would be accepted.[37] Credit was also established by religious donations, moral leadership and philanthropy, practiced by European and Indian merchants for centuries. In Britain educational improvement was championed by many merchants, encompassing inclusion, toleration and charity. Thomas Guy founded Guy's Hospital in 1721, for example.

Most merchants were multi-lingual. Numerous European specialised dictionaries were printed as commercial aids. Co-religionists and kin-groups reinforced trust, especially when geographically dispersed. Sephardic Jews were the most global, successful trading diaspora. Francesca Trivellato studied over 13,500 letters written between 1704 and 1746 by the Ergas-Silvera partnership in Livorno and Aleppo, most of their trade with Ottoman lands, especially its raw cotton, with fellow Sephardim in Amsterdam and London, Genoese and Florentines in Lisbon and a group of the Gauda Saraswata Brahmana caste in Goa.[38] Livorno's Jews were not directly involved with America but as Britain's main Mediterranean entrepot, they imported re-exports; tobacco, sugar, indigo, coffee and timber. British cloth and manufactured goods were re-exported to the Levant and North Africa. Mediterranean coral was sent to India for diamonds, increasingly an EIC trade with London, the world market for rough diamonds. In the 1730s Britain lifted restrictions on diamond trading and Brazilian diamonds were exported. Livorno's Jews continued this coral for Indian diamond exchange, relying on Portuguese Goa and Lisbon instead of Bombay.[39] In the 1740s they changed their Lisbon-Goa links to London-Madras, although coral supply gradually depleted. Livorno's success spurred Trieste in 1719 and Ancona in 1732 to become free ports. Jews and Greeks were the heart of Trieste's merchant class, 54 Greeks in 1752 rose to 752 in 1792 and 1,500 in 1821.[40] Increased trade even revived Venice's volumes, now confined only to the Adriatic; wine, olive oil, sulphur and currents.

Livorno was so successful that some Sephardic Jews returned from Amsterdam and North Africa to Livorno mid-century. In 1738, Livorno had 3,486 Jews, 5–8% of its population, the largest Jewish 18th-century Italian community. There was no ghetto, but a grand synagogue, equal rights with Tuscans and their own judicial system,[41] an Armenian church, three mosques and a Greek church from 1606 served 156 in 1810, toleration ensuring Livorno's success.[42] By contrast, in 1747, France targeting remaining Protestants, giving Catholic priests the power to place any 5–16-year-old Protestants in convents.

Chapter 5

War and Peace 1739–1775

'Our trade depends on proper exertion of our maritime strength…trade and maritime strength depend on each other.'

William Pitt

Without a customs service, Spain sold licences to *guarda-costas*, ill-regulated, peacetime privateer-smugglers. One off Cuba who sliced-off British Captain Jenkins' ear in a scuffle led to war in 1739. The Commons asserted 'the undoubted right of British subjects to sail their ships in any part of the seas of America.' Unease at Spain and France's seemingly better use of peace underlay the War of Jenkins' Ear. French industry supplied products to Spain and via Marseilles, the Levant. Increased French sugar production; 40% compared with Britain's 28% in the 1740s and its re-exports to Europe financed its military. Most European naval arms outside Europe were in the Caribbean because of its more valuable, voluminous trade. Moreover, French Indian trade overtook British sales in 1735, seven million livres in 1730, 17 million in 1733, nearly 20 million in the 1740s and over 25 million in 1756.[1]

Britain's American colonies' greater population was however, a powerful consumer market. Spanish America had most potential with its largely untapped demand for manufactured goods, insatiable slave appetite and apparently inexhaustible bullion supply. All trade was lubricated by Peruvian silver via Buenos Aires rather than Puerto Bello, produced at twice its 16th-century peak and Brazil's gold exports, peaking about 1741–60, an annual average of 14.6 tons, an 18th-century total of perhaps 800–850 tons.[2] Brazil-West Africa trade volumes in slaves for sugar and tobacco accelerated. Brazil-Lisbon trade averaged 609 ships in the early-1720s, rising to 945 between 1731 and 1735. Sugar's 100-fold rise from 1717–20 to 1766–70, reflected increased Cuban and St. Domingue production. Spanish American cacao exports similarly increased 17-fold, hides 18-fold and cochineal almost four-fold.[3] Before entering government in 1746, William Pitt studied French trade and industry statistics, increasingly convinced it posed the greatest danger and consequently that Britain must be supreme at sea.

After Austria's Emperor's death without heir, Louis XV attacked the Austrian Netherlands, France's centuries-old expansionist policy, again pitting her against Britain. The same allies joined the War of Austrian Succession (1740–48), subsuming the War of Jenkins' Ear, becoming four conflicts. The two most important were Britain against Spain for Spanish American trade access and Britain against France in North America, India and Europe: both commercially driven. In the Spanish Succession War, the French had agreed not to fight in India. This time they seized Madras, ordering its

Indian merchants to move to Pondicherry, while Calcutta expanded EIC trade fastest, then Madras and Bombay, as Surat's merchants continued relocating.

War in the Netherlands was again at French trade and industries' expense. Blockading French ports and controlling the Channel entrance, Britain crippled its sugar imports and re-exports. Two sets of sugar islands again tried destroying each other's production by burning cane, wrecking machinery and stealing slaves. France's Caribbean islands should have been isolated from British North American cargoes, but the Royal Navy could not stop American and Dutch merchant supplies. Nevertheless, in 1747 many Caribbean-bound ships from La Rochelle and 48 homeward-bound ships with coffee, sugar and indigo, valued at over £250,000 were captured. A 250-ship convoy from La Rochelle got through at the cost of six French escorts, but 40 were taken approaching the Caribbean and 100 French ships waited for escorts at Martinique for over a year, extremely damaging to French shipowners and traders. Effectively, French trade was brought to a standstill.[4] While resources drained away in Flanders, Germany and Italy, France laid-up her expensive fleet, re-adopting privateering. Captured French and Spanish merchantmen increased Britain's fleet by 20%. France's tax system was again unable to fund war, while Britain borrowed at 3%, half 1701's rate.[5]

The 1748 Peace of Aix-la-Chapelle made France restore all land conquests. Louisburg was returned to France and Madras to Britain. No islands changed hands. Dominica, St. Lucia, St. Vincent and Tobago were declared neutral. Freedom of navigation in Spanish America and expanding Honduras logwood camps were ignored and smuggling continued. Everyone expected another war. In 1749, Britain established Halifax, Nova Scotia, to counter Louisburg, although Canada's population was only about 55,000 in 1754.[6]

French trade quickly recovered, worth 221 million livres in 1735, over 500 million in 1752–54, a 'golden age' of French trade.[7] Bordeaux, France's main port for wine, brandy, sugar and coffee re-exports, attracted over 80 merchant companies from Amsterdam, Hamburg, Lubeck, Danzig and Stettin. Jean Christophe Harmesen for example, represented shippers and receivers in Danzig, Rotterdam, Sweden and Hamburg, importing French wine, sugar and indigo for Baltic timber.[8] About 150 Jewish merchants also established Bordeaux companies with subsidiaries in St. Domingue's Cap Francais and Port-au-Prince. One, Saloman Raba's from 1765, turned 80,000 livres capital into 4.3 million by 1785.

As North American settlers went inland, they found France's army along the St. Lawrence and Great Lakes attempting to link Quebec to Louisiana with forts in the Ohio Valley, claimed by Virginia. America's 1700–1750 population increased six or seven-times, a growing market for British manufactured goods and EIC exports, which increased 11-fold.[9] France aimed more at territorial control but lacked strong naval presence or maritime culture and attacking the Netherlands compromised trade, attracting multiple enemies; always self-defeating.

* * *

Madras-based merchants in the Bay of Bengal were influential. At Tenasserim, subject to Ayutthaya, Indian Muslims held prominent Court positions, managing shipping and trade. In the 1740s-1760s Indian merchants active in Kedah's administration, exported tin, elephants, ivory, betel nuts, gold, nutmeg, cloves, probably smuggled by Bugis merchants outside Dutch monopoly, for Indian cloth. British merchants also increasingly sailed from Madras to Kedah and Aceh, becoming close with their rulers, while Armenians were influential in Pegu.

By the 1740s Mughal emperors had little authority outside Delhi and Agra. Bombay's legal and naval security continued attracting Indian merchants. But EIC officials worried about French alliances with legacy-Mughal rulers including Hyderabad, part of Madras' hinterland, which directly threatened its trade. Conflict with them began in 1743. Hyderabad's Nizam granted the Compagnie and Dupleix territory, revenue and trade preference in return for French troops, so the EIC tried backing a pretender. London headquarters reprimanded them for acting 'as a military colony' rather than 'factors and agents of a body of merchants,' failing to appreciate French military intent. By contrast, France congratulated Dupleix on military success. A complacent 1754 EIC assessment of France's threat concluded 'the credit of the English as merchants is superior in India to…the French and they will always have the Preferences in all India Governments who are their own masters, so long as they preserve their mercantile reputation.'[10] India-based officials were less sanguine. EIC directors insisted troops only be used for defence, warning against Indian political involvement and territorial acquisition. But French factories at Hyderabad's Masulipatnam and villages around Pondicherry encircled Madras, cutting it off from inland weaving centres on which it depended.[11]

Robert Clive cut the noose around Madras and installed his Nawab, who had to pay the war's costs and British army maintenance. Madras added adjacent villages to its territory. Its income mainly from increasing customs dues was thus supplemented by land revenue. Dupleix by contrast sought to cover his administration's cost mainly by land revenue. While the EIC had to take territory to counter the French, it was more interested in cotton producing and finishing centres, differing outlooks: land revenue or trade! With armies and navies involved, as in the Americas, these were preconditions for a deadly Anglo-French struggle in India. Just as France in Europe was handicapped by an absolutist regime, a weak merchant class and an unreformed tax system, the French in India, J.H. Parry notes, were handicapped by concentrating on the wrong part. 'The Ganges and its confluents was worth conquering; the rest was not,' except the Malabar and Coromandel coast, stepping stones to Bengal and the Hugli.[12] Parisian Compagnie directors, alarmed at the wartime trade slump, removed Dupleix in 1754 and mistakenly appointed an inexperienced, arrogant general.

* * *

The Seven Years War (1756–63) resumed worldwide war for expanding trade. Austria, Russia and Sweden joined France, while Britain's trade wealth allowed subsidies to Hesse Cassel and Prussia, which received a four-year contribution equal to her entire revenue![13] France initially seized Minorca and stationed an army at Channel ports, threatening British control of two European choke points. Superior at sea, Britain had to employ more ships to protect commerce and prevent invasion. Martinique privateers initially caused havoc, but Prime Minister Pitt carried to office in 1757 due to merchant and popular pressure, impossible elsewhere, planned to attack it. The war also started badly for Britain in India. But Pitt's incisive global vision, 'the only man in the first rank of English politics who consistently thought in terms of strategic and economic value,'[14] used maritime power to reduce French and promote British trade in North America, the Caribbean and Indian Ocean and attacked France's coast to draw troops from Prussia and Hanover.

The strategy required adequate warships at sea for six months; efficient maintenance, repair, manning, victualling and healthy men. In 1762, 80% of its ships and men were at sea. France and Spain could not match it. With instructions to engage the enemy, crews were well-trained and battle-hardened. France had no private shipyard capable of building ships of the line. In 1750 it only had four drydocks, one abandoned, the others working poorly. Britain had 16 in 1700, 24 in 1800. The Navy Board responded to demand fluctuation by competitive procurement and new products like cheaper blocks designed by Southampton's Walter Taylor in 1759, not copied by France until 1795.[15] Their costly, inefficient, corrupt operations resulted in dirty ships and frequent on-board epidemics. British farmers supplied the Victualling Board by coasters, paid for by bills of exchange. Trade defence organisation was improved and the Admiralty, which had no French equivalent, coordinated with merchants about convoys. Sailing dates agreed with London merchants were communicated to provincial ports via newspapers, especially *Lloyds List*.[16]

Britain had more shipbuilding ports, trained shipwrights, a larger reserve of seamen, better access to Baltic timber and American masts. It started to show in 1758, even before Prussian subsidies took effect. In Canada, Louisburg surrendered, Fort Duquesne was taken, renamed Pittsburgh after Pitt. Quebec and Montreal's capture ensured its trade became British. By 1757 most French merchant ships in the Caribbean were captured or turned into privateers. Pitt ordered enemy islands captured, not just raided. West African slave port Goree's capture crippled France's slave trade. Guadeloupe was taken, supplementing British sugar and customs revenues. Dakar with gum and slave exports was captured in 1759. The only way France could win was by invasion, but its fleet was smashed at Quiberon Bay, while the coast was blockaded, paralysing its trade. Some off-shore French islands and most Indian trading stations were taken. Dominica was captured in 1761, Martinique, St Lucia and Grenada in 1762. The few French merchantmen still trading suffered rocketing rates on London's insurance market. Its trade crippled and naval budget slashed, France persuaded Spain to enter the war in 1762, due to grievances about Gibraltar and Honduran logwood camps. She had nothing to gain and much to lose. Britain took 12 ships of the line, a £2 million booty, Manila, a 2,000-ton galleon and Havana which, opened to British trade, flourished under British rule for a few months.

Britain's Newfoundland's cod fisheries and coastal coal trade were important nurseries of seamen. By contrast, France saw French Canada as territory to be harvested, especially for furs. Settlement was neither encouraged nor discouraged. Indecisive, Louis XV hampered himself by encouraging the nobility which Louis XIV had suppressed and appointing weak ministers, their turnover rapid on unpredictable whims. Seen as a weak bully and idler in France, Pitt by contrast saw commercial priorities with crystal clarity, that Guadeloupe produced more sugar than all British islands combined and was worth more than Canada, the British Caribbean more than North America. Indeed in 1773, British imports from Jamaica were five-times more valuable than North America. Nevis alone produced three-times more British imports than New York between 1714 and 1773 and Antigua three-times more than New England.[17] Sugar was 20% of all British imports, worth five-times its tobacco imports. Historians have discussed whether Pitt's motives were commercial or imperial, but from maritime trade's perspective, it is hair-splitting. In 1739 he had said 'when trade is at stake… you must defend it or perish.' Taking French territory created conditions favourable for trade and weakened France, Britain's political and commercial enemy.

*　*　*

Relations with Siraj ud Daulah, Bengal's 19-year-old Nawab, were difficult due to the EIC's right to trade free of tolls throughout Bengal, the details discussed for decades with his predecessor. The EIC ordered its employees not to trade in goods other than 'what are proper for Europe,' but they continued, disadvantaging native traders, reducing the Nawab's revenue. In 1756 with French backing, Siraj attacked and took Calcutta, about 100,000 people, famously locking its British residents in the Black Hole, then withdrew to Murshidabad to deal with Afghan invaders. Clive re-took it, restored EIC trading rights and prepared to expel the meddling French. Victory at Plassey in 1757 was decided by Mir Ja'far's defection, arranged by Clive, financed by Hindus, due to persecution and penal taxes.

French interference in Indian politics had forced Clive to act, leading to territorial control. Mir Ja'far became the new Nawab. The EIC got a saltpetre monopoly and reimbursement of war expenses, Clive £160,000 in presents and became Bengal's Governor in 1758. Within months of Plassey, the EIC confiscated cotton cloth made for the VOC and soon had the best weavers working for them, effectively ending competition in Bengal. Warren Hastings, who joined the EIC in 1750, British resident in Murshidabad from 1758, tried understanding India and Indians better. He investigated Bengal's abuses, fraud and illegal trading, threatening customs officials, thinking it shamed Britain's reputation.

In 1758 John Henry Grose, impressed with Surat, still an important port despite an exodus to Bombay, was nevertheless sceptical that merchant Abdulgafour 'drove a trade equal to the EIC' but admitted over 20 ships sailed annually, mainly 300–800-tonners, each trading £20–25,000 worth of cargo and was amazed how local merchants dealt with tens of thousands of pounds of cargo in half an hour.[18] In 1759 Bombay took control of it. After lifting the siege of Madras, the EIC took Masulipatnam in 1759. Pondicherry surrendered in 1761. British engineers destroyed its fortifications and France ceased being an Indian territorial power.

Mir Kasim became Nawab in 1760, rewarding EIC employees, but abolished all customs duties, negating EIC employees' advantages. Mir Ja'far was reinstated. Mir Kasim, the emperor and Oudh's Nawab invaded and were defeated at Buxar, the Ganges valley at EIC mercy. The Bengal Council chose the Nawab's ministers and regulated relations with the emperor. Some in London thought the EIC was taking unfair advantage, (see pages 40 and 87) but it had little alternative as weak, corrupt Indian polities disintegrated and France threatened. In India, these events however, were marginal as Sikhs, Afghans and Bhutanese invaded. The Marathas at their zenith were defeated by Afghans in 1761 at Panipat, who looted and enslaved women and children. A quarter of the Maratha army returned to the Deccan and defeated the Nizam in 1762, then descended into civil war. Poona-based Marathas, Haidar Ali of Mysore and the Nizam competed for EIC help against each other. Further pan-Indian political instability threatened.

When the British previously entered Delhi, they took presents to obtain trade privileges. This time they captured the emperor, who placed 'the empire', under British protection. The EIC received the *diwani*, Bengal and Bihar's land tax, thus the civil administration of 20 million people. Clive had bought EIC shares, which with news of his victories, doubled in value, the dividend increasing from 6% to 10%.[19] The *diwani* transformed the EIC. From 'quiet trade', early-17th-century EIC policy, they were masters of a rich province. After 1763, French and Dutch merchants traded freely but the EIC dominated in the richest part, its trade recovering quickly, although military expenses were high.

*   *   *

When in 1761 France and Spain allied, Pitt demanded war against Spain. Newly crowned George III refused. Pitt resigned. George's favourite Bute replaced him, stopped Prussian subsidies and moved for peace at almost any cost, yet within six months was at war with Spain. Pitt's priority was reducing French influence, Bute's was North America's safety. Board of Trade President Shelburne explained exports to it gave employment to millions of people in Britain and Ireland; thus 'of the utmost consequence to the wealth, safety and independence of these kingdoms.' A decisively won war, in which in its last four years trade increased 20%, including Guadeloupe's and Martinique's sugar revenues, led to the 1763 Peace of Paris, which returned Guadeloupe, the most productive sugar island, Martinique, most strategic, St. Lucia, necessary for Martinique's defence, which as Pitt complained was good reason to keep it, Goree's slave station, Spanish Havana and Manila. With American merchants, contrary to the Navigation Acts, buying French Caribbean sugar and selling provisions, keeping them would have brought the trade within them. Merchants, refiners and distillers were furious at the wasted commercial opportunities, which Bute's peace ignored. Pitt, backed by the City, denounced the islands' return because it gave France 'the means of recovering her prodigious losses and of becoming once more formidable to us at sea.'[20] Prophetic words! Pitt's brilliant achievements merited better returns. Appeasing aggressive European powers never worked for Britain.

Acquisition of French Canada meant America no longer needed protection. Whitehall knew it, so returning Guadeloupe and Martinique was doubly unwise. France was more concerned with getting back these productive islands than Canada, of little economic importance. Britain acquired Florida, the mid-west to the Mississippi, where France still had navigation rights and New Orleans. Spain agreed to tolerate Honduran logwood settlements. Britain also acquired St. Vincent, Dominica, Tobago and Grenada, enabling some sugar re-exports to northern Europe. British 1700–1748 sugar imports doubled, but quadrupled from 1748 to 1815, with a growing population and increasing consumption per head from four lbs in 1700 to ten in 1800, Europe's highest.[21] France re-built Caribbean trade, establishing French Guiana with displaced Nova Scotia's French settlers and started rebuilding Dunkirk, threatening southern England and the Austrian Netherlands and in 1769 gave Louisiana to Spain. Britain dominated Bengal and the Carnatic. Minorca was recovered and Senegal's factories, whose gum trade was important to English silk throwers, retained.

French Seven Years War trade which halved, recovered. St. Domingue boomed, producing two thirds of French sugar plus cotton and coffee, the latter 25% of French Caribbean export value in 1770 compared with 11% from British islands.[22] Following Livorno and Trieste's success, free ports in Dutch St. Eustatius, Danish St. Thomas and St. John and French Martinique, Guadeloupe and St. Domingue from 1763 were established. The 1776 British Free Port Act opened two in Dominica and four in Jamaica, hoping they would be more successful. They did not change basic realities. France's Caribbean islands were its economic crutch. Bute's concessions were wasted. American merchants continued trading with French islands, which could have been British. The Paris Treaty was not the landmark in the ascent of maritime trade it could have been. Most British assumed that France would resume hostilities and Britain's colonies would remain loyal. But prioritising North American security put those colonies on a collision course with Britain because of continued Navigation Act violations.

Despite Bute's mistake, British 1763–1775 politicians' limitations and EIC directors' caution, Britain's trade was huge. By 1765 it had large territories in Bengal, Bihar and around Madras. The Nawab of Arcot and the Wazir of Oudh were helpless clients. In effect, the EIC controlled the Carnatic and Bengal because EIC Indian officials reacted faster to developments and exploited opportunities. Even so, French sales climbed from 12.5 million livres to nearly 24 million after the war, including British tea imports: smuggled, due to high British duties.[23]

When Clive returned as President in Calcutta in 1765, he planned to take Bengal for the EIC. 'That critical juncture which I have long foreseen,' he wrote, arrived. 'The whole Mughal Empire is in our hands…we must indeed become the Nabobs [Nawabs]…in fact, if not in name.'[24] Ordered to reform the system by limiting presents and checking private trade abuses, Clive excluded EIC employees from inland trade, dividends recompensing them, and converted a Mir Ja'far gift into a fund for wounded veterans, but native traders were still disadvantaged. Clive wanted a permanent Bengal army. EIC directors reminded him, 'your employers are merchants and trade their principal object.' Clive instead wrote to Pitt explaining Britain's glorious future, replacing the Nawab and controlling Bengal's revenue which he thought over

£2 million, but identified the potential problem. 'So large a sovereignty may possibly be…too extensive for a mercantile company…without the nation's assistance to maintain so wide a dominion.' But it took time to realise how to do it. At this stage the government received £400 annually. EIC dividends rose to 12.5%. Clive returned in 1767 very rich, predicting his reforms would benefit Bengal's people.

EIC trade, increasingly important, was still a smaller import source than the Caribbean and lagged far behind North America as an export market. The *diwani* financed pre-ordered, low-priced Bengal cloth purchases. Cloth was also sent to China for tea shipments, which increased from 200,000 lbs in 1720, to 1,000,000 in 1730, 3,000,000 in 1760, 9,000,000 in 1770.[25] In the 1770s, the EIC also established direct relations with Coromandel's textile weavers. Local brokers, financiers and merchants lost autonomy and European competition was effectively eliminated. In 1773 it established a Bengal opium monopoly, auctioned to private merchants in Calcutta for sale in Southeast Asia and Canton.

Thereafter, substantial growth in Indian cloth, cotton and opium exports to Southeast Asia and China and tea exports swung EIC orientation to an India-China axis. Madras trade temporarily stagnated due to 1770s inland wars and associated agricultural crisis. Canton imports/exports were silver and cotton for tea, gold, tutenag (nickel-silver), mercury, alum and sugar. Growth is reflected in Malacca's records, which for 1700–1750 show an annual maximum of ten British private ships heading east, 24 in 1764, 50 in 1774. More went through the Sunda Straits. In 1772 Aceh imported 150 opium chests, Kedah 250.[26] In the 1770s-1790s British ships at Canton increased six-fold. The EIC continued sending yarn, cloth for export silk and saltpetre to Britain but private intra-regional trade with British, collaborating and competing Indians, Arabs, Malays, Bugis, Dutch and Portuguese far surpassed EIC trade from the 1770s. In 1760 the only large Bombay ships were EIC-owned, but in 1787 an observer noted 40 privately-owned Bombay ships with 60,000 cotton bales, half the total British exports to China.

Masulipatnam's merchants dispersed to Bengal or south to San Thome, Cuddelore and Porto Novo for Southeast Asian trade. They were called Kling, Kelang, Marakkayanis and Chulias (from Chola), their main trade with Perak, Malacca, Johor, Kedah and Aceh, the latter two Chulia strongholds where Indian cloth was exchanged for rattan, elephants, ivory, wax, fish, trepang etc. Mid-century Kedah was described as 'crowded with Indian, Arab, Portuguese, Dutch and English vessels.' In 1771 its Sultan agreed protection for the British and in 1783 a Chulia was the Sultan's merchant and minister.[27]

*   *   *

In 1769 Warren Hastings was appointed second in Council and in 1771 Governor of Bengal, his priority, restore prosperity and boost revenue. He declared 'dominion of all India is what I never wish to see,' because it would involve war and costly administration. Taking the Nawab's authority with the *diwani*, he reformed the courts, codified Hindu and Muslim law, moved the Treasury from Murshidabad to Calcutta and abolished all customs for a 2.5% duty, ending EIC employees' privileged positions, raising salaries to compensate. Salt, like opium, became an EIC monopoly and revenue collection was competitively tendered, curtailing the worst extortions, but did not assist local traders.

Hastings had three major disadvantages. First, Britain had not solved how merchants would run a large territory with responsibility to both directors and government. Second, despite being Governor-General, he was one of a five-man council, constitutionally unclear with ill-defined supervisory powers over EIC territories with high administrative and military expenses. Third, failure of the 1769 monsoon led to a 1770 famine, killing a third to half of Lower Bengal's population, perhaps ten million, heralding a 40-year economic decline, cutting revenue, reversing trade expansion, the *diwani* never approaching his £2 million estimate. Increased EIC dividends exacerbated the problem. Furthermore, high British tea import duties encouraged huge smuggling. In 1772 dividends were suspended and the EIC applied for a loan. The government loaned £1.5 million on condition it paid it £400,000 a year.

Distrust of monopoly as inefficient, resurfaced. When the two EIC's had merged in 1708, directors were prohibited from owning shares in its ships. Chartering was by open tender. Because of their specialist nature however, cartels were easily formed. By the 1720s the custom evolved for a ship's lifetime employment, replaced with a newbuilding on the same terms, resulting in artificially high costs, exacerbated by deliberate understating tonnage, causing a shipping glut and naval timber shortage, typical monopoly inefficiencies. A 1771 Act corrected the tonnage problem. Lurching toward more Parliamentary inspection of EIC affairs, the 1773 Regulating Act gave government access to all correspondence dealing with revenue, political and military subjects. It established a Supreme Court in Calcutta over EIC employees and allowed it to claim back duty on tea re-exported to North America. Due to high duties, over half the tea drunk in England was smuggled into England and America as large stocks of duty-paid tea accumulated in EIC warehouses. The government did not control the EIC. The Governor-General did not control his Council, Madras or Bombay. EIC directors had already disapproved of the Nawab's generous presents. EIC employees with no duties payable on inland trade, drove most local traders out of business, returning to Britain with large fortunes, attracting mounting criticism, especially Clive, who bought a country estate, Parliamentary membership and political influence. The self-perpetuating oligarchies of EIC chartered shipowners was abolished in 1796.

British public perspective changed, influenced by toleration, moderation, scientific progress and concern that political dominance should be balanced by responsibility to locals. Many thought the 1770s-1780s EIC engaged in extortion and oppression. Hastings partly restored Bengal's finances and reformed revenue administration but found his integrity impugned. Under intense criticism, Clive committed suicide in 1774. Edmund Burke believed in trusteeship and feared EIC misrule would damage India's society and economy. With Asia's riches and luxury, Pitt feared 'Asiatic principles of government.'[28] Despite disowning military conquest, it looked the only way to pacify aggressive Marathas, Mysore and Hyderabad. Mysore's French-officered army over-ran the Carnatic, entered Madras's suburbs as Arcot fell, while Hastings' skilful diplomacy split the Maratha Confederacy. Bombay invaded Mysore which abandoned the Carnatic to counter it.

* * *

British shipping displaced Dutch in whaling with larger ships, longer voyages and mechanical harpoons, not used by the Dutch, who also failed to participate in seal-hunting. They became conservative, unenterprising, lacking capital. Much VOC trade was unprofitable, it did not participate in Chinese trade, borrowed to pay dividends and the EIC broke its spice monopoly, stealing nutmeg and clove seedlings, propagating them in Mauritius and Reunion. In 1750 the VOC shipped half its 1650s volumes, but by 1757 controlled most of Java, administered by 'regents', descendants of sub-rulers and controlled coffee production and export. In Sri Lanka too they became landed rulers. The puppet Sultan of Johor sought Dutch help in 1755 to free himself from the Bugis who were defeated, but a *coup d'état* in 1760 restored their position and in 1782 Bugis raided Dutch islands in the Malacca Straits and had a thriving entrepot at Tanjong Pinang on Bintan Island until driven out in 1787.

*   *   *

The Middle East also descended into war. Persia's usurper Nadir Shah's violent reign from 1736 hindered trade. Silk exports, the original reason for EIC and VOC presence, greatly diminished. His 1747 assassination plunged Persia into turmoil. Internal and foreign trade collapsed. EIC withdrawal from Bandar Abbas was continually considered; to Bahrain in 1751, Qishm or Henjam in 1752, Hormuz in 1760 and Bushire in 1762 when the EIC agent thought it 'a nest of freebooters', withdrawing in 1769.[29] A 1753 dispute forced the VOC to quit Basra for Khark Island, but were forced out in 1766, due to violent tribal rivalry.[30] Persian merchants moved to Bushire, but by the mid-1760s, nine bandit gangs exacted dues between Bushire and Shiraz. In Oman, Sohar's leader forced the Persians out in 1744, starting Oman's successful Al-Busaid dynasty. Muscat's merchants, mostly Kachchhi, (from Kutch-see pages 93, 127, 141, 168, 194) sold silks, linens, spices, incense, coffee and foodstuffs. Sohar and Muscat were the main links to Indian ports exporting gums, drugs, hides, sheep and lamb skins, honey, wax and cattle, importing Indian cotton cloth, pepper, ginger, rice, tobacco, sugar, British cloth and cutlery. Mocha also thrived with coffee exports to Basra and Constantinople for carpets, silks and pearls.[31] By 1800 Oman was the Gulf's main economic and political power again.

In this 1739–1775 period, British trade increased rapidly in all sectors, <u>except</u> the Persian Gulf. Caribbean 1755–1775 sugar imports doubled, supplemented by mahogany and other tropical hardwoods for furniture associated with great cabinet makers, Chippendale, Adam and Sheraton. EIC tonnage also doubled, tea the most rapidly expanding cargo. Indeed, country house life was epitomised by imports. Tea, sweetened with sugar, drunk from Chinese porcelain on rosewood and mahogany furniture, smoking tobacco and drinking port, a far cry from life a century earlier, enabled by imports. American demand growth was especially strong in ironmongery, axes, hoes, ploughs and nails. Fisheries prospered. Newfoundland's surveyor calculated in 1740 that 20,000 tons of shipping and 8,000 people were employed sending fish to Spain and the Mediterranean. In short, expansion was broad-based, most with America, the Caribbean and Asia, long-haul trades, demanding increased shipping from 150,000 tons in 1748 to nearly 300,000 in 1775, despite war losses, increasing demand for Baltic hemp, flax and timber, nearly a third American-built.[32] Long-haul trade transformed Britain. In 1700 Holland was Britain's best export market. By 1760 it was tenth, volumes roughly constant. Dutch share of British imports fell from 14.6% to 3.6% between 1696 and 1772, exports from 41.5% to 12.7%, whereas France increased trade with Europe four-fold between 1716 and 1788, mainly re-exports.[33]

Chapter 6

British Port and Shipping Productivity

'By means of water carriage a more extensive market is opened to every sort of industry than what land carriage can afford.'

Adam Smith[1]

Until the mid-17th century, Britain's European-orientated trade favoured east and south coast ports, except Bristol with its cloth exports, tobacco, sugar and Gascon wine imports and Iberian, Irish, Icelandic and Baltic trade. Hinterland connections via the Severn with tributaries into the Midlands and Wales were important advantages. Trans-Atlantic trade encouraged west coast ports: Bristol, Liverpool, Glasgow and Whitehaven. Port volumes in 1700 were: London 140,000 tons, Bristol 17,300, Ipswich-Harwich 11,200, Newcastle 11,000, Yarmouth 9,900, Liverpool 8,600, Hull 7,600, Whitehaven 7,200, Exeter 7,100 and Lynn 5,700.[2]

In the 1720s Defoe thought Bristol 'the best port of trade in Great Britain, London only excepted.' Its 1700 population, 20,000, England's second city had a mile-long quayside. Glasgow, Liverpool and Whitehaven challenged Bristol in tobacco, but 15 sugar refineries gave it momentum until the 1790s. Sugar led to involvement in slave trading, officially excluded until 1698 by RAC monopoly, but routinely flouted, so when the Spanish Succession War ended in 1713, it expanded rapidly. In 1701–1705 nine ships left Bristol for West Africa, 42 in 1706–1710, 117 in 1716–1720, landing 57,862 slaves in the Americas.[3] It imported masts from Riga, planks from Danzig, bar iron from Sweden and exported ironmongery and tools to America and West Africa. Turpentine was refined from Carolina tree resin. Baltic hemp imports encouraged sailcloth and ropeworks. Soap, paper and chemical industries were established.

Bristol sugar merchant John Carey (1649–1720) in the 1690s thought slaves the means 'whereby our Plantations are improved [for]…great quantities of sugar, tobacco, cotton, ginger and indigo are raised, which being bulky commodities employ great numbers of our ships…[and] Handicraft Trades at home,'[4] although slaves were not the most valuable African export until 1700.[5] Ironic in modern terms, Carey was called 'the philanthropist', promoting workhouses for the poor, the main organiser of 'Bristol Corporation of the Poor' after 1696's Poor Act. Edward Colston (1636–1721), wine, fruit and cloth merchant, involved in slave trading, also philanthropically endowed schools, poor houses, alms houses, schools and hospitals, when Church and society accepted it.

With Chester's decline, River Dee channels too shallow, Liverpool's 17th-century merchants replaced its Irish cattle, sheep, pigs, grain, dairy products, tallow and yarn imports. Benefiting from Cheshire's salt mines, Lancashire's coalfields, Midlands' ironmongery, guns, gunpowder and clay tobacco pipes and the Mersey's deep-water entrance, its merchants became trans-Atlantic tobacco and sugar specialists. Liverpool's first tobacco consignment, 30 lbs, arrived in 1648. London's 1665 plague caused some merchants to relocate. Two sugar cargoes in 1666 initiated its first refinery. Sugar and tobacco imports rose rapidly in the 1680s. Its population trebled to over 5,000 in 1700. Cotton was imported from 1699 for Manchester manufacturers and a salt refinery established in the late-1690s. Merchants established Liverpool's Corporation in 1695 and Old Dock was opened in 1715 for Caribbean and African trade.

By 1704 Liverpool imported 760 tons of sugar and 470 lbs of tobacco annually. Routes north of Ireland were less exposed to privateers who hampered Bristol's growth and neutered Barnstaple, Plymouth, Exeter and Bideford where Walter Raleigh had landed his first tobacco, transported many indentured servants to America, imported Newfoundland's cod, 28 ships recorded in 1700. Plymouth's and Exeter's tobacco imports stopped by the 1740s, Bideford's and Barnstaple's shortly thereafter, concentrating on London, Glasgow, Whitehaven, Liverpool and Bristol. Liverpool's America-bound ships carrying salt, naval stores and ironmongery, sailed first to Cork for beef, pork, herring, butter and horses for Caribbean planters. Its first early-18th-century slaving voyage developed from selling cotton cloth, glass, copper, brass, especially Guinea kettles and Midlands' metal-wares to West Africa. There they loaded gold, ivory and slaves and via the Americas, returned with sugar, cotton, indigo, coffee, tobacco, rum and molasses. By the 1720s, over 40 slave ships annually cleared Liverpool. From the late-1730s, Liverpool's main import was raw cotton and main export cotton cloth to Africa and the Americas., Its population was 35,000 by 1750.

Inland on the Clyde, Glasgow was not an obvious port location, but Merchants House was built in 1659 and in 1668 the Council established a trans-shipment port 18 miles downriver, Port Glasgow. In 1669 a Glaswegian built the East Sugar House. North, South and West followed, using local coal for boiling. In 1674 the first tobacco arrived. By 1700 it had soap boiling, sugar refining, rope, candle, glass and cloth industries, exported from various 17th-18th-century-built quays. Theoretically, English Navigation Acts before the 1707 Act of Union limited its trading ability with English colonies but were circumvented and after 1707 no issue. Merchant-dominated, it rejected Stuart pretenders, supported the 1689 settlement and Church of Scotland. Greenock built a harbour in 1710 and in 1711 the famous Scotts of Greenock began shipbuilding, but Glasgow had early momentum for trade and industry. In 1707 there were 215 Scottish-owned ships, in 1712 over 1,100! The benefit of union was clear. Clyde-owned ships went from eight to 149 in the same period.[6] Defoe visiting in the 1720s described 'one of the cleanest, most beautiful and best built cities in Britain, London excepted,' with distinctive arcaded streets, piazzas and elegant public buildings, reflecting trade wealth and civic pride.

Northeast England's coal cargoes increased rapidly, mainly to London but also Rotterdam, Hamburg and Copenhagen, Britain's most voluminous, intensive trade. Cost advantages over London attracted shipbuilders, especially for colliers. Ownership spread along the east coast. In 1720 the *House of Commons' Journal* reported most Ipswich residents as part-owners of ships or colliers and fishing boat masters.[7] In

1733, 120 Whitby-owned ships were mainly 300–500-ton colliers. In 1701, 40% of leading provincial ports by tonnage, especially East Anglian, had either been coal ports or ports where colliers were owned, which increased to 50% in 1788. When late-17th-century grain exports to Europe began, Yarmouth was the main port, typically in 200–500-tonners, incentivising local ship ownership, which Defoe said supplanted Ipswich as a shipowning port.[8] It also smoke-cured 40,000 barrels of herring annually, exported to Iberia and Italy. London's timber imports were handled by a few timber merchants with factors in Norway. Most grain went to Holland, France and Norway. After shipping coal to London or north Europe, ships usually ballasted to Norway to load timber for east coast England, then loaded coal or grain for similar destinations, eliminating long ballasts. Grain exports peaked in 1751 with 1.6 million quarters, then declined as Britain's growing population consumed more, virtually ceasing in the mid-1770s. The collier fleet rose from 78,000 tons in 1702 to 125,000 in 1773.[9] Other coastal shipping doubled.

1700–1776 English export values grew 122%, manufactured goods 137%, over half for North America and Asia, in total £6.5 to £14.7 million, import values from £6 million to £11.2 million.[10] Bristol's population doubled between 1700 and 1750 to 100,000. Liverpool and Glasgow showed similar trends from smaller beginnings. Glasgow's 1720s-1770s imports increased 11-fold.[11] Liverpool doubled Chesapeake tobacco imports in the 1720s before losing ground to Glasgow in the 1740s. Liverpool was also the departure port for Lancashire's and Irish indentured servants until the 1760s. From the 1740s Liverpool and Glasgow outstripped Bristol. Whitehaven, where Christopher Lowther developed coal exports to Ireland from the 1630s, was Britain's sixth-largest mid-18th-century port with planned Georgian architecture. Defoe thought it England's 'most pre-eminent [coal] port...except Newcastle.' It dabbled in tobacco and slave trading in the 1740s, but with a less productive hinterland than Liverpool, concentrated on coal.

Remoteness of Liverpool and Glasgow from French privateers assisted in diverting trade from Bristol, which by 1800 fell to fifth-largest British port. Cotton cloth-making failed to develop around Bristol as in Lancashire and Glasgow. However, it pioneered a unique British development, provincial private banks, the first in 1716, around a dozen in 1750, ten-times more in 1784, 20-times by 1793, peaking at 650–700 in 1810 as Napoleonic War trade boomed (See Chapter 12). Shipping permeated banking, especially ship mortgages, credit in cargo transactions and finances for harbour construction.

Rivers were linked by canals by mid-century. Few important places were more than a dozen miles from navigable water. Liverpool's hinterland opened-up with the 1736 Mersey and Irwell Navigation, the 1757 Sankey Brook Canal from St. Helens' coalfields and Salthouse Dock in 1753, exporting Cheshire's salt, called 'Liverpool salt', to Newfoundland's fisheries and Europe. Nantes and Bordeaux were France's main slave ports but Liverpool's growing volumes exceeded them, although St. Domingue trade transformed Bordeaux. Liverpool financed 55% of British slave voyages after 1750, 75% after 1780, due to lower wages on heavily manned ships, although London financiers were also involved.[12]

In 1768–72 Liverpool undertook 460 slave voyages, London 205 and Bristol 135, its share about two-thirds in the mid-1780s, 85% by 1800. Eighteenth-century traders transported 1.3 million slaves in over 5,000 voyages, London's ships nearly 750,000 in about 3,000 voyages, Bristol's under 500,000 in about 2,000 voyages, averaging 230–260 per ship. Liverpool sent cloth, metalware, earthenware, gunpowder, firearms, shoes, purses, needles, silk, paper, playing cards and ironmongery to America and Caribbean markets, with sugar, cotton and tobacco imports, encouraged manufacturing, shipbuilding, banking, insurance, rope and sail making. Liverpool's population overtook Bristol's in the 1780s. St. George's Dock (1771) for the Caribbean, King's Dock (1788) for American and Baltic trade and Queen's Dock (1799) for Greenland Fishery reflected growing volumes. Exchanges, shipping and insurance offices, merchant houses and warehouses concentrated in a business area. Increasing London volumes meant large ships, unable to discharge at quaysides, instead lightered in the 'pool' adjacent to London Bridge, slowing discharge, encouraging west coast ports.

Glasgow's tobacco imports increased from eight million lbs in 1740 to 47 million by the 1770s, much for re-export, becoming Britain's main tobacco port. Of Britain's 1700 imports, 66% were re-exported, 85% in the early-1770s. Glasgow-Virginia voyages took 20 days less than London-Virginia. In 1732, two thirds of Glasgow's imports were organised by four families, the Dunlops, Bogles, Oswalds and McCalls, most of the rest by six other associations. Only a few from the 1740s, when tobacco took-off, were important in the 1790s, implying dynamic competition.[13] Firms such as Cunninghame, Spiers, Glassford, Buchanan and Simson, 'tobacco lairds' provided colonists with Glaswegian pottery, cloth and other essentials. Tobacco imports of 2.5 million lbs in 1715 became 13.6 million in 1745, 44 million by 1776, over a third of Scotland's imports by value; sugar, cotton and rum another 15%. In 1735, 67 ships sailed from Port Glasgow to the Americas, overtaking London as Britain's main tobacco port by 1760. This spurred banking, the Ship Bank and Glasgow Arms Bank in 1750 and Thistle Bank in 1761, all servicing trans-Atlantic shipping and trading needs.[14] By the 1780s its population grew to 48,000 with new streets, Virginia Street, Jamaica Street and Glassford Street, named after its trade destinations and tobacco merchant, who diversified into banking, dye-making and textiles. The 'lairds' spawned a prosperous middle class. Increasing Highlands' hardships led to emigration through Glasgow on its ships to Chesapeake colonies, two-way trade. Nova Scotia's settlement was mainly Scottish through Glasgow.

James Watt (1736–1819), son of a Glasgow shipbuilder, merchant, shipowner and instrument maker, was employed to repair a Newcomen steam engine in 1763. Knowing Glasgow University Professor Joseph Black's (1728–99) latent heat theories, he realised a separate condenser would increase power. With a 1769 patent he and Matthew Boulton (1728–1809) manufactured them. Ironmaster John Wilkinson, first apprenticed to a Liverpool merchant, improved cylinder boring, crucial for efficient engines. In 1770 the Clyde was widened and deepened enabling larger ships as industry developed, its harbour front designed by John Rennie and Thomas Telford, the period's greatest engineers. Merchants diversified into banking, coal mining, industry, engineering and financial services. British ports were the Industrial Revolution's front line.

Trans-Atlantic freight rates declined after Utrecht, because of peace and west coast ports' growth, reducing sailing times, increasing supply. After 1700, ship's wheels for steering, rotated a drum directing the rudder, replaced cumbersome, labour-intensive tillers. Rigging improvements, increasing numbers of sails per mast, reducing crew numbers, improving handling ability, especially sailing into strong westerlies, all improved efficiency. In 1725, a 200-ton tobacco trader had 25 crew, in 1765 only 14.[15]

Tobacco, increasingly tighter packed and hogs heads whose sizes changed, make it difficult to record accurate freight rates but they apparently fell from about 1s 3d/lb in the 1670s to 7d in 1720.[16] Sugar shippers increased casks' size and weight, as 1710–1730 sugar imports doubled. Caribbean freights were more stable, probably because ships necessarily carried more guns and crew than North American.[17] Carolina's rice freight rates show clearest evidence of productivity gains, apart from war-induced rises, declining from 100 shillings/ton around 1700 to 60 in the 1720s, 50–55 in the early-1750s, 40–45 in the 1760s and 32–38, even 20 in the early-1770s, with growing ship sizes, smaller crews and less arms. African slaving rates changed little as crew sizes were steady, needed to feed and control the slaves. On other trades, crew sizes declined especially on short-haul voyages. A 300-ton collier in 1757 claimed she was adequately manned with 11 including officers.[18] In 1700, Caribbean ships' ton/man ratio was about 9.5, 10.5 in 1750, 13.5 in 1774. Jamaica traders lagged initially but improved to 14.5 in 1774. For Chesapeake tobacco ships the figures were 10, 13 and 16 tons on the same dates or from 21 to 13 men.[19] Lighthouses were still infrequent, but reflectors installed after 1770.[20] Shipping in 1775 was double that of 1675 but employed only about 50% more seamen, most ships built cheaper in northeast England and America.

Gabriel Snodgrass, EIC chief surveyor (1757–1797) improved Indiaman hull designs and cargo-carrying ability, replaced some wooden fittings with iron and in the 1790s continuous upper decks replaced discontinuous ones. He boasted they were the 'safest ships in Europe' and the Navy would save labour and money copying them.[21] While Harrison worked on chronometers, most navigation was still made astronomically. Englishman John Hadley and American Thomas Godfrey independently in 1730–31 improved the sextant. Tapp's *Seamans Kalender* was superseded in 1765 by Nevil Maskelyne's *Nautical Almanac and Astronomical Ephemeris* with its companion *Tables for Finding Latitude and Longitude* requiring just a sextant and tables, locating the prime meridian at Greenwich, predicting star and moon positions up to his 1815 death.[22] All developments contributed to 25–35% cheaper freights by 1775, unmatched in other parts of the economy, combined with inland waterway improvements reducing inland transport costs, providing Britain's economy with cheaper goods and greater volumes, its merchant fleet growing from 3,300 ships of 260,000 tons in 1702 to 9,400 more efficient ships, almost 700,000 tons in 1776.[23]

London's trade growth increased specialisation and expertise of service functions; agents, factors, brokers, insurers, contractors and banks. West End banks serviced the gentry and aristocracy, City banks, merchants, traders, shipping and manufacturing interests. Shipping and trading profits financed new banks, which financed trade and shipowning; a virtuous circle.[24] London, central to Britain's commercial activity, in

1790 took 70% of all imports and sent 75% of re-exports.[25] Its million population in 1800 was nearly 10% of Britain's. It combined the role of main port, market, centre for finance, manufacturing and government. Britain's leading ports in tonnage owned were London, Newcastle, Liverpool, Sunderland, Whitehaven, Hull, Whitby, Bristol, Yarmouth and Scarborough,[26] still east coast weighted because of the Baltic's continued importance and growing northeast coal shipments to London and Europe. Increased efficiency and reduced shipping costs did not impact delivered prices by more than a few per cent but was vital because the accumulated capital drove later expansion.

Chapter 7

Historic Attitudes to Slavery and Serfdom

Slavery, with few exceptions, had always been seen as part of the social fabric, the world's natural state. Calvinist minister Francois Valentin's (1666–1727) *Oud en Nieur Oost Indien* called slave trading, 'the world's oldest trade.' Homer noted 8th-century BC Phoenician slave traders. Greeks shipped many from the Black Sea. Athens and Rome's slave population was variously estimated at around 15–35%. First-century BC Diodorus Siculus noted 'slaves who work in the mines…wear out their bodies day and night…dying in large numbers because of the exceptional hardship.' Classical writers debated how to discipline and treat slaves in moral, philosophical terms. Systems were different. Spartan helots were treated with casual brutality. Maritime-inspired Athens' talented slaves could take-over businesses. Jesus said nothing about it. Paul was indifferent, irrelevant to spiritual awakening. Early Christians accepted it. The Prophet owned slaves, urging but not commanding kindness and manumission. Owners were entitled to have sex with slave women, a common motive for purchase. Christians and Muslims only objected if co-religionists were enslaved by the other. In impoverished early-medieval Europe, slaves were the most commonly traded commodity. *The Domesday Book* recorded 10% of England's population as slaves. Feudal bonds resulted in similar conditions. Serfs were transferred with property. But slavery and serfdom died-out naturally in 12th-century northern Europe.

Baghdad's Abbasids had shipped huge numbers from East Africa for hard agricultural work, administration and the army. The Black Sea's Caffa's 14th-15th-century slave market was probably the world's most active, supplying the Muslim world and Mediterranean sugar plantations. In 1428, 10% of Majorca's population were slaves, their treatment enshrined in a legal code. War galleys were rowed mainly by slaves. Slavery persisted in Iberia, adjacent to the Muslim world. Catalan merchants bought them in North Africa, Barcelona and Majorca, the main markets for domestic and agricultural labour, owned even by artisans. However, 16th-century maritime Ragusa abolished slavery and Venice's galleys were rowed by freemen.

As 15th-century Portuguese sailed down Africa's coast they initially sought gold, then slaves for Mediterranean sugar plantations to replace Black Sea supplies, unobtainable after Constantinople's 1453 Ottoman conquest. As plantations migrated from Mediterranean islands to the Algarve, Atlantic islands, finally Brazil and the Caribbean, increasing sugar demand meant West Africa where slavery was endemic, became the natural geographical slave source, enriching 16th-century Benin, the 'Slave Coast'. Treatment varied. Dahomey's king slaughtered slaves in their hundreds or thousands in sacrificial rituals and earnt an estimated annual £250,000 selling them to European traders. In other areas slaves were treated like 'adopted children' with significant rights. Nineteenth-century African explorer Mungo Park estimated a 3:1 slave-freeman ratio, most inherited. New World demand expanded slave raiding hundreds of miles from shipment ports.

Spanish first used African slaves on Hispaniola in 1501 and Cuba in 1513, as natives died. The first slave base was Goree Island off Dakar in 1536. Angola was Brazil's main supplier. Conditions were dreadful. A 1627 account described them as 'crowded, in such disgusting conditions and so mistreated', collared and fettered, imprisoned below deck. 'No Spaniard... dares stick his head in the hatch without becoming ill... so great is the stench, the crowding and the misery.'[1]

Portuguese found slavery flourishing in the Indian Ocean. Manu had recognised seven types, including those captured in battle, those enslaved in return for food, those bought, those inheriting their status, those given away by parents. Muslims recognised four routes to slavery: capture in *jihad*, tribute, inheritance from slave parents and purchase.

Some Jesuit and Dominican friars denounced slavery as sinful but most early opposition came from Dutch and English. The early Dutch Republic declared slave trading immoral. William Usselinx, the WIC's driving force, believed it inhuman and uneconomic. Several Dutch cities banned it for moral reasons. Such ideals however, blurred as slaves in captured ships were sold on. In 1637, the WIC captured Portugal's slave port, El Mina. Others followed and by 1640 it was master of Atlantic slave trading. In England, despite William Hawkins dabbling in the 1530s, Elizabeth I declared, 'if any African should be carried away without his free consent it would be detestable and call down the vengeance of heaven upon the undertaking.' Slavery was un-English according to a shocked Richard Johnson who, while buying gold and ivory in West Africa in 1618, was offered slaves, explaining Englishmen did not buy and sell humans.[2] The 1618 Guinea Company charter did not mention slaves, trading mainly redwood and gold.

The VOC accepted Indian Ocean slavery, signing 1650–1675 treaties which included slave clauses. Animist, stateless and weak tribes of inner Sumatra, Borneo, New Guinea, Sulawesi and Mindanao had enslaved each other in low-scale inter-communal conflict for millennia, used as crew for 1st-millennium Madagascan settlers.[3] Frequent 17th-century Madagascan kingdoms' wars and militant Islamic Sultanates fed supply. Reunion and Mauritius plantations used mainly Indian slaves. Drought and famine in 1618–20 caused large Coromandel coast exports in 1622–23. In 1646, 2,118 were shipped to Batavia, nearly 2,000 from Madurai in 1673–77 in a long drought, more in 1688, caused by Aurangzeb's wars and poor harvests. Reportedly thousands of children were sold into slavery and exported by Asian traders from Nagapattinam to Aceh, Johor and other slave markets.[4] Makassar was the main transit port for Kalimantan's, Sulawesi's and other islands' slaves. Bali exported its own and New Guinea slaves. Of 10,000 brought to Batavia between 1653 and 1682, 41% came from Sulawesi, 24% from Bali.[5] Almost half Cape Colony's 1670–1700 slaves were from south Sulawesi, then supplemented by Indians and Madagascans. Slave trading increased with Omani and French plantations' rapid expansion. The VOC operated west Sumatran gold mines with 200–500 slaves and were over half of Batavia's late-17th-century population, used as domestic servants, concubines, for building roads and canals, growing crops, as miners, fishermen, artisans, shipyard workers and dockers. Africans were thought better at hard physical labour, Southeast Asians as artisans or domestic servants.

In the 1660s-70s over 2,000 VOC slaves worked fields around Galle and Colombo growing cereals, rice, cotton and tobacco. War and famine sporadically increased supply. Dutch Indian Ocean 1680s slave trade is estimated at 3,700–6,400 annually.[6] An estimated annual 9,500 were involved in 17th-century trans-Saharan trade, around 3,000 from East Africa and Red Sea, tiny compared with later Atlantic slaving. Tartar, Polish and Russian slave trades are impossible to gauge, annual estimates between 3,000 and 20,000,[7] much little-known, undocumented or ignored due to fragmentation and the more voluminous late trans-Atlantic trade, much higher Caribbean free-slave ratios and its massive demographic effects. It is not uncommon to see blacks in Oman, slave descendants, but not nearly as numerous as in the Americas. Nor is their trade as well-documented.

English Caribbean settlers needed labour to grow, harvest and process sugar, initially supplied by indentured workers, an extension of long-established English practice, working annual contracts at hiring fairs, offering young people the chance to learn basic, necessary skills, both parties bound by contract. Comparing notes at hiring fairs, an intelligence network of individual employer's merits gave protection as they worked to become tenants. For colonies, employers paid the servants' passage, an investment requiring longer service. Developed by the Virginia Company in the 1620s, men and women contracted themselves from three to nine years, then received a one-off payment, in Barbados ten acres. Many thought it an opportunity to free themselves from social and economic hardship. Generally treated worse than in England, sometimes close to slavery, Planter Richard Ligon thought it depended on the master, 'merciful or cruel', noting their 'wearisome and miserable lives.' 'I have seen an overseer beat a servant with a cane about the head till the blood has flowed for an offence that is not worth speaking of.'[8] Some signed-on again at the contract's end. Some worked them out, becoming wealthy buccaneers like Henry Morgan in Jamaica.[9] Others settled neighbour islands.

Although Atlantic slave trading ended-up an almost entirely African trade, many Irish prisoners of war were transported, sometimes for ten-years, some virtual slaves, the exact legal status unclear. By the 1650s, Antigua's and Montserrat's population were 70% Irish slaves. Cheaper than Africans, planters inter-bred them to produce better-priced mulattos. Prisoners after Penruddock's uprising of 1655 were sold as slaves. The 1660 Royal African Company (RAC) earned 25% of its revenues from slaves, the rest from gold and ivory. Re-founded in 1672 slaves constituted 60% due to growing Caribbean sugar production/export but could not meet demand, fed mainly by Dutch and interlopers.

North America's first slaves were landed at Jamestown by Dutch merchants in 1619, but for a century Chesapeake's economy was driven by indentured labour. As tobacco transformed the region and 1670s labour costs rose, slaves displaced them. Observing Caribbean sugar planters' achievements, who from about 1650 started copying Spain's use of slaves, it seemed logical to follow suit. In 1670 there were 2,500 negroes and

38,500 whites in the Chesapeake area; in 1700, 12,900 to 85,200, in 1730, 53,200 to 171,400, also shipped to Charleston for rice and indigo plantations.

John Locke's 1690 *First Treatise on Government* wrote, 'slavery is so vile and miserable a state of man and so directly opposite to the generous temper and courage of our nation that it is hardly possible that an Englishman, much less a gentleman, should plead for it.' People, he thought, were born free. Yet, he was an RAC shareholder and authored Carolina's Constitution in which free men had 'absolute authority' over their negro slaves. There were deep-seated ideals of freedom ingrained into the English body politic, but the logic of sugar plantations seemed to make slavery an unavoidable necessity. There was still much initial doubt about it. Barbados' Governor had to confirm its status in 1638, Massachusetts in 1641, Connecticut in 1650, Virginia in 1661, Maryland in 1663, New York and New Jersey in 1664.

English traders involved in the indentured servant trade switched to slaves, partly explaining Liverpool's transition. By 1700, 124,000 slaves had been shipped to French islands, about 500,000 to Brazil, about 450,000 to the non-Spanish Caribbean and 450,000 to Spanish settlements.[10] As sugar production rose, Jamaica's slave population grew to 80,000 by 1730. In the early-1730s a reported 40% died in the first two or three years, the rest one in fifteen a year.[11] From 1708 to 1735 Barbados' planters imported 85,000 slaves, yet their population only increased by 4,000. From the 1770s, slave imports accelerated as sugar production increased, although on-board mortality halved from early-17th-century levels to around 10% in the early-18th. Hundreds of thousands were re-shipped from Jamaica to Spanish colonies and Chesapeake Bay and from Dutch Curacao to Spanish America. In 1710, the slave-freeman ratio was 5:1, French islands more, St. Domingue in the 1790s, an unsustainable 16:1.[12] Brutality needed to sustain it made Caribbean slavery's only parallels, 8th-9th-century Abbasid slavery, those used in mines throughout history and contemporary east Europe's serfdom.

Indian cloth and tobacco were traded for slaves and Africans quickly developed specific demands. Slavers aimed to deliver them in decent condition to maximise profits, thus the imperative, fill holds quickly and sail. Provisioning was difficult, so small, fast ships were used, inefficient as sugar carriers. The so-called triangle trade was more complex than ships carrying slaves, then sugar or tobacco, then manufactured goods to Africa. Some did, but different crews were used for slavers and each route suited different ship types.

It is useful and no excuse to describe the social context. Death was prevalent and random. In 18th-century London slums three-quarters of children died before their fifth birthday. Despair led to gin consumption, illustrated by Hogarth. Smallpox was the biggest killer, typhus, malaria, malnutrition, tuberculosis, rickets, plague, chickenpox, influenza, dysentery and whooping cough ever-present threats. Seamen were especially vulnerable to typhus, piracy, scurvy and shipwreck. Today's easily treatable diseases were disfiguring, painful and life-threatening. Uncertainty about food supply was normal, hunger not unusual, famine not infrequent, war common. Traders endured disease-ridden bases in Southeast Asia, West Africa and the Caribbean. Slave ships' crew had high death rates. RAC records show 60% of their personnel in Africa died in the first year, 80% by the seventh, only 10% discharged from service alive.[13] Before 1700, 46%

of Jamaica's infants died before their fifth birthday, 60% thereafter, its success making it a hub for new virulent strains of fever and smallpox. One third of 20-year-olds did not make it to 30. Half those who did failed to make 40. One planter wrote of losing two wives and 16 out of 21 children to disease. Average marriages lasted only eight years before one partner died.[14] The rich were not immune. Queen Anne had 17 pregnancies. Only one lived beyond infancy, perishing from smallpox aged 11, the same disease that took Queen Mary. English life expectancy improved from about 35 to 42 by 1750 but was only 25 in France, in the Caribbean as low as ten.[15] French finance minister Necker (1777–1781) estimated that 25% of France's population died before the age of three, 25% before 25. In England and Holland surgical advances, use of quinine, improved water supplies, a better diet and soap helped population increase.

In England in 1697 the death penalty was extended for maiming cattle, destroying young trees, extortion and blackmail. Processions of condemned men to Tyburn often degenerated into drink-sodden carnivals. In early-18th-century Britain, aggravated capital punishment was discussed, by starving, hanging in chains, breaking on the wheel and whipping to death.[16] Later small felonies received the death penalty. Soldiers were regularly whipped and school boys flogged, which few thought unreasonable. Merchant seamen were pressganged and exploited. Early-18th-century Admiral Vernon noted, 'Our fleets are manned by violence and cruelty,' the pressganged 'in effect condemned to death…never allowed to set foot again on shore but turned over from ship to ship'. Naval stations in Jamaica and Antigua had especially high death tolls, seen as an unavoidable necessity, like slavery itself. Only after the 1797 Nore Mutiny were improvements made.

The number of Africans enslaved has been much debated. There were huge annual war-induced fluctuations in trans-Atlantic trade. Philip Curtin's and David Eltis' figures seem to be most respected.[17] They calculated between 1519 and the 1860s that 9.5 million arrived in the Americas, while 1.5 million died *en route*. About 60% were shipped between 1721 and 1820. David Richardson thinks British ships carried 3.4 million between 1662 and 1801, rising from 6,700 a year in the 1660s to over 42,000 in the 1760s then levelling out,[18] about half of trans-Atlantic shipments. French slaving accelerated due to booming St. Domingue production, the rest mainly Portuguese, Spanish and Dutch.

In central and east Europe, strict controls were gradually inflicted on peasants, their land taken, heavier obligations imposed and hereditary serfdom re-established between 1500 and 1650. Serfs used the lord's lands, under subjugation, needing permission to leave. Estate agriculture undermined medieval town privileges. Continental absolutism, slavery and serfdom were natural bedfellows. Russia's Romanovs, elected in 1630, established almost total enserfment. After the Thirty Years War in 1648 Austria's Hapsburgs turned inward and east, replacing Bohemian and Czech Protestant nobility with Catholic Austrians, reducing serfs to conditions hardly differing from slavery.

Peter's 200,000 peasant army, 100,000 special troops and western military advisors helped win the Great Northern War against Sweden's small population, but as people replaced land as the main taxation unit, life became harsher. Serfdom was not uniform throughout eastern Europe. Ottoman bureaucrats were slaves; but treated benignly.

Hungarian serfdom was brutal; landlords' abused property. Bohemian serfom only had to provide annual payments and labour, but was still miserable. In contrast, in 1648 in Putney, England, New Model Army junior officers debated concepts of freedoms, its limits, human rights and social justice.

Eighteenth-century serf conditions worsened. In 1721, Russian factory and workshop directors were empowered to take villages to work as serfs. The Czar granted estates for military service, usually 1,000 serfs ascribed to them. By the 1760s, 100,000 was common. In 1765 landowners were empowered to sentence under 45-year-olds to hard labour in Siberia. In 1767, rights of appeal against harsh treatment were withdrawn and serfs sold at public auction. Most Danish peasants were serfs. A 1733 decree tied them to the soil for 22 years after their 14th birthday. There was a deepening contrast between maritime trade's expansion, its effects on industry, knowledge, innovation and ideas, especially in Britain, and continental stagnation, between wide dissemination of news, ideas, the vitality of invention and commercial prosperity of worldwide trade and enforced conservatism in most of Europe. Peasants accounted for 75% of Prussia and Poland's population, 80% of France and 90% of Russia, degrees of freedom varying, but conditions wretched.[19] A recorded 73 Russian peasant risings between 1762 and 1769 culminated in Pugachev's rebellion, only finally suppressed in 1775. There were risings in Bohemia in 1775, Transylvania in 1784, Moravia in 1786 and Austria in 1789. Endemic in 17th-century France, due to high tax and arbitrary, inefficient government, they decreased thereafter; but over 100 are recorded between 1715 and 1785.[20] Danish serfdom was abolished in 1788 but conditions remained similar. It spread in Saxony, Brandenburg and Prussia, intensifying to increase grain output, the nobility tightening judicial and economic control. As Russia conquered Ukraine, free peasants were enserfed. A visiting Englishman in 1784 noted they 'have undergone a deplorable change…reduced by an edict of the…Empress to the condition of her other subjects.'[21]

Chapter 8

Enlightenment, Humanitarianism, Technical Advances and Abolitionism

"God said, 'Let Newton Be' and all was light."[1]

The series' previous books highlighted how maritime trade's inquisitive, problem-solving nature always coincided with intellectual and practical improvements, especially at its most voluminous and proactive; ancient Gujaratis and Tamils, Phoenicians, Greeks in Athens, Samos, Rhodes and Alexandria, eventually protected by Romans as maritime trade volumes reached unprecedented levels in the mid-2nd century before declining, in 11th-century Song China, halting in 1372 when private foreign trade was banned. Europe's post-Dark Age regeneration was led by its most active ports. David Hume's *Of Civil Liberty* thought similarly. 'If we trace commerce through Tyre, Syracuse, Carthage, Venice, Florence, Genoa, Antwerp, Holland, England etc., we shall always find it to have fixed its seat in free governments. The three greatest trading towns now in the world are London, Amsterdam and Hamburg, all free cities and Protestant cities, enjoying double liberty.'[2] In 1673 William Temple had identified Athens, Rhodes, Bruges and Antwerp; commonwealths or legal monarchies.[3] Seventeenth-century growing maritime volumes and geographical extent was, not coincidentally, accompanied by relentless technical innovation. The Dutch however, did not follow-up after 1672's 'Disaster Year' knocked confidence and creativity out of their commercial, scientific world. Calvinist orthodoxy opposed scientific rationalism. Dutch 17th-century liberty was anyway not intended for export. British entrepreneurs <u>did</u> continue it, differentiating Britain from <u>every</u> other country. The scientific revolution of rational Newtonian mechanics, problem-solving a by-product of increased maritime trade, invigorated British society, spawning industrial revolution. By the 1780s, everything was ready; increasing maritime trade, canals, mines, ironworks, steam engines, textile machinery, entrepreneurs and finance.

A search for technical improvements to produce cotton cloth equalling Indian quality bore fruit in Lancashire; Bury's John Kaye's flying shuttle (1733), Blackburn's James Hargreaves' spinning jenny (1764), allowing one operator to work scores of yarn-producing spindles and Preston's Richard Arkwright's 'water frame' (1769). The 1699/1721 Calico Acts were therefore repealed in 1774. The 'mule' (1779) used water to power weaving machinery. Cartwright's power loom (1789) set the pace of industrialisation and from 1790 steam engines allowed greater, cheaper production in cotton, then wool production, cotton requiring huge raw cotton imports. Multi-talented, progressive merchant Patrick Colquhoun in 1803 noted 20,000 manufacturers in wool and cotton export industries on north England's rivers and canals.

The value of British 1725–1750 exports to Asia expanded six-fold, the Caribbean two-fold, and North America four-fold and by 1773 six-fold since 1700.[4] North America's 1776 population of three million required woollen and cotton cloth, silk, linen, utensils, tools, firearms, tea, liquor, ironmongery, books, furniture, rugs and sails, distinguishing British trade from other European countries. Living standards were higher than Europe. Settlers wanted land, especially farms, producing a culture of consumption and self-reliant individualism. In 1775, 40% of British exports went to the colonies from 47 industrialising towns, also unique in Europe.

France's inability to embrace maritime trade, land-locked values and obsession with religious uniformity led to inherent financial and industrial disadvantages against Britain's merchant culture of compromise. Britain and northeast America's most significant 18th-century maritime legacy was toleration and compromise, necessary in maritime societies, which became responsibility for others and a totally new concept, humanitarianism. Improvement, a maritime dynamic, applied to improving land, pasture, food, machines and increasingly people. Uncultivated land meant uncultivated men. Native Americans were given a cow for eight wolves they killed to improve land and 'civilise' them. Many people lived 'in brutish, nasty condition' as William Petty said of the Irish.[5] 'Brutish' or 'beastly' were dehumanising words. Henry VIII had described rebellious Lincolnshire commoners as 'brute and beastly.' De-humanisation allowed Irish, African and native American enslavement. Similar terminology was used about potential tyranny. Edmund Ludlow thought the Civil War was about whether the king should govern by the rule of law or force 'like beasts.'[6] Edmund Burke blamed the French Revolution on *philosophes* and the 'swinish multitude,' the mob.

There were 17th-century indications in England of changing attitudes. John Donne's 1624 'No man is an island. Any man's death diminishes me because I am involved in mankind' was only possible in a world of connected productive trade in necessarily tolerant ways. Only in England could *The Merchant of Venice*, a Jew, be portrayed sympathetically.' Josiah Child's 1665 *Brief Observations* was concerned to better employ England's poor, both for the national good and compassion, proposing workhouses and hospitals to provide work. Charles Davenant, Inspector General of Exports and Imports, wrote similarly in 1698. Bristol's Carey, Child and Firmin founded institutions to help educate the poor.[7] Just before 1700 charity schools started teaching poor children, enabling them to earn a living. John Locke thought education would inculcate 'humanity' and 'compassion'.[8] The third Earl of Shaftesbury instead thought instinct and nature inculcated such feelings.

Many late-17th-century tracts described slavery's horror without calling for abolition. Quaker George Fox in 1671 Bridgetown Barbados, Nevis, Antigua and Newport, appealed in pamphlets to planters, to 'deal mildly and gently' with negroes, warning Governor Codrington that God would require an account of their treatment and criticised the Church for not converting them. 'Is not the Gospel to be preached to all creatures? And are they not creatures? And did not Christ taste death for every man? And are they not men?' Quakers emphasised personal religious, spiritual experience, espoused prison reform, social justice and more prominent roles for women. By 1680 there were about 60,000 English Quakers. Many emigrated to North America, especially Rhode Island and Pennsylvania, established by William Penn in 1682. Those in Philadelphia, the name from Greek for brotherly love, led the way. Christopher Codrington jnr. in the Leeward Islands in 1699 said he would 'endeavour to get a law restraining inhuman severities and punishing the wilful killing of Indians and negroes.' In the Caribbean, liberal ideas succumbed to 'the brutal reality of slave society.'[9] Sugar-planting, harvesting, crushing and boiling was hard, dangerous work. Because the free-slave ratio was so high, it relied on violence and fear. Sugar islands were different moral worlds. Nevertheless, Codrington's will aimed at slave conversion and better medical care. To many planters, they were property to use as they chose.

Scientific study of animals, birds and vegetation challenged the idea of a world made for man ruling other species, including maltreatment. Seventeenth-century bulls and bears were baited, tied to stakes and attacked by dogs before slaughter, geese webs were nailed to the floor and cock fighting was normal.[10] Pepys thought animal sports 'a very rude and nasty pleasure.' At Stamford's and Tutbury's annual bull running, bulls had ears cropped and nose blown full of pepper. In 1714 the *Stamford Mercury* criticised its 'barbarism and darkness of past ages,'[11] meaning its pagan origins <u>and</u> cruelty.[12] The Eton ram hunt in which a ram was clubbed to death was stopped in 1747. There had been no previous compassion for heretics and witches burned at the stake, criminals and the insane whipped. Animals were bled slowly, painfully to death in the belief it improved meat's quality. From the 1740s there was a growing stream of essays on animals' moral treatment, protests about cruelty and in the 1780s tracts persuading children to be benevolent to 'brute creation.'[13]

William Wollaston's 1724 *The Religion of Nature Delineated* argued that religion and morality were the same, religion 'the pursuit of happiness by the practice of truth and reason.' He wrote, 'It is grievous to see or hear any man or…animal…in torment.' Urban growth and keeping pets helped foster such feelings. The pointlessness of physical suffering, compassion to animals, slaves, criminals and the insane, previously and elsewhere unquestioned was new, peculiarly British. That man should kill animals without unnecessary suffering, that mankind could improve itself by ending flogging and public execution while reforming schools, prisons and the poor law became widespread.[14] England's and New England's 17th-century growth of libertarian ideas mutated into ethics based on human nature and progress.

Defoe pioneered the novel. Son of a small businessman and dissenter, staunch supporter of the political settlement, an example of how trade bred an articulate middle class, he championed trade, his 'beloved subject'.[15] His *Robinson Crusoe* (1719) described a man who, having made two slaving voyages, became a planter in Brazil. Returning to Africa he was shipwrecked, another opportunity to examine a relationship between a negro and Caucasian, following England's pioneering woman author, Aphra Behn's 1688 *Oroonoko, or the History of the Royal Slave* which, adapted for the theatre, played for many years. Defoe's 1722 *Moll Flanders* was heroine, thief and whore, imprisoned in a debtors' jail, which Defoe experienced when a business venture failed, and transported to Virginia.

Many middle-class men, products of a free, trading society, wrote plays and novels like Henry Fielding's *Tom Jones*, often with a prominent woman. Jonathan Swift promoted women's education, Ireland, even though he hated it, religious toleration despite his firm Anglicanism, was a pioneer abolitionist and wrote his epitaph; 'He strove with all his strength to champion liberty.' His *Gulliver's Travels* satirised man's ignorance and inflated ego, a story of two south Indian Ocean islands, Lilliput and Blefuscu, 800 yards apart, inhabited by people a twelfth of human height, both following the teachings of the same prophet, but at war over which end of their morning boiled egg they should break, one of the great satire's, impossible to have replicated in France; implicitly championing toleration.

Satire from Donne (1572–1631) to Dryden (1631–1700) had been powerful vehicles for questioning assumptions, used to poke fun at ostentation, vice, immorality, political corruption and religious differences and in John Gay's case, injustice and Italian opera in his much- imitated 1728 *Beggar's Opera*, a story of thieves, highwaymen and whores. Hogarth mirrored it in *A Harlot's Progress, The Rake's Progress* and *Marriage a la Mode*, a series of realistic, shocking, irreverent sketches. New thinking in science, novels, plays and philosophy matched industrial, technological invention.

Naval surgeon John Atkins' 1735 *Voyage to Guinea, Brazil and the West Indies* thought 'to remove negroes from their homes and friends where they are at ease, to a strange country, people and language must be highly offending against the laws of natural justice and humanity.'[16] *Rule Britannia's* (1740) author had earlier written of 'that cruel trade cost and inefficiency of slave labour', soon expanded upon by Adam Smith. In the 1760s Lieutenant Edward Thompson, well-used to Royal Navy whippings and executions, was shocked to see a young slave girl in Barbados tortured to death for 'some trivial domestic error'.[17] In ancient Athens and Rome, some masters treated slaves well and in the 2nd-century height and breadth of maritime trade volumes, Emperor Hadrian forbade slave castration and Antoninus Pius restricted slave torture.[18] But this movement sought abolition, not amelioration. The institution was wrong, not how people used it.

Glasgow University's influential Chair of Moral Philosophy, Francis Hutcheson's (1694–1746), *Concerning Moral Good and Evil* and lectures highlighted the growing importance of virtue and 'to be pleased with the happiness of others and uneasy at their misery,' stressing 'the sense of right and wrong', enunciating the principle of 'the greatest happiness for the greatest numbers.'[19] Adam Smith who studied under him, developed a passion for liberty, reason and free speech. Also Professor of Moral Philosophy, Smith was celebrated for his 1759 *Theory of Moral Sentiments* which tried explaining how moral judgements are formed.

Pennsylvania Quakers set new standards in dealing with native Americans. Although Penn was granted Pennsylvania, he chose to buy their claims. Quakers built schools, hospitals, asylums and voluntary benevolent associations, Many started manufacturing and commerce. From slavery being acceptable if slaves' material and spiritual needs were addressed, from the 1730s they opposed it. By 1756 only 10% owned slaves. In the 1758 Philadelphia annual meeting, slave-traders were excluded. In 1760 New England Quakers made importing slaves an offence. By the 1770s Quaker abolitionism was virtually ubiquitous. Many British visitors to North America were dismayed by racism, cruelty and violence, mainly in the south but also abuse of free negroes in the northeast.

Quaker ideas inspired John Wesley (1703–1791), founder of Britain's influential Methodists, who stressed spiritual salvation, Christian service, love of God linked to love of neighbour and justice; responsibility, sobriety, respectability, piety, establishment of hospitals, universities, orphanages, schools and soup kitchens, serving all people. Crowds of over 50,000 came to Methodist rallies after the 1740s and his 1774 *Thoughts upon Slavery*, that it was inconsistent with natural justice, had massive circulation, provoking a 1776 House of Commons debate. They produced huge volumes of books and pamphlets on Christianity, morality, natural history, Shakespeare, Milton, Spenser, Locke, medicine, grammar and electricity, to educate and enlighten, especially the poor, although Wesley thought the *Bible* and *Catechism* sufficient education for children. They distributed food and clothing, visited the sick and prisoners. It spawned Anglican evangelism. Both spread charity schools and Sunday schools, poor people's main source of reading, writing and arithmetic. Adam Smith reflected it in economic thinking. 'No society can surely be flourishing and happy of which the greater part…are poor and miserable.' Reformers' ideas varied, but with rationalism they began focusing on individuals' moral significance and well-being.

In the 1750s British public opinion started favouring abolition, hastened by changing attitudes in the maritime-inspired world, its main financial beneficiary, using reason, promoted by Quakers and Methodists, increasingly supported by the mainstream. Britain's government inched toward abolition in the 1770s-1790s. Laurence Sterne, author of *Tristram Shandy*, one of the great comic novels, wrote a 1776 denunciation of slavery, part of growing abolitionist literature. Wide publication of horrific incidents led to growing revulsion, allied with humanitarianism, which contemporaries called sensibility, formed from older ideas of liberty ingrained in the English psyche, newly harnessed in North America. Simultaneously, France supported slave trading, subsidising shipowners as booming coffee, cotton and sugar demanded more. Marxists however, contend that slave-trading was abolished because it was no longer profitable, so capitalists manipulated humanitarian sentiments; a ridiculous, cynical view, alien to facts and common sense. Merchants, slavers, shipowners, insurance brokers etc. were and are not mere instruments of their balance sheets and profit and loss accounts. Ideas influenced them. Diminishing genuine feelings distorts what happened and undervalues emerging humanitarianism as a supremely important event.

Apart from plantation slavery itself, was slave trading profitable? It is difficult to disentangle when ships also carried sugar, tobacco and rice. Revenues fluctuated, especially in war when merchants had ships captured or sunk. *The Davenport Papers*, the 1757–1784 ledgers of William Davenport and partners show examples of broken partnerships, failed ventures, fluctuating profit margins, high risk and uncertainty. One thorough analysis concludes an average 10.5% profit, only due to two voyages ending 72 others yielding only 4.3%.[20] 'It is a precarious trade, profits are sometimes good, sometimes not,' declared Bristol trader James Jones to a 1788 House of Commons Commission. Precarious meant West African delays, fever to the crew, on-board slave revolts, deaths *en route*, poor quality on delivery thus low prices and ever-present threats of war and capture. So why continue? Because merchants and shipowners are optimists and opportunists. Slaves were not the only Atlantic cargoes and shipowners, knowing freight markets fluctuate, tolerated low returns for exceptional profitable voyages, as *The Davenport Papers* show. West African gold, ivory, timber, dyewoods, gum, leather, malaguetta pepper and palm oil were as important and more valuable, while plantations depended on imported clothes, tools, food, leather and household goods.

In 1783 William Pitt estimated Caribbean slave trade profits accounted for 80% of Britain's overseas income, crucial to British prosperity.[21] *The Davenport Papers* do not support that, but as it was inextricably tied-up with sugar, coffee and cotton, hyperbole is understandable, but about 18,000 people <u>were</u> employed in manufacturing goods sold to Africa for slaves, about 4.4% of British exports.[22] Adam Smith argued that slavery was inefficient because it constrained individuals from acting in their own self-interest. 'A person who can acquire no property can have no other interest but to eat as much and to labour as little as possible.' But it cut no ice with planters who knew its inefficiencies, but saw no practical alternative. As a friend told William Wilberforce, Parliament had to act, not for national self-interest, but 'in some form of heroism.'[23]

Reformers used Britain's legal system. English Common Law was still not properly codified. From Sir John Fortescue's 1470 *De Laudibus Legum Angliae* (published 1543), Sir Edward Coke (1552–1634) justified Parliament's role to protect law and liberty, the essence of national identity against the Stuarts. Fortescue, shocked at the extreme poverty and misery of French peasants in 'the most fertile realm', eloquently expressed Anglo-French differences; England's king ruled under the law, France's king <u>was</u> the law. Little had changed since he saw conditions in the Hundred Years War campaigns! Montesquieu thought Britain the only nation where political and civil liberty was 'the direct end of its constitution.'[24] Uncertainty regarding Common Law's logical implementation was tackled by City merchant's son and barrister, William Blackstone (1723–1780) in his 1756 *An Analysis of the Laws of England* and his 1766 four-volume *Commentaries on the Laws of England*, still used in the 1870s. He argued the 'excellence of English government' was because 'all parts of it form a mutual check upon each other.'[25] The idea of checks and balances influenced the US Constitution. Blackstone's first edition emphasised 'liberty…deeply implicated in our constitution…the moment [a slave]…lands in England [he] becomes a freeman.' He emphasised Parliamentary sovereignty, treating the law in moderate, liberal, common-sense ways, espousing the principle, 'better that ten guilty persons escape than one innocent suffers,' first expressed by Fortescue's earlier work, but became known as Blackstone's ratio. *Commentaries* was a guide to implement evolving rational, liberal principles consistent with a maritime-inspired, pluralist society, allowing flexible responses to economic and social change.

In 1765 an 18-year-old black slave Jonathan Strong was brought to England and so badly beaten by his master David Lisle that, abandoned and close to death, he managed to find William Sharp's Mincing Lane surgery, which treated the poor for free. After four months in St. Bartholomew's Hospital, Sharp's brother Granville, earlier apprenticed to a Quaker linen draper, arranged employment for two years. Lisle accidentally saw him, kidnapped him and sold him for £30, payable once on-board a Caribbean-bound ship. Granville took the case to court. Strong was discharged as he had committed no crime. Lisle sued Sharp for depriving him of his property. Granville replied that any person who came to England automatically became free as he became a king's subject and therefore subject to *Habeas Corpus*. It was ruled that English Common Law made no provision for slavery.

Sharp's legal research found the precedent of an English captain bringing a Russian serf to England in 1569 in which a justice ruled that 'England was too pure an air for slaves to breathe.' In 1706 Chief Justice Holt ruled, 'as soon as a negro comes into England, he becomes free.'[26] Sharp tested his argument when another slave, James Somerset arrived with his master, escaped, was recaptured and confined in irons on a Caribbean-bound ship. Lord Mansfield, a natural conservative, disliking the institution, was well-aware of his 1772 ruling's economic consequences, pronouncing *Fiat justicia, ruat caelum*; Let justice be done though the heavens fall. He found no English law allowing slavery. He didn't say that slaves were free when they landed on English soil but that slave masters had no right to transport slaves from England. Both sides thought he had made slavery illegal in England.[27] Pennsylvania made it so in 1780.

While planters found ways round the judgement, like apprenticing slaves, the widely-reported Somerset case, Caribbean slavery's realities, boosted abolitionism. Thomas Day's 1773 *The Dying Negro*, the horrific story of a runaway slave, became a best seller. Sharp supported American independence and in 1789 joined the Society for Constitutional Information, for social reformers, supported Parliamentary reform and traditional English libertarian ideas. Plantation owner William Beckford, who unlike his pioneering ancestors grew-up in England, visited Jamaica in 1774, immediately detesting the cruelty inflicted on slaves and after a couple of years worried that he was becoming inured to it, one of many experiencing such feelings.[28]

In 1783 the slave ship *Zong* hit the headlines. Carrying 442 slaves, lost and short of water, the Master threw 133 into the sea, claiming the loss on his insurance policy, necessary for the crew's safety. Mansfield thought it 'very shocking,' and it heightened British humanitarianism. In 1784 Reverend James Ramsey who had lived in St. Kitts, published *An Essay on the Treatment and Conversion of African Slaves in the British Sugar Colonies and an Inquiry into the Effects of the Abolition of the Slave Trade*, arguing that immediate abolition would force better treatment. Ardent abolitionist Peter Peckard (1717–97), Master of Magdalene College, Cambridge (1784–85) and University Vice Chancellor set the Latin prize essay, *Liceat Invitos Servitutem Dare? Is it right to make slaves of others against their will?* In 1787 Thomas Clarkson, influenced by Quaker Anthony Benezet's tract on slavery and slave trading won it, accepting Peckard as 'first among the activists.' Re-written in English, it was immediately influential. In 1787 he, MP William Wilberforce, Granville Sharp and friends formed the Abolition Committee to campaign for it. In 1788 Peckard anonymously published a 100-page booklet, *Am I not a Man? and a Brother?* arguing greater commercial advantage would accrue from legitimate trade. The title became the movement's slogan.[29] Wilberforce proposed abolition to the Commons in 1791. Supported by William Pitt and Charles James Fox, it was defeated 163–88. He also sought general reform and enlightenment, lobbying for more churches, immersing himself in St. Bartholomew's Hospital affairs after discovering patient abuse and supported Jeremy Bentham's idea of model prisons,[30] while *The Times* began publishing abolitionist arguments more frequently.

As debate continued, public opinion was further mobilised. Clarkson promoted Asian sugar produced by free labour. He thought 300,000 people switched.[31] Although the aim was abolition of slavery, the first realisable goal was slave trading. Rhode Island banned its citizens from it. Tens of thousands of abolitionist tracts were distributed in England, read by an increasingly literate public. Clarkson toured, spoke to crowds, presented facts and arguments to Parliament. Petitions poured in from all areas and social classes. Public opinion counted! The *Société des Amis des Noirs*, founded by a French lawyer in London, did convert the Marquis de Lafayette and Vicomte Mirabeau, but as French sugar merchants enjoyed St. Domingue's boom and impoverished peasants were more concerned with daily needs, there was no chance of similar large-scale French support.

Medallions were produced indicating sympathy for abolition. Josiah Wedgwood in the 1750s led English pottery to new heights, experimenting in cream-ware, jasperware and basalt glazes, converting to coal as they required high temperatures, his techniques' popularity transforming Burslem's artisan works into the first pottery factory. He produced a seal showing a slave kneeling in chains with Peckard's *Am I not a man and a brother?* which were impressed on snuff boxes, bracelets and hair pins. Wedgwood estimated about 50 potteries employing perhaps 500 people around 1700–1715. By 1762 there were 150 employing 7,000 and by 1800, probably around 300 employing 315,0000. In 1785 Staffordshire potters' Committee of Commerce reported that five sixths of the area's earthenware production was exported to Europe. America took 1.2 million pieces in 1770, 17.5 million in 1835, to Europe's 10.8 million pieces.[32] Wedgwood transformed a peasant craft into an industry with a world market. A major backer of the Trent and Mersey Canal, connecting the factory to Liverpool, he also improved roads, canals, schools and built a village for his workers at Etruria, named after recently excavated Etruscan pottery. Interested in scientific progress, he was elected to the Royal Society in 1783 for inventing the pyrometer, which measured high kiln temperatures during pottery firing. Wedgwood touched all aspects of the enquiring, enlightened age.

Drawings of cramped stowage on slave ships made an instant impression. Poems were written, paintings painted, Parliament petitioned, even from Liverpool and Manchester, whose cotton imports and industry depended on slave-grown cotton. Facts were collected about British sailors' mortality on slave ships, much higher than onboard slave mortality. Wilberforce wrote 'This trade instead of being…a nursery of seamen, may be rather termed their grave; it consumes annually a quarter of those engaged in it,'[33] highlighting how little value seafarers' lives were valued; slaves more valuable! The 1788 Dolben Bill, passing narrowly, gave more ship space to slaves. Wilberforce told the Commons that better plantation treatment would lessen deaths and replenishment needs. Estates became better regulated and less cruel. In the 1790s British slavers transported about 400,000. In 1798, 150 ships left Liverpool for Africa, the most recorded. St. Domingue's 1791 destruction (see Chapter 12) and war pushed sugar prices higher, encouraging Caribbean and Brazilian planters' slave purchases as Cuban sugar exports became significant, importing 14,000 slaves annually, mainly in British and US ships.

As the movement grew and abolition seemed a matter of time, many Liverpool slave traders diversified in West African cocoa, ground nuts and gum, Senegal's major 18th-century export. Wilberforce tried demonstrating that slaving was only a 30th of Liverpool's total trade, West African imports and manufactured exports more beneficial and predictable. Clarkson believed its wealth was built more on its openness, salt exports, Lancashire's canals, increasing population and Manchester's manufacturing. Spearheading Parliamentary opposition, Liverpool's MP argued that abolition would destroy its economy, hurt Lancashire's manufacturing and British economic competitiveness, that French, Spanish, Portuguese and Dutch would take advantage.

Mansfield was also active in codifying maritime insurance law, establishing insurers' and insured legal rights so that underwriters, merchants and brokers understood the issues. He and underwriters developed the <u>science</u> of insurance, modern concepts of surveying, total loss, constructive total loss, laws and codes of salvage, adjustment, war risks, risks of carrying cargoes that might shift, liabilities according to the time a ship was in enemy hands, storm damage, codification, the roles of bills of lading and methods of ship construction. The 1906 Marine Insurance Act was a lineal descendant of his work. He and his successors made London paramount in maritime law and arbitration, most from non-British parties.[34] This legacy endures. Without maritime insurance definitions and forensic analysis, British commerce could not have generated the surplus capital necessary for further technical and commercial advances. Every damaged cargo, overdue ship, early arrival, grounding and sinking was recorded by *Lloyds List* from 1734, reliable information in war, after 1739 needed more than ever!

The EIC was also part of British Enlightenment, discontinuing Indian Ocean slave trading in 1764. Famine was a hazard of India's monsoon-dominated climate. For Mughals and previous Hindu states, it reduced revenues, but was never seen in the context of Court extravagance. The emerging British sense of responsibility and virtue meant opulence in such times appeared excessive and insensitive. EIC historian John Keay thinks the 1770 famine 'dates the first firm evidence of…company servants evincing a genuine concern for the lot of the peasant.'[35] In 1774 Governor-General Warren Hastings declared 'the practice of stealing children from their parents and selling them for slaves has long prevailed in this country,' which was a 'savage commerce,' the only way of 'remedying this calamitous evil,' abolish slavery.[36] The 1785 Indian famine, led to hundreds of children sold into slavery. Sir William Jones told a Calcutta grand jury, 'the condition of slaves within our jurisdiction is beyond imagination; deplorable and cruelties daily practiced on them, chiefly on those of the tenderest age and weaker sex.' Madras EIC official Samuel Baron increased grain shipments to Bengal to relieve the famine, hoping for a plentiful rainy season, despite shipments enriching merchants, as 'there can be no advantage more uncomfortable than that which arises from the poverty and misery of the poor.'[37] In 1787, Bencoolen's slaves were emancipated. No other European country had a groundswell of enlightened anti-slavery opinion or humanitarianism. In 1789 Cornwallis banned slave exports from Bengal. Madras followed in 1790. He wrote to EIC directors that he was considering abolishing slavery throughout EIC territories, without antagonising locals; seemingly gradual emancipation. In 1790 EIC directors commended him for prosecuting a master for transporting Bengali slaves to Ceylon.

Yet in a strange retrospective construct, this emerging humanitarianism is side-lined in favour of European, usually French Enlightenment led by *philosophes*, Voltaire, Diderot, Montesquieu, D'Alembert, etc. Equally strange, Scots like Francis Hutcheson, David Hume, Adam Smith and Thomas Reid, are included, as are German philosophers, Wolff, Lessing and Kant, but no English. Newton, Hobbes and Locke are mentioned as forerunners but, apart from Scots, it is apparently a purely continental phenomena and British-American abolitionism is ignored. Out-dated historical constructs tend to persevere long after logic has disproved them.[38] Gertrude Himmelfarb especially has criticised this Enlightenment interpretation, separating British, American and French political and social thinking. Scottish philosophers, economists and industrialists were from its vibrant ports, part of British Enlightenment, different from French *philosophes* and she notes, 'Britain had more moral philosophers, a very different breed.'[39] Voltaire's cry, *Ecrasez l'infame*, 'Crush the infamous' and Rousseau were anti-Church, anti-clerical and anti-government, whereas much British and American enlightenment was spread by dissenting Christian sects, mainstream Anglicans like Wilberforce, EIC officials, senior politicians and university dons; part of British society, working with, not against government. Himmelfarb thinks the Enlightenment's association with France and *philosophes* 'a puzzle'.[40] It probably started because French was the language of continental diplomacy, fashion and culture, one reason for Dutch decline, their establishment seduced by it. British thinkers she insists were consistently under-estimated, their ideas more durable. she aims 'to reclaim the Enlightenment…above all from the French who have dominated and usurped it.' Agreed. This series of books on maritime trade demonstrate that all maritime societies throughout history were forward-thinking, innovative and tolerant. In this period Britain added a moral aspect.

In the French Enlightenment myth, the *Encyclopedie* (1751–72) takes centre stage. Its inspiration was Britain's 1728 *Chambers Cyclopedia*, translated into French in 1743. Edited by Diderot, its 28 volumes, over 70,000 articles by over 140 contributors, aimed to be a compendium of human knowledge, abstract, theoretical, practical, mechanical, agricultural, scientific and technical, but was not as useful as British books which catalogued unfolding discoveries. Steam power efficiency had been tabulated from the 1710s. Lists and detailed descriptions of practices in farming, geology and water mill performance helped engineers and producers improve performance. Joel Mokyr calculates 18th-century scientific periodicals averaged 21 annually during 1700–1710, 34 in the 1720s, 77 in the 1740s and 531 in the 1790s, mainly in Britain, cataloguing 'useful knowledge'.[41] Unlike Himmelfarb, Mokyr joins all Enlightenments, their 'common denominator…the belief in the possibility of human progress…through reason and knowledge,' but as Himmelfarb explains, very differently. John Darwin, taking a global perspective, says enlightenment was the 'collapse of the scholarship monopoly of classical knowledge that remained so immensely powerful in Islamic and Confucian culture.'[42] Asking why, he answers 'the growth of trade…not just long distance…commercialisation was a political and cultural as well as an economic phenomenon. It unsettled old habits, promoted new tastes, created new discontents, disempowered old rulers and advanced new interests' and 'some parts of Europe were more successful than others at adapting to the demands of commercialisation and exploiting its benefits.'[43] Precisely; the maritime parts!

The *Encyclopedie's* mantra was reason, although not shared by Montesquieu and Rousseau. the latter dismissed by Voltaire as a Judas and by Diderot as an *anti-philosophe*.[44] It included an essay on slave trafficking as a violation of religion, morality, natural law and human rights but most *philosophes* thought it necessary. While Dr. Johnson pronounced a toast, 'to the next insurrection of the negroes in the West Indies,' Montesquieu condemned slavery in the name of morality, but maintained its economic justification; 'sugar would be too expensive were…it not worked by slaves.'

After the Great Northern War, Sweden regained strength by economic not military means, rational for a lightly-populated, maritime-orientated country, especially with timber, bar iron, hemp, tar and wax exports. Embracing science for national recovery, the Royal Swedish Academy of Sciences was founded in 1739. Uppsala University established chairs in physics and chemistry, essential in understanding blast furnace and forge technology.[45] Some historians think Rinman's 1789 *Bergwerks Lexicon* more practical than the *Encyclopedie's* <u>abstract</u> sections on manufacturing, because it analysed puddling, the most important 18th-century iron-making innovation.[46] Sweden's iron exports, especially to Britain, peaked in the 1790s as Henry Cort's puddling and rolling techniques were perfected, leading to huge expansion in malleable bar iron production. Cataloguing progress was not based on the *Encyclopedie* but incremental British reports. Equally important, between 1771 and 1815, four editions of *Encyclopaedia Britannica* were published, each with huge sales and with *Chambers Cyclopedia*, <u>unlike</u> the *Encyclopedie*, still today.

Britain's government gave Newton a knighthood, a lucrative government office and a state funeral, its politicians, merchants, colonists all steeped in ideas of freedom. In France however, Diderot was imprisoned, Montesquieu censored. Voltaire and Rousseau self-exiled in Britain. Inspired by British freedom they adopted some enlightened thinking. But without the idea of balance of powers, without Blackstone, Mansfield, maritime tradition, trade-created wealth, higher living standards, better food, consumer goods and schooling, a dynamic society and economy, they misapplied them. As Edmund Burke remarked, they displayed a bigotry of their own' and 'talk against monks with the spirit of a monk.'[47]

The French Enlightenment was patronised by Louis XV's main mistress, Madame de Pompadour. Voltaire directed his abstract thoughts at so-called Enlightened Despots, centralising their regimes of serf estates. He courted aristocrats and ministers, corresponding with Prussia's Frederick II, Diderot with Russia's Catherine II. Voltaire defended Catherine who 'seeks to destroy anarchy, the odious prerogatives of the nobles…[and] intermediate bodies.'[48] Like despots, *philosophes* had no regard for ordinary people, who lacked intellect to reason, were controlled by superstition and religion, which 'must be destroyed among respectable people…left to the *canaille*,' the rabble. Diderot thought 'common people…incredibly stupid.' 'The general mass of men are not made that they can either promote or understand this forward march of the human spirit.' They are 'too idiotic, <u>bestial</u>, too miserable and too busy' to be enlightened. Voltaire was also anti-Semitic, thinking Jewish expulsion from Spain deserved, as they controlled money and commerce.[49] Only Montesquieu believed in separation of executive, legislative and judicial powers, checks and balances, other *philosophes* that it threatened enlightened monarchs' power. Only Montesquieu grasped political practicalities.

Rousseau thought 'the common good of men did not necessarily mean of man', so education for commoners, unnecessary. Voltaire thought 'the cultivation of land required only a very common kind of intelligence', that 'these people did not have the capacity to learn.' 'It [is] essential that they be beggars.'[50] Holbach criticised Adam Smith's 'sympathy' for others' distress. The failure of Enlightened Despots as instruments of what passed for enlightenment led to Rousseau's idea of sovereignty of the people, the 'general will'; the alternative to enlightened despots. Used in the French Revolution, it was disastrous. All British improvers were far more important than French *philosophes*. The so-called Scottish Enlightenment over-contributed in many fields but was not separate, but culturally united and British. EIC officials felt responsibility for Indians over whom they ruled. They were curious about their culture, antiquity and languages and ameliorated slave conditions or freed them; practical application of real enlightenment.

Norman Davies's description of Europe's Enlightenment[51] highlights Polish educational projects including Europe's first ministry of state education in 1772–73.[52] Most Enlightenment discussion however is obscured by lack of definition. Was it a mainly French-inspired, pan-European or really a British-inspired rational, practical, scientific, industrial and moral movement? Poland's 1791 Constitution brought peasants into public law and enfranchised some of the middle class. Burke thought it 'probably the most pure…public good…on mankind…everything was kept in its place [but]…bettered…[and] not one drop of blood was spilled.' But Russia would not tolerate a constitutional, independent, adjacent Poland and annexed much of it while Prussia took Danzig, which being a free-thinking port, rebelled.[53] This partition was justified by Enlightenment because it 'rationalised' Europe; actually Russian propaganda, addicted to territorial conquest and elimination of other cultures. Bertrand Russell thought the Enlightenment a progressive development beginning in antiquity, rekindled after the Reformation, which although he did not link it, coincided with wider, more voluminous maritime trade. Protestant liberty to question gradually emerged. It was a maritime phenomenon, an extension of Europe's recovery from the Dark Ages. Wealth created in ports crept inland and as usual, ideas followed, some barely understood by continentalists.

British Enlightenment was another example of how maritime and continental societies are different. British and American abolitionists used reason and humanitarian feelings, allied with faith and morality. Wesley for example, argued that if 'religion and reason go hand-in-hand,' it could overcome wickedness and bigotry. British clergymen, far from resisting the unveiling of the universe's mysteries, embraced Newtonian physics to prove God's intelligent design. In Britain, education was independent after the 1689 Act of Toleration, while in France, priests continued controlling colleges. Technical creativity required political and economic, above all intellectual liberation.

All led to ways in which people thought about slavery and individual freedom, only possible in maritime cultures.

Abolitionism was part of greater enlightened maritime thinking. Raised by Quakers, James Cook (1728–1779) trained on east coast colliers, taught himself maths, charted the St. Lawrence during Wolfe's capture of Quebec, choosing a sturdy collier for his Pacific voyages, (1768–71, 1772–75 and 1776–79) the Royal Society's attempt to study its peoples scientifically, to find the southern Continent and expand British trade. The second voyage's aims were defined by the Board of Longitude, well after John Harrison's H4. Before the expedition, Royal Society President Lord Joseph Morton asked Cook and botanist Joseph Banks (1743–1820), later also President, to treat natives 'with utmost patience and forbearance' as 'the shedding of blood of those people is a crime of the highest nature. They are human creatures…the legal possessors of several regions they inhabit. No European nation has a right to occupy any part of their country or settle amongst them without their voluntary consent.'[54]

Results however were often unintended. Contact with native islanders produced a demographic disaster similar to 16th-century America. Britain reserved huge areas for native Americans, out-of-bounds to settlers; reversed after independence. Pitt's India Act prevented officials profiting at Indian expense, just as Lancashire's cotton started penetrating Indian cotton markets. By contrast, Calvinist Dutch shared Catholic Portuguese and Spanish belief in Europeans' right to exploit lesser breeds. In 1675 when Batavia's Governor-General sent food to relieve famine in Ceylon, he was censured. 'Feeding the people is really no concern of ours.'[55] When Dutch massacred most Chinese in Batavia in 1740 to forestall an imaginary rebellion, China's government was as indifferent as when Spanish massacred Manila's Chinese over a century earlier. Batavia's households had 50–60 slaves each for trifling domestic duties, the more slaves, the more prestige. Perhaps the cruellest slavery was in Dutch Surinam, triggering endemic revolts.[56]

Many British industrialists discussed scientific, cultural and philosophic issues at natural philosophy societies like the Lunar Society. Members included Mathew Boulton, James Watt, Josiah Wedgwood, Joseph Priestly, authors Anna Seward and Thomas Day, who wrote in 1776, 'if there be an object truly ridiculous in nature it is the American patriot signing resolutions of independency with the one hand and with the other brandishing a whip over his affrighted slaves.' They included painters, poets, architects and landscape gardeners, exchanging philosophical and scientific ideas, while trying to solve practical problems of technology, economics, manufacture, marketing and supply chains: bridging philosophy and practical knowledge.

Priestly, a natural philosopher, wrote over 150 publications on education, electricity, the standard text for a century, was credited with discovering various gases including oxygen, more famous at the time for inventing soda water in 1770. Other members were; John Smeaton (1724–1792), civil engineer who designed bridges, canals, harbours and lighthouses, eminent physicist and Royal Society fellow, winning an award for research into increased waterwheel and windmill efficiency; Erasmus Darwin (1731–1802), natural philosopher, physician, poet, abolitionist and botanist, grandfather of Charles who preceded the theory of evolution and survival of the fittest, asking 'would it be too bold to imagine that all warm bloodied animals have arisen from one living filament?' suggesting 'the strongest and most active animal…propagate the species.' He promoted women's education, was a prolific inventor, researched cloud formation and experimented with air and gases for clinical use; Richard Lovell Edgeworth (1744–1817), politician, writer and inventor; James Kier (1735–1820) chemist, geologist, inventor and industrialist in glass, chemicals and soap, working closely with Priestly on gaseous properties and with Darwin on botanical subjects; William Small (1734–1775) was Thomas Jefferson's professor; Jonathan Stokes (1755–1831) and William Withering (1741–1797) were physicians and botanists, the latter also geologist, chemist, discovering digitalis's medical uses and much other chemical and geological discoveries.[57] Boulton and Watt's 1775 steam engine company drove industrialisation. Wedgwood described Boulton, also a Kirwan's Coffee House Philosophical Society member, as 'philosophical'. Boulton thought Paris in 1786–87 a scientific, experimental wasteland compared to British cities.[58]

Northeast England's mines shipped coal to London, increasingly Holland, which in the 1720s imported 100,000 tons annually and other European ports, facilitating brewing, dyeing, sugar and salt refining, soap boiling, glass making, metal smelting and casting. Britain's northwest's coalfields were less favourably positioned. The Duke of Bridgewater (1736–1803) built a ten-mile canal in 1761 from Worsley's mines to Manchester's cotton manufacturers, halving its coal price, generating £80,000 annual revenue, spurring a 20-year canal-building boom to carry coal, ore and provisions by water, cheaper and more efficiently to industry. James Brindley (1716–1772), in contact with Smeaton, in 1752 designed a steam engine to drain Clifton's coal pits. Instead of locks, Brindley built a level canal with an underground tunnel and aqueduct and was influential in the 42-feet-high Barton Aqueduct over the River Irwell, with puddled clay for a watertight channel. He built 360 miles of canals including the 1777 Trent and Mersey Canal linking Liverpool to Staffordshire's potteries, promoted by Wedgwood and the Grand Trunk Canal through the Pennines, effectively linking the Irish and North Seas, enabling Lancashire's textile exports via Hull. Agriculture improved, providing for the growing population. The United Provinces 150 years earlier also had constitutional government dominated by a trade-dedicated elite, enforced by a dominant navy, low interest rates, manufacturing innovations, agriculture and transport, a free press and 'liberty to discuss new ideas and exploit new inventions.'[59] By 1800 British coal output exceeded Europe's seven-fold.[60] In 1784 Henry Cort was the first British ironmaster to sell the Royal Navy wrought iron for anchors. France's iron industry lacked technical innovation, the state its only market.

Interacting disciplines, inventions and thinking were industrial and enlightened. Engineering is not less intellectual or creative. British Enlightenment was home-grown and deep with literary and philosophical societies multiplying. By 1815 every important town had a library. Davy, Dalton and Stephenson were members of societies in Bristol, Manchester and Newcastle, searching for 'useful knowledge'. There were chemist, meteorologist and geologist Richard Kirwan (1773–1812); lecturer in natural philosophy and scientist Henry Moyes (1750–1807), John 'Iron-mad' Wilkinson (1728–1808), pioneer manufacturer of cast iron, who invented a boring machine for cast iron cylinders for steam engines and a blowing machine to increase furnace temperatures, involved in the first iron bridge at Ironbridge in 1779 and launched the first iron barge in 1787. He bought shares in eight Cornish tin mines, had a lead pipe works in Rotherhithe, built cottages for workers' families and financially supported brother-in-law Joseph Priestly. In 1796 he produced an eighth of Britain's cast iron. Joseph Black (1728–1799), son of a merchant specialising in Bordeaux wine imports was Professor of Anatomy and Chemistry at Glasgow University. Observing that heating boiling water increased steam, he funded Watt's early steam engine research. John Mitchell (1724–1793) was first to suggest the existence of black holes, that earthquakes travel in waves and how magnets are made. James Hutton (1726–1794) was geologist, physician, chemical manufacturer and naturalist, involved in building the Forth and Clyde Canal and the Royal Society of Edinburgh, Scotland's national academy covering sciences, philosophy, humanities, medicine and arts. The range and depth impresses; improvements in all fields, practical, moral, political, social, scientific and artistic, the tip of the iceberg of an enquiring maritime-inspired society, seeking improvements and better understanding of their world in virtuous, morally responsible ways.

Edmund Burke thought virtue and religious toleration the basis of liberty, supported American colonists' rights, urging his government, who suspended *Habeas Corpus* at home, to respect the liberty of both Americans and British and attacked corruption in India. Expected to support the French Revolution as many British celebrated the Bastille's storming, his *Reflections on the Revolution in France* argued that destruction of France's social fabric risked descent into barbarism and tyranny. Tom Paine earlier crystalised American opinion with *Common Sense* (1776), arguing that people could govern themselves without monarchy. His 1792 *Rights of Man* influenced by Locke's *Second Treatise of Government* countered Burke, that political revolution <u>is</u> permissible when governments do not safeguard people's natural rights; the only way to abolish despotic monarchy. His 1797 *Agrarian Justice* advocated an estate tax, inheritance tax and land value tax to fund old age and disability pensions. Burke thought long-term liberty was preserved by society's bonds, ordered society and <u>evolving</u>, interlocking liberties, obligations and institutions, not imposed from above, but grown organically, rather than abstract principles, which did not guarantee liberty. Paine later said that his religion was 'to do good', protect the weak, influenced by his Quaker father. Both expressed liberal, enlightened ideas but Paine in leaning towards French <u>abstract</u> idealism was proved wrong, Burke's gradual improvement, reform within the political tradition, right.

In economics Adam Smith argued that self-interested individuals advanced society's interests because of free market competition, that regulation, high import duties and monopolies pushed prices higher, benefitting a minority, not most people. 'Commerce which ought naturally to be, among nations as among individuals, a bond of union and friendship, has become the most fertile source of discord and animosity.' He showed that freely initiated trade benefited both parties, specialisation allowed economies of scale, improving efficiency and growth and was pro-abolition on moral <u>and</u> rational grounds. His *An Inquiry into the Nature and Causes of the Wealth of Nations* (1776), logical, rational and humane, was instantly successful. Its most novel aspect was that national power rested on the 'lower ranks', their well-being and wealth promoted by a progressive political economy, that self-interest in a free market and competition benefits all society, that monopolies were inefficient, protecting narrow interests, that society cannot flourish when most are poor and miserable; the <u>economic</u> counterpart to his 1759 ethical *Theory of Moral Sentiments*.[61]

Hume also contrasted the state's greatness and the subject's happiness. Jeremy Bentham's (1748–1832) *Theory of Legislation* (1776) similarly promoted reform on the principle of 'the greatest happiness to the greatest number', becoming known as utilitarianism, a label masking its part of a greater British enlightenment. Bentham disagreed with Blackstone, wanting a codification of common law, rather than Blackstone's defence of judge-made law, but it added to enlightened debate. His *Principles of Morals and Legislation* (1781) provided a scientific basis for legal, social and moral reforms, calculating the consequence of every piece of legislation on his principles' basis. Simultaneously, Pitt led efforts to liberalise trade and reduce tariffs.

The main so-called Enlightened Despots, Catherine, Frederick Il and Joseph II, paid lip-service to some flawed *philosophe* ideas while strengthening their power at the expense of Church, nobility and intermediate bodies. Frederick thought his subjects 'imbecile people', peasants and serfs 'cannon fodder'. Rigid social divisions meant merchants could not acquire land, everything organised for the army's benefit. Only Joseph abolished serfdom in his own lands but not labour service and limited noble's right to punish peasants. He dissolved 700 monasteries, using the funds to promote education and poor relief, but the main aim was strengthening monarchical power against the nobility and bishops who took oaths of allegiance, turning them into state servants. Montesquieu's and Rousseau's 'natural law' was used to justify ancient liberties of competing, privileged *ancien regime* groups; aristocrats and parlements. Joseph's successor restored serfdom. Russia saw its first university, library, theatre and museum; skin-deep events at best. In Spain, Charles III (1759–1788) tried rescuing his decayed regime by weakening the Church and monasteries, promoting science, trade and agriculture. A professional colonial administration was created, restrictions on internal trade removed, except for cotton, wine and silver. Duties were simplified and reduced; trade opened to all Spanish ports. Consequentially, between 1778 and 1790 Spanish colonial trade more than quadrupled and customs revenues increased to 1796, but in Spain 'free trade' meant <u>permitted Spanish</u> trade.[62] After his death, Spain relapsed. French Enlightenment achieved nothing except its baleful influence on the French Revolution.

France's *philosophes* disagreed with each other about many things but agreed that colonies drained resources, involving it in conflicts with Britain, territories like French Canada, administratively corrupt and loss-making. But France's Caribbean islands were hugely productive. In 1750 French Canada had 59,000 people against nearly two million North American British-origin inhabitants, <u>but</u> had 414,000 against 245,000 in the Caribbean. Some *philosophes* accepted this, but Voltaire especially thought France should play to her advantage, armies and land with no colonies. It would not have stopped war, because after 1688, fear of French control of the Netherlands, her centuries-old aim, always threatened British interests. Voltaire's traditional continental dominance was hardly enlightened thinking. Initially he looked to China for inspiration, seemingly a vast, harmonious, sophisticated meritocracy without hereditary distinctions, ruled by tea-drinking scholars. Chinese design in rugs, porcelain, gardens and furniture became fashionable, millions of porcelain cups and plates shipped every year. Canton's *hong* system restricted European vision to Canton's waterfront. Lord Macartney's 1792–94 mission penetrated the interior, noting its poverty and weakness. Gradually a realistic view, that its emperors were uninterested in material progress, emerged. Montesquieu, Rousseau and Hegel eventually realised it. Montesquieu thought it despotic 'whose principle is fear.' Adam Smith reflected that poverty and isolation masked lethargic despotism, lack of invention, military weakness and vulnerability.

Practical enlightenment was exercised by EIC slave emancipators, Josiah Wedgwood, Adam Smith and James Watt, whose son, visiting Paris in 1784 was shocked how nobles' coaches were driven with total disregard for people's safety. 'One would think that the common people here were looked upon as different creatures.'[63] In Britain, Parliament determined policy. No minister, even strongly Crown-supported, survived its displeasure. In culture, Bach, Hayden and Mozart were patronised by princes. Defoe, Swift and Fielding relied on a buying public.[64] Clyde-based inventive engineers developed steam engine technology, applying it to ship propulsion. Canal building, Lancashire's textile machinery improvement, Liverpool's port modernisation, inventive commercial and financial flair were examples of a burgeoning creative, problem-solving culture, where enlightenment flourished. Europe's so-called enlightenments were driven by a few writers. British Enlightenment went deep into society, novelists, philosophers, inventors, scientists in mechanics, medicine, political science, history, literature, ceramics, astronomy, geology, all aspects of intellectual and practical advancement and morality. Skin-deep French Enlightenment ended in a revolutionary *cul-de-sac*. British Enlightenment continued. Blackstone's influence lasted over 100 years in America and Britain. European humanitarianism never emerged organically.

Part Two

Revolutions

Chapter 9

The American Revolution and Atlantic Trade

Conventionally, America's War of Independence and *Declaration of Independence* were about noble issues; 'no taxation without representation', a slogan used for 30 years in Ireland. With only 10% of 1775's taxable males able to vote,[1] representation rhetoric was convenient propaganda. It was about smuggling; American merchants trading with non-British Caribbean islands, evading Navigation Acts with the French and Dutch Caribbean, exasperating British authorities. *Declaration* signatory John Hancock had 500 smuggling indictments against him.[2] Boston's economy heavily depended on avoiding duties. Thomas Hutchinson thought 75% of imported consumer goods illegal, especially Chinese tea, that people were so used to 'illicit trade [they]…see no evil in it.'[3] New England's Caribbean trade overtook its British trade in the 1740s. Britain showed flexibility, allowing South Carolina to export rice to the Mediterranean for fruit, salt and wine and New England's cod to Bilbao for wine fruit and iron, because while British 1700–1770 exports to heavily protected Europe increased 6%, to the Americas it rose 687%, from £461,000 to £3,628,000, stimulating British manufacturing.

The 1733 Molasses Act imposed prohibitive duties on French molasses. New England ports evaded it. Its cheapest fish went to Caribbean slaves, especially fast-growing St. Domingue. Timber, flour, bread, rum and meat were exchanged for molasses, sugar, cotton and salt. Connecticut exported vegetables, Maryland wheat, Pennsylvania corn and cattle. By the 1730s Barbados molasses cost 10d/gallon, Martinique's 4d. New England bought it. Barbados lobbied Parliament to tax it.[4] Martinique supplied Rhode Island's 30 rum distilleries. Of 14,000 imported hogsheads of molasses only 2,500 were from British islands. Rum was New England's most popular drink, 1760s annual consumption 3.75 gallons/person.[5] 1762–63's American trade with French islands was so blatant that insurance rates for St. Domingue voyages were openly quoted in Rhode Island.[6] Almost half North America's Caribbean imports in the late-1760s were from French islands.[7] Britain had won the Seven Years War with little help from American legislatures, reluctant to vote funds for over 30,000 British soldiers defending them, while supplying French islands and limiting British revenue, as the National Debt rose from £74.6 million to £132.6 million.

Illegal Caribbean trade hindered British naval supremacy, so it tried strengthening North American customs operations, changing from protecting trade and developing markets into a not unreasonable belief that colonists should contribute to their £225,000 annual defence costs. Grenville, following Bute in 1763, thought preventing conflict with native Americans would save money and show responsibility, so the 1763 Proclamation forbade westward expansion past the Alleghenies. But settlement was already well beyond. Many invested or speculated in land. In 1765 a Stamp Act charged a direct tax rather than customs duty. The Massachusetts Legislature objected, 'If our trade may be taxed, why not our lands? Why not the produce of our lands and everything we possess?' The 1765 Boston riots, directed at the stamp distributors and customs inspectors' houses, spread to other cities. British North American squadrons had to deter French attack <u>and</u> enforce the Navigation Acts, but getting convictions in American courts was impossible. Britain thought colonists' differences, state boundary disputes, religious and economic differences for example, would prevent a united rebellion. Non-British Caribbean trade provided the unity. South Carolina's Christopher Gadsen thought 'there should be no New England man, no New Yorker [etc.]…but all of us Americans.' Some New York merchants with full warehouses of British imports called for their cessation until the Stamp Act's repeal knowing its impact, because British exports to North America was 5.7% of all its exports in 1700, but 25.3% in 1772–73, a population about two million, with similar growth in American tobacco, grain, flour and meat imports. Twenty-five British towns dependent on exports to America urged repeal.[8] Concluding it unenforceable, it was repealed in 1766.

The 1760 Sugar Act taxed molasses, extended in 1764 to sugar and madeira, but reduced it to 3d/gallon. The customs service was enlarged and procedures reinforced, then reduced in 1766 to 1d. All were evaded and all northern colonies' legislative bodies protested. John Adams claimed northern colonies were being sacrificed due to strong Parliamentary Caribbean interests. The 1767 Townshend Act put duties on glass, paper, lead and tea imports, abolished in 1770 except tea. Without representatives in Parliament, legislative assemblies claimed there was no right to tax them. In 1772 an armed party organised by Rhode Island merchants captured and burned the Navy's *Gaspee* engaged in preventative duties.[9] Boston lawyer James Otis proclaimed, 'taxation without representation is tyranny.' Most unrest was in ports in Massachusetts, Rhode Island and Connecticut, whose merchants had most to lose. New York followed. Many customs officials went into hiding as demagogues portrayed resistance to taxation as a question of liberty against arbitrary rule.

Wealth of Nations compared Britain and North America, which, 'though…not [as]…rich…it is much more thriving and advancing with much greater rapidity,' with the world's highest average living standards. Five cities over 10,000 people were all ports; Boston, Charleston, New York, Newport and Philadelphia, whose 30,000 people, was the English-speaking world's second-largest city, with flourishing shipyards and Caribbean trade. Coal and iron helped it become an early industrial leader. Its merchant elite lived stylishly and sought greater autonomy. The south produced tobacco, rice and indigo. New England fished Grand Banks to Cape Cod, producing almost £300,000 worth of dried and salted fish annually. The colonies' most valuable exports were tobacco then flour and bread, then indigo and fish with shipbuilding a significant economic contributor, especially small, fast schooners to aid illegal Caribbean trade. It imported British textiles, ironmongery, furniture, tea, drugs and spices worth about £4 million in the 1770s. As American colonies prospered, they sought refined, expensive Indian cloth, replacing English and homespun. By 1770 nearly 60% of British cotton textile exports were North America-bound[10] and a third of British registered tonnage was built there.

The trigger for war was the innocuous 1773 Tea Act allowing the EIC to discharge tea in America without first landing it in Britain, reducing the American price but making smuggling unprofitable. Radicals seized on the small duty payable, which would, said John Adams open the door to 'Desolation and Oppression, to Poverty and Servitude.'[11] The first ship had its tea thrown into the harbour; the Boston Tea Party. The first Continental Congress met in Philadelphia in 1774, its leaders determined on independence. The 1775 Restraining Act, restricting New England trade to English ports and barring New England fishermen from the Grand Banks could not be enforced, solidifying opposition. While militants called it a prelude to tyranny, to moderates, minor grievances became major due to perceived British obstinacy. Tom Paine's 1776 *Common Sense* asked,' is it in the interest of a man to be a boy all his life?'

American rebels combined many strands of developing thought, individual conscience, natural law, natural rights, social contract, freedom, the danger of slavery, by which they meant themselves as slaves of Britain, just as Englishmen used the word in the previous 150 years as being potential slaves to Stuart and French Catholic absolutism; *'Britain, never, never, never shall be slaves.'* *Common Sense* proposed an independent republic in which 'the law is king'. Turning smuggling enforcement into tax, liberty and representation issues created a mass movement. The British Caribbean had similar tariff grievances, but North America no longer needed defending from France, whereas the Caribbean repeatedly proved vulnerable, their free population small. Canada and Nova Scotia, dependent on exports to Britain with <u>no</u> Caribbean trade, remained loyal, as did 500,000 in the 13 colonies.

Britain thought trading with French islands strengthened France's Caribbean-dependent economy, especially St. Domingue, which by 1767 had nearly 600 sugar works, 200,000 slaves producing 60,000 tons annually, twice Jamaica's. France dominated European sugar distribution Soil exhaustion meant British islands needed four-times the labour to produce similar amounts of sugar, making it 30% more expensive. In every other respect, France had unproductive industries and a stagnant economy.

Britain hoped native Americans might become useful trading partners, with rights, justice and protection. Its enlightened promise of liberty to slaves escaping plantations and reaching British lines frightened the south. In the rhetoric of freedom, Washington described the colonial governor who promised slaves liberty, 'arch traitor to the rights of humanity.' Slave owners as liberty's heroes? The revolution in the south crystallised around this huge issue.[12] Thus, American Independence was fought by the north to stop Britain enforcing Navigation Acts, smuggling, by the south to protect slavery.

But the 1776 Congress saw themselves as distinguished successors of liberty's defenders; *Magna Carta*, the English Republic, Glorious Revolution and Locke, who wrote about the pursuit of happiness. Massachusetts Governor Belcher in 1731 also spoke of laws to 'promote the happiness of the people.'[13] The *Declaration of Independence* and US Constitution were drafted by lawyers seeped in Blackstone's *Commentaries*, a result of growing political, commercial and legal stability and public perception about liberty and humanitarianism. 'We hold these truths to be self-evident, that all men are created equal and that they are endowed by their Creator with certain inalienable Rights, that among these are Life, Liberty and the Pursuit of Happiness.' It resonated internationally, although was suppressed in Spain.

While American resentment grew, Britain's sights were fixed on France and Spain, strengthening their navies including huge ships outgunning the best British by perhaps 25%.[14] France entered the war in 1788, bent on revenge, this time not simultaneously involving itself in continental war. Spain still regarded the Pacific as her private ocean, an extension of Spanish America, while Britain probed its trade potential, the Falkland Islands perhaps key to South America's west coast potential. Absolutist France used America's rebellion for liberty and supported Muslim Indian states, ignoring Austria's and Spain's offer of territory in the Netherlands and Brazil in return for intervention in Bavaria's succession war or support to destroy Portuguese independence. Revenge came first. French merchants hoped they might gain trade with an independent America. But debt-financed war again damaged its trade. Spain joined, hoping for Gibraltar, Minorca and Florida.

With Britain alone against American colonies, France and Spain, British Caribbean islands were vulnerable. In 1774 the Continental Congress banned their imports and exports, threatening them with famine. The Earl of Albermarle told King George, 'If we lose our sugar islands, it will be impossible to raise money to continue the war. The islands must be defended <u>even</u> at the risk of an invasion of <u>this</u> island.' North American privateers launched raids on British Caribbean ships. By 1777 about 250 were taken. If North America became independent, Britain's Caribbean islands, essential to national wealth, must be protected. On war's outbreak, Britain took St. Lucia. In Barbados, flour prices doubled. To the Caribbean they quadrupled. From 1773 to 1783 the slave population fell from 68,000 to 57,000. In the last three years many were near starvation. Jamaica's exports halved in the first year as freight and insurance rates rose. In 1778 France seized Dominica, in 1779 St. Vincent and Grenada, second to Jamaica in sugar production, its export value in 1773, eight-times Canada's.

Anglo-French wars were problematic for neutral shipping. For Britain, ships trading with France aided the enemy, therefore were the enemy, but Holland historically had traded with their enemies. Neutral Dutch shipping which supplied France with Baltic timber resented Royal Naval restrictions on it. In 1780 two Russian ships were seized by Spanish warships in the Mediterranean, suspected of carrying grain to Gibraltar. Russia declared that all neutral shipping should sail freely between countries at war. Denmark, Sweden and Holland formed 'the Armed Neutrality of the North', later joined by Prussia, Austria and Portugal

Britain, Spain and France claimed they respected neutrals, but Britain objected at what appeared outright support for America. Dutch St. Eustatius, nicknamed 'Golden Rock', thrived after becoming a free port in 1757 with over 100 Sephardic Jewish families and 200 warehouses, the key entrepot supporting American independence. In 1779 over 3,000 Dutch, Danish, French, British, Spanish and American ships called there, sometimes 20 a day. Its 1779 sugar production was 500,000 lbs but port records show 25 million shipped.[15] A Scottish traveller before the war noted French gloves and English thread stockings, embroideries, painted silks, muslins and clothes, all cheaper than at home. But it was arms and munitions it supplied that tipped the balance in America's favour. When Britain found it supplying American rebels <u>and</u> French islands, it declared war on the Dutch in 1781. Admiral Rodney took it, including 200 ships and cargo in harbour. It took six months to ship warehoused contents in a 34-ship convoy to Britain, preventing him support the British army at Yorktown or attack the Chesapeake-bound French fleet. Rodney wrote, 'had it not been for that nest of vipers…the American rebellion could not possibly have subsisted.' 'This rock had done England more harm than all the arms of her most potent enemies.'[16] He therefore fired the port. The Sephardim moved to St. Thomas.

Dutch trade ceased, its shipping blockaded in port, its fisheries eliminated, its shrunken navy held only Cape Colony, Ceylon and Malacca, with Nagapattinam and Trincomalee taken, its Asian trade challenged by the EIC which founded a factory in Penang in 1786. France was more successful. Between 1778 and 1782, 31 convoys left and 29 returned. Privateers captured over 1,000 British ships. France captured Tobago, Dominica, St. Kitts, Nevis and Montserrat. Spain recovered Minorca and captured Florida and New Providence. By 1781 Britain was reconciled to independence as it could still trade with it, the Caribbean and Canada could be retained and Indian trade was growing.

British Baltic trade was secure. Almost all British Asian and Caribbean convoys got through. Gibraltar was reinforced and resupplied. The Navy steadily expanded. The French fleet sent to invade Jamaica was trounced by Rodney at the 1782 Battle of the Saintes. British finances were stretched further than ever before. Taxes increased. The National Debt doubled to £240 million, three-times mid-century levels. Interest consumed two thirds of revenue. But France and Spain were in deeper trouble. French trade fell from 725 million livres in 1777 to 450 million in 1779, reviving somewhat thereafter. Spain's ports were blockaded, trade disrupted and business paralysed. France borrowed at 8–10% interest, Spain up to 20%, Britain at 3% since the 1730s. Vergennes, the French finance minister knew Britain 'has in its constitution…resources which are lacking to us.'[17] Parliament's demand for transparent accounts and reports, produced confidence, open and efficient tax collection methods compared with unscrutinised tax farmers.

In the 1783 Treaty of Paris, Canada and Newfoundland stayed with Britain. US independence was recognised with unrestricted St. Lawrence-Grand Banks-Newfoundland access. France gained Tobago and recovered St. Lucia: a tiny gain for years of expensive, damaging war. Britain recovered other Caribbean islands. Spain regained Minorca and Florida. The Dutch regained their Caribbean islands and Ceylon. New Englanders were barred from trade with the British Caribbean, a huge loss for them and slaves. Canada was unable to immediately provision it and food was imported from Ireland. Nevertheless, between 1780 and 1787, 15,000 Jamaican slaves died before Nova Scotia's and Newfoundland's fishermen filled the gap. Some loyalists went to the Caribbean to export salt as Cape Cod's price rose 16-fold at the war's end, some to Nova Scotia.[18]

French merchants expected increased trade with independent America, but Shelburne, who said he preferred 'trade to dominion,' recognised that North America was still commercially tied to Britain, so strongly in fact, it was not undone for a century. *Wealth of Nations* said if parts of Britain's empire 'cannot be made to contribute toward the support of the whole…Britain should free herself from the expense of defending those provinces.'[19] The 1786 Navigation Act encouraged British shipbuilding, confined colonial trade to British ships and applied more rigorous definitions to 'British-built' and 'British-registered'.

Plans to settle Nova Scotia and Canada proceeded and everyone wanted, in George III's phrase, 'to have as much possession of the West Indies as possible.'[20] Britain's territorial, merchant shipping and maritime trade losses were serious but within a year, trade almost at pre-war levels, thereafter expanding 6% annually. France had its pyrrhic victory, the war of revenge won at grave cost, its national finances in even greater disorder. Support to a republic espousing liberty and pursuit of happiness fed domestic resentment of aristocrats and monarchy. French expectations to gain American trade were disappointed. Britain's annual Caribbean trade value in 1783 was £4,250,000, over half with Jamaica, £2,000,000 with India and £882,000 with Canada and Newfoundland.[21] By 1800 America was by far the largest consumer of British exports, the economic consequences of independence to Britain minimal.

The US Constitution was ratified in 1788 on principles enunciated by Locke, similar to the decentralised United Provinces. One issue was unresolved. *Declaration of Independence* signatory Benjamin Rush thought it hypocritical to denounce their servitude to Britain 'while we continue to keep our fellow creatures in slavery just because their colour is different.' Pennsylvania, the strongest anti-slavery state, with Benjamin Franklin's help, led 'The Pennsylvania Society for Promoting the Abolition of Slavery'. By 1800 it was abolished in New England and Middle Atlantic states, Quakers prominent in underground railroad escape routes. Pennsylvania's 1780s legislature decreed negroes and mulattoes born after that date, free. The preamble explained, 'We esteem it a peculiar blessing that we [can]…add one more step to universal civilisation by removing…the sorrows of those who have lived in such undeserved bondage.' In 1783 Massachusetts Supreme Court ruled that the *Declaration of Rights* constituted slavery's abolition. Other northern colonies followed. Yet at federal level, abolitionist Alexander Hamilton was too concerned with abolition's potential adverse impact on US finance. New England denounced slavery while its ships sailed to Africa, supplying slaves to Spanish America after it opened-up to foreign traders. Jeremiah Thomson combined slave-grown cotton exports with his role in New York's Manumission Society. Southern slavery's continuation meant moral and economic choices were nuanced. As for John Jay's warning of white savagery against native Americans, the interior opened-up and colonists swarmed west with devastating consequences.

Chesapeake's 1775 tobacco exports employed 330 ships and 4,000 seamen but with exports halted during the war, Glasgow turned to textiles, especially linen. From 1800, it became important in bleaching, dyeing, printing, soap-making, glass, sugar and distilling, attracting Jewish, Italian and east European immigrants. From 1750 to 1800, due to Glasgow's re-exports, engineering, financial services and entrepreneurship, its population trebled. Backward and poverty-stricken in 1700, by 1800 Scottish ports were industrially advanced with scientific study and technological innovation united. Other British industries boomed. Imports rose six-fold, mainly Caribbean.

In 1775 British cotton imports were under 5,000,000 lbs, most from the French Caribbean via free ports. Better strains were introduced into British Caribbean islands and Guiana. In 1790, 33,000,000 lbs were imported, under half British-grown. America entered the market in the 1790s following Eli Whitney's cotton gin invention. In 1800 it supplied 16,000,000 lbs out of 55,000,000 British imports, the rest from the Caribbean, Levant, Brazil, India and Asia.[22] By 1805 America was Britain's main cotton supplier.

Freed from the Navigation Acts, American merchants developed old markets like the French and Dutch Caribbean and new markets with fast 'clippers' worldwide. Quaker-dominated Nantucket's whalers, whose main whale oil market was Britain, suffered during war. Acute shortage in Britain created opportunities for British whalers but Nantucket had the best harpooners. The 1786 Act for the Encouragement of Southern Whale Fishery allowed 'Protestant Aliens'. British whalers were in the south Atlantic by 1790, the first in the Pacific in 1789 was British with a Nantucket master, mates and harpooners.[23]

America's rebellion made Britain realise that colonies should be lightly governed. In 1783 only Nova Scotia and Prince Edward Island had representative governments. To attract and retain settlers they had to match US freedoms. New Brunswick, Ontario and Cape Breton were formed, the last two with representative government. Dundas, War Minister (1794–1801), argued that expansion should be commercial, with outposts, not territory. 'We must be merchants…our trade depends upon a proper exertion of our maritime strength.'[24]

Chapter 10

China, Northwest America and the Nootka Crisis

While Chinese trade held potential, the EIC sent only seven ships to Canton in 1751, eight in 1776, 21 in 1789, more than other Europeans, but negligible compared with hundreds crossing the Atlantic. Nevertheless, Britain's Chinese tea imports, 400,000 lbs in 1720 were 20 million lbs in the 1790s, 25 million in the 1800s, 35 million by 1835, providing 6–7% of Britain's revenue in about 1800. With silk and porcelain, it drained silver from Britain. At Canton's waterfront factories, foreigners lived only during the October-March trading season and women were banned. The *hongs* acted as brokers <u>and</u> superintendents, effectively price fixing. Their opulent lifestyle, bribing to maintain official favour, constantly needed loans. Foreign traders lent at high interest rates with inadequate security. In the 1770s the *hongs* defaulted. British government intervention recovered about 25% of arrears. In 1783 it renewed the EIC charter. The search for commodities that China wanted in sufficient volume continued. Indian cotton cloth, the main one. Sandalwood, sharks fin, birds' nests, sea slugs (trepang), spices, clocks, copper, whale teeth, tortoise shells, betel nuts and coffee did not fill the growing gap. Reaching the Pacific in 1743, Russians discovered that China paid high prices for sea otter, seal and fox fur, used for robe trimmings. In Europe and America, they were for coat collars and hats. With US ships excluded from the British Caribbean after independence, New England's enterprising shipowners sailed to Asia, the first, the *Empress of China* in 1784, carrying silver, lead and ginseng, returning with tea and silk.

By the 1770s the world's seas were better mapped than the land.[1] Asia's interior was a mystery to Europeans although the EIC learnt fast about Bengal. Despite administering extensive territories, trade remained its priority. Half Britain's tea imports were smuggled, but Pitt's 1784 Commutation Act slashed duties from 115% to just 12.5%, at a stroke killing smuggling, a huge commercial opportunity for the EIC. Official tea imports tripled between 1784 and 1794, reflected in a four-fold increase in EIC chartered tonnage in 1784, a third again the following year, with ships over 1,200 tons. Copper sheathing nearly doubled their lifetime, still mainly built at Deptford and Blackwall. There was huge unused space on the India-bound leg. The EIC argued that Indian demand for British goods was limited. Private traders wanting access, accused it of being more interested in *diwani* revenue.

British 1772–1798 exports to Asia and America doubled. To the Caribbean they quadrupled. While Asia was important to Britain, about 80% of British overseas investments were Caribbean-based. As late as 1812, exports to India were under half to Jamaica alone.[2] Clearly however, Asia's importance grew, while South America held great potential. Ideally Indian revenue should have paid for tea, but military and administrative costs rose and revenue surpluses were rare. Small quantities of local opium were exported by agency companies operating under EIC licenses, used to develop Chinese trade; Crofts and Kellican in Calcutta, Jourdain, Sullivan and de Souza in Madras and Scot, Tate and Adamson in Bombay, using their ships or freighting it on EIC ships. In the 1780s an estimated 75% of British and Indian goods reaching Canton were sent by private traders.[3] British tea demand outstripped Chinese demand for imports. About 90% of Britain's exports to China was bullion, some via Manila, but when Spain entered America's Independence War, supply dried up.

Would America's northwest coast, found by James Cook in 1774 and sea otter trading he described help? He bought pelts for 12 cents each which sold for $120 in China! No specific line denoted where the EIC monopoly ended. Did it include Pacific coast America? Not waiting for clarification and sensing opportunity, a Scot, Tate and Adamson ship in 1785 sailed from Bombay, Calcutta's Bengal Fur Society sent two ships and London's government-authorised King George Sound Company one. Selling the pelts in China profitably encouraged more ships. Canton agency Cox, Beale and Co. sent ships in 1788, more in 1789, partnering King George Sound Company. Thirty-five British ships traded trans-Pacific furs between 1784 and 1794,[4] competing with cheaper US-built ships.

Oil was vital for illuminating houses, streets and factories and lubricating machinery. Whale oil was most common, seal oil less smelly, more economical but available in much smaller quantities.[5] Baleen was used for corset stiffening, ambergris for perfumes. British whaling companies thus rapidly expanded throughout the Pacific from New Zealand to the northwest, where sealing supplemented whaling, the EIC collecting whaling license fees. New England whalers also became active in the Pacific.

The northwest Pacific thus became the simultaneous target of EIC-licensed private traders from Indian and Chinese ports, British and New England whalers and sealers and Russian fur traders while several Spanish expeditions between 1774 and 1789 from Mexico reasserted 15th-16th century claims with garrisons in San Diego, Monterey and San Francisco. By the late-1780s, Vancouver's Nootka Sound became the northwest's most important anchorage with all powers intent on occupation. In 1785 Spain dismantled a British fur traders' post, escalating tensions. In 1790 it seized three British ships, evicting traders and whalers. Britain threatened war, Spain backed down; the so-called 'Nootka Crisis' over. Spain recognised British traders and whalers' access between Spanish California and Russian Alaska, allowing lucrative fur cargoes to be shipped to China, driving sea otters to the brink of extinction, exports necessarily declining after 1810. Hawaii's sandalwood was also depleted by 1830. Britain's whale oil market declined with increased use of cheaper coal gas and paraffin. New England reasserted predominance. By 1850 over 75% of the world's whaling fleet was American.[6]

While investigating Chinese import potential, Britain tried addressing the unsatisfactory tribute/*hong* system. Having tried sending an ambassador in 1788, the 1793 Macartney mission to Peking aimed to normalise Chinese trade, establish embassies and operate beyond Canton. EIC officials warned, 'the Chinese government looks with contempt on all foreign nations. Its ignorance…gives it confidence in its own strength. It does not look on embassies in any other light than acknowledgement of inferiority.'[7] As predicted, Macartney was received with polite condescension and rebuffed. His gifts of Irish linens, Birmingham metals, Wedgwood pottery and optical instruments were accepted as tribute.

The Emperor wrote to George III that he understood the embassy was 'driven by the humble desire to share the blessings of our culture…yet the difference between our customs and moral laws and your own is so profound that were your envoy even be capable of absorbing the basic principles of our culture, our customs and traditions could never grow in your soil…Ruling over the vast world I have but one end…to govern to perfection…rare and costly objects are of no interest…I have no use for your country's goods. Our Celestial Kingdom possesses all things in abundance and wants for nothing…But since tea, silk and porcelain…are…necessities for…Europe…the limited trade hitherto permitted in my province of Canton will continue. Mindful of the distant loneliness of your island, separated from the world by desert wastes of sea, I pardon your understandable ignorance…Tremble at my orders and obey.' The request for a permanent ambassador was rejected. Two incompatible world views were starkly contrasted. Macartney noted China's weakness, the 'tyranny of a handful of Tartars over more than 300 million…Chinese,' predicting it 'may drift some time as a wreck,' but could not be 'rebuilt on the old bottom' and would be 'dashed to pieces' sometime in the future,[8] his maritime references contrasting with the emperor's 'desert wastes of sea.' The China problem was unresolved. *En route* to China Macartney stopped in Brazil, thinking its oppressive 'commercial regulations and restrictions' would prompt revolution.[9] Both his predictions proved accurate.

Chapter 11

Europe's 1780s-1790s.
Maritime-Continental Divide

In the early-1770s Crevecoeur's *Sketch of a Contrast Between the Spanish and the English Colonies* noted Spain 'looked on the obedience of a few as much more useful than the ingenuity of the many…the languor which corrodes and enervates the mother country enfeebles…those beautiful provinces.'[1] Catalonia and Castile were antagonistic, a progressive maritime region ruled by a backward, territorial monarchy. Seville, Barcelona, Valencia and Saragossa were potentially better capitals due to geographical position. In 1778, Cadiz' official Spanish American trade monopoly ended. Barcelona, already Spain's busiest port, hosted mainly foreign ships. American silver provided no economic stimulus, no benefit to colonists or Spain. Catalonia's cloth industry was optimistic about American potential, but Caribbean free ports opened South America to British competition, killing Catalan exports. For Spain it was too little, too late.

Travelling in Britain, Ireland and France, Arthur Young (1741–1820) published many agricultural commentaries. His 1787–1789 French visits found peasants poor, miserable with heavy tax and service burdens. He noticed France's admirable king's highways built for troop movement empty, contrasting with Britain's roads for business, peppered with inns to feed and rest travellers. French port's wealth did not penetrate inland. Young epitomised Anglo-French societal differences, experimenting with agricultural improvements on his family estate. Fellow of the Royal Society from 1774, appointed Secretary of the Board of Agriculture, he organised agricultural surveys and supported property rights to reduce poverty. 'Give a man the secure possession of a bleak rock and he will turn it into a garden; give him a nine-year's lease on a garden and he will convert it into a desert.' He thought Bordeaux merchants' 'extremely lavish' lifestyles, with the port unpaved, without quays, 'covered in detritus and stones' demonstrated lack of civic pride, unlike British ports. In 1730, Bordeaux' colonial trade was worth 8.6 million livres, Marseilles' 2.6 million, Nantes' 14.2 million and Rouen-Le Havre, two million. By 1788 those figures boomed to 112 million, 55 million, 47 million and 52 million. La Rochelle concentrated on Newfoundland, Bordeaux and Nantes on the Caribbean and re-exports, Le Havre on re-exports to Hamburg, Amsterdam and Stettin by 130 German firms. French ports and their merchants did not have Anglo-Dutch commercial values and in 1789, Bordeaux' 700 merchants were outnumbered by 1,000 officials, the ratio greater in smaller ports. Late into slave trading, Bordeaux' ships transported 150,000 in 1792.[2]

St. Domingue had 40% of France's trade. By 1788, it received 465 out of 783 ships, 320 of which went to Cap Francais, now Cap Hatien, 'Paris of the Antilles' with 20,000 people,[3] tiny purchasing power compared to North America; food, textiles, building materials, copper boilers etc., but did for the first time stimulate French production other than sugar refining, otherwise starved of capital, inefficient and burdened with layers of regulation. In contrast, British American trade was more voluminous and diversified. In 1788, 25% of French Caribbean export value was coffee, compared with 11% from British islands, 34,000 out of 39,000 tons from St. Domingue. It also doubled cotton exports from 1783 to 1789, mainly due to British demand, via free ports in Dominica and Jamaica. Bordeaux sent seven ships to Britain in 1785, 19 in 1789, of which 15 were Liverpool-bound. In 1789, a third of Britain's cotton imports came via Europe including Brazil's via Portugal and Demerara's via Holland.

Throughout Europe, weak middle classes and peasants paid tax to support aristocrats contributing nothing, unwilling to share power with wealth-creators. Caribbean sugar, coffee and cotton exports, refining and re-exports supported an otherwise unsustainable regime. Re-exports rose nearly four-times between 1716 and 1788, the value of all exports from 120 million to 500 million livres,[4] but reform was impossible, the king, nobility, clergy, tax farmers and parlements all unwilling to relinquish privileges, the system ossified, respect for Church and monarchy undermined. Turgot told Louis XVI, 'Your nation…is a society…of different orders [with]…very few social links…each one…concerned exclusively with his own interests,' unlike maritime-influenced societies where entrepreneurship ensured fluctuating fortunes, compromise and social mobility.

Britain still ran a Baltic trade deficit. In 1785 Hull imported Russian goods worth £1.3 million, only returning £500,000 exports, but John Newman, Russian consul there, thought Britain benefitted, because it employed 400 British 300-tonners with 7–8,000 seamen, imports contributing to industry and re-exports,[5] similar to the effects of Swedish iron described in Chapter 2 and reminiscent of Thomas Mun's 17th-century anti-bullionist argument, that bullion shipped to India returned much more value.[6] Early-1770s tobacco imports were three-times those of the early-1720s, with 85% re-exported, 25% of which went to France. Midlands' metalware exports rose ten-fold from 1700 to 1773,[7] supplemented by instruments, books, watches, jewels, pewterware, clothes, shoes and saddles. Agricultural workers constituted only 35% of the population by 1800.[8]

Pitt the Younger came to power in 1783 after the American War with the difficult task of reducing the debt. He succeeded through financial and administrative reforms, duty reductions on tea, wines, spirits and tobacco, increased revenues and 'the best of all causes, a general increase in the wealth and prosperity of the country.' He let sinecure offices lapse and appointed talented men like Richard Frewin at Customs who consolidated them in 1787. Customs and excise accounted for two thirds of government revenue.[9] Trade liberalisation favoured the most efficient. Pitt ensured that was Britain. Trade value to Europe nearly doubled. British exports to America rebounded and Lancashire's labour-saving textile machinery enabled effective competition in the previously French-dominated Levant. British merchant shipping rose; 615,000 tons in 1782 to 1,265,000 in 1788.[10]

Vergennes, who engineered the American War, prepared for the next with naval enlargement to 80 ships of the line, 50% of Britain's total, only 25% inferior in tonnage,[11] but still unable to man and pay for it. He recklessly added to France's debt, increased taxes, reduced customs and excise to discourage smuggling and barred US ships from importing anything but US produce. While Britain's Parliament scrutinised expenditure, France had little reliable information, its financial system again in crisis, unable to service its debt.

French Caribbean trade difficulties pre-dated US independence. One of Bordeaux' biggest traders, Francois Bonnaffee thought in 1774, 'trade with America is ruining small-scale shipowners,'[12] but post-independence, excluded from the British Caribbean, US merchants concentrated on French islands at French merchants' expense. They took 25% of US flour, 75% of its salted meats and 60% of its dried fish, enriching US merchants and plantation owners. French slave sales to plantations were for cash or promissory notes, unlike Liverpool's traders who settled in goods or negotiable bills of exchange. These factors led Bordeaux' Chamber of Commerce to record the 'thanklessness' of American business. 'There are barely ten shipowners in Bordeaux who have made a profit in their trade since the peace, the remainder…losses.'[13] Nantes had similar problems. Cap Francais, Port-au-Prince, the Cays, Point a Pitre, Santa Lucia and Tobago became free ports.

In India, the problem of managing the EIC as a territorial power was unsolved, while Mysore and the Marathas were still hostile. A 1781 Select Committee examined Bengal's justice administration 'and by what means the happiness of the natives may be promoted.'[14] Logically, Clive had been right to suggest that 'so large a sovereignty' in Bengal 'too extensive for a mercantile company,' but how to transfer without infringing EIC chartered rights? How could decline be avoided after territorial acquisition? Only through trade could revenue return to Britain. How to separate trade from revenue? Britain, always reluctant to accept territorial commitments, feared EIC revenue-control would give it too much patronage, enabling exploitation, corruption and fortune-seeking. Pitt's 1784 India Act solved some of these problems. Territorial expansion it declared, was 'repugnant to the wish, honour and policy of this nation.' The Governor-General became a royal appointment, accountable to ministers, with authority over subsidiary presidencies, supervised by a Board of Control. Commercial activity continued to be managed without government interference, effectively turning the EIC into a quasi-government department. Pitt hoped it would limit corruption. Muslim law was modified, replacing mutilation with fines. Slave trafficking was abolished.

Returning to England in 1784, Hastings found public opinion had turned against the EIC for perceived corruption. In 1787 he was impeached for high crimes and misdemeanours. However well-intentioned Burke was in leading it, Hastings was a scapegoat. He had successfully reformed the EIC, stabilised the northwest frontier and against a hostile coalition of Marathas, the Nizam, Tipu Sultan and French, skilfully divided them, concentrating on Muslim fanatic, the Tipu. He ruled mainly Hindus, 70,000 circumcised and enslaved,[15] wanting Islam imposed throughout India, 'the total elimination and destruction of the enemies of the faith.'[16] The Nawabs of Oudh and Carnatic were loyal because of Hastings. Under him, British influence penetrated Bhutan, Sikkim and Tibet as possible markets for English woollen cloth, potential openings to China. He learnt Urdu, Bengali and Persian to understand India's diversity.

Charles Wilkins, the first Englishman to master Sanskrit, translated the *Bhagavad-gita*. Hastings wrote its introduction. Under his patronage, William Jones founded the Asiatick Society in 1784, deliberately not called Oriental, wanting to study Indian culture on its own terms, not from European/Christian viewpoints. It was the main centre investigating India's geography, history, languages, economy and culture. Its works filled 13 large volumes. Hastings was an implementer of enlightened thought and after a long trial was acquitted.

The Tipu's 100,000-man, French-officered army took Bangalore in 1791, but surrendered in 1792, ceded northern Mysore to the Nizam and Peshwa and promised to pay 33 million rupees, two sons taken hostage until paid, while Bombay gained more territory. In the 1790s the Nizam and Marathas fought. The EIC ruled 40 million people paying £18 million in tax, a third of Britain's peacetime revenue and commanded a 180,000-man army.[17] With political chaos outside British territory, the EIC was forced into hostilities. As Sir John Malcolm noted, it employed Indians 'to conquer each other', commercial and political entrepreneurs! Wars against Marathas added to EIC debt, but loans, £20.7 million from Calcutta, £6.9 million from Madras and £4.4 million from Bombay, signalled they were considered investments protecting trade. Lancashire's cotton revolution altered Indian trade patterns from the 1800s. Raw silk, cotton, indigo and sugar replaced cotton cloth as India's staple export. It imported British manufactured goods, including cloth. But genuine feelings that Indians needed protecting from a powerful EIC continued.

Europe's economy had poor communications and restrictive tariffs. The Holy Roman Empire had about 1,800 customs barriers, Prussia about 70, with different weights and measures, stifling trade, industrial development and raising prices. Agriculture could not meet the needs of rising populations. In 1763–64 in Sicily 30,000 died, in 1770 in Saxony about 150,000 and in Bohemia 80,000. European textiles were produced in cottages or small workshops. Bohemia's was manned by conscripted labour, serfs, criminals and vagrants. In Abbeville's Van Robais textile mills 12,000 workers were subject to quasi-military discipline.[18] Only Britain and Holland applied scientific methods of crop rotation and cultivation and concentrated on trade and finance. Their nobles had no legal privileges, no tax immunity, no rights of jurisdiction, no feudal dues from dependent peasants. Only Britain had a well-informed middle class. Only Britain made substantial progress introducing labour-saving machinery and had a wide base of industrial activities, contributing to rising living standards. Samuel Johnson (1709–1784) claimed, 'The age is running mad after innovations.' Dutch trade was well behind British and French volumes, but Dutch investors owned 40% of Britain's National Debt.

Lancashire's cotton industry was still largely water-powered in 1780 when Boulton and Watt steam engines started in spinning and mining. In Europe, manufacturing was mainly state-sponsored. Eastern Europe's rich soil remained underexploited. Traditional, conservative cultures were uninterested in enquiry and improvement. Serf labour was far less efficient. Montesquieu, unlike Voltaire's pandering to despots, concluded, 'lands are well cultivated in proportion not to their fertility, but to their liberty.' Russia, Europe's main iron supplier, shipped around 26,000 tons to Britain in the 1790s. Poland's nobility had the right of life and death over their serfs. Only Hungary's nobility could own land. Successful British merchants married into the nobility who traded and invested in docks, canals and mines.

Hamburg was a larger sugar, coffee and indigo entrepot than Amsterdam. Leiden's cloth industry in 1790 produced 25% of its 1690 production, although diamond-cutting, papermaking, velvets, dyeing, brickmaking, brandy and tobacco held up and Delft pottery declined gently.[19] But the annual 500 ships built in 1700, especially in Zaandam's 60 shipyards with over 300, reduced in 1770 to 25–30 and ceased in the 1790s.

Pitt's Anglo-French tariff-reducing Eden Treaty (1786) led to increased British ironmongery, cloth and pottery exports. Birmingham's export-orientated manufacturing rejoiced in 'mutual friendship and harmony' but was fearful of continental trade impositions.[20] Increasing maritime trade, which led to industrial revolution, enabled Britain to break-out of previous civilisations' economic constraints. When Pitt reduced import tax on Portuguese wines to the same as French, they complained. But they were trifling problems compared with government finances. Finance Minister Calonne discovered expenditure exceeded revenue by 80 million livres, later revised to 110 million. Naval enlargement finally exposed the system's ineptitude and inflexibility.[21] Calonne wanted structural reform, taxes on land paid by all, no regional tariff variations, provincial tax exemptions and trade restrictions with consultative assemblies elected by all taxpayers. He first tried persuading the Assembly of Notables, not called since the early-17th century, who rejected it. Like his predecessors, it caused his downfall. His successor tried the Paris parlement, a civil and criminal law court which registered royal decrees, an administrative function. Membership was inherited, associated with land, so it rejected the land tax. Entrenched interests refused to compromise, a necessary feature of commercial societies. Rigid, flawed structures were bound to break violently rather than bend and adapt. The Estates General was called to find solutions. The Third Estate formed the Assembly, which assumed power with a reformed constitution, inspired by Britain and America, <u>but</u> without checks and balances.

Louis XVI gave it lip service but plotted against it. The Pope instructed priests to withhold allegiance. The Assembly was influenced <u>not</u> by practical, hard-headed reformers, but *philosophes*. Long-denied involvement in practical politics and law-making, Tocquville described 'their almost infinite detachment,' a 'kind of <u>abstract</u> and literary politics.'[22] The supposedly enlightened Physiocrats, financial theorists, regarded land as the only source of wealth, downgraded trade and manufacturing, had no concept of political freedom, wanting reason and natural law-based foundations. Rousseau's *Social Contract* (1762) began 'Man is born free but everywhere in chains', contrary to man born sinful, salvation only through God's grace, as interpreted by an omnipotent Church. New society he thought, should be governed for everyone's advantage by the 'general will,' blind optimism that individual virtue would combine to a societal one, a recipe for dictatorships, ignoring Locke, the 1689 political settlement and US Constitution. Necker championed an English financial model, produced the first budget, exposed Court extravagances but could not reform chaotic, unaccountable revenue collection. With an untrustworthy, duplicitous king and nobles in exile or revolt, constitutional monarchists were thwarted and reform abandoned.

Conflict became inevitable. France's 1789 crunch was not equivalent to England's 1688, because James II had fled and William III, already a constitutional monarch, accepted limitations on his power. Britain was commercially driven, France predominantly agricultural with a few ports grown wealthy on Caribbean imports and re-exports, faltering due to US competition. French ports had little influence on hinterland manufacturing, economic or social changes. No humanitarian abolition movement arose. Some wealthy merchants bought noble titles, but rather than influencing nobles to become more commercially aware, they imbibed stronger rigid, hierarchical values without the tempering effect of commerce, compromise and consultative politics. Burke, before the descent into the Terror, described the inherent dangers. Tocqueville likened the revolution to Islam's inception, 'flooding the whole world with its soldiers, its apostles, its martyrs.'

Most Assembly members were lawyers, 43% held government office, only 13% businessmen or merchants.[23] Rumours of royal and aristocratic conspiracy propelled the National Assembly. 'Men are born free and equal in rights', which were liberty, property, safety and resistance to oppression. Article Six declared 'the law is the expression of the general will,' idealistic, impractical words, contrasting with Blackstone and Mansfield's painstaking legal work. Internal customs were abolished, France administratively divided into 83 departments, the metric system instituted, tax exemptions abolished and a land tax implemented, much as Colbert and successors tried and failed to do. The Assembly had good intentions but established security committees with powers of search, arrest and imprisonment without trial used royal spy networks, instruments of control and suppression, as 'the general will'. Louis could choose his ministers who answered to the Legislative Assembly, which was sovereign, elected by males over 25 who paid taxes equivalent to three days labour. France's revolution started as an urban revolt of impractical professionals and officials with abstract ideas.

Chapter 12

The Revolutionary and Napoleonic Wars' Impact on Maritime Trade

The 1790 Assembly declared, 'The French nation renounces…any war…to making conquests and it will never use its forces against the liberty of any people.' Repeated in the 1791 Constitution, it was unrealistic because the Convention (formerly Assembly) declared that France extends 'fraternal feelings and aid to all people who wish to regain their liberty.' Minority Niçoise, Savoyard, Dutch and Rhenish 'patriots' invited France to 'liberate' them, evolving into Louis XIV's policy, eastward expansion to natural frontiers. Annexed territories and dependent republics were stripped of resources and heavily taxed, church lands, feudal dues and enemy property confiscated. France pre-empted Austria's and Prussia's war preparations, proclaiming liberation wars against all *ancien regimes*. Initial defeats pushed the 1793 Convention to abolish the monarchy. Vigorous new commanders annexed the Austrian Netherlands and occupied the United Provinces. Britain could not passively watch a hostile power hold the Channel choke point. France pre-emptively declared war, repudiated the Eden Treaty, banned British imports and invaded north Italy.

Merchant ships entering British ports in 1792 numbered 2,746 from the Baltic, 1,413 from Holland and Flanders, 975 from Iberia, 705 from the Caribbean, 219 from Canada, 202 from America, 176 from the Mediterranean, 77 from Africa and 28 from Asia, although the 700–1,500-ton Indiamen were much larger than others and carried far more valuable cargo.[1] Britain benefited from large, growing inter-Asian trade. No other nation had such extensive trade networks to protect. Most vital was control of the Channel and Baltic choke points.

In 1790–1791 St. Domingue's slaves rose-up, destroying 180 sugar factories, 200 plantations, killing 2,000 whites. France's richest colony was ruined. Marseilles and Bordeaux were blockaded. Pitt and war minister Dundas aimed to conquer French territory worldwide and destroy French naval and commercial power. St Pierre and Miquelon, Tobago, Martinique, St Lucia, Guadeloupe, Pondicherry, Chandanagore, Mahe, factories at Calicut, Surat and Masulipatnam were conquered, 32 French ships of the line captured or destroyed.

Swift had satirised rational, logical thinking when taken to the extreme in *A Modest Proposal* in which the answer to Ireland's problems was to eat its children and sell their bones, logical but inhuman and ridiculous. *Philosophe*-inspired revolutionary Marat ridiculously proclaimed, 'it is by violence that liberty must be established…the moment has come for the temporary organisation of the despotism of liberty in order to crush the despotism of kings.'[2] Cities and ports led by merchants rose against Paris' leaders, ever-more extreme as coalition armies advanced. The Convention gave absolute power to the Committee of Public Safety. Industries were nationalised, maximum grain prices set, bread rationed, essential food prices controlled, crops and cattle requisitioned and French produce export prohibited. By 1793 France was isolated from world trade, her shipping and commerce crippled, her ports ruined by trade collapse and naval blockade, further damaged by price controls. The only way of enrichment was European conquest and plunder. The Committee ordered a *levee en masse*, general mobilisation. Churches were stripped of gold and valuables. Robespierre guillotined anyone suspected of disloyalty, a general purge necessary, executions, violence and terror, before a virtuous republic could emerge. The conservative Vendee rebellion was crushed, fields and woods burned, villages razed and livestock slaughtered, ten-times more killed than the Paris Terror.[3]

Talleyrand, exiled in London, by contrast believed in partnering Britain in freer trade and joint opening-up Spanish America. He wrote, 'real wealth consists not of acquiring or invading the domains of others but in developing one's own.' The effect of 'all extensions of territory…is to increase the difficulties of administration and to diminish the happiness and security of the governed for the…vanity of those who govern.'[4] The French fleet was heavily defeated in 1794 but diverted British attention long enough for a 127-ship grain and flour-laden convoy to land, while Britain took Corsica and the Seychelles. The war followed familiar patterns, British maritime control and subsidies to allies. Both sides banned trade with the enemy, using privateers to attack enemy ships. Britain prohibited neutrals from carrying French cargoes. French ships sailed under neutral flags.

Blockaded Marseilles' trade was transferred to neutral Livorno. French-controlled United Provinces, re-named the Batavian Republic, declared war on Britain in 1795. Britain seized the Cape, coastal Ceylon including Trincomalee, Dutch posts in India, Malacca, Demerara and Essequibo, governors ordered by exiled William V in London, not to resist. Their once proud trade, shipping, shipbuilding and finance was wrecked, the VOC bankrupted. Amsterdam declined precipitously. France's aim of capturing the Low Countries since the 1290s had finally been achieved, with the same devastating loss of wealth seen, as when Champagne was annexed in 1248.[5] Britain seized Caribbean islands enabling 1792–1798 imports to increase over 25%.[6] Over half Hamburg's sugar imports had been French re-exports, but by 1795 most sugar and coffee arrived via Britain, sugar doubling in the decade, making it north Europe's main port. US ports also gained, their $20 million trade of 1792 became $94 million in 1801, accelerating post-independence momentum, at French expense in the Caribbean. It also re-exported to Europe, 192 US ships entering Hamburg in 1799.[7]

Napoleon Bonaparte emerged in 1795, winning battles in Italy, creating republics bound to France, plundering art, paintings and sculptures and taxing harshly. Ignoring traditional supply trains, revolutionary armies looted and stole, troops often billeted on locals forced to feed them. Napoleon in 1796 proclaimed 'The French army is coming to break your chains'. 'Liberty' rang hollow for peasants whose crops and livestock were 'requisitioned', usually without compensation. Driven by ego, like *philosophes* he despised *la vile populace*. In the 1804 *Civil Code*, the employers' word alone was accepted, property passed only to male heirs and married women judged 'incapable' of making contracts. Like <u>un</u>enlightened despots, he centralised with a state-directed economy. Road and canal building were started and weights and measures unified. He explained of each temporary peace, 'every treaty means no more to me than a brief armistice.' He was the 'ultimate territorial warlord,' representing 'France's warrior, agricultural past.'[8]

By 1797 French exports were 36% and imports 55% of pre-revolutionary levels, due to blockade and Caribbean trade collapse, especially St. Domingue.[9] With Martinique captured, its sugar was sent to Britain. In 1798 Guadeloupe was the only important Caribbean island left to France, but production fell, little reaching France until an 1801 expedition restored order.

Napoleon appointed to lead Britain's invasion, decided its navy made it impossible. But Malta and Egypt, which from the 1770s France studied annexing, would secure east Mediterranean dominance. Cairo's French consul in 1795 suggested Suez-built ships could carry troops to India in six weeks. Napoleon thus invaded Egypt. Admiral Nelson, guessing his destination, destroyed his fleet at the 1798 Battle of the Nile, then retook Port Mahon, Minorca and Malta. Napoleon's army was stranded. In 1799, he nevertheless wrote to the Tipu announcing 'my arrival on the banks of the Red Sea…to deliver you from the iron yoke of England,' pure bravado after the Nile defeat, letters intercepted in Mocha, and sent to the EIC.[10] Governor-General Richard Wellesley, on hearing that Mauritius was raising volunteers for the Tipu, took the rest of Ceylon in 1799, overran Mysore, during which the Tipu was killed, annexed Malabar and subordinated Hyderabad, ensuring Madras' security. Dundas sent 5,000 troops to India, a squadron to the Red Sea and occupied the Perrin Islands off Yemen to block further French moves on India.

Oman was a growing Indian Ocean economic power, Muscat the main Persian Gulf-India-Red Sea entrepot for coffee, cotton, timber, rice, sugar, spices and ghee. Sultan Hamed bin Seyyid (r. 1785–92) owned 50 ships. After Britain occupied Pondicherry in 1778 in America's Independence War, French traders turned to slave trading from Zanzibar and Kilwa for Reunion and Isle de France plantations. Kilwa's prosperity induced Oman to conquer it in 1780. Seyyid reduced duties on Hindus and Jews from 9% to 6.5% and gave religious freedom. Muscat was full of Arab, Jewish, African, Indian and Ottoman traders, the customs managed by a Kachchhi enabling an India-Arabia-Africa trade triangle. Surrounded by extremist Wahabis and Qasimis, Seyyid understood traditional Indian Ocean toleration was key to prosperity, protecting merchants who dominated coffee, grain and pearl trading. Oman's police protected Indian areas, including temples. The Gulf's British resident warned British merchants not to compete in pearl trading as they were no match for Kachchhi and other Indian specialists. Britain allied with him in 1798.[11]

A Hindu ruler was restored to Mysore with a subsidiary alliance, which entailed accepting a British resident and paying for British troops for protection from external and internal threats. French influence at the Nizam's court was eliminated. Almost 100 more subsidiary alliances were subsequently signed. Oman's Sultan heeded Britain's warning not to make it an enemy as its ships traded in Indian ports. A French envoy in 1803 was refused entry as Oman had 20 large ships in Bengal and Malabar.[12]

* * *

After the Egyptian debacle, First Consul Napoleon with virtually unlimited powers persuaded Czar Paul to revive the 1780 League of Armed Neutrality to protect their merchant ships. The issue of British ships stopping and searching neutrals was always controversial. Britain wanted to prevent Baltic naval stores from reaching France, but the League with Russia, Prussia, Denmark and Sweden, instead denied Britain Baltic access. With French annexation of the southern Netherlands and north Italian ports, Europe's market was effectively closed to British goods. Nelson's 1801 Battle of Copenhagen and Czar Paul's assassination however, led to his successor, pro-British Alexander, ending the Armed Neutrality, giving Britain renewed Baltic access.

Foreign Minister Talleyrand tried steering Napoleon towards peace and partnership with Britain; in vain. Britain's finance came from customs duties, income tax from 1799 and subscriptions to war loans. Its trade had increased 25% in the Seven Years War. In 1795–1799 it accelerated nearly 50%, from £78.2 million to £114 million, despite losing over 3,000 ships, and £151 million by 1815,[13] due to booming machine-driven factory cloth production, industrial revolution, lowering prices, increasing exports, allowing the National Debt to increase. Grain, sugar, tea, wine and timber imports doubled, raw cotton trebled, coffee increased seven-fold. Woollen and worsted exports doubled, cotton goods quadrupled.[14] France's maritime trade was destroyed, her Atlantic ports strangled. By contrast, Britain imported worldwide materials; unique in Europe. Prosperity returned to the British Caribbean, confidence shown by London's West India Dock, completed in 1802, the world's largest, enabling importers to better control supply, logistics and prices.

After the 1802 Peace of Amiens, Britain returned its conquests except Trinidad, Ceylon and Malacca. Pitt, no longer in power, was alarmed. Dundas thought it 'an act of weakness and humiliation', especially the Cape and Malta, *en route* to India. France was dominant in Europe. Its borders ran from the Rhine to the Alps with client republics in Holland, Switzerland, most of Italy and heavily influenced central German states. Napoleon declared himself Emperor in 1804. Previously neutral Livorno and Ancona were closed to British merchants. Locals were forced to repudiate debts to them and Portugal to close its ports to British shipping. War was declared in 1803. Neutral traders were not especially hampered, but had to prove to French authorities, the non-British origin of imports. The Elbe, Weser and Ems were closed to British ships and trade. But adaptable merchants shifted their trade, as will shortly be described.

Britain again subsidised a Russia-Sweden-Austria coalition, maritime dominance confirmed at the 1805 Battle of Trafalgar with 22 prizes, counting four attempting escape a month later, against no British losses; casualties 5,860 against 1,695.[15] Trafalgar also broke Spanish pretence to be a strong naval power. Its fleet was destroyed, the means of maintaining its empire gone. Most of its colonies declared independence after 1810; the export opportunity Britain sought. Britain dominated the oceans and was the heart of global trade. Napoleon taxed France tolerably, subservient republics rapaciously. Already in 1800, taxes and levies on the Netherlands accounted for 25% of French government revenue![16] Free from St. Domingue's competition, British colonies boomed. Former Dutch Guiana attracted huge investment, producing more cotton for Britain than Caribbean islands. The Cape was recaptured in 1806, this time permanently. But British exports to Europe fell from £10.32 million in 1805 to £5.09 million in 1807, under £3 million in 1808. Sugar accumulated in London warehouses, despite Paris' price being nine-times London's. In 1805 only 33% of British manufactured goods went to Europe, 27% to America and 40% to the rest of the world.[17] Blockade drove British exports to other areas, including Latin America, through Caribbean free ports, about £500,000 in 1792, probably £1 million by 1807, more via Brazil, Buenos Aires and Venezuela.

When Britain blockaded North France and the Low Countries, Napoleon responded with the 1806 Berlin Decree, placing Britain and Ireland 'in a state of blockade'. It was fantasy. It self-blockaded itself against British exports, the 'Continental System' from 1806, a deluded attempt 'to conquer the sea by the power of the land.' Responding to French prohibition of all British imports, Orders in Council instructed 'Any vessel coming from [a French] port shall be captured and brought in…with her cargo… condemned as lawful prize.'[18] Napoleon ordered seizure of British goods in European ports. But denying European markets to British imports meant he had to control any country not participating, meaning all Europe. Meanwhile, British exports to Bengal increased from £6 to £18 million.[19]

Alexander Baring thought there was little US smuggling to France, most Americans *bona fide* neutral. Distance from Europe did mean it was difficult to get current news in fast-changing situations. But James Stephens' 1805 *The War in Disguise* highlighted neutral shipping abuses, citing the *Mercury Roberts* sailing from Havana to Charleston. Interrogated by a British cruiser and released, it did not discharge at Charleston. With new papers it sailed for Europe. Stopped again, luckily by the same cruiser, the convincing papers were shown to be fraudulent. To Stephens, this must be the tip of the iceberg, although Baring disputed it.[20] Prohibiting trade with the enemy sometimes damaged British interests, so special licenses were occasionally issued before 1800. But 1,600 were issued in 1807, 8,000 in 1809, over 18,000 in 1810;[21] totalling 44,346 between 1807 and 1812![22] If stopped by British ships, the license was shown, if by enemy ships, alternate papers showing it was neutral. Insurance policies permitted their use, initially only to British merchants but soon to neutrals. Courts upheld them in insurance disputes to protect British trade. Chief Justice Mansfield in Fayle v Bouillon explained 'the words of the licence are as general as…possible…the very intention of government to encourage the importation of these goods from Russia, Prussia and Denmark…very good reasons for making this license so general.' In Feise v Bell, he explained the license's object was 'to find a market…abroad,' promoting British trade.[23] So simulated papers, ostensibly illegal, were used by merchants and insurers. The courts protected them, allowing recovery under insurance policies, provided the policies expressly allowed them. Protecting British commerce was essential for its economy. This legal fiction was, in the circumstances, common sense.

Ignoring the Navigation Acts, all cooperating European ships were allowed in British convoys, from British or friendly ports. Lloyds encouraged convoys, calculating 1793–1815 British annual merchant losses at 2%, in deep sea trades 5–6%, half from marine causes, half to enemy action. In the Channel in 1808, shipping losses were only 1.5%, never causing real anxiety. Convoys consisted of many foreign-owned, foreign-manned merchantmen, flying neutral, even enemy flags.[24] With high freight rates, shipowners willingly complied.

In France, false identities, accounts and bills of lading were common but worked against the regime. Bogus privateers with fictitious captures were actually imports. Before the 1807 embargo, America was Bordeaux merchants' main destination but most 1806–1813 passport destination requests were Baltic ports, where the Royal Navy escorted convoys of hundreds of ships, shipping British goods into French-controlled Baltic ports, then loading naval stores for Britain. British maritime control meant neutrals sided with them. Britain thus gained a huge shipping pool, enabling it to break continental embargo. France had to transport its materials by land and river, inefficient and expensive. Britain also took offshore entrepots like Heligoland in 1807 to trans-ship in and out of the Elbe, Weser and Ems rivers. The Channel Islands, Gibraltar, Corsica, Elba, Malta and the Adriatic's Lissa served the same purpose.

The 1807 Treaty of Tilsit, the high point of Napoleon's European control, divided it into two spheres. Russia was free to take Swedish Finland and attack the Ottomans in the Black Sea. Denmark and Sweden were coerced to join the blockade. Napoleon's sphere in western and central Europe oversaw French occupied Austria and Prussia, where family members became Kings of Westphalia, Holland and Naples. Prussia and Russia had to close their ports to British ships. Isolated Russian naval ships in the Mediterranean were captured by Britain, scuttled, abandoned or joined the French. Napoleon knew his system leaked. In 1808 he wrote to his brother, Holland's King Louis, 'If you need to sell your gin, the English need to buy it…make them pay in money…never in commodities.'[25] Deprived of German and Spanish wool, Britain imported Australian wool first in 1807. Judged better quality, demand soared.

Despite European dominance, Napoleon's failure was not understanding maritime trade's importance. Britain besieged Copenhagen in 1807 to prevent Baltic closure. Denmark had to surrender its fleet. The 1807 Orders in Council forbidding neutral states from trading with France was a body blow as it depended on neutral trade. In 1807, 43% of ships entering Bordeaux were foreign. In 1808 it collapsed to 2%. Few French ships risked putting to sea.[26] French ports suffered unemployment and misery, a risk for Napoleon, who while believing that maritime trade could be sacrificed in war with Britain, needed the support of elites, including merchants in ports! An 1808 license system tried placating them. Bordeaux got over a third. After 1810, it got 620 navigation permits, Hamburg five and Livorno, formerly neutral and thriving, now occupied, just one. Unlike British licenses, French ones were expensive, slow, bureaucratic and inadequate, increasing corruption. False declarations were common and controls weak, so in 1813 the Clamergeran firm declared a wine shipment three-times the size and seven-times the real value. Trade continued by bribing customs officials, especially outside France. In 1807 Hamburg's Senate and Chamber of Commerce spent about 1.5 million francs persuading authorities to ignore trade on the Elbe and 1,500 small ships entered Tonning, just north of Hamburg, with banned British colonial and manufactured goods. Between the 11th March and 6th June 1807, 281 ships left London for Tonning, 30% of all British exports to Denmark that year.[27] British naval and maritime trade supremacy accelerated because of Napoleon's continental blockade.

Britain also aimed to occupy strategic points for South American trade. Buenos Aires surrendered over a million silver dollars and much more valuable warehoused goods before the British evacuated.

Militarily, Napoleon's failure stemmed from Iberian occupation, meant to choke-off British trade. French troops sent to subjugate Portugal missed its fleet and Court, shipped to Brazil under British escort. Portugal revolted against occupation. Attempted overthrow of Spain's monarchy for Napoleon's brother Joseph triggered Spanish revolt. British resources were funnelled to rebels, who with Wellington, drained Napoleon's. British support helped open Spanish South American markets. French Caribbean islands were again conquered in 1809–1810. Freight rates rocketed. Baltic insurance rates more than doubled. Westphalian King Jerome told Napoleon of 'profound unrest…the example of Spain is being recommended…the underlying cause… not only resentment at foreign domination [but]…the ruination of all classes, the crushing burden of taxation, war-levies, the upkeep and quartering of troops and endless other vexations.'[28]

The mindset forged by the ideas behind the *Libelle*, Raleigh's 'he that commands the sea commands the trade and he that is lord of the trade of the world is lord of the wealth of the world' had been defined, developed and decisively launched in 1649 and 1688.[29] In Napoleonic war it came to almost monopolistic conclusion. Britain had half the world's warships, 101 captured between 1806 and 1810.[30] The Continental System hurt Britain, especially in the Baltic, but British courts and judges pragmatically helped create a reliable legal framework. British exports leaking into southern Baltic ports provoked Napoleon to occupy them. Wellington and Nelson get most credit in defeating Napoleon. Peter Padfield persuasively suggests Sir James Saumerez' equally important Baltic role has been unfairly neglected, supporting Sweden against Russia's invasion of her Finnish province, opposing French troops poised to invade Sweden from Denmark, keeping the Sound choke point open to British and neutral shipping, keeping Russian shipping in port and protecting convoys past Bornholm and Ertholmene Island, rather than the Sound, enabling British exports to flout blockade. Even though Prussia's and Russia's governments agreed to blockade, their merchants depended on trade continuing. After Tilsit, Russia ceased receiving British subsidies, ceased profiting from exports and her debt rose dangerously. Prussia, at war with Britain, depended on British trade. Saumerez reported in 1808, 'An immense trade is carried on by British merchants under HM's license with different ports of these countries. Both nations are…amicably disposed towards Great Britain and openly avow…peace and amity…[and] abhorrence of…alliance with France.'[31]

Saumerez blockaded Russia's squadron but did not attack her forts and fleet bases. In 1809 Baltic imports doubled and exports and re-exports trebled to £13.6 million, 25% of all British exports, much carried by neutrals. Baltic merchants colluded. Sweden conceded Finland to Russia and made peace. They had to agree to Napoleon's Continental System, but assured Saumerez they would assist him. In 1809 he seized Anholt Island, near the Baltic entrance, a new entrepot. Grain imports especially from Danzig rose in 1810 from £1.1 million to £2.7 million and timber from £0.5 to £0.8 million. Smuggling continued along the borders. Apart from Tonning, Altona,

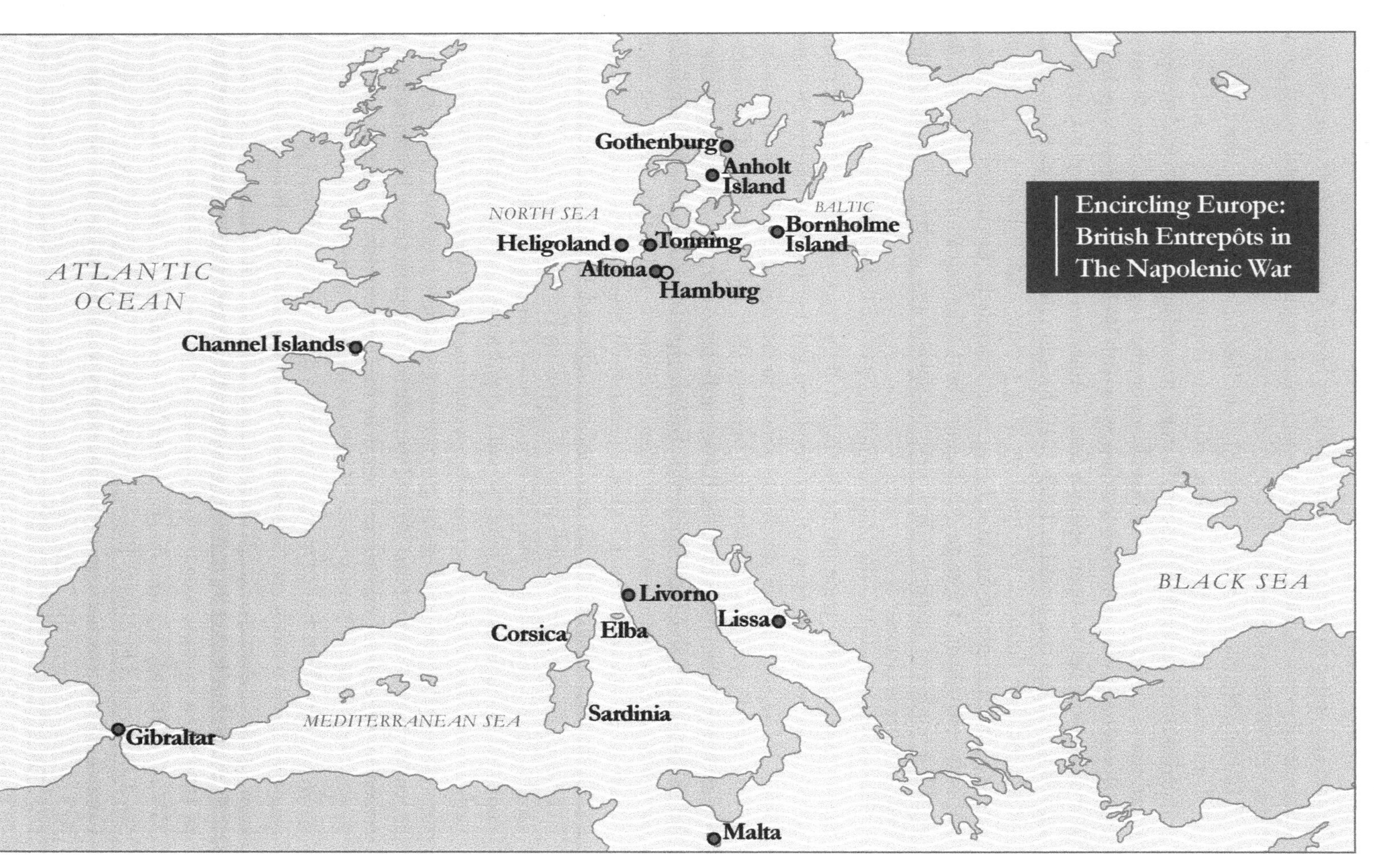

Encircling Europe:
British Entrepôts in
The Napolenic War
ATLANTIC OCEAN
NORTH SEA
BALTIC
Gothenburg
Anholt Island
Bornholme Island
Heligoland
Tonning
Altona
Hamburg
Channel Islands
BLACK SEA
Livorno
Lissa
Corsica
Elba
Sardinia
MEDITERRANEAN SEA
Gibraltar
Malta

a 15-minute walk from Hamburg, swelled with British colonial goods. Hamburg merchants lived there and kept trade flowing. Thousands of people crossed Hamburg's and Livorno's customs borders daily, each transporting small packs. In August 1810, 93,000 kilograms of goods was confiscated at the Hamburg-Altona gate, an estimated 5% of the smuggled quantity, essential for people's survival.[32] When Sweden was forced to declare war, Saumerez was again privately assured that hostility was a pretence. Trade continued and Swedish merchants supplied his ships. He maintained 1808–1812 Baltic trade through hostile waters, enabling regular, huge convoys. Between June and December 1809, 2,210 merchant ships were escorted through without loss, although in July 1810 Danish ships captured 47 off Skaw. Vinga Sound, 14 miles off Gothenburg was the British Baltic convoy's heart.[33]

France did not have the resources, ingenuity or merchant networks to enforce embargoes. Badly paid customs agents were easily turned. Livorno's police chief asked how he could prevent customs officers earning just enough to survive from refusing bribes quadruple their salaries. The Customs Director estimated that two thirds of his inadequate force were bribed.[34] Increasingly harsh measures like the 1810 Fontainebleau Decree, condemned armed smugglers to death, but juries were reluctant to prosecute influential merchants, especially in Livorno where local administration prevailed. Nevertheless, huge damage was inflicted on Italian and Baltic ports' populations. They survived by smuggling. In some ways, it was the making of 19th-century Hamburg, which developed direct trades with the Americas. Even Holland under Napoleon's brother imported British goods until 1810. Napoleon turned the war into one against maritime commerce, industry, bankers and consumers.

French occupation of southern Baltic ports did disrupt trade. Baltic imports dropped from £7.5 million in 1810 to £2.6 million in 1811, exports and re-exports from £11.2 to £2.3 million.[35] It coincided with a US ban on British ships and exports, which had comprised a quarter of all manufactured exports (See Chapter 16). Simultaneous collapse of Baltic and US markets led to industrial slump, coinciding with a poor harvest, raising bread prices, threatening Britain's economy, causing widespread unemployment, wage-cuts, rioting, machine-smashing and factory-torching by Lancashire's Luddites. Yet, in 1810 Napoleon authorised wheat exports, 13% of British consumption.[36] Had he banned it, Britain's social crisis would have intensified, further failure to understand maritime trade's power. French occupation of Italy meant Britain occupied Sicily which fed Malta, the Ionian Islands and Corfu as east Mediterranean bases.

The more the blockade leaked, the more Napoleon pressured his satellites, the more they resisted. Czar Alexander, tiring of a policy against Russian interests, profitable timber and naval stores exports, admitted neutral ships with British produce and refused to seize hundreds of neutral ships in Russian ports from Britain. Prussia, encouraged by Iberian resistance, looked to Britain for subsidies and arms for an uprising against taxes, indemnities, confiscations and French armies quartered on the population. Napoleon's Iberian venture drained resources. He still believed agriculture was 'the soul, the foundation of all national prosperity', foreign trade just 'profitable employment of the surplus of the national products…but much inferior to the others to which it was subservient.'[37] The Continental System was supposed to rely on a large

European protected market. Cotton cloth manufacturing <u>was</u> stimulated by British textile machinery imported before the Revolution and between 1802 and 1809, the St. Quentin Canal linked France to Netherlands' waterways and the North Sea. But compared to long-haul maritime trade, it mattered little. As the protective barrier was compromised, higher-quality, lower-priced British goods flooded in. French industry could not compete. It ruined French ports, shipbuilding, manufacturing and many export industries.

In 1790, 70% of British cotton imports came from the Caribbean. Increased cotton cloth production and overseas demand needed new cotton sources. Britain seized Dutch and French cotton-producing territory, Dutch Guiana, especially valuable. Eli Whitney's 1792 cotton gin (enGINe) revolutionised US harvesting by mechanising seed removal. Massachusetts-born, he thought it would reduce slave demand, hastening slavery's end. But <u>with</u> slaves, it slashed costs. Production and exports to Britain accelerated. In 1800 America supplied 16 million lbs out of 55 million, the Caribbean 15 million, the rest from the Levant, Brazil, India and Asia. By 1815 America supplied almost 50%, India and Asia just over 25%, the Caribbean only 7%. In 1820 total imports were over 140 million lbs, 75% American.[38] Manufactured goods, especially cotton cloth, dominated British exports from the 1780s. America more than fulfilled Shelburne's hopes, because after decades of evading or defying British trade policy, after independence cotton exports to Britain rocketed. By 1830, Caribbean cotton supplied only 2.5% of British cotton imports and was forced back on sugar.

By 1810 Britai produced 10–14-times more cotton yarn per hour than India, perhaps 400-times for finer qualities.[39] For 200 years India was the world's main source of high-quality cotton cloths, the most widely consumed manufactured product with perhaps 60% of 18th-century global manufactured exports, the world's textile workshop. But imported British cotton cloth boomed, growing from 81,800 yards in 1814, 1,913,800 in 1821 to 5,177,700 in 1835, at Indian cloth's expense.

By 1811 every French colony was in British hands. Spain's and Russia's ports were opened. Napoleon played his only hand, invading Russia to stop British goods leaking into Europe via the Baltic. After Britain's 1811 economic and social crisis, exports and re-exports grew again. 1793's imports, £19.3 million and exports/re-exports £20.4 million, in 1814 became £80.8 and £70.3 million respectively during 20 years of almost constant war. The most spectacular export/re-export increase was to north Europe; £2.3 million in the 1811 slump to £22.9 million in 1814.[40]

Wellington's depots, supplied by sea and river, allowed advances into Spain. Only 25,000 out of 450,000 men returned from the failed Russian invasion, only 10,000 fit for service; another army lost! Maritime trade's economic power cost him his position. As battles were lost, his empire disintegrated. Prussia and Russia were again subsidised by Britain. Wellington liberated Spain and Napoleon was deposed. The 1814 Treaty of Paris restored a Bourbon, Louis XVIII, and reduced France to her historic frontiers. Britain retained Mauritius, Tobago, St Lucia, Guiana, Heligoland, Malta, the Ionian Islands, Malacca, the Cape, Ceylon, Grenada, St. Vincent, Trinidad and Tobago for strategic and economic reasons, mainly off-shore bases as Dundas wanted. New naval bases were built in St. Lucia, the Cape, Malta, Corfu and Trincomalee. Trade not territory was the goal. America had showed territory was a liability. Castlereagh thought Martinique and Guadeloupe did not give France enough power to be dangerous. He tried persuading others to join the anti-slave trade crusade, bitterly resented in Nantes, Bordeaux and Le Havre, peace finally promising its resumption. America and Britain in 1814 pledged to 'use their best endeavours' to end it, a similar declaration signed by France, Russia, Prussia, Austria, Spain, Portugal and Sweden.

After Napoleon's escape and final defeat at Waterloo, the Congress of Vienna united the Netherlands and Austrian Netherlands, an attempt to counter France's archaic ambitions and eliminate the danger to Britain. Prussia gained Rhineland territories and trade was encouraged. Hundreds of principalities consolidated into 39 states. Norwegian timber exports to Britain led it to question union with Denmark. To avoid Swedish occupation of Jutland, it ceded Norway to them in a union of crowns with separate laws, parliaments, administration and currency. France had a constitutional monarchy, indemnities to pay, lenient compared to the damages suffered by conquered states. France's merchant marine had all but been destroyed.

Britain acquired empire by the necessity of defeating Napoleon, the incapability of legacy Mughal states keeping peace and security while keeping the seas and ports open for trade, promoting a world economy. Pitt and Dundas protected it by strategic naval bases, so her 26 colonies of 1792 grew to 43 by 1816, some substantial like parts of India, Ceylon, the Cape and Guiana, retained at merchant and manufacturing insistence, the commercial damage done by Bute's 1763 peace, undone.

The causes and results of the 1793–1815 Revolutionary and Napoleonic Wars were rooted in maritime trade issues with huge impacts on worldwide trade. They accelerated the growth and sophistication of marine insurance, which needed more surveying and risk assessment, better charts, technical manuals and chronometers. Britain directly administered some Indian territories and influenced 562 subsidiary states. The 1817–1819 Maratha regime of pillage ended in Bombay's annexation of the Peshwa's lands, many cotton-growing. With EIC monopoly in India ended in 1813, never having been proficient at selling British goods there, Liverpool and Glasgow sent agents to manage sales, becoming agencies like Alexanders, Colvins, Fergusons and Palmers and in the 1830s, Inchcape and Jardine Matheson, investing in ships, docks, sugar plantations and other Southeast Asian commercial opportunities.

Amsterdam ceased as a financial hub. Many Amsterdam bankers, merchants and capital fled to London. Half its remaining population were pauperised. Zaandam, Europe's first industrial zone, had one shipyard left. Aiming to reverse Britain's growing dominance, Napoleon actually catapulted it to the pinnacle of world power. British maritime trade and the resulting increasing customs, higher taxes on an increasingly wealthy middle class and a larger National Debt enabled Britain to pay subsidies in 1813–14 over £15 million; over £60 million throughout the war.[41] During it, Frankfurt's Rothschild brothers prospered by importing Lancashire's cotton cloth to Europe. They moved to London in 1814, financing Wellington's army and supplies.

* * *

Martin Stopford's study of shipping cycles from 1741 based on Newcastle-London coal freight rates show 1784–1791 rates at roughly nine shillings, the lowest before that, just over four shillings, the highest 13–14 shillings, but 1791–1814 rates peaked at an exceptional 19 shillings. Even when falling back in 1805 and 1810, it was still around 14–15 shillings.[42] Short-haul freight rate fluctuations are usually minor. These substantial ones imply that long-haul trans-Atlantic and Asian rates soared. Liverpool's 1807 cotton price was 27.5% higher than Charleston's, but in the embargo's final two months 293.3% higher, indicating rocketing long-haul freight and insurance rates.[43] Thomas Tooke said 1810 Baltic wheat cost 30–50 shillings/quarter to ship to Britain, compared with only 4s 6d in 1837.[44]

Kevin O'Rourke's study of the blockade's consequences in trade volumes and commodity prices show Britain's 1780–1830 prices except for 1811–1814 were all close to the long-term trend.[45] By contrast, French imports drastically reduced, especially in 1808–11. Sugar, cotton, pepper and coffee prices soared. Sweden's cargo volumes were little affected, timber and iron in high demand. US exports and imports declined massively after 1808 and collapsed in 1814 when volumes were only 10% of their 1820 levels, although this was also due to US policy (See Chapter 16). French and US imports halved between 1807 and 1814 and US exports fell over 36%.[46] Latin American trade was also severely disrupted. Independence struggles halved silver production/export in the 1820s from the 1780–1810 peak with worldwide consequences. British silver shipments to India and China dropped, replaced by British manufactured goods. Only Asian exports grew, averaging 4.6% annually during 1780–1829,[47] much more than previous years. Dutch Java enjoyed a sugar and coffee export boom after St. Domingue's revolt. When Holland was annexed in 1810, Britain occupied Java and Mauritius, welcomed as deliverers from French oppression.

Booming freight rates, insurance and license costs accounted for 25%-40% of British wheat prices in 1812, which were 57% higher during 1793–1815 than the previous 13 years and 47% higher than the next 15 years[48] especially during the 1807–1812 blockade when prices were 77% higher than the pre-war average, 66% higher than post-war average. Timber prices were affected partly by increased naval demand, partly by trade disruption. In 1802 Britain imported timber overwhelmingly from the Baltic which increased. By 1821 three-times more came from North America! Sugar was 43% higher than before the war, 66% higher than after, tea 16% higher than after the war, pepper 53% higher than before the war and 44% higher than after.[49]

Prices rose far more in blockaded France and Germany. Holland suffered worst. Sugar was an astonishing 577% higher in 1807–12 than before the war and 277% higher than post-war averages, partly by losing Guiana and Surinam to Britain, but more reflecting blockade, since its pre-war refineries relied more on French re-exports than Dutch plantations. Cotton was 39% higher than before and 90% after the war, pepper 167% and 61% respectively. French sugar prices were 190% higher during 1807–12 than post-war prices, cotton 169%, coffee 197% and tobacco 121%.[50] Sweden joined the Continental System by compulsion in January 1810. But during the whole 1807–12 blockade, textile prices were 118% higher than before the war and 70% higher than post-war averages, rye 67% and 77% and wheat 75% and 94% respectively, prices collapsing at the war's end.[51] When the blockade moved east, sugar and cotton prices rose in Germany. American textile prices relative to Britain more than doubled. Imported food prices rose everywhere, especially during blockade, 100–200% common, but in Britain while availability and prices were significantly affected, merchants navigated around the blockade. Protected French industries replicated formerly imported goods. At the war's end, they clamoured for tariff protection, mainly successfully. In America, lack of British textiles, helped kick-start its textile factories, assisted by tariff protection.

Spanish American viceroyalties and presidencies set-up juntas in the the king's name, but were virtually independent. In 1809 Spain decreed its colonies part of Spain, but refused American-born Spanish equal representation and did not allow them free trade, repeated in the 1812 constitution. By 1825 all but Cuba and Puerto Rico were independent. In Brazil, when the king returned to Portugal, Prince Regent Dom Pedro stayed as ruler but locals rose-up in 1822 and gained independence. Cuba prospered after 1790 with the opening of international trade and growing sugar exports to America. In the mid-1780s Latin America took 0.06% of British manufactured exports, 3.3% in 1804–6, 6.3% in 1814–16 and 15% in the mid-1820s. Britain's share of world shipping jumped from 25.3% in 1780 to 42% in 1820.[52] In 1814–15, probably half of Britain's Caribbean exports were for transhipment to South America. From the 1820s it dealt directly. British cotton cloth easily undercut local and Spanish protected goods' prices and quality. Mexican silver output fell from about 20 million piasters annually in the 1790s to around 16.4 million between 1807 and 1813, 11.3 million 1814–1820 and 8.8 million in the 1820s. Lack of South American representative institutions produced military dictatorships.

Despite Plassey and the *diwani*, as late as 1812, exports to India were under half Jamaica's. About 80% of British foreign investments were in the Caribbean. But its importance fell because US cotton replaced the Caribbean's as Britain's main source and South American trade became direct, while Britain's Indian trade value grew as British products gradually replaced silver shipments. These were watershed years for many trades with significant consequences.

Bordeaux, Nantes and Le Havre's trade was a trickle of former volumes. They could not reinvent themselves the way Liverpool and Glasgow did. British merchants returned to Livorno from Palermo, Messina and Malta, integrating the Mediterranean into the world economy. During the war, Scandinavian and Greeks replaced British ships trading with high freight rates in the Mediterranean (See Chapters 14–15). These prosperous merchant-led Greek years led to a developing national consciousness, which in depression and near-famine conditions which followed, unaddressed by Ottomans, led to calls for independence.

Napoleon believed Britain's weakness was dependence on foreign trade, but it was Britain's strength. French over-reliance on St. Domingue meant whenever at war, its concentrated interests were dreadfully damaged. Caribbean dependence meant it had to have a navy, an alien culture. British maritime culture was by contrast, deep-rooted, its *raison d'etre*. Napoleon also thought Britain's National Debt dangerously high, his aim to force financial overextension. But 18th-century financial stability proved Britain's greatest platform for world trade extension.

Waterloo heralded almost 100 years of peace and accelerating maritime trade. Proportionate to Europe's population, nineteenth-century battlefield deaths were seven-times less than the 18th-century's.[53] Indian dominion meant local armies disbanded, ending endemic warfare. The population rose but handloom weavers suffered as cotton cloth exports to Europe ceased. India still contended with periodic monsoon failures, famines, inadequate inland transport and lack of a capital market, but most British imports to India were subject to duty and Britain spent it on public works and infrastructure, encouraging private investments.

British trade was never crippled in war. It suffered, even when not directly involved, as in the 1700–1721 Great Northern War. Closed markets, loss of ships, high freight and insurance rates all affected it. But French trade could be halted by British naval supremacy. The Bank of England and National Debt made the City a capital market. Growing maritime trade, political and religious diversity encouraged industry. The merchant culture of compromise negated France's four-fold size and population advantage. Napoleon tried compensating for overseas trade by making Europe a French-dominated economic unit, hopeless when forced and Europe wanted British goods. France's inability to embrace trade organically and develop a strong merchant class, unused to representative institutions and compromise, led to inherent financial and industrial disadvantage.

Britain's 1763 supremacy was considerable; in 1815 unshakable, having destroyed French, Spanish, Danish and Dutch navies, its own was larger than the rest combined, increasing 32.8% from 1790 to 1815. Others declined by 38.3%.[54] The only other consequential commercial maritime power was Seyyid Said's Oman, its traders from the Gulf, East Africa, Red Sea, India and Southeast Asia. Britain sought few acquisitions in 1793, especially those of former allies, the aims domestic defence, Caribbean territory and South American trade expansion. Enlargement of Indian rule was unplanned and unintended. British natural instincts, informal trade empire, were correct, despite territorial gains in India. The end of Europe's national trade monopolies did not herald free trade. Tariffs replaced monopolies.

Chapter 13

Enlightenment Through the Wars

Slave trading evidence given to Commons' Committees after 1788 made Britain's public increasingly aware that slavery's economic benefits came at unacceptable human cost. John Newton's 1788 *Thoughts upon the African Slave Trade* told how he, a shipowner's son and ex-slave captain, was pressganged, escaped, recaptured, flogged, enslaved on a lime plantation, rescued and worked again on a slaver. He concluded it was 'unlawful and wrong' and to a 1790 Committee, thought Africans 'with equal advantages…would be equal to ourselves.' In 1789, Pitt supported a bill regulating the trade, telling Parliament, 'The nature and all the circumstances of this trade are now laid open to us. We can no longer plead ignorance…Let not Parliament be the only body that is insensible to…natural justice,' repeating that twice as many sailors died on slavers as other ships. In 1792 the Commons resolved slave trading's gradual abolition. The Lords rejected it. Volumes peaked in 1798 when 160 slave ships left English ports, mainly Liverpool, which annually sent 70–100 in the 1780s-1790s.[1] Sugar prices fell 50% by the early-1820s as cheaper Brazilian, Surinam, Mauritian and Cuban sugar undercut British Caribbean prices and Indian sugar imports rose as Britons began refusing Caribbean slave-grown sugar.

Britain was the world's leading slave trader, despite as Richard Johnson said in 1618, it was 'un-English' to hold slaves. Even in Liverpool, maritime minds were opening. Comedian George Cooke, booed at the Theatre Royal for being drunk, retorted he was not going to be insulted by a town whose every brick was cemented by African blood, echoing Reverend William Bagshaw Stevens' 1797 remark. That the audience applauded indicates readiness to support a moral stance, impossible in Le Havre, Nantes or Bordeaux. Eleven thousand people, 20% of Manchester's population, signed its first anti-slave petition in 1787.[2] There were 519 petitions to Parliament in 1792 alone, with 500,000 signatures, 'the greatest such demonstration of popular opinion British politics had ever known.'[3] In 1796 the Commons voted 93–67 for abolition but the Lords overturned it, just. Momentum continued building. Dundas admitted that the trade was 'founded on injustice and inhumanity' but 'this was not the time for abolition' because war with France from 1793 was a major threat, delaying it.

When in 1793 British authorities seized French Indian possessions, regarding themselves as guardians, they ended slave exports to French Indian Ocean islands. In 1796 EIC directors approved suppressing slave trading in Malabar and in 1805 Robert Farquhar proposed slavery's abolition in Penang; 'the greatest of all evils and the attempt to regulate such an evil is in itself almost absurd.' The EIC banned imports and sales of foreign slaves in Bengal in 1811. Richard Wellesley, EIC Governor-General from 1798, wrote in 1804, 'To facilitate and promote all enquiries…to enlarge the boundaries of general science is a duty imposed on the British Government in India.' He founded Calcutta's Fort William College to educate its employees. EIC London directors established Haileybury College and changed Fort William College into a school for Indian languages for Bengalis. He built roads and drainage to improve Calcutta to prevent it relapsing into 'its ancient state of filth and unhealthiness,' prohibited child sacrifice, directed British ministers in India learn Indian 'history, languages, customs and manners' and reduced *suttee*. General Charles 'Hindoo' Stuart even bathed daily in the Ganges, collected Indian art, recommended English ladies wear saris and criticised missionaries, without hindering his career.

Slaves who fled southern plantations and fought for Britain in the American Independence War were protected, first in Nova Scotia then in 1792 a free community of 1,196 settlers, sent in 15 ships to Freetown, Sierra Leone, comprising neat houses and public buildings, including Harmony Hall.[4] By contrast, in the Dutch Cape, slaves from West Africa, Java, China and Madagascar easily outnumbered Dutch, revolts controlled by draconian punishments, numbers maintained with supplies from Zanzibar from the 1770s. Taken in 1795, Cape Colony was returned at the Treaty of Amiens and retaken in 1805. This time the gallows and rack were publicly destroyed, torture ended, 'benevolence' announced towards indigenous and enslaved people and in 1809 a *Hottentot Code* prevented Boers enslaving those remaining.[5]

Napoleon tried reviving slave trading and reconquering St. Domingue in 1804, while abolition again passed the Commons, blocked by the Lords. Like a *philosophe*, Napoleon told his brother Jerome to ignore Westphalian public opinion. 'If the people refuse its own happiness, the people are guilty of anarchy and deserve to be punished.' He sent him the *Code Napoleon* and advised public trial, juries and serfdom's abolition: France's enlightenment's tool kit. Serfdom was abolished but feudal dues, rents and tithes continued, exposing its shallowness, the aim always centralising. France's enlightenment was a disaster. Arresting rhetoric, 'man born free is everywhere in chains,' disguised hollowness. Progress in solving practical scientific, technical and mechanical problems accelerated in Britain. In 1802, the first Factory Act, promoted by Robert Peel the Elder, limited child labour in cotton mills to 12 hours/day.

American Consul in Algiers William Eton, repulsed by Barbary states' slavery, thought it 'a copy of the very barbarity…seen in my…country…yet we boast of liberty and natural justice.'[6] Abolition of slave trading, although thought manageable, was a huge economic sacrifice. In 1804, 150 out of 1,000 British Caribbean ships were slavers,[7] America also abolished the trade in 1807, although not internally. Denmark abolished her tiny trade in 1803 because her government thought Britain was about to ban it. Britain thought Spanish America had insufficient slavers to sustain it and Portugal susceptible to British pressure. That proved too optimistic. Caribbean islands became dependent on foreigners supplying slaves and provisions. Despite US Quaker-led abolitionists, America's merchant fleet, the world's second-largest, met demand.

Abolition was <u>not</u> done because it was uneconomic. With unrivalled sea power, slave trading would have been more profitable. Moreover, abolition was enacted while new markets, Guiana, Trinidad and Cuba boomed, attracting slave investment. Yet it chose morality and virtue. This legislative enlightenment, hardly ever linked to mythical continental Enlightenment, needs contextual clarification.

That it happened in 1807, during war, the abolition of the institution itself in British territories in 1833 and in US southern states 30 years later, shows how maritime thinking evolved so fast from the 1760s, given it existed virtually unchallenged for most of human history. It could only have been done by a maritime nation and only enforced by one as strong as Britain. No continental country had a groundswell of enlightened public opinion against slave trading. Once abolished, the same humanitarian feelings fused with commercial desire to stop others gaining undue competitive advantage, establishing the West Africa Squadron in 1808, the 'Preventative Squadron', which for 50 years operated against slavers (See Chapter 25). In 1813 Stamford Raffles called for emancipation of Java's slaves, recently recaptured from the Dutch. East African, Madagascan and Indonesian slave traders were also suppressed. The 1811 Felony Act made slave trading by British subjects punishable by transportation to Australia. Some continued on non-British-flagged ships, but warships hunted them down. Slaving died in an atmosphere of rational, humanitarian disgust, an affront to enlightened British values.

The Manchester Chamber of Commerce representing the increasingly mechanised cotton industry embraced free trade. In 1800 Dundas proposed that Indian-built ships operated by regional traders should import to Britain. In the 1813 Parliamentary debates on EIC charter renewal, free traders and manufacturing interests broke EIC monopoly trade in India. The EIC successfully argued that Chinese xenophobia and Canton's *hong* peculiarities meant it should retain exclusivity in China and tea.

Britain's maritime culture of improvement was reflected in improving naval signalling, especially after US Independence. Captain Sir Home Popham's *Signal Book* enabled quick communications. France was slower. British blockading ships outside French ports for months in all weathers were, as in the 1750s-1760s, supplied with fruit, vegetables and live cattle from Plymouth-based ships. In 1795 the anti-scurvy policy of issuing lemons became official, following Dr. James Lind's 1753 *A Treatise on Scurvy*, never taken-up in French and Spanish navies, far behind in all disciplines.

In 1807, Napoleon urged his Interior Minister to ensure girls got a good education, 'not that girls should think, but that they should believe.'[8] Mary Wollstonecraft's 1792 *A Vindication of the Rights of Women*, proposing women receive the same education and career opportunities as men was too radical for its time, but French and English novels show different attitudes. Rousseau's *Emile* explains, 'A woman's education… must be planned in relation to man. To be pleasing in his sight, to win his respect and love…to make his life pleasant and happy, these are the duties of woman…taught while…young.' By contrast, Jane Austin's first three novels, written in the 1790s were concerned with moral responsibility and love as a guide to marriage. Women led boycotts of slave-produced sugar. While Europe was convulsed with war, Britain was convulsed with innovative industrial and intellectual change. Inventions, ideas and developing academia were expressions of liberated minds. In 1808 the first of many subsequent reductions in capital offences was introduced.

Other disciplines advanced. Since the early-18th century, smallpox was treated by inoculation with a mild dose, potentially spreading the disease. Edward Jenner (1749–1823), observed that milkmaids infected with cowpox, similar but less virulent, were immune from smallpox. In 1798 he began inoculating with it and by 1808 national vaccine centres were established in London.[9] He is perhaps responsible for saving more lives than any other person, laying modern immunology's foundations. In 1785 Scottish geologist James Hutton thought the earth's history should be understood as a gradual geological process over millions of years,[10] contradicting Christian ideas of a 4,000-year-old planet, challenged again in the 1830s when Charles Lyell published *Principles of Geology*. Thomas Malthus' *An Essay on the Principles of Population* (1798) theorised that populations grow faster than food supply and should be checked. Historians for the first time since Classical times began applying social, economic and cultural analysis. Edward Gibbon's 1788 *Decline and Fall of the Roman Empire* was critical of early Christians' role in its '*Fall*' compared with Clarendon's *History of the Great Rebellion* (1704), which assumed the establishment's authority. No less significantly, 1814 was the Marylebone Cricket Club's first season. Like previous eras of maritime trade-driven advances, art also pushed new limits. Between 1793 and 1814, J.M.W. Turner developed a style representing British maritime power, science, industry and technology.

The Manchester Literary and Philosophical Society from 1781 played a role in the northwest similar to the Midlands' Lunar Society. Its proceedings were first published in 1783, the first regular scientific journal except the Royal Society's *Transactions*. Members included self-made industrialist-philanthropist Robert Owen (1771–1858), who after seven years managing a Manchester cotton mill, bought one in New Lanark in 1800 to show employers that treating workers well was profitable, becoming a model business, providing health education, social security and temperance. His 1813 *New View of Society* stated 'we are advancing towards the dawn of reason…when the mind of man will be born again.' In 1817 he aimed at an eight-hour working day. The Newcastle Literary and Philosophical Society, founded in 1793, had prominent industrialists, engineers, scientists, philanthropists, naturalists, engravers and authors, including Earl Grey, the 1830–1834 reforming prime minister. Many debating societies, invaluable for scientists, industrialists, philosophers and intellectuals, discussed wide-ranging topics, spreading enlightened thinking. *Nicholson's Journal of Natural Philosophy, Chemistry and other Arts* (1797) accelerated scientific discovery. By 1815 the Royal Institution, Geological, Zoological, Horticultural and Astronomical Societies were founded. John Dalton (1766–1844), chemist, meteorologist and physicist researched colour-blindness and atomic theory, that elements are composed of atoms of identical size and mass which cannot be subdivided, combining into chemical compounds. He was first to publish an atomic weights table and was a fellow of the Royal Society and French *Académie de Sciences*.

Over the past couple of decades or so, some economic historians have debated the relationship between Industrial Revolution and Enlightenment, disadvantaged by failure to define either. In this analysis, Industrial Revolution was part of British Enlightenment, maritime-influenced, problem-solving, applying practical improvements. Indeed, proponent Joel Mokyr shows mainly British examples, knowledge-dissemination in newspapers, periodicals, pamphlets, lectures, books and coffee houses. Royal Institution public lectures on scientific and technological topics helped knowledge-diffusion and introduction of mechanical inventions and improvement.[11] Scientific, technological, agricultural and intellectual advances have always taken place in maritime-influenced areas. From the wealth created, culture, philosophy, architecture and engineering were improved. In this case, industrial development was triggered by domestic demand from an increasing wealthy middle class, created by trade. In contrast, poor continental peasants could not provide demand, nor time or incentive to invent or improve.

As with some historians' dismissal of inventive Phoenician engineers, highlighted in this series first book, some display arrogance about technical advances. One Mokyr critic writes 'the Industrial Revolution was largely made…by craftsmen with limited formal education solving basic technical problems.'[12] 'Basic' smears John Harrison's decades of heroic labour culminating in H4, one of British Enlightenment's greatest achievements. Technical advances were not basic but experience-driven, which until the mid-19th century, they always had been. Mokyr's critic continues, 'textiles accounts for at least 50% of productivity growth in England in the Industrial Revolution era. Yet the most important innovators of the British Industrial Revolution in textiles had little or no connection to the Enlightenment…the Industrial Revolution was not about designs for social engineering, the distinctive forces of the Enlightenment, but about cheaper production of textiles, coal, iron and motive power. Most of the focus of the Enlightenment had little bearing on this.' If the Enlightenment is defined as French or European, that may be, but Industrial Revolution and British Enlightenment were deeply connected with developments chronicled in preceding chapters, improvement, innovation, humanitarianism, trusteeship, welfare; only possible in maritime-influenced societies.

Even on Mokyr's critic's own terms, he is unclear. Do textiles really account for 50% of productivity growth? If so, in what period? Economic historians' use of numbers is often problematic when arguments are multi-layered and nuanced. Anyway, assumptions are critical. Richard Arkwright (1732–1792) and Samuel Crompton (1753–1827) whose roller (1769) and mule (1779) allowed finer, stronger yarns at lower cost with semi-skilled labour, were not moral or political philosophers, but mechanical philosophers. If the term seems strange, consider William Symington, key player in transferring steam technology to ships. 'My natural turn for mechanical philosophy led me to change my object and to direct my studies to the exercise of the profession of civil engineer,'[13] philosophy used in the way Wedgwood described Boulton (see page 68). Britain's post-Newton improvers saw things in mechanical terms. The technical imaginations of Boulton, Watt, Darby, Brindley, Smeaton, Trevithick, Kay, Arkwright, Hargreaves, Cort and Crompton demonstrate that creativity takes many forms. Crompton's spinning mule patent expired in 1783, leading to many cotton mills subsequently built, overtaking woollen cloth as Britain's main export. Arkwright's first mill at Cromford had workers' cottages and a public house.

If textile productivity is Mokyr's critic's main benchmark, Industrial Revolution, like Enlightenment, needs better definition. Steam power was surely the crucial element;

24 hours a day, all year, productivity, efficiency and reduced costs, without which it would _not_ have been revolutionary! By 1800, steam power drove cotton machinery, wool about 20 years later. It drained coal mines, enabling higher extraction rates, powered sugar, flour and malt mills, breweries and potteries. Richard Trevithick first made high pressure steam work around 1797–1799, built the first steam road locomotive in 1801, on rails in 1804. Malcolm Falkus thinks the most persuasive benchmark contender was pig iron production, smelted by coke, tripling from 1788 to 1806, contributing more than cotton cloth to national income, around 7%, supplying railways, shipbuilding, engineering, gas and water pipes. The 1806 export, 250,000 tons became two million in 1847, half the world's production, 3.07 million in 1854, 7.812 million in 1884, and 10.26 million in 1913, 30% exported in 1830, peaking in the 1870s with 70%, exports then stagnating.[14] Industrial Revolution cannot be defined or measured by textiles alone. It is clear however, that early-18th century Indian cloth import prohibition stirred a technical search for domestic solutions, Kaye's flying shuttle the first advance. Much enlightened pioneer thinking took place in ports or maritime-influenced areas, the direct results of maritime trade.

Canal engineer William Jessop (1745–1814) apprenticed to John Smeaton, was the West India Docks' chief engineer, designed the Grand Canal of Ireland, was consulting engineer for the Ellesmere Canal Co., appointing Thomas Telford (1757–1834) as resident engineer, linking ironworks and collieries to the Mersey with spectacular aqueducts using 'troughed' cast iron plates, enabling huge, spanned arches. Telford designed and built about 40 Shropshire iron bridges, influenced by the Darby's, improving spanning with half the weight. He worked on the Shrewsbury Canal, the Caledonian Canal, (1803–22) the Menai Suspension Bridge (1819–26) and St. Katherine's Docks. London's Pall Mall was illuminated by gas lights in 1813, coal gas widely available from the 1820s.

High-volume coal extraction needed safe lamps in methane-filled mines. Humphrey Davy (1778–1829), chemistry lecturer, President of the Royal Society and Geological Society fellow, invented the safety lamp using wire gauze to prevent the flame spreading. Michael Faraday was Davy's laboratory assistant. Direct links at multiple levels produced innovative problem-solving culture, not possible in France, Poland, Russia or China, but embraced in Belgium after 1830, when not under Spanish, Austrian or Dutch rule, but independent and British-influenced.

Boulton and Watt, steam engine manufacturers before 1815, employed many skilled workmen who released avalanches of invention and investment. Not all engineering improvements were British. Eli Whitney's was American. Robert Fulton, (1765–1815) a Pennsylvania-born engineer and inventor, who on a European tour, met the Duke of Bridgewater, published on canals, patented a dredging machine and probably using William Symington's ideas, built the first successful US passenger steamboat in 1806 for Albany to New York. He moved in enlightened circles, meeting US founding father Benjamin Franklin (1705–1790), inventor, political theorist, scientific writer, newspaper editor, first President of the American Philosophical Society who freed his slaves, becoming a prominent abolitionist. Some early chemists were French and German, but most first-half 19th-centuty inventors were British; practitioners of experimental science, making technological breakthroughs, descendants of prominent philosophical societies on all subjects, propelling British Enlightenment and Industrial Revolution.

As an Adam Smith disciple, Bentham continued advocating individual and economic freedom, separation of church and state, freedom of expression, women's rights, abolition of slavery, death penalty and physical punishment and like EIC officials and Blackstone was a doer. With Patrick Colquhoun and EIC official John Harriot, they tackled corruption in London's 'pool', establishing the Thames River Police in 1800. Bentham became a proponent of disabled and animal rights, foreshadowed in 18th-century Britain. He called Rousseau's 'natural rights' 'nonsense upon stilts' and during Greek independence struggles, complimented the framers of their 1822 constitution, as 'comfortable to the principle of the greatest happiness of the greatest number.'[15]

Arguably one of the British Enlightenment's greatest triumphs were in India. In 1815 Ram Mohun Roy assembled the *Almiya Sabha*, a reform discussion group. His 1818 *The Practice of Burning Widows Alive* stated that *suttee* was murder according to 'common sense of all nations.' Of the 1820–21 suppression of the Naples revolt, he wrote their cause was also his. 'Enemies to liberty and friends of despotism have never been and never will be ultimately successful.'[16]

The French Enlightenment's end in Revolution excesses is not quite the end of the story. Some bad ideas refuse to die. The Jacobin's heirs always claimed to speak for people from a position of superiority. Rousseau influenced Saint-Simon (1760–1825) and French socialists. De Tocqueville identified socialism as heir to pre-revolutionary France's bureaucratic spirit, denial of liberty, contempt for individuals, 'a new form of servitude.'[17] Even after the darkness that befell the 20th-century's first half, the detrimental effects of French Enlightenment did not cease. Disappointment with 1950s-1970s communist states led to thinking they had not been revolutionary or pure enough. One result was Mao's Cultural Revolution, a disaster in which tens of millions died. Another was Cambodia's elite studying in Paris, their Left Bank Marxist circle embracing callous elitism, contempt for the people. They especially idealised the creator and victim of the Terror who wanted to force people to be free, Maximilian Robespierre. The result was Pol Pot's Khmer Rouge government (1975–1979) and slaughter of almost half Cambodia's population, including all its intelligentsia. A visit to Phnom Penh's Khmer Rouge prison, actually a torture and death camp, is as sobering as one to a Nazi concentration camp.

Chapter 14

18th-Century Scandinavian Shipping

It is necessary to backtrack chronologically to explain emerging Scandinavian and in the next chapter Greek shipping. After mid-17th century military triumphs Sweden tried reducing dependence on Dutch shipping, especially for Portuguese salt. In the 1690s about 20 ships annually discharged bar iron, pitch and weapons in Portugal, returning with salt. During the 1700–1721 Great Northern War, the trade resumed on Dutch ships, but Sweden's 1724 Navigation Act allowed imports only on Swedish or the cargo-producing country's ships. Swedish ships passing the Danish Sound increased from 230 in 1723 to 480 in 1726. Dutch shipping passing the Sound collapsed from over 100 in 1720 to three in 1726.[1] Denmark-Norway's Navigation Act followed in 1742.

Denmark had three small Caribbean sugar islands, about 20% of its fleet engaged there in the 1780s. Copenhagen was central to Baltic distribution of colonial and south European products. It had Christianborg in West Africa, Tranquebar in south India and a trade enclave in Canton, from which its Asiatic Company's ships brought tea. It exported mainly timber and fish and supplied Iceland, Greenland and Faroe Islands with agricultural products. By the 1780s its merchant marine was Europe's fourth-largest, by 1800 about a third of Britain's, half France's just behind the Dutch.[2]

Swedish and Russian bar iron with Baltic grain, timber, tar, pitch and hemp were Baltic staples. Sweden needed secure maritime access to Finland and remaining north German territories. The Swedish East India Company (1731–1813) traded with China but had no trade stations and little Indian trade. Imports included Portuguese salt and Baltic grain but Stockholm and Gothenburg never achieved Copenhagen's redistribution role. Its merchant fleet was just under half the size of Denmark's, Europe's fifth-largest.[3]

Swedish shipping's long-haul origin was Portugal's dramatic 1690s salt price rises. Searching for cheaper Mediterranean sources, Swedish ships came into dangerous Barbary States' waters. Despot-governed Morocco, Algiers, Tunis and Tripoli sustained themselves through piracy against Mediterranean ships and villages, sometimes even northern Europe, enslaving and ransoming villagers and seamen. A continuing 17th-18th century problem, Cervantes and Defoe had been among their captures, both ransomed.[4] Spain, France and Sicily periodically sent fleets against them to get slaves released. England had forced Algiers to make a 1682 Treaty of Commerce, giving English ships freedom to trade without seizure or enslavement and supplying them with cattle. Still problematic for others, Sweden in 1729 signed a treaty with Algiers. In return for ships and substantial armaments, a Swedish consul sat in Algiers and 'passports' were issued to Swedish ships verifying they were Swedish-flagged and

Swedish-owned, thus exempt from attack and seizure. Treaties with Tunis followed in 1736, Tripoli in 1741 and Morocco in 1761. Denmark again followed Sweden's example.[5] Scandinavian treaties legitimised and regulated Barbary protection rackets by paying advance ransom for their ships' safety.

Scandinavian shipping's Mediterranean importance was aided by neutrality in Anglo-French conflicts as Ottoman opportunities increased, less belligerent than previously, with Trieste and Livorno free ports. Neutral shipping mitigated wars' damaging effect on trade volumes, meeting demand caused by rising populations and living standards. 'Passports' kept insurance premiums lower than for belligerents. Swedes also had smaller crews for high-bulk, low-cost iron, timber and salt, without military personnel or munitions. Furthermore, Swedish wages were 30–50% lower than British, French, Dutch, Venetian and Danish according to a 1768 report. That was a peaceful year. In war, the difference must have been larger.[6] These were useful advantages in the Mediterranean where, with Barbary ransom paid, there were few impediments to trade, Scandinavian ships as third-party carriers, a forerunner of today's non-national market. Geographically counter-intuitive as it seems, Scandinavian shipping's main 18th-century driver was Mediterranean trade, increasing from about 150 annual voyages in the 1740s-1750s, to 212 in 1764 during the Seven Years War, from 222 voyages in 1775 to 441 in 1782 during the American Independance War and from 257 in 1792 to 717 in 1804, during French Revolutionary War, as British merchant ships supported the war effort. Swedish ships increased in war, stagnated or declined in intervening peace and declined during the 1788–90 Russo-Swedish War when Danish shipping expanded at Swedish expense.[7] About a third of Swedish ships traded in the Mediterranean.

The *Pelikan*, a Swedish 183-tonner from Norrkoping, in 1775–1777 did not visit Sweden for 21 months, trading at Bordeaux, Ancona, Barcelona, Alicante, Genoa, Palermo, Cadiz and Setubal. Many stayed away longer and went further. US 1790s consular reports referred to Swedish ships carrying Mediterranean goods to the Caribbean and US.[8] Between 1732 and 1792 a third of north European ships arriving in Mediterranean ports were Scandinavian; 1,466 Swedish and 1,453 Danish, behind Dutch and British.[9] In 1787 over 20% of Copenhagen's merchant tonnage was in Caribbean trade, its most important destination.[10] Eighteenth-century Baltic volumes nearly doubled, 1,741 vessels passing the Sound up to 1750, mainly after 1721 but 3,176 between 1750 and 1800. Scandinavian and British ships increased while Dutch fell from 42% to 28%.[11] British share of Baltic trade rose from around 6% in 1660 to about 30% in 1760. The first Partition of Poland (1772) diverted grain from Danzig to Elbing, catastrophic for Danzig whose annual average of 11,000 ships fell to 65 in 1792, while increasing Swedish and Danish shipping challenged Lubeck and Hamburg as shipowner centres.

Chapter 15

18th and Early-19th-Century Greek Shipping

For centuries Greeks had been merchants and seafarers in Venetian, Genoese and Ottoman seas. Chios was Genoese for 200 years until Ottoman conquest in 1566. Syros and Andros were Venetian for 300 years until conquered in 1537 and 1566. Furthermore, Greeks monopolised 18th-century Ottoman naval bureaucracy. Anglo-French wars gave Greek shipowners, like Scandinavians, opportunities as neutrals to supply blockaded ports with goods and food. The thousands of Black Sea ships were mainly Greek-owned, many run from Istanbul's Galata suburb, some Armenian- and Jewish-owned, some in regulated grain movements and some in illicit trade.

Long-haul trade in British, Dutch and French ships benefitted from this Mediterranean-Black Sea distribution. British ships brought American fish, sugar, coffee and tobacco to Livorno, then shipped to the Levant and North Africa by Greek, Scandinavian and Tuscan ships, many with Jewish merchant intermediaries. Sicily still exported about 40,000 tons of grain annually, especially to north Italy, but drier climatic conditions reduced production and export. The 1747 Grand Duchy of Tuscany-Ottoman Treaty set duties on products traded between the two, benefitting Livorno whose warehouses stored grain until prices were right for Greeks to sell to the western Mediterranean.[1] East Mediterranean political divisions; Ottoman, Venetian, Genoese, Austrian and Tuscan, were commercially united by Greek merchants and ships.

The first large Greek Mediterranean merchant fleet was at Missolonghi and Galaxidi in the 1730s, near Ancona, Trieste and Livorno. Missolonghi's shipowners exported timber from Preveza. Ships from Hydra, Spetses and Psara took Thessaly's wheat west.[2] By 1764 Galaxidi had 50 small ships, totalling 10,000 tons with 1,000 seamen. Missolonghi had 80 ships in 1770. Aegean island families, friends, captains and seamen saved through years at sea, accumulating capital. Chiot merchants had commercial agents in all major Mediterranean and Black Sea ports, hiring Psara's and Hydra's ships for their cotton, silk, fruit, mastic gum, increasingly products from a wider area and were important grain brokers.

The 18th-century surge in Ottoman trade increased Greeks' role because they spoke Turkish and knew Turkish customs. Catherine II annexed Ukraine's rich, black earth, wheat-growing lands, important due to Mediterranean grain import needs. After the Russo-Turkish War in 1774, the Treaty of Kucuk Kaynarci gave Greek-owned, Russian-flagged ships Black Sea-Mediterranean navigation rights. Russia built Kherson, which from 1780 exported wheat and salt beef, the first legal cargoes into the Mediterranean since before the 1453 Ottoman closure. Russia encouraged emigration to Ukraine, 'New Russia', including Greeks. The population increased from 163,000 in 1782 to 3.4 million in 1856.[3] Ottoman officials could still be difficult, ships sometimes impounded if they felt rules were abused, but a small trade to Marseilles was established. Greeks in Trieste handled Austrian trade and were close with Greeks in Smyrna, Alexandria and Istanbul, as cargo volumes rose.

Kherson was not ideal, far from the coast, liable to flood into stagnant waters, breeding disease, killing two brothers of pioneering Marseilles' trader Antoine de St. Joseph in the 1780s. When Russia responded to the French Revolution by banning French products, he returned to Marseilles to write *Historical Essay on the Commerce and Navigation of the Black Sea*, an early-19th-century guide to its business.[4] Odesa, founded in 1794, quickly became the leading wheat exporter, attracting Greek, Albanian, Italian and Jewish merchants. It imported olive oil, wine, dried fruit, tobacco, cheese and wool from Greece, Italy and Spain on Greek and Italian ships. Greeks used Valetta, its merchant fleet increasing 70% to 120 ships by 1800.[5] Livorno was the main wheat entrepot.[6] By 1800 Greek shipping and shipbuilding emerged in Hydra, Spetses, Psara and Galaxidi.[7] Greek insurance companies, in Trieste by 1792, were established in Odesa in 1808. Greek masters, identified across the Mediterranean by language, religion, culture and business practices,[8] increasingly interacted with British as agents, vice-consuls and trade partners. Marseilles hosted 51 Greek merchants in 1799 and 345 in 1825 but suffered from intolerant Catholicism. Marseilles was against Greek independence. Only in 1861 was a Greek admitted to its Chamber of Commerce.[9]

War diverted Marseilles' trade to Livorno, whose ship calls jumped from 527 in 1791 to 1,135 in 1794. Greek and Scandinavian ships distributed British products; cloth, sugar, coffee and tobacco.[10] 1808–1814 were golden years for Greek shipping; 40 built on Hydra alone. By 1816 there were about 700 Greek ships but declined with peace and in Missolonghi's case, an oppressive local pasha,[11] but Greek ships still shipped Black Sea wheat. Being Ottoman and Venetian subjects, they operated ships under Ottoman, Venetian, Russian, Jerusalem and Ionian flags, the latter a post-1815 British protectorate, dominating inter-Mediterranean grain trades. British merchants, granted Black Sea access in 1802, mainly depended on them.[12] In the 1821–33 Greek War of Independence, the Greek fleet came from Hydra, Spetses and Psara. The Turks did not attack the ports, even poorly-defended Spetses or far-off Psara. Landlubbers lacked confidence for bold maritime moves, but the war was disastrous for Greek shipping, converted into warships, reduced to about 50 by the end, while a quarter of Chios' population were slaughtered and half taken to Smyrna's slave market.[13] Like support for Spanish colonies' independence, liberal Britain supported Greek independence and without declaration of war, Admirals Codrington and Rigny destroyed the Turkish-Egyptian fleet at Navarino in 1827. By 1828 southern Greece and central Aegean islands were free, official in 1830, its population about 800,000, while 2.5 million Greeks remained outside.[14] After the 1828–29 Russo-Turkish war, Greek-owned, Russian-flagged ships traded in Turkey.

Chapter 16

Growing Pains of the Early American Republic. Trade, War and Pirates

Post-Independence American merchant shipping grew quickly, especially in the Caribbean at French merchants' expense. Britain initially excluded American ships from British Caribbean trade and tried stopping them trading with Canada, but America still got most manufactured goods from Britain, which imported its tobacco, coffee and rice. British merchant tonnage surged; 900,000 tons in 1775, 1.7 million in the early-1790s. American merchants also directed their energies to India, East Africa and the Pacific northwest, discovering China's appetite for furs and ginseng. The Mediterranean was more problematic.

Iberia and the Mediterranean regularly imported American wheat, flour, maize and fish for wine and salt. Without British flag and naval protection however, American ships and seamen were vulnerable to Barbary pirates' seizure and enslavement, first in 1783. George Washington asked in 1786, 'In such an <u>enlightened</u>, in such a <u>liberal</u> age, how is it possible the great maritime powers of Europe should submit to pay an annual tribute to the little piratical states of Barbary?'[1] Like Denmark and Sweden, it paid them not to attack their ships. A US navy established in 1794, was initially not used in the Mediterranean. US consul Eton thought piracy hindered potentially far more lucrative trade. From Tunis, 250,000 hides were exported annually. There was inter-Mediterranean potential in wax, wheat, oil, barley, beans, dates, salt and livestock. Jefferson thought without Barbary pirates, US rice, dried fish, wheat and flour could employ 100 ships annually.[2] For them however, white slavery was as essential for their economies as black slavery was for the Caribbean and southern US, simpler and cheaper than enslaving negroes further south. Ransom provided revenue.

A 1786 a US-Morocco treaty agreed a $20,000 payment not to seize US ships and enslave seamen. Encouraged, the stronger Algiers declared war, seized US ships, demanding $1,000,000 for those captured. Immediate post-independece US had weak central government, paltry financial strength and no coherent foreign policy, so its seamen languished in Algiers for years. Attempted 1791 negotiations failed. In 1793, 11 more ships and 104 men were seized, prompting Congress to authorise six frigates. Algiers raised its price to $2,000,000 but in 1795 reduced it to $600,000. America agreed, remitting 10% deposit, encouraging its ruler, the Day, to raise it again by $200,000, some in ships, gunpowder and naval stores, which America again humiliatingly agreed, supplying the Dey with the means to threaten more ships. Tunis and Tripoli seeing that threat and violence paid-off, demanded similar sums, increasing demands to Spain, France and Venice. All complied. Sweden and Denmark because of their treaties refused, had ships seized and seamen enslaved. Eventually they had to pay too. By 1796 America paid 20% of its annual budget. Further demands were conceded. Jefferson's 1800 Presidential election campaign criticised US weakness, 'subject to the spoliations of foreign cruisers,' paying 'enormous tribute to the petty tyrant of Algiers,' but Tripoli seized more ships.[3]

Barbary enslavement involved men breaking rocks for harbour defences while women were concubines, maids and cleaners. In 1790, for about 3,000 in each Barbary state, fanatical religious motives made life miserable. The Dey of Algiers in 1793 told captured Americans, 'Now I have got you, Christian dogs, you shall eat stones.' They joined others, 'in more miserable condition than ourselves, with wretched habits, dejected countenances and chains on their legs, [in]…unutterable distress,' sleeping on stone floors, spending days breaking rocks and being beaten.[4]

America's critical post-independence issue was revenue. About 90% was import duties and tonnage dues. During Anglo-French wars, the choice between France and Britain in American politics was divisive. Alexander Hamilton and George Washington supported reconciliation. Jefferson, gentleman planter, slaveholder, believing black and white could never coexist peacefully, ambiguous about the Terror due to Republican commitment, *philosophe-* and physiocrat-follower, hating New England's shipowners and merchants, to whom he was in debt, thinking only farmers 'the chosen people', was against. Virginia's Madison whose 'pursuit of happiness' was managing slave plantations, wanted a French alliance and to 'strangle the former mother country,' with a 60 cents/ton duty on British ships, 30 cents/ton on French, economic war with Britain, which he said had 'bound us in commercial manacles and very nearly defeated the object of our independence.' Breathtakingly overconfident, he thought 'her interests can be wounded almost mortally…ours are invulnerable,' and that British Caribbean islands could not live without America's provisions but America, without British manufactured goods, could. War's legacy clouded judgements, especially in American states less involved in maritime trade. Barbary pirate difficulties should have been a reality check.

Federalists by contrast, guided by Hamilton believed in maritime trade, banking, manufacturing and financial stability, attracting capital for infrastructure, seeing British and US interests as complimentary, reconciliation thus necessary, economic war a grave danger to the young union. With Washington's support he won the Senate argument. British and French ships paid 50 cents/ton, US ships six. Enshrined in the 1794 British-US Jay Treaty, it re-established trading relations, opened British Caribbean ports to US ships and evacuated British redcoats from western forts, easing the post-independence legacy of mistrust, including 250 seized US ships and its pre-war debts to British merchants. Crucially, it recognised America's maritime trade's importance, especially with Britain where there were shared cultural values, social, religious, economic and linguistic. Ten years of prosperous trade followed. British 1793–1799 exports to America more than doubled, which by 1800 imported over 25% of British exports. Logic dictated mutually friendly relations.

Jefferson and Madison instead looked inland for the future, in 1803 negotiating with Napoleon 'the Louisiana Purchase', aided by Barings' finance, huge tracts of land, transforming a hitherto mainly maritime-orientated country based around wealthy ports into a continental power and sent Lewis and Clark to explore the route to the Pacific. America's 'Manifest Destiny' was the west, expansion to the Pacific and war with Mexico to secure Arizona to California; continental hegemony.[5]

During Anglo-French wars, US ships exported provisions to French and Dutch Caribbean islands. They and South America imported almost a third of US exports and in 1807, 40% of Caribbean trade was in US hands, especially Cuba's, which from 1792 to 1817 doubled its slaves. 1790–1807 annual US exports increased from $20 million to $48 million, re-exports from insignificance to $60 million, direct profits from trade from $6 million to $42 million[6] and 1792–1801 trade value from $20 million to $94 million.[7] US merchant shipping tripled to over a million tons, second-largest after Britain. The number of US chartered banks rose from three in 1790 to 212 in 1815. Manufacturing increased especially in New England and Pennsylvania. New England's textile industry expanded from 46,000 yards in 1795 to 2.35 million in 1815.

When European war restarted in 1803, Britain and France's more aggressive stance toward neutral shipping trading with the enemy inevitably brought potential conflict. As British ships stopped and searched US ships, relations deteriorated as some Americans thought Britain sought humiliation, fuelling patriotic feelings. British blockade of the French Caribbean, Atlantic and Mediterranean ports damaged US shipowners' interests while British deserter sailors who enlisted on US ships were retrieved by the Royal Navy by boarding US ships. Anyone not proving US citizenship were taken, inevitably some US citizens. But there was still the Mediterranean problem.

Jefferson opposed funds for a navy except coastal defence, a false economy. He described tribute as 'money thrown away. There is no end to the demands of these powers, nor any security in their promises. The real alternative before us is whether to abandon the Mediterranean or to keep up a cruise on it.' In 1801 he sent a squadron after Tripoli declared war, while the *George Washington* neared Algiers with partial payment of the earlier agreement; inconsistent signals to Barbary states.[8] They tried blockading Tripoli, but its small, shallow, fast ships meant it was not fully effective. They had more success in 1803–04 attacking its harbour and by 1805 it was forced to the peace table. America declared war on Algiers, demanded an end to tribute and American slaves released. Treaties were made with Tunis and Tripoli. Thus, US Mediterranean shipping continued.

In 1804 the British annulled the concession that US ships could enter the British Caribbean. US merchants suffered and impressment aroused strong feelings. In 1806 Congress passed the Non-Importation Acts, banning some British imports, boosting US manufacturing. Tensions reached breaking point when the *USS Chesapeake* was boarded by *HMS Leopard* searching for British deserters, in which three Americans were killed and over a dozen injured, US sovereignty clearly violated. Jefferson highlighted 'the great and increasing dangers with which our vessels, our seamen, and merchandise are threatened,' but underestimated maritime trade's power, already invigorating America's nascent economy, the reason Federalists were anxious about Jefferson's presidency. His 1807 Embargo Act prohibited all US ships from sailing! Treasury Secretary Albert Gallatin opposed it due to the economic damage and impossibility of enforcement. Besides, some US merchants had profited blockade-running goods to France, the full extent unknown, as earlier discussed. America's 1807 exports, $108 million collapsed, not to zero but $22 million, due to smuggling with adjacent Spanish and Canadian lands. Ships not in US ports continued third party trades. Livorno for example recorded 138 US ships in 1807, compared with 116 Greeks, temporarily no British, due to French blockade.[9]

With US ports closed to European ships and US exports prohibited to belligerents, ports and farms were paralysed. Many US merchants were bankrupted. Unemployment among seamen spiked, 500 ships idled in New York, exports collapsed: more costly than war. British policy remained unchanged. The 1809 Non-Intercourse Act banned trade only with Britain and France, less damaging but also difficult to enforce. In 1810, Macon's Bill No 2 re-opened trade with France or Britain if one repealed anti-neutral policies, naive in these exceptional times. The collapse of British-US trade coincided with declining Baltic trade in 1811 following French occupation of southern Baltic ports, causing Britain's industrial and social crisis.

In 1810 Napoleon tested Macon's Bill No 2, because American grain fed Wellington's Iberian troops in contravention of it. He announced he would repeal the Berlin Decree if America forced Britain to respect its neutral rights. President Madison, not understanding how maritime trade was economically beneficial and believing French victory imminent, that Canada whose population was 10% of America's could be overrun, that Canadian food had taken some Caribbean markets and that its masts were vital to Britain, despite warnings it was a trap, fell into it, imposing non-intercourse against Britain, demanded repeal of Orders in Council against neutral shipping having to go via British ports and declared war, egged-on by westerners annoyed at Britain's protective attitude to native Americans. Federalists, especially in New England, which heavily depended on British trade opposed him, believing France equally guilty of offending US neutrality. Earlier embargoes had manifestly failed. Madison said in 1795, 'of all the enemies to public liberty, war is perhaps, the most to be dreaded.' Yet after Republican refusal to recharter Hamilton's national bank in 1811, without one to finance it, a lesson only slowly learnt, only agreed in 1816, he declared war with a divided cabinet, militias refusing to fight outside their states and New England refusing support. Trade became smuggling; customs revenue was lost. Madison's war harmed only America and Americans.

Ostensibly about maritime rights, war began with invasion of Canada, potentially serious for Britain as its maritime provinces were a significant timber resource. Within a week of war's declaration, Britain, even before it learnt of it, suspended the Orders in Council, eliminating the supposed cause. Deaf to New England's maritime interests, ignorant of Jay Treaty benefits, jealous of their new national identity, especially the emotive impressment issue, fixated on old antagonisms, Madison's war became a dangerous, naive, blustering show of nationalism, an air of 'unfinished business'. On learning of the suspension, he continued, when it could have been presented as a bloodless victory!

In retaliation for Canada's invasion, Royal Navy ships from New Brunswick, Nova Scotia and Caribbean blockaded American ports, capturing ships. New England's fishing industry immediately lost Grand Banks access. America failed to prevent British supplies reaching Canada. New Brunswick and Nova Scotia merchants captured American ships and cargoes, swelling revenues. Ship seizures on the James, York, Rappahannock and Potomac Rivers seriously disrupted daily life. After Napoleon's defeat, more effective blockade ruined many businesses. Coastal trade virtually ceased, forcing land haulage, longer, more expensive, increasing prices. Most US navy vessels were blockaded. In 1813 the *Nova Scotia Royal Gazette* re-printed a letter from Baltimore; 'a besieged city…Nothing doing, all business at a stand…The price of everything almost doubled…our supplies by water totally cut off.'[10] Britain was hardly affected except Lancashire's cotton industry, starved of US cotton, imported Caribbean instead.

US flour exports to Iberia, almost a million barrels in 1812 dropped to 5,000 in 1814. Total exports, $45 million in 1811 fell to $7 million in 1814. As New York and New England hardened against war, some New Englanders contemplated secession.[11] Between 1812 and 1814 America incurred a $105 million debt, imports collapsed, customs and tax receipts declined, prices rose, insurance and transport costs rocketed. Its merchants had to suspend Mediterranean trade. Lloyds reported in 1814 that during the war, America captured 1,175 British ships, a third re-captured. It took 6,000 casualties, its navy lost 20% of its men-of-war. The Royal Navy lost more ships but that was only 1%. When news of the 1814 peace reached New York, sugar prices halved. In December 1813 only five US vessels cleared Boston. In March 1815, 144 did so, most for foreign destinations, boosting port receipts and the number of fishing licenses tripled from 1814 to 1816.[12]

No substantive issues prompting the war were resolved. Arguments over trade policies and maritime rights persisted into the 1820s. Madison led a divided US into an avoidable, costly war. He opposed the Jay Treaty and in 1807 as Jefferson's Secretary of State pushed through the embargo, which New England's Federalists repealed. He should have foreseen New England's refusal to commit militia, weakening American military efforts, sending a message of disunity, lengthening the war, draining America of treasure. Moreover, he refused to stop it when the alleged cause was removed. The burning of the White House seemed the ultimate self-inflicted humiliation. The peace treaty did not secure additional American maritime rights, nor gain Canadian territory. It is sometimes called America's forgotten war; with good reason. Although hailed as a victory, in reality it was its only defeat before Vietnam. It proved maritime trade's value to both nations, vindication of Federalist maritime commercial policies, which after 1815 was proved in spades.

Madison has been treated kindly by most US historians because of his role in drawing-up its Constitution, Bill of Rights, Louisiana Purchase and that after leaving office in 1816 it began an era of expansion and prosperity, albeit delayed by his recklessness. Muted criticism appears for his view on negroes as inferior and born for slavery, unlike Washington, the only founding father who freed his slaves. Madison's biggest failure however was not appreciating America's greatest immediate asset, its booming post-independence merchant shipping. He also opposed a survey for the future Erie Canal, the most important development in New York's explosive 19th-century growth. Adams and Jefferson avoided war with France and Britain, but he walked into Napoleon's trap, creating unnecessary American antipathy to Britain for almost a century, which twice almost caused war, the last in 1896, until Samuel Plimsoll dedicated part of his 1890s' campaigns (see Chapter 32) to withdrawing anti-British history books from US schools.

In 1815 two US squadrons were sent against Algiers. At the Congress of Vienna, Castlereagh's anti-slavery issue encompassed Barbary slaves, mainly Corsican, Italian, Spanish and Ionian Islanders, protection of which the Treaty granted to Britain. The Dey of Algiers received 1,000 Spanish dollars each for their release. Tunis and Tripoli released 1,600. Barbary piracy did not fully cease. In 1815, 158 people were snatched from Sardinia, in 1817 Tunisian pirates took ships in Hamburg and in 1825 Sweden, Denmark, Portugal and Naples still paid annual tribute. An 1827 crisis resulted in the 1830 French invasion of Algiers. Its piracy ended. The Dey was replaced, but only in 1847 was conquest complete, military *gloire* in Africa instead of Europe.

South America's independence wars involved blockades and privateers. In 1820 for example, 27 US ships were seized, prompting Congress to form a Caribbean squadron as over two thirds of US exports to South America were to Cuba.[13] A US ship was sent to the Pacific in 1817. Others followed in 1821 to form the Pacific squadron patrolling South America's coast to protect traders and whalers. In 1823 when Canning proposed a British-US declaration, warning against European intervention in Latin American independence struggles, President Monroe asserted unilaterally that it was a US sphere of influence. With a tiny navy this was Manifest Destiny bluster. Madison delayed the ascent of US maritime trade which between 1816 and 1860 increased 230%, mainly with Britain, but also Europe, South America and China.

Part Three

Maritime Enlightenment

B ritain emerged from Napoleonic War in 1815 commercially unchallenged, unassailable at sea. It imported raw materials, including from former French and Dutch Caribbean colonies, Ceylon, the Cape, Mauritius, Seychelles and the emerging Australian colonies. It sent manufactured goods to them, Europe, America and South America. Britain's export value increased from £38.9 million in 1825 to £60.1 million in 1845 and £90 million in 1896. Cotton cloth exports rocketed; 253 million yards in 1815, 336 million in 1825, 1.98 million in 1855 and 3.562 million in 1875.[1] By 1825 a third of Boulton and Watt's steam engines were sold outside Europe, while Britain built much of the world's railways. 1815–1850 was a period of extraordinary growth in British industrial production, trade volumes and wages. Atlantic trade set the pace in goods, money and people. Maritime trade value grew an estimated annual 1% from the 16th to 18th centuries, but 3.85% in the 19th and more in volume. Long-haul shipments carried about a million tons in 1800, 20 million by 1840, 80 million by 1870, enabled by ending near continual war, ushering-in a century of relative peace as the steam-driven revolution gathered pace.[2]

Pressurising others to abolish slave trading, in 1833 it abolished slavery itself. Maritime enlightenment did not end. Shelley's *Ozymandias* (1818) reminded Britain that nothing lasts forever. Much enlightened legislation, delayed by war, was implemented. The British political system responded well, the French not. Practical improvements were again largely British and American-driven. Some continued to use the term enlightened, others increasingly liberal, sometimes both for emphasis.

Chapter 17

Three Indian Ocean Choke Points

Increasing Chinese tea exports accelerated the EIC' search for secure bases *en route*. EIC official Alexander Dalrymple, thinking more trade could be conducted offshore with junks from <u>all</u> Chinese ports, surveyed Hainan and the Sulu archipelago, whose Sultan ceded Balambangan Island between Borneo and Palawan in 1762. He envisaged it as a free port, colonised by Chinese under British protection. Established in 1772 and initially successful, it failed due to the next governor's venality.[1]

In the 1770s Francis Light was told to encourage Malay Peninsula trade relations. The Sultan of Kedah, a Siamese vassal, asked for protection in return for Penang. Agreed in 1786, it developed as a free port for local tin, pepper and forest products for Indian cotton cloth. By 1804 its Georgetown settlement had 12,000 people, mainly Chinese, Malays and Indians. Adjacent land was bought in 1800 to feed them. Some Kedah merchants moved there. As a result, 85 ships calling in 1786 became 3,569 in 1802; important enough to become a separate British Indian Presidency in 1805.[2] Arthur Wellesley thought it a 'most desirable place to retain,' useful to shelter warships on convoy duty.[3] They took Ambon (Amboina), Banda, Timor and Ternate in 1801, cloves, nutmeg and mace islands. Cloves and nutmegs were already grown on Madagascar and Reunion. The British introduced them to Bencoolen and Penang, making useful contributions to the Chinese trade imbalance. Coromandel-Southeast Asia shipping was 72,700 tons Indian-owned, 84,150 British-owned and 16,050 by various Europeans.[4]

Stamford Raffles, starting in the EIC's London office in 1795 aged 14, was sent to Penang in 1805. He learnt Malay, studied local trade and noticed Sulawesi's and Borneo's Bugis' crucial trade role, concluding that Penang's future hinged on Malacca, which had controlled this choke point from the late-14th century, until Dutch concentration on Batavia led to decline. Raffles' insight however, contradicted post-1804 policy, to draw Malacca's population to Penang, as Malacca was to be returned after the war. He persuaded Governor-General Minto to reverse policy. In 1811 Batavia was taken. Raffles became Java's Lieutenant Governor. He thought Dutch monopoly, 'this withering policy', deprived its 'maritime and commercial people...of all honest employment...[who] sink into apathy...or...piratical attempts to recover by plunder what they had been deprived of.' He envisioned a liberal Southeast Asia, ending local wars, suppressing piracy and opening trade, because 'vexatious and tyrannical' Dutch control led to depopulation.[5] In EIC enlightened tradition he abolished its slave trade. Retaining government monopolies in spice, opium and tin, he opened other trades, tried reducing forced labour and following Bengal's revenue collection model, introduced land rents with taxes paid in cash, not in kind, encouraged peasants to grow and export coffee, rice and raw cotton with which to pay taxes and promoted British goods, especially textiles. He catalogued ancient monuments, including re-discovering jungle-covered Borobudur. Enthusiastic about Java, 'the Bengal of the East Indies,' 'the most splendid prospect,'[6] he could not make it profitable. Britain anyway was not acquisitive, just wanting to stop France using it. They returned it to Holland in 1814, but sensibly kept Malacca.

Raffles returned to England in 1815, wrote *The History of Java*, was knighted and became Lieutenant Governor of Bencoolen, unlike Java, he thought 'the most wretched place,' insecure, unprofitable and with minimal pepper exports, but unable to abandon it until a better location was found. Nevertheless, as in Java, he abolished slavery, encouraged education, cultivation where possible and made it a free port. He tried extending its territories in south Sumatra to command the Sunda and Malacca Straits. Bintan was again considered, provoking Dutch bans on British ships from their claimed Straits' islands, which were persuaded to sign treaties with them. Singapore had languished since destroyed by 16th-century Portuguese, inhabited only by Malay fishermen. Arriving in 1819, appreciating its strategic location, halfway from India to China, near the Malacca Strait choke point, Raffles thought, 'one free port in these seas must eventually destroy the spell of Dutch monopoly.' The local chief authorised a British factory subject to the Sultanate of Johor, a Dutch ally but riven by faction. Raffles recognised the exiled brother, who had Court support. A trading post was established. When declared a free port, 2,000 Malays and Chinese left Malacca and it grew vigorously. 'Our object is not territory but trade, a great commercial emporium and fulcrum,' he wrote, the aim, maximising <u>all</u> trade, confident that much would be British. The Dutch returned to Java in 1815, reversed Raffles' 'perverted liberalism', renewing segregation and monopoly.

In Singapore, Raffles established schools and churches, outlawed slavery, put toleration into all policy guidelines, established a local magistrate and police force and planned separate Malay, Chinese, Indian and British areas. Returning to England, he founded the Zoological Society of London and London Zoo. The Dutch claim on the Sultanate of Johor, including Singapore continued, a headache for Dutch and British diplomats, but as it grew exponentially, the Dutch conceded it and Malacca as *fait accompli*, swapped for Bencoolen in 1824. Singapore surpassed Penang as main regional hub in the 1820s and kept growing. Raffles concluded, 'the Dutch are no longer the exclusive sovereigns of the eastern seas.'[7] Canning, British Foreign Secretary (1822–27), saw British and Dutch as joint 'exclusive lords of the east.' In 1826 Singapore, Penang and Malacca were amalgamated as the Straits Settlements, Singapore, its fastest growing element and capital from 1832. Nineteenth-century Java became a productive exporter of planation produce <u>through</u> Singapore.

A free port, open to all nations, charging no duties, Singapore was a model of Britain's freer trade, inspired by EIC officials. With China's tea still an EIC monopoly, Singapore became its entrepot for tea, silk and porcelain. By 1830 much non-EIC trade had been captured by Singapore traders. Its population was 35,000 by 1840, a small minority British, most trade diaspora members, Arabs, Malays, Parsis, Bengalis, Klings,

Bugis, Javanese, Arwi, but <u>mainly</u> Cantonese and Fujian Chinese. Straits Settlements plantations and tin mines meant more Malays and Fujianese arrived.

*   *   *

Eighteenth-century Persian Gulf turmoil meant severely curtailed trade. Unstable Persian dynasties offered no control. After political stability was restored, the EIC's Basra factory was re-established in 1795. Bombay's 1800–1820 Gulf trade increased nearly three-fold.[8] A potential problem was the Qawasim, occupying the lower Gulf centred on Ras al-Khaima, which had 60 large ships, hundreds of smaller ones and about 20,000 men,[9] opportunistically trading or attacking shipping, competing with Oman, the Gulf's pre-eminent power and British ally under Sayyid Said (r. 1804–1856). An 1809 joint British-Omani raid destroyed 50 armed dhows and was taken decisively in 1819. Under the 1820 General Treaty of Peace in what became the Trucial Coast, after 'Truces', Gulf ships obeyed British rules with a register of size, cargo and destination produced on demand. Unfriendly ships could be confiscated. Bushire's British resident, where trade increased, was commercial umpire. Slave trading ended and peaceful trade established. Britain within a year, had secured Southeast Asian and Gulf choke points, making them safe for trade.

Sayyid Said oversaw Oman's commercial maritime empire from Muscat, entrepot for coffee from Mocha and Hodeidah, Southeast Asian sugar, pearls, salt, sulphur, copper, arsenic, saffron and incense, Indian timber and cloth. Kachchhi merchants were key. Seyyid controlled Zanzibar's trade with its clove plantations, the world's largest exporter. A British traveller in 1816 described 20 Omani 300–600-tonners trading dates, pearls and copper with India for muslin, spices, timber, rice, pepper and Chinese goods with Mauritius for cotton and coffee and Zanzibar for gold, slaves, ostrich feathers and ivory.[10] Over 100,000 slaves were annually shipped to the Gulf. From 1832 Muscat and Zanzibar acted as joint capitals, reflecting the increased importance of Zanzibar's cloves, coconuts, copra, hides, ivory, rhino horn, hippo teeth, tortoiseshell, ambergris and timber exports to the Indian Ocean, Britain and America, whose New England merchants were proactive, after post-independence restrictions on US ships in British India were lifted.

Britain seized Aden and Karachi in 1839 to prevent Egypt's Muhammad Ali, a French protégé, from penetrating the Red Sea, which increased importance with P&O's India route dramatically reducing sailing times (See Chapter 20). Britain thus secured the Red Sea choke point, after which Britain imported Ethiopian coffee. 1821–1857 imports rose from £2.7 to £3.3 million.[11] In 1846 Britain also acquired Labuan to close a 1,500-mile gap in the world-encircling chain of harbours, impossible without EIC employee control of intra-Indian Ocean trade in opium, cotton, spices and tin. Britain had the security to effectively sell its manufactured goods, which increased local trade.

Chapter 18

Port and Ship Productivity and Professionalism

Britain's 1785–1855 maritime trade value's explosive growth, from £17.2 to £123.5 million,[1] could not have happened without huge port and ship productivity gains. Efficiency increased enabling post-1815 shipping costs to dramatically fall. Guns were removed, crews reduced, convoys eliminated, insurance and freight rates dropped, ship sizes grew and steam-powered ships started revolutionising maritime communications.

1745–1795 coastal trade doubled, accelerating 25% between 1792 and1795 alone![2] London was still Britain's busiest port, despite west coast ports' growth. Manchester, its next largest city, was just 6.25% of London's size whose 1700 population, about 500,000, rose to 900,000 in 1800, 10% directly involved with port activities. Supply networks ran deep inland. Irregular dock work depended on seasonal cycles dictated by harvests and winds. London's 'pool', with space for 545 ships hosted over 3,600 by 1795. The 'pool' became a huge traffic jam, some ships waiting days or weeks to discharge. The 1,400-feet quay-length contrasted with Bristol's 4,000 feet. Operations were slow and security poor, subject to pillage and fraud by criminal gangs, partly mitigated by the Thames River Police. Larger ships discharged downriver into barges at Wapping, Woolwich, Deptford and Blackwall. Given Britain's increasing manufactured exports and raw material imports, backed by its successful financial and service sector, London's port was totally inadequate.

On the Hull Dock Company model, the West India Dock Co. was financed by over 350 investors, City merchants, shipbuilders, shipbrokers and banks. Completed in 1802 on the Isle of Dogs, two main docks berthed 600 ships. A high security wall surrounded five huge warehouses. All in-bound Caribbean ships for the next 20 years had to discharge there. Wapping's 1805 London Dock, similarly financed, eventually expanded into six basins, 90 acres for 430 ships, four-story warehouse space for over 200,000 tons of goods.[3] Cargoes included tobacco, hides, horns, coffee, spices, cork, sulphur, indigo and copper. Blackwall's 1806 East India Dock, financed by banks, EIC directors and City merchants covered 30 acres with parallel import and export docks connected by locks to the river, handling 250 ships simultaneously. All encouraged ancillary industries.

Commercial Road (1802–1804) and West India Dock Road (1806–12) sped high-value goods to the EIC's five-acre City warehouse at Cutlers Gardens off Bishopsgate, employing 400 clerks and 4,000 warehousemen. Surrey Dock, for timber and the East Country Dock for Baltic goods became operational roughly simultaneously. The Commercial Dock Co., formed to buy the Greenland and adjoining Norway dock for expanding Baltic trade, reduced pillage. The 1809 Baltic Dock Co. stored timber.

These ambitious moves showed confidence in trade's continued growth and eventual victory over Napoleon. Canals were built from Limehouse to Blackwall around 1800 to save navigating around the Isle of Dogs and in 1820 Regents Canal connected the Grand Junction Canal at Paddington with the Thames at Limehouse. Islington's City Road Basin handled incoming inland freight.

Huge productivity gains resulted. By 1824 with booming volumes, 1,700 merchants, bankers and traders and 1,600 shipowners agreed to build St. Katherine's Dock, due to 10% import growth between 1823 and 1824, an extra 200–300 ships in one year![4] It opened in 1828 for 1,000-tonners. A million square feet of warehouse storage enabled valuable ivory, shells, marble, wines, perfumes and spices to be craned from hold to warehouse directly in 20% of the usual time but was already too small for increasing volumes and ship sizes. The New York Line, started in 1833, used it for a weekly service of 500-ton packets but was inadequate for its 1846 more frequent service with larger ships. Nevertheless, in 1851 *London Labour and the London Poor* wrote, 'before…eight days were necessary in summer and 14 in winter to unload a ship of 350 tons…the average time now occupied in discharging a ship of 250 tons is 12 hours and one of 500 tons, two or three days.' The deeper Royal Victoria Dock with almost 100 acres of water further downriver was opened in 1855, featuring finger jetties projecting from the main quays to help deliver cargoes quicker, a tidal basin, lock and direct railway connection for fast distribution. Southampton had already responded in 1840 when P&O (see Chapter 20) agreed carriage of cargo from London's Southampton Railway Company, a precursor of modern 'intermodal' supply chains, enabling expansion of services to Australia and South Africa in 1845 and 1856.

Liverpool's West African and US connections enabled diversification after slave trade abolition. Niger River delta's palm oil became a major import after 1807, Europe's largest volume, for candles, soap and grease for industrial machinery. Liverpool's dock revenue almost quintupled between 1801 and 1814. By 1815 docks and warehouses covered 17.3 acres.[5] Canals already connected Cheshire's salt mines and Staffordshire's potteries with the Mersey. In the 1830s railways linked it more extensively. European emigrants came to Hull, then by rail to Liverpool, Britain's main US emigration port. Rising trade required Prince's Dock in 1821, over 11 acres, Brunswick Dock in 1832, Waterloo, Trafalgar and Victoria Docks in 1834–36, Clarence, Stanley and Albert Dock in 1846, surrounded by warehouses with numerous wet and dry docks and the largest floating quay; by 1866 over 247 acres, the most advanced interconnected dock system. Herman Melville in 1849 said, 'For miles you may walk along that riverside, passing dock after dock, like a chain of immense fortresses.' In 1907 Walter Scott described a 'seven-mile sequence of granite-tipped lagoons.'

Liverpool's expertise, enterprise and capital developed trades whose value multiplied ten-fold from the 1820s to 1850s. Cotton imports from 1801 to 1850 rose from 54,000 to 360,000 lbs, US wheat imports, 8,000 to 75,000 tons and was the main manufactured goods exporter to Asia after EIC monopoly was lost. The Liverpool-Manchester railway first carried passengers and goods in 1830. Liverpool had the first trans-Atlantic steamer in 1833. As Britain's main export port, in 1857 it handled over 45% of Britain's trade value, London 23%, then Hull, 13%.[6] In 1800 about 4,000 ships called, by 1871 over 19,000. Regional prosperity ensued. Britain's maritime strength however ran deep and included many smaller ports. Bideford shipowner Thomas Burnard's (b. 1796) family for example had shares in 102 ships, owning 32 outright, trading to the Mediterranean, Azores and Canada.[7]

The 1790 Firth of Forth and Clyde Canal linked Glasgow with Scotland's east coast whose jute bags, linen and iron goods from Dundee went west. It witnessed some early steamship trials. Dundee's remodelled 1770 harbour by John Smeaton introduced water tunnels to tackle silting. In the 1820s it was expanded with King William IV Dock, then Victoria and Camperdown Docks. After dredging, early-19th-century Glasgow's quay length was 7,629 feet, the 14-acre harbour increased to 51 by 1851.[8] Steam-powered ships began a revolution. The expiry of Watt's patent in 1800 released targeted, inventive energy. Lord Thomas Dundas, as Governor of the Firth of Forth and Clyde Canal, was responsible in 1800 for building the *Charlotte Dundas*, the world's first practical steamer, with a William Symington-designed engine. In 1803 it towed two 70-ton barges 20 miles to Glasgow. Cheaper than wood, iron had greater structural strength, lasted longer and could be built larger, all productivity gains. Wrought iron, invented in the late-18th century, four-times stronger than cast iron, made possible iron bridges, buildings, railways <u>and</u> ships which endured engine pounding.

In Glasgow in 1812 Henry Bell built the 28-ton *Comet*, the first commercially successful steamer, bankrupting Glasgow-Greenock coaches within a year.[9] Steamships were initially used short-haul due to frequent refuelling. In 1815 steamships sailed between Liverpool and Glasgow. David Napier (1790–1869), a Clyde foundry owner's son built the *Comet's* boiler, pioneering marine engineering as a distinct profession. With a new wedge-shaped bow his 1818 *Rob Roy* ran Dublin-Greenock voyages, formerly almost a week's voyage in 26 hours, then to Belfast, then between Dover and Calais. By 1820, 34 steamers sailed between British ports or crossed the Channel. The first iron-hulled ship crossed the Channel in 1821 then serviced French rivers. Building progressively larger ships with more efficient engines for Irish Sea packet services, in 1822 Napier boasted that his *Superb* performed Greenock-Liverpool for three years without 'a single article of her machinery…ever given way, [despite] the worst of weather.' Cousin, Robert Napier (1791–1876) made improvements for the 1823 *Leven*, assisted by works manager David Elder and built the largest steamship, the 560-ton *United Kingdom* in 1826. He invested in companies buying his ships, encouraging larger-scale Clyde-based marine engineering; 'the father of Clyde shipbuilding.' The Lairds, originally Greenock-based, moved to Birkenhead where William established an iron works in 1824 and with son John built an iron barge in 1828, an iron paddle steamer in 1833, the first with watertight bulkheads for added strength and safety and the first iron steamer for Savannah in 1834. Their ships quickly developed excellent reputations. Sailing ships also continued efficiency gains. Improvements in Indiamen design paid-off because Indian trade competition encouraged speed. In 1817, 13 Indiamen astonished the shipping world by sailing from Canton to the Channel in 109 days.[10]

Steam tugs increased port efficiency and voyage times, negating the need to wait for favourable winds. Improving turnaround times made shipping more efficient, each ship capable of many more voyages. Even though trade volumes grew fast, more efficient ship supply outweighed it. Thus, after the Napoleonic freight boom, low 1818–30 rates prevailed, then rose until an 1841 slump. Increasing steamship use stimulated coal mining. Bibby Line established coaling stations in Iberia and Italy. In America, only harbour tugs, Ohio, Hudson and Mississippi riverboats and Great Lakes-Ohio-Mississippi canalboats used steam with impetus to push west. By 1817 one was on Lake Ontario, by the mid-1820s, five.

Commercial dealings also became more organised and efficient. London's various late-18th-century coffee houses and taverns, meeting places for commercial specialists, became more ordered. Those interested in naval stores met at the Virginia and Maryland Coffee House, renamed in 1744, the Virginia and Baltic. The Jerusalem attracted Asian traders. Tallow, sheep and cattle fat in various grades was used for machine lubrication, soap and candles. Its traders met at the Grecian. Imports from St. Petersburg, Riga and Archangel grew from nothing in the 1750s to 11,473 casks in 1774, and 66,525 in 1815. 'Ton Tallow' became the standard unit for measuring freight. Hemp imports, 426,000 hundredweight in 1820, rose to 667,141 in 1823, further increasing the Baltic's importance. The Royal Exchange's East Country Walk became the Baltic Walk. Increasingly Baltic merchants met at the Baltic Coffee House, having dropped 'Virginia'.[11]

In 1823 to exclude speculators and maintain reputation, Baltic Coffee House membership was restricted to 300 traders paying annual subscriptions, with rules, regulations and a code of conduct drawn-up by Russia merchant and economist Thomas Tooke (1774–1858). It concerned 'greater security of the money advanced' and 'more adequate protection against fraudulent conduct of foreign merchants.'[12] The Baltic Committee became arbiters of business ethics. Coffee house in name only, it followed Lloyds, which in the 1760s-1770s had changed into a Royal Exchange-based organisation, restricted to specialists. The same happened to the Jamaica Coffee House which specialised in Caribbean and Madeira trades, the St. John in Iberian and Ottoman trade, the North and South American Coffee House in American trade. *Robson's London Directory* (1838) defined 32 broker-types of various commodities. Shipping and insurance were classified together. Eight out of eleven general and commercial brokers and all eleven Russian brokers gave the Baltic Coffee House as their address. In 1848, as part of growing professionalism, it presented a common front to Crimean linseed growers over adulteration. Pandia Ralli, a Chiot grain merchant/ banking family member, the first Greek Baltic member in 1837 and brother Stephen suggested the Marseilles' analysis system at all import ports, agreed in 1863.

Chapter 19

Trans-Atlantic Trade and the Rise of New York

Due to Napoleon's 1806–1812 Continental Blockade, New Brunswick's timber exports to Britain rose from 5,000 to 100,000 tons, 240,000 tons in 1819 and by 1825, 417,000 tons; more than all North American exports 50 years earlier and 74% of total timber imports in 1819–23.[1] Backhaul passenger and cargo space to North America was therefore cheap. Furthermore, British raw cotton imports rose from 24,000 tons in 1801 to 120,000 tons in 1821, increasingly from America with manufactured goods and emigrants back. Lancashire's cotton textile manufacturing assisted Liverpool's adjustment to slave trade abolition.

Madison's 1812–14 war stimulated Canadian shipbuilding. Entrepreneurs built ships and traded them, enriching the region. In 1840 Prince Edward Island for example had 192 ships, about 22,000 tons, in 1850, 254 ships of 32,000 tons. Typically loading timber or grain for Liverpool, they sold them via British brokers, occasionally sailing to the Caribbean, Australia, New Zealand or China, before finding buyers. This Canadian industry disappeared towards the century's end due to Scandinavian, Italian and Greek competition with cheaper crews in niche trades where speed was unimportant. Opening-up Canada's interior awaited powerful St. Lawrence steamships. The London-subsidised Rideau Canal provided the trigger.[2]

In 1815 Thomas Arnold won an Oxford prize for an essay encouraging migration. Malthus noted US population doubling every 25 years, but after 1815 it doubled in a decade due to natural increase and high immigration, mainly from Britain. There were about 500,000 British 18th-century emigrants. Between 1825 and 1842 almost 900,000 Europeans entered America, extraordinary acceleration, more in 16 years than the previous 216,[3] driven by cheap back-haul freight rates, hopes of better lives, stories of abundance, lack of servility, absence of game laws, freedom to hunt in extensive, untapped lands and to daily eat well. Most went to America but 40,000 to Canada, most on returning timber ships,[4] cheap but uncomfortable. Between 1714 and 1837 Hanover was British. Its ports of Bremen and Verden and connections with Hamburg probably encouraged German emigration.

Emigration was risky. Between 1832 and 1838, 252 trans-Atlantic ships were wrecked, reducing to 50 between 1846 and 1852.[5] Irish emigration was mainly from Dublin or Cork to Liverpool to take emigrant ships. On cramped sailing ships without ventilation, bathing or laundry facilities over six weeks, disease spread quickly. In 1847, potato famine year, trans-Atlantic emigrants' death rate from disease was 16%, children especially vulnerable. On one 1852 voyage to Victoria, it was 25%.[6] Nevertheless, emigration rose; 68,000 in 1846, 118,000 in 1847, 151,000 in 1848, 180,000 in 1849, 184,000 in 1850 and 219,000 in 1851. A Parliamentary Act of 1848 introduced minimum standards for ventilation and cleanliness. Inman Line in 1852 started specialising in steerage class passengers. The fare, slightly more on steamships, meant better treatment and only a two-week passage.

After Madison's war, US raw cotton exports to Britain resumed. New York firms controlled purchases, southern planters increasingly in debt. Britain's total 1821–1857 cotton import value soared from £4.3 to £24.6 million, surpassing Caribbean sugar as Britain's most valuable import about 1825.[7] Sugar also increased from £5.7 million in 1821 to £12.3 million in 1851,[8] as consumption per head doubled. In 1833 nearly 850,000 bales of cotton were discharged in Liverpool, about 49,000 in Glasgow and 40,000 in London.[9] By 1859 Britain imported two million bales a year, almost 90% to Liverpool. Between 1816 and 1850 Liverpool overtook London in tonnage, although not in ships.

Wall Street's origins were from its marine insurance, then securities in the 1790s. America's fourth-largest 18th-century port, New York lagged Boston, Charleston and Philadelphia, the latter over 100 miles upriver, not always ice free. Deep-drafted New York was ice free, sheltered by Staten Island. As London-based investors financed much US development, New York's closer, more frequent connections gave it advantages. It had a stock market from 1817, great commercial companies, shipowners and banks. It coordinated trade and supplied credit to the south. The over 300-mile-long Hudson River accessed the interior and was closer than Boston to southern cotton. Overwhelmingly however, the Erie Canal, built 1817–1825, was key to New York's explosive growth. Connecting New York to Lake Erie, thus mid-west agricultural products, it lowered Buffalo-New York freight rates by 90%.[10] In its first year, its 185,000 tons of eastbound cargo triggered a US canal-building boom, which by 1840 constituted 3,326 miles,[11] overtaking Britain's 3,100 miles of 1815. New York thus became the hub for British ships discharging goods and immigrants.

Southern US cotton monoculture needed the mid-west's meat and flour. Previously shipped via the Mississippi to New Orleans, the Erie Canal diverted it to New York. Ships from the south discharged cotton in New York for export to Britain, then loaded mid-west agricultural produce and manufactured goods for the south, eliminating ballasts. In 1817 coastal shipping was reserved for US-owned ships. In 1845 the Erie Canal carried a million tons, in 1852, two million and by 1880, 4.6 million,[12] attracting Boston merchants to New York. In 1821 Boston exported $12 million and New York $13 million. By 1860 Boston increased to $17 million, New York to $145 million, its 1790 population, 33,131 increased to 813,669.[13]

New York-London packet services began in 1816, mainly US-built and run, growing in size, number and regularity, becoming the world's busiest long-haul ocean route. The first regular service was Black Ball Line from 1818, with New York-built 400-tonners. Instead of the master waiting until enough cargo and passengers were loaded, it initiated a 'line' of ships sailing on known dates to established ports with passengers, valuable cargo and mainly post. The innovation of speed, comfort and predictability brought competition from Boston and Philadelphia. Baltimore's *Nile's Weekly Register* thought, 'Such steadiness and dispatch is truly astonishing and in a former age would have been incredible.'[14] Red Star Line followed in 1822 with two ships, prompting Black Ball to double her ships and sailings. Blue Swallowtail Line followed with four monthly departures from each port.

In the 1820s there were 36 liners employed, becoming more luxurious with mahogany dining tables, pillars, sofas and plush draperies. Blue Swallowtail Line added a library, cabin doors, washstands doubling as desks, Turkish carpets and a piano in the ladies lounge. East River shipwrights developed longer, thinner hulls and sharper bows for speed. In the early-1820s New York's Edward Collins started packets to New Orleans and in 1836 launched Dramatic Line to Liverpool, the first over 1,000 tons, with cabins on deck for light, air and less smells, setting new standards of elegance in food, wine and décor. In their first decade they averaged 24 days out and 38 home, by 1839 only 20.5 and 30.5 days.[15] An 1836 Parliamentary committee heard that US ships were better built, preferred by shippers and insurance companies with US captains more educated and competent, its seamen more efficient and better paid.[16] By the 1830s they carried 75% by value of US exports and 90% of imports. By 1840 it had 2.14 million tons against Britain's 2.72 million.[17]

New York became the major US import/export and domestic distribution hub as trans-Atlantic ships became larger. In 1834, 1,950 entered carrying 465,000 tons of cargo. In 1860, 3,982 carried 1,983,000 tons, their size growing from 300–400-tonners in the 1820s, 1,000-tonners by 1838 and about 1,750-tonners by 1854.[18] In 1800, 9% of US trade went through New York, by 1860, 62%, its share of imports from 23% in 1811 to 51% in 1825 and 68% in 1860. It was the entrepot for Cincinnati- and Chicago-processed food to London and Liverpool,[19] eclipsing Philadelphia in the 1830s, shipping most southern produce with shipping agents, commodity merchants and bankers, the centre of commerce, canal, coastal and international shipping. In the 1830s with a Wall Street bull market, New York enjoyed a building boom, adding an average ten miles of developed Manhattan streets annually.

Before 1820, cotton was compressed by jumping on bags, giving about five lbs/cubic foot density. Bales and screw presses increased it to 8–12 lbs. In the 1840s steam presses improved it to 20–25 lbs. New Orleans grew from 17,000 people in 1810 to 169,000 in 1860. Charleston's imports rose 50%, but New Orleans 700% between 1824 and 1839, with most manufactured goods from the northeast arriving in New Orleans for onward distribution using 727 steamboats in 1855.[20]

In 1820 over 9,500 of New York's population were engaged in manufacturing, over 3,000 in commerce, by 1850, 43,340 in manufacturing, 11,360 in commerce. From the 1830s factory-produced ready-to-wear garments appeared, partly because of US and Caribbean slaves, first from imported British cloth, about a third of US imports, until tariff-protected domestic cloth competed. In 1860 sugar refineries' 1,494 workers made $19 million, while 26,875 garment workers, almost 30% of manufacturing employment, $22.3 million.[21] Elias Howe's 1846 sewing machine lowered costs especially after Singer popularised his adaptation.

The third-largest industry was printing and publishing. In important ports throughout history, transfer of ideas was as crucial as goods. Early-19th century British authors were pirated in America which refused to recognise foreign copyright. New York and Philadelphia competed to publish British novels. New York received them quicker and more regularly due to frequent liners, distributing to consumers via coasters and the Erie Canal. It joined other major ports as wealth-creation hubs, encouraging learning, literacy, intellectual curiosity, immigration and advancement. Its 100 millionaires by the 1840s, increased to 1,368 by 1890[22] with a prosperous middle and working class. US foreign trade value rose from $134 million in 1830 to $318 million in 1850, tripling again in the 1850s, 60–70% through New York. Between 1816 and 1845, Liverpool's traffic tripled to about 1.3 million tons,[23] while New York's rose 2.5-times to about 500,000 tons, but between 1845 and 1860 it tripled again, an expansion of seven or eight-times since the 1820s. In 1824 the port was seven miles long and by the 1840s there were 60 East River and 50 Hudson River wharves. British-US dependency, especially Liverpool-New York, happened despite US protection of young industries with import tariffs, 35% on British woollen textiles by 1828, 50% by 1832, some products as high as 100% by 1842. Smaller volumes of Parisian fashion items went from Le Havre to New York and southern ports. The first Liverpool-New Orleans packet line started in 1851. By the mid-1850s New York had 16 to Liverpool, three to London, three to Le Havre, two to Antwerp and one each to Glasgow, Rotterdam and Marseilles.

Chapter 20

Ocean-Going Steamship Development

Packet ships were essential for government. Quicker delivery meant better informed decisions. Monthly Admiralty mail ships operated to Iberia and America since the mid-18th century but often took 21 days to Iberia, 30–70 days to America and lost business to private US trans-Atlantic packets. Enterprising partners formed the Peninsula Steam Navigation Company and bought a beached schooner in the 1820s for cargoes to Portugal. It bought a steamship in 1828 and by 1837 had seven. Quicker and cheaper than Admiralty ships it was awarded the Iberian mail contract. Government subsidies were vital for steamship development, giving financial incentive to innovation. Sailing from London to Falmouth, then Vigo and Lisbon, steamships enabled regular timetables. Within a year it was invited to take mail to Malta, Alexandria and within two years, Egypt to India. EIC Indiamen took almost a year for a Britain-India-Britain round voyage. The EIC, slow to develop steam, refused to relinquish its Bombay monopoly but allowed a Suez-Aden-Galle-Madras-Calcutta service. 'Oriental' was thus added to 'Peninsula', becoming the Peninsula and Oriental Steamship Company, P&O.

It was a huge technical, logistical and financial challenge to develop ships with enough power and coal-carrying capacity. It ordered two 2,000-ton paddle ships with 60 cabins and 150 berths, three masts, two funnels and comforts such as warm showers. Coal was only mined in quantity in Britain and America, so was shipped in sailing ships to coaling stations around the Cape to Aden and Galle, enabling a 25-day Calcutta-Suez service, transforming EIC officials' wives and families' lives, despite the uncomfortable Alexandria-Suez desert crossing.[1]

Napoleon's Egyptian invasion had weakened Ottoman control. Albanian warlord, Muhammad Ali (1769–1849), sent by them to expel the French in 1801, tried modernising Egypt's economy, encouraging agricultural and irrigation projects on nationalised land: cotton, sugar, rice and indigo for export. Alexandria, little more than a village with virtually no long-haul trade, revived with his encouragement of Greek, Turkish and Jewish immigration. Screw propulsion using Archimedes' principles was patented by Francis Smith in 1836. After many improvements, the appropriately named *Archimedes* outran sailing packets by 1846.[2] Paddle-wheel steamers could not berth alongside quays, making loading/discharge inefficient and carried less cargo. Screws stayed submerged, wasted less energy, consumed a third less coal, which enabled larger ships. Brunel's observation that resistance of ships in water increased less than size increased, incentivised more powerful engines and higher steam pressures.

P&O built barges and a steam tug with screw propellers and advised Ali, with whom they had good relations, to build a railway to Suez. It offered tickets to Malta, Athens,

Smyrna, Rhodes, Constantinople and Jaffa with sight-seeing Holy Land excursions, the start of cruise ship tourism. To reach Bombay, passengers used EIC ships or sailed to Calcutta on P&O ships, then Bombay. Its 1845 offer to run a Bombay-Australia service, focused attention on the unpopular EIC route and was finally awarded Suez-Bombay, giving it a near-monopoly of steamships in Asia until the 1860s. The mail contract to India was crucial for Britain's government and British trade. Charles Wood, Secretary of State for India explained in 1866, 'Increased postal communication with India implies increased relations…increased commerce, increased investment of English capital, increased settlement of energetic middle-class Englishmen, [whereby]…the wealth and prosperity of England…are greatly increased.'[3]

Isambard Kingdom Brunel's stellar reputation was based on his London-Bristol Great Western Railway, Bristol's merchants' attempt to compete with Liverpool and Glasgow. The first purpose-built trans-Atlantic steamship was his 1,200-ton *Great Western*. Wooden-hulled with iron straps, paddle-wheeled, supplemented by sails on four masts, connected London by rail to its 1838 Bristol-New York route. Junius Smith's British and American Steam Navigation Company competed with the 1,800-ton *British Queen* in 1839. The *Great Western's* five round voyages in 1838 and steady P&O advances led the Admiralty to invite bids for a trans-Atlantic contract. Great Western wanted a later start. St. George Steam Packet Co. offered a Cork-Halifax service, both deemed inadequate and rejected, but improvements continued. By the 1840s, Clyde, Mersey, Tyne and Thames shipbuilders regularly built iron steamships.

Nova Scotia-based Samuel Cunard was son of one of 50,000 loyalist Pennsylvanian Quakers bringing discipline, money and energy to Halifax. After working for a Boston shipbroker, he persuaded his father to open a ship agency and merchandising firm for Caribbean trade. Halifax, the main supply and staging base for British forces during Madison's war, imported flour, meal, corn, pitch, tar and turpentine from New England, which opposed it. By its end, Cunard bought and sold ships and cargoes, obtained a Boston-Halifax-St. John Newfoundland Royal Mail contract and a reliable reputation. On his father's death, his brothers joined the renamed Samuel Cunard and Co., trading timber and fish with the Caribbean, building and owning, ships, dealing in whaling, banking, iron and coal mines. In 1825 he sailed to London to ask the EIC for a tea agency, leading to direct shipments from Canton, quarterly tea auctions and re-exports to Newfoundland, New Brunswick and the Caribbean.

Halifax-St. Lawrence voyages were usually foggy and in winter, ice-strewn, taking regular tolls of ships and men. The Lower Canada Assembly, wanting reliability and safety, turned to Clyde steamship knowledge, but no Canadians were tempted until 1830, when a joint Lower Canada-Nova Scotia subsidy attracted Cunard and 169 investors to build the *Royal William* in Quebec from Clyde plans, the crankshaft forged by Robert Napier,[4] but severe weather and the 1832 cholera epidemic reduced demand and it was sold.

Cunard heard about Britain's trans-Atlantic tender after it closed. Believing 'steamers properly built and manned might start and arrive at their destinations with the punctuality of railway trains on land,' he caught the next packet to Britain, impressing the Admiralty by wanting more than a monthly service and to compete with New York sailing packets. His *Royal William* and coal mine experience persuaded it to award twice-monthly services with 1,120-ton, 420-horsepowered ships, a link to Boston and agreement that when technology allowed, further improvements would be made.[5]

David and Robert Napier's apprentices led steamships' technical advances. David Tod and John Macgregor built engines and after 1836, hulls. Tod specialised in engines, Macgregor in hulls. Following Birkenhead's Lairds, successful pioneers of iron hulls, they strengthened and subdivided them with watertight bulkheads. The Glasgow and Liverpool Royal Steam Co. commissioned the 1841, 800-ton, 380-horsepowered *Royal Princess* which set the Glasgow-Liverpool speed record and continued building larger, more efficient ships. At high speeds, fuel costs rose dramatically and were therefore limited to either short-haul voyages, subsidised mail, passengers and high-value freight.

Napier, recommended for Cunard's engines, found Glasgow investors to help him, including those running the Glasgow-Liverpool route, Caribbean and iron merchants, cotton and insurance brokers, textile manufacturers, ships agents and himself, Glasgow's commercial heart. Boston, being overtaken by New York, made an irresistible offer of pier and dock facilities with quick transfer to railroads. The *Britannia* was the first Liverpool-Halifax-Boston crossing in 1840 in 14 days 8 hours, two thirds faster than the latest sailing packets,[6] doubling Boston's throughput in the first year.

As Brunel planned another 1,200-tonner, the *Great Britain*, rapidly developing iron hull, screw and boiler technology persuaded him to modify the plans to 3,400-tons. Continually changing propulsion, size and other design aspects, compromised the ship. Launched in 1843, *The Times* thought it 'of vast importance', but was only ready in 1845. Six masts, one funnel and a 360-passenger capacity, it was the first iron-hulled, screw-driven ship to cross the Atlantic. With disastrous performance on only two round voyages in the first year, it was a financial disaster. By 1847 the company was bankrupt, the ship sold to work mainly under sail, an emigrant carrier in the Australian gold rush until 1876, averaging 60 days out, 60 back, shipping 15,000 emigrants and the first English cricket team in 1861, but ended as a coal hulk.

Unlike Brunel, Cunard took no risky leaps, embraced recent technical changes, learning from others' mistakes. His smaller, faster ships used less fuel and in the first two years averaged 13.25 days to Halifax and 11.2 days to Liverpool.[7] When Smith's 2,360-ton *President* sank in an 1841 storm, his company soon followed into bankruptcy. By 1845 Cunard carried more passengers than sailing packets, but lost money underestimating winter storm severity. Fares were raised and the government subsidy increased, because its ships sailed 'with regularity almost unexpected and wholly unsurpassed.'[8] After the *Great Western* was sold, Cunard briefly had a trans-Atlantic steam packet and passenger monopoly. The Admiralty subsidised four more ships, around 30% larger and more powerful, again breaking the trans-Atlantic speed record. Collins' Dramatic Line took risks with larger, faster, more luxurious sailing packets and the New Orleans-Liverpool Line was profitable, but he relied on sailing ships, reaching their zenith in the still-revered, fast, elegant clippers. Cunard's ships, however, overtook his trans-Atlantic business because US shipbuilders could not match the dozen or so Clyde-based designers' and shipbuilders' experience and knowledge.

Incremental technical breakthroughs included larger hatches by the 1840s, enabling faster loading and discharging with hydraulic cranes, developed by Tyneside's William Armstrong, improved in the 1850s. Boiler pressure increased from six pounds/square inch in the 1810s to 60 in the 1850s. In the 1840s, Robert Napier built three ships with a new steeple engine design, which Tod used for his 1850 *City of Glasgow*, a 1,600-ton trans-Atlantic steamship, screw propulsion's breakthrough ship, more room for passengers and freight with 52 first class cabins, 58 second class and 400 steerage, effective competition against US sailing packets.[9]

Colliers also improved efficiency. Jarrow's Palmer Brothers' screw-propelled 1852 *John Bowes* did ten sailing colliers' work due to two technical breakthroughs. First, one 60-foot hatch loaded from a chute and discharged at 650-tons/day. Second, previously colliers paid for, queued and loaded sand or shingle ballast for the return, then discharged it in the northeast. After discharging coal *John Bowes'* ballast tanks were filled instead with water and pumped off before loading. Much faster, it made 30 trips annually. Copied for coal to Europe, the Black Sea and Argentina, they returned with grain.

Dramatic Line's wooden-hulled 2,800-tonners performed poorly in Atlantic gales, frequently withdrawn for repair with schedules adjusted. Cunard maintained reliability. Losing money, Collins approached Congress for a larger subsidy, which it doubled. In 1854, his *Arctic* sank. Sixty-one out of 153 crew survived, including four out of five officers, but only 23 of 281 passengers, many prominent names and no women or children. Its reputation plummeted.[10] By 1854, Cunard had 70% of trans-Atlantic mail revenues and in 1855 commissioned the iron-hulled 3,600-ton paddle steamer *Persia*, the world's largest ship, surviving a maiden voyage iceberg collision due to strengthened bow and watertight bulkheads. Re-taking the speed record, 9 days 16 hours out, 8 days 23 hours back, it was the most popular trans-Atlantic steamer. Eight Cunarders requisitioned for Crimean War troop and horse transport reduced trans-Atlantic services, allowing Collins a comeback, but an 1856 disaster forced him to sell-up. *The Times* explained, Cunard 'always avoided alluring novelties' and 'sacrificed show to substance…speed to safety [and]…gradually increased the size and power of their ships but only so much as experience showed to be advantageous.'[11] Cunard pulled well ahead. His Clyde-built ships incrementally improved technologically and in luxury.

John Elder (1824–1869) following father David by 1854 developed the compound engine. Passing steam through two cylinders increased power, saving 30–40% fuel. Contributing to Cunard's and others' success, it further enhanced the Clyde's reputation, enabling further screw propulsion development. Employing 4,000 men, in British enlightenment tradition, Elder contributed to a sick fund, school and houses. His brother Alexander joined Birkenhead's Lairds as superintendent engineer for the Africa Steamship Company in 1852.

The *City of Glasgow* was sold to Liverpool's Richardson Brothers for exports to Philadelphia. Originally Quakers from Belfast's linen industry, five brothers ran Belfast, Liverpool, New York and Philadelphia offices, freighting cargo in sailing packets. William Inman formed the steamship group inside the company. Lancashire cotton interests were major investors. David Tod also bought shares, the Napier-

Cunard model. Inman Line ships increased in size and power, a third cheaper than Cunard's. John Richardson opened an 1847 model linen factory near Belfast, providing workers' housing. He was, with many Quakers, active in Irish famine relief, opening soup kitchens, donating food, clothes and seeds for new crops. Richardson's Quaker principles prevented him contracting his ships as Crimean War supply and troop ships. The partnership dissolved. Inman took charge, chartering his three ships to the French government. The US service was suspended for 18 months. Thereafter with Dramatic Line's demise, Inman saw opportunity in New York, a larger, growing market, part-competing with Cunard, although Inman's ships, two knots slower, catered more for emigrants. During the 1850s Cunard expanded to other British ports and Halifax-Bermuda. Meanwhile a mail contract to South Africa was awarded to Union Steamship in 1857.

Chapter 21

Opening China to Foreign Trade

Thirty-five per cent of Surat's exports went to Arabia and Persia in 1802, about the same to Bombay, most of which also went to the Red Sea and Persian Gulf.[1] As Surat declined, before Bombay's rise, the most significant west coast maritime area was Kachchhi (Kutch), trade ties existing with Oman since antiquity.[2] Its main port Mandvi had banks, marine insurance and shipbuilding. Its merchants lived and worked in Muscat and advised the Sultan. From 1785, with Oman's reassertion of influence in Zanzibar they also dominated its Indian trade, some in Bombay and in 1802 one controlled Muscat's customs. Muscat was the main Gulf entrepot in pearls, rice, wheat, sugar, ghee oil, lead and arms, organised by Kachchhis.

As Surat's merchants, especially Parsis, moved to Bombay, they brought Gujarati cotton and Bengali and central Indian opium contacts. Their work ethic, entrepreneurial talents and shipbuilding were admired. Bombay, Calcutta and Madras were different to previous Indian ports because merchants traded freely without negotiating their status with Mughal officials. English Common Law's fairness empowered Indian merchants and capital. They were natural British allies. Parsis like Dudy Nasserwanji consolidated shipping and cotton interests. From 1800 to 1813, 33 out of 129 Bombay-registered ships shipped raw cotton to China,[3] whose cotton was more expensive. South China's famine encouraged farmers to grow grain instead, enabling the trade.

Opium, cultivated for centuries in Anatolia, traded in the Mediterranean, used in China since the T'ang dynasty, probably introduced by Arab or Persian traders, was noted by Portuguese writer Pires in Malacca in 1512.[4] Dutch traders became involved in Bengal's exports in the early-1600s. In 1793 Calcutta's eastward trade was worth five million rupees, three of which was opium, about 4,500 chests, half sold in Southeast Asia, half in China.[5]

The EIC assumed control of Bengal's opium growing and production in 1797. After the 1813 EIC monopoly revocation, British and Parsi traders were licensed to ship it, especially trademarked *Patna* and *Varanasi* brands, sold at auction and shipped from Calcutta. Non-EIC *malwa* opium from western and central India was EIC-licensed and shipped from Bombay, returning with tea, silk and chinaware. Cotton and opium exports gradually reorientated Bombay's historic Gulf-Red Sea outlook to Asia. Hirji and Maneckji Jivanji, among the first Parsis to establish business in Canton, owned ships and adopted the surname Readymoney. Like many maritime merchants they established charitable works. The EIC tea monopoly was increasingly difficult to protect because India-Canton trade was private.

Agencies like Forbes and Co., Bruce Fawcett and Co. and Parsis like Dudy Nasserwanjee and Framjee Cowasjee became export partners. William Jardine after an 1802–17 EIC career, partnered Cowasjee, shipping *malwa* opium to China and Jamsetjee Jeejeebhoy and James Matheson, successor to the Cox-Beale partnership, which like most Canton agencies, turned to opium, transhipped in the Pearl River estuary and Lintin Island rather than Whampoa, the usual discharge port, up-river, past bribed customs officials. Clippers, narrow-hulled with massive sails, pioneered by Americans in 1812 to outrun British blockading ships, enabled two or three annual India-China round trips. The first from Calcutta in 1830 reached Macao in only 22 days, enabling building costs to be amortised within a year. Exports grew from about 9,000 chests in 1800, about 10,000 in 1825, to 40,000 by the late-1830s. Bombay, Calcutta, Canton and Hong Kong thus became increasingly interconnected and opium revenue, the largest source after land taxes, was used to build Indian canals and railways.

Following Britain's 1793 Macartney embassy, Lord Amherst's in 1816 investigating the possibility of normal commercial relations, was harassed, humiliated and expelled. The emperor it said, considered himself 'Lord and Sovereign of the world. Was it possible to submit calmly to such…irreverent arrogance?' But for the moment, Chinese rules were followed. The silver flow into China increased from three million ounces in the 1760s to 16 million in the 1780s, but thereafter two million taels of silver flowed out. Powerful mandarins supported legal opium purchase by barter for tea to reduce prices and stop the silver drain but were defeated at Court. Opium overtook cotton's export value in 1823. By the early-1830s about nine million taels were paid from China.

No moral repugnance had ever been attached to opium consumption, used as a relaxant and pain killer, invaluable before anaesthetics. Coleridge took it when sick and Wilberforce used it as a sedative and pain-killer. Friends noted how large quantities restored his health quickly and effectively. Gladstone (1809–1898) took laudanum based on tincture of opium in his coffee.[6] English horticultural societies awarded prizes for the best domestic plants. Usage was only questioned after Thomas de Quincey's 1822 *Confessions of an Opium Eater* described the pleasures and pain of opium, especially the pleasures. 'Oh! Just, subtle and mighty opium…that with thy potent rhetoric stealest away the purposes of wrath.' Freely purchased in Britain until the 1868 Pharmacy Act, European countries restricted it much later, San Francisco in 1875, fuelled by anti-Chinese immigrant sentiment about opium dens, but throughout America only in 1907. Until insulin's 1921 discovery, it was used to treat diabetes.

Grown in China for centuries as a medicine and painkiller, its import was outlawed in 1729. No one was sure why and was not rigorously enforced. All Chinese exchanges were abnormal. This seemed just another quirky, arbitrary irritation. It was expensive, consumed by mandarins, added to tobacco and smoked, as the Dutch had done, a social drug. Like alcohol, few became harmfully addicted. Tobacco, more addictive, has killed far more people. William Jardine thought investing in opium was 'the safest and most gentlemanly speculation' and James Matheson, 'morally equivalent' to selling brandy and champagne in Britain. An opium ship master's diary records, for 2nd December 1832, 'Employed delivering opium briskly. No time to read my Bible.'[7] The Emperor and mandarins were concerned about opium's damage to the trade balance, because while other imports gradually rose, 1821–1837 opium sales increased five-fold to around 1,400 tons. British consumption was however higher.

Eighteenth-century China had been peaceful. South American maize, sweet potato and peanut imports helped increase its population. This caused pressure on land, deforestation, river silting, flooding, food shortages, internal migration and over 15 major uprisings between 1795 and 1840, the cost of suppression, significant. In denial about the maritime world, it viewed these internal threats more seriously. Many Chinese migrated, mainly to Southeast Asia, especially Singapore after 1824. As South American independence dramatically reduced world gold and silver supply, Indian opium for silver and tea seemed an obvious exchange. By 1828 more silver left China than entered. With EIC monopoly abolished in 1834, more traders entered Canton, increasing opium sales.

Between 1830 and 1860 Bombay export values rose six-fold, opium ten-fold.[8] Parsi merchants specialised, working closely with EIC and agencies. Other Gujarati and Marwari businessmen went inland, financing opium, cotton, grain and oilseed growing. In 1838 Surat's Nowrojee Jamsetji sent his son and nephew to learn about steamship design and Ardaseer Cursetjee, head of Bombay's dockyard, from 1848 produced boilers and small engines, although not whole ships.

When his father died, Jamsetjee Jeejeebhoy (1783–1859) moved to Bombay, dealt in pearls, rice, cotton, cotton cloth, cochineal and dates, his business enhanced by marrying Bombay merchant Framjee Pestoujee's daughter. In 1804 he met William Jardine, both having established contacts in Canton, Calcutta, Madras and Bombay and Jeejeebhoy in Colombo, Penang and Sumatra. Between 1805 and 1817 he bought west coast Indian-built 500–1,200-tonners to ship opium and cotton to agencies in Canton, Macao and Hong Kong. In the 1820s there were ten agencies in Madras, 15 in Bombay and 46 in Calcutta.[9]

A seventh of EIC revenue derived from manufacturing and selling opium. Trans-shipping via Singapore in 1822 increased its importance. In 1827 Matheson founded the first English language newspaper, the *Canton Register*, printing local shipping news, opium prices and free trade articles. In 1830 Jardine Matheson and Co. sent about 5,000 chests annually to Canton, others sailing it on to Manchuria. American merchants' inferior, cheaper Anatolian opium competed. In 1828 British imports into Canton were 1.7 million Mexican silver dollars-worth of woollens, 400,000 of other goods, 3.4 million of Indian raw cotton and 11.2 million Indian opium. Exports were 85 million in tea, 6.1 million silver and 1.1 million raw silk: <u>still</u> more export value than imports.[10]

In 1830, free traders led by Jardine, successfully petitioned Parliament for a 'new commercial code' to replace the EIC's China monopoly. Jardine criticised both EIC and *hong* monopolies, arguing for access to China's internal trade and a permanent offshore base. Taiwan and Lintin were suggested. Opium was not the reason for wanting access to China's market. Manchester's Chamber of Commerce thought nowhere potentially better for all 'legitimate and mutually advantageous trade.'[11]

In 1833 the EIC lost the China monopoly and Palmerston sent Lord Napier as Superintendent of Trade to try to end the *hong*/tribute system. Told to observe Chinese laws and customs, to extend trade by treaty and insist Britain be recognised as China's equal, they were rejected. From 1834 Jardine joined EIC calls to send warships to

China to force it open. In the 1830s Manchu officials again debated legalisation <u>or</u> how to ban it. The emperor backed mandarin Lin Tse-hsu's aggressive ban.

European traders lived in many Chinese ports without legal recognition. Palmerston thought there were two ways, withdraw or 'bring the Chinese government to reason with vigorous measures.'[12] As for opium's illegality, it was China's job to control its coast and their corrupt officials. Merchant expectations were high. Palmerston wished to 'assist the commerce…by opening new markets for our trade.'[13] 'We must look again to Africa…especially to India and China.' 'The sun never sets upon the interests of this country.' But in 1839, Lin Tse-hsu destroyed almost £2.5 million-worth of opium and besieged Canton's British residents. This led to the first Anglo-Chinese War. Colloquially known as the Opium War, Britain just wanted more general, normal, orderly trade in more goods, more ports, with consuls defending British subjects. Canton could not access large populations in central and north China. Palmerston in 1841 reiterated, 'It is the business of the government to open and secure the roads for the merchants.' With tea volumes increasing, mid-18th-century 400–500-ton Indiamen became almost 1,500-tonners by the 1840s. Twenty ships annually rose to over 300. Between 1821 and 1857 British tea imports rose from £3.1 to £7.1 million.[14]

Palmerston thought China wanted domestic opium protected from imports which drained silver from China and thought Lin's actions unlawful. The war had British critics, albeit a minority. Gladstone opposed it as 'unjust and iniquitous' and Thomas Arnold, influential Rugby headmaster, called it 'a national sin,' a war 'to maintain smuggling…of a demoralising drug which the government of China wishes to keep out.' Palmerston was unmoved. No one he said, could 'say that he honestly believed the motive of the Chinese government to have been the promotion of moral habits,' but the balance of payments deficit. John Quincy Adams thought opium 'no more the cause of the war than the throwing overboard of tea in Boston harbour was the cause of the American revolution…[it] is the kowtow, the arrogant and insupportable pretensions of China that she will hold commercial intercourse…not upon terms of equal reciprocity but upon the insulting and degrading…relations between the lord and the vassal.'[15] Foreign Secretary Lord Aberdeen explained, 'a secure and well-regulated trade is all we desire.' Confucianism however, shunned trade, industry and economic development, promoting a static social order.

By 1841 British forces occupied Canton and by 1842 the Grand Canal and many other ports. Significantly, the 1842 Treaty of Nanking did not mention opium. An indemnity and compensation were paid, duties reduced. With *hong* monopoly abolished, Canton's and Macao's merchants had to trade normally. Amoy (Xiamen), Foochow, Ningpo and Shanghai were opened to trade and residence with rights for British to be tried by British courts, becoming economic centres unhindered by officials. Palmerston thought it would 'form an epoch in the progress of the civilisation of the human races.'[16] Hong Kong was ceded to Britain, declared a duty-free port and grew fast as a Chinese trade entrepot. In many ways it was a return to normality, large foreign trading communities in China since at least the 3rd century, encouraged during Song and Yuan dynasties. Banks, merchant houses, insurance brokerage companies followed, including Dutch, French, German, Parsi and Sephardic Jewish businesses.

Hong Kong and Singapore opened China and Southeast Asia to worldwide maritime trade. Hong Kong's 1844–1861 ship calls quintupled from 538 to 2,545, tonnage from 189,257 to 1,310,388. By the century's end over 11,000 ships called annually with over 13 million tons, the empire's third port after London and Liverpool. In 1838 Sir John Bowring thought it 'another example of the elasticity and potency of unrestricted commerce, which has more than counterbalanced the barrenness of the soil…[and] disadvantages of the climate.'[17]

Opium quality mattered. In 1845 Jeejeebhoy wrote to Matheson about a superior product. 'I regret I could not procure more and you can expect very little of this in the future…[so do not] part without the Chinese pay handsome prices, otherwise hold [a] little longer,' and occasionally chastised Jardine for not getting better prices. With freer trade and improving technology, Jeejeebhoy's ships became uncompetitive.[18] He sold them and invested in insurance, railways, land and banks. His charity helped debtors, educated paupers, built public buildings, hospitals, schools of industry and art. Knighted in 1842 at the EIC's recommendation for charity to widows, orphans and the destitute, he became a baron. Elphinstone rhetorically asked where else could boast of 'a citizen who has devoted a quarter of a million sterling to purposes of public charity and benevolence,' for the poor and suffering of all creeds: maritime enlightenment. Jeejeebhoy and other Parsis were convinced that free trade's effects were entirely benign.

Shanghai's people were more welcoming than Manchu authorities, renting premises, profiting thereby. Jardine Matheson opened there in 1844. Jardine observed he lived in a Chinese treaty port with property protected, 'business conducted easily and usually with singular good faith,' praising Chinese courtesy, 'the reason why so many of us keep coming back and staying so long,' rejecting accusations of smuggling, like Jeejeebhoy, simply a legitimate issue of Chinese demand and Indian supply, contrasted with Chinese government hypocrisy. Jeejeebhoy thought British intentions, 'the advancement of her native [Indian] subjects',[19] empowered Indian entrepreneurship. Indeed, a key to British power in India was empowering Indian financial and merchant commercial life, ignored by land-hungry Mughals. John Stuart Mill's *Representative Government* thought British rule the only path to social progress. Partnering and empowering Indian entrepreneurs helped Indian trade outstrip Caribbean trade.

The 1844 Treaty of Wanghia gave America the same rights as Britain's Treaty of Nanking but forbade opium, completely disregarded by US merchants who increased their influence. Boston, Baltimore and New York shipowners imported tea, silk and porcelain, driving US trader expansion throughout the Pacific, especially after California's 1846 annexation. They even competed to ship tea to Britain. At Shanghai they carried almost half the trade.[20] More aggressive than the British, they wanted all Asian ports open. American Commodore Perry forced Japan to open in 1852–54. Whaling's extension into the north Pacific meant safe harbours and supply stations were needed. The 1854 Treaty of Kanagawa affirmed that US consuls could protect stranded seamen and supply US ships at Shimoda and Hakodate. Secretary of State Daniel Webster said it was 'the last link in that great chain, which unites all the world by the early establishment of a line of steamers from California to China.' US merchants, scouring the Pacific for goods that China wanted, led to consulates in Fiji in 1844 and Samoa in 1856.

In 1845 there were, at any one time, an estimated 80 clippers carrying opium to China, tea from it, a quarter Jardine Matheson's.[21] In 1851 there were more Parsis in China than British. Palmerston thought the treaties needed constant surveillance, 'gingering up', because if China resumed its former 'tone of affected superiority we shall very soon be compelled to come to blows…again.'[22] In the 1850s China increasingly became a market for British cloth and manufactured products, but treaty ports did not develop as hoped. Shanghai at the Yangtse's mouth was the most successful, accessing populous, tea-producing central China. Other ports were too few and too far from main population and production centres. There were disagreements regarding coastal trade and foreigners were not allowed up the Yangtse, where large inland populations lived. The British triumphed militarily, technically, commercially and industrially, so the methods employed were naturally British. As Philip Curtin notes, 'Normally communities of a trade diaspora learned about the culture of the host society, not the other way around.'[23] That gave merchant societies throughout history their toleration, openness to new ideas, the vanguard of progress. Chinese isolationism made this impossible. Tea clippers sailed from China to the Thames in about 90 days. P&O's faster steamships were in India, Ceylon, Penang, Hong Kong and in 1848 a feeder service to Macao and Canton and 1853 from Singapore to Australia.

Commercial treaties of 1858 and 1866 opened Japan to unrestricted maritime trade, but imposed low tariffs exposed its backward agrarian economy to industrialising maritime nations, ruining rural handicrafts. Chinese cotton yarn was stronger and easier to weave, its sugar cheaper, imported kerosene cheaper than vegetable oils, imported woollens cheaper and warmer than domestic silk. It led to over 200 rural uprisings.[24] Japan's government responded, building sugar refineries and spinning mills.

Following many Chinese 1795–1840 uprisings, the Taiping Rebellion (1850–1864), an anti-Manchu peasant revolt, history's largest civil war, destroyed 600 cities, killing about 20 million people. The Nien rebellion (1853–68), a Muslim revolt in Yunnan (1853–73), a Miao rebellion in Kweichow (1851–72), involved seven million revolting against misgovernment.[25] When Taiping rebels threatened Shanghai in 1853, Chinese customs passed into foreign control, from 1873 managed by Sir Robert Hart with 89 European staff, mainly British, answerable to the emperor. Famous for its efficiency and incorruptibility, it helped keep Chinese finances afloat. Treaty ports and Hong Kong were havens of peace and security. Hong Kong's Chinese population rose from 40,000 in 1853 to 85,000 in 1859. Tea and silk were diverted from Canton to Shanghai and Foochow, which were linked in 1855 by Russell and Co's. regular steamship services, America's first permanent firm in China. Domestic rebellion and poverty encouraged further mass emigration to Californian and Australian gold fields, Malaysian tin mines, Singapore, Batavia and Bangkok. In 1858 about 20% of Shanghai's opium imports were in American ships, which shipped out emigrants. Hong Kong was the main centre for this *coolie* traffic. Between 1855 and 1859 over 80,000 left Hong Kong for worldwide destinations. Between 1847 and 1862 US traders shipped 6,000 to Cuba annually.[26]

Britain thought non-adherence to the Treaty of Nanking's terms and victimising Chinese merchants trading with British merchants a continuing problem. To protect them, Britain granted their ships British registration. In 1856 Chinese authorities seized the *Arrow* flying the British flag whose registration had expired. Hong Kong's governor without consulting London, ordered Canton's bombardment. Palmerston supported him but the Commons narrowly resolved he had over-reacted. Palmerston called an election in which it loomed large, winning an increased majority. Britain did not want to repeat Indian take-over, but an attempt to poison Hong Kong's Europeans persuaded Palmerston that China needed a 'drubbing' once a decade to keep them in order, using it as the excuse for the 1857–1858 Second Anglo-Chinese War, to extend trade inland.

The Treaty of Tianjin gave Britain, France, America and Russia rights to establish diplomatic legations in Peking. Twelve more ports opened for foreign trade, including Kowloon, next to Hong Kong and Taiwan. Foreign ships were permitted to navigate the Yangtse and foreigners given the right to travel internally. Some deluded mandarins persuaded the weak emperor to continue war. The British diplomatic envoy's entourage were arrested, some slowly tortured to death. The end however, was inevitable and a small Anglo-French force destroyed the Manchu army. Peking was occupied and the emperor's summer palace burned, leading to some reforms; too little, too late. The emperor fled.

Anyone could bring *malwa* to Bombay, ship it with P&O and sell it in Hong Kong. Jardine-Matheson were gradually forced to diversify. Baghdad Jew David Sassoon started shipping opium in 1830. By mid-century his son Elias' firm was the leading agency and started Bombay's textile mills. Another, Silas Hardoon later became a Shanghai millowner and married a Chinese Buddhist, such inter-cultural relationships only possible in the tolerant maritime world.

The 1860 Convention of Peking, signed with the emperor's brother, reaffirmed the previous treaty, opening Tianjin. Kowloon was ceded to Britain, opium legalised, freedom of religion and British ships' right to carry indentured Chinese to the Americas granted. Western merchants could trade with the Yangtse's great Hankowen tea centre. Over 40 British firms including Parsis operated from Hong Kong. By the early-1900s they had breweries, cotton mills, railways, ferries and insurance companies. Coastal shipping and Chinese trade grew, especially opium and cotton imports, despite continuing rebellion. British exports to China and Hong Kong were £1 million in 1854, £5.4 million in 1860 and £10 million in 1870.[27] Until the dynasty's end however, it rejected reform. Only 195 miles of railway existed in 1894, contrasting unfavourably with India's British-built networks.

Chapter 22

The Free Trade Debate and
Repeal of the Corn Laws

Britain exported grain to Europe until the 1760s. As its population rose, seven million acres were enclosed between 1760 and 1815 and 200,000 from 1815 to 1845, shrinking Britain's agricultural workforce. London's growing food demand was met initially mainly from southern England, Cheshire for cheeses, Wales for pigs and Wiltshire for bacon. Corn Laws aimed to stabilise grain (corn) prices. During poor harvests, low import duties encouraged imports. When good harvests reduced prices, producers got export subsidies. They prevented grain prices rising too high for the poor or too low for landowners to grow. Sporadic grain and flour imports during poor harvests from the 1720s became about 3–4% of consumption after the 1774 Corn Law, encouraging imports to supply the growing population.[1] From 1780 Britain became a regular net importer, mainly from the Baltic. From 1791, the Commons received petitions from London, Norwich, Somerset and Dorset merchants complaining of grain shortages. Bridport requested to be made a 'granary port' to enjoy 'greater connection with America' and Bristol wanted to import its grain.

From 1785 Britain addressed the issue by re-orienting Ireland's economy. Previously Belfast's linen and cotton, Cork's salt pork and beef provisions to army, navy and merchant ships and Liverpool's increasing livestock imports were the main exchanges. But by 1815, Ireland supplied 57% of Britain's wheat, 70% by the mid-1820s and 90% by the mid-1830s. By 1845, 40% of Ireland's wheat production went to Britain. In the 1830s-1840s, around 100,000 cattle, 200,000 sheep and lambs, 400,000 pigs, butter, cheese, lard, animal skins, honey, glue, seed, horses and 60–90 million eggs annually were sent. Ireland contributed about 75% of Britain's food imports in 1825, despite British 1800–1853 agricultural productivity increasing 70%.[2] This seemingly mutually beneficial arrangement meant Irish peasants gradually became dependent on potatoes. Coastal shipping to London was an annual three million tons by 1840, mainly coal but including 200,000 tons of grain. Meanwhile, North American river and canal steamboats from the 1820s and railways from the 1840s, enabled mass transfer of bulk goods from the interior to east coast ports. By the 1840s, Irish food was insufficient for Britain's growing population.

Pitt tried liberalising trade after 1783 with the Commutation Act and Eden Treaty, but 1793–1815 Anglo-French war made European grain supplies problematic and expensive. Grain export and its use in distilleries was banned and import duties eliminated. In 1800 good harvests reduced prices and in 1804 Parliament passed a Corn Law with a sliding scale, giving farmers minimum 63 shillings/quarter when

1690–1790 prices had averaged only 40, encouraging domestic output, some on previously uncultivated land, increasing agricultural employment. Wheat prices were over 100 shillings/quarter when Napoleon sold to Britain in 1809–10.

Pitt's trade liberalisation effectively made free trade Tory policy and Lord Liverpool's government from 1812 was faithful to it, <u>except</u> agricultural protection. Tax on land effectively taxed grain. Logically imported grain should also be taxed. Adam Smith said duties were justified if contributing to national defence. Farmers made good profits, landlords high rents. Historically, high prices prevented agricultural depression, which would occur if free trade allowed cheap imports.

Napoleon's June 1815 defeat was unexpectedly decisive. Before it, a Corn Law prevented wheat imports unless the domestic price was above 80 shillings/quarter. As prices fell from 120 to 70, wheat imports were initially eliminated, warping the aim, price stability, to protection. Cultivated land opened during war became uneconomic and lapsed. The timing was also unfortunate because Britain's 1811–1841 population rose from 12.6 to 18 million,[3] and Indonesia's 1815 Mount Tambora eruptions caused the 1816 'Year Without a Summer', reducing crop yields, causing famine. Wheat prices rose to 100 shillings/quarter, as wages were depressed, leading to discontent and disorder.

There was country-wide urban and rural unrest. London rioters broke into Foreign Secretary, Castlereagh's home. *Habeas Corpus* was suspended and martial law provisions enacted. Thomas Tooke's 1820 *Petition of the London Merchants* stated, 'freedom from restraint [will]…give the utmost extension to foreign trade and the best direction to…capital and industry' and 'the maxim of buying in the cheapest and selling in the dearest…is…the best rule for the trade of the whole nation.'[4] The *Petition* was respected but political consensus, that domestic agriculture should be protected, remained. Tooke later wrote *Thoughts and Details on the High and Low Prices of the Past Thirty Years, History of Prices* and the 1823 Baltic Coffee House's *Constitution*.

Adam Smith's disciple David Ricardo (1771–1823) came from a Portuguese Sephardic family, via Livorno. Becoming Amsterdam stockbrokers about 1680, they helped finance Dutch Seven Years War defence. Frequent trips to London led to relocation about 1760. His 1817 pamphlet *Principles of Political Economy and Taxation* argued that each country should specialise in what it did best, rather than protect inefficient industries and thought wages 'must' fall with grain prices, which they would if more was imported. Entering Parliament in 1819 advocating free trade, his 1822 *On Protection to Agriculture* thought reforming the tax system was necessary before free trade. Like today's US, EU and Japanese farm lobbies, landowners argued that farming was unique; the nation's food producer must be protected, that free trade would create reliance on foreigners, endangering national security. Free traders claimed agriculture was like any other business, the danger of dependence exaggerated. Less restricted trade would encourage food exporters to engage in mutually profitable trade. Britain could depend on food imports in war because it would profit exporting countries. Hadn't Russia resisted Napoleon because he attempted to prevent their profitable exports? Hadn't Napoleon permitted grain exports to Britain when prices were high? Ricardo died in 1823 but had many followers. The influential *Leeds Mercury* campaigned against the 1815 law, arguing it increased industrial wages, making manufacturers uncompetitive in world markets. *The Sheffield Independent,* (founded 1819) and *Manchester Guardian* (1821), were also radical free trade supporters, established with cotton manufacturing money and William Cobbett's *Political Register* claimed a 40–50,000 circulation compared with provincial papers' 2–5,000.

Economic recovery and declining social discontent eased fears of social revolution. Lord Liverpool, Prime Minister 1812–1827, favouring free trade, said in 1812, 'the less commerce and manufacturers were meddled with, the more likely they were to prosper.'[5] His reforming ministry in 1822 had Home Secretary Robert Peel, son and grandson of cotton manufacturers who sponsored the first Factory Act in 1802, Huskisson, MP for booming Liverpool as President of the Board of Trade, Robinson as Chancellor and after Castlereagh's suicide, Canning as Foreign Secretary. Huskisson's predecessor Thomas Wallace said he aimed to relieve British shipping 'from every vexatious and unnecessary burden, to simplify laws of navigation, to recommend a system of trade more adapted to an age in which we live and the <u>enlightened</u> and <u>liberal</u> principles that characterise it…to render this island the universal emporium of trade and to see the City of London, the metropolis…of the commercial world.'[6] Huskisson's 1823 Reciprocity of Duties Act allowed foreign ships to trade directly at the same duties as British ships if reciprocity was guaranteed, leading to 15 agreements between 1824 and 1829. Merchant shipping increased almost 50% in the next 20 years. Duties on bar iron and cotton were reduced 70%, raw silk 90%, spun silk 50% and 30% on French silks, hitherto prohibited, were imposed. Prosperity resulted. Radicalism declined. Peel abolished the death penalty for over 100 crimes. His 1823 Gaols Act made gaolers government-paid rather than prisoner-paid, separated men and women, instituted inspections and prisoner education. In 1824 Trade Unions became legal, reversing the 1799–1800 Combination Acts, thought, like suspending *Habeas Corpus* in 1794, necessary in war. In 1825 duties on plantation-grown hemp, iron, coal, rum, books, porcelain etc. were abolished. Government policy was that no industry would have more than 30% duties. Huskisson told the Commons in 1825, 'we furnish…the world with all the leading articles of manufacture…I am not afraid of…being overwhelmed with foreign goods…our manufacturers supply cheaper and better.'[7] Customs revenue rose 64% between 1821 and 1827.

Canning, son of a failed merchant, was raised by his merchant uncle. Strongly supporting Pitt during the war, he worked in the Foreign Office, the Board of Control for India, had been Treasurer of the Navy and Foreign Secretary, who after the 1807 Franco-Russian Tilsit pact, planned the Copenhagen attack. He supported South American independence movements, recognised Colombia and Mexico because British capital was already invested in mining and territory and later Brazil and Argentina, declaring, 'Spanish America is free; and if we do not mismanage our matters sadly, she is English.' He meant commercially dominant and British! In 1825 he received the first Latin American state minister and persuaded Portugal to recognise Brazil. Robinson's 1823 budget paid off much National Debt and halved the window tax. The next reduced or abolished many duties on imports, his third cut duties and tax further.

Meanwhile, the Manchester Chamber of Commerce, representing industrial interests, in 1824 pointed 'to the overwhelming restriction under which the commercial interests of this country are placed by…the Corn Laws.' Its 1825 meeting resolved 'removal of the restrictions on importation.' There were many strands of thought within the freer trade movement, considerations of grain prices, effects of manufactured goods' demand on wages, employment and rents, principles of economic freedom, in some cases, political reform. Some believed free trade would increase textile demand or stunt foreign textile production. Many businessmen believed in their duty to help the poor and that Corn Laws imposed an unjust tax on food. Some paid higher than average wages. Others sponsored the 1833 Manchester Statistical Society, which conducted investigations into factory labour conditions. Consumer cooperatives, building and friendly societies and other self-help groups started there in the 1820s. Manchester was not only the cotton industry's heart, but one of reform and enlightenment.

Prime Minister from 1827, Canning brought some Whigs into government; further years of significant reform. In 1829 Peel founded the Metropolitan Police, Britain's first, more efficient than local spies, watchmen and yeomanry, defining ethical requirements of officers. Crime dropped and other cities formed police forces. Huskisson's 1828 bill replaced the 1815 Corn Law tariff with a sliding scale similar to 1804, enabling rising imports. In 1828 legal disabilities on non-conformists were abolished. In 1829 all offices except Lord Chancellor and Viceroy of Ireland were opened to Catholics, although the Irish franchise narrowed, raising the question of electoral reform. Pitt the Elder had earlier warned that Parliament must reform itself to prevent it being done from outside 'with a vengeance'. Pitt the Younger wanted to abolish 36 once substantial constituencies which subsequently declined to a few electors but still chose two MPs, 'the rotten part of our constitution,' but was defeated in Parliament in 1785. This too was delayed by war. Thereafter, popular pressure for reform increased, especially from growing cities like Birmingham and Manchester. In 1830 the Commons had over 150 MPs who were nominees of 84 landed magnates, another 150 who were influenced by 70 others. The issue dominated political life until the 1832 Reform Bill. House of Lords rejection triggered a fierce reaction. With King William IV's support, they submitted, abolishing 56 'rotten' boroughs, 30 more reduced to one seat. The franchise increased from about 430,000 to about 800,000, reflecting trade and industry as important as land, brought a large Liberal majority under Lord Grey and more reforming legislation.

In 1830 US ships were admitted to the British Caribbean. In 1833 the EIC lost its China monopoly and slavery was abolished in British territories. No society had ever had to adapt to problems associated with fast industrial growth and burgeoning cities. Humanitarian concerns increasingly addressed them. The 1833 Factory Act forbade employment in textile factories to children under nine. Those under 13 could work maximum nine hours a day, those under 18, maximum 12, a weekly maximum of 48 with regular meals, education and state inspections. Most employers did not oppose them. Subsequent Acts over the next 20 years improved conditions, including in mines in 1844, restricting work to men, until the ten-hour day was conceded plus regulations for ventilation, sanitation and guarding machinery. The 1834 Poor Law was much influenced by Bentham's 'greatest happiness for the greatest number' principle. The 1835 Prisons Act established inspectors. The 1848 Public Health Act addressed bad urban housing, overcrowding, inadequate sanitation and water supply contamination because Manchester's, Liverpool's and Glasgow's 1811–1831 populations had doubled. The 1831–32 great cholera epidemic killed 32,000, a third in London. An 1848–49 outbreak probably claimed 80,000. In 1849, Dr John Shaw demonstrated the connection between water supply and cholera. Further Acts followed, tightening regulations. In the 1830s, local governments were given powers over poor relief and the first grants made to public education. Reformist governments flexibly adapted to societal changes, unlike Europe. Independent newspapers like *The Times* and *Morning Post* supported Tories, *The Morning Chronicle* and *Examiner*, Liberals.

The idea of responsible self-government for settler colonies, part of free trade/ liberal thinking, nascent from Burke's late-18th century ideas, was first suggested in 1829 for Upper Canada and finally introduced by Gray in 1847, <u>not</u> influenced by the famous but flawed 1839 Durham Report. Elgin presided over the change, staying as Governor for five years, signing free trade and reciprocal trade with America in 1854, after which its economy recovered from 1840s depression. The idea spread to New South Wales, Victoria, Queensland, New Zealand, the Cape and Western Australia.

The Anti-Corn Law Association was established in London in 1836. Most 1830s domestic harvests were plentiful, prices low. Corn Laws did not top political agendas. But in 1837, prices began rising. Richard Cobden, first apprenticed to his calico merchant uncle, established with his brother, a Manchester printing factory. After travelling in the US, Middle East and Europe, he became convinced that Britain needed to sell its manufactured goods cheaper, that wheat prices, determining bread prices, on which much of the poor's wages went, needed reducing. The general assumption was that Corn Laws increased bread prices which meant wages had to be conceded, increasing manufactured goods' prices, eroding their competitiveness. German, French and US competition was gaining ground. Workers were emigrating to America, where food was cheaper. German and French wages were half Britain's because bread was cheaper. The movement's aim was to alarm politicians that Britain was losing industrial supremacy and Corn Laws urgently needed repeal. British mainstream economic thought since 1649 was its future wealth depended on trade. That meant industrial exports, agriculture less important. Imported wheat would lower bread prices, wages, thus manufactured goods prices, encouraging more exports. By 1840 Britain sent a third of its exports, mainly cotton cloth and clothing to America. Cobden's visit convinced him of its rising competition.

Manchester cotton interests shared these ideas and in 1838 founded the Anti-Corn Law League, an organised pressure group with a powerful propaganda machine, paid for by subscriptions which financed workers, speakers and its own building, Free Trade Hall.[8] It was unique in Europe, because merchant values of compromise were understood and institutionalised. The Manchester Chamber of Commerce's philosophy was that their fortune was governed by foreign trade. It asked for free trade between England and Ireland, opposed restricting ship sizes in EIC trade, opposed unnecessary quarantine regulations, expressed alarm on reports of higher duties on US raw cotton imports, urged extending cotton growing in Egypt and India and opposed duties on non-British sugar and coffee because it reduced 'demand for our manufactures.'

Between 1838 and 1846, Cobden, John Bright, son of a Quaker, Rochdale cotton mill owner and many others toured Britain, speaking to millions supporting free trade and condemning protection. Large London meetings were held almost daily.[9] Cobden and Bright became national figures.

Most thought Repeal would reduce wages, although John Bowring and Cobden argued it would stimulate manufacturing and factory employment. In 1842 he explained, 'In every period when wages…dropped…manufacturing interest dropped…I hope manufacturers…[take] a rather more <u>enlightened</u> view of their own interest than conclude that the impoverishment of the multitude…great consumers…could ever… promote the prosperity of our manufacturers.' After Repeal, the textile industry did expand more rapidly. One reason was free trade but also increased demand, railways and steamship efficiency. All promoted economic expansion.[10] 1840–1860 cotton cloth exports were double 1820–1840, all exports, four-times greater.

Rowland Hill thought Britain's quickly developed 1830s rail system would reduce postal costs, a shilling paid by recipients. Cobden helped persuade Parliament to pass the penny post in 1840, a powerful weapon as the League targeted adult male voters after the 1832 Reform Act. *The Anti-Corn Law Circular* and *The League,* daily and weekly respectively and many pamphlets were circulated targeting religious and humanitarian feelings, with mottos like 'Give us this day our daily bread.' Bright claimed Jesus Christ would have preached against the Corn Laws, their repeal Cobden said, the most important event since his coming. They focused on returning a free trade majority in the anticipated 1848 election, objecting to protectionists at annual register revisions, creating thousands of new free trade voters in urban constituencies enfranchised by the Reform Act. Parents were urged to buy property for sons, so they could vote, as Cobden said, to 'defend himself and his children from political oppression.'[11] Bright, more radical, saw it starting franchise extension.

They thought free trade an issue of liberty and morality, the alleviation of the poor's hardships, not just economic practicality. Edward Baines, *The Leeds Mercury* editor wrote 'Free trade means perfect freedom for every kind of industry…includes liberty to every man to employ his money or his labour in the way that he himself thinks most advantageous…to buy and sell wherever he can…with the greatest profit.'[12] Others believed Ricardo, that free trade would give worldwide buyers and sellers strong economic interests in peace, repeated by Bowring and Cobden's 1842 pamphlet *Free Trade as the Best Human Means for Securing Universal and Permanent Peace.* Tennyson, echoing the idea, 'saw the heavens fill with commerce, argosies of magic sails…till the war-drum throbb'd no longer.' Bright asserted freedom to exchange produce was a fundamental right; 'there was not liberty without this liberty…simply the liberty to live.'

Arguments conducted amid growing industrialisation and urbanisation, with unskilled or semi-skilled work, some by woman and children, led to pockets of extreme urban poverty. Rural poverty was dispersed and probably as bad, but less outwardly shocking. Disraeli's *Sybil; or The Two Nations* (1845) recorded the widening class gap 'between whom there is no intercourse and no sympathy; who are ignorant of each other's habits, thoughts and feelings…fed by different food…ordered by different manners.' Factory reform until the 1850s was confined to textile mills and coal mines, only extended to workshops in the 1860s. Lord Ashley, Earl of Shaftesbury campaigned for the 1847 Ten Hour Act, actually 10.5, ten achieved in 1874. The tradition of enlightened industrialists continued. Titus Salt (1803–1876), the first to use alpaca wool he found in a Liverpool warehouse, Bradford's largest employer in 1850, consolidated his five textile mills in Saltaire on Owen's New Lanark model: houses, alms houses, bath houses, hospital and churches, his motives economic, using economies of scale and religious/humanitarian, workers living healthy, virtuous, godly lives. Prussian Prince Puckler-Muskau thought some urban conditions terrible but generally better than Europe's. Most gained more working within the system than working against it.

Arguments against landed interests potentially led to subversive stances on game laws, aristocrats, military, universities and Church of England, which didn't support the movement. A.W. Paulton insisted the free trade movement, a contest between '30,000 landowners and 26,000,000 men.'[13] The *Anti-Bread Tax Circular* criticised Parliament as a 'landowners club…passing laws to enrich themselves by the impoverishment of the millions they pretend to represent.'[14] Most arguments were economic. How would the revenue from customs, 38% and excise 37% in 1846 be compensated?[15] Leaguers said refusing imported grain prevented exporters obtaining capital to buy British manufactured goods. Increasing manufacturing would ensure Britain's future prosperity, but which parts? Industrialists and landowners claimed to defend workers' and farmers' interests, yet agricultural wages were also low, despite supposed Corn Law protection.

During the 1842 economic recession and poor harvest, Manchester's Chamber of Commerce reported on 'late lamentable commotions' driven by hardships, praising workers' 'heroic fortitude.' Importantly, Prime Minister Peel persuaded his cabinet to halve 1828's grain import duties' sliding scale. Over 1,200 tariffs were reduced: Canada's wheat to a shilling/quarter, raw materials to 5%, semi-manufactured goods to 12%, foreign manufactured goods to 20%. He introduced the first peacetime income tax, 7d per £ on annual incomes over £150 for three years to cover reduced duties, in many ways more significant and dramatic than 1846 Repeal. In 1843 with the League's help, *The Economist* was founded to promote free trade. Important questions were if Britain unilaterally repealed the Corn Laws, would exporting countries reciprocate and open their home markets to British manufacturing exporters? Would free trade damage national security by reliance on imports? How would Britain obtain food in wartime? Charles Villiers MP initiating annual Repeal motions from 1838 wanted 'the community to enjoy that which is needful and desired at the lowest costs and at the greatest advantage?' Parliament's anti-Repeal majority fell year-by-year.

A cold, wet 1845 summer produced poor harvests, resulting in a potato blight in England, Ireland, Belgium and Germany, inducing hardship everywhere but famine in Ireland, which gave Peel the excuse for Repeal, Whig leader Russell already pledging support. Peel argued that free trade allowed Britain to retain world trade pre-eminence whether other countries reciprocated or not, that increasing trade, industrial wealth and income tax would offset lost tariff income, that no tariff exceed 10%, reducing them on sugar, silk, spirits, butter, cheese, hops and fish and abolishing them on meat, potatoes, vegetables and other non-grains, to benefit industrial and working classes.[16]

Repeal, passed in 1846, was phased-in over three years. The Duke of Wellington persuaded the House of Lords to accept it, demonstrating Britain's political flexibility. Landowning lords voted seemingly against their interests because they understood the consensus for gradual reform. Standing against it risked Chartists' more radical, disruptive reforms. By 1846, tariffs were anyway a minor real issue, symbolic only, the main reductions effected in 1828 and 1842. As Peel said, it was a decision between 'continued relaxation of restriction or the return to restraint and prohibition…advance or recede.'[17]

Between 1816 and 1821 the government sent grain to Ireland during food shortages. At the potato blight's first appearance, Peel sent it to stabilise food prices. There were no excess deaths in 1845–1846 but in free trade debates, intervention was increasingly viewed as inappropriate. Russell's government which followed, tried countering famine by public works because Peel's intervention upset grain producers. In early-1847, deaths soared. Lord Lieutenant of Ireland, Bessborough said 'I cannot make up my mind entirely about the merchants. I know all the difficulties that arise when you… interfere with trade, but it is difficult to persuade a starving population that one class should be permitted to make 50% profit by the sale of provisions whilst they are dying of want of these.'[18] By January 1847 public works had clearly failed, replaced by soup kitchens. Import restrictions were suspended. Food prices fell, too late to help hundreds of thousands who died. Emigration soared. Twenty thousand left in 1843 before the crisis; between 1847 and 1855, 1.187 million![19]

Douglas Irwin examined Peel's ideological evolution. Initially adopting 'without… much serious reflection, the opinions generally prevalent' about agricultural protection, in 1839 Peel defended the Corn Laws against Ricardo's arguments, that they did not draw resources from industry whose profitability grew fast, that they were not responsible for price volatility and that demand for British manufactures would not suddenly rise if the Corn Laws were repealed. On economic theories, 'its brightest luminaries…have failed to throw light on the obscure and intricate question of… those special burdens upon agriculture which entitle it to protection from foreign competition' and the 'higher considerations involved than those of mercantile profit,' were economic distress of the rural poor.[20]

In 1841, he said. 'If I could…believe that an alteration in the Corn Laws would be an effective remedy for those distresses, I would be the first to step forward and… would earnestly advise a relaxation…if necessary, a repeal.' In 1842 when persuading his cabinet to halve duties and introduce income tax, he thought they were entitled to a fair trial.[21] 'I believe that on the general principle of free trade…that all agree on the general rule that we should purchase in the cheapest market and sell in the dearest, but the Corn Laws and Sugar Duties are exceptions to the general rule.' His criteria was national welfare. 'The only protection which can be vindicated, is that… consistent with the general welfare of all classes.' Support was insurance against foreign dependence. Removing it would add to agricultural labourers' burdens. Manufacturing had expanded while co-existing with Corn Laws. He quoted Huskisson who guided 1820s tariff cuts; 'all general theories, however incontrovertible in the abstract require to be weighed with a calm circumspection.' Are these not the words of practical wisdom?'

In 1843 he had seen 'nothing…to change my opinion' and in 1844 still maintained agricultural protection for 'considerations of justice,' in 1845 saying 'I think experience has shown that a high price of corn is not necessarily accompanied with a high… wage. But I believe it would be impossible to show that the rate of wage varies with the price of corn.'

Peel changed his mind before the potato blight, acknowledging Ricardo's and Cobden's 'abstract reasoning', but acted 'upon the results of enlarged experience.'[22] Having 'the means and opportunity of comparing the results of periods of abundance and low prices with periods of scarcity and high prices…I do not believe after the experience of the last three years that…wages varies with the price of food.' Paternalistic Tory tradition for labour welfare changed his mind, eventually concluding Corn Laws did labour harm, pragmatic evaluation to lessen distress, a high point of economic enlightenment.

From different positions Peel and Wellington arguably saved Britain from revolution in 1848. When Disraeli, became Prime Minister, seeing the evidence, did not attempt reintroduction. Tariffs on wine, sugar, coffee, tea and rum persisted for a few decades, so Repeal did not introduce free trade. The League highlighted the significance of 1846, but the process began in the enlightened 1780s. Freer trade had other consequences. As British Caribbean sugar became less competitive, its export value fell from £6.25 million in 1814 to £3.75 million in 1830.[23] The 1846 Sugar Duties Act meant British Caribbean sugar producers competed with Cuban and Brazilian slave-grown sugar. British Caribbean economies collapsed. By 1850 estate prices were 10% of 1840, parcelled into smallholdings for ex-slave subsistence farmers. British exports to the Caribbean halved between the 1820s and 1860s. Those to India, Australia, Canada, New Zealand, Hong Kong and Singapore rose significantly.

Repeal focused attention on the Navigation Acts. Why should shipping enjoy protection if agriculture didn't? John Lewis Ricardo, David's nephew, told Parliament it was 'better to send forth our ships free as the winds…with liberty.[24] In 1849 they were repealed. An 1859 shipowner's meeting at the bottom of a freight cycle demanded return of colonial trades to British ships. *The Times* described them as 'political and commercial fossils…political antiquarianism,' not representative of the free trade spirit or most shipowners.[25] In 1840 there were over 1,100 items subject to import duties, by 1860 only 50. Britain succeeded in avoiding revolution while France had two in 18 years because Britain's governing classes were closer to economic life than France's or other Europeans, operating in a commercial world of clear argument, compromise and national interest. Income from shipping continued covering the difference between import and export values. 1815–1820 shipping earnings averaged £9.92 million annually against a £7.22 million balance of payments deficit, 1841–1845, £11.7 against £5.9 and 1876–1880, £54.2 against £24.9. In short, shipping earnt Britain the money needed to import raw materials, food and luxuries. In 1859 *The Times* wrote, 'Free Trade is henceforth …an article of faith.'[26]

By contrast, continental Europe's developments will be briefly recapped. In 1815 the *ancien regime* was restored on its ruined economy, reaction against French Revolution excesses. Louis XVIII dreamed of imperial power, sending an expedition to Annam in 1816, Napoleonic-like thirst for *gloire*, unsatiated. All European princes except Turkey and Britain joined the Holy Alliance, enforcing absolutism. Theocratic origin of kings and pope was stressed; hierarchy, obedience, divine revelation; not discussion, toleration, individualism and free enquiry. The Papal States and Inquisition were re-established. Jews were forced back into ghettos. More liberal though still onerous policies of pre-revolutionary popes were reversed. Jews were barred from public office, from friendly relations with Christians and had to wear yellow badges. Frequent police visits to Rome's ghetto seized women and children for baptism.[27]

Enlightenment/liberalism however, could not be forgotten, especially with forces unleashed by industrialisation. Europe was still mainly agricultural without cheap, fast transport. Farmers used traditional methods. Bad harvests caused crises in 1817–18, 1826–29, 1836–39 and 1840–50. As Britain moved towards freer trade and efficient ships, Europe was rigidly protectionist. Famine caused thousands of deaths. Fear of famine was constant. Typhus, plague and cholera epidemics were common. Censorship, summary justice and lack of press freedom provoked violence. In 1830 Paris was seized and Charles X abdicated. Under the Duc d'Orleans, toleration was allowed, censorship abolished, the franchise slightly widened, but elections were usually rigged. Belgium revolted against Dutch control. Industrialisation spread there and to adjacent German and French regions, financed by the Rothschilds. Spinning and weaving were mechanised in Ghent and Brussels, metal industries established at Namur, Charleroi and Liege, contrasting with most of Europe. By 1836 Britain produced ten million tons of iron, Belgium under three million, France one million.

Napoleon's territorial simplification, foreign rule and Ottoman decline awoke national consciousnesses. In absolutist Russia, serfdom compensated for poor yields and techniques, exporting huge wheat volumes despite famines with unorganised internal markets, no railways or banking system. Annexed parts of Poland were subject to Russian terror. Russian Minister of Education Uvarov under the slogan, 'Orthodoxy, Autocracy, Nationalism' tried restricting university education to nobles and excluding 'dangerous' subjects from the curriculum. Historian Granovsky in 1849 wrote 'The dead are the lucky ones…Russia is nothing but a living pyramid of crimes, frauds and abuses, full of spies, policemen, rascally governors, drunken magistrates and cowardly aristocrats all united in their desire for theft and pillage…supported by 600,000 automata with bayonets.'[28]

Trieste, Austria's window on Mediterranean trade, flourished as a free port, especially after 1797 when Venice lost independence. In 1805, 537 ships were registered there, mostly Venetian-owned.[29] It copied Livorno's success with toleration and security, abolishing the ghetto in 1785, hosting Armenian, Greek, Jewish, Serb, German, Dutch, British, Albanian and Turkish merchants, stimulating intellectual and cultural life. But this maritime culture did not penetrate inland where serfs worked vast estates. The German Confederation of 39 states, all virtually absolutist, was overseen by aristocratic, authoritarian Austria's lethargic bureaucracy. Karl Friedrich Nebenius, author of Baden's 1819 customs initiative with the German Confederation explained, '830 toll barriers…cripple domestic traffic…to trade from Hamburg to Austria, from Berlin to the Swiss Cantons, one must cut through the statutes of ten states…and ten-times pay the tolls.' In the 1820s-1830s more states joined the Prussian-led customs union, forming the Zollverein in 1834. By 1836 it had 26 million people in 25 states. From 1840 it encouraged trade and industry especially in the Rhineland, where businessmen led a liberal movement. Railways spread faster than in France, assisting industrial development with some German companies leading mechanical research.

In 1837 Austria gave Trieste's Austrian Lloyd Co., 60% owned by Vienna's Rothschilds, a bi-monthly contract to Constantinople and Alexandria via Corfu, Patras, Athens, Crete and Smyrna for mail, bullion and passengers. By 1838 it had ten ships, competing with P&O's Trabzon route and had regular contact with America, Brazil, Egypt, Britain and Greece. Outside vibrant Livorno, other Italian states were retrograde, Church-influenced and inward-looking. In Sardinia 64% of men and 77% of women were illiterate in 1815, little better in 1865.[30] The King of Naples thought railways useful for rapid troop assembly and safeguarding sovereignty but 'under no circumstances for the convenience of the public.' Pope Gregory XVI feared they would spread ideas rather than goods.

It took until the 1820s for French trade to return to 1789 levels. Bordeaux recovered with wine exports, not sugar. The government opened a Marseilles-south Italy steam packet route in 1831, opposed by conservatives.[31] In 1840, the French Chamber of Deputies debated creating <u>state</u> steamship companies to New York, the Caribbean and Rio. One thought, 'fire is a thousand times more expensive than wind…that God gives freely to every sail.'[32] Nevertheless, in 1847 the government supported the ill-managed Compagnie General des Paquebots Transatlantiques, far behind Britain, Hamburg and Bremen. French franchise extension was neutered. Economic crises worsened. Land tax increased and salaries were cut, leading to insurrection, brutally repressed in some areas. Protectionist laws were passed. The king chose ministers who rarely met. Central government bureaucracy ensured nationwide uniformity, contrasting with America and Britain where elected councils ran local affairs. Railways were delayed until government-organised. Industry was subject to its influence and interference. Scientists, engineers and architects went into government service rather than private companies. De Tocqueville warned revolution would happen again because of central bureaucracy's cloying effect. French wages declined and working conditions worsened. Saint-Simon's *De la Reorganistion de la Societe Europeanne* (1814) conceived an authoritarian, socialist, technocratic state, suppression of inheritance, common education and reformed religion to improve 'the lot of the poorest class.'[33] Rousseau-inspired egalitarian Proudhon went further with 'property is theft.' A reactionary government produced an extreme over-reaction, again!

The 1846 potato crop failure in Belgium, Holland and Germany led to business decline, financial chaos and a crescendo of reform calls. Unbending French royal opposition led to regime collapse, failing to promote talent or compromise to avoid breaking. European discontent, personal insecurity and police states triggered huge protests, demands for constitutional reform or government change. Disruptive ideas like nationalism, restrictions on church and state, universal male suffrage, liberalism and socialism gained traction. Kaiser Friedrich Wilhelm IV promised a Prussian Assembly, encouraging German nationalism but refused to create a liberal state. A

Viennese Constituent Assembly was set-up by middle class liberals, workers and students. Budapest, Prague, Tuscany and Piedmont revolted against Austria but were defeated. In 1849 Mazzini led democratic revolt against the Pope in Rome, defeated by France; every 1848 revolution a failure. Widespread repression and disillusionment fuelled trans-Atlantic emigration.

Chapter 23

Worldwide British Investments and Settlements

British investment created trade. £10.4 million in 1815 increased 150% in 1816, mainly in America, by 1850, £208 million, by 1913, £4.1 <u>billion</u>, crucial in its 1830s canal construction and 1840s-1850s railways, mining and ranching.[1] Bankers like Barings and Rothschilds also helped stabilise war-torn Europe, imposing Britain's financial model of state debts, funded by national assemblies, transparent budgets and central tax-collecting bureaucracies. Baring controlled French finances after Talleyrand and Wellington imposed a British-style constitution.[2] Rothschild explained to Prussia that France's loan was because representative government was security, absent in autocracies, found instead in Prussia's royal estates. This started the international London-centred bond market. Five Rothschild brothers operated from London, Paris, Vienna, Frankfurt and Naples. After 1820 most loans passed through their hands. Profits were invested in railways, mines and Austrian Lloyd, for example. Prince Puckler-Muskau thought Rothschild was 'without whom no power in Europe today seems able to make war.'[3]

Banks' main pre-1815 role in maritime trade had been financing loans for trading voyages. Merchants borrowed to buy a cargo, shipped and sold it, then repaid the loan, the cargo being the security. Most were based on personal relationships with clients. Shipping and trading profits established many London and provincial banks. In the emerging industrial economy, British banks and shipping were essential in developing sophisticated overdrafts, mortgages and shareholdings. Credit and the number of banks increased massively until the ultimate lender and borrower no longer knew each other. Realising the need for strong banks with branch networks, the 1826 and 1833 Bank Acts encouraged joint stock banks outside London. Barclays and Lloyds adopted the model in the 1860s.

In the 1820s, voyages from Britain to Australia and New Zealand took around 200 days in 300–400-tonners carrying about 150–200 passengers. In 1852 a 1,600-ton clipper carried almost 1,000 emigrants to Melbourne in 68 days, due to improved understanding of Indian Ocean winds. Perth, Adelaide, Auckland, Wellington, New Plymouth and Nelson were thus settled.[4] Huge distances between them encouraged shipping. In the 1840s, Hobart had four shipyards. Sydney built 164 ships between 1837 and 1843 and owned 259 in 1846. Tasmania had 41 whaling stations, Sydney more, New Zealand even more. New South Wales's (NSW) 1839–1848 wool exports grew four-fold as better breeds increased productivity and improved screw presses reduced the bales' bulk. Half the world's 1820s newspapers were in English, circulation increasing massively. California exported cattle, hides and tallow already in the 1820s, supplementing whale, seal and sea otter furs. About 40, mostly US ships, annually took settlers to California between 1840 and 1847, returning with hides.[5] Seven San Francisco banks and 80 manufacturing enterprises operated in 1850.

British banks followed British settlements. Between 1828 and 1841, £16 million was invested in Australia, only recently a reviled penal colony, more than <u>all</u> British overseas investment 25 years earlier![6] In Latin America £20 million was invested by 1825, three-times US investments, with nearly 100 companies.[7] Buenos Aires hosted 3,000 British residents. South American 1825–1828 defaults resulted in investments redirected to the US, especially the west, but in 1837 nine banks there defaulted. They eventually met their responsibilities. Capital flows revived in the 1840s, South America only in the 1870s when Argentine growth accelerated, due to grain and livestock exports, boosted by refrigeration and British-built railways. In the 1840s, South American trade with Britain averaged £5.7 million a year, compared to £2.6 million Turkish and £1.6 million Chinese, but still held potential.

After the EIC lost monopoly, much capital was invested in Indian railways, cotton plantations, coal mining, paper, iron and steel. India's first cotton mill started in 1854. There were 271 in 1914, many Parsi-owned, although jute mills and tea plantations, starting in the 1830s were British-inspired and owned.[8] Chinese seeds planted in Assam produced 216,000 lbs in 1850, 6.25 million in 1871. In 1831 Bengal had 1.3 million acres of indigo plantations and 300–400 indigo factories, exported to Britain, much for re-export. Mid-century German manufactured dyes became more competitive and acreage fell.[9] Indian coalmining started in the 1770s, accelerated in the 1830s, sent to Singapore, Madras, Ceylon and Penang for steamships, production rising from 15,000 tons in 1831 to a million in 1880 and 12 million by 1912 but Mysore's coffee plantations ceased in the 1870s-80s because of cheaper Brazilian coffee.

In the 1850s, NSW's and South Australia's population doubled, Queensland's tripled, New Zealand's quadrupled, doubling in the 1860s, triggering aboriginal conflicts. Searching for exports, Queensland experimented with ginger, arrowroot, tobacco, coffee, sugar, cotton, quince and cinnamon.[10] California and Victoria settled on wool and wheat. Victoria started wheat exports in 1867 and South Australia shortly thereafter. Australian wool seriously penetrated the British market in the 1840s. By the early-1860s it sent 20–30,000 tons annually.

Chapter 24

The 1853–1856 Crimean War's
Impact on Shipping

Napoleon's failed Egyptian adventure highlighted Britain's vulnerable Red Sea route to Asia. After 1815, France still harboured North African imperial ambitions, sending technical and military assistance to Egypt's Muhammad Ali. Britain took Aden in 1839 to secure the route. Palmerston expelled him from Syria in 1841. 'The mistress of India', he declared, 'cannot permit France to be mistress of the road to her Indian dominions.'[1] Its defence began in the Bosporus, especially with increasing Black Sea grain imports after Corn Law liberalisation. Ali promoted maritime interests, inviting Greeks to Alexandria to create merchant shipping, improved shipyards, encouraged irrigation for agriculture, especially cotton for export to Britain, reviving Alexandria.

Inter-Black Sea trade grew strongly after the 1768–74 Russo-Turkish War, when Russia gained Crimea and the Black Sea's north and east coast. Caffa, peopled mainly by Greeks, Jews and Tartars and Trabzon, formerly Trebizond, still mainly Greek-speaking, revived and regular sailings between Caffa, Istanbul, Sinope and Trabzon started. Only in 1829 did Turkey agree regular access to foreign ships.[2] Kherson and Odesa exported wheat to Genoa, Marseilles, Livorno and some to northern Europe. Greek merchants dominated Black Sea exports from all ports, many of which were improved and dredged, enabling 1831's 228,000 tons to become 12 million by 1910.[3] Taganrog, into which 3,000 miles of navigable Volga and Don rivers and tributaries flowed, was the area's largest port, its merchants, intermediaries between inland suppliers and foreign buyers.

In 1836 a British steamship entered Trabzon and a regular route opened to Istanbul. In the mid-1840s P&O opened regular Trabzon-Southampton voyages, essentially cotton cloth, tea and sugar for Persian silks, textiles, carpets, dried fruits, spices, perfumes, wine, opium, indigo, liquorice, grain, cotton, wool, linseed, tallow and tobacco.[4] Dardanelles transits increased from 250 in 1842 to over 1,700 by 1852. Turkish grain exports, negligible in the 1830s, were equal to Russia's by 1851. Its £3 million exports in 1838 peaked at £11 million a decade later, part of Palmerston's plan to regenerate the 'rotten empire', preventing Russian or French encroachment towards India, increasing India-China trade and Australia's potential.

More Russo-Turkish antagonism led to fighting in 1853. Russia sunk the Ottoman fleet and threatened large tracts of territory. Britain and France decided the threat to the Bosporus and Istanbul required preventative war. Blockaded Russian wheat drove-up prices. Russia anyway banned its export in 1854, secured for its troops. With European grain demand high due to poor 1853–1854 harvests, treaties between Greece, Russia and Turkey allowed Greeks to ship grain to neutral countries. Istanbul, Livorno and Syros were entrepots, sold to northern Europe when prices suited.

Cephalonia's Vagliano brothers became Taganrog's largest grain and linseed exporter, one of three main ones. Maris Vagliano bought 18 ships between 1822 and 1830, nine between 1844 and 1850 and 20 between 1851 and 1860. Cephalonia, an Ionian Island, a post-1815 British protectorate until incorporated into Greece in 1864, had the largest merchant fleet, about 1,000 ships, concentrating on Black Sea and east Mediterranean cargoes. After independence, some Greek merchants moved to London into shipping, banking and grain sales, led by the Ralli brothers (see pages 175–176). The Radocanachi, Vagliano and Milas families followed due to increasing British grain imports. The Vaglianos' 1851 profits of 360,000 roubles rocketed in 1861 to 2.5 million and in 1863, 2.9 million. They owned 24 ships by 1860.[5] The trend was clear, although during the war, with Russian ports blockaded, exports were just from the Ottoman Danube basin, forcing Britain to buy Canadian wheat. Because Baltic timber exports were compromised, Canadian timber exports and shipbuilding also increased. Coming shortly after the 1849 Canadian-US reciprocity (free trade) agreement, it boosted Canada's economy.

Not so for Australia. Its first dedicated mail service started in 1844 in sailing ships. Scheduling was difficult. Freight was needed to make it pay. Following Victoria's and NSW's gold discoveries and mass immigration, a campaign for regular British steamships started. The 1852 *Sydney Morning Herald* thought monthly sailings would 'reduce the distance between us and old England by at least one half,' economically better for both. In 1854 the telegraph connected Britain to Bombay, Calcutta and Madras (see Chapter 26). From seven steamships in 1838, P&O had 42 larger, more efficient ones by 1855 with screw propellers from 1851. The Australian Royal Mail Steam Co., awarded the mail contract from 1852, collapsed after two years, due to poor management and inadequate coaling arrangements. P&O's twice-monthly Singapore-Australia service from 1853 ended without notice due to Crimean War troop carrier demand. It frustrated Australia's colonies but P&O was lucky. Singapore-Sydney was unprofitable, despite subsidy, as was its 3,500-ton *Himalaya*, which the Admiralty bought and after the war used to ferry troops to India until 1898. News of Britain's declaration of war reached Sydney 90 days later, via the Cape by the General Screw Steam Shipping Company's *Queen of the South* from London.[6] This company's Australian lines were also unprofitable and needed for war. Sailing packets run by Black Ball and White Star Lines from Liverpool resumed deliveries via the Cape. The *Sydney Morning Herald*, wanting regular steamship services, sympathised with 'the mother country in her efforts to repel the barbarism of the north. Australia is too patriotic not freely to bring her quota of sacrifice to the national cause, and she waives for the present what is most important…to her…frequent communication with the parent state.'

Five firms with mail contracts provided 30 mail steamers, over 53,000 tons, including P&O, Cunard, South American and General and Royal Mail Steam Packet Co. Eleven Cunarders were used, two as hospital ships. Another 76,000 tons of steamships and 93,000 tons of sail were hired. The operation helped change the Royal Navy's conservatism into appreciation of steam. It began building small gunboats with heavy canon commanded by young men. Addressing British shipping to Australia, which the Crimean war interrupted, Britain proposed a jointly subsidised scheme to South Australia, Melbourne and Sydney with branch services to Tasmania and New Zealand. Awarded to a company that failed to meet schedules, in 1859 P&O took-over.[7]

Blockade forced Russia to end the war. Malta's increasing use as a Royal Navy base and coaling station limited commercial opportunities. Grain storage from the Black Sea to Britain became redundant as quick steamship-driven Black Sea-Britain sailing times meant less deterioration. Steamships also ended Livorno's entrepot role for sugar and cocoa for Sicily and Italy and cloth to North Africa. By the 1860s only one Greek was among the 30 wealthiest Livorno merchants. George March, US minister in Istanbul in 1857 thought 'Greeks…the Yankees of the Levant…mostly Chiot, [with]…branches in all the chief ports in Europe, the US and South America…who by their industry and…fair dealings, do honour the Greek name and the cause of modern Greece.'[8] With northern Europe the main market, more established themselves in London. Hundreds of Greek grain traders were involved in banking and exporting in Odesa and Taganrog. In 1860, 66% of the top 20 trading firms in southern Russia were Greeks, the rest mainly German and Sephardic Jews.[9] By the 1860s Taganrog had wide, paved roads, schools, hospitals, library and opera house. In Galatz and

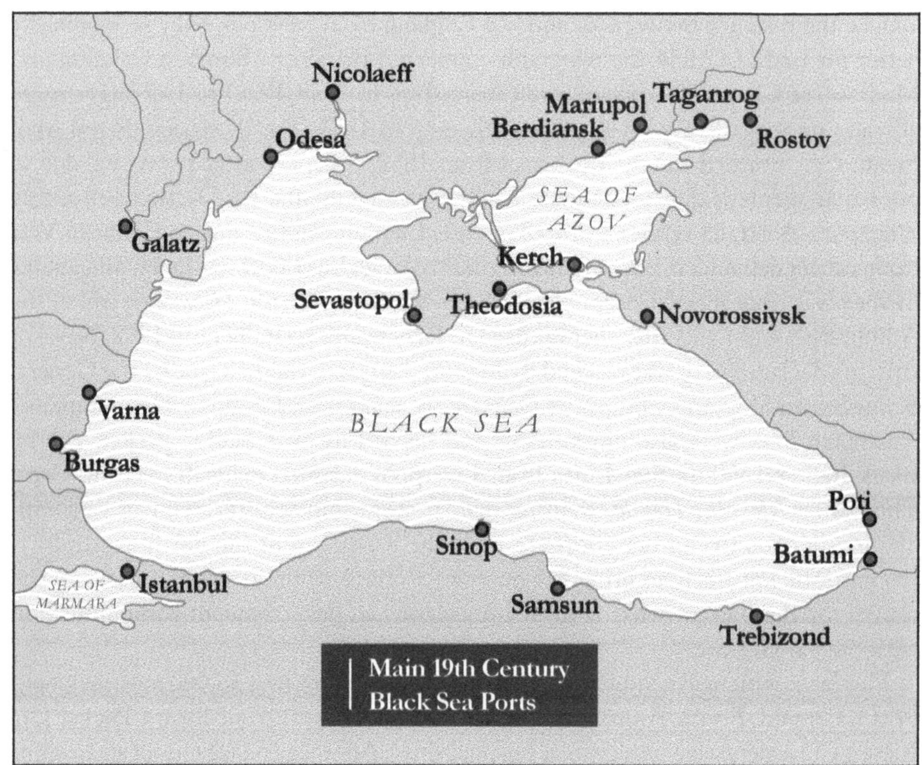

the Lower Danube, Greeks concentrated on coastal and river shipping rather than competing with British steamships to north Europe.

That Britain and France allied in the war needs brief comment. After a failed coup against Louis Philippe in 1836, Napoleon's nephew went to London, Brazil and New York, meeting political, industrial and intellectual elites and researching Britain's economy. Another failed coup in 1840 led to imprisonment, where he wrote the widely circulated *L'Extinction du Pauperism* (1844), a study of poverty and France's working class, which he thought should have rights, education and a banking savings system. Escaping from prison, he returned to Britain. Elected President in the 1848 revolution, he dissolved the Assembly and declared himself Emperor Napoleon III: an unlikely agent of progress. But he had learnt much from his travels. In 1852 he declared, 'We have immense unploughed territories to cultivate, roads to open, ports to dig, rivers to be made navigable. We have in front of Marseilles a vast kingdom [Algiers] to assimilate into France. We have all the greatest ports in the west to connect with the American continent by modern communications which we still lack.' In short, he initiated infrastructure for economic growth, stock market, investment banks, a modern merchant fleet, ports, canals, roads, railways and education. In 1852 France had just 3,500 kilometres of roads. By 1870, it had 20,000 linking ports, capital and neighbour countries. In 1855 the private Compagnie Generale Maritime began the first commercial service to the Caribbean and California with sailing ships, then Greenock-built steamships.

Marseilles and Le Havre were rebuilt. By 1870 France had the second-largest merchant fleet after Britain. Marseilles' population rose from 195,200 in 1851 to 313,000 in 1872 as trade boomed, encouraging supplementary industries. He backed the Suez Canal, funded by shares on the Paris stock market. Land was drained for farms and forests. Paris sanitation, water supply and traffic were improved, two railway stations, opera and parks, inspired by London's were built. His vision was sometimes clouded by uncommercial, continental, prestige motives, *gloire*, the attempted Mexican puppet state, takeover of Cochin China (Vietnam) in 1862 and Cambodia in 1863, the creation of the National Museum of Archaeology and excavation of major Gallic War sites to show how Roman conquest civilised, which vainglorious Napoleon III's arrival would herald. But he also built Parisian clinics for sick and injured workers, instituted legal assistance to the poor, subsidised workers' housing, encouraged a state insurance fund, in 1864 gave workers the right to strike and greater education for both sexes, finally wrenched from the Church, enabling the teaching of art, science, music, history, economics and languages, which it fiercely opposed, but enabling literacy rates to soar and in 1860 signed the Cobden-Chevalier treaty, reducing tariffs (see Chapter 32). These measures dramatically changed France's economy. From 1852 to 1871 industrial production increased over 70%, agricultural production a little less but still spectacular, spurred by new techniques, encouraged by agricultural schools, the last endemic famine in 1855. Rather than the *philosophes*, Napoleon III deserves to be called France's first flame of enlightenment; perhaps the only 'Enlightened Despot.' His reign ended in 1871 Franco-Prussian war defeat, after which French support for freer traded faded.

Chapter 25

Combatting Slave Trading and Promoting 'Legitimate' African Trade

'Exchange of commodities may be accompanied by…diffusion of knowledge… commerce may go freely forth, leading civilisation with one hand…peace with the other, render mankind happier, wiser, better.'

Palmerston (1842)[1]

Once Britain abolished slave trading, apart from humanitarian instincts, it was in her economic interest to persuade rivals to abolish it too, so pressured others to follow. The prospect of British naval power stopping slave traders created a mini-boom after 1807 as Brazil and Cuba stocked-up, 42 ships arriving in Rio in 1810, the most recorded.[2] In 1810 Portugal agreed to restrict its trade to its colonies. In 1813 Sweden outlawed it, the Dutch in 1814 and France agreed abolition within five years. Newly-created Venezuela banned it in 1811, Buenos Aires in 1812 and Simon Bolivar outlawed slavery itself. Failing to get anti-slave trading clauses in 1815's peace treaties, Britain negotiated bilateral treaties and increased slave patrols. West African anti-slave bases, Sierra Leone in 1808, Gambia in 1816 and Gold Coast in 1821, intended as bases for legitimate trade, proved disappointing. From 1819 the Preventative Squadron forced anti-slavery treaties on coastal chiefs and hunted Portuguese, US and Cuban slavers. In 1817 in return for British payments for three years eastern Madagascar's king ended its trade. In 1820 Spain agreed rapid abolition for £400,000 compensation, although trans-Saharan trade continued. In 1820 President Munroe joined the crusade, dispatching forces to intercept US slavers. Sensitive to its ships being boarded by British patrols, Britain agreed not to. Thus, ironically, US- and French-flagged ships, also exempted, were preferred by slavers.

Like high tariffs and bans, traders circumvented them if profitable. Ending slavery itself was needed, the movement's actual goal. Wilberforce led again, in 1816 explaining, 'It is in no case safe that a man should be entrusted with arbitrary power' but slavery 'conspires to provoke an abuse of arbitrary power.'[3] The Anti-Slavery Society (1823) emphasised guilt, Christian duty and concern for human suffering. The 1832 Great Reform Act brought many new MPs committed to it, achieving it a year later, for £20 million compensation to slave owners. There was no British economic self-interest to abolish slavery. 1816–1867 anti-slavery patrols cost £12.4 million, at their height taking half the naval budget or 2% of GDP.

A unique problem was Mauritius, newly British, with several thousand French and 60,000 slaves. Insufficient ships patrolled the coast and by 1819 slave numbers reached 80,000 despite the Madagascar treaty. In 1828 a new governor threatened to bring troops from India if there was any more trouble and the 1833 Act banning slave-owning was enforced by £2 million compensation from British taxpayers, 50% higher per head than Caribbean slave-holders. Indian contract labourers from 1835 replaced them, by 1837, 20,000, by 1860 over 60,000.[4]

Seyyid Said's Muscat was crucial for Gulf trade. His navy and trader's ships needed timber and repairs in Bombay, but slave trading provided 25% of his revenue, protected by his Bombay-built navy. He reluctantly signed an 1822 treaty prohibiting slave sales to Christian countries, giving the Royal Navy the right to seize Omani ships carrying slaves off East Africa.[5] Oman had coveted Mombasa for a century but as Seyyid's warships threatened, it offered itself to Britain with half the port revenue. A visiting British captain agreed, installing a governor. In 1826, not wanting to confront Seyyid, a crucial ally against Russia, or alienate Indian slave-owning princes, Britain withdrew, allowing its capture.

An 1832 Liverpool trader steamship venture, 400 miles up the Niger bought palm oil at almost half the coastal price. After Palmerston sent a small force to Lagos to eject Portuguese slavers, the region interested William Laird's young son, McGregor, who started the African Steamship Co. in 1852, which in 1861 provided over 10% of Liverpool's palm oil imports, when Britain annexed Lagos. By 1871, five river steamers traded annually £55,000; by the late-1870s, £300,000.[6] It was tiny in the bigger picture, but progress in converting slaving to productive trade.

Abolition sparked the Great Trek from Cape Colony from 1835 to 1845. Like Americans who thought Britain soft on native Americans, Boers were appalled at attempts to improve negro status. Half descendants of Dutch farmers, half Huguenots and Germans, hard Calvinists, their culture clashed with British business. Voortrekker leader Piet Retief wrote in 1837, 'it is our determination…to preserve proper relations between master and servant.' His sister wrote of 'the shameful and unjust proceedings with reference to the freedom of our slaves…it is not their freedom that drove us to such lengths, as their being placed on an equal footing with Christians.'[7] The British annexed Natal in 1843 to keep Boers off the coast. Two inland Boer republics were recognised in the 1850s.

After 1833 it became more difficult to source West African slaves but with Caribbean and Spanish American demand, Mozambique became a new source, an estimated 90,000 transported before 1811, 386,000 after![8] French sugar island plantations took around 15,000 annually from Mozambique from the 1820s to about 1845 but Portugal ceased in 1842, France in 1848, substituted with indentured labour from India and China. Palmerston tried ending Arab slave trading by treaties backed by naval patrols. Seyyid moved to increasingly prosperous Zanzibar in 1840 to oversee slave-based clove plantations, including 12,000 on <u>his</u>.[9] Zanzibar still exported about 15,000 slaves annually to Arabia, not enforcing the 1845 treaty allowing coastal trade but not to Arabia and Asia.[10] But mid-century, it and neighbouring islands also engaged in legitimate trade, 80% of the world's clove exports, ivory, for piano keys, cutlery handles, chessmen, napkin rings, furniture inlay, billiard balls and firearm handles, plus tortoiseshell, rhino horn, hides, beeswax, coconuts, copra and copal for varnishes and palm oil, importing brass, guns, cloth, beads and rice from Britain, India and New England.[11] Britain soft-peddled with Seyyid because, as Indian Viceroy Lord Auckland warned, rapid suppression might cause 'even our old and faithful ally...to be estranged from us.'[12]

American merchants were also active in Zanzibar in the 1820s, importing textiles, gunpowder and arms and exporting ivory for piano keys as it produced 500,000 pianos annually by 1900. A US consulate was established in 1837. Kachchhi merchant Jairam Shiji controlled the customs and labour from ship to customshouse. Consul Richard Walters, a Salem merchant, encouraged business. In the early-1830s three-quarters of ships in Zanzibar were US-registered, with Jairam, unofficial broker for Salem merchants. Bostonians and New Yorkers followed.[13] New England's cloth exports replaced Indian cloth, already undercut by British cotton exports to India, which grew from 81,800 yards in 1814 to 1,913,800 in 1821 and 5,177,700 in 1835. Thariya Topan moved from Kachchhi in 1833 and became Zanzibar's leading merchant, working with Jairam despite being Muslim, Jairam a Hindu, and had good relations with the US Consul, British and Hamburg companies. In 1859 New England merchants took 68% of East African copal. US cotton cloth dominated Zanzibar's imports with 51% compared with 29% Indian and 20% British. In retirement, Topan built a school and was knighted in 1890 for anti-slavery services, British contemporaries noting his 'honesty and strict business integrity.'[14]

Mid-century, Zanzibar's exports were worth about a million silver dollars annually, a quarter with America, slightly less with Britain.[15] When Seyyid died, the Oman-Zanzibar Sultanate split, the latter the hub of a vast Indian Ocean and inland trading empire with Kachchhi merchants moving between Zanzibar, Bombay, Mandvi, Muscat and Trucial states. They financed caravans of elephant tusks and up to 30,000 slaves annually. Oman's commercial expansion lasted until the 1870s with around 300,000 slaves imported for domestic labour and date plantations. Zanzibar was also hub to a booming 1875–1910 arms trade, resold in the Gulf, Afghanistan and Northwest Frontier.

Palmerston, variously Foreign Secretary or Prime Minister between 1830 and 1865 was much influenced by his Edinburgh University teacher, Professor of Moral Philosophy Dugald Stewart: in Adam Smith tradition, a free trader and abolitionist. As an architect of British commercial expansion, Palmerston was serious about suppressing slave trading and Britain's moral weight through trade, which 'begets kindly feelings';[16] economic interest _and_ moral imperative. 'Treaties for the suppression of the slave trade...promote the greater interests of humanity...rid mankind of a foul and detestable crime...Virtue carries...its own reward and if the nations of the world could extirpate this abominable traffic and...Africa...be left free...to peaceful and innocent trade, the greatest commercial benefit would accrue, not only to England, but to civilised nations which engage in maritime commerce.' Slave treaties were, he said 'indirectly...for the encouragement of commerce.'[17]

In 1850–51 British warships entered Brazilian ports, seizing and sinking slave ships, after which slave depots were closed, although slavery survived until 1888. Palmerston thought ending Brazil's slave trade one of his greatest achievements. Like Wilberforce,

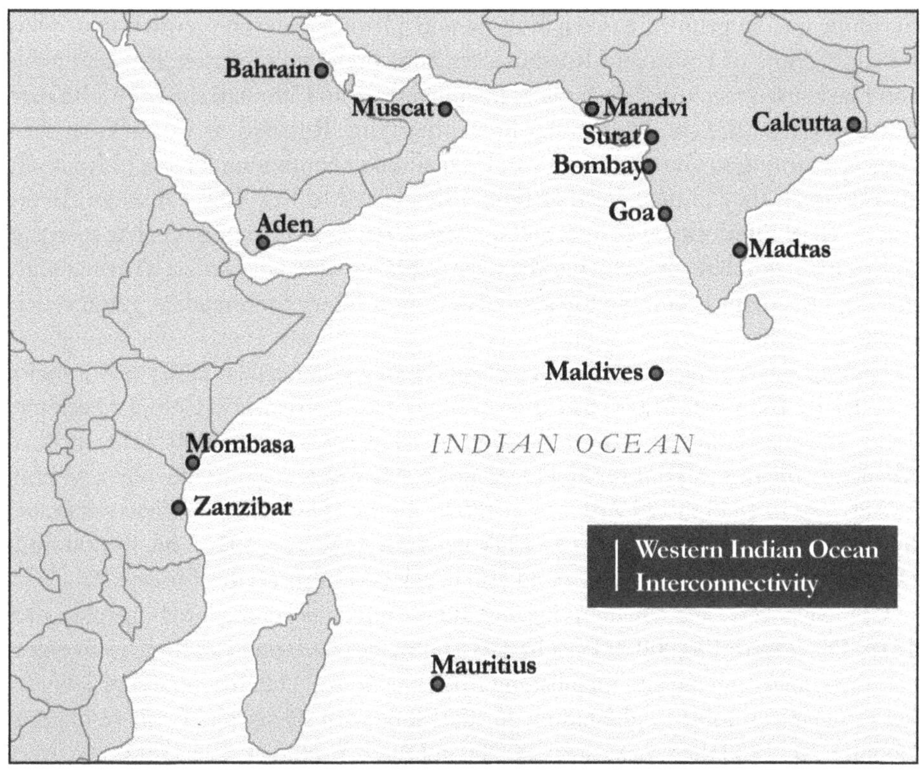

he championed prison reform, education and charity for improving the poor's living conditions. By the 1850s around 25 British ships, supported by some US naval ships and nearly 1,000 *Kroomen*, West African fishermen, risked death from disease combatting slaving, mortality 5.5% compared with 1% for Mediterranean squadrons. Between 1807 and 1860 they seized about 1,600 ships and freed 150,000 slaves, its best year 1837 with over 8,600, perhaps 10% of the total: a great deterrent.[18]

African leaders who refused agreement to British anti-slave treaties were also targeted. Dahomey's 1840's King Gezo declared, 'the slave trade is the ruling principle of my people…the source of the glory of their wealth…the mother lulls the child to sleep with notes of triumph over an enemy reduced to slavery.' In 1850 the Manchester Chamber of Commerce induced Palmerston to send a mission encouraging cotton cultivation, 'legitimate commerce'. In practice, trans-Atlantic slaving only ceased in the 1870s. In Africa, legitimate trade was only slowly established. Stopping slave trading was not always straightforward. Aden-based ships liberating slaves could not land them in Africa to be re-captured and were sent to Bombay, working low caste jobs. Many British captains, risking death from malaria and yellow fever, started believing their mission hopeless. After Seyyid's death in 1856 his successor was indifferent to trade. Said Azzan bin Qais (r. 1868–71) was religiously zealous. Oman became an Islamic police state. Its revenue plummeted and slave patrols intensified.

*   *   *

Serfdom was so grim in eastern Europe and Ottoman slavery gentler, that many female 'victims' of Polish and Russian slave raids preferred the latter. Prussian noble von Haxhausen recounted six females liberated from an Ottoman slaver by a Russian warship. Given the choice of going home, marrying Russians or Cossacks of their choice, returning to Germany with von Haxhausen or continuing for sale in Istanbul's slave market, they immediately, unanimously elected to be sold.[19] Ottoman slavery had no racial inferiority overtones and numerous routes to manumission like marriage to free men, purchase or outliving the master. Slaves were not bred as a permanently inferior race, many becoming top administrators, military commanders, grand viziers or sultan's wives.

Ending slavery meant alternative cheap labour was needed. India was a major supplier. By 1838 over 25,000 had gone overseas despite Glenelg's (Colonial Secretary 1835–1839) attempts to stop it, peaking in 1858–59 when 53,000 went, most to Mauritius, the rest to Trinidad and Demerara.[20] Mauritius' sugar production rose from 35,580 tons in 1843 to 129,210 tons in 1863.[21] In the 1860s-1870s Indians emigrated to Natal's sugar estates, 60,000 to Fiji's between 1879 and 1916 and 19,000 built Uganda's railways, while Queensland also developed sugar estates for export.

Chinese poverty and rebellions meant Chinese migrants poured into Singapore after 1819. There were 100,000 in Peru by 1852 on sugar plantations on three to five-year contracts, many staying and establishing small businesses. Dutch conquest of Sumatra led to sugar and tobacco plantations in the 1860s with substantial Chinese migrant labourers. By 1900 there were over 500,000 in Dutch Southeast Asia, Gold's discovery in California in 1848, Australia in 1851 and British Colombia in 1858 provided further impetus. By 1880 over 100,000 Chinese, mostly men, lived in western US states. Their immigration was suspended in 1882.

Some Chinese, Indian and Southeast Asians intending to go to Singapore or Batavia, boarding French, Dutch and British ships, instead found themselves Mauritius or Reunion-bound as indentured labour. Mauritius' indentured labour's economic success led to over two million Africans, Chinese, Indians, Japanese and Southeast Asians being transported to the Caribbean, South Africa, Ceylon, Burma, Malaya and South America between the 1830s and 1920s. Public outcry in Britain and India about *coolie* trade led to its suspension in 1838 and government-supervised resumption in 1842.[22]

Free Trade's focus on prices conflicted with humanitarian support of former slaves and colonial sugar and coffee imports. Equalisation of sugar duties from 1846 reduced prices, opening Britain's market to cheaper slave-grown sugar. British Caribbean plantations re-imported about 36,000 liberated Africans from St. Helena and Sierra Leone, about 100,000 Asians in the 1840s and developed new plantations in Mauritius, the main British-owned sugar exporter by 1860 with 136,000 tons a year. Caribbean coffee exports fell from 292,000 hundredweight in 1827 to 63,500 in 1845 as other producers like Ceylon and Brazil became competitive.[23]

Chapter 26

Mid-Century Shipping

Eighteenth century Atlantic and Baltic trades were still mainly controlled by merchants and partnerships, which built ships <u>and</u> provided the cargo. Masters or 'supercargoes' handled business on shipowners' behalf, buying and selling cargoes with discretion where to sail. Ships operated in areas they knew well. Late-century, trader and carrier started to separate. The word 'shipowner' first appeared in shipping registers in 1786. An early-19th-century General Shipowners' Society emphasised members' business was <u>just</u> running ships.[1] Specialisation, increasing numbers of shipowners, growing importance of Scandinavians and Greeks in Mediterranean-Black Sea trades, accelerating trade-growth and steamships led to shipping services' growth; banks, insurance brokers, underwriters and shipbrokers, centred in London.

Commercial risk is borne by traders and shipowners, ship safety by seamen and underwriters. Explosively growing trade volumes in a deregulated commercial environment meant casualties inevitably increased, but some owners neglected safety. The 1831 *Rothesay Castle* loss led to the 1836 Select Committee on Shipwrecks. A *Register* published by Lloyds from 1760 to ensure structurally sound ships with experienced masters, in 1834 became *Lloyds Register of British and Foreign Shipping* with 63 surveyors employed to ensure its Rules were followed. By 1840, 15,000 vessels had been surveyed. In 1852 it opened a Canadian office, then others abroad. Without it, the transformation that maritime trade propelled would have been more problematic. In 1853 of 10,050 *Lloyds Register* ships, 62 were iron sailing ships and 133 iron steamships. The 1845 and 1854 Wreck and Salvage Act and 1857 International Code of Signals addressed safety issues, which from the 1850s *Lloyds List* increasingly referred regarding crew, navigation and pilotage. Nevertheless between 1861 and 1870, 5,826 British wrecks cost 8,105 lives.[2]

US segregation also caused problems. In 1847 black US abolitionist Frederick Douglas took a Cunarder to Britain but had to take steerage. When returning, Liverpool's Cunard agent made him eat meals alone and not mingle with saloon passengers, causing uproar in Britain that racial segregation was practiced on British ships. Cunard responded, 'No one can regret more than I do the unpleasant circumstances respecting Mr. Douglas's passage, but I can assure you that nothing of the kind will again take place in the steamships with which I am concerned.'[3]

Without state support, Bremen and Hamburg companies were quicker with steamships than French. Independent-minded, outside the Zollverein, they distanced themselves from agrarian, militaristic, autocratic Prussia. They imported British, South American and US goods and exported emigrants, especially after the failed 1848 revolutions dashed reform hopes. In 1847 Hamburg merchants started Hamburg-

America Line in Hamburg-flagged 700-ton sailing ships with 20 cabins and 200 steerage passenger capacity. After Inman's emigrant steamships, it modernised. Bremen, trading with America since independence, established Bremerhaven at the Weser's mouth in 1827 for larger, deeper-drafted ships. It contracted two 2,100-tonners from Caird, in 1856 starting a 16-day New York run compared with sailing ships' over 40 days, then two larger ships. Herman Meier who worked at his family's Bremen-America packet line since 1834, helped start Bremen Bank. In 1857 he raised capital to amalgamate three Weser steamboat lines into North German Lloyd Line, the name Lloyd, like Austrian Lloyd, pure marketing, conferring vintage and legitimacy. He built 2,700-tonners at Caird and Jarrow's Palmer Brothers in 1858.[4] German international shipping was born from Hamburg-Bremen competition. As Prussia's Otto von Bismarck pulled 18 states and free cities together in the Second Reich, they sensibly opted out.

Brunel's last ship, the 1857 *Great Eastern* tried solving how to sail to India via the Cape without coaling stops. A 22,500-tonner, six-times larger than the largest ship until the 1907 *Lusitania*, double-hulled with watertight compartments, six masts, a 24-feet diameter screw propeller <u>and</u> 58-feet diameter paddle wheels, it had luxury passenger capacity for 4,000 or 10,000 troops. Three years to build, it ruined the builder. Belfast-based Edward Harland thought Brunel took a 'more gigantic stride than was warranted,' despite agreeing that size was needed for comfort at sea, his priority.[5] Making few trips to New York with a fraction of passengers needed to break-even, it demonstrated that change should be fast, but incremental.

Early-19th-century electromagnet, battery and wire improvements, enabled long telegraph lines to transmit messages. In the 1840s, American and British inter-city cables were laid and Morse Code messages sent. In 1850 a Cross-Channel one was laid from a steam tug, working briefly before fouled by fishermen. Better ones were laid in 1851 to France, Holland and Ireland, within the Mediterranean and across the Black Sea. Julius Reuter opened his Royal Exchange-based Submarine Telegraph office in 1851, most customers wanting Black Sea grain information, Britain's main source with Greek-owned shipping vital. He also offered Liverpool cotton prices, twice-weekly European grain exchange prices, steamship arrivals, political and commercial news.[6]

In 1854 New York businessman Cyrus Field suggested a trans-Atlantic cable, 2,000 miles long, ten-times deeper than any existing. Businessmen, shipowners and traders invested in it 'for the good of the world', according to glue magnate investor, Peter Cooper.[7] The *Great Eastern* was ideal to lay it. Laid at the third attempt in 1858, it went silent later that year, just after signalling the Indian Mutiny's near-end. Countering orders for two regiments to board at Halifax for India saved Britain £50–60,000, a seventh of the cable's cost. Investors tried again. Of 350 shares, Field held 61, London investors 110, Liverpool 86, Glasgow 37 and Manchester 28, all having interests in shrinking the Atlantic. Rapid technical advances were made between 1857 and 1865, among which, William Thomson (later Lord Kelvin, the first scientist elevated to the peerage) in electro-magnetism and Henry Bessemer's 1858 steel process, significantly reduced prices. The *Great Eastern* was the only ship capable of carrying and laying the much heavier cable. An earlier broken one was also found and completed. In 1869 a French company used the *Great Eastern* to lay one from Brest to Massachusetts. Scrapped in 1887, it bankrupted seven owners, missed the emigrant market, but its five cables were vital. In 1869 a Suez-Bombay cable and in 1871 an India-Singapore-Australia cable virtually encircled the world. In the 1830s, a Britain-India-Britain round voyage took two years. By the 1850s steamships cut it to about three months, bunkered at Galle, which annually imported 50,000 tons of British coal. By the 1870s cables enabled daily messages, making business more efficient.

British pioneer shipbuilders like Napiers, Elders, Lairds and Brunel were practical men, not theorists, without formal education, relying on apprenticeships, experience, rule of thumb and eye, but knew more was needed as only intermittent engineering courses were offered at University College and Kings College London, full-time departments at Glasgow and Edinburgh until the 1850s, none at Oxbridge. In 1856 The Institution of Engineers in Scotland was founded, soon adding 'and Shipbuilders'. The 1860 Institute of Naval Architects was started in London by John Russell (1808–1882), shipbuilder and keen technical education advocate who worried that Britain was ignoring it, (see Chapter 46) in 1869 published *A Systematic Technical Education for the English People*. The first President of the Scottish group, William Rankine, Glasgow University's Regis Professor of Civil Engineering and Mechanics wrote a textbook on shipbuilding, applied mechanics, civil engineering and steam engines, the standard authority for 40 years,[8] then concentrated on hull design, helping keep Glasgow in British engineering's and shipbuilding's forefront. Another 1864 Russell-prompted school became the Royal Naval College. William Fronde's work on hull forms enabled shipbuilders to precisely predict the engine power needed. In 1813–14, 5% of British shipping was launched on the Clyde. By the 1860s-70s two thirds of British iron ships were Clyde-built, more than every German shipyard.[9]

*   *   *

Oslo had many owners but few charterers, New York many charterers but few tramp owners, but London, from where the cable network radiated, financed, owned, insured, bought, sold and chartered ships, increasing shipbroking's importance. Many shipping and shipbroking companies started in the 1840s-1860s. Formed in 1849, Houlder Brothers' partners travelled widely for new business, including Hawaii for copra exports.[10] Leon Benham of Horace Clarkson and Co., (founded 1852), rowed out to meet London's incoming ships in his early years,[11] but the telegraph meant brokers learnt about ship positions and cargoes from further afield. A typical day started reading overnight mail and telegrams, monitoring ship's positions, finding onward employment. They visited the Baltic or Jerusalem Coffee House to find cargoes, informing clients by telegram. Cheyney, Eggar and Forester evolved from colliery agents. Lambert Brothers were originally coal exporters, Watts and Watts and John I. Jacobs originally shipowners and Mathew Wrightson, insurance brokers.[12] John Glover originally from South Shields established Glover Brothers in 1853 after quitting a slower-moving broker. Galbraith's founder was a Scottish ship's master in 1847, which added insurance broking. Profitable, they bought a small steamship and with

Glasgow shipowner Robert Henderson started refrigerated cargo from New Zealand: the Albion Line. They also formed the Irrawaddy Flotilla Co. The British Burmese Steam Navigation Co. opened-up Burma. James Denholm formed J&J Denholm in 1866 with a 122-tonner, took coal to the Caribbean, sugar and resin back, grain to Spain and flour back.[13] This was a time of opportunity.

Outbound coal, the gold rush, Crimean War, free trade, Scandinavian and Greek shipping, trade growth and submarine cables meant London's shipbrokers quickly became internationally connected, market experts on whom owners and charterers relied for ship and cargo availability and market guidelines. Goodliffe and Smart thought the key 1850s routes were Black Sea grain, Mediterranean grain, flour, sulphur, salt, wine, oil, timber and corkwood, Baltic timber, grain oilseed, tallow, flax and hemp, North Sea timber, central American mahogany, dyewood, sugar, South American coffee, hides and sugar, Pacific guano, nitrate of soda and saltpetre and Asian rice, teak, cotton, sugar, coffee, oilseed, jute and general cargo. New York brokers added locally-controlled cotton, tobacco, naval stores, grain and flour.

Navigation Act repeal in 1849 encouraged competition. Freight rates fell from 1848 to 1851, rose in 1852 with an Australian demand surge after the 1851–52 gold discovery. Between 1852 and 1855 over 313,000 passengers left Britain for Australia.[14] The market peaked in late-1853 and first-half 1854 with Crimean War preparations including east Mediterranean and Black Sea-bound coal and Pacific guano discoveries, slowed thereafter, rebounded in 1855 then fell until 1860–61. Goodliffe and Smart's 20th January 1853 circular noted, 'It is seldom that at this season we [can]…give so encouraging an account of the freight market' because Australian trade and poor harvests 'has caused a very active demand for tonnage and…general improvement in the rates of freight.' Informative market reports became normal. Unlike the war-dominated 18th-century, post-1815 freight cycles were created by worldwide supply and demand issues. Glover Brothers' 2nd January 1860 circular asked, 'Will freights be better in 1860 than in 1858 or 1859?' pointing to earlier causes noted above, hoping the next 'may be…complete settling down of the European nations to industrial pursuits.'[15] In 1857 the Baltic Coffee House was renamed the Baltic Exchange. It had a sale room for grain, linseed and tallow sales, rules for ethical, gentlemanly behaviour and mechanisms to solve commercial and legal disputes. From 1858 *George Dornbusch's Floating Cargoes Evening List* gave grain cargo information.

*   *   *

Ships of the 1850s, except the *Great Eastern*, averaged three-times larger than the 1820s. Britain built them cheaper in New Brunswick in timber and on the Clyde in iron. Wooden ships were cheaper, American clippers, faster. Iron steamships completed about three-times more annual voyages, were less prone to damage, weighed less, were more waterproof, reducing cargo damage. Iron-hulled sailing ships with up to five masts competed with steam for years on appropriate trades. America could not overtake British shipbuilding due to constantly improving engines.

New Bedford, Massachusetts' main whaling centre and richest US city per capita, grew 14-fold between 1816 and 1850. Variously graded whale oil lubricated new machinery and lit rooms. Baleen or whale cartilage was used for umbrellas and corsets, ambergris for perfumes. In 1846 Americans owned 640 whaling ships, more than the rest of the world, the economy's fifth-largest sector, depicted in Herman Melville's *Moby Dick*. In 1859 America produced 2,000 barrels of petroleum, 40 years later however, that amount every 17 minutes, while 1860s-1880s average wages grew by a third. US whaling collapsed. Countries with lower wages like Norway took greater market share. Capital was instead invested in railroads, oil and steel. By the end of *Moby Dick*, young men previously lured to the sea by lack of alternatives, went into factories. America's fifth-largest 1850s industry was virtually dead by the 1880s.[16]

Wooden shipbuilding thrived in mid-19th-century Baltic, Canada, America and Mediterranean, especially in Syros. Having helped break Napoleon's Mediterranean blockade Greek shipowners began coalescing there, the maritime hub of the young Greek state, with shipbuilding, banking, repairs, insurance, sales, purchases and chartering for inter-Mediterranean and Black Sea voyages, mainly grain to Malta, Livorno, Syros, Genoa, Marseilles or Spain, sometimes West African trades, even emigrants to the Americas.[17] Greek shipping's international pioneers were John and Stratis Ralli who in 1818 went to London from Livorno. Brother Augustus was already in Marseilles and in 1824 Pandia joined in London. Stratis went to Manchester, John to Odeśa in 1827 and Tomazis to Istanbul, a network ideally placed to trade growing volumes of British and Mediterranean goods, widening their horizons even to India and US cotton exports. In the 1850s they employed 4,000 clerks and 15,000 workmen, only Rothschilds substantially richer.

In 1845, 15 of Syros' 20 most prominent merchants were Chiots. Theodore Rodocanachi's company was Odesa's largest, in 1847 handling 3.5 million roubles worth of goods, mainly wheat and linseed to Britain. The Zizinia Brothers were next largest importing Egyptian cotton, wheat, maize, linseed and barley. The Chiot network controlled nearly 40% of Odesa-Britain trade in the mid-1840s. In 1868, of the 1,000 people involved in trade, banking, manufacturing and services in Istanbul, 348 were Greek.[18] Chiot merchant education was commercial. They adopted the host city's nationality but retained Greek identity.

John Ralli loaded Black Sea wheat cargoes, bought from peasants by local agents, often in advance, posted the bills of lading and cargo samples to Pandia, who sold them on the Baltic Exchange. The master, not knowing the buyer, sailed to pre-arranged 'ports for orders' to learn the discharge port, until replaced by wireless. Pandia was a member of the 20-man Committee in 1854. After 1857, two of the Baltic Company's 12 directors were a Rodocanachi and a Ralli and 37 shareholders were Greek, mainly Chiots, 7% of Baltic Exchange membership in 1886, 18% by 1893.[19]

The Vaglianos operated from Istanbul from 1849. In 1858 Panagi Vagliano opened a London office to represent them, two Danube-based grain merchants and other Greek owners.[20] Another brother went to Marseilles in 1869, the region's main Black Sea grain recipient, where over 20 Greek families were established in the 1830s. The Rodocanachi, the largest of 20 Greek Marseilles' companies in 1840 had 48 ships. Unlike

British merchants, Marseilles' merchants resented Greek competition, as 1840–1860 Marseilles-based Greek-flagged ships more than tripled, while after 1850, only two Marseilles' firms chartered more than ten ships annually.

The Chiot network, about 60 families, was the largest and richest, shipping bulk grain, wool, cotton, linseed and tallow with branches in Marseilles, Livorno, Trieste, Alexandria, Syros, Istanbul and Smyrna. In the 1850s there were 58 Greek companies in London, Manchester and Liverpool. The *Liverpool Journal of Commerce* indicated Greeks largely controlled Liverpool's 1850s east Mediterranean trade, the largest, the Rallis.[21] Greeks handled over a third of east Mediterranean and Black Sea cargoes between 1830 and 1860, competing with other Europeans and Jews. Greeks promoted British cloth in the Black Sea, easier to sell than French. British cloth exports to Ottoman-controlled regions increased from 9.5 million yards in 1820 to 194 million in 1850 and 670 million in 1870, 20% of exports.[22]

Non-Chiot George Papayanni established a Liverpool-based company in the 1840s. Unlike most Greeks concentrating on tramp sailing ships, his brother Basil in 1860 bought five steamships with British finance, running a regular Liverpool-Black Sea line, one of four main ones with British masters and crew, an important information source when most Greeks started transitioning to steamers in the 1880s. But Stepans Xenos who bought ten, also in 1860, had to sell them five years later because of lower freight markets.[23] From the 1860s, the Vaglianos operated their and other Greek owners' chartering, insurance and sale and purchase. By 1875 they had 60 sailing ships, plus a few dozen more client-owned under their control, the largest London-based Greek fleet from 1870 to 1905 and were the biggest 1860s-1880s Azov grain traders, replacing the Rallis and Scaramangas. An £8 million 1881 turnover compared with Schroders £4 million and Rothschilds £12 million.[24] Russia's 1861 serf emancipation, poor harvests, Danube and US competition led many landowners to sell to Jews, about 75% around Odesa. Jewish brokers and grain specialists like Paris' Louis Dreyfus and Berlin's M. Neufeld worked with Chiots. Mari Vagliano, other Greek and Jewish merchants founded the Azov-Don Bank.

The British merchant fleet grew from 2.3 million tons in 1814 to a more efficient 5.7 million in 1860. The US fleet was second, tripling to 2.4 million tons to 1860, together over half the world's merchant fleet. British steamers dominated trans-Atlantic passenger and freight traffic by the 1860s. America's population rose to 23 million by 1850 compared with Britain's 27 million and France's 34 million,[25] increasingly demand. Post-famine emigration fell from 219,000 in 1851, averaging about 75,000 by the late-1860s.

In 1862 Cunard launched the 3,900-ton paddle steamer *Scotia*, the fastest to date, but paddle ships were already obsolete, screw propellers essential for efficient ocean-going steamships. John Napier built Cunard's first screw ship, the 2,500-ton *China*, for 160 first class and 770 steerage passengers. On Cunard's 1865 death, his and Inman ships sailed bi-weekly at similar speeds. George Thomson, Robert Napier's assistant manager and brother James, built fast screw ships, some for Cunard's auxiliary Caribbean trade and Australia's mail.[26]

Rapid engine design advances meant steamships became competitive in long-haul routes. In 1840, the 1,139 grt *Britannia* (gross registered tons-See Glossary-Tonnage) made eight knots at 38 tons/day in boilers under nine pounds pressure, generating 400 horsepower, carrying 225 tons of cargo and 90 passengers. In 1855 the 3,300 grt *Persia* made 13 knots on 150 tons/day with 1,100 tons of cargo and 180 passengers at 25 pounds pressure generating 1,000 horsepower. By 1874 the 4,556 grt *Bothnia* made 13 knots on 63 tons, 3,000 tons of cargo and 340 passengers.[27] Robert Napier's pioneering efforts, insistence on quality, technical innovation and encouragement of other leading shipbuilders and engineers led the Clyde to become the world's best, busiest shipbuilding centre. The EIC's Sir James Melvill in 1856 told Napier he was 'the man who, above all...[gave] practical effect to the invention of Watt, and has passed to the world the great blessing of steam navigation.'

Part Four

Limits of Enlightenment

Second-half 19th-century global trade growth was seven-times faster than the first; from 20 million tons in 1840 to 140 million in 1884, annually averaging 4.2%.[1] Tonnage clearing British ports increased eight-fold between 1845 and 1900.[2] British shipping's 1840s-1890s horsepower trebled. By 1870, British maritime trade was more than France, Germany and Italy combined and four-times America's. World volumes increased 400% as freight rates halved.[3]

Ton-mile ratios also increased as long-haul trades to the Americas, Asia, Australia and New Zealand grew. Britain's service sector was larger than manufacturing, had higher employment, growth and largest per capita incomes.[4] Britain's imports exceeded exports but were more than covered by shipping receipts, London's most important 'invisible' until the 1870s when overseas investment returns took over. British ports handled 40% of world trade. By 1890 over half the world's tonnage was British-owned, which in 1913 carried about two thirds of the world's foreign trade.[5]

Between 1870 and 1910, the world fleet doubled from 16.7 million grt to 34.6 million. In the 1870s one in three British ships were steamships, in the 1890s, five in seven, assisted by American, European, Indian and Japanese coal discoveries. Continual engine refinements and lower steel costs increased ship sizes, enabling economies of scale and efficiencies, ushering-in the era of cheap, safe travel as more safety measures were implemented. Steam and sail co-existed in different trades until sail finally ceased in the late-1930s. Industrially, Britain peaked in the 1860s compared with others, importing half the world's raw cotton, responsible for 66% of trade in manufactured goods.[6] While maritime trade always encouraged innovation and recently moral enlightenment, towards the century's end, disquieting ideas started coalescing, as Britain's manufacturing lead eroded.

Chapter 27

Evangelical Christianity

Expanding maritime trade, conditional on toleration, started encountering the religious vanity of evangelical Christianity, changing some British perceptions. The EIC had excluded missionaries from India but the 1813 Charter renewal specified a duty of religious and moral improvement. Belief in protecting disadvantaged peoples remained. Mid-century British politicians and merchants, trying to improve Indian peasant conditions and repressing slave traders were confident improvers. Their philosophy, private enterprise, free markets, liberty to think, speak, worship, enquire, invent, trade and self-help were, Britons thought, the keys to success. Intellectual enlightenment accompanied trade growth, prosperity, political and economic freedom. But in 1833 EIC-licensing of missionaries was abolished. Evangelicals got an Indian Church, bishops and missionary freedom. Calcutta's bishop wrote an 1819 hymn, 'From Greenland's icy mountains, From India's coral strands, They call us to deliver, Their land from error's chain.'[1] Conversion they believed, would enlighten people to discard alien religions. This implied superiority based on wealth, material progress, scientific knowledge, arms and constitutional government. As Britain became more powerful, respect for Indian, Chinese and other civilisations diminished.

Desire to improve in general became one to improve others. Warren Hastings was happy to leave Indians to their rich culture and religions, but missionaries were sure of Christianity's superiority, proven by commercial success. Keeping mistresses in 18th-century Britain was not uncommon, easily transferred to India, a means of increasing local knowledge, free of racial and cultural prejudice. The 1770s-1780s EIC encouraged soldiers to marry locals to build-up the army. But Cornwallis' and Wellesley's priorities were efficient administration. In 1791 Anglo-Indians were prevented from holding civil or military office. Although mistresses were still kept, intermarriage virtually stopped by 1800, limiting previous inter-racial contact, increasing distance between ruler and ruled.[2]

Protestant missionary movements from the 1790s; the English Baptist Missionary Society from 1795, the Scottish Missionary Society from 1799 were partly by-products of anti-slave trade evangelism. Unlike Jones and Hastings, evangelicals did not try to understand India. William Carey's 1793 remark that 'no people can have more surrendered their reason than the Hindus,' was not common thinking then, but increasingly became so. Thomas Thomason in 1814 thought, 'we have annihilated the political importance of the natives…without giving them anything in return.'[3] Wilberforce after 1807, self-proclaimed guardian of Britain's worldwide moral duty, thought Hindu gods 'monsters of lust, injustice, wickedness and cruelty,' Hinduism a 'great abomination'.[4] EIC official Charles Grant, infused by evangelical Methodism, thought it caused Indians to be 'degenerate and base', that India was 'given to us not merely that we might draw annual profit…but that we might diffuse…the light and benign influence of the truth.'[5] Christian conversion would restore them 'use of their reason.' The magnitude of British power, the huge gap between it and others, its industrial products, exports, navy, internal stability and avoidance of revolution, convinced many that Protestantism was responsible. God was on their side. Even the secular believed Protestant Christianity the secret of greatness. Changing attitudes to Indian culture and religion began driving a wedge between Europeans and Indians at <u>official</u> levels. By contrast, there were many productive Anglo-Indian <u>commercial</u> partnerships.

British government's humanitarian impulses were strong with 1830s reforming, enlightened ministries. Idealisation of Pacific Islands' noble savages shifted to 'anxious, even guilty concern,'[6] as they died of European diseases and were debilitated by rum, firearms and European import dependence. Tahiti's population shrank from 40,000 in 1770 to just 9,000 in 1830.[7] The British and Foreign Aborigine Protection Society was founded. Buxton's 1837 Select Committee Report on aborigines asserted the duty to safeguard native rights, proposing a share of revenue set-aside for education and religious instruction, concluding that British policy should be 'to carry civilisation and humanity, peace and good government and above all, knowledge of the true God to the uttermost ends of the earth.'[8] Traders in India however, continued business as equals.

Glenelg's (Colonial Secretary 1835–1839) morally based policy feared for South African natives and ordered settlers to abandon Queen Adelaide Province, the only time government refused to accept annexations by 'men on the ground,' insisting on Australian native rights, ordering inquests when any were killed. In 1837 he wrote, 'It cannot be too strongly impressed on every European that the lives of the natives must be considered equally as valuable and entitled to the same protection as…European settlers.'[9] He urged not offending Canada's native cultures, 'to protect and cherish', establishing an 1843 Commission of Enquiry into their state. New Zealand was reluctantly annexed, the 1840 Treaty of Waitangi guaranteeing North Island's Māori's full possession of their lands and fisheries as British subjects to avoid Australian or American natives' fate. But London's enlightened directives were ignored by missionaries and settlers. Deprived of land, they were decimated by disease.

Charles Darwin, naturalist on *HMS Beagle* in 1831 studied South America's animals, birds and insects, leading to his 1859 *On the Origin of Species by Natural Selection*. Alfred Russell Wallace reached the same conclusions virtuously simultaneously, coining the phrase, 'survival of the fittest.' The London Missionary Society's David Livingstone (1813–1873) encapsulated enlightenment's continuation <u>and</u> limits. After his mid-century African expeditions, he lectured on legitimate trade's importance in replacing slaving. His motto was 'Christianity and Commerce,' in the native's interest. Having learned African languages, he listened to witchdoctors, how medicinal plants, like quinine from a Peruvian tree bark could treat fevers, using it in mixtures, eventually marketed by Burroughs, Welcome and Co., later leading to the discovery of the mosquito-malaria link. Yet rigid Christianity led him to reject Darwin's theories.

Macaulay began his *History of England* in the late-1840s, 'The history of our country during the last 160 years is eminently the history of physical, of moral and intellectual improvement,' giving it a duty to improve others. In 1848 Palmerston declared, 'our duty, our vocation, is not to enslave but to set free…we stand at the head of moral, social and political civilisation. Our task is to…direct the march of other nations.' Evangelical Christianity's and the Oxford Movement's influence led to a deeply conservative, religious society.[10]

Muslim acceptance of slavery, Hindu lingums and multiple sexual positions depicted on Chola temples were officially and religiously seen as degenerate. Trade, technology and especially Christian conversion would effect moral change. John Bowring (1792–1872), Canton consul in 1849, Superintendent of Trade in China and Governor of Hong Kong, allowed Hong Kong Chinese as jurors and lawyers, but asserted 'Jesus Christ is Free Trade and Free Trade is Jesus Christ.' Cables, steam engines, missionaries, sailors in preventative squadrons were 'co-operators with God' for the 'restoration of the world.'[11] The difference with 18th-century enlightened beliefs was Christianity was increasingly seen as the crucial element. Discernible from the 1790s, by the 1840s it was widespread, increasing with technological and commercial dominance, but totally absent from Jeejeebhoy's, Jardine and Matheson's partnerships for instance, built on mutual respect. But this 'background noise' to commerce became louder.

Thomas Babington Macaulay (1800–1859) introducing western education to India, asserted in 1835, 'all the historical information…collected from all the books written in the Sanskrit language is less valuable than the most paltry abridgement used at preparatory schools in England,' and in 1836 that with English education, idolatry would disappear from Bengal's respectable classes within 30 years by the natural operation of knowledge and reflection. James Mill's (1773–1836) *The History of British India* (1818), standard reading for those joining the Indian Civil Service, denigrated Hinduism. 'Deficiencies' were blamed on environment, curable by education. By the 1860s belief in the equality of mankind disappeared.[12] Belief in Caucasian superiority was the fertile soil in which the Aryan invasion myth germinated.[13]

John Stuart Mill (1806–1873), EIC employee (1823–1858), Liberal MP (1865–1868) and abolitionist wrote *On Liberty* (1859) which addressed the limits of power legitimately exercised over individuals on the principle of utility. People should be free to do as they wish, unless harming others, but benevolent despotism was legitimate in dealing with the less civilised if the aim was improvement. From Bentham's 'greatest happiness principle,' he thought moral pleasures superior to physical. He believed in free markets but accepted interventions on utilitarian grounds, like alcohol taxes. A liberal philosopher, he nevertheless equated successful nations with moral worth. He proposed female voting, proportional representation and, against the trend, that the universe is not governed by an omnipotent, loving God. Embodying maritime commercial values, he wrote 'The economical advantages of commerce are surpassed in importance by those of its effects which are intellectual and moral. It is hardly possible to overrate the value of placing human beings in contact with people dissimilar to themselves with the modes of thought and action unlike those with which they are familiar;' stressing trade as 'one of the greatest instruments not only of civilisation in the narrowest, but of improvements of culture in the widest sense.'

America was also affected by evangelical Christianity. De Tocqueville's 1835 *De La Democratie en Amerique* noted New England's deeply held principle of liberty, yet blasphemy and adultery were capital crimes. Hunt's *Merchants' Magazine* from 1839, contained an article entitled *Commerce as Connected with the Progress of Civilisation*. An article in 1856 by President John Tyler wrote of ships' cargoes as 'the means of civilisation and refinement,' <u>but</u> he meant Bible distribution. As the Black Sea opened after the Crimean War, many articles questioned Turks', Egyptians' and Levantines' commercial acumen. Regarding US slavery, only a minority of northerners were abolitionists.

Chapter 28

The Indian Mutiny/Great Rebellion.
Erosion of British Confidence and Enlightenment

The Indian Mutiny or Great Rebellion (1857–58) triggered by perception that new ammunition used either pig or cow fat, insulting Muslims or Hindus, drew on resentment of missionaries' alienating message, non-Christian societies' wickedness. British soldiers' arrogance and to some, Governor-General Dalhousie's high-handed rule, adding princely states where no heir was immediately apparent, disregarding previous generations' concentrating not taking territory, were also factors. Taking 18 months to suppress, it knocked British confidence in themselves as improvers and in Indians as people capable of improvement. Canning, the first post-Mutiny Secretary of State for India confessed 'the sympathy for which Englishmen…felt for the natives has changed to…repugnance.' Even Macaulay had thought eventual independence desirable and inevitable, but the Mutiny shook some British faith in Indians' capability. Cobden was dumbfounded that 'after a century of intercourse… [Indians] suddenly exhibit themselves greater savages than…North American Indians.' Perceptions of 'mild Hindus' were replaced by assumptions of deceit and cruelty. Nevertheless, government maintained a sense of responsibility for peasant welfare, concentrating on honest government and raising living standards.[1] Secretary of State for India, Cranbourne (later Lord Salisbury) in an 1874 famine, got a £6–10 million loan for famine relief and banned food exports.

Disturbances in 1865 Jamaica led to martial law and floggings, dividing opinion and loyalties. *The Times* was disappointed that hopes for self-government were dashed. Mill wrote that but for a royal enquiry, 'I should be ashamed of my country.'[2] Debate and self-criticism meant enlightenment was alive. An 1865 Commons Select Committee recommended withdrawal from commercially unsuccessful West African slave bases except Sierra Leone, but public opinion did not allow it. Nevertheless, racial attitudes hardened, mainly because of the Mutiny, missionaries its main cause. Furthermore, continental racism started infecting some attitudes. Darwin thought racial differences minor, but French Count Gobineau's 1853 *The Inequality of the Races of Mankind* promoted inferiority. After reading it in 1866, Charles Kingsley no longer believed in mankind's equality, that 'science' proved racial differences[3] and was sure Irish and Catholic countries could never run a constitutional government, although Mill continued to believe in education's power.

Colonial Secretary Kimberley in 1873 directed that 'except in quite subordinate posts we cannot safely employ natives.'[4] Railways were built for military and commercial reasons with investors given 4.5% returns and guaranteed exchange rates. By 1882 the subcontinent's network connected most major cities.[5] British and Indian merchants built large factories, tea plantations, the fifth-largest railway and telegraph network, banks, ports, universities and hospitals. India's first cotton mill started in 1854. In 1865 there were ten, mainly in Bombay, by 1914, 271, employing 260,000, most Parsi-owned. British-owned jute spinning in Calcutta started in 1855. In 1870 it had five mills, by 1913, 64, employment rising from 5,000 to 215,000. Moreover, by 1900 most British tea imports came not from China as in 1800 but British-owned Indian plantations.[6]

The 1858 Queen's Proclamation that Britain would 'no longer impose our convictions on any of Our subjects', showed respect, especially as proclaimed in Allahabad where the Yamuna and Ganges converge, where the once mighty Sarasvati joined, *Triveni Sangam*, Three Rivers, Indian civilisation's heart, where during the *Magh Mela*, tens of thousands bathed chanting Vedic hymns.[7]

An 1894 biography of the EIC's Thomas Munro (1761–1827), who fought Haidar Ali and Tipu Sultan, administered northern districts ceded by the Nizam of Hyderabad and in 1820 was Madras' Governor-General noted that between Munro's 1780 arrival when Haidar Ali was devastating the Carnatic and his 1827 death, there were 'great changes…The country has been opened-up by the railways and telegraph wires and the people…modernised by schools and colleges. Almost every town which Munro visited…has now a railway station or is within a few hours' drive of one and each has its English school, its dispensary or hospital, its post and telegraph office, its magistrates court and its police station.' His name was still revered. A clergyman noted 'old natives…cherish his memory as…their greatest benefactor. In the Ceded Districts boys are still named after him, Munrolappa.'[8]

Reaction to the Mutiny was not even. <u>Official</u> belief in trusteeship continued, official self-confidence partly shaken, but businessmen like Parsi Jamsetji Tata continued investing opportunistically. Realising cotton exports to China were more profitable than opium, changed in 1859. When prices rocketed during America's Civil War, he travelled to Britain with his cotton. Unlike official positions in Bombay, business clubs were open to Indian businessmen. In 1869 he bought a bankrupt Bombay oil mill, converted it to cotton cloth, learnt in Britain, hiring Indian and English employees, then a larger one in Nagpur selling its products throughout the empire. Diversification initiated a famous, still-growing business empire.

Chapter 29

The US Civil War (1861–1865)

By 1860, maritime trade and tariff protection had transformed America's northern states into an emerging industrial powerhouse. But the south only had 8.2% of national manufacturing,[1] 29% of its railroads and 13% of its banks. Cotton production, 750,000 bales in 1830, rose to 2.85 million in 1850, its exports America's most valuable. Slaves from 700,000 in 1790 increased to 4.5 million in 1860, half the south's population. The north had 40% of its people in agriculture, the south 84%, but northern agriculture was mechanised, producing 80% of US wheat, 87% of its oats. Chicago, Cincinnati, Cleveland and Detroit had food processing, machine tools and railroad equipment factories. North and south were classic juxtaposed continental, backward and agricultural, as favoured by Jefferson and Madison, and northern maritime-influenced, commercial, increasingly wealthy and urban.

It was no accident. The 1789 Tariff Act provided 80–95% of government revenue up to 1860,[2] protecting and nurturing northern industries from cheaper imports, especially British cloth, encouraging US shipbuilding and shipping. Washington's Farewell Address explained the Union's *raison d'etre*, an economic trade-off, northern maritime trade and manufacturing and southern agriculture. In 1795, 92% of imports and 86% of exports were in US-flagged ships. Shipowners and merchants tenaciously competed in China, the Caribbean and Zanzibar. US shipowner earnings rose from $5.9 million in 1790 to $42.1 million in 1807, exactly why Madison's war was so unwise![3]

Tariff levels flip-flopped depending on the party in power and interest groups' relative strengths, but was the most important domestic issue, dominating federal government revenue. Post-Madison 1816–1824 tariffs were higher than Hamilton's but then increased 40–100% on cotton cloth, paper, glass, woollens and iron imports. The south, resenting expensive imports of machinery and manufactured goods, wanted low, balanced tariffs and land sales in the west, the north high protective tariffs and free land in the west, although New England's merchants also disliked high tariffs.

The Erie Canal-inspired rise of New York as entrepot for US east coast ports hurt Charleston. As the northeast industrialised, New York's 1810–1860 population increased ten-fold. Charleston's did not even double.[4] The divide was reflected in Congressional voting. In the 1824 tariff, the House of Representatives' Atlantic states voted 60–15 for, the south 64–3 against.[5] Northerners dominated New Orleans and Mobile trade in the 1830s as northern states became important cotton markets, negotiated through New York, most British-bound cotton passing through it. Northern merchants were less active in Charleston, whose society's mainstay were absentee planters. The south, complacent and hierarchical, failed to effectively colonise the west.

The 1828 Tariff of Abominations enflamed north-south arguments, exacerbated by New York's growth. The south became militant. Calhoun in 1831 thought it 'a fixed and hopeless minority.' In 1832 South Carolina declared the 1828 and 1832 tariffs illegal within its borders. President Andrew Jackson threatened force to enforce federal law. The 1833 Compromise Tariff promised gradual tariff-reduction to 1842 to 20% on dutiable imports, implemented slowly, mostly in 1842 itself.[6] In 1844 Calhoun thought 'tariff takes from us the proceeds of our labour, abolition strikes at labour itself.' Most abolitionists however were a northeast evangelical or Quaker minority. Tariffs increased again, were reversed in 1846, lowered again in 1857, the south constantly unsure and defensive. New England's tariff-protected industrial sector emerged from the 1840s with westward migration an expanding demand base. Almost 90% of immigrants settled in free states, vastly outnumbering the south's free population. In 1790 north-south populations were about equal. By 1850 the north had 13,527,000, the south 9,612,000. Britain's cultural connections were in the north, two maritime-inspired regions. The south by contrast was a slave monoculture society, proud but without maritime instincts to control its exports and shipping, agricultural slaveholders in an industrialising country with advancing liberties. It relied on the west for wheat and livestock, the north for clothing and machinery, while planters were increasingly indebted to New York merchants who bought and shipped its cotton.

In 1854 the proposed admission of slave-free Kansas and Nebraska to the Union led to the Republican Party's formation. Their people did not want to live beside negroes. Lincoln said new western territories should be for 'free white people' and 'cannot be…if slavery be planted within them…New free states are…for poor people,'[7] but denounced slavery in 1854. Preventing slavery's spread was for most, preventing negroes living closer to them, not a moral objection. Lincoln in 1860 favoured tariff increases, slavery's <u>containment</u> and national control of banks. South Carolina again threatened secession, supported by Georgia, Alabama, Florida, Mississippi, Louisiana and Texas. The *Natchez Free Trader* in 1861 thought, 'the south needs no Custom House and will thrive on free trade as the north can never be without it.'[8]

In 1860 Georgian politician, Robert Toombs explained, 'The material prosperity of the north was greatly dependent on the Federal Government, that of the south, not at all. In the first years of the Republic, the navigating, commercial and manufacturing interests of the north…[sought] profit and aggrandisement at the expense of agricultural interests. Even the owners of fishing smacks…obtained bounties…The navigating interests begged for protection against foreign shipbuilders and…competition in the coasting trade. Congress granted [it]…Not content with these…advantages, they have sought to throw the legislative burthens of their business…upon the public…the cost of lighthouses, buoys and the maintenance of seamen…above two million annually… they pleaded…the infancy of their business…But when these reasons ceased, they were no less clamorous for government protection.' The south sold cotton in unprotected world markets. US consumers bought in a highly protected one, which as Calhoun said, made 'the poor poorer and the rich richer,' the south increasingly culturally and economically marginalised. Toombs thought northerners taxed southerners, 'exactly as…Britain taxed our ancestors.' Tariff policy did not cause war, a states' rights issue like former secessionist threats, but hugely contributed to north-south division. Britain dominated overseas investment in America and took nearly half its exports. Of foreign tonnage entering US ports in 1860, 80% was British, leading *The Times* in 1851 to conclude it 'more closely united with this kingdom than any one of the colonies.'[9]

Seven of the 15 slave states seceded to form the Confederacy, almost immediately halving import tariffs. By contrast, the north voted 96–15 to erect the world's highest tariff walls against British competition, the border 7–9 against, the south 1–39 against. Thereafter, low-tariff southern senators withdrew, Republicans took control and the Morrill Tariff passed, increasing from about 17% to 26%, some products higher. Implemented in 1862, it remained for the rest of the century, continuing southern degradation. Free trade dominated British political thinking. Palmerston told Adams 'We do not like slavery, but we want cotton, and we dislike very much your Morrill Tariff.' He thought the north just as accountable as the south for slavery, slave traders safe under US-flagged ships.

In 1833 Liverpool imported nearly 850,000 cotton bales, Glasgow about 49,000 and London 40,000.[10] By 1859 Britain imported two million, almost 90% to Liverpool. America supplied 75–84%, fluctuating year-by-year.[11] Other European cotton industries also depended on it. With war looming, Britain sought other supplies. Apart from Indian, Brazilian and Egyptian imports, missions to Dahomey, Liberia, Sierra Leone and Mozambique were sent before 1859, because cotton textiles employed four million people, about 16% of Britain's population, was a third of its exports and a major factor in Liverpool's prosperity.

Southern leaders believed that 'King Cotton' would sustain secession. South Carolina's Senator Hammond boasted in 1858, 'without firing a gun, without drawing a sword, should they make war on us, we could bring the whole world to our feet…you dare not make war on cotton…Cotton is King.' Southern leaders believed they could coerce Britain's support by embargo; 'King Cotton Diplomacy', arrogance born of ignorance, a terrible mistake.

Anxious about possible war, British manufacturers stockpiled a million bales from previous years' bumper crops, delaying Lancashire's 'cotton famine' until late-1862. Exports to Europe dropped from three million in 1860 to just half a million. Cotton's 1860 ten cents/lb price rose to $1.89 in 1863–64. India, Egypt, Argentina and Brazil increased production, India by 700%. The south's embargo was really the north's blockade of the south: Lincoln's Anaconda Plan. Declaring the sides belligerents rather than insurrectionists enabled him under international law to stop and search neutral ships suspected of violating blockade. French cotton merchants and manufacturers initially pressed Napoleon III to recognise the Confederacy and some Liverpool merchants, thinking it a free trade issue, called for recognition, but after Lincoln's blockade, that meant war with America, which no one wanted.

Two Confederacy agents sent to assess the chances of a British-Confederacy alliance were intercepted by a US ship. Isolated, uninvolved in maritime trade and shipping, they did not undertake diplomatic offensives. Their world was closed, convinced that Europe would cave-in, but Palmerston pre-war had urged neutrality. When in 1862 it appeared the Confederacy might win, Birkenhead's Lairds built blockade runners and some Liverpool merchants started the National Line to take cotton from an independent Confederacy, but when abolitionists forced Lincoln's hand to declare emancipation, the war became a moral issue in Britain. Mill wrote of his 'happiness to have lived to see the termination of slavery.'

The most important Civil War battleground was the sea; US Navy blockaders against blockade-runners, mainly Bermuda-, Bahamas- or Havana-based British-manned steamships carrying cotton, tobacco and turpentine out, rifles, ammunition, medicine, brandy and coffee in. Captured ships were confiscated. If successful, investors gained windfall profits. Initially perhaps one in ten were caught, one in three by 1864, an increasingly successful deterrent. Hull-based shipowner, Z.C. Pearson bought or part-bought 13 blockade-running steamships and seven sailing ships, lost many and was bankrupted by 1864.[12] Texas cotton adjacent to Mexico, shipped from Mexican ports, was a small, lucrative trade. The south's army was nearly always short of supplies in the final two years, the Union Navy increasing year-by-year. In 1863 it won control of the Mississippi and New Orleans. As more territory was won, blockade became more effective, cotton export almost totally choked-off.

Hard-hit British cotton workers opposed slavery, despite their unemployment peaking in 1862 with 60% idle. Manchester's sent Lincoln support, hoping 'erasure of that foul blot on civilisation and Christianity, chattel slavery…will cause the name of Abraham Lincoln to be honoured and revered by posterity…[with] Britain and the United States in close and enduring regards.' He replied, 'I know and deeply deplore the sufferings which the working people of Manchester…endure…Your decisive utterances…sublime Christian heroism…re-inspiring assurance of the…ultimate and universal triumph of justice, humanity and freedom.' *The New York Times*, 26th November 1862, reported 'tailors, shoemakers, bakers, milliners, beerhouse keepers… whose customers mainly belong to the working classes…[were also] on the Books of the Guardians and the Relief Committees…208,621 persons receiving parochial relief…four times…last year' with 'no hope that the sufferings…will have an early termination. Should this war be immediately settled, it would take months before our spindles and looms can be again humming.' In 1863 US merchants sent the first ship with provisions for Manchester's Central Relief Committee.

As workers were paid by the piece, incomes were slashed and did not always suffer in stoic silence. Riots erupted in 1863, Confederate flags flown in some towns, complaints that more charity had come from outside than from millowners. Glasgow's smaller cotton industry was also hit. Ever resourceful, it added locomotive manufacturing and engineering to its increasing shipbuilding, while Liverpool's traders sought new opportunities. In 1866 Hatton and Cookson found a river route to West Africa's Oguwe, gradually building a trade in rubber, ivory, palm oil and gum,[13] more legitimate trade.

Paternalistic millowners helped workers. Relief committees were established, soup kitchens, schools and tickets for presentation at local grocers started. Some workers left for Yorkshire's woollen mills. Some emigrated to New York where factory labour was needed in the war effort as steamship lines reduced fares. Australian and New Zealand governments offered free passage. Some towns diversified into hat making. Too late, the 1863 Public Works Manufacturing Districts Act allowed authorities to borrow for public works like municipal parks, sewers, canals and roads. Some southern sympathy in Liverpool due to close commercial ties led to building Dixie Line ships to Spain, named *Richmond, Virginia* and *Jefferson Davis*. Cobden the pacifist deplored the war but Bright's Quaker principles strongly opposed slavery.

By 1863 Indian, Egyptian, Turkish and Brazilian cotton shipments increased. India's *Surat* cotton was least suitable for machinery, producing only 40% of previous throughput. Surging prices however, brought Bombay merchants substantial wealth, like cotton, bullion and stock trader Premchand Roychand,[14] giving Bombay its enduring commercial, speculative spirit. India-wide cotton was funnelled into it. Exports rose from 490,000 bales in 1859 to 890,000 by 1865. Parsis, Jews and Bahtias commissioned steam-powered mills employing 13,000 in ten mills in 1865, by 1900, 73,000 in 80 mills in Bombay, 193 in India. An 1860 Bombay newspaper boasted of £250,000 invested in a fortnight to establish manufacturing. 'Bombay has long been the Liverpool of the East and she is now to become the Manchester.'[15]

Governor-General Dalhousie's (1848–56) first 320 miles of railway-building in 1853 was to prevent famine, but the Manchester Chamber of Commerce in 1861 resolved a £5–6 million annual loan to finance Indian roads, canals and railways, completing aborted post-Mutiny transport projects, to increase cotton exports. By 1867 it reached nearly 1,170 miles. The Civil War's end in 1865 reduced prices. Abdullah (later Sir Albert) Sassoon, son of Baghdad-born refugee David, who arrived in Bombay in 1832 as a commodity trader, was one who profited in cotton weaving and built the Sassoon Docks in 1875, then schools, hospitals and the David Sassoon Mechanics Institute and Library. As imports from non-US areas, including India, increased, British workers' conditions improved. By early-1864, imports kept mills operating three days a week, by year-end, four and a half, normal working in 1865 and by 1870 US cotton production exceeded 1860 levels. By the 1870s-1880s Lancashire's cotton workers produced a consumer society, paying to watch football, music halls and Blackpool holidays.

Before the war a third of slavers were built in America, fast ships to outrun patrols. With many southerners in US government, not all their anti-slave patrols had been pursued vigorously. Few slave ships were detained by US ships, most by British. But after 1862 Lincoln offered Britain mutual right of search and declared fitting-out slavers in New York illegal.[16] The focus on slavery prompted the Dutch to abolish it in their colonies in 1863. Spain outlawed slave trading in 1867, slavery in Puerto Rico in 1873, Cuba in 1886. Brazil followed in 1888.

The war benefitted most sectors of the Union economy, with the world's largest railroad system, leather, weapons, food, textile and iron production. New York's stock and bond transactions were second to London. National debt rose from about $65 million to $2,755 million,[17] but was easily serviced. The south's economy worsened. It took a decade to recapture replacement Brazilian, Indian and Egyptian cotton supplies. By 1870 America provided 40% of Britain's wheat imports and substantial increases in flour, lard and meat. A Cincinnati trade analyst wrote, there is now secured a market for our pork in Great Britain and on the Continent of such magnitude that…the amount consumed heretofore in the southern states sinks into comparative insignificance.'

However, the war meant US Pacific-China trade and cotton cloth exports to Zanzibar, 2.5-times the value of British pre-war exports, collapsed. British and Indian cloth took their market, ending US merchant shipping dynamism. Confederate raiders had sunk around 110,000 tons and forced US owners to transfer to other flags. A post-war issue was the Confederacy's order of two John Laird ships, which had sunk over 150 Union ships. It was resolved when Britain impounded two more during the war and by a post-war $15.5 million arbitration award. Well behind British shipbuilding, especially iron steamships, America fell further behind. Its 2.4 million tons in 1865 dropped to 817,000 in 1890, the same as 1807. By 1900 US-flagged ships carried only 9.3% of its seaborne trade. Britain dominated steam shipping even more than it had sail, but invigorated by northern industry, US GNP grew at twice Britain's rate thereafter.

Chapter 30

The Suez Canal and its Consequences

French official Ferdinand de Lesseps, researching ancient Egypt's canals in 1854 got permission to cut a Suez Canal. Napoleon's former threat to India via Egypt and French Madagascan influence caused Palmerston's opposition, but British merchants supported it. New York merchant Emanuel Weiss thought it a French plot against British interests and that Greeks would gain most; 'three quarters of the trade in Egypt, nay all of Turkey, is in the hands of the Greeks…it would be foolish…to make them grow and prosper faster.'[1] Britain's Egyptian investments had increased; cotton-growing from 1820, irrigation, banking, railways, a Cairo stock exchange and P&O's Alexandria-Suez land route for passengers. Export values, Egyptian £1.43 million in 1863 rose to £11.42 million in 1866. As the Canal was cut, stimulated by Lancashire's 1861–1865 cotton famine, prices soared. Alexandria boomed.

Khedive Ismail borrowed to finance the Canal, increasing national debt from Egyptian £3.3 million in 1863 to £91 million in 1876. Completed in 1869, it reduced the distance from Britain to Bombay, Hong Kong and Singapore around 3,300 miles, to Australian ports 545–680 miles. After the American Civil War, cotton exports resumed, Egypt's exports and prices fell. More ships still used the Cape route because the Canal was built for steamships, only gradually replacing sail on long-haul routes.

Alfred Holt, from his brother's Liverpool-based Lamport and Holt, bought two ships in the early-1850s, chartering one to the French government for Crimean War duties, then ran Liverpool-Caribbean trades, which no unsubsidised steamers had previously done. The problem of running steamships to Asia that the *Great Eastern* tried solving with size was solved with John Elder's two cylinder or compound engines, the most important advance since Boulton and Watt. Re-using steam produced much higher pressure, increasing power, efficiency, cargo and passenger space, reducing coal-use by 30–40%.[2] In 1868, 60% of the 7.5 million tons of ships in Europe, North America and the Mediterranean were steamships, but only 12% long-haul and Europe-Asia only 2% of the 1.1 million tons. Much of that was Alfred Holt's Blue Funnel Line started in 1866 with *Agamemnon, Achilles* and *Ajax*.

Competing clipper ships performed China-Europe in about 90 days. Holts advertised 76 days, not always fully loaded as 1866–1870 freight markets were low. Much responsibility rested with the Master's discretion and ingenuity. The first *Ajax* voyage from Shanghai for example, sailed only a third full but the Master's decision to call unscheduled at Port Elizabeth was fortuitous, loading a full cargo of wool and in 1868 *Agamemnon* loaded at Hankow, 700 miles up-river, both initiatives much appreciated by Holt, who was confident of the Canal's significance. 'We shall benefit by it more than all other nations of the earth put together.'[3] His five ships used it immediately, unlike P&O which had heavily invested in the overland route; docks, warehouses, coal dumps, Alexandria and Suez hotels, farms to feed passengers, Nile steamers and railway. After a year they reluctantly decided to scrap unsuitable ships and built new compound-engine ships. Their 44 ships averaging 1,857 tons in 1870 increased to 50 ships of about twice the size and by 1884 the Canal was dredged to take them.[4] By 1883 Holt had 26 ships, mainly built by Scotts of Greenock. It invested in the line with agent W.H. Swire, his three original masters and several Liverpool families.

The Canal signalled the end of tea clippers. The famous *Cutty Sark*, launched also in 1869, was capable of just one annual round voyage. In 1877 it changed to tramp cargoes; Welsh outbound coal, jute from Manila to New York and in 1883 Australian wool to Britain, not time sensitive cargoes. The Canal boosted Singapore. In 1869, 264,790 tons of steamships and 347,596 tons of sailing ships called there. By 1876 that transformed to 1,291,304 steam and 163,385 sail.[5] With Batavia silting up, its trade to China ceased. Tanjung Priok as replacement was not built until the 1880s. Singapore therefore became the conduit for Dutch plantation produce and Malay tin and rubber to Britain. Steamship calls at Jeddah also rose from 38 in 1864 to 205 in 1875.[6] By 1904–05 Muscat hosted 834 steamships, catching the 1,297 sailing ships, exporting fruits and dried fish to China, importing rice, sugar, tea, coffee and textiles, Kachchhis still its main traders. Much Southeast Asian regional trade was conducted by Bugis trading from creek to creek, island to island, exchanging sandalwood, spices, shells, dried fish, copra and coconuts for Lancashire cloth.

Colombo also developed with 18 jetties exporting cinnamon, coffee, tea, coconut and rubber and was a crucial coaling depot, by 1910 the world's seventh port in tonnage. Karachi was transformed by surging cotton demand during America's Civil War. Its trade tripled from 1854 to 1864, then slumped, before being boosted by the Canal and railways. Calcutta exported growing jute volumes. Mombasa became East Africa's main port for industrial imports and raw material exports, Zanzibar still a centre for Kachchhi traders. In 1886–87, 44% of its exports and 40% of its imports were to and from India.[7] Aden-based Parsi, Cowsaji Dinshaw ran India-East Africa steamers, mainly Bombay-Zanzibar. Mediterranean trade also benefitted. Between 1869 and 1899, Trieste quadrupled volumes; coffee, tea, pepper, rice and cotton.[8]

Many US clippers were withdrawn from China after 1865, repositioned for US cotton export resumption. This and increasing trade made 1873–1875 freight rates double those of 1869. Despite buying five new ships, by 1875 Holt had reserves of £280,000, enough to buy six or seven more.[9] To secure sufficient cargoes, partnering with Butterfield and Swire in China and Japan, and Mansfield, Bogart and Co. in Singapore were crucial, especially John Swire's understanding of likely Chinese trade developments.

Before 1869 more sailing ships were built than steamships, but after, apart from two years, this reversed. Some British shipowners like Hull's Thomas Wilson, West Hartlepool's James Pyman, Newcastle's Edmund Watts and London's Pickernell Brothers pioneered unsubsidised steamships, financed by provincial banks. For mail, passengers and perishable cargo, speed and regularity were especially important. Steamships surpassed sail on Atlantic short-haul routes before 1869 but Suez encouraged them on Asian routes. Mail times to Australia halved to about 60 days by the 1850s due to steamships. They halved again in the 1870s through Suez with better engines, lowering insurance premiums. British steam tonnage overtook sail in 1883, which declined after 1890, as triple expansion engines made the economics increasingly attractive.

In 1870, 486 ships of 654,915 tons passed the Canal, in 1899, 3,607 of 1,3,815,992 tons. Annual receipts reached over £3.6 million,[10] but too slow to save Egypt's finances. Because sailing ships could not use the Canal, it showed insufficient returns in the first years to pay the Khedive's debts and he was forced to sell his 44% stake. Disraeli discovered he was negotiating with two French groups. A Rothschild loan enabled an 1875 purchase for £4 million, preventing French control, a long-term investment returning £86 million in dividends between 1895 and 1961.[11]

Canal ownership had significant consequences for Turkey and Egypt which Britain wanted as reformed, reliable allies to protect and increase trade and counter Russian aggression. Palmerston had forced Turkey to relinquish monopolies and accept free trade between 1838 and 1841, expanding trade and agricultural production. The same policy was followed in Egypt. Trade, prosperity and enlightenment would march hand-in-hand. British and Greek merchants did grow Turkish and Egyptian trade but Ottoman conservatism, antique administrations alien to enterprise and good governance and Russian intrigue blocked reform,[12] while in 1875 Britain found Egypt's financial system extravagant, corrupt and wasteful. Both went bankrupt in 1876. Meanwhile, the 1878 Treaty of San Stefano created a large Bulgaria and gave Batumi to Russia. Odesa and other Russian ports prospered. Turkish ports remained undeveloped. Rostov exported grain. Novorossiysk, founded in the 1830s, rapidly became a major export centre. Batumi soon eclipsed Trabzon and railways revived Kherson and Nikolaev. Between 1850 and 1900 their population grew three-fold, Odesa's six-fold and Rostov's ten-fold.[13]

Frustrated by continued Turkish decline and Russian aggression, Disraeli thought Russian expansion to Istanbul threatened Egypt, thus Russia was the key to India, not Egypt and the Suez Canal,' dismissing as 'moonshine' the idea of occupying Egypt. Cyprus, 'the key of western Asia' thought Disraeli, was occupied in 1878, as a precaution.[14] After Egypt's bankruptcy, Anglo-French control tried imposing financial discipline. That led to a revolt under army officer Urabi Pasha. By 1881, 2,250 ships out of 2,727 transiting Suez were British. Thus, strategic emphasis moved to the Canal. Gladstone told Parliament, 'for India, the Suez Canal is the connecting link' and 'the great question of British interest,' because, as Dilke explained in 1882, '82% of the trade passing through the Canal is British…[and] the Canal is the principal highway to India, Ceylon, the Straits and British Burma where 250 million people live under our rule and also in China where we have vast interests and 84% of the external trade of that still more enormous empire…[and] one of the roads to…Australia and New Zealand.'[15]

Chinese opium imports, mainly from India, peaked around 13 million lbs in 1879,[16] worth £10 million annually in the 1880s compared to £3 million Lancashire cottons. As early as 1830, 700 indigo factories in Bengal and Bihar supplied Britain with blue dye. Indian and Ceylonese tea and rubber plantations were developed for export to Britain, by 1887 employing about 500,000 in India. Burma became the world's leading rice exporter due to British-financed infrastructure. Following Siam's 1855 Treaty with Britain, Bangkok became a major rice exporter, growing 856-fold between the 1850s and 1913, mainly to Malaya and China.[17] In the 1880s Britain had about 20% of its overseas investments in India, which took about 19% of British exports and was key to other Asian trade. Growing trade revenue paid for the 250,000-man Indian Army, used to clear obstructions to other trade or potential trade areas.[18]

Britain took 80% of Egypt's exports, mainly cotton, and 44% of Egypt's imports were British.[19] British investors held the largest share of Egypt's government bonds and loans for harbour and railway projects. In 1878, trade valued at £91 million passed the Cape, £65 million through the Canal,[20] but increasing steamship use meant 1880s Suez trade exceeded Cape trade in value <u>and</u> volume. Egyptian misgovernment however, continued. An 1882 Anglo-French bombardment of Alexandria after 50 Europeans and 250 Egyptians were killed failed to solve the problem. Urabi declared *jihad* on the British. The Khedive fled, anarchy threatened, endangering the Canal. Pressed by financiers, bond holders and other commercial interests, Prime Minister Salisbury ordered occupation to prevent chaos. Consul General Sir Evelyn Baring was tasked to solve Egypt's finances. Envisaged as temporary occupation, it turned permanent as Baring warned that solvency would take time and quick withdrawal would lead to anarchy. Evacuation was therefore impossible. Britain had to protect the Canal. In the general disorder, Egypt's power in Sudan collapsed as Mahdist forces took control. General Gordon, sent to deal with it <u>and</u> end slavery, still a British moral imperative, was killed. Restoration of order however, had to wait.

Chapter 31

The Two-Way Boom. Old World Emigration. New World Food and Wool

This chapter concentrates mainly on emigrants, merchant ships, food and wool import numbers. Chapters 34 and 35 examine the shipping logistics involved. Corn Law Repeal did not immediately result in cheaper grain, mainly due to the Crimean and US Civil War. Britain imported 2% of its grain in the 1830s, 24% by the 1860s, 45% in the 1880s, 80% by 1913 because British wheat production peaked in 1845, the next highest in 1864, declining thereafter.[1] Grain prices plummeted after 1876 because of huge imports from the New World, Black Sea, mainly Odesa, and Baltic, mainly Cronstadt, St. Petersburg's port. Pre-Crimean War, Britain's most valuable Black Sea imports were tallow, flax, linseed oil and timber, after, grain; 123 shipments averaging 205 tons in 1853 and 290 averaging 334 tons in 1855,[2] giving opportunities to Greek shipowners. Exports to France and Italy grew about 25% in the 1840s-1850s, to Britain 700%![3]

However, Britain's main wheat supplier after 1837 was America, surging during the Crimean War to around 100,000 tons until around 1860,[4] increasingly from Chicago, via the Erie Canal and New York. After 1857 bulk grain replaced sacks, loaded by steam-powered bucket chains into ship's holds, increasing efficiency and volume. Canadian exports became significant from the 1850s-1860s. Californian wheat was exported to Britain in about 500 iron-hulled sailing ships annually, about a million tons, peaking in the 1880s.[5] British manufactured goods and capital returned. Five banks opened in San Francisco during the Civil War and by 1891, over 20 British marine insurance companies.

Britain's meat arrived live for slaughter from Ireland on steamships, Scotland on railways and from the 1850s the Low Countries, sharply increasing in the 1860s. US exports of cured meats, salt beef, bacon and salt pork to Britain, 20,000 tons in 1860, reached 400,000 tons in the 1870s, as New England meatpacker Gustavus Swift moved to Chicago and improved refrigerated railcars, cutting costs by 80% over live animals. Chicago's 1870s-1880s meatpacking centralisation made meat cheaper and shipping space was saved. All efficiencies and economies of scale lowered prices. Migrants and capital poured out of Britain. Food poured in from America, Russia, Australia, New Zealand and Canada.

Irish emigration accelerated from 20,000 in 1843, with the potato blight 105,000 in 1847 and with its aftermath 220,000 in 1851; an 1847–1855 total of 1,187,000, compared with 919,000 Germans.[6] To meet Irish demand Inman and Cunard began calling at Irish ports. Thereafter Liverpool handled over 60% of 1850–1874 British emigration. London was next biggest and main port for Australia, then Glasgow, then Southampton.[7] The 1855 Passenger Act specified minimum rations, space and sanitation. Fierce competition meant prices fell. In 1825 a Liverpool-US ticket cost £20. In 1863 steamships asked £4.15, mid-century sailing ships only £3.00.[8] By 1870 virtually all US and Canadian immigrants went by steamship, the voyage seven to ten days and by the 1890s, third class cabins started replacing steerage. Between 1850 and 1914, Europe's population increased from 266 million to 450 million, 70% in 64 years, despite increasing emigration, which between 1800 and 1840 was a million, 1840–1914, 35 million; 29 million to America alone, enabled by improving steamships' efficiency and safety.

Twelve million Britons emigrated between 1815 and 1890, mainly to America, four million to Canada, 2.5 million after 1880. By 1900 two thirds of the English-speaking world lived outside Britain. By the 1880s most Germans left from Hamburg and Bremen on German lines, other Europeans from Antwerp and Le Havre. East Europeans replaced Germans in Liverpool, especially Jews after Russian 1881–82 pogroms. British merchant ships totalled 1,876,000 nrt in 1850, 4,684,000 in 1870 and 12,168,000 in 1880: explosive growth. Latin American immigration, meagre before 1850, surged strongly from 1871 to 1914. From 1894 to 1900, a million Italians left for the New World, 2.5 million from 1900 to 1907. In the 1880s Irish emigration was 141.7/thousand, Norway's 95.2/thousand and between 1900 and 1910 Italy's, 107.7/thousand. This favourably affected European wages. Britain's 1870 wages were 60% of America's, Irish 44% and Norwegian 26%. British wages rose 43% to 1913, Irish wages from 73% of British wages to 92% and Norway's from 48% to 95%.[9]

Railroads opening-up America's west enabled high-volume food exports, with mid-western population growth explosive. Chicago's population tripled in the 1850s, again in the 1860s, 80% in the 1870s, doubled in the 1880s and by 1890 it was 1.1 million. By 1890, 25% of British meat imports were from America.[10] Mid-western farmers depended on Britain's market and Britain on American food, supplemented in the 1850s by Canadian and Australian wheat. America sent 40,000 tons of cheese and butter in 1863–64, over 75% of its cheese output and from the 1870s Canada sent cheese, bacon and livestock. In the 1870s Canada's beef, cheese and bacon replaced timber as its main export by value, cheese its leading export in the 1890s, over 100,000 tons in 1903, displacing US cheese from the 1880s. In 1877 Canada shipped 20,000 live cattle to Britain, 315,000 in 1920.[11] Pork product exports rocketed from half a million lbs in 1909 to 51 million in 1910 and 254 million in 1919. 1860s-1890 freight rates declined 50%-75% due to larger ships and better engines, enabling North America to compete with closer but inefficient Russian serf-grown grain. In 1910 America sent 400,000 tons of beef to Britain. British meat imports increased five-fold between 1870 and 1900, improving diets of all classes. By 1914 almost 40% of British meat consumption was imported.

Britain's 3,750 tons of wool imports in 1800, rose to 14,419 in 1830, most from Germany and Spain, to 66,250 in 1860, 26,400 from Australia. As mass-market carpets created new demand, by 1886 Australia's rose to 179,169 tons out of 266,294,[12] first on clippers, by 1890 on iron-hulled sailing ships and steamships about equally. In 1851 a million tons of ships traded in Australia, 40 years later 16.2 million, the freight to Britain about the same as Scotland to London 100 years earlier.

South African wool exports, 2,700 tons in 1850 rose to 11,000 in 1860, 22,000 in 1875, enabled by regular steamships from the 1850s. In 1862, 1,140 ships of 386,000 tons called at Cape Town and Durban. Between 1873 and 1883 manufactured goods and about 25,000 immigrants were discharged, and wool loaded. Imports rose from £2.5 million in 1871 to £9.3 million in 1882. Durban's 1890–1904 population tripled to 64,000 and Cape Town's doubled to 170,000. Australia's first refrigerated meat arrived in Britain in 1880 when its two million people had 65 million sheep and eight million cattle. Meat export values rocketed from £200,000 in 1890 to £2.2 million in 1900, £13.2 million in 1913. Between 1870 and 1900 Britain's frozen meat imports increased five-fold, enriching the poor's diet.[13] Australia diversified into dried fruit, canned meat, about 10,000 tons in 1883, metals and sugar from the 1920s.

As wheat imports surged, British prices fell under 47 shillings in 1878, 31 shillings in 1886 and 27 shillings in the late-1890s, British farm workers migrated to cities or emigrated. In the 1870s over 50% of Britain's grain imports came from North America, 70% by 1900.[14] The US imported more goods and capital than exports until 1873, New Zealand until 1886, Australia until 1891 and Canada until 1913, as new agricultural lands opened.[15] Erie Canal volumes peaked in 1885, value falling from the 1850s as railroads took high-value goods.[16]

After about 1900, America's larger population and higher living standards absorbed more produce. Dominion food exports gradually replaced it; their main business feeding Britain! Australia supplied 20.8% of British butter imports in 1913 and 51% in 1925. New Zealand overtook Canada as Britain's main cheese supplier in the 1900s. Between 1880 and 1916 Britain imported 225 million frozen mutton and lambs, 150 million from Australia and New Zealand, 70 million from South America, mainly Argentina. By 1914 Dominions supplied almost half Britain's wheat imports, 82% of its cheese and 75% of its mutton and lamb.[17] Between 1910 and 1912, 60% of all settler colony exports went to Britain, which imported over 80% of their wheat and 45% of their dairy and meat products; an outsourcing of basic food supply unique in history.[18]

After ending slavery, Brazil lowered customs duties and encouraged British capital. In 1914 four-times as much was invested in Brazil than America, 1.5-times more than other foreign capital. British ships carried 40% of its coffee exports, mostly to America. British banks held 30% of Brazil's banking assets. It was Britain's largest South American market until about 1880. Argentina and Chile had small populations, poor communications and political instability. Argentina's post-1860s British-financed railways however, made a huge impact, enabling wheat exports of four million bushels in 1884, by 1890, 59 million, by 1900, 71 million and by 1913, 103 million.[19] Ronald Hyam thinks by 1880, Argentina's grain, mutton and beef more important to Britain's economy than Egypt, China or Canada.[20] Capital, business and skilled workers poured in; a world economic wonder. Buenos Aires grew from 30,000 people in 1880 to 1.3 million in 1910.

Danish 1850–1870 butter and cheese exports to Britain tripled and in 1882 a group of dairy farmers organised a cooperative to buy milk-separating machinery to sell cream and butter. Success led to 500 more. Similarly in 1887 a group of Jutland pig farmers built a meatpacking plant with government assistance. Denmark's 442,000 pigs in 1871 grew to 2.5 million by 1914: pork and bacon exports from 11 million lbs to 300 million and by the 1930s, 731 million, almost half the world's pork trade. Instead of tariff protection, Denmark's enlightened government gave targeted loans for factories, equipment and vehicles.[21]

Between 1865 and 1913, while Europe's wheat imports more than tripled, Germany and France increased wheat production about 1.5-times, protecting agricultural interests. India exported 80 million bushels in 1905,[22] planned and organised by British and Indian interests who saw exchanging British manufactures and Indian raw materials as mutually beneficial, first cotton then wheat, dependent on railway expansion from 1855 between agricultural areas and Bombay, Calcutta and Karachi, progressive, enlightened <u>commercial</u> interests contrasting with <u>official</u> post-Mutiny distrust.

Chapter 32

The British-Driven Shipping Market

In 1859 manufacturing interests asked Palmerston to send Cobden to persuade Napoleon III to reduce Anglo-French tariffs. France's cotton industry wanted protection from British cloth, but its wine, silk and furniture producers supported lower tariffs. The 1860 Cobden-Chevalier Treaty slashed them. Chevalier, Professor of Political Economy and National Assembly deputy, earlier described Britain's free trade policy as 'one of the greatest events of the century. When such a powerful and <u>enlightened</u> nation not only puts such a great principle into practice…and known to have profited by it, how can its emulators fail to follow?'[1] French tariffs on coal and most manufactured goods were reduced to under 30%, some to 10–15% after 1865, dramatic but nowhere near British reforms. 1859–1869 British export values to France and French wines to Britain doubled.[2] Gladstone in 1860 reduced the number of import duties from 419 to 48. Between 1860 and 1875 duties on sugar, timber, paper and some minor items were abolished. After 1875 tobacco, tea, spirits and wine duties accounted for 95% of customs revenue, produced in Britain, purely for revenue. France still had hundreds of tariffs, but reductions were positive. Italy, Switzerland, Norway, Spain, Austria, Bremen and Hamburg followed. Tariffs as high as 50% fell. Some disappeared.

* * *

Until 1860 steamships were mainly passenger, mail or liner ships, advertising a port schedule for numerous small-volume cargoes. Tramp shipowners by contrast advertised their ship to cargo owners or traders to charter it from port to port or for a fixed period. Most long-haul, bulk tramps were sailing ships. Tyne and South Wales' coal were the usual outbound cargoes, Britain the world's main supplier, 1.4 million tons in 1840 to 49.3 million in 1887, much more than grain.[3] Chilean copper, wheat, fertilisers like nitrate of soda, saltpetre and Peru's guano were major homebound cargoes. As late as 1880, 73% of Britain's merchant fleet was tramp sailing ships, most only embracing steam thereafter due to improved engines. From 1861, petroleum in barrels was exported from Philadelphia. Cattle and frozen meat trades took-off from the 1870s-1880s. Mutton was easily frozen but not beef, so live cattle were shipped until the late-1890s. However, chilled beef at 30–32 degrees Fahrenheit retained quality on arrival.

Marine cables transformed shipping's development. They reached Paris in 1851, New York in 1866, Bombay in 1870 and Sydney in 1876. Cables were expensive, $1.25 a word in the 1860s and although trans-Atlantic message costs fell to 0.5% of the 1866 price, other areas were high until the 1890s, when a shipping clerk's annual wage was about $100 and the world's cable network complete. Clarksons' 1869 accounts show it spent more on telegrams than wages, so Baltic Exchange face-to-face negotiations, terms cabled as little as possible, were vital. In 1860 it had 760 members, 1,164 in 1873, including many Scandinavians, Greeks, Maltese and Italians.[4]

Baltic Exchange brokers centralised international shipping in London. Clarksons' Henry Benham travelled to Italy, France, Germany and Norway, learning each language. In the early-1860s it had Norwegian, American, English and Italian departments, the latter headed by an Italian. Charles Northcote and W.S. Lindsey formed joint ventures with Norwegian and Swedish owners, establishing favoured broking positions. Competing, Clarksons bought shares in Norwegian, then other ships, for exclusive broking rights. By 1873 it had interests in 114 ships from Italy, Germany, Norway, Sweden, Britain and America and a significant insurance department.[5] It and Galbraith, Stringer and Pembroke hired Norwegians. Clarksons invited sons of shipping families to spend a training year or two with them, known as 'Clarksons College' in Norway, enhancing business relationships. Expanding with German, Norwegian, Swedish, Finnish and steam departments, it was among many growing shipbrokers. Gunder Aas headed its Norwegian department, corresponding with Norwegian owners in Norwegian until the 1890s.[6]

Norway's 1.4 million people in 1850 were over-represented in shipping. Most lived on the coast, used the sea for transport, exporting timber and fish and importing grain and salt. British free trade, Navigation Act repeal, the telegraph, mass manufacturing and railways enabled Norway's shipping growth. By 1875 it had 8.5% of the world fleet. Thomas Fearnley in 1864 went to London's Rucker, Offor and Co., cultivating Norwegian shipowners before returning to Christiania (Oslo) to act as broker/agent, taking shares in ships giving him exclusive chartering rights and was joined by others, the start of Fearnley and Eger, a leading Norwegian broker, taking advantage of the North Sea telegraph from 1872, working with Gunder Aas and others. In 1871–1875, 88% of its business was timber, 44% to Britain, 12% to France, 10% to Holland, gradually diversifying into wood pulp and coal.[7]

Despite London's service centralisation, Glasgow and Liverpool were major shipowning centres and at Liverpool's Exchange, an 1870s visitor watched 'a crowd of merchants and brokers…like a hive of bees…with the latest telegrams, notices of London stock and share lists, cargoes, freights, sales, outbound and homebound ships, times of sailings, state of wind and weather:' a world of metal merchants, commodity brokers, underwriters and bankers.[8] A 1907 Liverpool history boasted it was among the world's three or four great ports, handling 25% of British imports, owning a third of British shipping, a seventh of the world's, overseeing 34% of British trade in 1913, signs of invincible virility.

Glasgow hosted City, Anchor, Albion, Glen and Clan Lines, the British Isles Steam Navigation Company, British and African Steam Navigation Co., Clyde Screw Steam Packet Co., and J&J Denholm, which by 1882 owned 12 wooden sailing ships, mainly trading to the Caribbean, gradually replacing them with steel-hulled steamships. Liverpool was home to African Steamship, Blue Funnel, Lamport and Holt, Blue Star, Bibby, White Star, Castle Line and Australian Navigation, among others. Solicitor Ralph

Ward Jackson aimed to build in West Hartlepool an east coast rival to Liverpool. Coal Dock was opened in 1847, Jackson and Swainson Docks in 1852, attracting capital and businesses, when coal demand seemed insatiable. Strong demand for pit props ensued, Baltic imports. Timber merchants imported props. Coal merchants shipped worldwide, including the Baltic. By 1860 West Hartlepool had thriving shipyards, iron works, foundries, rope, paint and cement works from chalk brought back as ballast. Foundries supplying anchors, cables and brass products opened. In 1854 its trade value exceeded Newcastle's.[9] Jackson's West Hartlepool Steam Navigation Co. soon took advantage of Baltic trades in Hamburg, Gothenburg and Cronstadt. By 1867 it had four 450–600-ton compound engine ships and five in Queen Line. Furness Line was also established there in 1877. Walter Runciman's 1889 South Shields Shipping Company, moved to Newcastle in 1897, changing its name to Moor Line.

A brief representative description of a much larger suite of shipping companies shows a huge range of trades, backgrounds and experience. Robert MacAndrews and Co. was founded in 1853 as shipbrokers and shipowners, a family tradition dating from 1770 when William MacAndrews started in Liverpool selling Spanish fruit, imported in small schooners. It bought its first steamship in 1857 and by 1900 had 30, mostly Spanish-flagged. Union Steam Collier Co. was started by P&O's Arthur Anderson bringing coal from South Wales to meet Southampton's needs. Renamed Union Steamship Co., it won the mail contract to Cape Colony and Natal in 1857. From 1852 Donald Currie's Castle Line competed. He built sailing ships, operating from Liverpool and London via the Cape to Calcutta, carrying emigrants to South Africa, from 1871 in steamships, which bought George Payne's Cape and Natal Line, carrying unsubsidised mail. It charged a third the price of official mail but without guaranteed sailing and arrival dates. Calcutta was phased-out and new ships achieved shorter times. The government contracted with Castle and Union Line, which merged at the century's end. Lamport and Holt, founded in 1845, traded to India and South Africa but specialised in South America, especially River Plate, carried mail for British and Belgian governments, operated coastal services for Brazil's government and carried frozen meat and coffee. T&J Harrison (from 1853) imported brandy and wine from Tonnay-Charente, boosted by Cobden-Chevalier's reduced duties on French wine and spirits and British coal. It encouraged them to buy two steamships for that and larger sailing ships for India and Caribbean trade, also replaced with steamships after the Suez Canal opened.

Two industrious shipping clerks, Shaw and Savill in 1859, chartered and bought mainly iron-hulled sailing ships for New Zealand's emigrant trade, gunpowder in lower holds, emigrants on tweendecks in hammocks or cabins, successful enough to buy, 25 years later, Albion Shipping Co. Despite the 1852 emigrant clipper's 68-day voyage to Melbourne, New Zealand on slower ships could take 120 days or more. If unlucky with winds and sea states, provisions could run low. A passenger on a 150-day 1879 voyage recalled, exceptionally it must be stressed, the galley producing rat pie,[10] but by 1890 with triple expansion engines, ships sailed to New Zealand without coal replenishment. Return cargoes were initially difficult to source, but typically hides, wool, Newcastle NSW coal to Chile's coaling stations then Chilean nitrates to Britain.

For the brave, there were opportunities aplenty. The shipping industry was driven by Britain; shipbuilding, coal export, steamship design, proliferation of lines, emigration, the 13 Passenger Acts from 1803 to 1870, gradually tightening regulations covering on-board conditions, the sheer volume of imports, exports and shipping services; arbitration, shipbroking and insurance.

*   *   *

Antwerp, neutered as a port since 1648 with the Scheldt's closure to navigation[11] was opened after long negotiation in 1863, beginning its modern growth. Rumanian ports were developed after 1878 independence, the Black Sea's second-largest grain exporter with 30–40%, the fastest growing Black Sea region with Azov and the Caucasus. The 1883 trans-Caucasian railway made Novorossiysk an important grain, oil and cement port. Batumi, acquired from Turkey, grew due to Baku's oil exports, 500,000 barrels in 1873, four million in the early-1880s, dominated by Robert Nobel, brother of Alfred, famous for dynamite and prizes, prompting Rothschild to set-up there, a third the size of Rockefeller's Standard Oil.

In 1888 Rothschild and Nobel established shipping companies in London and developed tankers, the first a Tyne-built sailing ship in 1863. Marcus Samuels' company, Shell, shipped oil through the Suez Canal to India, China and Japan in the 1890s. By 1885 over 1,000 mainly sailing ships carried US oil to Europe. By the mid-1890s most US oil was carried in steamships. Rockefeller, alarmed by Rothschild's erosion of his near-monopoly tried playing the anti-Semitic card, warning of 'Hebrew influence', which *The Economist*, reflecting British tolerance, cautioned 'should [not] count against it.'[12] Almost 80, 200–400-ton tankers operated from the Black Sea and US to Europe by 1891. Royal Dutch, a Dutch Southeast Asia-based competitor, became close with Shell and merged. By 1908 Anglo-Persian Oil also discovered large Middle East reserves and was the main shareholder in Burmah Oil, established to export Burmese reserves. The *Anastasia's* trading history demonstrates oil's early impact; 1881–83 Black Sea grain to Britain, backhauling Cardiff/Swansea coal to Syros and Smyrna, two temporary lay-ups with intermediate inter-Mediterranean-Black Sea trades, then 1894–1896 Batumi-Alexandria consecutive voyages with oil.

Denmark's Mads Christian Holm was employed by a Jutland shipbuilder, then as a ship's carpenter. After a voyage to Boston, he got a shipyard job in 1847. During California's gold rush he joined a San Francisco-bound ship, made money building houses, invested in a new Oakland shipyard in 1854, before returning to Denmark. In 1871, he invited others to share in a 1,000-ton Clyde-built iron steamship, the *Norden* for Baltic cargoes. Her first voyage carried coal to Copenhagen, then Russian wheat, oilcakes, rye and flax to Antwerp, then to the eastern Mediterranean, took wheat from Taganrog to Bristol, two voyages from Archangel with oats and linseed to Britain, then a three-month charter via Brazil and the River Plate, three years later through the Suez Canal to Hong Kong and Shanghai, two years in regional trades before returning with NSW coal to Suez and Rangoon rice to London. In 1880 it took a Russian government cargo from Cronstadt to Vladivostok, spending another year in regional trades. This abbreviated history of one ship shows the widening horizons that submarine cables, steamships, burgeoning trade volumes and Suez Canal offered enterprising young men.[13]

Another was Prussian-born Robert Ropner. Deciding to emigrate to Australia, he arrived as first stop at booming West Hartlepool in 1857. Finding employment with Appleby's, exporting coal, he launched a steamship in 1868 jointly with Appleby, the first of a significant fleet, forming Ropner Shipping Co. in 1874. In 1888 he bought Stockton Shipyard. Cardiff and London offices gave easier access to outbound coal and in-bound Black Sea grain cargoes, traded on the Baltic Exchange. With a profitable fleet, he kept buying!

*   *   *

Wooden ships tended to be repaired and sold-on. In competitive, often low markets, ships were usually loaded full, sometimes dangerously so, especially tempting on short-haul voyages. Despite *Lloyds Register*'s 1835 load-line guidance of three inches of freeboard per foot of hold depth, some owners disregarded it and over-insured their ship and cargo, knowing that if it sank, they would profit. The 1850 Merchant Shipping Act was the culmination of government realisation and enlightenment that it must ensure safety of life and property at sea, establishing the Marine Department within the Board of Trade, certifying masters and mates, gradually increasing responsibility over dangerous cargoes, seaworthiness and seamen's welfare, applicable to ships in British ports; thus, felt worldwide.[14] But marine casualties grew, some due to overloading and/ or unseaworthiness. Samuel Plimsoll, elected to Parliament in 1865 on an enlightened platform; franchise extension, secret ballots, financial reform, unrestricted free trade, repeal of the game laws and abolition of religious tests, from 1868 campaigned for safer ships, 'those in peril on the sea,' against unseaworthy ships and greedy, unscrupulous shipowners. James Hall of shipbuilder/shipowner Palmer and Hall fought for load-line legislation. Plimsoll gave public and Parliamentary expression to his expertise. In 1871 the Board of Trade recorded 856 British merchant ships lost within ten miles of the coast in strong breezes and another 149 in moderate gales that should not have affected seaworthy ships. Between 1861 and 1870, 5,826 ships were wrecked close to the British coast with 8,105 deaths. Further out, half the 17,086 wrecks occurred in fine weather. Despite increasing lighthouses and buoys, deaths were higher than in other occupations.[15]

Everyone knew sea travel's dangers. The 1818 British and Foreign Sailors Society, formed to cater for sailors and families, was followed in 1824 by the Royal National Institute for the Preservation of Life from Shipwreck and the Royal National Lifeboat Institution, the 1827 Destitute Sailors Asylum, the 1830 London Sailors Home, the 1839 Shipwrecked Fishermen's and Mariner's Royal Benevolent Society, the 1856 Mission to Seamen and the 1860s Society for Improving Conditions of Merchant Seamen, which reported to the Board of Trade in 1867 that life expectancy 'does not extend beyond the forty-fifth or perhaps even the fortieth year' because of being 'broken down in health soon after the age of thirty-five.'[16] Victualing, accommodation, bathing and toilet standards were especially criticised.

The 1871 Merchant Shipping Act made the Board of Trade responsible for detaining suspected unseaworthy ships. Five crew members could detain it but were liable for costs if surveyors found them mistaken, deterring many. An 1873 Act gave the Board power to survey ships suspected of defect or overloading. Its surveyors detained 440 ships in the first year, only 16 of which were allowed to sail. But not all ships had to be surveyed. An 1866 Board of Trade enquiry into the *London* recommended a load-line, but subsequent Parliamentary questions revealed the difficulty of adopting 'any general rule applicable to all ships.' Thus, the government did not follow up.[17]

There was a chasm between the best and worst owners. Cunard's motto had been 'safety first, profit second.' Aberdeen-based George Thompson lost only one ship out of 22 over 30 years. He named a three-masted iron clipper for Australian emigrants *Samuel Plimsoll.* Cunard's head, John Burnes was supportive and Liverpool steamship owner David MacIvor wrote to *The Times* attacking the 1871 and 1873 Merchant Shipping Acts as inadequate. He later said of Plimsoll, 'Many vessels have been lost which ought not to have been lost…Mr. Plimsoll compelled attention to the subject… he has unhappily been right.'[18] Holts, Bibby, Cunard, White Star, P&O, the main lines, especially passenger lines were enlightened regarding maritime safety. But the 1873 Royal Commission found W.J. Fernie's Merchant Trading Co., owning 73 ships in ten years, had lost 18 due to unseaworthiness, coal catching fire and overloading, highlighted by seamen's anxious letters to families before sailing. By contrast, ex-merchant seaman George Reid working for guano charterer, Gibbs and Co., did not charter ships without surveys and load-lines. In 1873, there were 12 Liberal and six Conservative shipowner MPs. Plimsoll took special aim at Liverpool's Edward Bates and Sons, whose old steamers, converted to sail, had a terrible record of ship losses and crews incurring scurvy.[19]

Greed, highlighted by Plimsoll, should not however be over-emphasised. Ship development was fast, technical problems often discovered only after accidents and enquiries. Iron ships threw magnetic compasses off-course until remedied in the 1870s. Double bottoms built for extra strength and safety, raised the centre of gravity, increasing instability, which some thought one of the main causes of iron ship accidents. In 1863, 20 countries, led by Britain, agreed 'Rules for the Avoidance of Collision at Sea.'

Plimsoll's campaign mirrored anti-slave trade and anti-Corn Law campaigns, meetings throughout Britain with prominent supporters like Florence Nightingale. *The Times* in 1873 wondered why 'seaworthiness of vessels carrying passengers or even government stores, [had]…a most careful supervision…[but] over…merchantmen, none…With just a little thought some measure could be framed.' While the Royal Commission deliberated, Plimsoll forced a division, only losing 173–170. *Punch* thought to lose so narrowly when MPs awaited the report, 'was to carry it. The House, like the country, has made up its mind against toleration of floating coffins.'[20] Yet the Commission recommended no change. Why?

An enlightened idea was laws not being unduly prescriptive. Disraeli on a different subject in 1875 said, 'permissive legislation is the characteristic of a free people. It is easy to adopt compulsory legislation when you have to deal with those who only exist to obey. But in a free country and especially…England you must trust to persuasion and example.' John Glover, shipbroker and new shipowner in 1873 published a pamphlet, *The Plimsoll Sensation. A Reply*, arguing it was already illegal to send unseaworthy ships to sea and that existing laws should be enforced. When the 1912 *Titanic Enquiry* pointed to inadequate lifeboat numbers, Joseph Conrad wrote, 'It is the same psychology which…before Samuel Plimsoll uplifted his voice, sent overloaded ships to sea. 'Why shouldn't we cram in as much cargo as our ships will hold? Look how few, how very few of them, get lost." Newspapers reflected public support for Plimsoll, whose campaign seems to have led the Board of Trade to be more diligent in surveillance of potentially unseaworthy ships. More cases were revealed.[21]

The *Alcedo's* owner knew his ship was unseaworthy but insured and sailed it. He was fined and imprisoned, proving that existing laws could work, but fuelled public anger. Newcastle's Davidson and Charleton thought Plimsoll 'bigoted and prejudiced' but did not 'defend every individual shipowner.' The movement changed the way society thought about seamen, from rough, drunk, frequenters of brothels, to family men trying to support families. The Earl of Shaftesbury noted that philanthropic legislation 'extended to miners, colliers…factory children and to emigrant ships', but not yet to sailors.[22]

Plimsoll also wanted grain cargo regulations to eliminate dangerous stowing and shifting cargoes, deck loading regulations and compulsory ship surveys. The 1875 government bill, heavily amended with many of Plimsoll's demands, still gave owners the right to put load-lines where they liked. But it was progress, prohibiting bulk grain to be over a third of the cargo, officers appointed who could detain unsafe ships, a quarter of the crew had the right to get the ship surveyed and it became a misdemeanour to send or attempt to send unseaworthy ships to sea. Public pressure forced an 1876 bill for compulsory surveys and a government load-line, defeated because British ships might become uncompetitive. Plimsoll replied that Canadians issued certificates and deck loading had been banned in 1839 and, he thought, unjustly repealed in 1862. The 1876 bill allowed deck loading to three feet, gave further safeguards to seamen's welfare, forbade loose grain loading and winter timber deck cargoes, allowed detention of unsafe ships and made load-lines compulsory, although still where owners wanted.

Plimsoll thought if 'zealously and faithfully administered' it 'will be found to remedy the evils which affect our sea-going population,'[23] retiring from Parliament in 1880. When Joseph Chamberlain became President of the Board of Trade, he made further progress; the 1880 Act for the Safe Carriage of Grain Cargoes, the 1882 tables of freeboards as overloading guidance, the 1884 Act preventing ships' over-insurance and in 1885 compulsory load-lines for different ship types and sizes, which the Board of Trade regulated in 1890. Foreign ships leaving British ports were required to bear the same load-lines, encouraging international standardisation, although Germany only made it compulsory in 1908, France 1909, Holland 1910, America in 1917. The 1906 Merchant Shipping Act recognised the need for seasonal load-lines. Only in 1930 did 30 countries sign a convention for a fixed Plimsoll Line. Only in 1935 did America necessitate it for protected domestic trade.[24] Other safety measures were implemented. In 1916 every passenger ship over 3,000 tons had to have a wireless and direction-finding equipment.

* * *

Accelerating trade led to further improvements and efficiency gains in London. Millwall Docks opened in 1868 with the first pneumatic grain discharge system into a 24,000-ton granary. The 1884 Royal Albert Dock was an extension of Victoria Dock, its entrance too narrow for the largest ships. Designed for 12,000-tonners, over 16,400 feet of quays handled mainly grain, chilled and frozen meat, tobacco and generals with single-story transit sheds rather than warehouses for fast turnaround. Tilbury Dock, 25 miles downriver, was opened in 1886.

Manchester's business community, unhappy with dependence on Liverpool, sometimes found it cheaper to import goods via Hull. In the 1870s they proposed a canal from the Mersey to avoid Liverpool's dock dues and railway costs. The 1885 Manchester Ship Canal Act led to its eventual opening in 1891, fully in 1894, the world's eighth-longest ship canal, enabling Manchester to become Britain's fourth-busiest import port by 1903.[25] It was never the commercial success its sponsors hoped because sailing up a long canal lost valuable time and Liverpool's commercial expertise understood where to pitch rates. Northeast shipowner and merchant James Knott's Prince Steam Ship Co. however, supported it, importing Egyptian cotton, returning with manufactured goods. Sunderland's Pinkney family's Neptune Steam Navigation Co. secured America's first cotton directly to Manchester, tapping northwest investors and in 1898 Christopher Furness started Manchester Liners. Trafford Park became Europe's largest industrial estate, its 1898 grain silo, Europe's largest.

Chapter 33

The Scramble for Africa

Gladstone's government had no territorial ambitions. Britain's West African anti-slave enclaves might one day be commercially worthwhile. South Africa, which up to the 1870s had little trade or revenue, was held for the same reasons as Egypt, to protect the route to India. Discovery of Transvaal's huge gold deposits in 1886 led to large-scale immigration and a railway boom. Capital flowed in, mainly British. By 1890–91 it produced 25% of the world's gold. France however, still seeking *gloire*, wanted an African and Indo-China empire. Displeased by British actions in Egypt, where it had enjoyed the Khedive's favour, it occupied Tunisia in 1881.

Britain still hoped Turkey would guard the Bosporus against Russia. Prussia's defeat of Denmark, Austria and France made the new German state another major European continentalist power with global territorial ambitions. In 1886 Chancellor of the Exchequer Randolph Churchill told Germany's ambassador that Britain would 'never give up India and…stay in Egypt for a long time.'[1] As all powers increased their navies, Britain feared simultaneous war with Russia and France. Baring, reflecting mid-century optimism that free trade, good governance and reform would improve peasant conditions, did not want to return Egyptians 'to a corrupt and incompetent class of native leaders.'[2] That meant eliminating corruption, establishing revenue surpluses, reducing taxes, developing agriculture and public works. Achieving near solvency, economic gains were too slow to stop opposition. Africa's diseases, endemic tribal warfare, difficult communications, poor purchasing power and commercial enterprise was, for Britain, no place for costly territorial expansion. But Egyptian occupation, meant as temporary, triggered what became known as the Scramble for Africa.

By 1887 Salisbury concluded that propping-up Turkey as Egypt's defence was defunct. Britain had to occupy Egypt because of the Canal's importance. German interest in East Africa also concerned Britain, which meant up to the Nile's headwaters in Uganda. The 1890 Anglo-German Agreement reflected East Africa as more important than West Africa, because of India, the Canal and the Cape Town-India submarine cable turning at Zanzibar, which supplied two-thirds of the world's ivory.

Britain recognised France's position in Tunisia, Algiers' hinterland to the Upper Niger, Madagascar and West Africa, for recognition of Britain's Zanzibar and Pemba protectorate. Salisbury thought he gave 'a considerable stretch of country…but it is necessary to judge land…by its value.' If Britain got East Africa, then France could have the Sahara![3] Italy, wanting Abyssinia, was persuaded to ignore Sudan. Cecil Rhodes' British South African Company drove into Rhodesia to encircle the newly rich Boer republics, but his Cape to Cairo colonial dream was not British policy. As French and Belgians advanced in central and West Africa, Kimberley asked 'whether these African disputes are really worth taking seriously.' He told France's ambassador they were 'barren deserts or places where white men cannot live'.[4] African partition was therefore driven by Britain's trading interests and inability to find popular, skilful Egyptian collaborators to protect the Suez Canal. Weighing the risks of Turkish decline, the rise of aggressive European powers and distrust of Egyptian fanaticism, British politicians thought first of commercial interests, secondly prestige; France's, Germany's and Italy's, purely land-grabbing prestige.

France had most of Mauritania, Senegal and hinterlands. London and Liverpool merchants pressed the government to prevent French encirclement of their Nigerian, Gambian and Sierra Leone bases. But Indian security was paramount. Liverpool's Chamber of Commerce in 1892 complained that from 1882, Germany and France outstripped Britain. 'The Gambia has dwindled, the Cameroons has been lost, two foreign powers have intervened between Lagos and the Gold Coast…wherever…a preponderance of British trade existed…British interests should have been secured.' But for Salisbury, Gambia and Sierra Leone had barely enough revenues to cover administrative costs. The trade value was not worth it. Cotton, coffee and indigo had been tried and failed. Only on the Niger had effective administration been established.[5] British concern was Mediterranean and Asian trade security. Although trade prospects were better in West Africa, Salisbury concentrated on strategic goals. Kitchener's 1896 Sudan conquest was the climax of protecting Mediterranean-India trade routes.

Spain had invaded Morocco in 1860 and by 1907 it was under French-Spanish control. In 1912 the Sultan agreed a French protectorate. In 1911, Italy landed troops in Tripoli and occupied its ports. Germany had <u>never</u> dealt with the issue of slavery. Apart from Bremen and Hamburg, it remained unenlightened. In German SouthWest Africa colonists stole Herero tribal land, triggering rebellion. The Herero were massacred. Some fled to the desert where between 1904 and 1907 official 'Cleansing Patrols' hunted and killed them, ethnic cleansing, seamlessly carried over to post-1939 colonisation of eastern Europe.

Thus, Britain concentrated on securing two choke points for maritime trade, while France, Germany, Belgium, Italy, Spain and Portugal grabbed territory of dubious value, creating colonial African empires, Belgium's and Germany's ruled with barbaric brutality. Britain, the least land-hungry, had around 35%! Earlier British politicians acted from positions of strength. These were acquired, anxious that dominance was eroding.

Chapter 34

Liner Shipping Competition

Close liner shipowner-shipbuilder relations continued. Harland and Wolff's best initial customer was Liverpool's Bibby's Mediterranean Line; building 20 gradually larger ships.[1] Gustave Shwabe helped Edward Harland's shipbuilding and Thomas Ismay's lines to South America, Australia and New Zealand. Harland and Wolff bought shares in his White Star Line for New York-Liverpool; its first ship launched in 1870. Trans-Atlantic transit records fell to under eight days, and in 1872 the US Post Office gave it a mail contract, at which time only Britain, America, France, Germany and Belgium were industrialised, producing 80% of the world's manufactured goods, British trade worth £547 million, French £227 million.

US Civil War spurred industrial production. Fourth behind Britain, France and Germany in 1865, by 1890 it almost equalled Britain, France and Germany combined! As kerosene, refined from Pennsylvania's oil, took whale oil's market, Clement Griscom exported it in barrels to Britain in 1861. He proposed that J. Edgar Thomson's Pennsylvania Railroad Co., the world's largest company, start Red Star Line to ship it and other products, return with emigrants and rail them west. Its Jarrow-built ships pioneered tanks for bulk oil plus conventional holds, first class cabins and steerage passengers.[2] Intense competition with subsidised French and German lines and Liverpool's faster mail lines left it unprofitable.

Two of Scotland's Henderson brothers started Montreal's Allen Line, which carried Canada's mail with two more in Liverpool. Glasgow's Anchor Line from 1856 ran sailing ships in Mediterranean fruit trades, then steamers to New York, but both lost ships on the dangerous northern Great Circle route. Liverpool's National Line originally conceived as cotton carriers with an independent Confederacy, after 1865 concentrated on large, slow steamships for cotton and emigrants. Profitable and paying dividends, by 1871 it had 12 Mersey-built ships.[3] One of its managers, Stephen Guion founded Guion Line, its first steamer entering New York in 1866. By 1870 he had eight 3,000-tonners.

In 1873 Cunard, Inman, White Star, Guion and National carried over 236,000 passengers. Cunard's 72,600 and Inman's 63,700 led. In the 1870s Cunard, uniquely had an unbroken safety record, but lagged in speed and luxury, until fresh management raised money for large, fast, luxurious ships. Henry Bessemer's 1855 invention lowered steel-making costs. Later improvements reduced them more. By the late-1870s steel was still twice the price of iron but 14% lighter, saving fuel and space.[4] Steel hulls overtook iron around 1880, helping reduce fuel consumption. Steel boilers allowed higher steam pressure, enabling compound engines to maximise effectiveness, ships three-times more powerful than ten years earlier. In 1881 the east-west trip was completed in under seven days by ships with electric lights, before most had them on land.[5] In the 1880s Elders' new Fairfield works employed 7,000 men and introduced triple expansion engines, unbroken progress from Glasgow's branch of Britain's Enlightenment.

French and German lines challenged British trans-Atlantic supremacy by government-subsidy. Pennsylvania Railroad Co. and Standard Oil's International Navigation bought Inman Line, then three more British lines to build twin triple expansion engine, twin-screwed, 20,000-horsepowered 10,500-tonners, monuments to creative engineering, which made New York in under 5.5 days. Forty records were broken between 1884 and 1894 by Clyde builders.

In the 1880s, central and southern Europeans, fleeing poverty and persecution took steamships from Genoa to North and South America on older, smaller ships, many originally from Russian Black Sea ports to Genoa for onward transport. Italians mainly left from Marseilles as Messageries Maritime had the South American mail contract from 1857. As demand increased, Fabre started Naples-New York and Genoa-Montevideo-Buenos Aires services. Bordeaux was France's third emigration port, mainly to Argentina favoured by Spanish and Italians. Greeks also emigrated from the 1880s, mainly from Fiume. Central and southern Europeans constituted only 8% of US immigrants in 1880, but 72% in 1900! In 1880 there were only 20,000 Italians in New York City; by1908, 500,000. In 1889 there were under 500,000 Jews in America. In the next 15 years, 1.5 million entered.[6] Total US immigrants, under 370,000 annually in the 1890s, became over a million in the early-1900s, peaking at 1.3 million in 1907, many on minor lines in overcrowded, older ships.

In contrast to liberal Britain, many Russians visiting the Black Sea were shocked by cosmopolitan ports. An 1891 guidebook reflected prevailing anti-Semitism. 'Unfortunately, Novorossiysk is…far from being completely Russian…and [in]… neighbouring villages, foreign elements, Greeks, Germans, Armenians, Czech-Catholics, usually foreign subjects, are very strong, as are local foreigners.'[7] Ethnic purity was not Black Sea reality. Russia expelled Tartars, Circassians and Chechens. Jews fled frequent pogroms. Escape, even in poor quality ships, seemed the best chance for better lives. Even if official papers allowing legal emigration were obtained, most preferred being smuggled due to untrustworthy officials.[8] Russia was <u>never</u> maritime-orientated, <u>never</u> enlightened, <u>never</u> humanitarian-influenced.

Many European crews had ethnic and religious prejudices, especially against Jews. German lines for a time refused to carry them. Others put them in separate compartments.[9] but facing discrimination, many went via Hull to Liverpool or London. About 100,000 stayed, transforming London's East End and despite some tension, assimilation was complete by 1939. During Russia's 1882 pogroms, Liverpool's Jewish Board of Guardians assisted over 6,000 transit refugees.[10] Most went to America, but a significant minority to South Africa, 1880s passenger numbers rising from around 7,500 annually to about 16,000, triggered by Transvaal's gold, for which between 1891 and 1900 Union Line built 12 passenger ships, Castle Line 24 with generous third and steerage class capacity.

On the Liverpool-New York run, huge improvements in size, power, speed and first-class luxury were seen. German lines' Fairfield and Caird-built ships never matched the size and speed of Liverpool's lines until 1880 when Bremen-America Line's Herman

Maier ordered a 'paragon of strength and speed' at Fairfield.[11] Impressed, Cunard asked for a version. Intense competition in engine and hull design, speed, safety and size were mirrored in luxury and style, almost every new ship lauded as the best so far, the final Fairfield-built ship for North German Lloyd in 1888 a 5,700-tonner for over 1,000 passengers with a further-improved triple expansion engine. It and Hamburg-America Line carried most German emigrants, other Europeans from Antwerp and Le Havre.

Bismarck finally bullied Hamburg and Bremen into the Zollverein and eyeing imperial expansion in Africa and China, Maier was forced to run subsidised German-built mail steamships of specified size and speed; a 'contract for our slavery.' Vulcan was the first German yard to build a major ocean-going steamship. In the 1880s when German emigration accelerated, Jewish ship agent Albert Ballin persuaded Carr Steamship to add emigrant accommodation by economising on first class, enabling cheaper emigrant fares than Hamburg-America or Lloyd, resulting in Hamburg-America buying Carr. Ballin became passenger department head. They built at Lairds, but at Bismarck's urging in 1886, one at Vulcan for a subsidised line to China to assist territorial ambitions. German merchant tonnage overtook American in 1884 and French in 1889. In the 1890s Lloyd became the world's largest steamship company, until Hamburg-America took over.[12]

Germany industrialised fast at government dictat, importing shipbuilding materials duty free. Government railways transported them to shipyards at cost and built harbours and docks. By 1892, Essen's Krupp supplied Fairfield with large steel plates for rudders for two Cunarders that British mills could not. The Institute of Naval Architects held its first meeting in Germany in 1896. Its president thought Britons and Germans 'the two great commercial races of the world', praying it 'remain…friendly and peaceful rivalry.' In 1897 Vulcan launched the 28,000-horsepowered *Kaiser Wilhelm der Grosse* which set trans-Atlantic records, the most innovative liner since Harland's 1870 *Oceanic*; four funnels, six decks for 2,184 crew and passengers. Hamburg-America's 33,000-horsepowered *Deutschland* beat its record in 1900. Shipbuilder Robert Caird thought it 'humiliation' that 'crack German mail steamers are so enormously ahead of our latest and best.'[13]

After the retirement or death of British liner pioneers, Thomson's takeovers were amalgamated in 1892 as America Line. To secure US mail subsidies, he agreed to build two in Philadelphia's Cramp shipyard, the first US-built fast mail steamers since Collins' liners, with 20,000-horsepowered quadruple expansion engines. In 1899, he merged American Steamships with Baltimore's Atlantic Transport Line and in 1901 bought British Leyland Line from Ellerman, acquired on its founder's 1892 death, White Star, the Atlantic's most profitable line and started merger talks with the two German lines. The British, losing industrial supremacy, saw Atlantic shipping also apparently falling to America and Germany. Responding in 1902, Britain's government gave Cunard a large subsidy for two 59,000-horsepowered newbuildings.

With few university engineering opportunities, Charles Parsons, interested in steam engines, studied maths at Dublin and Cambridge and after an engineering apprenticeship, set-up an 1889 company manufacturing dynamos and turbines, later the Marine Steam Turbine Co., running the 44.5-ton model *Turbinia* at the 1897 Grand Naval Review. At over 32 knots it could not be caught. Parsons sold the turbines to

Cunard's two new ships, increased to 68,000-horsepower, resulting in the *Mauritania* and *Lusitania*, for which the Clyde was dredged. In 1907 the speed record was broken, four days 20 hours out and four days 23 hours back, a record lasting 22 years. After ten years, Britain took back what Germany briefly grabbed.[14]

* * *

Late-19th-century North Atlantic shipping, based on westbound passengers and eastbound grain, cotton, meat and cattle, worked contrary to normal liner economics. In the 1880s-1890s, most north Atlantic shipping was liner-based, even though tramps dominated other bulk trades, because cattle and passenger transport needed regularity. Lines concentrated on either cattle or passengers. Both had large lower hold spaces where heavy bulk commodities were carried, supplementing revenue and ensuring stability with lower drafts. Refrigerated meat shipments were pioneered from America. The Bell-Coleman system reduced costs, trialled by Anchor Line in 1879. Australian frozen and chilled meat followed in 1880, New Zealand in 1882 and Argentina in 1883, transforming New World agriculture, further stimulating emigration. North America's live cattle exports grew to about 400,000 annually in the 1880s with British consumers paying premiums for fresh meat. In 1886, having left his load-line and safety campaigning, Plimsoll campaigned for better cattle conditions. His 1890 *Cattle Ships* described overcrowding, goring and trampling in storms, although contradicted by an official report. Lamport and Holt, London Steamship Co., Warren Line, National Line, Hill Line, Leyland Line and Allen Line were notable carriers. Inman and Cunard, passenger specialists, did not carry cattle, using the extra space for refrigerated and bulk cargo, normally only carried economically on tramp vessels as full cargo. A Cunarder for example, left New York in 1882 with 28,539 bushels of wheat, 1,495 sacks of flour, 1,606 cotton bales, 220,127 lbs of bacon, 47,625 lbs of ham, 34,580 lbs of tallow, 5,600 lbs of lard and 86,836 lbs of cheese.[15] With regular sailings, they carried huge annual volumes. What made this commercially viable?

The New York Shipping and Commercial List (3rd June 1882), stated, 'an indication of the depression is…Liverpool steamers have taken grain free…in preference to buying ballast.' White Star's Thomas Ismay explained in 1890, 'Since the introduction of carrying cattle…so many ships are engaged…they now compete with us for the deadweight…necessary to give stability to those ships. We should have been very much more in pocket if there had never been a beast brought over the Atlantic…for our cargo we make very little…we are bringing our grain over freight free.'[16] Refrigerated cargoes were charged 30–50% higher than non-refrigerated, but because liners depended on passengers, refrigerated freights were still low. In short, because of cattle and passengers, liners carried <u>most</u> US grain. Tramps were not entirely displaced. In 1895, for example, 16 million out of 78 million bushels of wheat went as full cargoes on tramps, in 1896, 40 million out of 123 million.[17] Partly due to this dynamic, early-1860s to early-1900s US grain freight rates declined 44%, liner rates 60%.

* * *

Liner economics were more conventional elsewhere. In Asia, Holts faced competition from Glen, Shire, Ben and Castle Lines, which starting later, introduced newer, larger, faster ships. Ben Line's origins were an 1825 Leith shipbroking firm, which in 1829 bought a ship to carry marble from Livorno to Leith, then Scottish coal to Canada and timber back, several subsequent ships Canadian-built. Their 1850s exploratory voyages to Asia and Australia led to two ships for emigrants out and wool back. They also shipped coal to Chile, guano to Mauritius then sugar to Britain. Using the Suez Canal, they built steamships from 1871.

Holt was slow to adopt steel hulls and triple expansion engines. Competition came from subsidised mail carriers like P&O, Messageries Maritime, the Dutch KPM and Sir William Mackinnon's British India Steam Navigation Co. (BI). Established in 1856, it operated feeder routes from P&O into Persian Gulf ports and the British-controlled Euphrates and Tigris Steam Navigation Co. to Baghdad. In 1882 it had 108 ships.[18] In East Africa, Mackinnon's Imperial British East Africa Co. in 1913 absorbed Bombay and Persia Steam Navigation Co. founded by Bombay Muslims in 1877 for the hajj. Heavily subsidised KPM helped extend Dutch rule over Southeast Asian islands with sailings to China, Japan, Bengal, Australia and Thailand. Shire Line founded in 1861 by Captain David Jenkins, initially concentrated on the Caribbean with sailing ships, then Asia, buying a steamship in 1872. Her maiden voyage was to Singapore, Hong Kong, Nagasaki, Kobe and Yokohama, by 1890 regularly sailing from Hamburg, Antwerp and London. Glen Line, founded in 1869 by James McGregor, partner in shipping-shipbroking firm Alan C. Gow and Co., also saw the Suez Canal's potential. His first steamship made its maiden London-China voyage in 1871. By 1882 it operated 15 against Holt's 23 and was quicker to build large triple expansion-engine ships in the 1890s.

Contrary to intense trans-Atlantic competition, John Swire's China Navigation Company and Russell and Co. cooperated, pooling earnings and equalised savings into what became Conferences. Holts believed in competition and free trade, but after initial reservation, copying the Calcutta-Europe Conference in 1875, established the Far East Conference in 1879 to fix rates, in Swire's words, so 'we may not ruin each other' in years of depressed rates when compound engines made scheduling more reliable. By the late-1880s with larger, faster ships they were staunch upholders of it. Conferences' *raison d'etre* were that liners carried hundreds of different commodities for many small shippers, increasing handling and stowage complexity, thus costs. Customers needed regularity. Seasonality, market cycles, changes in supply and demand and cutthroat competition meant extremely volatile freight rates endangered regularity. Conferences guaranteed regularity and regulated competition. Freight rates, number and times of sailings and ports served were fixed, even revenues shared and loyalty discounts given to regular shippers. Subsequent Conferences covered Australia in 1884, South Africa in 1886, West Africa and Brazil in 1895 and the River Plate in 1896.

Some Manchester merchants however, supported the 1882 China Shippers' Mutual Steam Navigation Co., from Glasgow and Liverpool in 1884. Holts responded, also loading in Glasgow. Seeing the Conference's benefits, China Merchant joined in 1885, a year after Ben Line. In 1893 North German Lloyd and Kingsin, a German line taking pig iron to Japan and in 1994 Rickmers joined, as each saw the logic. The Homeward Conference did not hold-up as well, incurring frequent rate-cutting wars but held together intermittently in 1885–1887, 1893–1895 and 1897–1911. The China Conference was suspended between 1887 and 1893 as legality was investigated by a Royal Commission before acceptance in 1891, partly due to cotton shippers' support, telling it 'Holts have done more for the China trade than any other firm.'[19]

Competition also came from newly industrialising Japan. The 1868 Meiji Restoration ushered-in vigorous reform, much by trial and error, copying what it thought the best western examples; German army, constitution and education which emphasised technical subjects, British navy, railways and empire. Armaments and military expenditure thus increased. Japan colonised Hokkaido, annexed the Ryukyu Islands and planned to capture Taiwan. Unable to charter foreign ships as troop carriers, vetoed by European powers, the government bought 13 steamships, entrusting them to the Yataro family company, Mitsubishi, which was transformed from a small coastal operator into a large international operation.

Strongly increasing trade volumes underpinned Japan's heavily subsidised merchant fleet. Like German lines to Asia under Bismarck, they wanted links to future colonies. A marine training school and a Yokohama-Shanghai service was established, competing with US-controlled Pacific Steamship Co. In 1876, P&O tried competing but withdrew after six months.[20] In 1882 the government provided half the capital for a second line, Kyodo Unyu Kaisha. Heavy losses resulted in amalgamation in 1885 as the state-subsidised Nippon Yusen Kaisha (NYK). In 1884 Japan leased Nagasaki's shipyards to Mitsubishi, then sold them to it. Regime supporters, families like Mitsui, Mitsubishi, Sumitomo, Yasuda and Kawasaki had widespread interlocking banking, industrial and commercial firms called *zaibatsu*, intimately connected with government-sponsored industrialisation, promoting economic and military power.

After NYK's creation, Mitsubishi pursued trading, mining, shipyards and banking. Mitsui Busan (1876) was established by the Mitsui family at government request for import and export. The government-supported Yokohama Specie Bank (1880) provided financing, the foundation of future trade. NYK's routes were mainly around Japan, China, Korea and Asiatic Russia. The growing economy attracted others and by the early-1880s, 70 companies had over 100 steamships, most uniting in 1884 in Osaka Shosen Kaisha (OSK), government-subsidised from 1887, including routes to Korea. Most NYK and OSK ships were British-built. Japanese companies were encouraged not to compete with each other. European and US mail lines were subsidised. Japan's subsidy was exceptionally large, spent mainly on its Shanghai link, for imperial ambitions but also to promote trade, income, employment and shipbuilding.

Canadian Pacific which built the Montreal-Vancouver railway, began a Vancouver-Yokohama -Hong Kong route in 1887, adding to the growing network. Japan needed lines to Europe, centre of world trade and shipping and rapidly growing America, for trade and partly for emigration, which NYK had done to Hawaii on tramps. By 1892, fast-expanding NYK started a Bombay-Kobe service with India's Tata group, shipping raw cotton to Japan's growing cotton textile industry. It planned six ships of 3,100 grt to London, two 8,500 grt to Seattle and three 2,500 grt for Melbourne and asked for a subsidy.[21] With a trans-Nicaragua Canal planned, extensions to New York were considered. Until 1896 Japanese-built ships averaged under 250 grt, imported ships nearly 2,000 grt. In the 1890s it had 11 small shipyards with meagre output, compared with the huge Yokosuka Naval Shipyard, its workforce greater than all merchant yards, demonstrating Japan's government's real priorities.[22] Most Japanese believed in protection. Even the liberal *Tokyo Economic Journal*, which supported free trade and competition, excluded shipping from 1894.[23]

During the 1894–95 Sino-Japanese War, provoked by Japan, NYK bought nine more ships, the government 14, added to NYK's fleet at the war's end for an 1896 European service competing with British, German, French and Dutch lines. Taiwan, the Pescadores, Liaotung Peninsula and northern China were captured. China had to recognise Japanese commercial privileges in China and Korea. Mitsubishi retained the ships and shore facilities, a pattern of government initiative, then selling to investors at below cost, like glassmaking in 1885 and cotton mills in 1886–87.

NYK joined the Far East Conference to stabilise rates. The 1911 agreement between the Outward China Conference and NYK formalised various post-1887 agreements. Lines running from Britain's east coast were P&O, NYK, Glen, Shire and Ben Lines, from its west coast, Holts and China Steam Ship, which Holts bought in 1902 after a sharp recession, after overextending itself with three 9,000-tonners when Holt's largest was 7,000 tons. Holts' Blue Funnel was dominant to Asia, but all Conference members gave shippers regular services, rate stability, protection for small shippers, allowing shipowners reasonable profits, which unrestricted competition could not. Liverpool's Conference charges and services satisfied most merchants, contributing to Manchester's port's unfulfilled potential.

Britain's steel production grew from 300,000 tons in 1870 to five million tons in 1900, 20% exported, much used in shipbuilding. In 1900, 739,000 tons of shipping was built and registered in Britain, its total over 11.5 million tons. Between 1894 and 1902, 22 large steamships were added to Holt's fleet as Malaya's, Singapore's and Dutch Southeast Asia's exports to Britain and British to Asia virtually trebled: cotton goods, including heavy machinery, locomotives, railway materials, bicycles, soap, sewing machines, whisky, brandy, beer, tobacco and chemicals. Encouraged by 1885's 'Safety' bicycle and Dunlop's pneumatic tyres, Malay rubber exports, 100 tons in 1905 grew to 47,000 in 1914, of which Holts carried 12,000 tons. By the late-1920s with surging automobile production, rubber exports were over 400,000 tons. Dutch Asia's plantation-grown tobacco production also grew. Indian and Ceylon tea replaced Chinese. Holts' 1913 Australian and Javan earnings were similar to its China and Japan service, the whole fleet 'on the crest of a wave of unparalleled prosperity.'[24] Since 1901 it trebled earnings, not always year-by-year which market volatility prevented, investing in larger, faster ships, Asian wharves and warehouses. P&O also prospered, despite only using twin screws from 1903. In 1910 it bought Blue Anchor Line, taking emigrants and general cargo to Australia, returning initially with wool. In 1914 it merged with BI, its 131 steamships of 598,203 grt, against P&O's 70 ships of 548,564 grt.

Indian exports doubled from 1883 to 1913. India's one cotton mill in 1856 blossomed by 1914 to 246, exporting 198 million lbs of yarn, the world's fourth-largest cotton industry and second-largest jute,[25] merchant-driven enlightened progress. Trade growth spawned other European lines; Dutch East Africa Co. in 1903, Sweden's Johnson Line in 1904 to South America, Norway's Mexico-Gulf Line in 1908 and several others to South and North America, Africa, Asia and Australia.

* * *

West African trade was less voluminous than trans-Atlantic and Asian trades but liner economics like Asia's. Macgregor Laird's 1852 African Steamship Navigation Co. with a ten-year mail contract, ordered five ships from brother John and set-up brothers William and Hamilton as Liverpool agents. It sailed from London via Plymouth to Tenerife and a dozen or so West African ports, returning with palm oil, gold, gum, ginger, timber, pepper, arrowroot, palm nuts, beeswax and ivory. Imports peaked in 1890 with 14,349 hundredweight.[26]

In 1856 Laird used the Niger to develop trade with the interior, introduced direct sailings from Liverpool and in 1864 took-over Dominion Line and Beaver Line to Canada. Their significant employees were John Dempster, Alexander Elder and John Holt. The rival British and African Steam Navigation Co. from 1868 was supported by Glasgow and Liverpool merchants, but as in Asia, Conference cooperation in freight, passenger rates and sailing dates was agreed in 1870, the mail contract shared from 1873, as African Steamship sold its older ships and bought more efficient ones.

In 1878 Alfred Jones set-up a shipping-insurance broking firm and bought and chartered ships for West Africa. Elder and Dempster offered him a partnership in 1879 and retired in 1884. Jones took-over and by 1891 controlled both African Steamship Co. and British African Steam Navigation Co. Ltd. as Elder-Dempster Line with 90% of the trade. German competition from Hamburg's Woermann Line was regulated in 1895 by a Conference in which it was not allowed to call at British ports, but Elder-Dempster could call at European ports. US-West Africa trade was funnelled through New York and Liverpool, much like wheat, effectively freight-free across the Atlantic, creating a regular, reliable service at stable rates, ensuring profits, but low enough to discourage competition, with US goods sold competitively. Elder-Dempster acquired the Antwerp-Congo mail contract, bought two south Wales coal mines and increased efficiency by using owned boats for offshore discharge, establishing integrated transport and storage infrastructure with coaling stations, banking and credit facilities, enabling ocean-going ships to concentrate on major ports, leaving smaller ships servicing others. He expanded into Jamaica with Elder and Fyffes Ltd, revitalising Jamaica's banana trade, increasing imports to Britain, brought tourism to the Canary Islands and helped its banana industry. Between 1885, when Jones orchestrated the West Africa Shipping Conference and 1909, when he died, Elder-Dempster's fleet doubled and was dominant.

It should be stressed that Macgregor Laird, John Dempster, Alexander Elder, John Holt and Alfred Jones developed important trades in areas British politicians thought lacked commercial potential. Appropriately, Jones was knighted for services to Britain's West African colonies and Jamaica; significant in replacing slave trading with legitimate, wealth-creating trade. Like many merchants he was also a philanthropist, instrumental in founding Liverpool's School of Tropical Medicine.

*   *   *

In the Atlantic, Asia and West Africa, British, especially Liverpool-based entrepreneurs successfully pioneered and developed 19th-century maritime trade, shipping new and traditional products, enriching lives in areas they traded. Rapid technical developments and efficiencies allowed huge leaps in ship sizes. In 1889 Inman's *City of Paris* was the world's largest ship at 10,650 grt; by 1906 Cunard's *Mauretania* was 37,938.

Chapter 35

Tramp Shipping and the City

British-German liner rivalry in size, speed and comfort dominated shipping headlines. In 1912, BI and P&O's fleets were almost 500,000 tons each while Holts/Blue Funnel led in book value at £8.1 million with dividends seven-times higher than P&O.[1] Holt, Inchcape, Philipps, Jones, Ellerman and Runciman were well-known and government-connected. But liner companies only represented 25% of British shipping's tonnage. Tramping was much larger. City banks, insurers and shipbrokers serviced tramp owners large, small, British or foreign.

The Baltic Exchange, focused on grain and shipping, trialled the Edison and Bell telephone in 1879. It competed with the Jerusalem Subscription Room and Exchange, a more general shipping market, overtaken by London Shipping Exchange in 1892, with 1,500 members. In 1894, Baltic Exchange membership dropped as some shipowners felt grain interests were prioritised. C.W. Kellock, originally Liverpool brokers, started ship auctions at the Shipping Exchange in 1895.[2] In 1900 it and the Baltic Exchange merged, housed in a building in 1903 on St. Mary Axe, a tiny City street, where now stands the building nicknamed the Gherkin.

Concentration of grain and shipping functions transformed the warren of streets around St. Mary Axe into the nucleus of world shipping: shipowners, brokers, agents, banks specialising in ship finance, trading and insurance companies. Lloyds moved to adjacent Leadenhall Street in 1928, concentrating it further. In 1866, 170,000 people commuted into the City and 93,000 lived there. By 1911, 384,000 commuted and 20,000 resided, transformed from 18th-century bankers and merchants living and working in the same building. Between 1855 and 1905 many City buildings were rebuilt, increasing floor space by 50%, the maritime sector a third of City firms. Baltic Exchange membership rose from 760 in 1860 to 2,377 in 1913. In 1909 there were 10,500 City businesses connected with international trade, most around St. Mary Axe or close to the docks or Customs House. British re-exports peaked in the 1860s. London developed expertise in petroleum, pharmaceuticals, coffee and rubber, controlled 30% of world coffee and imported 7% of world rubber for its own consumption, but re-exported 45,000 tons in 1914, dominating distribution, including to America.[3] Amsterdam, Rotterdam, Antwerp, Hamburg and New York challenged in different commodities, Antwerp in ivory for example. In 1900 London handled 20% of British exports by value, by 1913 over 30%, growing from £19 million in the 1850s to over £100 million in the 1910s.

In the 1850s there were 61 Greek merchant companies in London, Manchester and Liverpool.[4] By the 1890s Ionian Greeks dominated Greek shipping, as their grain trading decreased. Bulgaria, independent by 1885 increased grain exports seven-fold from 3% of Black Sea exports in 1885 to 7% by 1894. With improved engines, steamships gradually took over Black Sea trades. In 1880 sailing ships took about 75 days from Britain to Odesa, steamers 20 days. Shorter voyages diminished grain deterioration risks. By the mid-1880s, over half the Vaglianos fleet was steam. Up to 1910, they financed 14 undercapitalised Cephalonia, Chios, Andros, Syros and Leros shipowners to buy steamers with loans up to 50% of the ship's value at 7–8% interest, the ship as collateral. From 60,000 nrt in 1835, Greek-owned shipping rose to almost 600,000 in 1914.[5]

By 1901 Greeks had 158 steamships and 1,152 sailing ships. Black Sea grain exports boomed, Greek shipowners gradually moved from Constantinople, Taganrog, Smyrna, Marseilles, Odesa, the Danube and Syros, centralising in Piraeus and larger owners in London, taking advantage of cables, information, expertise and shipping services, including many names familiar to later shipping professionals; Livanos, Embiricos and Lykiadopolu, for example.

By 1914 London and Piraeus were Greek shipping's maritime centres. Many Greeks sold at high prices during the Boer War and bought at subsequent lower prices. The Vaglianos had only three sailing ships left in 1900 and Greek-owned steamers surpassed sail by 1903. By 1910, 60% of Greek shipping was steam. Norway lagged with 59%, America, 56%.[6] However significant for the future however, Greek-owned tonnage could not compare with British-owned fleets; Furness Withy of Hartlepool in 1910 had 95 ships of 178,837 nrt and Hain of Cardiff were fourth-largest with 36 of 93,169 nrt, Turnballs of Whitby were eighth with 29 of 65,150 nrt. The Vaglianos, largest Greek shipowner, had 30 of 42,857 nrt.[7]

Burrell and Son was formed in 1850 in Glasgow. William joined in 1876, establishing worldwide agencies to secure onward cargoes prior to discharge, increasing efficiency and profitability. With a gift for selling high and buying low, he bought 17 ships in a severe 1894 recession, sold when freights recovered and bought 32 more in the 1905–1911 low market, becoming one of the largest tramp companies, each ship operating as a single company, the model Onassis later adopted. He sold all during the Great War at three-times newbuilding prices, devoting his time to collecting art and in enlightened merchant tradition, donated much to Glasgow with money for a dedicated museum and smaller donations to various provincial galleries.

* * *

The 1894 Merchant Shipping Act created better forms of ship mortgage registration, providing mortgagees with the power to sell ships without taking possession, easing bank fears of becoming unwitting shipowners.[8] Some banks were better informed and braver than others in shipowner loans, when future earnings depended on volatile markets and values, always difficult to determine. Banks around St. Mary Axe specifically catered to shipowners, shipbrokers, Greek shipping representatives, masters aspiring to ownership and traders needing credit for physical and future commodity trades. They built considerable expertise.

Between 1860 and 1900 British mineworkers increased from 307,000 to 820,000, annual coal production from 80 to over 225 million tons, 25% exported, accounting for 40% of all tramp shipping, 60% of all British shipping in 1913, when 13.7 million tons of cargo left Cardiff, 10.5 million of which was coal, its peak. Shipping it from Newcastle and Cardiff to distant coaling stations earnt shipowners £25 million in 1914.[9] Cardiff's 1859 Bute Docks' coal and ore exports made it the world's busiest port for a few years, outstripping Liverpool and London and a major shipowning port.

Australia, Japan, Korea, China, Taiwan, India and Indonesia also mined coal; Japan 21 million tons in 1913, exporting over three million. Australia's huge coastline, small population, underdeveloped roads and rail meant its coastal cities depended on shipping. Newcastle NSW, the port and state's name emphasising coal's importance, with place names like Swansea, Hexham and Morpeth, originally mined coal by convict labour. Interstate cargoes were recorded as exports before Australia's six states federated in 1901,[10] serviced by many companies with Newcastle coal interests, which in 1902 formed the Australian Steamship Owners Association. In 1913 over two million tons were exported from Newcastle and Port Kembla, about 20% to New Zealand, some to New Caledonia's nickel smelters and 50% to San Francisco and Chile's coaling stations in sailing ships along the roaring forties. From Chile, ships carried nitrates for fertilisers to Europe, increasing 12-fold from 1880 to 1913.[11] Newcastle was San Francisco's major supplier with 107 sailings in 1881 and 56 in 1908, declining when the Panama Canal opened in 1914. Chile still took 700,000 annually before 1914, where Brown Collieries had a sales office, sail remaining competitive into the 1920s, but Brown warned in 1915 that oil-fired ships were increasing and coal-burning decreasing.

In the 1880s, British newbuilding sail and steam were equally divided and in the 1890s four-masted steel barques were built for grain. Steamship tonnage from 1890 to 1914 increased from 12.9 to 45.4 million grt, greatly overtaking sailing ships. Norway was fourth maritime nation in 1890 after Britain, America and Germany. With insufficient capital for extensive steamship ownership, Norwegian owners only acquired them and steel sailing ships in the late-1890s. Their fleet grew 30% between 1906 and 1913, about 65% in British coal and Baltic timber trades, but crucially developed niche, third-party trades. In 1911, 67 Norwegian steamers were chartered in Caribbean-US fruit trades, some on Newfoundland and St. Lawrence iron ore and Nova Scotia coal to Europe.[12]

The Suez Canal, increasing sizes, cargo-handling and steamship improvements reduced freight rates and sailing times in an 1870–1914 worldwide fall in shipping costs, liner and tramp, with greater volumes and varieties for expanding European, US and Japanese economies.

Chapter 36

Tariffs and Territorialism

British enlightenment continued with pioneer works in comparative law and anthropology. Dickens depicted a vast social and human panorama, supplemented by Thackery, Eliot, Trollope, Carol, Lear, Tennyson, Bronte, Hardy and many more. In the 1860s Lister devised antiseptic surgery. Edwin Chadwick pioneered urban sanitation. The franchise was gradually extended and national education established, made compulsory in the 1890s. Miners achieved an eight-hour day. The world's 34.5-million-ton fleet in 1910 was employed more efficiently than the nine million of 1850. But there were disquieting developments. The dangerous Gothic myth of Germany's supposed tragic past, continually invaded and fragmented was born. Chancellor Bismarck declared a Second Reich; 60 million people against France's 40 million, hitherto the most populous European country. The Papal State was abolished in 1870 but the Vatican's propaganda machine, 500 periodicals by 1910, mobilised against secularism and liberalism. Jewish restrictions in Rome continued. The Jesuit bi-weekly *Civilta Cattolica* began an anti-Jewish campaign, promoting 'exceptional laws for a race…so exceptionally and profoundly perverse', that even if converted, enveloped the economy, encouraging European anti-Semitism,[1] already rife in Russia, whose economy was retarded and social structure dangerously imbalanced. Moreover, the Cobden-Chevalier impetus to reduce world tariffs reversed from 1879, becoming protectionist.

Booming trade and growing industrial activity made 19th-century western Europe and America richer. Cotton cloth dominated British exports. In 1800, 62% of 52 million lbs of imported cotton was exported as cloth, in 1840, 50% of 452 million, by 1912 an incredible 85% of 2,038 million. Woollen cloth exports grew more slowly. In 1913 about 70% of British exports were cloth, iron and steel products and coal; a strikingly narrow base.[2] New industries embracing newer technology, like chemical dyes, pharmaceuticals, telephones, lifts, cameras and electric motors were developed by Germany and America where scientific and technical educational institutions were created specifically to catch Britain's industrial lead. Technological schools were especially successful in Germany from the 1870s. Unlike the Joseph Black-James Watt, Glasgow and Edinburgh University collaboration on steam engine research, few connections between British scientists and manufacturers allowed Germany to lead in chemicals, which by 1900 produced almost 90% of world dyes. In 1886 Germany imported over 1,000 tons of natural indigo, by 1896 none, exporting 256 tons of synthetic indigo. In 1902, 80% of colours used by the Bradford Dyers Association were German-made.[3] British schools and universities mainly concentrated on the classics, nurturing civil service mandarins after the Northcote-Trevelyan reforms of 1854 (see

Chapter 46), rather than technical or chemical engineers, neglected in Britain but promoted in America, Germany and Japan. Andrew Carnegie who built America's steel industry pioneered in-house scientists. Germany's economy became Europe's most advanced but retained a social structure of rich landowners and industrialists and poor peasants and workers, unsolved in 1848.

British industries depended on imported raw materials, 100% raw cotton, 90% lead, tin and copper, 80% raw wool and 60% copper.[4] India-Dundee jute shipments from 1840 developed quickly, benefitting Bengal and Assam, where in the early-20th century three million acres were cultivated for Dundee manufacturers of sacks, twines, rope, carpet backing and mattresses. British export-growth slowed after the 1870s. In 1900 British exports were worth £291,192,000, mainly due to coal export growth, compensating for stagnating textiles and iron and steel decline. Trade, as a proportion of national income, 50% in 1875 fell to 42% in 1900. The trade deficit grew; about £16 million in the mid-1820s, about £28 million in the mid-1850s, about £62 million in the early-1870s and £134 million in 1913, still covered by shipping, banking, insurance and especially foreign investment returns, which rose from about £200 million in 1850 to about a billion in 1870, two billion in 1880 and four billion by 1913.[5]

By 1914, 10% of Britain's income was foreign investment returns, 20% of the world's total. Overseas railways constituted 40%, then mines, plantations, harbours and docks, mainly in America and the Dominions, but also India and Argentina for wheat, Malaya for tin mining, Siam for teak and Rhodesia for copper, enabling purchases of British rails and rolling stock. About half Britain's commercial exchanges and investments outside Europe were with the Americas, the rest with Australasia and India. Argentina, Chile and Uruguay were dominated by British capital. The Dominions with stable governments, enterprising populations and representative institutions favouring progress were better guarantees for capital and property, their business the most profitable, causing few problems. By the 1870s, 10% of immigrants to NSW, Queensland and California were Chinese, nearly 20% in British Colombia. In the 1880s, British emigration was urged to the Dominions, rather than America. Between 1891 and 1900 only 28% of British emigrants went to the Dominions, the rest mainly to America. But from 1901 to 1910, 63% of three million were Dominion-bound, 78% in 1913. Canada introduced preference for British goods in 1897 with a 25% rebate, increased to 33.3% in 1900, by New Zealand in 1903, South Africa in 1904 and Australia in 1907. British industry and exports increasingly concentrated on accessible colonial markets.

Overall trade volumes increased 400% from 1870 to 1914 but America and Germany with state support, currency union, high tariff barriers and scientific education for industry were catching Britain's manufacturing and trade dominance. After 1850, retail banking spread rapidly in France, Germany, Belgium and America, increasing capital markets' support of industry. By 1899 Britain's share of the world's manufactured exports halved to about 33%. German manufacturing output increased from 13.2% of world output in 1870 to 15.9% in 1906–10, while America at about 23% from 1870 to 1900, boomed to 35.5% in 1906–10. German industrialists acquired political influence which Britain's lacked. Lorraine's iron ore and coal-rich Ruhr, Saar and Upper Silesia fed German steel production, doubling every decade between 1870 and 1910. In the early-1870s, Britain made four-times more iron and twice the steel as Germany. By 1910–14 Germany made about twice as much iron and steel and exported more. US steel production overtook Britain about 1890 and in 1900 was over double Britain's.[6] Between 1870 and 1914, US GNP increased five-fold, Germany's 3.5-fold, Britain's doubled. Germany's home market was much larger than Britain's, America's even larger. Their companies benefitted from economies of scale. America had capital, food and raw materials. Wall Street's volumes approached the City's. The Chicago-Liverpool meat price differential reduced from 93% to 16% and Boston-Manchester textile prices, 13.75% to 2.6% as shipping costs fell and American and German economic power grew.

Germany led steel, chemical and electricity industries, accounting for about 70% of its exports in 1900. American manufactured exports accounted for only 30%, due to huge agricultural exports. Rudolf Diesel patented an oil engine in 1892 and by 1900 several marine diesel engine builders included Burmeister and Wain, MAN and Sulzer. More efficient than steam, they allowed more cargo space, the first diesel-powered ship built in 1910 in Amsterdam, a tanker for Anglo-Saxon Petroleum, a Shell subsidiary, burnt two tons of oil for every 11 tons of coal and required 16 rather than 30 crew.

In the 1850s-1870s, 40% of British exports went to Europe and America. By 1910, because of high tariffs, it was under 30%, gradually shifting to colonies, Latin America and Asia. By 1914, 40% of Britain's cotton goods went to India, probably 75% to the underdeveloped world, unlike 1850 when 75% had gone to Europe and North America.[7] Naturally therefore, as British export focus shifted, Germany, France, Japan and Italy saw British colonies as captive markets, so aimed to copy it, to increase African and Asian colonies, captive markets, but also prestige, whether economically sound or not, Britain's guiding criteria. Britain, the least acquisitive, had in the 1850s-1880s acquired Burma, to protect northeast India and tin-producing Malaya, the large tin-plate industry increasingly dependent on it. Fiji which offered itself was accepted in 1874 to protect sugar plantations and eliminate labour traffic abuses. Altruism continued. Carnarvon's policy for the Gold Coast, for example, in 1874 was 'not a desire of selfish interests or the ambition of larger empire…it is simply and solely a sense of obligations…[and] duties.'[8] Between 1874 and 1902 Britain added 4,750,000 square miles of territory to its empire, almost 90 million people.

Britain worried that while practicing free trade, competition was conducted unfairly by protectionist tariffs, first felt in Europe's reaction to cheap food imports, where more people farmed. After Cobden-Chevalier, Europe's tentative 1860s-1870s liberalisation sharply reversed. Grain prices halved from the early-1870s to mid-1890s, causing Europe's tariff protection backlash. Germany imposed protectionist tariffs in 1879. Bismarck thought Germany's future power lay in protected home markets, state-organised national resources and higher tariffs to increase government revenues, heightened further with the 1902 Bulow Tariff, benefitting grain-growing Junkers, but depriving peasants with cows and pigs of cheap feed grain. In 1892 over half Europe's 53 trade treaties expired. France's 1982 Meline Tariff doubled rates. Further increases followed.[9] Swedish, Italian, Austro-Hungarian and new Balkan countries' tariffs rose in the 1880s. US protectionists' rationale, protecting infant industries evolved to include mature ones. The 1890 McKinley Act, especially damaged British textiles, rails, pig iron and Welsh tinplate, 75% of which had been exported to America. The 1897 Dingley Act and 1909 Payne-Aldrich Tariff followed. Falling revenues from them necessitated federal income tax, very poor policy. In Britain 'unfair' competition caused escalating labour disputes. Already in 1886 Manchester's Chamber of Commerce debated 'that having waited in vain 40 years for other nations to follow the Free Trade example…the Chamber thinks the time has arrived to reconsider the position.' It was only defeated 22–21. Protectionist tariffs reinforced the trend of protective maritime trade blocs.

In Japan, hundreds of foreign experts advised on science, education, engineering, finance, military and naval affairs and Japanese were sent abroad to learn. Initially forced to have low tariffs as it industrialised from the 1860s, it also became protectionist after 1911. By 1914 Russia's average import duties on manufactured goods were 84%, America 44%, Japan 30%, France and Sweden 20%, Austria-Hungary 18%, Germany 13%, Argentina, Brazil and Mexico 15–26%, the Dominions 28–70%, Belgium and Switzerland 9%, and the Netherlands 4%. Britain, its colonies and China, where from 1863 to 1908 the Inspector General of Customs was British, maintained free trade. Britain underwrote an international system of stable exchange rates, was the largest creditor, providing capital and naval power, ensuring trade lanes stayed open. Its respect for contracts helped create a healthy business climate. High tariffs wounded but did not kill global trade because Britain was the greatest trading nation and food importer. But America, Germany and Japan choked Britain's exports, overtaking its industrial dominance. Arguably, Britain might have benefited by retaliating, but chose liberal, enlightened free trade.

All competitors were territorially bigger than Britain. Largest was Russia, which in the second Anglo-Chinese War took more territory and built Vladivostok's naval base. Economically and socially backward, lacking capital to support industrialisation, like pre-revolutionary France, reform, if possible, threatened domestic upheaval and/ or economic dependence on commercially advanced countries. Alexander II started in 1861, emancipating serfs, 80% of the population who had to make 50-year compensation payments to serf owners. Payments lagged and were reduced in 1886, when a state bank was belatedly established. Its military did not keep pace with western technical advances. Continual problems with Baltic ethnic minorities and central Asians led to uprisings. Terrible living conditions, high tax, frequent strikes and agrarian disorders added to a lethargic, inefficient, corrupt bureaucracy which produced radicals, socialists, anarchists, liberals and nationalists. America and Britain were anxious that Russia, asserting itself in Mongolia and Central Asia, would acquire large parts of China as the trans-Siberians railway pushed east. Russian War Minister Kuropatkin, warned of 'a yellow peril' as Chinese immigrants moved into Siberia.

Other European countries also expanded territorially. The Dutch started early after Java was returned in 1815, Sumatra in 1817, Aceh in 1907 and earlier claimed western New Guinea. France's 1830s-40s conquest of Algiers was followed in the 1850s by Vietnam and Cambodia, recognised in 1885, and tried creating spheres of influence over Guangdong, Yunnan, Syria and Mexico. Under Russian pressure

Japan returned the Liaotung Peninsula, captured in the 1894–95 Sino-Japanese War, only to have Russia take it. Japan doubled its army and fleet and was victorious in the 1904–05 Russo-Japanese War. Manchuria was to be a raw material source for expanding industries. Korea was annexed in 1910, its people and resources ruthlessly exploited in a brutal regime in which Koreans had to change their names to Japanese, extreme continentalist uniformity, similar to Hokkaido's colonisation when the Ainu language was banned, like Russia whose language was imposed on ethnic minorities, 56% of its empire's people. Most Jews were forbidden residence in western Russia, onerous restrictions imposed on others with 1881–83 and 1903–06 pogroms spurring emigration. Polish, Finn and Latvian minorities were targeted for Russification. All were disquieting, illiberal developments.

China's, Turkey's and Egypt's failure to reform weakened them. Indian Viceroy Curzon (1898–1905) thought Chinese private enterprise 'killed by official strangulation' and John Stuart Mill of China and Egypt, 'their people were halted for want of mental liberty and individuality.' In 1876, 12 out of 20 highest taxpayers in Hong Kong were European firms, by 1881 only three, the rest Chinese, having escaped China, where belief in its superiority was shaken by the Sino-Japanese war. Yet reform was shunned, money to build an 1880s railway diverted for a new summer palace. In 1900 India had 35-times more railway mileage. China's weakness triggered another European scramble. Germany seized Jiaoshou, Russia Liodong, Britain Weiheiwei and the New Territories next to Hong Kong. France leased Guangzhou. Britain disliked territorial control but feared being overtaken. Inevitably the Manchu fell in 1911.

America had pushed west, fought Mexico for Texas, acquired California in 1848 and bought Alaska from Russia. An 1876 US House Committee asserted, 'the Pacific Ocean is an American Ocean…the future great highway between ourselves and the hundreds of millions of Asiatics who look to us for commerce, civilisation and Christianity.'[10] Hawaii developed sugar with American capital. 1870–1890 acreage rose ten-fold, entering America duty free. The 1890 McKinley Tariff replaced sugar duties by domestic subsidies, great incentive for planters to suggest annexation. President Theodore Roosevelt's 1898 war with Spain ostensibly supported Cuban independence, but really wanted captive trade, first attacking the Spanish Philippines, due to its strategic value in opening China to US imports. It took Puerto Rico. Guam, Hawaii and Cuba came under *de facto* US protection. Roosevelt's imperial expansion was cloaked in a 'civilising mission', the 'great work of uplifting mankind.'[11] He supported Panama's independence from Spain, after which it granted America the right to cut and operate a canal with full control over the Canal Zone. Begun in 1904, it opened in 1914. Foreign policies aggressively sought unilateral advantage, not international cooperation. Henry Cabot Lodge attacked free traders in jingoistic, racial terms. 'The disciples of the Manchester School…think…the price of calico more important than a nation's honour, the duties on pig iron of more moment that the advance of the race,' blustering in a dispute over Venezuela's boundary, a position ridiculed by free traders seeing cooperation with Britain beneficial instead of risking war over areas of negligible value, hurting many US economic interests.

Responding to rising economic competition, the growth of large territorial powers and rush for extra-European territory, some Britons concluded, 'only by gathering together the several nations of the empire can we cope in the international balance of power.'[12] Charles Dilke's 1868 *Greater Britain* concerned relations with Dominions. Joseph Chamberlain, Colonial Secretary (1895–1903) strongly advocated Imperial Preference, an imperial customs union to protect industry from foreign competition, raising revenue to finance social reform, welding the empire together. He prized West African territory 'for its own sake as an estate for posterity.'[13] He wanted to build roads, railways and harbours, creating wealth, progress and social justice for Britain's overseas subjects. Alarmed at Caribbean sugar industry decline, he tried modernising and diversifying its economy by developing citrus fruits and bananas. Elder-Dempster shipped them to Britain. Small nations were 'destined to fall into a secondary and subordinate place. But if Greater Britain remains united, no empire in the world can ever surpass it in area, population, in wealth or the diversity of its resources.'[14] Leo Amery in 1904, thought 'successful powers will be those…[with] the greatest industrial base.' Distaste for taking and ruling territory, concentrating on trade, assuming colonies would govern themselves when ready, dangerously morphed into pride in empire. Curzon thought, 'we do not want to occupy, but we cannot afford to see it occupied by our foes.'[15] Moreover, like the 1970s debate on EEC membership, Imperial Preference and EEC advocates conceded that food prices would rise but be offset by long-term export rises. Both were wrong.

In India paternalistic, efficient administration was emphasised. The Suez Canal made travel to India almost routine, London-Bombay just 15 days. British wives' lives revolved around home, club and church, distinct from Indians. Exclusiveness, protecting 'civilised standards', fostered racial prejudice. Indians became divorced from British rulers. Ronald Hyam concludes, 'white wives blighted racial harmony,' while Sarawak's good race relations was attributed to their absence and much inter-racial sex.[16] Racial attitudes hardened elsewhere. Explorer Grant Speke who discovered the Nile's source, thought in 1863 that 'to say a negro is incapable of instruction is a mere absurdity for those few…educated in our schools have proved themselves even quicker than our own in learning.' When he met a 'very pretty woman' in Buganda in 1860 he offered her his arm 'and we walked along…as if we had been in Hyde Park… flirting and coquetting all the way.' His companion danced with a bare-breasted queen mother.[17] By late-century all that vanished, finally capped by the 1909 *Crewe Circular* warning officials not to take mistresses, still practised by traders, less prejudiced than the Colonial Office, influenced by the 1880s Purity Campaign, partly missionary-inspired to maintain an 'imperial race', beliefs reinforced by conceits like sun helmets protecting supposedly thinner British skulls housing larger brains.[18] Elgar's *Land of Hope and Glory* (1902) was an anthem to empire, <u>not</u> the benefits of trade, masking self-doubt caused by failing industrial supremacy. Meanwhile, a third of early-20th-century Liverpool's population, about 200,000, were Irish and Blue Funnel's Chinese crew who settled, created Europe's oldest 'Chinatown'.

Ideals of trusteeship continued, but force was empire's ultimate guarantor. Lugard explained 'ascendancy must at any price be maintained just as…with a <u>brute beast</u>…

even…physical force,' sentiments unheard a century earlier.[19] British disappointment with Egypt's elites also hardened racial feelings. Gladstone's sympathy with oppressed nationalities evolved into Cromer's distrust of subject races.[20] But no enlightenment penetrated French Indochina, unashamedly based on racial superiority, brutal Russian, Prussian or Japanese regimes or King Leopold's Congo. Curzon described the British Empire as 'Under Providence, the greatest instrument for good the world has ever seen.' John Stuart Mill and earlier generations would have substituted 'maritime trade' for 'British Empire' But territory acquired to protect trade became an end in itself, Empire Day celebrated from 1902. With manufactured exports stagnating or being overtaken, because Britain was not matching Germany's, America's and Japan's technical education, pride in trade supremacy was replaced by mistaken pride in empire, outside of which, Curzon thought, was unreformable, Islamic influence, ignorance and despotism too widespread. Despite Kipling's belief in the empire as a force for good, his *Kim* reflected on India's ancient wisdom and missionaries' arrogance. *Recessional* anticipated decline. 'All our pomp of yesteryear is one with Nineveh and Tyre.'

Racial awareness, always different in America with its acceptance of slavery until the 1860s, was also heightened. California's 1852 population was 10% Chinese when the Chinese Exclusion Act restricted immigration to Europeans. Benjamin Harrison's 1888 acceptance speech spoke of his 'duty to defend our civilisation by excluding alien races.' Europeans and Americans increasingly believed in British, American and European racial superiority. Joseph Chamberlain thought Britons 'the greatest governing race the world has ever seen.' Japanese resented European racial profiling them as inferior, but thought Chinese and Koreans far inferior to them. Dominions enthusiastically embraced the idea of an extended Britain. New Zealand marketed its lamb as 'British from New Zealand.' British culture was diffused by ships carrying books, mail and newspapers. Australians were 'more British than the people of Great Britain,' said Prime Minister Billy Hughes.[21] From the 1880s, Dominions established 'great white walls' encouraging British, Scandinavian and German immigration, kindred races, and in the 1890s, Celts, embarrassing Britain by explicit discrimination, but Dominions wanted to be better British.

The Conservatives split over Imperial Preference in 1905, including Churchill who joined the Liberals. 'Dear food for the millions, cheap labour for the millionaires.' At the 1906 General Election it was rejected. A free trade, Liberal, reforming ministry's achievements in a retreating enlightened world were impressive, coinciding with economic revival and stability. Churchill explained, 'to keep our empire we must have a free people, an educated and well-fed people,' thus 'we are all in favour of social reform.' Subsidised school meals were introduced in 1906 and compulsory school medical inspection in 1907. Imported Chinese labour for South African mines was stopped. India was offered 'order plus reforms' to prepare for future self-government, Basutoland, Bechuanaland and Swaziland were withheld from the Union of South Africa in 1910 to safeguard Africans from Boer dominance. Cotton, palm oil, groundnuts, cocoa, rubber and coffee were promoted in Africa, but <u>not</u> technical education in Britain! Lancashire cotton interests pressed for Nigerian railways to cotton districts. Oil was prospected and tin sought. Cotton was grown in Sudan and Uganda, sisal in Kenya.

Cocoa exports increased from the Gold Coast and Nigeria from 110,000 hundredweight in 1906 to 882,000 in 1913. West African palm oil production doubled and by 1910 the Gold Coast, the largest cocoa grower, produced 40,000 tons annually. Fifty-five companies were floated for African rubber interests. Maritime trade volumes and diversity were unsurpassed.

Migration continued to rebalance labour supply, lifting European wages. New technologies offered more efficiencies. The 1907 *Atlas of the World's Commerce* opened, 'At no period in the world's history has there been commercial expansion of such stupendous growth as at the beginning of the 20th century.' The 1910 election again pitted the Tariff Reform 'crusade' against Free Traders, so arousing the electorate that turnout was 87%, the issue as in the pre-1846 free trade debate, the effects of foreign competition, this time more acute with some closure of manufacturing. By 1902, J.P. Morgan also controlled all but two of Britain's largest trans-Atlantic shipping lines, but other lines, tramp shipping, shipbuilding and shipping services were still mainly British-dominated. Britain's pre-war 41 million people were better fed, clothed and housed with greater life expectancy, 53 compared with 36 in 1750 and average living standards double those of 1850.[22] In 1914, refrigerated shipping enabled Britain to import 20 lbs of beef and mutton per head. Globally few places were unaffected by distant markets and capital. New technologies offered efficiencies. British investment continued to be mainly overseas because as emigration increased, capital followed, for railways, farms, mining, more lucrative than domestic investment.

However, European high tariffs, rivalry for colonies, French animosity to Germany for the loss of Alsace and Lorraine and German ambition fuelled by the Gothic and Aryan racial origin myths were a dangerous European cocktail. It need not have been fatal. The world was growing richer by booming maritime trade and despite relative retreat, was led by Britain. In 1910 its merchant ships constituted about 40% of world tonnage, Germany about 8%. In 1911, British shipyards' built 1,804,000 grt, 68% of world output. Shipping employed 119,000, shipbuilding 115,000, fishing 53,000, ports 167,000, navy and dockyards 93,000, totalling nearly 4% of British males.[23] In a rare outbreak of US relative economic liberalism in 1912 President Wilson reduced tariffs to 16% by 1920. The value of 1913 British imports and exports was £5,186 million, 80% more than only 20 years earlier.[24] In index form, world trade from 7–8 in 1810, was 100 in 1880 and 200 in 1910.

But Kaiser Wilhelm in 1890 inherited the power Bismarck gathered, supreme political, military and naval command. Authoritarian, illiberal and arrogant, his advisers were German Junkers, warrior, philistine landowners, who like Bismarck aimed for continental hegemony. Interpreting Boer War army defeats as weakness, he decided on confrontation to replace Britain as major world power. For Germany, Austria-Hungary, Russia and Turkey, war was part of their territorial culture, dangerous with so much to lose. Like Napoleon, Wilhelm derided Britain as commercially-driven. It was in no nation's interest to confront British naval supremacy, which worked to keep the seas free for everyone's trade, increasing wealth, wages and populations. African partition had eliminated possible causes of conflict there. Britain allied with Japan in 1902, France in 1904 and Russia in 1907 to dissuade German aggression. German meddling in Transvaal, where it had no legitimate interests, was worrying, but its post-1898, hostile, expensive fleet-building programme challenged British naval domination. Britain needed it to protect extensive maritime trade. Germany did not. Lacking overseas coaling or oil bases for re-fuelling, Germany's navy could not cover the Atlantic. German rail subsidies had diverted traffic from Antwerp and Rotterdam to Bremen and Hamburg, the latter becoming Europe's greatest port. Germany had much to lose.

Kipling feared war as early as 1897. Churchill, Fist Lord of the Admiralty, thought Autumn 1914 the likely start, when Kiel Canal enlargement enabled German dreadnought battleships to pass. With oil-fuelled naval ships producing more power, increased manoeuvring, faster acceleration and less crew, he ordered immediate oil conversions. Oil became the world's economic foundation, its transport in tankers vital. Churchill noted, 'If we cannot get oil, we cannot get corn, we cannot get cotton, we cannot get a thousand and one commodities necessary for the preservation of the economic energies of Great Britain.' The Admiralty took a controlling interest in Anglo-Persian Oil. The German ambassador in London thought 'a defeat in the North Sea means the end of the British Empire. A lost battle on the continent is a long way from the end of Germany.'[25] Wilhelm rejected suggestions to mutually reduce naval build-up as 'measureless impertinence.' His ambassador claimed it 'a question of national honour and dignity.' Like pre-1789 France, the burden of building a new fleet without taxing aristocratic wealth, fell on ordinary people. Russia increased its army. Its railways enabled rapid build-up on German borders. Austria-Hungary prepared to strike at Serbia, Russia's ally.

Britain had to out-build Germany. Her trade depended on it. Hamburg-America Line's head, Albert Ballin, recognised it and sought agreement. But he and Chancellor Bulow who sought compromise were rebuffed. Social Democrat August Bebel secretly wrote to the Foreign Office. 'To reform Prussia is impossible; it will remain the *Junkerstaat*...German Naval Law of 1900 [accelerating naval construction] was directed against...England alone.'[26] In this atmosphere, British political confidence, receding after the Mutiny, with Asia's and Egypt's reluctance to embrace liberalism, was replaced by anxiety. Like Venetians and Dutch prior to decline, Britain had huge territorial commitments. Social and political reform continued, but Britain was less technically and commercially innovative. Technical education and foreign languages were neglected, although atomic science was researched by Rutherford, while trams, bicycles, underground railways and automobiles entered daily life.

The 1830s-1840s Anti-Corn Law Leaguers thought free trade would lead to world peace. In that the Great War's background was increasing tariffs and territorialism, they were not entirely wrong. Its only cause was Wilhelm's arrogance. Its trigger was Austro-Hungarian instability, Russia's territorial meddling and the crumbling Ottomans, all continental countries for whom trade was relatively unimportant. Russian, Austro-Hungarian and Balkan disputes had nothing to do with trade. Many believed that because Britain and Germany were each other's biggest trading partners after America, war was economically illogical. The City was incredulous as to its insanity, markets only showing nervousness from 19th July. The decision was taken by a Berlin military cabal who believed in war's nobility: archaic Prussian military values, ignorant of the positive impact on Germany and the world of maritime trade's huge recent progress. Germany declared war on August 1st to stamp its jackboot on lesser nations, which had for centuries, supposedly humiliated it. Born in three quick wars, rapidly gaining economic strength, it initiated another one for world domination, not an 18th-century war over trade, but a re-run of Napoleon's land grab, plunging the world into chaos: a mini dark age.

Part Five

Descent into Darkness.
War, Depression, War

Chapter 37

'The lamps are going out all over Europe.
We shall not see them lit again in our lifetime.'

British Foreign Secretary, Sir Edward Grey

For Germany's gamble to succeed, it had to be, as with Danish, Austrian and French wars, quickly successful. Apparently confident, Von Moltke told Austro-Hungary's Chief of Staff, he would not fight Russia alone as he hoped to defeat France in six weeks, but must have had doubts, warning Wilhelm it would not be settled by a decisive battle but a 'long wearisome struggle with an enemy who will not be overcome until his whole national force is broken...a war which will utterly exhaust our own people even if we are...victorious.'[1] Wilhelm rejected an international meeting, prepared to sacrifice decades of huge economic gains for possible military glory.

Andrew Lambert[2] explains that after 1815 Britain had sought to neutralise European threats by vigorous economic growth through global trade and the permanent removal of France, the original threat, from the Scheldt estuary, the only place from which invasion could be realistically attempted, an economically wise strategy, disciplined by the massive financial legacy of 18th-century wars ending in 1815. It was he argues, Wellington's strategy; to concentrate on naval strength and the Scheldt.

The debt, 200% of GDP in 1815, fell substantially as the economy grew. The decision to send the British Expeditionary Force (BEF) , created in 1907 as an instrument of maritime strategy to France was taken by an *ad hoc* committee dominated by soldiers while politicians forgot Wellington's strategic principles and instead of concentrating on British interests, focusing on the Scheldt and using its greatest asset, the Navy, it subordinated itself to French interests. In 1916 Britain built a huge army to pursue continental war, further abandoning the sound military strategy.

Implicitly the correct strategy would have been to send the Navy to the Baltic to neutralise Germany's navy and the Scheldt. Britain won therefore at hugely unnecessary cost in blood and treasure and a debt burden that changed Britain for ever.

The maritime trade aspects of the war that <u>was</u> fought however, were as follows. On the first night, the five German Channel cables were cut,[3] while Britain's cable network and Royal Navy protected British and prevented enemy trade. The three German lines' 29 ships in the West African Conference were sunk, captured or took refuge in neutral ports. The West Africa and Far Eastern Conferences ended. After eliminating Germany's Indian Ocean cruiser *Emden* in 1914, British shipping in Asia was relatively safe. German African and Pacific Island cable stations were destroyed, the last in Southwest Africa in May 1915, when most of its ships were sunk, its ciphers broken and maritime trade blockaded. Japan invaded its Asian colonies immediately. Meanwhile, German armies were bogged down in static trench warfare.

Many British merchant ships were requisitioned including by December 1914, 100 P&O and BI ships. Sixty carried Indian troops to Europe, others converted into armed merchant cruisers, protecting trade and patrolling the China Sea.[4] Holts had to reduce China, Java and West Australian services, which ended in 1915. By late-1917, 78 out of 83 of its ships were requisitioned.[5] Fearful of sugar shortages, Britain centralised sugar chartering through Holts and required it, Shire and P&O to bring oil from Singapore in ballast tanks. Requisitioning, especially after 1917 when U-boat warfare intensified, meant British exports fell.

France blockaded Austria-Hungary's Adriatic ports. Neutral ships destined for Rotterdam and Copenhagen with Germany as end-user were examined in the Orkneys. By July 1915 no neutral shipowner knowingly accepted goods for Germany fearing costly voyage disruption. P&O's *India* was sunk in 1915 as she stopped and searched neutral vessels. Nevertheless, Lord Inchcape told shareholders of the service's 'unfailing regularity'.[6] German and Austro-Hungarian trade was paralysed. Their $169 million trade with America collapsed to about a million in 1916, while Denmark, Holland, Norway and Sweden increased their US trade from $187 million to $279 million,[7] indicating Germany was partly supplied indirectly. Mines and U-boats made the Baltic too dangerous for British ships. Closing the Dardanelles in Autumn 1914 meant Black Sea markets were lost, but war increased demand for maritime transport and many ships, including Greeks, were chartered by the allies, especially for inbound grain, iron ore and phosphates and outbound coal.

In May 1915 Cunard's *Lusitania* was torpedoed and sunk with many American lives lost. An American journalist thought it sunk 'Germany in the opinion of humanity.'[8] There were too few U-boats to seriously disrupt US and Canadian wheat supplies on requisitioned ships until 1917, despite some casualties. Poor pre-war freight rate weakness reversed and shipping revenues rose. By 1916 some complained that shipowners made excessive profits. Neutrals made the most. Richard Holt told shareholders that they had not squeezed regular shippers, charging 'very moderate freights while mounting the most regular service' that requisitioning and labour shortages allowed.[9] As war continued, almost all British and most neutral shipping was taken under government control. The 1916 Battle of Jutland ensured the expensive German navy never exited the North Sea. To feed and supply itself, it therefore planned to turn parts of eastern Europe into slave colonies.

Lloyd George, Prime Minister from 1916, thought shipping 'the most vital and vulnerable point in the issue of victory or defeat.' Non-requisitioned allied ships were required to carry government supplies at 'Blue Book' rates. But in 1917 wholesale requisitioning under a Shipping Controller in a new Ministry of Shipping demanded, 'You are to continue to manage and run those vessels as if they were not requisitioned… [but] you will hand over to the government the profits you make.' Richard Holt thought it a step too far, took the Controller to court and won.[10] Meanwhile, German shipyards built up to seven U-boats a month, 187 operational by January 1917, calculating they could sink 600,000 tons monthly and stop more sailing. In February, 209 British, allied and neutral ships were lost to U-boats, mines and surface raiders, 532,856 tons, in

March 599,854 tons.[11] Admiral Jellicoe projected 900,000 for April, fearing German victory. 1917's first six months losses were 2.75 million tons. Norway lost 889 ships during the war, mainly in the 1917–18 U-boat offensive. British 1916–1920 food prices rose to nearly three-times pre-war prices, causing government intervention for the first time.

A striking strategic aberration was that convoys were only organised in mid-1917, not fully until the year's end. Inventor Edison recommended modifying their routes and fitting ships with radios. Monthly losses fell to 400,000 tons. Allied ship production increased and German fuel and raw material shortages bit hard. Surprisingly, many liner companies continued publishing sailing dates and ports of call. P&O's 7,979-ton, 18-knot *Persia* for example, was announced leaving London on 18th December 1917 for Marseilles and from there on the 25th for Bombay and Karachi. Off Crete on the 30th, it was torpedoed and sunk with 335 out of 501 lives lost.[12] British blockade of Germany was made more difficult by Germany's defeat of Russia, which slid into revolution.

The Zimmerman telegram, inciting Mexico to war with America and more American ships sunk resolved President Wilson to war. Its army was transported to Europe on merchant ships and liners without loss. By 1917 there was widespread German malnutrition, scurvy, tuberculosis and dysentery. In November 1918 acute shortages brought workers onto the streets. Morale collapsed and Wilhelm fled. Maritime blockade was pivotal to German defeat, deprived of coal, non-ferrous metals and fertilisers, leading to food shortages. It was lifted after the Treaty of Versailles was signed, although food imports were allowed under allied control until then. In Belgium, northern France and Poland where Germans confiscated the harvest, the situation was certainly worse. German propaganda used the delay, designed to get German agreement to peace, as inhuman, deliberate starvation. While there were deaths, they were self-inflicted. Deliberate starvation was another German myth.[13]

The British free trade economy in 1914 was unique, its major industries, textiles, coal, engineering and shipbuilding, produced mainly for export. It had huge imports, serviced in British-built, -financed and -insured ships. Its £4 billion overseas investments far exceeded other nations, impressive relative to gross domestic product of £2.3 billion, which assisted exports.[14] Britain's industrial lead had been overtaken but merchant and banking firms' networks, shipping facilities and companies made London the world's financial capital. Liverpool and Glasgow competed for the title 'second city of empire.' Without war Britain would not have continued to supply two thirds of the world's cotton cloth, 80% of its coal and half its shipbuilding, but war smashed what could have been managed <u>relative</u> decline.

Given Britain's dependence on maritime trade and international finance it is unsurprising that war badly shook its economy. Sinking 40% of Britain's merchant fleet was the largest loss of capital equipment, the death of 745,000 under-45-year-olds, including 37,500 officers, the largest loss of well-educated men. Nearly a third of Cambridge graduates who served were killed, 1.65 million were wounded, many so seriously, they never worked again, a generation of potential leaders, inventors and entrepreneurs wiped-out.[15]

Marine losses were unevenly distributed. Elder-Dempster lost 42 ships. Because of its Asian concentration, Holts only lost 18. Due to their 1915/1917 take-over of Indra Line and Knight Line, both Asian trade specialists, they ended the war with more ships than in 1914 and made decent wartime profits.[16] During the war, P&O acquired New Zealand's Union Steamship, Hain Steamship Co. and James Nourse Ltd, 107 ships, over 370,000 tons, but lost 58 ships in 1917–1918. Acquisitions however, meant its 1914 total of 1.1 million tons became 1.5 million in 1918.

The standard freight index, 100 in 1869 which sunk to 50 in 1910, was 751 in 1918.[17] Holt's dividends rose from £106,334 in 1913, 1914 and 1915 to £212,668 in 1917 and 1918. Earnings of £482,072 in 1914 rose to just under £3 million in 1917. Moreover, it built ships in Hong Kong and in 1915, opened new routes to the west coast and via the Panama Canal to New York, and connected Manila, Hong Kong and Japan.[18] It continued building wharfs and 'godowns' in Hong Kong and Shanghai and made investments in small British shipbuilders and repairers. British shipowners however, were unprepared for peace in a world of damaged production centres and changed markets. Norwegian and Greek third-party carriers were better placed. Greeks had sold nearly 30% of their pre-war tonnage, 114 steamships, at high wartime prices, compared to 147 losses, earning about £30 million from freights, sales and indemnities.[19]

Chapter 38

Imperfect, Unstable Peace

Britain's 1914 £650 million national debt rose to £7,435 million in 1919. Some loans, like those to Russia had to be written-off. It acquired costly territorial Middle East mandates and took-over some German colonies. Its manufacturing had been dislocated and markets lost. Its shipping companies tried maintaining pre-war markets rather than meeting the many technical, financial, competitive challenges and opportunities. Britain was psychologically changed in 1918. The confident, outward-looking maritime emphasis was replaced by introspection and anxiety.

Norway and Greece had much less trade, few major ports, their fleets mainly tramps which can respond faster to change and were more open to worldwide opportunities. But British tramp shipping companies in 1914, most of British shipping, also declined or disappeared, succumbing to difficult markets and low-cost Greek and Norwegian competition. After 1918 few British tramp companies were formed. Liner companies survived by amalgamation. Between 1918 and 1923, P&O bought Orient Line, Khedevial Mail Line, General Steam Navigation Co and Strick Line; about 500 ships.[1]

Politically, Lloyd George argued against the Versailles punitive peace. But France resisted revisions needed for democratic German recovery, to neuter political extremism seen in Russia. Keynes criticised Clemenceau for wanting a Carthaginian peace. America, strongest, fastest-growing economy and largest creditor was reluctant to play the international role vacated by Britain's former enlightened leadership and unwilling to join the League of Nations it sponsored. The USSR became centrally planned. Black Sea exports reduced. Turkey deported Armenians in 1915 and over the next few years, Greeks, Jews and other foreigners were ethnically cleansed. Smyrna never recovered from the 1919–22 Greco-Turkish War. Rotterdam overtook Hamburg as Europe's largest port.

US immigration in 1913 was 1.2 million. In 1921, unemployment led to it being restricted to 3% of each nationality resident in America in 1910, tightened in 1924 to 2% of each nationality resident in 1890. Substantial European emigration to Central and South America continued until the early-1930s. Canada's halved between 1913 and 1929. Trans-Atlantic passenger trade collapsed, thus lines like Cunard suffered most and started catering for industrialists, bankers, businessmen, actors, designers, politicians, and sportsmen. It partly recovered in the late-1920s despite fierce competition. Between 1924 and 1929, Cunard had about 20% of North Atlantic traffic, White Star, 7%, the French Transatlantique Co., 7% and two German lines about 11%.

Resource-rich America with high tariff barriers created badly imbalanced international trade which in 1921 was 22% lower than 1913, reaching pre-war levels only in 1924. Europe also continued high tariffs. France's in 1918 were four-times higher than 1914.[2] Average food import tariffs rose to 53% in France, 59.5% in Austria, 66% in Italy and 75–100% in eastern Europe. US farmland had expanded during the war to meet European demand. As Europe's agriculture recovered, US exports fell, prices plummeted, many farmers became indebted or lost their farms, but US industry thrived. Post-1920 Republican administrations reverted to high tariffs. The 1921 Emergency Tariff Act and the 1922 Fordney-McCumber Tariff made European exports to America difficult. Britain, with two million unemployed, enacted the 1921 Safeguard of Industries Act, not as severe as European or US actions, but a break with free trade. Most nations' tariffs were higher than before the war, exceptionally so in America, Argentina, Australia, Canada, Italy and Spain. Nevertheless, maritime trade grew from 270 million tons in 1923–24 to 308 million tons in 1929.[3]

New York's financial centre rivalled London. Huge American factories created massive economies of scale for consumer goods; automobiles, typewriters, tractors, vacuum cleaners, refrigerators, sewing machines etc., production four-times greater than any other country.[4] By 1929 both Ford and General Motors produced 1.5 million automobiles. No European or Asian firm made over 80,000. The world's twelve largest automobile firms, nine farm machinery producers and five office machinery firms were American. Americans bought 25-times more cars in 1929 than any other country's consumers. Domestic steel consumption supported 62 steelworks producing over 500,000 tons, 18 of which produced over a million. Germany had eight over a million tons and Britain three over 500,000.[5] *The Times* recorded America 'risen from…a simple commercial force to…in financial control of the world.' Safe, it thought, behind tariff walls, it launched a huge export drive and retreated into isolationism, reinforced by Prohibition from 1920, rejected by only two states, Rhode Island and Connecticut, outposts of maritime common sense, temporarily overwhelmed by continentalist, puritan uniformity. As with all bans, it encouraged smuggling, rum from the Caribbean, cognac via St. Pierre and whisky via Nassau, until Prohibition's 1933 suspension.

Making little war contribution, Japan gained Germany's Asian colonies and markets British lines could not service. London lost South American financial markets to New York, Chinese to America and Japan. Australia, Canada and South America had become more industrialised needing fewer British imports. Worse, Britain's enlightened India policy involved 'progressive realisation of responsible government… as an integral part of the British Empire,' enabling India's legislature to control tariffs, raising them against British goods, especially cotton cloth, which in the 1890s had been 40% of Britain's cloth exports, 19% of all British exports and 20% of its overseas investment. Consequently, in the late-1920s British cloth exports were under half 1913's. Japan's cotton cloth exports to India rose from 1% in 1913 to 21% in 1918, at Britain's expense, whose share of Chinese imports fell from 16.5% to 9.5%,[6] while US cotton exports to Latin America rose over 75%. Chinese 1914–1922 textile looms tripled, mainly in Japanese-owned factories,[7] spurring Chinese and Japanese growth. Japan's 240,000-ton 1914 pig iron production increased to 583,000 in 1918, its exports to America rose five-fold. From a 1.1-billion-Yen debtor, by 1920 it was a 2.7 billion creditor. Foreign Minister Kaoru Inoue who wanted a 'European-style empire on the Eastern Sea,' thought the war 'divine aid.' Japan's *zaibatsu* extended manufacturing, banking, insurance, mining and shipping control, especially Mitsui and Mitsubishi, closely associated with the military oligarchy, enabling rapid capital accumulation and technological modernisation. Manufacturing output rose over 50%, exporting to Australia, India, Southeast Asia, Africa, Latin America and especially China. Every country was protectionist. Lack of international cooperation made the world dangerously imbalanced, feeding national prejudices.

Germany, stripped of Alsace and Lorraine, had to pay reparations, from which France wanted to repair its devastated northeast. Considered excessive by some, Germany was destabilised, contributing to hyper-inflation, eliminating savings, reducing the middle class to poverty, destroying respect for government. The 1924 Dawes Plan reduced German payments and gave a loan; welcome US re-engagement with Europe.

Many ships were built in busy British shipyards in the 1919–20 boom at high prices. The Clyde launched a third. The freight index, 751 in 1918, was still 602 in March 1920, but fell to 166 a year later due to oversupply. The Inter-Allied Commission asked Lord Inchcape to sell 196 government and 300 enemy ships, 3.3 million tons at collapsed prices. P&O bought 98.[8] But in 1921, Britain and America launched millions of tons of ships, war loss replacements. The fall was predictable. Walter Runciman had sold his ships at the top of the market, including Newcastle's Moor Line to Cardiff's Edgar Edwards. At the post-war boom's peak there were 150 Cardiff-based shipping companies, after the crash just 77.[9] The world's 49 million grt in 1914 became 61 million by 1922. A 7,500-ton steamship valued at £45,000 in 1914 and £232,500 in January 1920 was worth £105,000 in December, only £70,000 from 1922 to 1930.[10] Birkenhead's Cammell Laird produced the first all-welded ship in 1920, but riveting remained the preferred building method. In 1925 Furness Withy caused an outcry by ordering five ships at a German yard, due to price. Some British shipyards amalgamated but structures and practices remained. Depressed demand discouraged investment in more efficient production. Foreign yards from lower bases, took advantage. The cards were especially stacked against Liverpool due to collapsed emigration, export decline, Japanese competition, Indian boycotts of British goods and NYK's new services, monthly to New York, between Taiwan and Java via Singapore and Hong Kong, to Australia and Liverpool.

Greek shipping, under half its 1913 size through losses and wartime sales, expanded with the increased capital. Foreign banks started lending to them. Not all succeeded. Nicholas Ambatielos contracted nine newbuildings in 1919 without specific delivery dates. When delayed, he was ruined.[11] Rethymnis and Kulukundis (R&K) established in London in 1921, bought many second-hand for clients, a role the Vaglianos pioneered, a few at post-war high prices but most after 1922, close to the market's bottom, taking shares in clients' ships, acting as agents for chartering, insurance and sale and purchase. By 1938 it operated 50 ships, 230,000 grt, 12% of the Greek-owned fleet, representing 12 Piraeus companies.[12]

British coal exports, 73 million in 1913, valuable outbound bulk cargoes, fell due to new fuels and new coal sources. Wage cuts and unemployment resulted. 1929's coal exports were only 84% of 1913 and by 1937 just 57%,[13] Diesel motorships, more expensive to build but cheaper to run in fuel and crew, became attractive. Anglo-Persian Oil's British Tanker Company used them from 1929, generally favoured for tankers, refrigerated ships (reefers) and tramps but not appropriate for short-haul north European routes.[14] British owners continued using steamers because of cheap, plentiful, local coal as outbound cargo. Nations lacking coal embraced diesel engines. Harland and Wolff bought the British rights to Burmeister and Wain's design before the war and built some in the 1920s, while Doxford developed one independently. Diesel engines accounted for 27.8% of British 1920–1939 output, but 41.9% foreign output.[15] British Tanker Co. and Anglo-Saxon Petroleum had British shipyard-built tankers, but Unilever built eight in Germany in 1936–37 and Hunting three in Denmark and Sweden.

British shipping company fortunes fluctuated. Runciman cleverly bought again in 1923. For P&O, 1918–28 was profitable due to renewed passenger services to Australia and New Zealand, but Glen Line paid no dividend after 1923, Lamport and Holt after 1925, while P&O reduced theirs in 1926. Holts' Chinese trade was twice as profitable as others despite collapse into warlord factionalism after 1925, because by 1928 there were over 90 treaty ports, a dozen served by regular lines, reaching previously untapped populations and commodities. Moreover, 1922–1928 rubber exports to Europe increased by a third and Japan-Southeast Asia trade rose.[16] Japan's intentions were imperial. Its 1917–1921 naval programme absorbed a third of its budget. Responding, America transferred most of its fleet to Hawaii's Pearl Harbour.

Many Norwegian ships were laid-up in 1921–23, owners bankrupted, shipyards closed, losses absorbed by banks. Survivors bought increasingly diesel-powered 10–12,000 dwt drybulk ships from British, German, Swedish and Danish shipyards, overtaking Dutch merchant tonnage in 1925; from 1.9 million grt in 1920 to 2.8 million in 1928.[17] World oil transport rose from 14 million tons in 1914 to 60 million in 1931. A few Norwegians who before 1914 bought tankers with long-term charters to oil majors, like Hans Westfal-Larsen and Knut Knutsen, continued the policy. They, Wilhelm Wilhelmsen, Ivara and Fred Olsen ran liners, but tankers became their speciality, as oil discoveries in Mexico, Venezuela and the Middle East increased opportunities. Norwegian-owned tankers doubled between 1914 and 1920, again from 1920 to 1925 and every year to 1931, reaching 1.45 million dwt. With 75% of tankers, oil company-owned, Norwegian owners dominated independents. Its 1914 tanker fleet, 1.5 million tons rose to 11.4 million in 1939. In 1926 Anglo-Saxon sold some with ten-year charter-backs, 22 to Norwegians, two to Germans and two to British. In 1927 Anglo-Saxon tendered for newbuildings with ten-year charters, almost all covered by Norwegians, built at Swedish yards, mainly Gotaverken, with 70% credit, partly paid for by selling 24 older steam tankers. In 1930–31, British yards delivered 78 tankers to Norwegians; 'Norwegian Tanker Year' according to *Motor Ship* magazine, all fixed to oil companies. Shipyard credit against long-term oil major charters gave 20–21% returns when equity rises are considered, begging the question why more British owners did not follow this route, British shipping's main inter-war mistake. By 1939 Norwegians owned 2.12 million dwt, leading the world, when half the world's tonnage was diesel-powered, the only part of inter-war shipping and trading with positive figures, making Norway fourth-largest maritime nation after Britain, America and Japan with 4.8 million grt, 7% of the world fleet.[18]

Shipping was Norway's only internationally important industry, attracting most entrepreneurs. Lacking large foreign trade, Norwegians and Greeks were more aggressive than British owners, even ordering without long-term charters, working on narrower margins, taking greater risks, borrowing heavily, sometimes with government assistance. With high US and European tariffs, British companies increasingly concentrated on colonial markets. Apart from tankers, Norwegians favoured reefers and heavy-lift ships, third-party niche markets. In 1914 Norway's home market employed 60% of its ships, in 1939 barely 25%. Fiell Line's 1920s Great Lakes-Europe ships shifted in winter when the St. Lawrence froze to Palestine's orange exports; the Jaffa Line, while pre-war Caribbean-US fruit ships spread in 1932–33 with Halfden Bugge's regular California-Europe Fruit Express Line's reefers with Sunkist cargo guarantees. One niche Scandinavian business was Gustav Erikson's, who ran over fifteen 3–4,000 dwt sailing ships with Baltic timber to South Africa and Melbourne, returning with Australian wheat to Britain, outbound coal and inbound Chilean nitrates until 1939.

*　*　*

Mid-1920s US prosperity, optimism and financial leverage induced a huge stock market bubble which burst in 1929: the Wall Street Crash. By 1932 US industrial production was half 1929 levels with corresponding unemployment. Five thousand banks collapsed. Others called in loans from Europe. Worldwide depression resulted. Between 1929 and 1932 GDP fell 17% worldwide, <u>26%</u> in America. 1924–1929 world trade had risen 30%. By 1932 it was back to 1921 levels, but the world's fleet had grown to nearly 69 million, a vast oversupply of faster, more efficient ships. 1931–1934 maritime trade fell a disastrous 26%, ship values 60%. In 1932, 25% of Norway's fleet, 294 ships, 1.4 million dwt and 17%, 3.5 million grt of British shipping, was laid-up. Global laid-up tonnage rose from three million grt in 1930 to 14 million in 1932. Massive scrapping resulted. Ships worth £200,000 in 1914–15, were bought for just £5–6,000 by 1933.[19] From 1918 to 1939 about 40 British yards, 35% of British capacity, closed. Some amalgamated. Northeast England with 2% unemployment in 1913, had 30% in 1932. Impoverished Jarrow shipbuilding workers marched to London in 1936 following the 1934 closure of its main employer, Palmer's, established in 1851, which had launched over 1,000 ships. Workers in Midlands and southern-based automobile factories, chemical and electrical industries by contrast, were relatively prosperous.

The infamous 1930 Smoot-Hawley Tariff, meant to relieve American farmers, included many industrial goods. It raised average tariffs to almost 60%, with many non-tariff barriers, despite opposition from all leading American economists, Ford and other large producers. Effectively America aimed to flood the world with cheap exports but prevent it selling anything back, a deeply flawed idea which provoked European boycotts of American goods and retaliatory tariffs, Mussolini's Italy to 100%, virtually halting its American car imports. France and Germany also targeted its cars and radios. Smoot-Hawley failed to halt the agricultural crisis, lift prices or improve domestic employment and dramatically worsened international trade and relations as the world headed for national self-sufficiency: autarchy. Pre-war protectionism was potentially dangerous but did little damage until the 1920s-1930s. America not only failed to replace Britain's stabilising role, it shattered trust in trade reciprocity.

Atlantic trade suffered most. American imports from Europe declined from $1,334 million in 1929 to just $390 million in 1932 while American exports declined from $2,341 million to $784 million and hugely imbalanced. Rubber imports from Southeast Asia increased and intra-Asian trade was still profitable. China's foreign concession territories introduced electricity, telephones, cars, running water and a commercial infrastructure amid political chaos. Blue Funnel ships sailed from Birkenhead with 1,500 tons of cargo, not 6–7,000 previously loaded, as profits fell from £848,829 in 1929 to £423,570 in 1930 to just £156,579 in 1931, recovering in 1932 to £483,275.[20] Atlantic-focused Cunard's losses increased from £533,000 in 1931 to £927,000 in 1932. The French Transatlantique Co. lost 30 million francs in 1930 and 236 million in 1931, saved from bankruptcy by government, as it laid-up 52 of its 98 ships. A million American passengers to Europe fell to 460,000 by 1934.[21] British exports fell from £729 million in 1929 to £389 million in 1932.

P&O paid no dividend between 1931 and 1935. Holts reduced then suspended their 1931 payment, cut pay, jobs and reduced the 1929–1933 Java voyages from 33 to 22, the New York service from 30 to 13, the Australian fortnightly service became monthly, even suspended for a few months.[22] Many companies, if surviving, remained depressed for a decade. Holts resumed dividends in 1933 as China and Southeast Asian routes were profitable, but 1929–1936 trans-Atlantic and trans-Pacific trades were loss-making, over-tonnaged by subsidised fleets. The government forced a Cunard-White Star merger in 1934 in return for a £4.5 million loan to build the *Queen Mary* and *Queen Elizabeth*. By 1933 British shipping's invisible earnings were 40% of 1920s levels, by 1938–39 still only 60%.[23]

In the 1919–22 Greco-Turkish War, Black Sea grain was halted, replaced by American, Canadian, Australian and Argentine. Greek Black Sea ships started competing in Argentina-Europe trade, previously dominated by British ships. Black Sea grain exports after 1925 surpassed pre-war levels, encouraging ship purchases in the 1920s, more in the 1930s when prices were exceptionally low. By 1929, 900,000 nrt of Greek ships entered the River Plate.[24] From 1914 to 1938 Greek shipping went from 13th to 9th position, 3% of world tonnage: 16% of bulk tramps, compared to Japan's 11%, Norway's 8%, all growing at British expense, down to 39%. Eleven London Greek shipping offices in 1914, grew to 17 in 1938 handling nearly 1,000,000 grt, 48% of its fleet. Unlike Britain, America, Germany, Italy, Japan and France subsidised their merchant fleets. Canada and Australia had government-owned lines in the 1920s and Australia reserved coastal trade for domestic ships.

The fastest growing pre-war shipping company was Sir Owen Philipps' Royal Mail, absorbing Lamport and Holt in 1910, Elder-Dempster in 1911 after Alfred Jones' 1909 death and Union Castle in 1911, then Glen Line, Shire Line and in 1917 MacAndrews.[25] Considered good buys for a well-run line, they adopted diesel engines.

By 1929 his 140 companies, over 700 ships, over 25 million grt, 15% of the British fleet, was the world's largest shipping conglomerate. The crash and depression caused the ennobled Philipps, Baron Kylsant's shipping empire's 1930 bankruptcy. Dubious accounting practices led to trial and imprisonment. R&K and other Greeks made huge purchases of Kyslant's and other ships flooding the market at historic low prices. Kyslant's failure discouraged British investors. In 1932, Elder-Dempster was hived off with 55 ships to Holt who also bought Glen and Shire in 1935 from the Trustees at half the price offered in 1930. He modernised with eight fast new ships,[26] necessary because the fleet was ageing due to hesitancy to order newbuildings.

Between 1935 and 1939 British, Greek, Norwegian, Dutch, French and Italian shipowners combined into a Minimum Rate Scheme administered by the Tramp Shipping Cooperation Committee for Argentina, Canadian and Australian grain,[27] although there was no guarantee they would find charterers and some discounted to secure employment. Buenos Aires-based tobacco merchant Aristotle Onassis, faced with falling sales, noticed cheap ship prices. After spending six months with the Dracoulis Brothers' London office he bought two ships for £3,750 in 1932, the bottom of the market. Stavros Niarchos, in the family grain business from 1929, convinced that shipownership could save Argentine and Baltic grain freight, also bought in the Depression.

Britain's pre-war rough balance between imports and exports, balanced by invisibles changed. Imports were maintained or grew but exports declined. With American and Japanese commercial invasion of traditional British markets, Britain seemed to have no alternative but revive Imperial Preference, rejected in 1906. The 1931 Import Duties Act fixed 10% tariffs on foreign manufacturers, reaffirmed at the 1932 Ottawa Conference with large Imperial Preferences. Dunlop supported it because mass production required a 'secure market of sufficient volume.' ICI sought a 'self-sufficient economic system' as 'an exclusively British trading area.'[28] Imperial Preference's impact was economically small, but unlike pre-1914, by 1934 the empire took 44% of British exports, a pattern continuing into the 1960s, ending free trade orthodoxy, reinforcing the flawed idea of protected blocs. China's nationalist government battered by warlords, Japan's army and silk and tea export collapse, turned to western economists and engineers to help banking, tax, transport and communication systems in cities and treaty ports, which were relatively prosperous. Most peasants however were victims of soil exhaustion, erosion, flooding and exploitative tenancy.

1929–1935 were the worst sustained shipping years ever experienced. President Roosevelt's 1934 Reciprocal Trade Agreements Act was the first step to return to economic integration, mutually beneficial lower-duties up to 50%, ending disastrous, beggar-thy-neighbour tariffs. Secretary of State Cordell Hull, like many southerners, hating high tariffs, thinking a 'prohibitive, protective tariff is a gun that recoils upon ourselves,' his warnings previously unheeded, spent 1934–1939 negotiating them. Furthermore, between 1935 and 1937, five million grt of ships were scrapped, allowing better supply/demand balance. Tankers started recovering in 1936 and by 1937 oil's 490 million tons surpassed 1929's volume.[29] But much political and economic damage had been done. 1937's drybulk volumes were still lower than 1929 or 1914, the world fleet almost stagnant; 64.4 million grt in 1922, 67.4 million in 1939.[30] Oil transport however, for heating, propulsion and automobiles increased 150%; 107.3 million tons in 1922 to 268 million in 1938, 20% of total seaborne trade. Drybulk trade declined 15%.

The 1935 British Shipping (Assistance) Act provided subsidies if freights dropped below sustainable levels. A scrap-and-build scheme was introduced if built in British yards. Compared to subsidised foreign shipowners, it was too little, too late. Kylsant had many diesel-powered ships but in 1939 British owners only had 25% compared with Norway's 62%, Denmark's 52% and Sweden's 46%.[31] Britain's 1,500 ships of five million grt compared with Norway's 600 ships of three million. Safety requirements continued improving. Radio transmission enabling the *Titanic* to transmit SOS before sinking in 1912, became mandatory on passenger ships and in 1929 on all ships over 1,600 tons.

In the 1930s, NYK introduced six heavily-subsidised, 18-knot liners for New York. Southeast Asia's tin, rubber, copra, palm oil, dyes, tobacco, rice, timber, sugar and coffee trades, which collapsed in the Depression, recovered in the late-1930s. There were few new inter-war British shipowners. Vestey's chilled Argentinian beef to Britain business moved to Australia, because of Imperial Preference. Queensland specialised in chilled beef, 94% to Britain in 1938, 52% of all its chilled beef imports. Britain also took 94% of Australia's butter and 97% of its cheese. By 1940 Australia and New Zealand exported 620,000 tons of meat to Britain in large reefers. In 1913 Liverpool handled 31% of British trade, by 1938 only 20.8%, while London's increased to 38.1%.[32] Glasgow's, Hull's, Dundee's and Manchester's trade also reduced, unbalancing Britain's economy to the southeast.

Hamburg registered over two million grt in 1930, half Hapag's. Blohm and Voss was Europe's largest shipyard. In Germany's 1930 election, Communists got 13.1% and Hitler's Nazis 18.3%, as it pressed to end reparations and lift military restrictions. By 1933 the Nazis got 40% and seized power, Germany again ruled by a fanatic. Hitler gave it another dangerous myth, that in 1918 they were close to Paris, held Ukraine and the Baltic States and should have and could have won the war if not cheated by Jews and Communists. In 1933 Jews and foreigners in Hapag were purged, self-inflicted harm when trade networks depend on multiple nationalities and local knowledge. In Russia, marginal to maritime trade, Stalin's ruthless collectivisation probably cost three million lives. In 1939 Europe had fewer constitutional states than 1921.

By 1934 Britain's largest tramp company was Ropner's 50 ships of 240,000 grt. But in sharp contrast to 1914, liners dominated British shipping. In 1939, P&O had 371 ships of 2,133,000 grt, Furness Withy 129 of 1,099,000, Cunard 64 of 821,000 and Holts 115 of 744,000.[33] With renewed trade growth, 1937 freight rates finally surpassed 1929 levels and the 1938 freight index rose from 80 to 143, declining again with new deliveries, but the maritime world continued creativity, advances led by British and US scientists. The City's position as a maritime trade hub strengthened. In the 1920s, the Baltic Exchange daily traded 250,000 tons of grain, worth around £2.5 million. Its face-to-face freight market was indispensable to tramp owners. But British shipping fell from 48% of world tonnage in 1914 to 32.5% in 1937.

*   *   *

Japanese exports to America, 15% of all exports were killed-off by the Smoot-Hawley Tariff. Unemployment rose to a million, remedied by military-colonial expansion in China, another protected trade bloc. Manchukuo, Japanese Manchuria, was established in 1932, ruled by the army, a market of 30 million people and huge mineral and agricultural resources. Contrasting with everywhere else, 1931–1935 Japanese steel exports rose 900%, machinery 600% and automobiles 540% mainly to its Chinese and Korean colonies.[34] 1930–1936 exports increased from Yen 1,435 to 2,641 million, led by textiles, especially cotton cloth, cutting hard into Lancashire's exports.[35] The *zaibatsu* supported territorial expansion, bigger markets and more raw materials. Banks and trading firms built large European-style buildings on Chinese ports' main streets. Chinese workers were kept on starvation wages. Japan's army lived off the land. It and the navy consumed 60% of government expenditure. It left the League of Nations in 1933, no longer tolerating criticism of its Korean and Manchurian actions, taking Shanghai, killing or wounding 250,000, then Nanking in an orgy of terror, rape and massacre. Within a year, Japan controlled all eastern China. Resistance was met with the three 'alls'; kill all, burn all, loot all.[36] In 1935 Italy attacked Ethiopia, like Germany and Japan, its imperial land-grabbing ambitions unfulfilled. Britain's not closing the Suez Canal to Italian troops, demonstrated weakness to aggressors. Germany sent troops to the Rhineland in 1936 to test France, which also did nothing. In 1938, with all China's ports under Japanese control, Britain and America which had supplied Japan with cotton, petroleum, steel, machinery, metals and timber, half of all American exports to Asia, embargoed them. Southeast Asian oil, metals and rubber were mainly under British, American and Dutch rule. Japanese conquest of them needed America's Pacific fleet eliminated.

Richard Holt had told shareholders in 1932 that company prosperity depended on peace, thus final settlement of reparations. War debts must be made so 'debtors can pay what is due from them without exhausting their vitality' and 'monstrous tariffs, prohibitions and other interferences' be eliminated.[37] But it took the League of Nations until 1938 to recommend urgent tariff relaxation. Too late. A week later Hitler annexed Austria. Britain could never solve the problem of defending itself <u>and</u> empire especially with German and Japanese air power. Isolationist America was committed to neutrality. Britain had to work for peace.

Realisation that war was coming began dawning on Britain and France. From late-1937, Sir Frederick Leith-Ross, the British government's chief economic advisor, realising Nazis prioritised prestige over economic well-being, urged plans for a Great War-like blockade plan, using Britain's overseas business network in world ports for intelligence-gathering. The Navy had advance warning of possible contraband-carrying ships. Nor was the City caught out as in 1914. Holts prepared themselves, fitting 'defensive armour' on some ships as early as February 1938.[38] Germany was not as rich as 1914 when it had plentiful gold, foreign currency and good credit ratings, but geared itself into an almost self-sufficient war economy, imports reduced, with price and wage controls, strategic materials stockpiled and heavy investment made in synthetic *ersatz* industries to make textiles from cellulose, rubber and oil from coal, sugar and ethyl alcohol from wood. A week before Germany invaded Poland, it announced food, coal, textiles and soap rationing. Germans knew war was coming.

Chapter 39

The Second World War

Two days after Poland's invasion, Anchor-Donaldson Line's *Athenia* was torpedoed and sunk, resuming Great War tactics, strangling British trade and communications. At the outbreak, 30% of German merchant ships were at sea and sought shelter in neutral ports. Perishable cargo rotted and strategic goods went undelivered, but like Napoleon and the Kaiser, Hitler's priorities were land-based. As in the Great War, Britain's fleet at Scapa Flow blocked the North Sea. Merchant ships were examined there, Gibraltar, Malta, Haifa, the Channel and Aden. Intelligence-gathering and Contraband Control information collectors had been efficient. Neutral ships were surprised at British knowledge. Most neutral captains voluntarily stopped at Contraband Control ports. Leith-Ross also collected trade statistics for bordering countries so that if exceeding peacetime levels, action could be taken. In the first four weeks, the Royal Navy confiscated 289,000 tons and the French 100,000 tons, including petrol, sulphur, textiles, food, copper, virtually all cargo types; in the first 15 weeks 870,000 tons, 10% of Germany's peacetime imports. Following British requisitions, the 1940 Anglo-Norwegian Agreement requisitioned 150 tankers and 450,000 grt of dry cargo. Shipowners were paid 'Blue Book' rates, allowing 5% return on capital.[1] Convoys were immediately introduced on some routes, although lacked sufficient escorts. U-boats targeted those sailing independently, in the first six months sinking 164 ships, although only seven in convoys.[2]

Norway's inter-war merchant ship replenishment meant it had 2,000 in 1939, only exceeded by Britain, America and Japan. Scandinavia, Belgium and Holland continued trading with Germany, according to a frustrated Churchill, 'hoping that if he feeds the crocodile enough…[it] will eat him last…that the storm will pass before it is their turn to be devoured.' As in the Great War, Swedish iron ore was shipped to Germany, about a third of its consumption through Norway's port, Narvik, protected after defeat of France, Norway and Denmark. Britain imported wheat from Halifax and seized more contraband than ships being torpedoed. Neutral ships joined allied convoys; Norway's four million grt and Greeks' 1.8 million, important contributions. Occupied countries' shipping offices, including Greeks, re-located mainly to London, a few to New York, partly because Greece's government tried taxing shipowners' freights, 'the taxation of the wealthy', requiring declaration of foreign assets, whether under Greek or foreign flag.[3] By late-1939, at least 19 German merchant ships scuttled themselves. In early-1940 Hitler ordered the rest, about 60 in South America, incurring huge port costs, to return. Few did, but U-boats sank allied ships. The Balkans supplied grain, meat, metals, minerals and oil from Romania. Britain agreed Iranian oil supply and all Norway's whale oil surplus. But, as in the Great War, exports suffered, falling 37% compared to 1935. Gold and dollar reserves were almost exhausted.

Admiral Doenitz deployed 100 U-boats in 'wolf packs' to attack Atlantic convoys. Britain rushed to build escorts after the allies lost 1.7 million tons between March and May 1940. Attempted destruction of the RAF accompanied bombing of London, Liverpool, Southampton and Portsmouth docks. Despite severe damage, discharging war goods and food continued. The RAF attacked ships and barges assembled at Antwerp, Ostend, Calais and Boulogne preparing invasion. Late-1940 victory at Taranto cut Italy off from 80% of its imports. Like the Anglo-Norwegian Agreement, in the 1941 Anglo-Greek Mutual Aid Agreement, Britain chartered all Greek ships over 4,000 dwt. During the 1940 Battle of Britain, Norwegian tankers carried a third of Britain's petroleum imports. Ministry of Shipping's control meant, unlike in the Great War, London's shipbrokers lost their income, their enterprise and efficiency replaced by chartering committees. Breaking Germany's codes enabled convoys to route away from U-boat packs. July-December 1941 tonnage losses halved in first half 1942, still heavy, almost eight million tons.

US public opinion under Roosevelt became less isolationist, more realistic in needing to spend more on defence against Japan's threat. Churchill thought only US shipping food and materials would prevent Britain's defeat. In late-1940, it finally turned from neutrality into the 'arsenal of democracy', without declaring war. In March 1941 Lend Lease was passed, sending war materials while U-boats sank 500,000 tons of shipping a month. The military costs of Japan's war in China were crippling. Pre-war, it depended on US scrap, aluminium, nickel and oil. Roosevelt in 1941 embargoed oil and froze Japanese assets in America. In December 1941, Japan attacked Pearl Harbour's US Pacific fleet while consolidating Southeast Asian gains; French Indochina, Malaya, Singapore, the Philippines and Java. Germany also declared war. Japan tried shipping rubber to Germany but were captured *en route*. Japan's *zaibatsu* moved into heavy industry, the big four controlling the wartime economy, producing bombers, fighters and ships. Japan was not a pure military dictatorship. The *zaibatsu* were as much in control.

The allies concentrated first on Europe. America's Board of Economic Warfare bought strategic materials to supply allied needs and dealt with neutral Portugal, Spain, Sweden, Turkey, Argentina and Switzerland, all different cases geographically and in sympathies, by diplomacy and veiled threat. With Channel shipping unsafe many convoys were directed to the Mersey and Clyde. All remaining Dutch, Belgian, Norwegian and Danish ships joined British convoys. Like Napoleon's conquered territories, they were plundered. Locomotives, rail cars, machines, instruments, clothing, tools, soap, art, even door knobs were looted. Farmers were forced to sell animals and food. Annual crop percentages were soon replaced by random, all-encompassing seizures. European industry and agricultural resources were bled to feed Germany's war machine, causing famine and death. German labour shortages were solved by virtual enslavement of occupied labour. Greece's food was taken, people's suffering relieved, despite past enmity, by Turkey, which sent food and medicines, but by January 1942 up to 2,000 daily died in Athens and Piraeus. Britain and America lifted the blockade for <u>humanitarian</u> reasons; the eventual death toll, over 70,000. Poland, Yugoslavia, Czechoslovakia and Holland were pillaged. By November 1943 the allies believed Germany had appropriated over $12,800 million which continued. German supply problems were partly solved by capture of wheat-rich Ukraine and Donetsk's industrial region, producing 80% of Soviet steel, coal, manganese and aluminium and Caucasus oilfields. Russia relocated some industries further east, retreating using 'scorched earth'.

By January 1943 Germany had 409 U-boats. In February-March four convoys lost 38 out of 191 merchant ships with only three U-boats sunk. March losses shocked the allies into closing the 'air gap' where merchant ships were unprotected by aircraft, with long-range patrols from Newfoundland. and Iceland. U-boat losses rose immediately, 31 in the first 22 days of May before being recalled. Germany's target of sinking 1.3 million tons/month became unrealistic.

A vital component of eventual victory was the efficient supply of food and materials in mass-produced US and Canadian ships, prefabricated and welded, which allowed lighter, stronger hulls; about 490 16,500-dwt T2 tankers, 2,770 Liberty 10,500-dwt tweendeckers and 500 slightly larger, faster Victory ships. Welding, adopted in the Great War, quicker than riveting, required less labour and training. British yards' 277 Empire ships, of which Germany sank 50, continued riveting,[4] a foretaste of post-war managers' and unions' unwillingness to address a fast-changing world.

German labour shortages grew acute, so increasingly relied on slaves. Britain and America disrupted industrial production by bombing factories and oil fields, initially ineffective and costly in aircraft and crews, but more significant after allied victories at El Alamein and Stalingrad. In mid-1944, the second front opened in Normandy. Blockading Germany did not work as well as in the Great War because it controlled more European territory, but its effects were cumulative and as before, victory was achieved by maritime control. Retreating Germans destroyed port facilities until coordinated resistance led to Antwerp's lightening liberation, <u>almost undamaged</u> on 4th September. With the Scheldt estuary secure in November, Liberties and Empire ships reinforced allied troops through Antwerp. As they closed-in, thousands of Dutch died in winter famine. Sweden felt safe enough to stop supplying iron ore. Japan was also blockaded, the 6.1 million tons of Japanese shipping regularly sunk, reduced to under five million by late-1943, just over 2.5 million by late-1944, 1.5 million by the war's end, strangling its economy, inability to import enough oil and other resources, a major factor in defeat. As Japan's defeat loomed, the *zaibatsu* protected their ownership of the industrial economy.

Part Six

Re-Emerging Enlightenment

Chapter 40

Recovery. 1945–1960s

America already recognised inter-war mistakes. John Bell Condliffe in 1941 explained, 'If an international system is to be restored, it must be…American-dominated…based on *Pax Americana*.[1] The Roman maritime world flourished under *Pax Romana*, the 1815–1914 world under *Pax Britannica*. During the war American industrial production surged almost 50%. Its industrial rivals were in ruins. Responsible American power was needed. At the 1944 Bretton Woods Conference, its Treasury Secretary stated the aim, 'a dynamic world economy in which the peoples of every nation will be able to realise their potentialities in peace and enjoy the fruits of material progress.' By its end, the World Bank and International Monetary Fund (IMF) were founded, groundwork laid for the General Agreement on Tariffs and Trade (GATT), which met every few years to reduce tariffs. By 1951, pre-war barriers were largely demolished. Nations were encouraged to transform their economies through trade; a new economic environment based on world financial institutions, stable currencies, capital investment in underdeveloped regions and liberalised capital flows. Wealth-creation depended on maritime trade and efficient shipping. International regulations, developed at Britain's initiative since the mid-19th century, needed an international body to effectively promote it. Formed in 1948, a London-headquartered United Nations (UN) body now called the International Maritime Organisation (IMO) provided inter-government regulatory and technical cooperation for the highest practicable maritime safety, efficiency, seafarers' welfare, passenger safety, rules for carriage of dangerous cargoes, traffic routing, collision avoidance, training certification, pollution avoidance and much else as the post-war world revolutionised ship design, size and cargo volumes. Its motto was 'Safe, secure and efficient shipping in clean oceans.' It had a long, difficult birth, only 21 countries ratifying by 1958, but is now considered the most successful, best-run UN body.

In 1945, America was the dominant world power, with 75% of the world's gold and greatest creditor nation. Britain, in 1913 the largest creditor, became the largest debtor, its emergency $3.75 billion loan finally repaid in 2006. Britain still led in shipping and shipbuilding, <u>but</u> with 19th-century structures. Liverpool's city and docks were badly bomb-damaged, a third of the berths unusable. America refused French reparation demands, fearing a repeat of 1918–21's mistakes. The 1948–51 Marshall Plan, a comprehensive programme to rebuild Europe, enlightened self-interest, dispensed $12.5 billion. The Organisation of Economic Cooperation and Development (OECD), a conduit for Marshall Aid, generated European industrialisation, establishing markets for American goods. The USSR refused to join, brutally occupying eastern Europe. Its economies struggled under central control, widening economic division. With most ports ruined, undamaged Antwerp in January-June 1945 discharged 1,710 ships, 4.87 million tons to aid recovery. Its Compagnie Maritime Belge (CMB), whose origins were from early-century Belgian Congo Elder-Dempster exports, having diversified into port services, benefitted from Antwerp's good fortune. It fitted Victory ships with reefer spaces, vegetable oil tanks and passenger cabins and provided US and Congo sailings.

As in 1918, Britain lost many lucrative export markets and imports had risen. Stationing troops in Germany, Austria, Italy, Cyprus, Palestine, India and Malaya, the army devoured half the defence budget. It scrapped most aircraft carriers. It helped stabilise a damaged world, still a great power, but economically ruined. Unlike the post-Great War boom, bust, hesitating recovery then depression, post-1945 western Europe's economy expanded. Pre-war trade levels, 490 million tons, were surpassed in 1948. The 1951 *Economic Survey for Europe* predicted 40–60% industrial production growth by 1960. Because of the Marshall Plan, it was surpassed in under five years, the momentum continuing. Maritime trade volumes rose; 500 million tons in 1950, 800 million in 1955, 1.86 billion in 1967, 3.2 billion in 1973, especially oil. In 1948 world shipbuilding output was 2.48 million grt, in 1958, 9.27 million, inducing complacency in British shipyards. Strong maritime trade growth meant post-1945 ships, liners, tramps and tankers, few ships over 20,000-dwt, began diversifying in type and increasing sizes.

Britain lost over 11 million tons of merchant shipping during the war, 60% of 1939's ships. Unlike the Great War, there were no windfall profits to fund post-war shipping. Of Holt's pre-war 77 ships, 38 remained, a third still coal-burners. Of P&O's 371 ships, 2.2 million tons, only 1.2 million survived.[2] Holts bought three ships from the government and ordered eight diesel-powered newbuildings. Over 2,400 Liberties survived the war. A third formed America's Naval Reserve, the rest sold in 1946, offsetting British shipyard delays caused by post-war labour and materials shortages. Holts, needing more ships for their Asian lines, bought 14. It should have bought more when freight rates were buoyant, prices cheap and shipping space short. Ben Line did and captured more Asian trade; expansion, not just restoration.[3]

Greeks lost 70% of their 1.8 million grt in the war, which Manolis Kulukundis thought could be replaced by Liberties and T2s, bought 25% in cash, the balance by US credit with Greek government guarantees.[4] Greeks bought 526 Liberties, British 200 and Italians 98. Shipowners like John Fredriksen, Aristotle Onassis, Stavros Niarchos, George Livanos, the Gouldandris brothers, the Andreadis, Tsaviliris, Lauro, Grimaldi and Bottiglieri families started or extended their fleets with Liberties, fundamental to subsequent shipping recovery, generating sizeable incomes in a good market. Excluded from Greece's government scheme because he was an Argentine citizen, the soon-to-be-famous Onassis bought ten Liberties and T2s. The Liberties cost $600,000 each. Onassis had $3 million capital, the balance a US bank loan against five 12-month charters to the French government, the hire paid directly to the bank. When rates rose in 1948–49, he sold seven for a million each. The T2s cost $1.7 million each in 1946, secured by three-year charters, which rapidly repaid the loans.

Oil's importance in the world economy saw 1915's 2.4 million dwt of tankers increase to 8.2 million in 1925, 13.5 million in 1935, 21.7 million in 1945 and 64 million by 1961. By 1963, a billion tons was transported annually.[5] America imported mainly from Venezuela, Japan mainly from Indonesia, both increasingly from the Persian Gulf, the main exporter. Greeks previously mainly operated bulkers but rising oil demand and tripling 1948–1951 freights led them into tankers, led by Niarchos, Onassis and London and Overseas Freighters (LOF), Liberty profits providing the capital. When Congress in 1948 stipulated further Liberty/T2 sales until March 1949 only to US citizens, Onassis, Livanos, Niarchos and Kulukundis formed US companies. With oil companies and law firms' support, they appeared to be US-controlled. Onassis bought 14 T2s and nine Liberties. Between 1946 and 1951 he bought 56 second-hand ships, but from 1951 only newbuildings at US, German and French yards, including 16 whaling ships between 1950 and 1956 in Germany, which in 1938–39 had 56 whalers, the third-largest fleet after Norway and Britain. With newbuildings and converted T2s, Onassis' whalers ruthlessly broke most rules regarding territorial waters, seasons, permitted captured species and numbers, a whale massacre as whale oil prices rose, selling out to Japanese owners in 1956.

Oil companies dominated by Chevron, Esso, Gulf, Mobil, Texaco, Anglo-Dutch Shell and Britain's BP, the Seven Sisters, made deals with Saudi Arabia, Kuwait and Iran for supplies to service European and Japanese economies. After 1948 America became a net importer. In 1950 a barrel of Middle East oil cost $1, freight to Europe also $1. Thus, shipping continued as core oil company business, owning and chartering from independent shipowners, mainly Greek and Norwegian, typically 5–7-year charters, some longer, enabling finance. Onassis' ships had separate companies, ring-fencing potential financial or legal issues.

Greeks especially used Panamanian or Liberian registry. Panama, a *de facto* US colony due to US Canal Zone control, from 1916 allowed foreigners company control. Large US, especially oil companies used them from the 1920s: a low-cost alternative to US registry. Liberian registration/flag was established in 1948, also US-administered for the same reason. Honduras, Bermuda, Isle of Man, Cyprus, Malta and many others followed. America imported oil and exported government cargoes in American-owned ships, registered in Panama, operated with little tax, low registration fees, fewer regulations and cheap foreign crews. By1949, 50% of Greek-owned ships were foreign-registered and by 1957, 87%. During the 1950s, Greeks operated 80–90% of Liberian-flagged ships and 45% of Panama's.

Southern Russia's Greek merchants had relocated during the 1917 revolution, Istanbul- and Smyrna-based Greeks in the Greco-Turkish War, so by 1938 there were 320 Greek shipping companies in Piraeus and London, rising to 350 in 1958, over 800 in 1975, the largest owners in London. London Greeks ran foreign-registered ships' commercially from London, technical operations from Piraeus. London offices acted as their agent, minimising legal and tax issues. British owners did not embrace these cheaper costs. In 1957, over 400 tramps were still British-flagged.[6] The London-based International Transport Workers Federation (ITF) in low markets threatened foreign-registered ships with boycott and their safety standards improved. Over half the world's fleet sail under what are now called international registries, breaking the link between shipowner, shipping company, flag and nationality, serving international trade, not one country. Most opened London offices to liaise with the IMO and ITF.

*   *   *

Japanese occupation left Asia devastated. A Blue Funnel master in 1947 wrote of Shanghai's 'chaotic state', the collapsed exchange rate, life's essentials meagre and expensive, destitution rife.' In Yokohama, US forces 'control everything, labour, ships' movements.' Much was destroyed by bombing, 'little or nothing…for sale', Kobe 'a shell of its former self,' although Holt's Hong Kong warehouses were intact and in Singapore, little expense was needed to re-start operations.[7] In 1946 George Holt, thought it 'well on the way to recovery'. Swires' Shanghai damages were however huge, its wharves, warehouses and buildings destroyed or damaged and Hong Kong's buildings, go-downs, the Taikoo Sugar Refinery and Dockyard ruined. A 1951 UN report on Southeast Asia noted millions, 'near the borderline between hunger and famine.'[8] In China, communist-nationalist civil war resulted in Shanghai's exports dwindling to a fraction of the 1930s. But other volumes increased. 1949's Suez Canal tonnage increased 36% during 1948.[9] Newbuildings, Liberties and acquisitions enabled Blue Funnel weekly sailings by 1950, halved the fleet's average age, were faster with better cargo-handling equipment than most competitors.

Supreme Commander General McArthur dismantled the Japanese army except self-defence and banned former officers from political leadership. He promoted free speech, civil liberties and local democracy, redistributed land to tenant farmers and maintained Emperor Hirohito as figurehead with a democratic parliament, which renounced war. Strengthening rather than punishing was partly due to fear of growing Chinese and Southeast Asian communist insurgency, thus the attempted break-up of *zaibatsu* was abandoned, so despite Japanese wartime barbarity, America supported Japan's economic recovery. Its Ministry of International Trade and Industry (MITI) prioritised steel, automobiles and shipbuilding.

Without German and Japanese competition, fully laden British outbound ships compensated for homebound raw material shortfalls from devastated economies. British lines re-supplied Asia until 1953 when German and Japanese lines re-entered the Far East Conference. Holts tried excluding Mitsui because merchants and shipowners disliked Mitsui's roles in trading and shipping. The 'Mitsui Fight' resulted in liner rates falling 20–30% as costs rose and profits were squeezed. It joined in 1955 under NYK's wing. Meanwhile, many ships installed radar, radio telephones, RDF equipment and Japan pioneered 'all automated' ships with smaller crews.

In 1951 American Daniel K. Ludwig's National Bulk Carriers set-up Japan's first shipyard for large bulkers and tankers at Kure's former naval yard, building 52 ships, 2.36 million dwt until 1962, copied by other Japanese yards, some on greenfield sites, using US pre-fabrication and welding with Japan Development Bank finance. All aided rapid growth, as post-1945 shipping demand grew; the foundation of Japanese 1950s-60s centrally guided shipbuilding, mainly bulkers, ore carriers and tankers. By contrast, British shipbuilders with full order books, concentrated on labour-intensive passenger and cargo liners, most contracts 'cost-plus', with delivery up to three years. Japan maintained protectionist tariffs to develop industries like motorcycles, which undercut Britain's unprotected industry, which was bankrupted. Electronics and automobiles followed.

After Japanese forces in Korea were removed, America and Russia divided it at the 38th parallel. American forces withdrew in the late-1940s. The north attacked in 1950. America returned, pushing back beyond the 38th parallel. Post-1949 Chinese communist forces supported the north, full-scale proxy US-China war, sparking huge raw material demand, especially petrol, therefore tankers. Maritime trade grew 16% in a year. 1944 Liberty ships worth £110,000 in June 1950 became £500,000 in December 1951, a year later £230,000.[10] With Japan becoming America's wartime base, economic growth was significantly stimulated. The war ended in 1953. Viewing Communist China (from 1949) as a Cold War adversary, America embargoed it. China anyway traded little, carried mainly by liners, Glen's perhaps most and Greek tramps. British exports to Asia significantly declined after 1953, especially textiles, as Japanese and Indian competition increased, while Asia's rubber, tin, hardwoods, palm oil, minerals, sugar, tobacco, fruits and Australian wool, wheat and meat exports grew.

America granted Philippine independence in 1946. India and Pakistan became independent in 1947, adopting socialist economic models. India's Nehru thought the state should occupy 'the commanding heights of the economy', which bred inefficiency and corruption. Both countries stagnated. P&O passengers to and from India fell. The Dutch tried re-establishing imperial power, but in 1949 conceded Indonesia's independence to Sukarno's dictatorship: more slow growth and corruption. In 1950, Holts partnered Philippine's De La Rama Steamship and Swedish Asia Company in De La Rama Line between the Philippines and Hong Kong to US west and east coasts. Holts also ran the Malaya-Indonesia-Jeddah hajj. Chinese communist-backed anti-colonial Asian uprisings led to Malaya's 1948–1957 'Emergency'. France reluctantly recognised independent North and South Vietnam in 1954. Indonesia's army crushed a 1965–1966 communist insurgency with over 250,000 deaths. Authoritarian regimes in both Koreas, both Vietnams, the Philippines, Burma and Southeast Asian communist infiltration meant lethargic economic performance, <u>except</u> Japan, Hong Kong, Taiwan and Singapore after independence from Malaya.

Post-Korean War freight rates fell. General Nasser's 1956 Suez Canal nationalisation triggered a British, French and Israeli invasion, but intense world, especially US, pressure forced withdrawal. Nasser blocked the Canal with concrete-filled ships. Tankers sailed via the Cape, triggering a tanker boom. Interscale surged from 62 to 456 in December 1956. Onassis reputedly made $60 million in six months. As combination carriers switched to oil, bulker rates also improved. In liners, a Blue Funnel 10,000-tonner, pre-closure's 122-day round trip, over half in port, made £37,593 profit. The next via the Cape took 12 days more, netting £51,354, the highest for that ship since the Korean War.[11] *The Times* echoed what many believed; 'a nation of low technical skills such as the Egyptians couldn't manage [the Canal].' Oil companies also believed it. In 1956 they time-chartered 200 tanker newbuildings for 1959 delivery, including many Norwegians who in 1960 owned 542 tankers, most 16–20,000-dwt. Closure also encouraged shipowners to build bigger. A 122,000-dwt tanker was launched in 1959, economies of scale reducing Persian Gulf to Europe, US and Japan freight rates. But Suez reopened in 1957. Rates plummeted, coinciding with record deliveries from 1955–1956 orders. The drybulk market also fell, 62% between late-1956 and late-1957.

* * *

In Australia, about two million tons of coal was annually shipped interstate, mainly from Newcastle for power, railways and from 1951, South Australia's Whyalla Steelworks, but strong unions discouraged investment. Half Australia's early-1950s 250,000-ton annual exports went to New Caledonia's nickel smelters, the rest to New Zealand and nearby islands. Japan produced 50 million tons of steam coal annually, gradually dwindling, ending in the 1980s. It imported coking coal for steel mills, built on coastal sites with deep-water terminals, automated cargo handling and fast discharge from east coast America's Hampton Roads. A 1956 miners' strike forced Japanese steel mills to buy Port Kembla's coking coal. Reduced domestic mining also meant industrial demand for Newcastle's steam coal. Port Kembla's 40-year-old jetty loaded 15,000-tonners at 2,000/eight-hour shift, unions reluctant to work at night. A 1961 steel mill/trading house delegation told NSW's Coal Board and suppliers they needed to seriously improve loading facilities if Port Kembla's 600,000, Newcastle's 750,000 and Sydney's 300,000-ton exports were to increase. They responded. By 1963 Port Kembla and Sydney loaded 30,000-tonners at 10,000/day, each with 1.2 million tons annually. With draft-improvements and new loaders, by 1967 Newcastle's exports reached three million to Japan, Sydney 2.2 million and Port Kembla 1.8 million. Japanese steel mills and industries were directly responsible for Australia's improved port and mining developments.[12]

Queensland started exports in 1959 from Auckland Point with Japanese, American and Australian investors. By 1967 shipments reached 1.7 million tons and in 1968 US-owned Utah Developments, which already developed iron ore and salt mines, so had good Japanese mill and trading company contacts, started exports through Gladstone, 2.3 million tons in 1968, four million in 1969 with a second loader, 5.5 million in 1970, about half NSW coal exports to Japan.[13] Japanese mills used the newbuilding long-term charter model with Japanese ships and as Japanese-flagged and -crewed ships became expensive, Hong Kong-owned ships with open registries and Chinese crew. Growing Asian interaction led to more liberal Australian immigration policy. In 1966 it overturned 1901's Immigration Restriction Act, ending 'White Australia', with migrants selected for skills, not race or colour. By 1973 Australia fully embraced multi-culturalism; another example of maritime trade encouraging toleration.

* * *

P&O recognised before many others that colonial-based liner shipping was doomed. Its bold 1955 move to order twenty-five 20,000-ton tankers for 1958–1960 delivery was compromised by the Suez crisis, modified to fourteen 35,000-tonners. As Britain's dominant independent tanker company, it highlighted others' hesitancy compared to Greek, Japanese and Norwegian owners. In 1960, over 75% of British-flagged tankers were oil company-owned but only 37% of the world's, most of the balance Greek, Japanese and Norwegian-owned. Most British owners ignored new opportunities and ship-types, just like post-1918. As Shell tried interesting British owners in tankers, British Iron and Steel Corporation tried in bulkers, built to its designs. Some like Furness Withy and Denholms did contract, but most missed the opportunity. Belgian steel mill Cockerill however, signed a 20-year contract of affreightment (COA) in 1963 with CMB for a 57,775-dwt newbuilding ore carrier.

In 1950 the largest Norwegian owners were Wilhelm Wilhelmsen, Fred Olsen, Fearnley and Eger, Lief Hoegh, Olsen and Ugelstad, Klaveness, Ivaran and Norwegian-America Line. About 60 operated tankers. From 1946 to 1962 Norway's merchant fleet accounted for two-thirds of new jobs created. In 1965, 85,000 Norwegians comprised over 5% of the world's seamen from a country representing 0.1% of world population, more in shipbuilding and equipment, the maritime sector employing 10% of its mid-1960s male workforce.[14]

By 1964, P&O had 89,000-ton tankers and bulkers, freezer trawlers and roll-on/roll-off ships (ro-ros).[15] By 1966, 250,000-ton tankers, (Very Large Crude Carriers, VLCCs) were common, a 326,000 dwt (Ultra Large Crude Carrier, ULCC) launched in 1968, while engine and hull design, rudder, navigational and automation improved enabling reduced crew sizes. Concern with increasing sizes was encapsulated by the 1967 *Torrey Canyon* disaster, spilling 120,000 tons of oil either side of the English Channel, prompting the IMO to re-address pollution, developing measures to prevent accidents and minimise their affects.

Gulf Oil booked six 276,000-tonners for 15 years for 1968–1969 delivery, Shell and BP, 175–190,00-tonners.[16] In the early-1970s, about 27–36% of tankers were oil company-owned, 45–52% long-term chartered, the rest spot-chartered as needed. With long-term oil contracts, some Greek and Norwegian owners made fortunes, including Onassis and Niarchos. British yards were slow with new designs or larger ships. European and Japanese industrial growth also drove coal and ore shipping, propelling Greek-owned tramps from 2.93 million dwt in 1950 to 12.2 million in 1960, 30.9 million in 1970, Japanese 1.6, 6.9 and 27 on the same dates, Norway's 5.4, 11.2 and 19.3. British grew slower 18.2, 21.2, 25.8 while US merchant shipping declined; 27.5, 24.8 and 18.5.[17]

* * *

Holts modernised in the late-1950s and 1960s, building in Japanese shipyards. When other British lines' outlook was bleak, Chairman Nicholson told shareholders in 1961, 'Hong Kong's zestful commercial activity is unabated', was 'pleased by the strong position in Japan' and optimistic about Malaya and Singapore. Indonesian independence left Holts as main Indonesia-Europe carriers, but operating, handling and capital costs rose, ship life expectancy shortened as technical advances were made.[18]

In 1962 passenger accommodation was removed from Asian lines, needing fewer crew, reducing costs. In 1965 it acquired Liner Holdings which owned Elder-Dempster, Henderson Line's Burmese trades, Seaways Car Transporters, African Container Express and various West African property and agency interests. Unlike tankers and bulkers, whose increasing sizes could be loaded and discharged faster, larger liners could not, because stowing many commodities took planning and time. Standardised pallets from 1959 tried addressing this. In 1965 Manchester offered discounts for palletised cargo, claiming 75% increase in handling rates.[19]

Despite Southeast Asia's slow growth, Blue Funnel (Holts) and Glen recovered profitability, although Holts managers' meetings increasingly discussed Asian political instability, discouraging newbuilding investment, while conscious of the need for fast ships to compete with Ben Line. Glen ordered four 11,500-dwt, 20-knot ships in 1960, delivered in 1962–63, two from Holland and two from Clyde-based Fairfield, the only British yard to match Dutch prices, a recurring theme. In 1964, two orders were placed with Mitsubishi, 12–20% lower than British yards. Mitsubishi's ships were built on time. British ones suffered delays and poor quality.[20]

*   *   *

Mao Tse-tung's 1958–1959 Great Leap Forward was disastrous. The 1958 uncollected harvest created mass famine with over 30 million 1959–1962 excess deaths. Deng Xiaoping criticised ideological fanaticism but was dismissed. The 1966 Cultural Revolution threatened civil war. Other countries continued high tariffs, Pakistan 90% in the early-1960s, Argentina's 1939 tariff of 30% increased to over 140%.[21] In contrast Indonesia's General Suharto deposed Sukarno in 1966, reversed self-sufficiency policies, cut import tariffs, relaxed foreign investment regulations and reduced licensing. In Chile after a 1973 army coup rid it of a bleak communist future, General Pinochet reduced tariffs from 94% to 10%. His otherwise brutal regime and Suharto's corrupt but gentler rule laid solid economic foundations for growing wealth-creating enterprise and trade.

France, Germany, Italy and Benelux countries joined the 1951 European Coal and Steel Community, becoming the 1957 European Economic Community (EEC), a Zollverein-like common market surrounded by a tariff wall protecting uncompetitive industries and agriculture with increasing economic and political union, the aim to prevent another European war. Distrusting political union and continental power, Britain proposed a looser Free Trade Association and in 1960 joined Denmark, Norway, Portugal, Sweden, Austria and Switzerland in the alternative European Free Trade Association (EFTA) without political control. In 1950 Europe took only 10% of British exports. Australia was as economically important to Britain as the six Coal and Steel Community members. New Zealand was more important than Germany. Britain's 1950–1970 share of world exports fell from 25% to 8% and trade denominated in sterling from 50% to about 20%.[22]

Wartime necessity transformed Britain's liberal economy into a centralised, bureaucratic one. By 1944 Britain's exports were 31% of 1938 and the state controlled much of the economy. Clement Atlee explained, 'it is necessary that the government be given <u>complete</u> control over persons and property.' Contradicting Palmerston's 1833 enlightened statement, 'the province of a wise government is…not to insist on knowing better than those they govern,' Atlee's economic advisor Douglas Jay wrote 'the gentleman in Whitehall really does know better what is good for the people than the people,'[23] reflected in the 1944 Education Act, the post-war National Health Service and welfare state as the 1945–1951 Labour government nationalised electricity, communications, coal, railways, even road transport and Thomas Cook, the travel agent, attracted by Russia's planned economy, the inefficiencies of which were not yet fully apparent. Immediate post-war British political thought about future direction was confused. Churchill and Macmillan, concerned about European collapse, optimistically thought Commonwealth and European imperatives could be reconciled, with Britain leading, but as Marshal Plan-driven Europe recovered, the threat of Russian expansion dominated, while Britain's new <u>planned</u> economy multiplied bureaucrat numbers.

Among those persuaded that the 1914–1945 disaster was caused by nationalism were Woodrow Wilson, John Foster Dulles, Jean Monnet and Harold Macmillan. America thought a United States of Europe could be created. Monnet and Macmillan saw new world institutions, UN, World Bank, IMF etc. as global directors to be managed regionally. Atlee, Bevin and Churchill distanced themselves from such ideas because of Europe's vulnerability to extremism. Standing aloof from European entanglements had worked. Intimacy with nations so recently enthusiastically undemocratic was dangerous. The war confirmed their faith in British institutions and that they shared more with English-speaking democracies than Europe. In 1905 Churchill had railed against Imperial Preference, that Britain 'should be free to purchase its…food…in the open markets of the world…[not] walled off like a medieval town victualled for a siege' and Bevin thought the nascent EEC 'a Pandora's box full of Trojan Horses.' Britain's post-war mind-set was conditioned by pre-war trade blocs, the result of high tariffs and misplaced desire to keep the empire for prestige. The Federation model for Australia, Canada and South Africa had made sense. West Indies and Central African Federation, imposed from a Colonial Office making itself a role to buttress unprofitable empire did not, while European Federation was unattractive for free trade-minded Britons.

Macmillan, who Richard Crossman thought clever but 'intellectually reckless', misled the Commons saying EEC membership involved no loss of sovereignty and only minor commercial changes.[24] Anthony Sampson's biography of him is generously subtitled *A Study in Ambiguity*. Macmillan thought Britain could lead a regional European group, so with the EEC resisting joining EFTA and concern about economic performance, applied for EEC membership. Civil servants, believing their own propaganda that Whitehall knew best, increasingly conflated <u>their</u> interests with Britain's, seeing opportunities with European bureaucracies, blind to rapidly growing global maritime trade opportunities, where Britain had advantages.

Some have re-written this episode as low-growth Britain with debilitating strikes, trying to tie itself to a strong economic body. As Alan Sked explains, individual <u>states</u> guided economic recovery like Erhard's 1948 German supply-side reforms, not the EEC, which concentrated on agriculture and fisheries. Besides, France was defeated in Vietnam in 1954 and Algeria in 1958, politically unstable, 'almost visibly collapsing' according to Dulles. Germany was occupied and divided. Macmillan's idea that Britain could lead might indeed have been feasible if met with EEC compromise about Commonwealth ties. Britain's growth rates sometimes lagged Europe, sometimes led. In the 1960s western Europe's was 3.5%, Britain's 4.5%, in 1959 and 1963 almost 6%. Britain's defence spending and bad industrial relations hindered growth, but defence spending would reduce with decolonisation, exactly like 1783. Britain had been overtaken by America, but catching pioneers is normal in economic modernisation and throughout this book's period, Britain was the most global of the world's powerful states.

General de Gaul however, attempting post-1945 French resurrection after Algerian and Vietnamese defeat, bitter at 1944–45 liberation by Anglo-US forces, could not tolerate British leadership, explaining that unlike existing members, Britain was a maritime state which would disrupt 'European Europe'. At the 1963 press conference announcing his veto, he asked, as Britain was democratic, had nuclear weapons, cheap Commonwealth food and was a global power, why did it want to join? The question was never satisfactorily answered.[25] Macmillan renewed the application, again vetoed by de Gaulle, because he said the British were 'worn-out…driven by desperation.'

Looking for French *gloire* within Europe after colonial defeat and solve the 'German problem', the Franco-German 1963 Elysee Treaty (reaffirmed 2019), agreed that their bureaucrats would fix EEC direction, a political project more than a customs union. From then on, if Britain joined, it had no chance of leading it. Besides, the EEC parliament was like Bismarck's Reichstag; without power, without ability to raise issues, already decided by France and Germany. Absolute power resided with the unelected European Commission, dominated by French and German hegemonists. British EEC entry should therefore have been a dead letter.

*   *   *

In the late-1950s, Japan built nearly three million tons of ships annually, twice Britain's total. Greek and Norwegian bulker and tanker owners worked on narrower margins and borrowed heavily. British shipowners disliked debt, had high overheads and were risk averse. The 1969 Rochdale Report found they had little debt, remembering the depressed 1930s when indebtedness was dangerous, whereas Greeks and Norwegians built large fleets on finance, some from British banks situated around St. Mary Axe. Meanwhile, Japan's economy was boosted during the 1960's Vietnam War.

In the 1960s-1970s, western Europe, North America and Japan generated 60% of world trade, which grew from 360 million tons in 1946, 990 million tons in 1959, to 1,790 million in 1966, 2.6 million in 1971, to 3,247 million by 1974; unprecedented, accelerating volumes. The Suez Canal was again closed in 1967 at the Arab-Israel War's outbreak and did not re-open until 1975, aiding all shipping markets. The energy sector drove momentum. Oil rose to 57% of seaborne volumes by 1970.[26] Communications kept improving; in the late-1940s, telexes, direct dial telephones, air travel, from 1969 satellite navigation on ships and 1970s faxes all made business easier, faster and communication more efficient.

Chapter 41

Specialisations and the Container Revolution

Between 1964 and 1973, crude oil ton-miles increased by 328%, while coal and iron ore ton-miles rose by 183%. Ore, grain, bauxite/aluminium and phosphate, 40% of drybulk tonnage, meant bulkers became ubiquitous. As volumes rose, other specialised ships appeared; the first chemical parcel tanker (1954), liquified petroleum gas carrier (LPG) (1950), car carrier (1956), open-hatch forest product carrier (1962) and liquified natural gas carrier (LNG) (1964), their sizes growing quickly. Norwegians liked investing in specialised ships; car bulkers, open-hatch bulkers, tankers, ro-ros, cruise ships and especially LPGs and LNGs from 1970, developed from Kvaerner's patented spherical tank, carried at minus 161 degrees Celsius, built by Scandinavian, German and Japanese, some against 20-year COAs.[1] In 1954 Volkswagen agreed a five-option-two-year contract with Sweden's Wallenius for cars to the Great Lakes and grain back. By 1965 it employed 40 ships, 80 by 1969 when output reached 1.425 million cars. Retailing at $1,800 each, $60 shipping costs made them competitive. Japanese manufacturers initially relied on liners at $220/car until Nissan used Anders Wilhelmsen in 1968 and later Lief Hoegh's ro-ros.[2] Erling Naess specialised in combination carriers, ore-oilers and ore-bulk-oilers (OBOS) from 1965, the 10–15% higher building price covered by eliminating ballast legs. By 1972, Norwegians controlled over five million tons, 18% of the world fleet. Star Shipping, Joachim Grieg, Gearbulk and Lief Hoegh's open-hatch bulkers broke British owners' west coast US-Canada forest products stranglehold to Europe by backhauling cars, similarly grain and cars to and from Japan with 36,000-dwt bulkers with hoistable car decks in the 1970–1980s. Norwegians introduced Scandinavia's ferry idea to the English Channel. Thoresen Carferries started in 1964 between Southampton and Cherbourg, merging with Townsend Carferries as Townsend-Thoresen, finally as P&O European Ferries, with extensions to Iberia in 1966. In 1969 Norwegians I.M. Skaugen, Anders Wilhelmsen and Gotaas-Larsen formed Caribbean Cruise Line, followed by Princess Cruises and Royal Viking Lines in 1970. Norwegians had 15 cruise ships by 1973. They also concentrated on North Sea oil, the first drilling rig and supply ships in 1971.

Liners carried finished and semi-finished goods. For efficiency, some shipowners like Fred Olsen favoured pallets for fruit loading, moved by forklift trucks, others ro-ros. Liners had vegetable oil tanks, refrigerated holds, heavy lifting gear, ro-ro decks, complex and expensive to build, load and discharge, because cases, barrels, drums, sacks and pallets needed securing with ropes and timber dunnage. Ships called at eight to ten ports per trip, spending much time in port. In heavily unionised Australia, Blue Funnel ships were inactive at weekends and nights, 50–60% of voyages in port. A 1954 study of a 5,015-ton Brooklyn-Bremerhaven shipment found 194,582 items from 151 cities in transit sheds up to a month, $5,000 of dunnage used in over six days loading, four days discharging, half the voyage in port, the last cargo arriving at its destination 33 days after docking with cargo handling accounting for 36.8% of the costs.[3]

American businessman Malcolm McLean made the breakthrough that slashed liner shipping's inefficiencies. Selling his trucking company for $6 million to buy T2-owning Pan Atlantic Tanker Co. in 1956, he converted one to carry sixty 35-feet containers from Newark to Houston, instead of inland trucking, which had grabbed the market during the U-boat threat. Cargo packed inside locked containers was better protected from damage or theft than loose cargo. Handling costs were 16 cents/ton compared to $5.83 breakbulk. Although initial routes were short-haul, the implication was large long-haul routes could make huge economies of scale. Another was converted in 1957, to carry 226, the first fully cellular ship, meaning vertical guides kept containers stacked, limiting movement at sea. They were loaded/discharged by shore cranes and delivered to receivers in 90 minutes, showing how one containership could replace eight conventional ships.[4]

In 1961, even with increasing ship sizes, ocean freight accounted for 12% of the value of US exports and 10% of imports. Since the average US import tariff was 7%, high freights were more effective trade barriers.[5] McLean's renamed Sea-Land in 1962 started a California line with ships carrying eight-times more cargo than his first. When Bull Line serving Puerto Rico collapsed, Sea-Land took-over. The resulting cost savings allowed opening of new factories, an early glimpse of containerisation's cascading economic benefits. In 1964 McLean sold and leased back nine containerships, using the cash to convert others, adding 18 in four years. By 1967 Sea-Land carried 1,800 containers a week in 19 ships, half to Puerto Rico.

Matson Navigation from the late-19th century had built a business in tankers, Hawaiian oil storage, passenger ships, hotels, sugar plantations and shipping Hawaiian sugar and pineapples. It pioneered California-Hawaii containerships in 1958, which by 1960 were loading 400 tons/hour. Only 2.5 days of each voyage was in port instead of 7.5 days. McLean's 35-feet container sizes were determined by his tanker sizes. Matson found 20–25 feet more efficient.

United States Lines (USL) rivalled Sea-Land. The US Maritime Association (MARAD) started discussions on standardising container sizes in 1958. By 1964 it decided on eight feet by eight feet six inches by 10, 20, 30 and 40 feet, effectively becoming just 20 and 40 feet, TEUs (twenty feet equivalent unit) and FEUs (forty feet equivalent unit), which continued to be subsidised. Sea-Land continued using 35-feet units, thus ineligible for US subsidies.

In 1960, British lines thought containers could not be economic in long-haul trades, based on carrying them on conventional liners' deck and that cargoes like wool would not containerise, but gradually changed their minds. Australian Steamships Co. ran a weekly Fremantle-Melbourne service in 1964, the first purpose-built cellular containership, important due to Australia's high handling costs, congestion and bad labour relations. In 1966 there were five container lines, mainly US-based, by December 1967, 38 worldwide, most with converted ships, but 107 specialised newbuildings were on order. Refrigerated containers started in 1969.

For a fully cellular container system to become internationally standard, massive capital and coordination was necessary. The first trans-Atlantic service started in 1966 by Sea-Land from Newark to McLean's Rotterdam trailer terminal, Bremen and Grangemouth. With 250,000 American soldiers in West Germany, military goods dominated westbound cargoes. Eastbound whisky, previously easily stolen on the dockside or broken *en route* was shipped from Grangemouth in steel tanks for bottling in America.[6] Only large shipping companies could afford semi-automated £250,000 gantry cranes handling 15–30 containers/hour, dramatic productivity gains over general cargo. An annual 100–200,000 tons became two million![7] Containerships needed about two and a half sets of containers, each costing £1,000 for simultaneous land, sea and port use. Liner company responsibility started and ended at the ship's rail, but containers integrated seamlessly with road, rail and distribution depots; the greatest savings made when containers were loaded early in the logistics chain and unpacked close to the destination; 'intermodal' in industry jargon. Initial focus was trans-Atlantic. Container trades would involve fewer, larger ports with extensive waterfront areas and huge cranes, but such investment was beyond most shipping lines' resources. Thus, some European companies formed consortia. British companies were quickest, the first, Overseas Containers (OCL), a 1965 P&O-Holts-British and Commonwealth-Furness Withy joint venture.

Manufacturers found container shipping faster and cheaper. Eliminating special packaging, damage and theft made insurance cheaper. McLean used <u>his</u> freight forwarders, <u>his</u> containers, <u>his</u> railcars, railed to <u>his</u> Newark railyard in time to meet inbound ships. Trans-Atlantic routes were the first long-haul commercial focus. In the rapid Vietnamese War military build-up, McLean solved congestion in its shallow ports in late-1967 by containerships to Subic Bay, Philippines, then smaller ships to two Vietnamese ports where he installed shore cranes, saving half the previous costs. In 1970 America calculated that had this been done in 1965, $882 million would have been saved.[8] Responsibility for transportation to inland destinations enabled containers' re-use. As Japan's 1960–1973 industrial output quadrupled, backhauling electronics, cars and industrial equipment gave two-way revenues. Matson joint-ventured with NYK in 1967, which sailed its first containership to America in 1968. Sea-Land ran six sailings from Yokohama to the west coast as other Japanese owners entered. OCL planned containerising UK-Australia shipments, investing £45 million in six 1,300 TEU containerships, equipment and containers, starting in 1969, then targeted Asia. An estimated £700 million was invested in 1966–1970 containerisation. OCL continued with five 2,300 TEU, 27-knot, German-built ships in 1972 for $60 million.[9]

Holts diversified further from 1969 to 1972, tankers, bulkers, an NYK-partnered 215,000-dwt ore-oiler, P&O-partnered chemical tankers for Asian palm oil shipments to tank storage terminals in Antwerp, Rotterdam and Liverpool, offshore services, LNGs and various stakes in shipping and air service companies. Not all were successful, but they were proactive, acquiring William Cory & Son in 1972. Originally an 18th-century London coal importer, by the 1870s Cory's handled over 50% with its own tugs, barges and wharves and between the wars expanded in France, North and South America and South Africa, switching from coal to oil distribution. By 1960 it managed warehousing, transport, forwarding, harbour, towage, shipowning and general distribution; a complimentary company also adapting and growing in fast-changing times, valued at over a third of Holts.[10] OCL accelerated containerisation in 1972–73, almost 90% done by 1978, with Nicholson, Conference Chairman from 1969 to 1972.

* * *

Containerisation's ability to dramatically affect how ports developed was first seen in Newark, whose share of New York's 1956–1960 traffic rose from 9% to 18%. Sea-Land's 1962 New Jersey's Port Elizabeth terminal's volumes soared. New Jersey's share of New York's general cargo reached 63% in 1970. Brooklyn's tonnage fell and longshoremen's employment dropped 91% between 1964 and 1976.[11] Factories moved out of New York for lower tax and energy costs because of easy inland container transport. Philadelphia built a terminal only in 1970, New Orleans in 1971, so Newark dominated early east coast container shipping.

Similarly, Los Angeles was the main west coast container port and modernised, but San Francisco refused Matson's request to build a terminal, so it built in adjacent Alameda, near Oakland. When Sea-Land started a west coast service, Oakland spent $600,000 deepening the harbour and upgrading berths. Surplus spoil from the recently-dug Bay Area Rapid Transport Transit tunnels provided a 140-acre, 12-berth area for cranes, containers and ships. Throughput of 365,085 tons of non-military containers in 1965 rose to 1.5 million in 1968 and three million in 1969, 60% of its cargoes containerised. San Francisco did not respond, so American President Line and Johnson Line moved to Oakland.

In Britain, port work irregularity had created trade union militancy and frequent strikes. A million man-days were lost from 1948 to 1951 and 1.3 million in 1954.[12] Containerisation meant hundreds of liner companies disappeared with tally clerks, warehousing and stevedores' skills in stowing, weight distribution (trimming), avoiding cargoes tainting each other, bracing dunnage to protect cargo and avoid shifting at sea. Stowage plans were masterpieces of draftsmanship, the product of decades of inherited knowledge. Despite being unhealthy, dangerous work, pride in these skills and fear of job losses made containerisation, which January 1966's *Economist* called a 'hurricane from America,' fiercely resisted. McKinsey's 1966 report to the British Transport Docks Board warned, 'Containerisation is…not a possible or potential long term future development. It is already well advanced and proceeding at pace…so far… seriously underestimated by virtually all those sectors that will be most affected,'[13] predicting widespread shipping company consolidation, smaller operators marginalised, with fewer ships needed and high capitalisation.

Like US ports, containerisation was key to European ports' fate. Rotterdam, destroyed in 1945, was rebuilt, by 1962 the world's largest port by tonnage and spent $60 million building the European Container Terminus. By contrast, London's docks were small and fragmented. A 1965 cabinet committee thought 'the movement of goods in and out of the country…one of the least efficient parts of the economy,' because they had been developed piecemeal.[14] It wanted a national plan and deep-water port like Rotterdam.

McKinsey advised building Tilbury which had the potential to tranship to Europe's smaller ports. Its five container berths each with 20 acres were ready in 1968. But the Transport and General Workers Union (TGWU) banned working containers: a profound act of self-harm. OCL had to use Rotterdam and Antwerp until 1970 with greater costs. Southampton won the Asian container link. Meanwhile, the owners of Felixstowe, a tiny port 90 miles northeast of London with 90 permanent workers, no general cargo or militant unions, agreed with Sea-Land to spend £3.5 million, under an eighth of the government's Tilbury outlay, to instal a crane and other improvements,[15] enabling a Sea-Land Newark-Rotterdam-Felixstowe service from July 1967.

Responding, the TGWU allowed only USL at Tilbury. In its first call, it discharged and loaded containers in 12 hours, but by 1968 Felixstowe had two or three North Atlantic sailings a week and several feeder services, handling 18,252 loaded containers: by 1974, 137,850. From obscurity it quickly became Britain's largest container port. In 2013 it handled 42% of Britain's containers by adding a third rail link for surging volumes. London's main conventional docks closed from 1967 to 1970. The TGWU lifted their ban in April 1970, then went on strike for double pay. Its short-sightedness ruined London as a great port, Tilbury unable to fulfil its potential. Liverpool's Mersey Docks and Harbour Board was also ruined. Obstructive trade unions in ports and shipyards generated negative images of maritime industries, discouraging investments. Seaforth's three 1972 government-financed container terminals replaced ten conventional Liverpool docks, which closed. Manufacturing fell 10%. Manchester, Britain's fifth-largest port closed in the 1970s, containerships avoiding the time-consuming canal.

Britain's government, terrified of the TGWU, made little preparation for containerisation. Rotterdam, Antwerp and Bremen without self-destructive union hostility prepared well. Sea-Land's 1966 container shipments to America's Okinawa base prompted Japan's transport ministry to plan 22 container berths in Tokyo and Kure while Sea-Land developed Yokohama. Australia invited bids in 1966 for a Sydney terminal. Taiwan planned terminals in five ports. After its 1965 independence, Singapore rebuilt its conventional berths into a container feeder centre serving regional ports. By 1982 it handled a million TEUs, the world's sixth-largest container port. In 1996 more passed through than Japan. By 2005 it was the world's largest.

* * *

OCL pioneered but other European lines also formed consortia. Blue Star, Ben Line, Cunard, Ellerman and T.&J. Harrison formed Associated Container Transportation for Australia. Blue Star independently set up for west coast North America. Furness Withy's Manchester Liners inaugurated the Montreal route. European consortia were; ACL (Holland-Amerika Line, Compagnie Generale Transatlantique, Cunard, Swedish-Amerika Line, Transatlantic Steamships and Wallenius), Hapag-Lloyd (Hamburg-Amerika and Norddeutchsher Lloyd) and Dart (CMB, Bristol City Line and Clark Traffic Services).

Sea-Land's 1965 $102 million ship revenues became $227 in 1968 with expansion to Europe, Japan and Vietnam. Most were conversions carrying a few hundred containers. British companies' 51 containerships in 1971 were not far behind US companies' 75. Many consortia changed shareholdings, consolidation the tendency. The consortium idea transferred to a British shipping effort to establish strength in large bulkers and OBOs; Seabridge, using government tax and depreciation allowances. At its 1975 peak, it owned 1,750,000 dwt with 375,000 dwt chartered, mainly 120–165,000-tonners, carrying 20 million tons of cargo. It was dissolved in 1980, due to low returns following the 1973–1979 oil shocks (See next chapter). Early OCL losses due to investment, experimenting and remaining conventional liners became profits in 1972. Hapag-Lloyd also lost money until then. Even Sea-Land had difficult years, but as the economy grew most containerships traded profitably. Furthermore, the amount of liner cargo capable of containerisation surpassed expectations, rising 40% in 1973.[16] P&O continued diversifying, buying Bovis property group in 1974. British shipping companies were playing catch-up, but given the fast-changing circumstances, quite skilfully.

US carriers were richer, all except Sea-Land subsidised. All had military shipments giving them advantages. McLean, knowing he needed more money, sold to US tobacco giant Reynolds Industries, which generated huge cashflows. Shipping investments could provide corporate tax shelter. Within Reynolds, McLean in 1969 ordered eight 33-knot containerships, still 35 feet (1,900 TEUs), at $32 million each, with $435 million of equipment and in 1970 bought American Independent Oil to provide it with fuel.

Japan-California container volumes were two-thirds of trans-Atlantic volumes in 1969 but Japanese exports, 27.1 million tons in 1967 rose to 40.6 million in 1969, the first full year of California container services. Within three years, 30% of Japanese exports to America were containerised and half to Australia. Television exports climbed from 3.5 million sets in 1968 to 6.2 million in 1971, tape recorders 10.5 to 20.2 million. In 1969 only 9% of Hong Kong-west coast trade was containerised, in 1970, 37%. Japan's five-year plan involved a 50% expansion of its tankers, ore carriers and containerships. Japanese-built ships needed just 5% deposit, received a three-year interest holiday, bank loans at 2% and repayment over ten years at 5.5%. With such favourable terms, by late-1970, 158 ships were on order in Japanese yards. Regular Japan-US east coast routes began in 1970, with 30 ships by 1973.[17] Japan-Europe containership lines began in 1971.

The 1970s saw Cambodia's murderous Khmer Rouge, but more significantly the rise of Asia's tigers. After Japanese 1910–1945 exploitation and Korean War, South Korea recovered slowly. Dictator Park ruled harshly but 1960–1975 manufacturing doubled, copying Japan's *zaibatsu* model; in Korean, *chaebols*, 30% of which in 1981 accounted for 60% of GNP, the top ten *chaebols* 29.3% of 1983's exports. Exports in 1969 were 2.9 million tons, six million in 1973. Hong Kong's 1970–1972 textiles, toys and electronics export value rose 35%. Taiwan's 1970 $1.4 billion exports rose to $4.3 billion in 1973. It was similar in Singapore, while by 1970 most of Australia's imported general cargo was containerised, not from 11 European ports as before, just Tilbury, Hamburg and Rotterdam.[18]

* * *

Maersk originated in the 1880s. Between the wars, it had tankers, a Danish shipyard and ran worldwide lines. From 1964 it developed pallets, loaded through side ports by forklift trucks, invested in VLCCs in the late-1960s, a ULCC and off-shore activities in 1974. It was unique in having been run by only two men in over 100 years, a private company without the inconvenience of shareholders or risk of take-over. In 1968 McKinsey spruced-up their 1966 container report for Maersk, whose Asian offices recommended continuing with side-loading pallets for less-developed ports, so delayed ordering containerships until 1971, an 1,800 TEU ship for 1974 delivery. By 1972 over 27 containerships were deployed on Europe-Asia services and over 30 European ports had container-handling terminals, but had not reached the Middle East, so Maersk built craned ships carrying general cargo and 628 containers on deck and hatch covers, a well-received, interim solution. For Europe-USA-Asia routes, more container ships were ordered, with feeder ships from Hong Kong, Taiwan, Singapore, Nagoya and Tokyo.[19]

Between 1976 and 1979 Dubai built Jebel Ali container port. Oil-rich Saudi Arabia without modern ports, imported via it. In 1985 a free trade zone was added, enabling shippers to store goods tax-free, transhipping to secondary destinations, becoming the Persian Gulf hub, re-exporting also to East Africa's and south Asia's inefficient, state-owned ports. Its container throughput reached 913,363 in 1990. Its operator, Dubai Port World became a worldwide terminal operator. By 2015 Jebel Ali's three terminals could work ten of the largest ships simultaneously, more throughput than New York and Los Angeles combined and kept expanding, turning Dubai into the region's logistic and financial hub (see Chapter 46).

From 1968 to 1975, 406 containerships were delivered, most twice the size of 1967's. Sharply rising oil prices in 1973 made ships reduce speed to conserve fuel, reducing voyages, tightening the market. Freight rates soared. Sea-Land made $142 million profit, but worldwide recession followed. Manufactured exports fell in 1975 for the first time since the war. Maritime trade fell 6%. Containerships were built for speed when fuel was cheap but with bunker prices rising from $22 to $70/ton they were unprofitable, yet 272 were delivered between 1976 and 1979; the 1980 fleet ten million tons, because the 1973–74 collapse of tanker and bulker rates (see next chapter) left shipyards short of orders, allowing Maersk and Evergreen, neither of whom had containerships before 1973 to buy cheap newbuildings. Thus, despite rising fuel costs, the cost of shipping cargo fell rapidly. In 1976 *The Financial Times* thought 'the revolutionary impact of containerisation, the biggest advance in freight movement for generations, has largely worked itself out.'[20] Actually, it had only just begun! First seen in Puerto Rico, it enabled manufacturers to outsource operations to countries with lower labour costs, accelerating Taiwan's, Hong Kong's, Korea's and Dubai's development. By 1981 Maersk's 25 containerships made it the world's third-largest containership company, with almost 5% of the world fleet, only Sea-Land and Hapag-Lloyd larger. Evergreen with 15, was eighth.

Chapter 42

Two Oil Shocks, Shipping Depression and Economic Liberalism

In 1973–1974 the Organisation of Petroleum Exporting Countries (OPEC), Saudi Arabia, Iran, Iraq, Kuwait and Venezuela, quadrupled oil prices. Previous shipping optimism had resulted in newbuilding orders rising from under 15% of the fleet in the mid-1960s, 37% in 1972, to 49% in 1974![1] The total fleet, 338 million dwt in 1970, grew to 553 million in 1975 but the oil price hike crashed the world economy. Shipping markets collapsed, tankers immediately, bulkers slower, partly due to Persian Gulf, Red Sea and Nigerian building material imports for newly rich oil exporters with inefficient port infrastructure. Up to 100 days congestion resulted. As combination carriers switched from oil to drybulk, it collapsed too. The 1975 reopening of the deeper-drafted Suez Canal further increased supply, allowing 150,000-ton laden and larger ballasting ships to pass. Shipowners like Colocotronis collapsed. Some Norwegians were 'stabilised' under bank control and some banks suffered liquidity crises. Shipping mortgages in mid-1976 totalled $25 billion, $13 billion for ships on order, but because of containership demand, by 1980 it reached over $100 billion. Hundreds of liners were laid up or scrapped. Drybulk trade grew 30% from 1973 to 1981 but oil decreased 44%. Tanker tonnage peaked at 335 million in 1978 then fell sharply. The hiatus affected most shipping markets until 2000.

Norwegian tanker-ownership meant that in 1976, over 26% of laid-up tonnage was Norwegian-owned. Norwegians continued investing, <u>but</u> in offshore oil as the OPEC shock led to exploration of new sources; North Africa, Nigeria, Russia, Alaska, the North Sea and by late-1974 they held stakes in 54 drilling vessels, by late-1975 over 100, plus assorted anchor handling tugs, pipelaying barges etc., the world's second-largest investor after America.[2] These shorter tanker routes switched emphasis from VLCC/ULCCs for long-haul Persian Gulf routes to smaller tankers. Norway's 1970s car/bulk carrier fleet evolved into roll-on/roll-off PCC's (Pure Car Carriers), offering quicker turnround, almost immediately copied by Japanese and Korean owners for their exports.

P&O's 1974 £48.5 million profits dropped to £22.7 million in 1975. Its 178 ships in 1974 became 89 larger ones in 1980.[3] Of its £41 million 1981 profits, its OCL share counted most. In 1980 Furness Withy was taken over by Hong Kong's legendary shipping tycoon C.Y. Tung, who owned 150 ships, 11 million tons during his lifetime, including the 564,763-dwt *Seawise Giant*, the world's largest. Rumours circulated of other tycoon take-overs. One for Cunard's owning group, was rejected. Public ownership was the Achilles Heel of much British shipping, their fate in shareholders' hands, especially institutions which disliked volatility. Property expert Jeffrey Sterling was appointed to P&O's board, becoming Chairman in 1983, merging his Sterling Guarantee Trust into P&O in 1985, theoretically a good fit with P&O's road haulage, containers and ferries and Sterling's warehousing. 1985 produced record profits; £125 million. They bought Holts' 53% of OCL, making P&O Containers Britain's largest containership owner. Similarly, Belgium's CMB also diversified; container terminals, stevedore companies, tugs, towage, salvage, offshore, multipurpose ships, liners and bulkers, having signed a further 20-year COA with steel mills Sidmar and Cockerill.

*　*　*

On the political front, after de Gaulle retired, Pompidou became French president. Macmillan's protégé Edward Heath renewed the EEC application, even though there was no chance of British leadership after the Franco-German Elysee Treaty. He believied membership at <u>any</u> price would remedy British 'decline', although Britain's economy had grown every year since 1945, in 1973, 7.4%! Heath, stuck in 1930s-1950s regional trade bloc ideas, did not appreciate how quickly the world was re-globalising. Pompidou, alarmed at West German resurgence agreed entry. The EEC's economic purpose was <u>not</u> promoting an open, global economy, the post-war vision. Heath should have heeded de Gaulle's accurate assessment of its maritime-inspired past, his 1967 rejection and scorn. The EEC should have heeded his warning that due to these cultural differences, Britain would prove 'a disruptive presence'.[4] Heath's chief negotiator Con O'Neil warned the EEC's objective was <u>power</u>, 'none of its policies…[were] essential to us, many…objectionable,' but Heath promoted its common market aspect, never mentioning 'ever closer union' or the Elysee Treaty; essentially a continentalist bear-pit, nor how much it would cut Britain from world economic development. He swallowed the detrimental Common Agricultural Policy (CAP), operating from 1967 to restrict imports, raising consumer prices and surrendered rich British fishing grounds. Maritime historian Peter Padfield calls it 'the great betrayal' of Britain's liberal, free trade past to join an illiberal, protectionist, Franco-German-dominated bloc, contrary to much the world's increasing liberalism. Multiple studies show CAP resulted in lost GDP, higher food prices, expensive surpluses dumped on world markets, bringing argument with America, squeezed out of an important market, forced to compete with 'dumped' grain, damaging global welfare by misallocating resources.

Britain did not need closer political association with Europe. Anglo-French cooperation had produced the Concord jet in 1969. Britain did not share Europe's agricultural interests. When Britain realised Heath's deception, push-back would be inevitable, because not only was Britain's maritime-inspired past ignored, but British public opinion's power, seen in abolitionist, free trade, Plimsoll and Imperial Tariff campaigns. Indeed, the issue caused more dissention in British politics than any other, the fall of four Prime Ministers; Thatcher, rejecting aggressive Brussels integration efforts, toppled by her Europhile cabinet, Major and Cameron failing to get EU compromises and May, bizarrely that withdrawal meant greater integration!

But that was the future. Immediately CAP membership increased British food costs 40%, led to stagflation, strikes and a 30% wage explosion. In the referendum to confirm it, the government mounted a huge publicity campaign, stressing faster EEC growth, concealing European law's supremacy, proclaiming Britain could veto things affecting her national interest. In a year of strikes and 27% inflation, most support came from the prosperous south but the vote in general reflected unenthusiastic acquiescence. Between 1945 and 2008, Britain only had four full years of economic contraction, all between 1974 and 1981, partly due to the oil shock, partly EEC-entry shock, just before Europe's economies stagnated.

There was immediate conflict between British sugar cane imports from Commonwealth countries and EEC protection of the 4% of its farmers growing sugar beet, which, even after subsidies, was over 50% more expensive. The 1975 Lome Convention's Sugar Protocol denied efficient cane sugar-producers like Australia, access. Some African, Caribbean and Pacific countries were given quotas at engineered 'intervention' prices, and some not, resulting in an immediate UK import reduction of 500,000 tons, excess sugar dumped on world markets, depressing prices, disadvantaging developing countries and Britain, distorting markets so much that world prices were usually below most sugar cane production costs. Most Commonwealth countries were excluded, but former Belgian and French colonies included, clearly indicating where bear-pit power resided. Commonwealth governments recorded 'strong dissatisfaction' before its 1980 signing. London sugar refineries despite a massive take-over to consolidate were closed in 1979 with 4,600 jobs lost,[5] as Britain sacrificed worldwide connections on the altar of European integration and subservience.

EEC-British trade had grown before entry; 14.5 million tons in 1965 to 31.5 million in 1973,[6] part of post-war recovery. But northern British ports were detrimentally affected by entry. In the 1960s, Liverpool still handled about 23% of Britain's manufactured exports, a decade later just 10%. Between 1966 and 1985 its share of British ship arrivals halved, Dover's increased 4.5-fold,[7] especially after joining. In 1981, Liverpool slumped 19%, the number of calls down 957 from two years before. Tate and Lyle's Love Lane sugar refinery, closed in 1981, 'a victim' of EEC membership, said its chairman.[8] The Toxteth riots followed. Trotskyists took over Liverpool's local council, deterring potential investment, collapsing employment. Two world wars, 1930s depression and containerisation damaged Glasgow, Liverpool, Tyne and Wearside, skewing Britain's economy to the Midlands and southeast. EEC entry increased that imbalance, this time self-inflicted. Britain had to have a $3.9 billion IMF loan. Export competitiveness fell 25% from 1979 to 1981. In 1985 Felixstowe berthed 496 containerships, Southampton 272, London 156, Liverpool just 76. Financial services concentrated in London. In 1987 the last deep-sea containership sailed from Greenock.

CAP encouraged sugar beet over-production, tariffs effectively excluding imports. Mauritius with 90% of its agricultural land devoted to sugar tried diversifying into textiles. The EEC thought it threatened EEC-made textiles and tariffed them out. Mozambique's 2004 sugar production costs of £154/ton, compared with the EU's £364, could not sell to the EU, ensuring developing nations' workers' poverty; a blot on an otherwise gradually enlightening world. America lobbied for years against the Lome

Convention, insisting it breached WTO rules.[9] The detrimental effect on northern British ports was potentially partly offset by North Sea oil and gas, which by 1981, provided export surpluses. By 1983 it was the world's fifth-largest producer, peaking in 1985. However, British shipyards hardly participated in drilling rig construction, three out of 119 in 1974, while 29 operated in British waters, although Furness Withy's 1982 £11 million shipping loss was offset by offshore's £14.5 million profit.[10]

Meanwhile Conferences weakened. Singapore rubber traders avoided them to Europe saving 40% and Australian dairy producers 10% to Japan. Malaysian palm oil exporters in 1973 won a two-year rate freeze and in 1975 the Australian Meat Board got rate reductions by concentrating its US-bound exports on just four lines.[11] Taiwan's Orient Overseas (C.Y. Tung) was the first independent running Asia-Newark at 10–15% under Conference rates. Korea Shipping (KSC) ordered containerships in 1973 and did not join. It and Evergreen won about 20% of North Europe, 40% of Mediterranean and 35% of trans-Pacific routes by 1981. Taiwan's Yang Ming started a Europe service in 1982 and Maersk left the Conference. Yet in this ultra-competitive environment, the EEC interfered, using its competition law to examine shipping pools, where owners place ships with a central administration, where it was irrelevant, and Conferences whose influence was waning.

Furthermore, EEC interference sometimes ignored international agreements. Its 2005 ship pollution directive was contrary to IMO's MARPOL regulations. IMO Secretary-General Efthimios Mitropoulos diplomatically explained that universally applied standards were 'an absolute requisite…a patchwork of different standards and regulations in different parts of the world is clearly unworkable.' Moreover, 'criminalisation of seafarers involved in accidental…pollution…[was] counterproductive.' Five years imprisonment or $1.9 million fines hardly encouraged 'seafarers to cooperate fully and openly with casualty enquiries or accident investigations' and 'if too harsh a line is taken, we may discourage exactly the sort of high-calibre people that we need in positions of responsibility for safety and pollution prevention.'[12] Maritime common sense rebuked heavy-handed continentalist interference.

Two months later the EU's planned take-over of representation of separate states' IMO representatives was fiercely opposed by the International Chamber of Shipping and most national shipping boards as a threat to IMO independence and effectiveness by stifling informed debate, 'the essence of the IMO' according to Hong Kong Shipowners Association director Arthur Bowring. Technical competence rebuked a political power-grab,[13] and still does. A 2020 EU seminar paper accepted that with further applications failing, its aims were unlikely short-term, but has not given up.

*   *   *

In Australia, Utah Developments ramped-up Queensland coal exports, loading Capesizes (150–200,000-dwt) in 17-metre-deep Hay Point in 1971. Gladstone followed in 1986. Hay Point shipped 12 million tons annually to Japan, Rotterdam and Europe's new Taranto, Fos and Hunterston's deep-water steel mill terminals, enabling Capesizes to cross-trade Brazil/Japan or Hampton Roads/Japan with Australia/Europe backhaul, some spot, many on long-term COAs. Without bunker escalation provision, the 1973–74 oil price shock forced them to seek *force majeure* relief. Oil price rises meant power stations switched to burning coal, increasing Australian coal exports via a second Hay Point jetty (1976), Abbot Point (1983) and Dalrymple (1984), with Gladstone continuously improved. During the 1970s, BHP grew by acquisition and in 1984 Utah Mining became the largest Australian coking coal exporter. Weipa exported Queensland's bauxite and Port Hedland its iron ore.[14] The main carriers in long-term coal and iron ore COAs were *zaibatsu*, Bergesen, NBC, Ludwig, C.M. Lemos, Erling Naess, London's Anglo-Nordic (including P&O) and Seabridge. *Zaibatsu* had the advantage of being integrated industrial, financial and shipping groups. For example, Kawasaki's shipyards built for K-Line, given long-term COA's by Kawasaki Steel, financed by the group's bank: *zaibatsu* in action.

Between 1973 and 1990 South Korea, the world's fastest growing economy and by 1989, tenth-largest steel producer, powered by shipping and shipbuilding, transitioned to democracy from 1987 to 1992. Before 1976, US-Asia container traffic contained more US exports but Japanese, Korean, Taiwanese, Hong Kong's and Singapore's export expansion in electronics, footwear, textiles, clothes, toys, sports goods, tyres and cars quickly equalised and surpassed it. Containerisation was a major factor in Asian trade growth. Singapore also built massive oil storage, refining capacity, tanker loading and discharge terminals, for regional oil products and petrochemical distribution. Hong Kong's prosperity was due to economic liberalism, China's free port trade entrepot with low taxes, rule of law, protection of private property, its currency tied to the US dollar. Taiwan enjoyed large US and Japanese investments. Technically-trained engineers and economists became heads of ministries. 1980s economic growth averaged 9%. Taiwanese capital was invested in China, especially Fujian where wages were 10% of Taiwan's. With 20 million people in 1993 it was the world's 13th-largest trading nation. In the 1980s-early-1990s it also transitioned from one party rule to parliamentary democracy.

Economically liberal Asian tigers showed that exchange controls and trade barriers hindered economic growth and spawned political liberalism, powered by population growth, a significant latent demand factor. The world's 1950s population, about 2.5 billion was by 1985 nearly five billion, much of the increase Asian. Thailand's 1960 population, 25 million became 55 million in 1988, Bangkok from 1.5 to 7.6 million. Indonesia's 1960 population of about 80 million was 190 million in 1988, the Philippines 25 to 65 million.

Maersk converted its semi-containerships to fully cellular when markets were ready, running Japan-Indonesia for example since 1952 with breakbulk, then pallets, then semi-containerships and finally in 1981 fully cellular. World containership capacity rose; 195,312 TEUs in 1970, 568,363 in 1975, 1,354,012 in 1980 and 1,849,227 in 1984.

The improved drybulk market from 1977 was boosted in 1979 as inefficient Soviet collective farming necessitated massive grain imports, while increased Hampton Roads coal exports to Japan caused up to six months loadport congestion. But the most consequential 1979 event was the Iranian Revolution when oil prices rose from $11/barrel to nearly $40. World GDP growth dropped from 4.75% in 1978 to only 1.2% in 1982. More power stations switched to coal as bulker tonnage overtook tankers and more LNG and LPG carriers were built. Oil demand fell 10%, the trade from 1.4 billion tons in 1979 to 900 million in 1983, inducing a severe recession when a 280,000-dwt tanker worth $28 million in 1979 was sold for $3.5 million three years later and an eight-year-old 318,000-dwt was scrapped for $4.65 million. Forty million dwt of tankers were laid-up in 1982, 52 million in 1983.[15] The market only started recovering in 1986. Shipping costs became even less critical to oil's delivered price. OPEC's share of world 1979–1985 production fell 45%, non-OPEC increased 26%. By the early-1990s, 70% of tankers traded spot compared to 20% in the early-1970s.[16] Higher fuel prices incentivised efforts to increase fuel efficiency, about 25% by reduced steel weight, improved hull coatings and engines. South Korean shipbuilding's advance and global recession forced Japan to shut 50 of its 138 drydocks by 1980.[17] Over 100 shipyards closed, especially in Europe. In the 1980s, Japanese and Korean shipbuilders had about 33% market share each, China, 7–10%.

During the 1980–1988 Iran-Iraq War, tankers were attacked. Lloyds recorded 1,546 commercial ships damaged or sunk. Loucas Haji-Ioannou specialised in Gulf loading. His special security systems lowered otherwise punitive insurance rates, enabling super-profitable voyages, adding 27 ships between 1982 and 1985, becoming by 1990, the largest independent shipowner; 50 ships, 7.5 million dwt. John Frederiksen also sent tankers to the Gulf, the profits of which founded large tanker, drybulk and offshore drilling fleets, more examples of how wars make and break fortunes.

Steam coal for power stations meant increased Australian, US, Canadian and South African volumes. In 1984 Japan started a ten-year plan to subsidise 20 ports on greenfield sites, from 1983's 15 million tons, to an expected 22 million by 1985 and 53.5 million by 1990,[18] planned like steel mills with long-term COAs with Japanese-owned, Japanese-built ships for Australia-Japan consecutive voyages, indicative of how the world economy was swinging from Atlantic to the inter-dependent Pacific and from oil to coal. Korea, Taiwan and Hong Kong also commissioned 1980s power stations importing Australian coal.

Chinese coal exports from 1980 and Indonesian from 1987 competed, forcing NSW port upgrades. Newcastle in 1982 and Port Kembla in 1983 loaded Capesizes on 15.2 metres. In the late-1990s Australia exported 85 million tons of coking coal and 77 million steam coal, supplying nearly 50% of Japan's and 83% of Asia's coal, while Australian dollar weakness induced European shipments to resume.[19] World seaborne steam coal trade increased from 150 million tons in the late-1980s to 283 million in 1999, mainly in Asia.

1981–84 freight rates were exceptionally low, but 1984's economic growth did <u>not</u> lead to drybulk recovery, mainly because Japanese shipowner Sanko ordered over 120 bulkers in the low market. Thinking it privy to future Japanese economic growth, other owners also bought, swamping the market with 20.7 million dwt, bankrupting Sanko, delaying drybulk recovery until 1987, the nadir August 1986 when a four-year-old panamax sold for $6.2 million. A five-year-old equivalent in 1980 had cost $22 million.

* * *

Container shipping grew faster than bulkers or tankers. In 1982 USL which McLean joined in 1977, ordered 14 containerships for $770 million for a round-the-world service, calling at hubs only. At Maersk's 1984 Algeciras hub, containers transferred to geared feeders for West African ports, aiding their development. By late-1985, Evergreen became the world's largest container operator with 95,000 TEU capacity, USL had 66,000, Maersk 65,000 and Sea-Land 51,000. Consolidation continued. Maersk bought Norfolk Line from Unilever and in 1987 all CMB's Chargeurs Reunis' and Franco-Belgian Services' volumes. Its fortnightly service through Suez quickly became weekly but in the depressed early-1980s, high-speed, high-consumption containerships were hard-hit. Pacific Far East Lines, Seatrain Container Lines, McLean Industries and USL went bankrupt. Japan's Yamashita Shinnihon had to merge with Japan Line, which in 1989 was taken over by Mitsui-OSK (MOSK). While British shipping companies dwindled, P&O had substantial container and bulker fleets and P&O European Ferries was the third-largest cruise ship fleet. Belgium's Bocimar emerged as a large independent bulker company carrying 30–50 million tons annually and bought LNGs. Between 1982 and 1993, 37 carriers left trans-Atlantic container trades, but Maersk re-entered in 1998:[20] inspired timing.

*   *   *

India's 1950–1970 foreign trade declined, with a tepid 1970–90 revival. Bureaucracy strangled private businesses. Millions of man-hours were wasted getting licenses and permits to start or proceed with business, breeding corruption. Government monopolies in oil, steel, airlines, electricity, newsprint and high tariffs encapsulated self-reliance. It produced everything inefficiently. Gradual tariff reduction, market-directed exchange rates and opening to foreign companies from 1991 gradually freed it, reviving trade, especially with China. Since 1995 its educated, entrepreneurial middle class grew 6.3% annually, now 31% of the population and growing.

In 1982, oil and gas comprised 82% of Indonesia's exports. Coal production, under a million tons in the early-1980s was first meaningfully exported in 1987. By 2002, production exceeded 100 million tons, exports enabled by new state-of-the-art, private Capesize ports and because of the 'bar' caused by fast-flowing tropical rivers depositing silt beyond the coast, offshore floating cranes and loading stations. Overall, the developing world's average tariffs fell 34.4% in the early-1980s, 21.9% in the early-1990s, and 12.6% in the early-2000s,[21] all with beneficial consequences. Indonesia's poverty rate, 45% in 1970, dropped to 11% in 1996 with a 1966–1997 GDP growth of over 50% per annum: the power of maritime trade!

In 1960 Japanese car output was 482,000, 8% of which was exported. By 1980 it produced six million, 54% exported. Criticism of its protectionism while flooding the world with cars, bikes and electronic goods led to car import tariffs reductions to zero in 1978, but only when domestic makers were strong enough to defend themselves. Most non-tariff barriers remained, like complex vehicle tests with copious documentation for each. Frequent rule changes without notice caused delays, making imports prohibitively expensive, so foreign market share remained under 2%.[22] Its 1982 whisky tariff was

68%, protecting domestic makers, much less on gin where there were none. Registering import rights took up to six years at huge costs. Thus, products sold worldwide were prevented from sale in Japan, making a mockery of trade reciprocity. So, while Japan became a maritime nation, its sense of responsibility which should have accompanied it, followed slowly, forced in 1981 to double aid to developing countries, still well behind others' aid-GNP ratio and spent little on defence. When 1950s-1960s growth rates of 10% dropped to 5%, living standards stagnated because distribution, service and farming sectors were so inefficient, the latter heavily subsidised and protected.[23] In 1990 its economic bubble burst. Recession followed.

Australian mineral exports kept growing led by coal and iron ore, especially to Japan, Korea and Taiwan, exports to Asia growing 400% between 1980 and 1991. New Zealand's 1991–92 exports were 34.8% to Asia, 15.3% to Japan alone, 16.6% to the EEC whose regulations it described as worse than the Soviets and 12.8% to America. In the Philippines, dictator Marcos was ousted in 1986. Corrupt oligarchs remained but in 1992 it removed foreign exchange regulations. 1990s Vietnam reformed along capitalist lines and grew rapidly. Bangkok became prosperous. Asian economic liberalism, industrialisation and democracy produced prosperity.

In America and Britain, President Reagan and Prime Minister Thatcher cut taxes, deregulated and reduced government spending. Thatcher privatised government industries including British Telecom, gradually reducing communication costs. Privatisation of the Central Electricity Generating Board was copied in developing countries. Between 1990 and 2010 many Independent Power Projects (IPPs), privately-owned power stations were built, the huge capital cost typically repaid to lenders by 15-year guaranteed electricity sales, most with 15-year coal import contracts. In 1980 Reagan persuaded Congress to let truckers negotiate rates, previously state-imposed and the 1980 Staggers Act deregulated US railroads. Inland transport costs fell, saving shippers and consumers about 16%,[24] encouraging container lines to sign ten-year railroad contracts. Consequently, by 1987 a third of Asia-US east coast containers were railed from west coast ports, freeing more ships. The 1970s World Bank and Asian Development Bank poured $1.3 billion into port projects in developing countries.[25] In 1981 Thatcher sold 21 British ports. Others followed, some to leading containership owners. By 2000, half the world's containers passed through private ports. Reagan and Thatcher are controversial figures in their countries, but for world economic and shipping efficiency, pioneering the privatisation model enabling electricity provision to impoverished people in developing countries and reducing consumer prices everywhere, their enlightened impact was considerable. In 1993 Peel Ports which owned the port of Liverpool bought the under-used Manchester Ship Canal believing it could relieve road congestion and in 2011 invested £50 billion in seven load/discharge terminals for all types of cargo, which continues to grow.

*   *   *

In 1973 four million TEUs had been shipped, in 1993, 26 million. As freight costs fell, the shipping component of foreign-made TV and phone retail prices became insignificant. Computer programmes and yard-handling improved, terminals became bigger and cranes faster. It was cheaper to move containers from Asia to Europe than short-haul inland. By 1993 most breakbulk routes were containerised. Maersk 'route-shared' with P&O and Sea-Land but Reynolds sold Sea-Land in 1984, explaining to stock market analysts that its investors disliked 'a capital-intensive, cyclical transportation company.' CSX bought it and sold it to Maersk in 1999. NOL, Singapore's national carrier, bought APL. P&O merged with NedLloyd in 1996, because both shareholders were unhappy with returns. In 1999 Maersk also bought Safmarine's liners, bulkers and reefers. Evergreen took Lloyd Triestino. D'Amico took Italia. Dozens of mergers and buyouts were a constant feature, while a new carrier entered. Founded in 1970, Aponte family-owned Mediterranean Shipping Company (MSC) bought second-hand ships. By 1987 it had 154,100 TEUs, its first newbuilding in 1994. In 1998 it had 220,745, fourth-largest after Maersk's 346,123, Evergreen's 280,237 and P&ONedlloyd's 250,858. With huge Asian trade growth, ten of the top 20 container companies in 1999 were Asian. The top 20 controlled 37% of global capacity in 1989, 53% in 1999, 83.7% in 2003,[26] aggressive consolidation, exactly as McKinsey predicted, with 2003 world trade ten-times larger than 1975.

In poor 1980s markets, P&O's over 20 bulkers of 110,000–210,000 dwt sensibly had COAs with mines, steel mills and power companies. When markets improved after 1987, the same strategy gave shareholder certainty but limited profitability and in 2000, 50% option 50% was sold to Sammy Offer's private Zodiac Maritime, which had ridden the volatile but more profitable spot market. That public companies are not the right vehicle for shipping companies was already widely accepted. John Hadjipateras, Greek Shipping Cooperating Committee Chairman, in 1992 blamed British shipping's decline on most being public companies, decisions made by boards of directors. 'Shipping doesn't work like that,' he said, meaning it needs entrepreneurial freedom. Furthermore, sons of British shipowners, unlike Greeks, did not follow the family profession and many companies did not diversify or adapt from imperial routes quickly enough.[27] By contrast, CMB in 1991 was bought by the Saverys family's Bocimar, which moved quicker and more purposefully. Divesting itself of liners, its LNG/LPG arm named Exmar, grew quickly.

In Asia, in 1986 South Korea's trade deficit turned to surplus. By 1988 it was tenth-largest trading nation with per capita income eight-times higher than 1960. Its $3 billion 1997 trade surplus was $108 billion by 2014. Indonesia followed Taiwan and South Korea into democratic transition after Suharto's 1998 fall. Thailand and the Philippines followed, also with liberal economic policies and low tariffs. Singapore's container and oil product distribution port attracted shipping companies and shipping services. Prime Minister Lee saw the maritime sector as developmentally vital, explaining, 'We must attract more international shipowning and ship-operating companies,'[28] extending tax and other incentives, attracting shipping and trading companies to set-up. In 2005, it was the largest container port, third-largest refining and largest bunkering port, as China's volumes rose.

* * *

In the early-1980s, grain traders with COAs started demanding 'wash-out' clauses, so if grain prices or freight rates were unfavourable, they could avoid shipment by paying an agreed lumpsum compensation. This evolved in 1985 into freight futures, the BFI (Baltic Freight Index), a basket of the main handy, panamax and Capesize routes, daily collected by the Baltic Exchange from expert broker panels, audited by it and published as an index (BIFFEX), the future value of which could be traded. Without vested interest in market levels, it was ideally independent. In 1989 Capesize, panamax and handy indexes, BCI, BPI and BHI were established. With no physical delivery, settlement was in cash. In 1992 this developed into Forward Freight Agreements (FFAs) for individually traded routes, far easier for route specialists. As markets and sizes changed, they were adjusted with market agreement. Shipping thus joined other commodity markets in having an efficient, flexible futures market to hedge physical positions, its popularity seen by turnover; in 1992, $0.5 million freight was covered, 1993, $48 million, 1994, $70 million and 1995, $273 million, when tanker FFA's tentatively started. By 2003, 41 daily route indices from different panels from 25 companies, were published, including tankers and gas carriers with nearly 3,400 annual trades.

In 1991 Norway became third-largest shipowner after Greece and Japan, falling to fourth in 1999 as Hong Kong/China overtook it, continuing concentration on smaller, specialised, expensive ships, well-protected niche trades, Greeks and Chinese on tankers and bulkers. In 1999, 135 million dwt of Greek-owned ships were worth $18 billion compared to Norway's 52 million dwt worth $23 billion.[29] Fleet expansion was timely. In 1990 world trade was worth under $7,000 billion, in 2000 about $13,000 billion.[30]

*   *   *

Containership sizes increased. By 2000 over 5,500 TEUs ships were built. Experts thought 18,000 TEUs feasible and Korean shipyard Samsung progressed a 12,000 TEU design as trans-Pacific volumes especially increased, the largest ships first deployed there. Ships of 12,500 TEU were 11% and 24% respectively cheaper per container than 8,000 and 4,000 TEU ships. Major ports' average handling speed was 34 containers/hour/crane but Sea-Land's Hong Kong terminal averaged 46, so big improvements were possible. Optimism reigned. By February 2005 Maersk-Sea-Land was the largest containership operator with 349 ships of 912,810 TEUs. In 2006 it bought P&ONedlloyd, shareholder dissatisfaction with volatility again the problem. MSC climbed to second with 251 of 639,404 and Evergreen third, 154 of 423,635. The world's largest liner routes were North America-Asia and Asia-Europe, much more voluminous than Europe-North America, where 19th-century lines and long-haul containerisation started. In 1992 Hong Kong's s annual TEU throughput was eight million, Singapore and South Korea's Pusan 7.5 million, Shanghai 5.6 million and Rotterdam 4.1 million, demonstrating the rapid, shipping-led rise of Asian economies.

*   *   *

Fearing British politicians and civil servants' indifference and ignorance of shipping's importance to Britain, in 2000 'Maritime London' was established, representing all London's maritime activity, the world's largest maritime hub in legal, insurance, broking, surveying and countless other support services, the aim to keep it strong, despite cost pressures and challenges involving Asia's economic rise. Brazil's Docenave, Australia's BHP Billiton and Rio Tinto had already relocated their sales and chartering offices to Singapore, nearer Asian buyers, which with government encouragement, attracted many major shipowners, shipbrokers and shipping lawyers to open or grow offices. Some Greeks had relocated to Piraeus after the junta's fall and Athens' infrastructure upgrade. But most, <u>hundreds</u>, stayed in London. Maritime London's 2004 *The Future of London's Maritime Service Cluster: A Call for Action* demanded ending 30 years of Treasury speculation of taxing shipowners' worldwide earnings and instead introduce tax incentives to buy ships as in Germany, Norway and Japan or examine Singapore's tax encouragements to attract foreign trading and shipping companies. Shipping contracts are governed by English Law. The IMO, ITF and International Association of Classification Societies (IACS) were, it argued, London-based, all liaising with flag states' London offices. In 2008, London's 400 shipbroking companies generated substantial revenues. With 17% of world insurance premiums, it was pre-eminent despite US, German, Scandinavian and Japanese competition and had the largest Protection and Indemnity (P&I) insurance with UK P&I Clubs accounting for 62% of the world market. London banks had 13% of world ship finance, down from 16% in 2006, although loans rose to $391 billion with surging shipbuilding. Lloyds Register classified 18% of the world fleet, the second-largest. City UK's 2011 report showed Britain's maritime sector generated £1.5 billion in GDP, providing 12,000 jobs, raising tax revenue of £483 million and £2.2 billion overseas earnings and with multiplier effects through the economy, totalling £6.1 billion GDP contribution, employing 117,000.[31] How Maritime London's efforts were rewarded is seen in Chapter 46.

Chapter 43

Decline and Fall of British Shipbuilding: An Analysis

In the 1890s Britain launched over 75% of world tonnage, northeast England the most, with apparently awesome productivity. An 1888 steel, triple expansion-powered 5,000-tonner for North German Lloyd was built in 98 days with 40 first class cabins, 16 second class and 2,000 third class, all electrically-lit.[1] A century later, British shipbuilding was virtually dead. What went wrong? Clearly two world wars' economic and psychological shocks were important. But it went deeper. Despite William Rankine, Glasgow University's Professor of Civil Engineering's (1855–1872) work, most universities did not promote engineering and few British shipbuilders sent apprentices to Royal Naval College's architect lectures, which were attended by foreign students. Many yards had at least one foreign scientifically educated draftsman. There were exceptions. William Denney and Bros. (1811–1963), which built over 1,500 ships, including the first steel ship in 1878 and first steam turbine ship in 1901, published papers on hull forms in the 1870s-1880s and funded the first commercial tank in Dumbarton. But most relied on apprenticeships, learning on-the-job. Evening classes were useful but not as much as scientific training. By contrast, post-war Japanese yards recruited graduates as foremen, trained workers and developed new systems, copied by Asia's tigers where engineers and economists headed ministries, directing economic progress.

During World War II, America built diesel-powered, welded, prefabricated, cheap Liberties, but Britain's equivalent Empire ships, their name showing misplaced pride, were rivetted and coal-burning, obstinate reluctance to modernise. Post-war complacency with full order books also contributed. Between 1937 and 1946 British shipyards' building cost index rose from 28 to 73, by 1956 160: totally uncompetitive.[2] In 1950 British yards made half the world's ships, 103 million tons, its main competitors defeated, but stagnated during rapid global growth.

In 1999 Sir Robert Atkinson, ex-Chairman of the nationalised British Shipbuilders Corporation (1980–1984) analysed British shipbuilding's decline. Britain's pre-war shipping was based on three pillars: passengers, liner services to colonies and America and coal exports in tramps. Its share of tonnage built declined from 44.7% in 1902, 32% in 1931, 22% in 1948, 12% in 1968 to 2% in 1988, because these pillars disappeared.[3] In 1897, Cardiff shipped 12 million tons, Swansea four million. Diesel and oil-fired engines negated this advantage. Passenger shipping limped along from 1950 when they carried three-times more passengers than aircraft. In 1955 a million crossed by sea and 750,000 by air, but in 1965, 400,000 by sea and <u>five million</u> by air.[4] Passenger liners were either scrapped or converted to cruise ships, P&O's in 1969. Given its inheritance, it could not have competed effectively, he reasoned but British shipyards were badly managed, working conditions addressed by management, usually only after strikes. Redundancy given with little or no notice fuelled labour and union militancy leading to strikes just before already delayed launches: deliberate blackmail, effective anarchy. Management and workers were too conservative, resisting change and unenterprising. In the 1950s-60s, financial control, production and labour relation weaknesses were highlighted but went unaddressed. With a substantial share of world shipbuilding and a growing market, it might have competed, only if comprehensively reformed; impossible with poor management and militant unions. Subsidised European yards without these disadvantages declined slower.

Furthermore, British shipbuilders built mainly for British shipowners, exporting only 20%: fatal complacency. Between 1958 and 1963, 17 British yards closed but world shipbuilding accelerated. Japan's share increased from 8.2% in 1954 to 39.5% in 1964, when six British yards closed, four more in 1965, which would have been five had the government not tried reconstructing Fairfield. The 1966 Geddes Report recommended amalgamating 60% of yards into five groups. But poor management and labour relations remained, taxpayer money injected to prevent insolvency, not modernise. By the mid-1960s it was too late to re-equip and catch-up. Building large tankers in the early-1970s when Japanese yards built faster and cheaper was mistaken. British liner companies adjusted to container shipping challenges much better.

British yards did not build tankers and bulkers, increasingly demanded in the 1950s-60s, nor containerships and cruise ships in the 1960s-70s. Sweden set-up new yards to build large tankers for a world market, not just Scandinavians. Of OCL's first six ships, five were German-built and Cunard's first early-1970s purpose-built cruise ships were from Holland and Denmark, while Finland's Wartsila became the leading high-value cruise ship supplier. In 1949, Britain had 44% of Norway's market, by 1958 just 8.5%. British owners' loyalty also wore thin. By the late-1950s, 28% of British-registered ships were foreign-built.[5]

Scholars have identified yard structure, the small scale, craft-based working, trade union militancy, management failure and lack of investment in equipment. All reinforced each other. Labour-intensive liner production was not easily deployed on bulkers and tankers. When markets fell, labour was laid-off, increasing militancy. 1945's full order books came with bitter memories of 1930s depression. Yards were unprepared for a long expansionary period, maintaining traditional methods, building bespoke ships in twos and threes for British clients rather than standard mass production of ships, reducing costs, increasing productivity. *Zaibatsu* industry, finance, shipbuilding and shipping integration, described in the last chapter with the Kawasaki example, also applicable to NYK and Mitsui, was also vital.

Malcolm Falkus' analysis points to British shipbuilders' small, fragmented, under-capitalised character. In the mid-1960s Mitsubishi's capacity alone equalled nearly 50% of Britain's main yards. Their order book equalled total British capacity. Holts were scathing about British yards, especially Vickers' absenteeism, poor time-keeping which Vickers made 'no effort…to correct,' time wasting, bad organisation, poor discipline, 'weakness in leadership', planning 'especially weak', 'no team spirit between management and men', senior managers never seen in the yard, from when they used German, Japanese, Dutch and Scandinavian shipyards.[6]

Atkinson also criticised politicians. In 1968 Prime Minister Wilson granted £250 million to British shipowners without commitment to scrap and build in British yards. Owners took British flag to obtain the grant, built in foreign yards and when the grant ended, switched back to open registries. British taxpayers indirectly subsidised foreign yards![7] The 'botched' 1977 nationalisation of 25 British shipyards was done by a union-influenced government, thinking only of jobs, pooling inefficiencies, without understanding the enormity of the task, proper analysis or strategy to solve deep-seated problems. Politicians and civil servants lacked understanding of industry and commerce. An admiral and civil servant without business knowledge or experience were appointed to run this complex giant, against stiff foreign competition; the 'ineptitude…almost criminal.' After Britain joined the EEC, its detrimental shipyard size proposals, Atkinson said, 'should not have been agreed.' Whatever was done, he thought, decline was inevitable, but laments 'a cultural and national problem of [not] taking manufacturing seriously.'[8] With further hindsight, one sees governments wasting taxpayer money, propping-up a dying industry.

And yet there was one success. London Greek owner LOF in 1957 bought 50% of Wear-based Austin and Pickersgill (A&P), which built Liberty replacement 14,000-dwt tweendeckers, SD14s, marketed to Greek owners. Between 1968 and 1985, it and its licensees built 211 profitably. When the right product was aimed at the right market, success followed, giving Japan's slightly larger Freedom design serious competition. In 1970, British yards' output of 1,327,000 grt was far behind Japan's ten million as British shipowners bought 913,000 grt from British yards and 1,551,000 from foreigners.[9] A&P apart, there was no clear strategy beyond survival. Already by the 1960s, Japan built almost 50% of world shipping; 15 million tons in 1974 and with open registry ships, controlled half the world's merchant shipping. When South Korea started industrialisation, it copied Japan's model, prioritising steel, shipbuilding and shipping companies to promote economic growth. A&P was nationalised, probably detrimentally, in 1977 and closed in 1988 following EEC negotiations to reduce capacity, which Atkinson criticised.

British 19th-century pioneers can perhaps be compared to Japanese and Korean post-war builders with modern equipment and working practices, both innovating. Japan's government insisted that Kure's technology be shared with other yards, developing standard designs. Its well-educated naval architects and marine engineers led numerous design improvements, from less resistant hulls to lighter engines. Undoubtedly cheap finance, initially cheap labour and subsidies helped. Korea's path was similar. Heavily subsidised Pohang Iron and Steel, opened in 1972, provided cheap steel. Korean shipbuilding had been insignificant. Hyundai Heavy Industry built power stations, oil refineries and industrial plants. Founder and CEO Chung Ju-yung in the early-1970s also wanted to build the most modern shipyard and ships. Recognising that bulkers and tankers, the latter 21.5% of merchant ships in 1960, but 75% of all newbuildings by 1970, was the main market, he thought them conceptually simple;

assembling steel units into a large tank with engine added, drydocks like building a large swimming pool. Initially seeking joint ventures, Japanese yards refused to help a potential competitor. Barclays Bank however, impressed with Hyundai's track record, agreed finance if a buyer was found for ships in an unbuilt yard. Greek shipowner George Livanos offered two 260,000-dwt tankers at $31 million each, well below market prices, with punitive terms if not delivered within 2.5 years from 1972, before the yard was built!

With hard work, low wages, tax holidays, low-interest government loans, national pride and ambition, they were delivered in 1974. Such was the demonstrable progress that eight more orders were received in 1973. As Korean industries developed, imports were encouraged in Korean-built ships. By the 1980s, Korea's shipbuilding was about equal to Japan. After the 1979 oil shock, they built off-shore platforms. Shipping's largest names, Angelecoussis, Bergesen, Sea-Land, Shell, BP, Lief Hoegh, Salen, Niarchos, Canadian Pacific, even normally loyal Japanese owners built there. By 1983, continuous capacity expansion made Hyundai the world's largest shipyard. It built LPGs from 1985 and LNGs from 1991. Its Marine Research and Welding Research Institutes' cutting-edge tank-welding technology in 1995 developed automatic welding robots for LNG tanks' curved surfaces.[10] Facing such vision, dynamism, well-targeted government assistance and good management in efficient greenfield sites, British yards could not have resisted.

Chapter 44

The China Phenomenon

'Let China sleep, for when she wakes, she will shake the world.'

Napoleon Bonaparte

'A more extensive foreign trade…could scarce fail to…improve very much the productive powers of its manufacturing industry.'

Adam Smith

Moderate Chinese Foreign Minister Zhou Enlai arranged President Nixon's surprise 1972 China visit. Deng Xiaoping was purged again in 1976. Moderates regained power in 1978 and China reformed. Deng pragmatically dismantled collective agriculture, incentivising peasants and encouraged foreign investment. Hong Kong businessmen took advantage of lower labour costs and 97% of its toy factories relocated to adjacent Guangdong.[1] Average incomes tripled by the early-1990s, lifting 170 million peasants from extreme poverty.

Until the mid-1990s Chinese maritime trade was globally insignificant. Opening its economy to foreign investment and encouraging bank loans to buy houses, cars and infrastructure projects worked much faster than expected. In 1978 there were no privately-owned cars in China; by 1993 over a million. Its trade leapt from $30 billion in 1980 to over $135 billion in 1992, its economic annual growth over 10%. A huge, hitherto dormant market accelerated. Because China had been so backward, Hong Kong's manufacturing and trade benefited as the world's fourth-largest financial centre after New York, London and Tokyo and had many prominent shipowners. A 1990 Sino-British agreement returned it to China in 1997 as a Special Administrative Region with separate economic, political and legal systems for 50 years. Many distrusted China, which warned it would not tolerate dissent. Jardine-Matheson immediately moved its headquarters to Bermuda and 1,000 residents a week emigrated to America, Canada, Australia, Britain and Singapore.

Memories of disastrous 1974–1987 and unspectacular 1990s shipping markets led to newbuilding under-investment. But in the 1990s, while Japanese industrial output flatlined, America increased 50%. Annually, Europe grew about 1.5%, Asian tigers over 10% and bulk volumes 10% from the late-1990s, mainly steam coal as the world's main energy source. However, in the 1997–1998 Asian crisis, industrial output fell 6%, many Asian IPPs were postponed or cancelled, four million tons of Capesizes scrapped and newbuilding panamax bulker prices fell from $28 million to $19 million, inducing owners to order 25.3 million dwt, beating the 1980s Sanko-inspired ordering boom. The 2000 Dot.Com crisis deflected attention from Chinese plans for many large steel and power plants and unprecedented infrastructure investment. In 2000, all shipping sectors rose. Clarkson Research's general shipping index, rarely passing $16,000/day in the 1990s, hit $19,900 in August 2000, the best since 1973.

Like Japan's and South Korea's industrialisation, Chinese imports were mainly iron ore and oil. They had planned their shipping; capacity contracted in advance. China did not, giving full reign to private enterprise and the free market. China's size magnified the effects, especially iron ore imports for steel production, which rose from 70 million tons in 1992 to 180 million tons in 2002 and 242.4 million in 2004, incredible acceleration and signs of things to come. Its total 2000–2004 imports rocketed from 296 million tons to 633 million. Meanwhile its low-priced, mainly containerised exports, rose 25% annually. Following its 2001 membership of the World Trade Organisation, its 2001–2008 manufactured exports increased 464%.[2]

Asian imports in the 1990s grew 5.1% annually compared to developed economies' 2.65%, which still accounted for 57% of world seaborne imports. But the tide was turning. China turbo-charged already substantial Asian maritime trade. Furthermore, its bullish forecasts turned out to be chronic underestimates. Becoming a net oil importer in 2001 with 1.5 million barrels/day, in 2003, it predicted three million in 2010. Only a year later they surged to 2.5 million, about 23 VLCC equivalents because Chinese car production boomed while rail congestion meant coastal power stations had to import. The 2010 figure was almost ten million. Predicted 300 million tons steel production in 2010 reached 500 million by 2007. Because it also used domestic ore, its 2007 imports were 'only' 382.8 million, compared with all Japanese, Korean and European imports of 320.8 million! In 2008 they rose to 442.5 million! Container volumes to Europe and America doubled from 2002 to 2005, when it was calculated that America had 475 automobiles per 100 people, China six, with similar deficiencies in other consumer goods: significant potential growth. European 2002–2005 container liftings rose from 58 to 72 million, North American 33 to 45 million, Asian 138 to 203 million, Hong Kong and China alone, 56 to 90 million.[3] In 2003 two million TEU ships were ordered, a record.

Familiar with market cycles, reliant on Chinese forecasts, few foresaw post-2004 growth acceleration, although Clarkson analyst Tom Cutler thought if 2024 consumption grew 15% from 23% in 2003, it meant 40 million tons more, with only 29 Capesize newbuildings due. Maquarie Bank's Jim Lennon compared China's prospects with Europe's and Japan's post-1945 growth, lasting over 15 years, that Japan's, Korea's and Taiwan's example suggested over a decade's rapid growth, needing huge investment responses from suppliers.[4] These were accurate forecasts.

Needing time to build ships, the market was unprepared for the demand surge. 1970s-1990s Tubarao/Japan Capesize iron ore freight rates had fluctuated from $5 to $15/ton, depending on market levels and bunker prices. From 2002 it rose, peaking at $46 in winter 2004–2005, fuelled by 6% industrial output growth with only 3% and 4% fleet growth in 2004 and 2005. By late-2004 with markets hitting new highs, Clarkson Research wrote 'an industry which for 50 years [with]…rates…never far above operating costs has suddenly hit the stratosphere,' adding, 'Economic theory does not set any limit where rates can go.' Compared with idle steel mills, 'a few extra dollars/ton freight is easily absorbed.' This again was accurate. Few expected how much.

Capesize rates had never exceeded $30,000/day. In the 2004–05 winter they peaked at $105,000/day, then fluctuated between $20,000 and 60,000/day for a few months. In 1996 there were only three Chinese Capesize ports: Beilun, Quingdao and Yantai. In 2005, only 40% of Chinese imports were in Capesizes. By 2006, there were 19 Chinese Capesize ports, in 2009, 27. Nevertheless, booming imports led to 7–10 days congestion, further constraining supply. Average annual 2002–2007 bulker earnings grew 45.6%, tankers 10.1%. Japanese, Korean and Chinese shipyards were full. China expanded existing yards and built over 20 greenfield ones. As more people prospered, diets improved. In 2003–2004 China imported 31% of world soyabean imports, in 2007–2008, 46%!

In 2000, without large Chinese container ports, Hong Kong served almost all China's manufactured exports. By 2006, Hong Kong's TEU throughput was second to Singapore, but with China catching-up, Shanghai was third, Shenzhen fourth, Busan fifth, Taiwan's Kaohsiung sixth, Rotterdam seventh, Hamburg eighth, Dubai's Jebel Ali ninth and Los Angeles tenth because world trade in manufactured goods surged 120%, mainly from China. Between 1990 and 2015 Britain lost almost half its manufacturing, Japan a third, America a quarter, most to China. In 2004 American factories made 222 million tyres, in 2014 only 126 million, substituted by Chinese.[5]

In 2011 Shanghai became the leading container port with 30 million TEUs. Singapore had 29.5 million. In 2013 Shenzhen was third. By 2014, seven of the world's ten largest container ports were Chinese! As shipping drove Asian prosperity in previous decades, Chinese containerised exports dominated Asia's. No European port was in 2014's top ten list, despite what in other times would have been considered robust growth. For example, in 1960 Hamburg handled 11 million tons of general cargo, 40 million in 1996, 88% containerised, over 100 million by 2014. Maritime transport costs were so insignificant that companies outsourced manufacturing to world locations with the cheapest labour, creating complex just-in-time supply chains. By 2015 the world handled 580 million TEUs annually.

China's steel industry consumed energy voraciously. With 13% of world coal deposits, in 2002 it produced 1.1 billion tons, burnt in rapidly proliferating power stations. By 2006 it produced 1.9 billion, exported to industrialising Asian neighbours. But from 2002 coal exports fell and it started importing, especially from Indonesia. 2002's 7.6 million tons of steam coal, became 41.8 million in 2008. It imported 1.7 million tons of coking coal in 2002, a little more in 2007, but then took-off to 32.5 million in 2009. Japan, Korea and Taiwan turned to Australia for their imports, a reversal so sudden that Australian ports became exceptionally congested. Newcastle especially tended to congest, but in June 2007, 82 bulkers queued to load, over 145 in all Australian ports, coinciding with the worst storms in 30 years, inhibiting loading, restricting ship capacity, further escalating freight rates. Mining companies incurred demurrage bills estimated at $830,000/day,[6] leading to deepening Newcastle from 15.2 to 16.5 metres, completed in 2009. Simultaneously, China exported steel and cement it could not absorb, about 72 million tons of steel in 2006, further fuelling the boom. Capesizes were normally

Chinese Capesize Ports

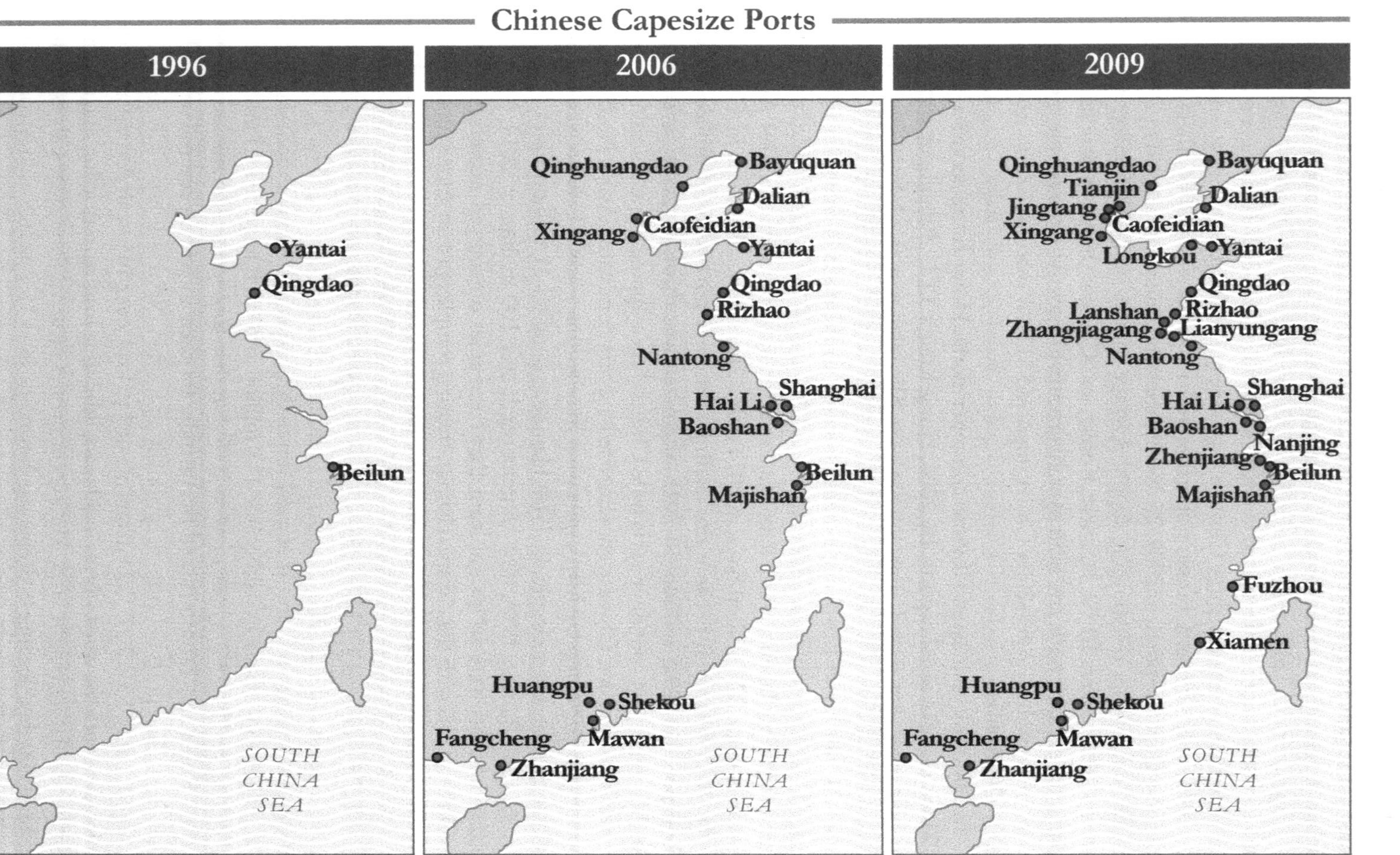

scrapped when 20–25-years-old, depending on market conditions and if the 20-year Special Survey cost was affordable, but unprecedented high rates meant scrapping fell from 10.6 million dwt in 2004, to 5.7 million in 2005 and 6.6 million in 2006. Scrap prices rose from $350/ton to $500/ton over 2006, while owners exceptionally paid even the 25-year Special Survey costs, charterers exceptionally chartering them. No wonder. The average 2005 Capesize Tubarao/Beilun & Baoshan freight rate, $29.23 and 2006 of $27.85, rose to $59.40 in 2007, peaking in May 2008 at $101.20! This led to exceptional solutions involving tankers.

In 1989 the *Exxon Valdez* had spilled 11 million gallons of oil off Alaska after grounding. To prevent further pollution events, Congress' 1990 Oil Pollution Act phased-out single-hull tankers from US waters by 2010 while the IMO required more stringent assessments. In 2003, following other spills, it also mandated single-hull tanker phase-out, over-riding market mechanisms for the first time, although some traded beyond 2010 with flag, state and port permission, mainly in West Africa and developing Asia. To solve this phase-out problem and booming iron ore freight rates, in 2005 China's Heibei Ocean Shipping, under classification society supervision and rules, converted a single-hull VLCC into a VLOC (Very Large Ore Carrier). Despite a December 2007 VLCC super-spike of $220,000/day, other Chinese and some foreign owners followed with about 30 more, conversion costs amortised by Chinese steel mill COAs, as spot Capesize rates peaked at $235,000/day in mid-2008.

The boom had other consequences. Since containerisation, reefer containers gradually took reefers' market, which in 1993 still had two thirds, but by 2003, fuelled by Asian demand, reefer containers carried 70%. With soaring bulk rates, reefers turned to drybulk: fertilisers, fishmeal, sugar etc. Newbuilding orders were spurred in all sectors. In 2003 Maersk owned 280 containerships, ran terminals in 30 ports, owned two factories making containers but thought it needed increased capacity and ordered seven ships for Asia-Newark and eight bigger ones for Asia-Europe, crewed by only 13, making a container slot 18% less costly than on Maersk's 11,000 TEU ships. Built with subsidies in Denmark, the first was the 2006 *Emma Maersk* at 15,500 TEUs.[7] After acquiring P&ONedLloyd in 2006 for $2.8 billion, Maersk had over 600 ships, 1.7 million TEUs, 16.2% of world capacity, twice MSC's. The acquisition was difficult due to incompatible computer systems. It temporarily lost money. But most lines were very profitable. In mid-2007, the container fleet reached ten million TEUs, doubling since 2000, as the orderbook hit five million TEUs, over three million in 2007 alone, many the new giants. All containership growth in the 50 years since 1956 was delivered from 2005 to 2010! World GDP grew 5.3% in 2003, 4.9% in 2004 and 5.4% in 2006, Asia and Africa especially strong. Chinese exports rose from $226 billion in 2001 to $1.9 trillion in 2011. Its share of textile exports to America and Europe, 17% in 2005, rose to 40% by 2010,[8] when half as many containers again were moved than in 2006, and at much lower cost.

The August 2007 credit crisis created a sense of unease. Looking back, a five-year old panamax worth $14 million in 2001, was $92 million in February 2008. A newbuilding Capesize, $37.5 million in 2000 and delivered a year later commanded $151 million in March 2007. An Aframax tanker newbuilding, also ordered in 2000 for $37.5 million, delivered a year later, commanded $92 million in March 2007, both earning handsomely since delivery. Chinese demand still seemed insatiable. Because China's remaining iron ore reserves had less iron content, in May 2008 Jim Lennon predicted imports, which jumped from 34 million tons in October 2007 to 46 million in May 2008, 35% in seven months, crude oil 31% in the same period, would soar from 2008's projected 431 million tons to over 800 million in 2015![9] He was again proved correct.

Brazil and Australia's supply response was as impressive as demand. In 2002 they shipped 35 and 44 million tons respectively to China, by 2009, 165 and 266 million, necessitating new mines, automated drilling equipment, railways, trucks and port infrastructure; huge capital outlays. Western Australia's mines transported ore in 2.5-kilometre-long trains with 225 wagons, each carrying over 100 tons to 160–220,000-tonners, loaded by very few, well-paid, non-unionised crane drivers in 24–30 hours. Brazil's Ponta da Madeira invested $10 billion in 2008, adding 100 locomotives and 600 wagons to its existing 182 and 10,000, with trains lengthened from 220 to 330 wagons. A new berth handled two 380,000-tonners with 16,000 tons/hour shiploaders, aiming to increase export capacity from 85 million tons to over 200 million by 2012. In 2007 shipowners ordered newbuildings worth $123 billion, Greeks $36 billion, Chinese $16 billion, Korea and Japan $21 billion. But the huge order book and sense of gathering storm reduced 2008 orders.

Nevertheless, apart from 2008 deliveries, 164 Capesize newbuildings were due in 2009, 349 for 2010 and 219 for 2011, totalling 840, compared with 641 delivered in the previous 18 years! Mid-2008's orderbook was 49% of the fleet. Shipping professionals knew the boom could not last, the orderbook dangerously large. But what could go wrong and when? US banking problems, first apparent a year earlier, proved more serious than first thought. In September 2008 Lehman Brothers went bankrupt, triggering the Great Financial Crash. Normal short-term credit, necessary for trade, was withdrawn. Freight rates crashed as most steel mills struggled to sell steel or accommodate contracted iron ore in their stockpiles. Investors willing to pay $160 million for a second-hand Capesize a week earlier, evaporated. The Capesize index, $231,000/day dropped to under $2,100 in a couple of months. The actual market was even lower. The index reflected fixtures, but with almost all Capesizes laid-up, those still trading waited days or weeks for a cargo. The whole drybulk market as measured by the Baltic Dry Index, 11,793 in May was 663 by December; 94% down.

In early-2009 however, China realised that with collapsed ore prices and freight rates, it could close low-quality domestic mines and in 2009 imported an astonishing 185 million tons or 39% more iron ore than in 2008, creating Chinese port congestion, about 90 ships waiting in July. Despite worldwide recession, with EU steel production down 72% year-on-year, Japan's 44%, Chinese imports catapulted Capesize rates to about $90,000/day mid-year and were volatile but strong throughout, depending on Australian and Chinese port congestion. Less spectacularly, India's 2009 steel production surpassed America's. Developing countries including China had 85% of the world's population. India's ports, privatised from 1999, provided with new cranes, berths and yards, were deepened. India was unlike centrally-directed China, but IPPs with long-term steam coal imports, doubled to 150.5 million tons, many to Capesize ports in 2010–11. Mundra handled 60 million tons, Gangavaram 35 million.

In 2008, 850,000 TEU capacity was ordered, deliverable in 2009–2011. Falling freights meant despite a 7% volume increase, in 2011 hundreds of containerships were laid-up. Maersk lost $2.1 billion in 2009, with recovery a $2.642 billion profit in 2010 and a $550 million loss in 2011. It nevertheless ordered more newbuildings. Tim Harris, former P&O CEO admitted 'Maersk took a long-term view, not driven by short-term returns to shareholders…western stock markets like…predictability.'[10]

In the 1980s, six over 300,000-tonners had been built for Ponta da Madeira's and Rotterdam's 23-metre draft berths, too big for spot market trading but ideal for core consecutive voyages to European steel mills. By 2004–2005 standard 160–185,000 Capesizes after discharging in Asia, unable to find Australian or South African backhaul cargoes not only ballasted to Australia, but back to Brazil. Australian ports' proximity enabled lower freights, thus higher prices. This presented Brazilian miners with a problem and opportunity. The average Brazil/China Capesize rate in 2000–2003 was $12.20, Australia/China $6.40, a $5.80 differential, but average 2004–2008 rates were $42.30 and $17.50, a $24.70 differential. This led Brazil's Docenave (now Vale) to encourage more Chinese large ports as it commissioned thirty-six 400,000-tonners, a record drybulk size, for 15-year Brazil/China consecutive voyages from 2010, drastically reducing the differential.

*   *   *

Inevitably China's economic growth slowed from over 10% to about 7%. Maersk thought container trades would rebound in 2009, as it did with drybulk and built 18,000 TEU ships. Competitors CMA-CGM and MSC ordered more. The weight of deliveries gradually drove freight markets to below operating costs by 2015. Despite slow steaming to save fuel, adding voyage time, thus decreasing supply, 2015–2017 markets were disastrous. Older ships rushed to demolition or lay-up. High-profile Korean shipowner Hanjin went bankrupt. Japanese rivals NYK's, MOSK's and KLine's container departments exceptionally joint-ventured. Failing to staunch the haemorrhaging, they merged into Ocean Network Express (ONE) 'so none of us become zero', they quipped, hoping cost-cutting would achieve closer to breakeven. CSAV and UAS joined Hapag-Lloyd. Maersk swallowed Hamburg-Sud. Still, many ships were under-utilised. Under pressure, Maersk sold its considerable banking and retail assets. Tentatve recovery started in 2017. For survivors, in 2019 all sectors started breaking even.

With growing ship sizes and trade volumes, Panama's Canal Authority from 2007 invested $6 billion on a second canal with wider, deeper entrances and larger locks, aiming to double capacity by 2016. Many questioned its wisdom. Large containerships still discharged on the west coast and railed containers east, but increased volumes meant the new canal succeeded so well, there was often 7–10 days waiting after 2020, enabling Panama to auction the earliest access, which for containerships carrying valuable goods was several hundred thousand dollars, for LNG ships up to a million following the gas price spike after Russia's 2022 Ukraine invasion. Smaller ships used the original canal.

*   *   *

To demonstrate speed of change, China produced 6% of world steel in 1980, 9% in 1990, 16% in 2000, 48% in 2009 and <u>73%</u> in 2021! It imported 665.4 million tons of iron ore in 2011, 794.9 million in 2013, 939.7 million in 2015, 1,058 million in 2017, more than <u>world</u> imports five years earlier and 1,107 million in 2021, 693.9 million from Australia, 237 million from Brazil, since when it has plateaued, fluctuating up to 1,219 million in 2024 and an estimated 1.185 million in 2025, out of the world's 1.597 million. Japan produces 8% of world steel, Europe 6% and South Korea 5%. Europe's iron ore imports by contrast declined from 120.4 million tons in 2017 to 86.4 million in 2024. China's coking coal imports rose from 43.2 million in 2017 to 62.4 million in 2024, while Europe's declined from 48.5 million to 37.8 million, China's steam coal imports for its multiplying coal-fired power stations, from 174 million in 2017 to 358.9 million in 2024, over 195 million from Indonesia. Europe's declined to 55.9 million as it prioritised renewables (see next chapter).

Bulk tonnage swung from Atlantic predominance until 2002–2003 to the Pacific, 67:33 by 2013. Energy was also supplied by 90.4 million tons of LNG in 2018, 38% more than 2017 and 122.4 million in 2021 with LPG rising from 18.8 to 24.5 million tons. Chemical imports also soared. In 2000 Japan's automobile makers had no Chinese factories. By 2009 a seventh of their global production was from Chinese joint-ventures. In 2010 China overtook America as the world's biggest automobile market. By January-March 2023 it was the largest exporter with 1.07 million.

Chinese crude oil imports grew from 148.1 million tons in 2007, 415 million in 2017 and to 503 million in 2024. Vietnam's industrialisation had similar transformative effects, exporting over 30 million tons of coal in 2006–07, but began importing, peaking in 2021, 18.5 million tons of iron ore, 9.3 million coking coal, both gently declining thereafter but 25 million team coal increased to 60.8 million in 2024.

In contrast to China's relentless import growth, Japan's 2011–2021 iron ore imports fluctuated between 113 to 126 million, reducing to 102.2 million in 2023 and 96.4 million in 2024. South Korea's rose from 56.3 to 74.1 million in 2021 to 68.3 million in 2023 and Taiwan 18.9 to 25 million in 2021, 21.2 million in 2023 thereafter declining slightly to 19.8 in 2024. Japan's steam coal imports rose gently from 119.5 million in 2010, peaking at 132.6 in 2017, plateauing around 113–126 million thereafter. South Korea's peaked at 116.7 million in 2017, gently declining thereafter, 85.9 in 2024. Asian grain imports continued growing from 177 million tons in 2014 to 279 million in 2021, of which 156 million was Chinese. Japan and South Korea then plateaued, while Vietnam's doubled to 17.5 million, then stabilised.

In the Gulf, in the early-1990s, to capture more value, Saudi Arabia's and Kuwait's refineries exported oil products, not just crude. Furthermore, because aluminium production consumes huge electricity, Bahrain used its oil to start production in 1971 from imported bauxite. Saudi Arabia and the UAE soon copied it, making the Gulf a significant importer/production centre. Gulf iron ore imports, mainly Bahraini, also increased from 2010's 20.5 to 22024's 36.3 million, as many Gulf countries broadened their economies.

2000's seaborne trade almost doubled in 2018 to 11.9 billion due to Asian economic expansion. Worldwide 2020 covid lockdowns, extending deep into 2022 in China, caused supply chain interruption and congestion. Containerships spent 13.7% longer in port in 2021 than 2020, especially severe in China, Long Beach-Los Angeles and northern Europe, limiting supply. From 2015–2017's containership despair, the market reached new heights with record profits. In late-2020, a 4,400 TEU ship commanded $25,000/day for 6–12 months, a year later, $100,000. In 2022 Russia invaded Ukraine, which together provided 30% of world wheat and barley, 20% of maize, 50% of sunflower oil and substantial amounts of fertilisers. Ukraine's second quarter wheat exports dropped 87%, a food security threat to developing countries. Egypt, the world's biggest wheat importer, normally importing 85% from Ukraine and Russia, switched supply to India: China to the EU, Africa to Brazil and America. Ukraine's 17.4 million tons of iron ore shipments to China collapsed. Europe's reduction of Russia's piped LNG caused a massive spike in LNG rates, $250,000/day for five years in 2022, an extraordinary windfall for owners lucky or clever enough to have one or more free. By 2024 rates had fallen to around $30,000/day.

Massive Indonesian coal exports transformed its economic fortunes. It became democratic from 1998–1999. In 2020 and 2023 it banned raw nickel and bauxite export to promote processed exports, the value for which in electronic vehicle production for example was far greater. As President Widodo said, 'we don't want to sell raw materials [but]…something semi-ready,' continuing Asia's sensible economic development.

In 2021 Chinese shipyards built 44% of the world fleet, Korea 32%, Japan 18%. China's fleet reached 225.1 million grt by 2021, mainly bulkers, but increasingly containerships at 39.9 million. In November 2022 China's 139 shipyards' orderbook was 1,816 ships, including 579 containerships and 524 bulkers, only 41% for Chinese owners, the rest foreign including an impressive 51 containerships for MSC, which overtook Maersk as the largest container carrier. Unlike its competitors it also bought second hand ships, an astonishing 470 from 2022 to 2025, huge scale its defence against uncertainty. In mid-2025 it claimed 922 ships, by end-2025, it added another 50 to reach 972 of 7.14 million TEU capacity with another 2.05 million on order. Its mid-2025 market share was 20.5%, Maersk had 14.2%, CMA-CGM 12.2%, quadrupling in 16 years and COSCO 10.4%. By December 2025 the total order book was a hefty 34% of the fleet. China continued to dominate new buildings in 2025 with 53%, South Korea 29.1% and Japan 13.1% but China had over 60% of orders made that year.

The biggest post-1945 change was Europe's relative decline and Asia's accelerating rise. In 1959 Asia, Latin America and Africa together generated under 10% of world manufacturing. Container shipping was central to the change, reflected in the following tables, the first in millions of tons.

	Tanker	Bulk	General/Containerised cargo	Total cargo
1970	1,440	448	717	2,605
1990	1,755	988	1,265	4,008
2000	2,163	1,186	2,635	5,984
2010	2,752	2,232	3,423	8,408
2020	2,918	3,196	4,531	10,645

The following table shows the Asia-centric acceleration in millions of TEUs.

	Trans-Pacific	Asia-Europe	Trans-Atlantic
2008	19.2	19.1	5.8
2022	32.7	26.3	8.9[11]

Spreading economic liberalism, especially in Asia enabled the 1990–2015 world economy to double. World poverty halved, life expectancy and literacy improved as two billion people gained electric power, a function of IPPs, an insufficiently recognised Thatcher legacy. By 2015 worldwide container liftings were 837 million TEUs, 1,013 million in 2019, China's share 203 million in 2015, 263 million in 2019. Between 1980 and 2016 average EU incomes rose 66%, America and Canada 84% and China, 1,237%.[12] In 2021 the top five container exporters, almost half world volumes, were China with 30% alone, America, Vietnam, South Korea and Japan.

To understand how maritime trade growth, especially China's, drove Asian economies in this century, UNCTAD's Liner Shipping Connectivity Index demonstrates world shipping access for manufactured goods. The selected countries demonstrate the main trends.

	2006	2011	2022
Bahrain	7.11	16.88	36.17
Belgium	72.4	78.6	86.98
China	100	129.23	171.93
France	56.98	63.18	74.61
Germany	75.59	80.68	85.21
India	42.24	49.09	61.52
Japan	72.69	76.58	79.39
Malaysia	63.95	87.79	98.96
Oman	22.95	40.52	53.67
Netherlands	71.25	79.59	90.58
Philippines	19.77	23.49	25.33
Saudi Arabia	39.5	52.32	70.25
Singapore	81.58	93.89	111.06
South Korea	68.17	90.69	111.82
Thailand	36.09	38.85	69.59
UAE	47.44	61.72	74.69
UK	78.8	81.2	89.82
Vietnam	20.55	49.34	78.77

Notice China's widening lead as the most connected country. Singapore, Malaysia, Thailand and South Korea continued developing, Vietnam the latest tiger with the largest increased which continues. India's port upgrades enabled increased regional connectivity. Middle East countries have developed quickly. Europe and Japan grew slowly. World population growth, from five billion in 1980 to about eight billion in 2022 is partly a fundamental demand-driver and partly caused by increased maritime trade and wealth, total trade in all products increasing from about four to 12 billion tons, especially drybulk, from under one billion to over three billion. In 1995 the largest container ship carried 4,000 TEUs, in 2025 over 24,000, with 28,000 on drawing boards. In 2024, seven of the top ten container ports were Chinese; Shanghai 47.28 million TEUs, Singapore 37.29, Ningbo-Zhousan 33.36, Shenzen 30.4, Qingdao 24.6, Pusan 22.07, Tianjin 21.03, Los Angeles 19.04, Hong Kong 16.58.

The 2005 'Trans-Pacific Partnership', Brunei, Chile, New Zealand and Singapore aimed to lower tariff and non-tariff trade barriers. In 2008, Australia, Canada, Japan, Malaysia, Mexico, Peru, America and Vietnam joined negotiations. America's 2017 withdrawal triggered agreement with the remainder, 2018's 'Comprehensive and Progressive Agreement for Trans-Pacific Partnership' (CPTPP). The eleven signatories represented 13.4% of global GDP, a huge free trade area. Its requirements to share information on state-owned enterprises and detailed standards for intellectual property (IP) made China, who later applied, ineligible due to widespread belief it organised IP theft. Japan's Shinzo Abe suggested Britain, exporting over £1 billion of goods, holding £98 billion investments and trading £110 billion with CPTPP members, join after leaving the EU and was ratified in 2023. Taiwan, the Philippines, UAE and several Latin American states subsequently applied. As the EU continues protectionism, almost every other region grew faster and 2000–2020 British trade with the Americas, Asia and Africa grew faster than with the EU when still a member (see Chapter 46).

Replacement of expensive telex communication by free e-mails and competitive mobile phone charges from the 1990s meant daily face-to-face Baltic Exchange contact became redundant. But as custodian of the internationally trusted Freight Indices, its importance changed as volumes grew, expanding to 33 bulker and 25 tanker routes. The LNG, LPG, container and air freight routes were little used, but drybulk is voluminously traded and tankers significantly. Drybulk volumes, $273 million in 1995 continued growing. The yearly average since 2012 have been: Capesize $19.2 billion, panamax $14.8 billion, Supramax $3.4 billion,[13] another demonstration of the ascent of maritime trade.

America's concern over China's trade and shipbuilding dominance led to President Trump's 2024 election tariff pledges which also cited unfair EU tariffs and regulatory barriers. With China accounting for 30% of US container imports, in April 2025 he imposed tariffs on all countries, most on Asia and the EU, 59-20%, even 10% on countries without imbalances and 50% on all steel, aluminium and automobiles, levels not seen since the 1930s. This time however, 90% of global maritime trade did not involve America. China retaliated. Within days America had 145% on Chinese and China 125% on US imports with America threatening punitive port charges on Chinese-built ships irrespective of ownership. Initially rocking stock and bond markets,

US-China container traffic dropped 43% in May, affecting US imports of clothing, furniture, mobile phones, computers, sports equipment, bicycles, toys etc. although some was re-routed through Southeast Asia, disguising origins. Trump dialled back, threatened, ratcheted up and eventually made deals.

After threatening the EU with 50% on its $600 million exports to the US, it settled at 15%, up from 4.8% with promises of EU investment in America. In 2010 the EU's economy had been slightly bigger than America. By 2025 it was 25% smaller, with almost no economic growth for 25 year, its per capita GDP $40,800 compared with $81,70 in America, a failure if its protectionism. Vietnam and Taiwan agreed tariffs of 20%, Indonesia 19% with guarantees to buy US energy and Boeing aircraft, Japan and South Korea 15%, the latter in return for investment in US shipbuilding. Despite the confusion the US economy grew. US tariff revenue surged fourfold to $24.2 billion by June but China stopped buying US soybeans, a trade worth $12 billion in 2024. In October they agreed a ceasefire. Tariffs were eased, punitive charges on Chinese ships reduced. China agreed to buy US soybeans, stop fentanyl shipments and resume rare earth exports. India initially replaced some Chinese exports but because it bought huge quantities of sanctioned Russian oil (see next chapter), 50% tariffs were imposed on its exports.

Asian container lines were hard hit, especially COSCO. Japanese and Korea lines volumes and rates were slashed to under half. By the end of 2025 the situation was unresolved but America continued to try and rebalance and counter Chinese trade and shipbuilding dominance, although with Chinese prices competitive it attracted three out of every four orders by the end of the year when China's trade surplus exceeded $1 trillion, its declines to America balanced by increases to the EU, Latin America and Africa. By December 2025 Greek owners had 16.4% of the world fleet with 398 million dwt, Chinese owners 14.4% and Japanese 9.9%, a total of 40.7% for the top three. In container shipping MSC in December bought a 2500 TEU ship, built 2005 for $29 million and a 2001-built for $17 million; very full prices for overaged ships, but instant capacity coped with various logistical changes caused by the tariff turmoil, control of capacity critical.

Chapter 45

Going Green

Fossil fuels transformed mankind's living standards, but many were concerned with their role in climate change. In 1954 scientists told Congress that the Arctic would be ice-free in 25-50 years, but when global temperatures reversed in the 1970s some warmed of a coming Ice Age. A resumption of warming persuaded the UN in 1989 to warn the world had ten years to stop human-induced warming, that island nations like the Maldives would drown, coastal flooding and crop failures would cause chaos. By the 1990s the Centre for Biological Diversity said the Arctic would be ice-free by 2012, the BBC by 2013.

Increasing global concern led to the 1997 Kyoto Protocol between many countries which took the first measures to reduce carbon dioxide (CO_2) which was blamed, especially coal. They agreed to make way for renewables and LNG, whose negligible early 1970s fleet grew to 16 million dwt in 2008. The pressure increased. In 2006 and 2009 Al Gore predicted a 75% chance of an ice-free Arctic within seven years. In 2008, NAS's James Hansen predicted Lower Manhattan under water by 2018, due to fossil fuel burning. Kyoto however, did not apply to India, Brazil and Indonesia.

Steam coal shipments, drybulk's fastest growing sector, doubled from 242 million tons in 1995 to 490 million in 2005, driven by Japan, then Korea, Taiwan and since 2006 China, faster than iron ore trade's growth. As China supercharged its economy with coal-fired power stations, Europe increasingly demonised coal as global warming's main source. In the third post-war energy directional change, <u>not</u> driven by markets but policy, it was decided that fossil fuel dependence be reduced.

Europe led the green agenda. Its steam coal imports peaked in 2006 at 162.9 million tons, by 2023 only 62.5 million, of which Germany imported 18.6, Holland six, Italy 6.2, Spain 5.5, France 3.1 and Portugal zero. Britain reduced most, from 44.4 million in 2006 to two million in 2023, zero by 2025. Asian imports by contrast accelerated; China 241.7 million in 2021, to 313.4 million in 2023, Vietnam 25.3 in 2021 to 34.2 in 2023. Developed Asia's imports are declining very gently: India's are in the 140–192 million range depending on domestic coal use.[1] Realistically, there are too many Asian coal-fired power stations, in 2025, 3,269 in China alone, having added two per week in 2024 with 800 more planned after 2025, to switch to alternative fuels. In 2022, it was calculated that China's industrialisation discharged more CO_2 into the atmosphere in the previous <u>eight</u> years than Britain had since 1780! 2024's world coal output, a record 8.8 billion tons, of which 1.55 billion was shipped, was driven mainly by Asian, especially Chinese, demand, low-cost energy, fuelling growth. Coking coal imports for steel decreased slightly in Europe and rose slightly in Asia. World oil consumption in 2023 and 2024 was 101.89 and 103.75 million barrels/day respectively, buoyed by Chinese and increasingly Indian demand. Almost 40% of 2024's seaborne trade involved energy. But while Britain and Australia, the most zealous net-zero proponents, dismantled base-load power plants, harming their economies, China released as much CO_2 in 12 days as Australia does annually.

In the increasingly feverish 'climate change' atmosphere, shipping itself was attacked as a similar CO_2 emitting culprit as aviation: an absurd comparison. According to Clarkson Research, shipping's CO_2 emissions are 2.3% of world emissions; the most CO_2-efficient transport. Shipping carries 90% of world trade, a vastly bigger industry. Modern ships emit about five grams of CO_2/ton-mile, large trucks over 50, aeroplanes over 500, high altitude emissions having multiplier effects. Nevertheless, shipping consumes 250 million tons of fossil fuels emitting nearly a billion tons of CO_2 and greenhouse gases annually, <u>but</u> makes minor contributions to marine pollution, the majority from land-based discharge, sewage, industrial effluent etc. The shipping industry however made early efforts to reduce emissions.

The first LNG-powered ship was launched in 2000. In 2006 the Baltic-North Sea-Channel Emission Control Area reduced fuel sulphur levels. In 2009 Maersk, Shell and *Lloyds Register* worked for two years on biodiesel. NYK put solar panels on a ship and recovered waste heat on another for electricity supply. Beluga Skysail pioneered a towing kite, which in favourable conditions reduced fuel by a third. In 2014 MOL, previously MOSK, fitted a car-carrier with solar panels which charged batteries enabling diesel generators to stop in port. In 2020, Clarkson's CEO told shareholders that shipping's CO_2 output had reduced about 14% since 2008 by more efficient ships and slow steaming, despite moving 35% more cargo while UNCTAD calculated that 2012–2022 CO_2 emissions fell 21% for containerships, 18% for bulkers, only 1% for tankers. All improvements were market-driven. For example, after the 2008 Global Financial Crisis, shipbuilders delivered their orderbooks, but had to design more fuel-efficient engines to entice buyers. Thus, a 2008-built 83,000-ton bulker consumed about 32.5 tons of Intermediate Fuel Oil (IFO) at 13 knots fully laden, a 2020-built 86,000-tonner, only 26.5 tons.

The green debate often generates more heat than light. In 2021 an ill-informed *New York Times* article entitled *Tasked to fight Climate Change, a Secretive UN Agency does the Opposite,* wrote 'the IMO has repeatedly delayed and watered-down climate regulations.' The IMO is <u>not</u> secretive. With an imposing London headquarters overlooking Parliament, keen to promote its message and mission, <u>with</u> member states agreement, it directed maritime improvements since 1958, transforming merchant shipping into a safe, responsible, world-changing industry. Few ships now sink. 'Losses' are usually damaged ships beyond economic repair, 'written-off' by hull insurers. Lives are lost in all industries, but those in shipping are modest, despite huge fleet growth, the trend down. IMO regulations have prevented accidents and pollution through rules regarding oil tank cleaning and waste disposal, the 1973/1978 Convention for Prevention of Pollution from Ships (MARPOL), continually updated and strengthened, a compensation system for pollution's financial victims, the 1988 Global Maritime Distress and Safety Management Code, training certificates, Certificates of Financial Responsibility and the 1996 Code for gas monitoring equipment. In the 2000s it enacted conventions on ballast water management and maritime security, so that international shipping operated with minimal environmental impact, which with maritime safety is the IMO's mission.

From 2008 its Working Group on Greenhouse Gas (GHG) Emissions from Ships addressed the issue. In 2016 it introduced IFO sulphur limits, applicable from 2020, from 3.5% to 0.5% and for gas oil to 0.1%. Since it is a lubricant, this involved significant engineering solutions. Non-compliant ships fitted 'scrubbers' to extract sulphur from heavy fuel or burned more expensive low-sulphur fuel. With substantial reductions achieved, in 2018 it set ambitious targets to reduce GHG emissions; 40% by 2030, 50% by 2050 compared to 2008 levels. Resulting uncertainties about how targets would be met, future technical developments and regulation changes induced shipowner caution in newbuilding orders, falling 45% in 2019.

One result of Russia's invasion of Ukraine was after European sanctions, pipelined Russian oil fell from three million tons in February 2020 to one million in January 2023. To avoid western P&I insurance, Russia used four-times as many old ships, which might otherwise have been scrapped, bought by obscure Chinese-run, Hong Kong-registered companies, by mid 2025, 435 crude tankers or 16% of the crude fleet, sanctioned, a 'dark fleet' disguising their positions by disabling transponders when near Russian loadports, many overdue inspections, with sub-standard maintenance, dubious insurance status, increasing emissions and chances of oil spills. The tanker market is split between those not shipping Russian exports and 'dark fleet' sanction-busters. In 2022 Chinese imports from Russia in such ships increased 19% to 1.9 barrels/day and India 800%, to 900,000 barrels/day. Member states are duty-bound to enforce IMO regulations, but some ships trans-ship at sea and dishonest organisations fraudulently register ships without knowledge of their governments. The IMO hunt and highlight them as 'false flags', but it is a regulator. Member states are supposed to police them.

A significant emissions reduction effort was the IMO's 2023 'Energy Efficiency Existing Ships Index', which monitored energy consumption and carbon emissions, assessed by a Carbon Intensity Indicator (CII). Started in 2024, ships calculated A-E ratings based on previous year's emissions. While welcoming emission reduction ideas, many shipping professionals thought the approach problematic. Shipowner Oldendorff's widely read paper; *CII is not the answer. What do we do now?* encapsulated it, stating the way 'to reduce emissions [was] Not with fancy formula…but…actual and meaningful reductions.' The critique highlighted some unintended consequences, penalising port time or Panama Canal waiting time, where bulkers often waited 7–10 days, consuming <u>less</u> fuel, time in bad weather, also unfair. Long ballasts were not penalised, so efficient trading discouraged. Transhipment vessels, which travel little, suffer under CII even though they significantly reduce emissions by loading larger ships, increasing economies of scale. CII did not benefit larger ships and short voyages, producing less emissions. For example, ships carrying 90,000 tons emit 45.14 carbon/1,000 tons carried at full speed, 38.26 at super-eco slow speeds, whereas those carrying 185,000 tons emit only 25.97 and 22.22 respectively. Furthermore, shipowners should not be concerned with CII's implications of how ships are traded when time chartered. Oldendorff concluded that owners should not focus on CII, but build economical ships, leading to premium rates, encouraging modernisation, in short, market mechanisms that always encouraged efficiency. Since its publication, a suggested charter party clause assigned joint charterer-owner responsibility to the agreed CII target.

Most thought alternative fuels the long-term answer, but none are available in quantities needed for global bunkering. LNG, methanol, ammonia and hydrogen were only available at main hubs. But IMO targets made an impact. Almost 40% of 2022's newbuilding orderbook and 50% of 2024's were multi-fuel capable ships, especially LNG as major bunker ports considered supplying it. LNG reduces CO_2 emissions up to 25% over IFO or marine gas oil, produces significantly lower sulphur dioxides, nitrogen oxides and particulates, is abundant and has well-developed global supply chains. Despite requiring three-times the space, it may achieve an interim, if not permanent solution. Qatar's 1996 production, zero, rose to 134 billion cubic metres in 2021 and with Australia and America, are the main producers.

Other alternate fuel's availability, scalability and sustainability are questionable. Ammonia and hydrogen produce no emissions, but production is energy inefficient, yielding fuels with less energy than used to produce them. Ammonia is mainly used for fertiliser production. Competition might lead to higher prices for it and food. Widespread use of either needs new global production, storage, distribution, safety and infrastructure logistics. In 2023 millions were raised to investigate green methanol, needing green hydrogen made by electrolysis using green power (solar, wind, nuclear) added to CO_2 and water vapour but it has a low flashpoint. It and ammonia are toxic and corrosive, requiring specific storage, handling and safety. The density of IFO (380) is 960–991 kg/m3, methanol 748, hydrogen 704, ammonia 688 and LNG 422, so all need much larger storage tanks. Furthermore, even without trade growth, 150 million tons of green methanol will be needed, equivalent to 8.2 billion MWh, twice 2024's industrialised energy consumption. There are also price issues. In December 2022 very low sulphur fuel was about $635/ton, IFO (380) about $515/ton. Assuming green hydrogen costs $2.50/kilogram, ammonia would be $1,239/ton, methanol $1,400/ton. Thus, grey methanol would have to be used, which produces more emissions than LNG. These issues were probably behind Maersk's policy reversal. Previously championing methanol, in 2024 it planned to order at least 22 LNG dual-fuelled 16,000 TEU ships. Other shipowners reached similar conclusions. Although MOL pioneered some ammonia-powered ships, produced from solar energy, LNG seems to be the general direction of travel as an IFO alternative.

Many innovative improvements were introduced in the 2020s. Oldendorff promoted a new bow shape and a duct and rudder bulb which optimised water flow, thus fuel savings. MOL built bow sails, shown on the book's back cover, which with bow strengthening cost about $10 million, claiming 5–8% fuel savings on north-south Pacific routes and 12.75% on trans-Atlantic laden voyages. Ambitiously it aims to have 25 Wind rotor-sail-equipped ships by 2030, 80 by 2035, each with five, deck-mounted rotor sails. Engineering company ABB in 2023 announced a propulsion system, Dynafin, ready in 2025 they said, comprising five fins protruding from the hull, mimicking a whale's tail movements, claiming 22% reduced consumption Caro

Carriers SG markets various IMO GHG 2050-compliant LNG-powered battery-driven ship-types, claiming its VLCC performs an impressive 12 knots on 10–15 tons or 15.5 knots on 15–20 tons, improvable with wind power. In 2023 MOL operated 16 LNG-fuelled car-carriers and bulkers carrying coal to Japanese coal-fired power stations plus two ferries and five methanol-fuelled ships. Hydrogen power is workable on shuttle trades but requires large storage with significant energy to liquify the gas. In 2017 CMB's hydrogen-fuelled cross-Scheldt ferry *Hydroville* enabled commuters to avoid environmentally damaging traffic jams. Hydrogen-powered container handlers replaced diesel-powered ones in Kobe's Container Terminal in 2022 with planned rollouts in other ports. In 2023 MOL ordered a hydrogen-powered 100,000 dwt bulker for Southeast Asia/Japan shipments. Given the scale of the challenge these were important initial initiatives for which in 2025 the IMO initiated seafarers' training and safety guidelines on alternate-fuelled ships.

Further initiatives concerned onboard carbon capture systems. Warstila advocated solvents although their longevity in 2025 was unknown. Norway's Solvang's new buildings included technology removing nitrogen oxide, sulphur dioxide and particulates, estimating a four-year payback of capital without any cargo capacity reduction. A suggested simple solution was to pump engine emissions into containers containing lime. That takes 1–2% of cargo space and begs the question what to do with the collected CO_2. One idea was injecting it into concrete. The research is at an early stage and faces questions of scalability and retrofitting existing ships. The IMO plans to include suggested technologies into their regulations. By 2050 however, these carbon capture ideas might reduce emissions by 5% at best and many questions remain.

Into the mix in the late-2010s came potentially game-changing marine nuclear power. Over 30 western, Russian and Chinese companies researched it. Many decided Molten Salt Reactors using liquid fluoride or chloride salt fuel and coolants were best. Known since the 1950s but only pursued academically because oil was cheap and decarbonisation unheard of, it was increasingly researched in the 2020s as more efficient, cheaper and safer, accelerating development comparable to 1870–1900s steam engine progress following the compound engine. The logic is compelling for both floating offshore reactors and nuclear propulsion for ships. In energy density/efficiency, green ammonia and methanol produce 19 MJ/kg, conventional IFO (380) 42 MJ/kg, meaning more storage will be needed, quite apart from their higher cost. But nuclear produces <u>80 million</u> MJ/kg! If the system overheats or loses power the molten salt drains into a reservoir where it cools and solidifies, stopping the nuclear reaction, so-called Ultimate Safe Reactors (USRs). Core Power, a company at the cutting edge, which in 2023 advertised '30 knots for 30 years', in 2024 thought after 30 years, 90% could be re-used in a newbuilding, an <u>appreciating asset</u> rather than an expense.

Nuclear is the only reliable, emission-free energy source. It could produce green hydrogen and other alternative fuels. Nuclear-powered submarines and warships have been used for decades. Factory assembly and mass production of small units sent to approved shipyards could reduce construction times and costs. Since the largest 16% of ships emit 80% of shipping's GHGs, a few, large nuclear-electric ships could make a big difference. There are about 26,000 shipping companies, 11,000 of which only have one ship. The initiative is thus being taken by industry giants, partnering with engineering entrepreneurs, nuclear reactor designers, the insurance industry, shipbuilders, classification societies, the IMO, regulators, banks, etc. to create a workable cost-effective solution. Banks and shipyards have thought about new finance models for the heavy initial costs. For example, a 15,000 TEU methanol-powered newbuilding would cost about $200 million with a probable 25-year fuel bill of about $2.7 billion and about 100 days lost to bunkering; a nuclear-powered newbuilding about $1,000,000 but no fuel costs, double the voyages and revenue, selling power to loading/discharging ports.

So much for logic. The hurdles were public perception with terminology such as spent fuel incorrectly called nuclear waste. Some environmental organisations however revised earlier concerns regarding cost and safety. Nuclear is the largest clean energy source in America, France and China, generating about 10% of global energy. Germany's nuclear phase-out was increasingly seen as a mistake costing consumers 600 million Euros according to a 2024 *RealClearScience* article. Unlike wind and solar, nuclear operates full time and occupies 360-times less land than wind farms for the same output. Twenty million shipments of nuclear material are made annually, mainly medical equipment but including reactors and their parts, all safely. Maritime nuclear energy should be addressed without negative bias. Eighty percent of land-based reactors' costs can be eliminated if operated offshore. A commercial anxiety for shipping companies considering nuclear-powered newbuildings is the possibility of a country banning them, mid-life, mid-COA. This may mean US and European offshore nuclear reactors start first. Russia started in 2019, with more under construction. In 2024 Maersk, Lloyds Register and Core Power started collaborating on nuclear propulsion.

Before commercial nuclear ships can operate however, intergovernmental agreements on safety, security, licensing and common liabilities needs to be made, but governments act slowly and America will not deal with what they believe is an aggressive, dangerous Chinese government on this issue. Yet China dominates maritime trade volumes and cooperation between flag states, regulators, shipbuilders, classification societies and insurance companies are needed for standardised nuclear units.

The transition from wind to steam took over 50 years, containerisation 40 years. Decarbonisation, more challenging if fully implemented, will take decades. The 2050 target, modified in 2025 to 'by or around 2050', will be missed due to the 20–30-year ship's life. Ships ordered in 2024–25, probably deliverable in 2028–29, should operate well beyond 2050. Shipping professionals envisage a multi-fuelled future shipping industry, but because of the huge challenge, no one is clear exactly how it will look. A realistic technical date for commercial molten salt-powered new building orders is about 2035, the less favoured heat-pipe reactors a few years earlier, although they are quite suitable for offshore power plants.

* * *

While shipping and the IMO's little-known efforts accelerated, general climate alarmism, which headlined agendas before 2020, crumbled thereafter, mainly due to rising energy prices and the emergence of Artificial Intelligence (AI) needing vast quantities of energy that wind and solar could not satisfy. Repeated predictions of catastrophes which never happened and increasing scientific challenges to the CO_2 doctrine also contributed. Moreover, most countries did not pursue damaging climate policies. For Britain and Australia which did, with less than 1% of global emissions, reductions were meaningless.

Paradoxes in climate policies were increasingly highlighted. The world would not feed itself without yield-enhancing LNG-made fertilisers. More materials were annually mined than everything extracted until the 1950s, worsening as energy and carbon-intensive electric car production required four-times the copper and other metals as petrol cars. Swathes of Indonesian rainforests were destroyed by nickel mining for their batteries, the run-off killing fishing grounds, the nickel plant itself creating a toxic micro-climate. China discharged six-times more CO_2 than Britain in 2000, 33-times by 2021, partly by British reductions, mainly Chinese growth. Britain's 2021 emissions were 5.2 tons/head, equivalent to the 1850s, China's over eight, as it manufactured renewable batteries and wind turbines mainly using coal-fired power stations. These emitted 15 billion tons of CO_2 annually, 25% of the world's, Britain only 400 million, down from 817 million in 1990, a 44.1% reduction compared to America's 2.6%. China's increased 426%. In 2024 China's coal consumption rose 6% to 4.9 billion tons, 56% of the world's, 3.59 million imported.

Fracking, a 21st century technology, designed to liberate vast pockets of trapped oil and gas, smashed the idea that the world would run out and renewables were the only answer. With it, after 2008, US gas prices fell from $9 to $3/cuft. Extracted at 6-10,000 feet it did not affect the water table, thus US environmentalists embraced it as an ideal transition fuel as it powered a manufacturing renaissance.

Britain's government by contrast penalised domestic car manufacturers if consumers did not buy electric. Chinese imports were anyway cheaper. It refused to frack British LNG condemning consumers to energy costs seven-times that of China, Russia and India which in 2025 dominated world steel and metals used in batteries, four-times US prices, when in 1980 they had been similar, and twice European prices. In acts of official vandalism, Britain's government poured concrete down exploratory onshore wells, costing $80 million each to drill, disincentivising energy firms whose profits were taxed at 78% compared to America's 40%, forcing them overseas. Ineos for example, in December 2024 increased US investment to over $3 billion and imported fracked US LNG, paying tax to America, not Britain. By 2025 its refinery incurring CO_2 costs had to be subsidised to avoid financial difficulties. Shipping LNG involves liquefying and re-gasification, using up to five-times more emissions. Such deceptive virtue-signalling exported emissions and cut British revenues. In 2025 Norway drilled nearly 40 North Sea exploration wells some of which inevitably captured gas in adjacent British areas. Britain drilled none, despite an estimated 20–24 billion barrels there, compared to the 48 billion extracted since 1970, and imported half its oil and gas from Norway, £20.6 billion-worth in 2025, further enriching its Sovereign Wealth Fund (see next chapter). With improved technology Norway plans to re-open closed wells after 2025.

Additionally, Britain's Drax power station, formerly Europe's largest coal-fired one, burned wood pellets, a third less efficient than coal, 6.4 million tons annually, equivalent to 27 million trees, shipped mainly from west coast America. Pellets stow at 53 cuft/ ton compared with coal's 37-39. Using US draft-restricted ports needs more voyages than coal, previously available locally. Bizarrely classified as 'green', Drax received £500 million annual subsidies, but was fined £25 million by regulator Ofgem in 2024 for using unsustainable timber sources, not sawdust as initially intended. With outdated prejudice against nuclear, Whitehall stalled auctions for modular nuclear reactors for a decade. Britain's 2000-2025 energy policy was an incoherent, self-defeating shambles. Energy costs made exports uncompetitive. Deindustrialisation resulted. America, between 2020 and 2024 spent billions on wind and solar power until President Trump who thought climate alarmism 'the greatest conjob ever perpetrated on the world,' ditched net-zero, supported nuclear and pressured the UN-sponsored climate agenda.

This was not just party politics. Many scientists <u>not</u> funded by CO_2 advocates had challenged climate alarmism. Nobel-winning chemists and physicists thought CO_2, 0.0391% of the atmosphere, of which around 3% is man-made, was essential for life. Climate science pioneer Svante Antheius (1859-1927) was positive about its effects. Ivan Giaever (1929-2025) thought 'global warming…a non-problem' and climate catastrophism 'a new religion.' Kary Mullis (1944-2019) thought predictions 'wrong by a large factor.' John Clauser (b 1942) said 'there is no climate crisis.' Emeritus Prof. Paul Loftus stressed CO_2 was 'the basis of life on earth.' In some verdant peaks of geological history CO_2 was four-times today, so 'climate is not terribly sensitive to CO_2' and '100% change in CO_2 only makes 1% change in flux…It's very basic physics… There's really no threat…It's all a made-up scare story.'

Dr. Patrick Moore, founder of Greenpeace, called climate change hysteria, 'complete fabrication,' CO_2 the most important nutrient for life on earth, that 'it is a good thing we are putting more CO_2 into the atmosphere because it was running low' and science has not proved CO_2 'is causing the earth to warm…in 50 years we will look back in dismay at this hysteria.' Windmills' bases, made with 300 tons of iron ore and 170 tons of coking coal, mined in Australia or Brazil, shipped to China and transported to Europe, burned more energy in manufacture and transport than they ever produced. Moreover, demand was so great that plantation-grown balsawood, used in blades, was inadequate, encouraging illegal rainforest logging.

Physicist professors William Happer and Richard Lindzen said CO_2 was irrelevant. Gregg Braden rejected human agency because geological history showed sometimes high temperatures corresponded with low CO_2, sometimes the opposite, because over 90% of CO_2 comes from oceans, caused by tectonic and volcanic activity. Dr. Mototaka Nakamura ridiculed climate models based on guesswork, ignoring oceans, the sun and cloud cover. Prof. Ian Plimer said no one had ever shown that human emissions drove temperatures, which ice core data indicated rose first, followed by CO_2 centuries later, greening the planet and that climate alarmism was 'the great CO_2 fraud.'

Geologists found today's CO_2 levels low compared with the last 600 million years. Greenland ice cores (drilled 2007-2012) to the last interglacial period, about 125,000 years ago, showed it about eight degrees Celsius warmer than today, but Greenland did not melt and life flourished. Since the Ice Age the earth warmed and cooled in cycles. This 'Climatic Optimum' was about 2-4 degrees warmer than now. Within that, about 10,900-9,700 BC was an abrupt cold period and about 6600-6400 BC it was 1-3 degrees cooler. Iron Age Europe around 900-300 BC was colder before the Roman 250 BC-400 AD warm period. The 536-540 cold years caused famine, pestilence and depopulation. Medieval warm years saw Vikings settle Greenland, raising wheat, barley and livestock. Then it cooled, warmed and cooled about 1600-1850, the so-called Little Ice Age. Since then, it warmed and cooled within a stable band. The world is about five degrees <u>cooler</u> than 2,000 years ago. Measuring temperatures against the 1850s, the coldest period since the Ice Age, therefore made little sense. Cold spells were always worse for humanity than warm ones. Sea levels have risen <u>regularly</u> about 1.8 millimetres annually since the 1850s.

Dr Roy Spencer's peer-reviewed study found 65% of warming since 1895 explained by urban expansion. Another showed rising CO_2 levels drove a 30% rise in global plant growth since 1990, that the post-Ice Age world was much greener, meaning more CO_2 and since 1750 natural CO_2 rose four-times more than human input, part of a recurring cycle. Another found water vapour as clouds drove 95% of the atmosphere's radiative effect, CO_2 contributing only 4-5%. It concluded, moisture, clouds and natural dynamics run the climate, not CO_2. But these it seems are minor variables. Astrophysicist Dr Willie Soon put it simply. Climate is unsurprisingly overwhelmingly driven by the sun and past climate swings like the Little Ice Age are in line with solar variability, not emissions. The CO_2 obsession, he said, is political. CO_2 is taxable. He described an 'iron triangle' of government funding, compliant scientists and media amplification creating a dogma. Priorities should be adaptability and affordable energy. Critics claimed many of these studies were funded by fossil fuel interests. Many were, but does not necessarily invalidate them and CO2 advocates were funded by their vested interests too.

1979-2025 South Pole temperatures were flat. The 2025 Arctic Sea Ice Minimum was 4.6 million square kilometres, 350,000 more than 2024 and 180,000 above the 2011-2020 average. Despite warnings, glaciers in 2025 were the same size as in 1990, polar bear numbers increased, tornados and hurricanes declined, the Great Barrier Reef over 2021-2025 posted record coral cover, the Maldives and Mount Kilimanjaro's ice cap were still there. Unlike other branches of science, climate zealots did not re-examine the evidence, but sought to silence those challenging the CO_2 claims. To demonstrate Dr. Soon's media point, in 2006 the BBC's climate correspondent Roger Harubin thought the science 'settled'. Criticisms were to be downplayed. In 2018 Director of BBC News Fran Unsworth wrote scientists agree that 'humans have changed the climate but specifically how is more difficult to evidence.' Editors were therefore told they need not balance their coverage with alternative views and report human-made CO_2 warming as fact. With opinion having dramatically changed, in 2024-25 it sounded like propaganda, suppressing scientific enquiry. Little reported by western mainstream media, independent and fossil-fuel funded scientific opinion relied on increasingly penetrative social media, especially influential podcasts.

In 2021 Bill Gates, who had called global warming 'one of the greatest challenges humans have ever taken on,' in 2025 a day after UN Secretary General Antonio Guterras <u>again</u> warned of 'devastating consequences' of inaction, backtracked. 'People will be able to live and thrive in most places on earth for the foreseeable future,' that prosperity is the best defence and closed his climate policy office. Director of the Global Warming Policy Foundation, Lord Mackaulay concerned climate policy reflect economic reality, thought him 'absolutely right.' Climatologist Prof. Judith Curry sensed 'climate alarmism fatigue.' Prof. Lindzen thought Microsoft's huge AI energy needs persuaded Gates and that zealots proclaiming the science 'settled', wrong as 'science is a mode of enquiry' not 'a belief structure.' Since then, the Net-Zero Banking Alliance collapsed after every major US bank quit. Shell and BP returned to oil and Ford stopped electric vehicle development.

Cost was key in collapsing support. In 2020 almost half Britons told TV money pundit Martin Lewis that they would pay higher taxes to tackle climate change. By 2025 it fell to 13%, while opposition soared from 30.4% to 72.6%. Reflecting this change, the governing Conservative Party which in 2020 set ambitious targets, in 2025 opposition, abandoned them as Britain's Frawley Oil Refinery complained spending £70-80 million on CO_2 costs, expected to be £150 million by 2030: totally unsustainable.

The Daily Telegraph (3rd November 2025) said net-zero challenges could not remain 'taboo', a day later that the UN's COP climate summit was a pointless junket without China's, Russia's, India's and America's heads. It reminded readers that as taxpayers they had paid £136 million to fund a complex off-set system in Brazil, whereby polluters buy carbon credits from tree-planting to cancel real emissions, while Brazil itself, unlike Britain, planned 20% increased oil and gas drilling by 2030. COP's final communique did not mention fossil fuels, which a despondent BBC reported 'drives global warming', ignoring the avalanche of scientific papers arguing the opposite, betraying its mandate for impartiality.

Britain shut its last coal plant in 2024. In 2025 however, other governments were rethinking. New Zealand's Resources Minister reigned back on fossil fuel elimination. Queensland, Australia's main coal producer, scrapped plans to shut coal-fired power stations, saving $26 billion. Germany announced plans for 20 gas plants by 2030, a stable base load. Spain, in a backlash against the early-2025 grid blackout, extended the lives of fossil fuel plants. The EU dropped its pledge to ban sales of new petrol, diesel and hybrid cars by 2035. Japan, Korea and ASEAN, southeast Asia's 650 million strong economic bloc, had paid lip-service to the agenda but continued coal use. ASEAN's rising energy demand was 96% coal-fired with no planned change. China's 2025 coal production increased to almost five million tons. Thus, in 2025 the 14.2% of global energy from renewables was barely above 2007 levels. In 1995 fossil fuels supplied 76.6% of global energy. In 2024, it was almost the same, 76.4%, despite trillions spent on renewables and thousands of European jobs lost. With India, China and Southeast Asia soon producing two-thirds of emissions, global AI energy needs soaring, much of the world backtracking and 2024-2025 CO_2 emissions at record levels, transition to renewables to near the 2050 deadline, seemed impossible.

* * *

As for shipping companies' efforts, with only about 2.3% of global emissions, they seemed detached from this rapidly changing wider scenario. The IMO's Net-Zero Framework (NZF), approved in April 2015 by its Marine Environment Protection Committee, aimed to raise $15 billion/year for a Net-Zero Fund starting in 2027 from $180-380/ton charges on CO_2 for non-compliant ships, rewarding efficient ones with tradeable credits; a credible incentive framework. IMO Secretary-General Arsenio Dominguez thought it significant in 'efforts to combat climate change.' Expected to pass in October 2025, US opposition caused a 57-49 vote against. China and Saudi Arabia backed the US. Greece and Cyprus abstained, breaking EU unity, postponing another vote for a year.

This put the UN-sponsored IMO in the forefront of a global power struggle. Shipping companies' expensive initiatives, encouraged by its NZF, were cast in doubt. For example, at this time, about 40 ammonia-powered ships, 15-20% more expensive than oil-fired ships, were on order and over half of 2024-2025's container orders were for alternative-or dual-fuelled ships. Whether 2025 is a turning point cannot be predicted at the time of writing. The IMO plans resuming NZF, aiming for reductions relative to 2019 of 21.5% by 2030. Although most shipping companies at the end of 2025 continue to assume net-zero will happen, without IMO power to levy fines, it may not.

Vested interests unexpectedly thrust maritime trade into the centre of an ideological war about the science and propaganda of climate change, but ultimately, as always, about money and power, issues traders and commercial shipping companies have always had to navigate.

Maritime Decline Comparisons and Perspectives. Ingredients of Success and Failure

'The farther back you can look, the farther forward you are likely to see.'
Winston Churchill

Competing with pioneering Britain, America, Germany and Japan caught and surpassed it by avoiding its mistakes, discovering domestic coal, concentrating on technical education, creating more efficient technology. Do features of British maritime decline have parallels with declines described in this and previous volumes? Most successful, wealth-creating societies were merchant-dominated or merchant-influenced. Examples include Phoenician Tyre, Sidon and Byblos, Carthage, Miletus, Athens, Alexandria, Oc-eo, Palembang, Dorestad, Quentovic, Venice, Genoa, Bruges, Antwerp, Amsterdam, Malacca and post-1649 England/Britain. Phoenicians were conquered and as Sephardic Jews are unique. Rhodes, Carthage, Athens and Alexandria were conquered by Rome. It protected traders, but frequent civil wars weakened the structure, while adoption of Christianity as the state religion hastened decline.[1] Dorestad and Quentovic did not survive Charlemagne's heavy-handed rule and Viking attacks. Egypt's early-11th century Fatimid rulers were Shia fanatics and probably mad <u>but</u> did not interfere in Jewish-organised trade which increased. Non-interference is a key theme in success, but enlightened governments proactively <u>encouraged</u> merchants' wealth-creation. The first Song emperor in 987 lured foreign traders with better facilities and <u>protection against bureaucrats</u>. By the 13th century, Chinese merchants and ships dominated Asian maritime trade, its industry flourished in the world's most advanced civilisation. Its 1372 maritime trade ban precipitated an exodus of craftsmen and enterprising merchants, causing China's subsequent decline. The Hanseatic League, an early trade enabler, became a rule-enforcer, contrary to members' interests,[2] which thus disintegrated. Lubeck repelled merchants by religious intolerance. Portugal's commercial mechanisms were monopolistic brutality, using trade-generated wealth to fund religious-inspired conquest of Morocco. Failure led to 1580 union with Spain's extreme continentalism and conflict with Dutch sea power, badly wounding it.[3] Wars triggered Venice's, Holland's and Britain's decline. Their empires encumbered them, deflecting them from what made them great; maritime trade from which they <u>deliberately</u> turned. Why and how?

Venice was state-run and protectionist, unable to adapt in quickly changing times. As a Spanish vassal, Genoa's maritime inclusiveness disappeared with its shipping, trade and glass industry, becoming Spain's banker until the 1630s. Venice's elite moved from trade to landed investments, the Dutch into fixed assets including Britain's national debt, away from economic dynamism towards caution. After 1713, Dutch third-party trade, industrial dynamism and economy stagnated. In 1697 Peter the Great studied Dutch shipbuilding. Holland built 300 ships in 1707, nothing after 1793.[4] Like 20th-century Britain, it did not adapt. Holland's post-1690 Heren XVII gentrified, embraced French fashion, became continentalist, bureaucratic, impeding efficiency, like post-1945 Britain. Dutch fishing declined, especially whaling, again not adapting, overtaken by more efficient British whalers. Britain's healthy 20th-century fishing industry was destroyed by Heath's EEC entry terms. In 1780 Dutch maritime trade was still impressive but declined compared to British, French and Baltic competitors. Many 18th-century Dutch farmers left due to high taxation.[5] Throughout his account of 18th-century Dutch society, Charles Boxer points to a 'conservative, unenterprising mentality [in]…trade and industry.' Its elite deliberately orchestrated the change of direction, stability for themselves, sharply contrasting with 17th-century confidence and enterprise. as did Britain's 20th-21st-century political establishment, high tax and over-regulation also impeding efficiency and stifling initiative. Can the causes be more precisely identified?

Wool's importance in exports from the 1170s led English monarchs to vigorously defend merchants from the 1270s as France's aim to conquer Flanders impacted its wool then cloth exports. *Magna Carta's* (1215) clause 42 equated merchants' and public interest as the same. Trade and government interests were integral in the Hundred Years War, the government borrowing from the Company of the Staple and frequently consulting the Assembly of Merchants. Kings also defended England's Baltic trade. Even Henry V fighting in France found time to support it against the bullying Hansa who sought English merchant exclusion. The importance of maritime trade became <u>visionary</u>, encapsulated in the 1430's *Libelle of Englyshe Polycye*, recommending Channel control for peace, prosperity and trade which it described country-by-country, product-by-product. It influenced maritime trade advocates like Hakluyt, Cecil, Selden and Pepys. Robert Sturmy's extraordinary 1457 expedition to secure Mediterranean alum for England's cloth industry had high-level political support. Genoa's sabotage of it was met by stringent government reprisals.[6] Political weakness during and after the War of the Roses prevented effective support but gradually strengthened under the Tudors, especially Edward VI and Elizabeth. Thomas Gresham, formerly the Mercer's chief merchant in Antwerp, advised in 1552 to export <u>all</u> cloth through the Merchant Adventurers in return for loans, which broke Hansa merchants' stranglehold.

Sixteenth-century English merchants with government encouragement explored White Sea, Mediterranean, Caribbean, African, Asian and American trade opportunities with the important innovation; the joint-stock company. The early Stuarts antagonised them by ignoring this <u>vision</u> just as volumes and opportunities increased. From 1640 Parliament re-set the agenda, vigorously supporting traders, especially after 1649, well-expressed by Council of Trade member Slingsby Bethel; 'Nothing makes countries rich but trade and nothing increases trade but freedom.' A petition to Cromwell during the Commonwealth complained, 'It is no wonder that these Dutchmen should thrive…

their statesmen are all merchants…they understand the course of trade…do everything to further its interests.' He confronted them and established a civil service with City merchants sitting on committees for finance, trade and colonies. Trade and freedom were confirmed in the 1688 Glorious Revolution. In 1689 there were 15 joint-stock companies worth £0.9 million. By 1695 there were 150 worth £4.3 million. Government encouragement continued in the 18th century, especially long-haul American and Asian, championed by Adam Smith who noted that China could arrest decline by promoting maritime trade. Corn Law debates focussed on how to keep industry competitive and promote trade. The Cobden-Chevalier Treaty demonstrated vibrancy. So, from the 1270s until the 1860s maritime trade was England's/Britain's visionary purpose. But from the 1870s it lost priority and intent. Why and how?

Britain lost many tramp shipping companies after 1918 through to the 1980s because some 2nd/3rd generation family owners were less ambitious or capable, managing their companies more as hobbies than cutting-edge businesses, investing in property, bonds and shares, like Venice's post-1453 and Dutch post-1673 merchants. In different ways Harrisons, Reardon Smith and Ellermans fall into this category. Amid 1930s depression British shipowners failed to take advantage of tankers with long charters and minimal risks. Greeks and Scandinavians more successfully directed sons to grow family businesses. Apart from this social explanation, perhaps reflecting lack of national direction and issues addressed in chapters 36–43, politico-economic problems developed between government and businesses.

Britain's civil service was reorganised by the 1854 Northcote-Trevelyan reforms, prompted by Crimean War supply scandals and perceived Chartist threats. The model was China's imperial examinations, which concentrated on Chinese classics, rewarding conformity, caution, tradition and conservatism. Britain's senior civil servants are thus called mandarins. Having seen since the 1793 Macartney mission, China's insular mandarins failing in fast-changing maritime and industrialising times, recognising cascading wealth creation by engineers and industrialists; Crompton, Watt, Boulton, Wedgwood, Arkwright, Wilkinson, Telford, Stephenson, Napier, Elder, Brunel, et. al., it is extraordinary that Parliament chose this induction method rather than continuing visionary trade expansion, which needed continued industrial progress, thus technical education for innovation and exports, as its competitors were doing, to catch Britain's lead, as highlighted in Corn Law debates. Instead, induction exams were heavily biased towards Oxbridge classicists, especially Oxford's 'Greats' course; classical history, moral philosophy, Roman law, Greek and Latin translations, designed to produce intelligent, reliable men to preserve traditional values in times of political and social uncertainly, especially the expanding franchise.[7] Unlike Glasgow and Edinburgh Universities, Oxbridge did not teach technical, scientific or commercial subjects and was restricted to Church of England members. The 1855 Administrative Reform Association by contrast, argued for commercial training for civil servants. Bentham-follower Edwin Chadwick thought merchants and bankers needed 'good handwriting…arithmetic… business and accounts,' not classics. Prime Minister Russell and Lord Mounteagle opposed Northcote-Trevelyan, the latter because China was not enlightened. Others feared Prussian autocratic bureaucracy. Shipbuilder John Russell who wrote the 1869 *A*

Systematic Technical Education for the English People and Glasgow University's William Rankine promoted technical education. Palmerston thought scientific understanding central to progress but after Northcote-Trevelyan, it was shunned: Britain's biggest, most far-reaching 19th-century mistake. By contrast, Germany, America and Japan foresaw technology, economics and scientific education as <u>essential</u> for industrial exporters, promoted it and succeeded in catching Britain.

Implemented in the 1870s, this was the time Palmerston-like talk and action of making pathways for merchants ended. Numerous 1860s-1870s proposals to include technology, science and maths in induction exams were shelved, the classics re-emphasised. Disraeli thought it would lead to fossilised thinking. Chinese mandarins had over-regulated state monopolies and knew nothing nor cared about the maritime, industrial world. China's already catastrophic decline should have warned that countries run by well-educated, self-satisfied mandarins, ignorant of trade, technology or wealth-creation, self-destruct. In 1683–84 Pepys, noting that Spanish 'men of the sword' were employed at sea without knowing anything about it, thought 'Never were a people so overrun with fools.' Northcote-Trevelyan did precisely this, ignoring what the well-expressed petition to Cromwell said, that Dutch success was because their statemen were merchants. As Northumberland told Cecil in 1552 regarding the Merchant Adventurers, government and trade 'are of two natures,'[8] a perennial problem, but one they discussed within the context of commercial encouragement. The James Watt-Joseph Black collaboration and Dundas, war minister whose family sponsored new steamship developments were examples of Britain's establishment's close relationship with its technical and economic life. After Northcote-Trevelyan however, it became divorced from both.

It caused much concern. From the 1850s 'technical educationalist' reformers sought scientific and technical education in schools. While many regarded the 1851 Great Exhibition with complacent satisfaction, Prince Albert overseeing it was less sanguine. In 1845 he helped form the Royal College of Chemistry, later the Royal College of Science, because he perceived growing foreign threats and believed in educating working people and improving attitudes to business. Lyon Playfair, Professor of Chemistry, MP and advocate of technical education told the School of Mines, 'Euripides and Thucydides cannot make power-looms and spinning-jennies…dead literature cannot be the parent of living science or active industry.' In *Industrial Education of the Continent*, he proposed technical education as part of most schools' curriculum, a national one not yet existing. He thought the 1867 Paris Exhibition where British entries won few prizes demonstrated scant British progress since 1851. Many government commissions recommended widening secondary education's curriculum to include science, overseen by a ministry, as in Europe. The 1869 Taunton Commission recommended technical education for factory and workshop masters and managers,[9] because while European and American workers progressed in 'proportion to their…education and training,' British workers and managers did not understand fundamental scientific principles, impeding 'their inability to originate invention and improvements.' It concluded, 'complacency reigned.'[10]

An 1868 Commons Select Committee established to examine the problem represented only traditional manufacturing, not emerging industries; anyway, was ignored. The 1870–1875 Devonshire Commission reported science in schools was 'extremely unsatisfactory…a national misfortune' and minimum seven hours a week should be devoted to it. Industrialists' concerns that Britain was not keeping pace led to the Yorkshire College of Sciences (later Leeds University) which welcomed students to focus on technology. Despite mounting evidence from abroad, <u>caution</u> was still urged. Pressured by Glasgow merchant and MP Samuelson, his Commission on Technical Instruction thought many youths labelled dunces at school could become capable if schooled in technology and business and that Britain should copy European models of national technical education because foreign engineers, designers, draughtsmen and foremen dominated British factory life, just as foreign electrical appliances and dyes appeared in shops. It called for state-funded, national technical schooling which had enabled European catch-up, including technical drawing, maths and modern languages to replace Latin and Greek and that local authorities establish secondary and technical schools. It kept the issue alive but apathy and inertia, especially in the civil service, were stronger. In 1884 the Marquis of Hartington thought the 'subject of technical education has now been for so long before the country [it] would be very little short of a scandal if we failed to promote it.'[11] *The Times* prevaricated, proclaiming technical training 'indispensable' in commercial rivalry (December 14th,1883), then foreign competition 'much exaggerated' (October 8th,1884). The 1889 Technical Instruction Act had too many funding obstacles for success.

Prevailing free trade, free choice thinking was against state intervention in people's lives. A Ministry of Education, resisted for over 50 years as too intrusive, too prescriptive, was finally established only in 1899. The 1900 Paris Exhibition's US education exhibit so impressed the Director of Manchester's Technical School, demonstrating the gulf between foreign and British attitudes to manufacturing, education and trade, that he had it transferred to Manchester for a time. Influential politician Haldane thought Britain should put herself in the same educational position regarding technical training as her competitors. Joseph Chamberlain agreed that British education needed raising to German levels, which America fast approached; the 'application of the highest science to the commonest industries and manufacturers.'

Andrew Pears, head of his family's soap business, in the 1890s paid for local schools to teach technical subjects and languages. The Education Department's mandarin reformer Michael Sadler, admiring German technical training, concerned about inadequate British commercial and industrial training, initiated 11 volumes of reports detailing foreign educational successes, among which his impressively-argued *The Unrest in Secondary Education in Germany and Elsewhere* called for more and better education, 'better' defined as preparation for all kinds of <u>business life</u>, that reform was 'urgently required' to meet current needs and those 20–30 years hence. He approved of Pear's initiative, but his well-prepared scientific, technical and commercial agenda lost out to traditionalist Robert Morant's classical public-school model.[12] In the resulting 1902 Education Bill, Local Education Authorities imitated public school education, classics and character-building, reinforcing anti-commerce, anti-science biases, denying industry its human raw materials, blunting incentives for Britain to adapt and compete. Moreover, the Education Department gave schoolchildren an Empire Day holiday, started in 1902, indoctrinating imperial pride with a motto, previously a continentalist, absolutist theme, 'One king, one flag, one fleet, one empire.' 1902 was also when 'Land of Hope and Glory' was written; a symbolic date perhaps, when centuries of trade encouragement gave way to imperial glorification. The Imperial Tariff movement was caused by effective foreign competition driven by technical education. Germany's 180,000 dye workers, a £120 million industry in 1913, led the world when Britain had one Chair in Organic Chemistry, which was moribund!

Despite growing realisation from the 1840s that technical education was desirable, civil service inertia, ingrained in classical education, a largely uninterested government elite and British inclination not to over-regulate quashed the 1850s-1902 debate about educational reforms to boost technical competence. Some commentators think the task to promote it was too big, but intervention on utilitarian grounds had been accepted for decades, employers' rights curtailed, employees' working hours restricted, urban safety and sanitation measures introduced. The 1850 Merchant Shipping Act and subsequent legislation imposed sensible safety interventions. Plimsoll continued fighting non-interventionism and with Joseph Chamberlain's help, won. Resistance to national technical and commercial education hindered extracting potential from Britain's people. The political/bureaucratic establishment's failure, encapsulated in the induction system to the 'reformed' civil service was the key blunder. Its result was failing industrial supremacy, replaced by the misguided promotion of imperial pride.

Ronald Hyam explains that political decisions were made in small, bureaucratic groups 'frequently disdainful of business interests,' mainly concerned with 'high politics', with only a vague duty to 'promote trade.' Relevant training was minimal, the aim survival politics, responding to immediate problems, ignoring trading interests when inconvenient, lobbies and public opinion treated with suspicion or contempt.[13] Clashes with business thus occurred early. Majority government-owned Anglo-Iranian Oil's chairman had 'fire-eating contempt for civil servants,'[14] who hated Castle Line's founder Sir Donald Currie (1825–1909, founded 1853) for commercial relations with Germans, quite different from previous encouragement.

Until the 1930s most believed prosperity resulted from limiting government intervention. Depression and war changed this. By 1945, Labour lawyer Sir Hartley Shawcross proclaimed, 'we are the masters now;' lawyers, bureaucrats etc. devoted to public spending, intervention, planning and regulation, thwarting policies against their interests, much like Soviet bureaucracy. The post-1945 creed was everything could be solved by benevolent state direction by well-meaning Whitehall officials, satirised in the 1962–77 radio comedy *The Men from the Ministry,* all incompetent and TV's *Yes Minister,* the art of obstructing government wishes. In the 1950s, Technical Schools were built, like Thomas Linacre School, Wigan (1953) with huge technical workshops, <u>enlightenment</u> apparently rediscovered a century too late, but in the early-1960s they were merged with grammar schools with their classic-led curriculum, then comprehensives, deleterious to technical, indeed all education. Oxford University's 1960 Chancellorship's election was still held in Latin, still deemed necessary to study science at Cambridge until a few years later!

Adam Smith thought parts of the empire that couldn't contribute should be freed, Disraeli that 'wretched colonies...millstones round our necks.' Dominion emigration and trade changed that. Pride in empire, which in official late-19th and 20th-century minds compensated for German and US catch-up, was promoted. When almost bankrupt in 1945 it was obvious that Britain could not spend 10% of its GNP on defence, but officials and many politicians thought colonies gave Britain prestige, a mistake earlier made by continental powers when Britain prioritised trade, not empire.

Hyam's account of John Bennet's 1940s-1960s Colonial Office career shows Whitehall inertia, thwarting intelligent analysis, logic and Disraeli-like common sense. Realising that Britain's great power status was finished, its empire over-extended, Bennet concluded it must purposefully decolonise quickly, enabling future friendships, not wait until revolts forced independence. Regarded as too clever, he was side-lined, his sensible, proactive options not even presented to government. Although Britain decolonised more elegantly than France, Holland or Portugal, it did so without commercial purpose, making taxpayers fund post-war empire on ludicrous bureaucrat-inspired schemes, mass egg production in Gambia and groundnuts in Tanganyika, for example. The Colonial Office's merger with the Foreign Office was the final blow for Bennet, their suave, arrogant diplomats obsessed with Europe, he thought.[15] Just as 40 years of French wars killed Dutch political willpower, German wars, Britain's centralised reaction and fantasy of imperial pride distorted Britain's political direction. In both education and decolonisation, civil service inertia trumped enlightened reform.

Anthony Sampson's 1982 updated *Anatomy of Britain* described post-war civil service deterioration, multiplying 20-fold to 1980, controlling roadbuilding, hospital management, nationalised industries and scientific research. By early 1960's, the Treasury's Richard Wilding thought it 'a gently ossified muddle staffed by intelligent, urbane but managerially innocent mandarins.'[16] Harold Wilson thought 'whichever party is in office, the Treasury is in power.' The 1966–1968 Fulton Committee found civil servants educated in studies without business knowledge, not tasked for second-half 20th-century problems, excluding engineers, scientists and other specialists. Yet Whitehall doggedly defended the status quo. The Fulton Report was quietly shelved, scientific advisors downgraded, denied ministerial access, as industrialists became exasperated at lack of interest in manufacturing. Cover-ups were routine. Appointed by Heath as chief advisor for state interventions, arch-mandarin Sir William Armstrong's nervous breakdown was covered-up, retiring as Midland Bank Chairman, the instincts to keep heads below parapets at Fortress Whitehall. Alan Cottrell, 1975's Chief Scientific Advisor noted, in 'conflict between commercial considerations and social and political ones… commercial ones almost always go to the wall.'[17] The Auditor General and most of his department lacked professional training in auditing! Home Office inefficiency and secrecy was well-known but ignored. Franklin Roosevelt had thought all bureaucracy inefficient, 'unwieldy, expensive…[meaning] higher taxes.'[18] Post-1945 British bureaucrats proved it in spades.

Departmental budgets were benchmarks of success, not efficiency. A 1982 Select Committee reported 'the amount of money spent…far more important to the Treasury than how effectively.' On leaving Whitehall, officials moved to supposedly autonomous bodies; the British Council, Arts Council, Ombudsman's Office or large companies wanting access to corridors of power, not their non-existent commercial talents. By contrast, more French and American businessmen moved <u>into</u> government, assuming responsibility for projects, rare in Britain. Sampson's critique was coruscating. Had he compared it with newly industrialising nations' bureaucracies, not his remit, it would have been more so.

When Japan's 1850's economy opened and radically restructured, it rationally took what it thought best from Europe, significantly German education and British empire. Post-1945, it abandoned empire. Japan's post-1945 unifying <u>vision</u> was state-guided catch-up by MITI and the Economic Planning Agency from 1955 when priorities shifted from recovery to growth. In the 1970s, most science students were on average two years ahead of European and Americans. Japan's 1946–1976 economy increased 55-fold, no miracle, but carefully planned, by the late-1970s GNP equivalent to Britain and France combined.

Japan's small, elite, inexpensive civil service, scientifically and technically trained, were initially sent to foreign universities and Japanese research centres, honing specialisations, studying foreign tax regimes, laws, businesses, market trends etc., remaining with the same ministry for life, planning for agreed national economic, educational and health goals, implemented where possible by the private sector, unlike Britain's post-1945 ideological mistake. Japan's better-informed officials worked <u>with</u> industry and traders, conceiving, discussing, persuading, encouraging, continuing the diligent search for knowledge and intelligence, a totally different background and approach than Britain's, with less arrogance and vastly superior outcomes. Korea, Taiwan and Singapore copied the model's parts suiting their circumstances. Singapore was expelled from Malaysia in 1965 but due to its economically liberal policies, in 2025 its GDP per capita was 70% higher than Britain's, low taxes a crucial component, the highest 24% on earnings over £570,000 equivalent, corporation tax 17% and no capital gains tax, government spending just 15% of GDP, under a third of Britain's. Britain's bureaucracy had no purpose except self-perpetuation: increasing regulation and personnel. Its politicians refused to learn from recently successful countries.

Despite claiming to know best, when windfall North Sea oil flowed in 1969, unlike Denmark and Norway, Britain's commercially naïve government gave generous concessions to foreign companies and unlike Norway, the UAE and Saudi Arabia, did not set-up a Sovereign Wealth Fund. In 2025 Norway's was the world's largest, equivalent to £1.2 trillion, growing annually more than the government spends on schools, hospitals and welfare because it invests for purely commercial considerations. Britain extracted more North Sea oil and gas but the state squandered it.

The 1974 oil price shock drove America to find ways of becoming energy self-sufficient, while Japan planned to make oil producers dependent on its <u>technical</u> assistance in an overall programme providing reliable, long-term, multiple energy sources. No such <u>vision</u> penetrated Whitehall. After Sampson's book's, Thatcher fought inefficiency. Marks and Spencer's Derek Rayner's Efficiency Unit reduced 1979–1996 manpower 32%, 27,000 forms scrapped, 41,000 redesigned, but without constant vigilance, inefficiency increased thereafter.

There was considerable 1970s-1980s Conservative Party debate about education, fuelled by concern of children not fulfilling their potential in comprehensive schools, following industry complaints about employees lacking numeracy, literacy and technical knowledge; the 'skills crisis' especially in engineering, compared with American 'Special Schools' emphasising science and technical subjects. New peace, urban and women's studies were criticised as undermining basic skills; a continuing theme that more technical training would help Britain compete economically. The Education Department resisted, although one of their arguments, shortage of specialist teachers, should have been a wake-up call! The resulting 1984 Business Technology Educational Council agreed university-acceptable qualifications and the 1988 Education Reform Act authorised City Technical Colleges, intended as 'beacons of excellence,' independent of local authorities, bridges between education and industry. Only 15 were established, inadequate without further measures. Meanwhile, a legislative, bureaucratic straitjacket was imposed on state schools, failure hidden by easier exams with higher results. Civil servants still lack technological awareness. In 2024, the Institute for Government reported only 23% of recruits had science, technology, engineering or maths degrees, compared with 44% nationally, still too few, with a dearth of maths skills in the Treasury.

Robert Atkinson's 1999 criticisms of British politicians regarding shipyards, that of not taking manufacturing seriously was one of many, but the situation worsened. Parliament became dominated by lawyers and career politicians only experienced in party apparatus or local government, few involved in manufacturing, none in maritime trade, the last shipowner MP, Leonard Ropner, (1923–1929, 1931–1964) grandson of Robert. Like the 1789 French Assembly, lawyers and government officials' domination was a recipe for political and commercial naivety. Britain's 18th-19th-century Parliament was unique in having land <u>and</u> commerce represented, thus generally competent economic policy. Near disappearance of Parliamentary commercial expertise was catastrophic because there was none among officials. As political quality declined, civil service power grew, increasingly unproductive despite computerisation, on retirement handed titles and/or quango posts without responsibility for outcome. In 2010 the Constitutional Reform and Government Act, civil servants were made independent of ministers. Efficiency declined. Decisions were outsourced to ideologically-driven bodies which lacked accountability or commercial ability. In October 2025 the BBC reported civil service numbers 35% more than in 2016. Britain's 2025 ruling party had <u>no</u> MP with business experience.

Britain's maritime services sector however, despite higher costs, maintained its leading position due to unprecedented increasing <u>world</u> trade volumes, open registries, primacy in insurance and arbitration, both 18th-century Mansfield legacies, English law applicable to international shipping and favourable tax treatment of resident, foreign, mainly Greek shipowners.

In 2002, Home Office Minister John Reid said his department was 'not fit for purpose.' Many subsequent examples of incompetence made it accepted as normal, never reformed. In 2023 former Bank of England chief economist Andy Haldane thought the Treasury also 'not fit for purpose', urging its breakup. As civil servants identified their own well-being with the state's, they not only became <u>indifferent</u> but <u>hostile</u> to commerce, like Britain's former competitors; Portuguese merchants' 1689 plea, 'merchants are so little-favoured and commerce despised' (page 26), the post-

1690 Heren XVII exclusion of merchants from the Assembly, divorced from trade, commercial instincts dying, 16th-17th-century Spanish colonial centralisation, slow in service, meticulous in meddling and the 1716 French Council of Trade identifying overcomplex regulations, control and restraint, hindering merchants (page 8), when English/British expansion was self-motivated, commercial, unhindered and encouraged.

In the 2008 Financial Crash, Britain's government took a majority shareholding in Royal Bank of Scotland (RBS) to prevent bankruptcy. Its large, successful ship finance department had nothing to do with the crisis. Nevertheless, it was instructed to cease. As it wound-down the portfolio, potential buyers knowing it had to sell, declined to pay full price, apparently unforeseen by commercially innocent bureaucrats, while decades of expertise were lost, future business gifted to foreign banks. Furthermore, post-1914 British policy allowed wealthy residents including London-based Greek shipowners, underpinning its maritime services, only pay tax on worldwide income when brought into Britain. Their employment of many maritime professionals encouraged other service industries, earning far more revenue. But with 'generalist' civil servants frequently swapping departments, unwilling to engage with commercial specialists, despite Maritime London's efforts, Treasury ideas about targeting their world income, floated since the 1970s, continued. A 2002 Cambridge University study estimated if implemented, shipowners were likely to relocate to Switzerland, which made pragmatic deals, like those once accepted by the Treasury and 4,500 jobs would be lost.[19] Even Gordon Brown finally accepted the logic, but George Osborne's 2015 budget tried trapping them, demonstrating incomprehension of how world shipping works and ignorance about the reasons other countries tried attracting them with favourable tax treatment.

Most left, as they, the Cambridge study and Maritime London predicted, many closing their London offices completely, losing thousands of jobs and skills. Like Tilbury anti-container strikes, it was an unnecessary act of self-harm. Willingness to move as economic opportunities and threats appear define merchant activity and values. Penalised merchants <u>always</u> move; Yemenis and Omanis from antiquity throughout history to India to form Mappila and Arwi communities, Persians to India from the 7th century to become Parsis, Chinese after 1372, Jews from Iberia to Holland, Britain and the Americas, French Huguenots to Britain, Holland and Switzerland. Hansa restrictions and high Hapsburg taxes were among the reasons for Bruges's decline and the rise of Antwerp about 1480, its merchants and industry moving to more promising locations, assisted by the flight of Mediterranean capital and expertise in Ottoman-Christian warfare. Antwerp's 1480–1564 golden age as Europe's economic heart was wrecked by Philip II's religious myopia and attack when 150,000 economically productive people moved to Amsterdam heralding its spectacular rise as Europe's shipping, shipbuilding, trading and banking capital. In Portugal's Indian Ocean entry, Calicut's merchants moved to Cochin and Surat, Hormuz' to other Gulf and Red Sea ports and Malacca's to other Southeast Asian ports, the Malacca-Cambay connection replaced by Surat-Aceh to avoid Portuguese *cartaz* impositions. Surat's 18th-century merchants moved to Mandvi, Muscat and especially Bombay, Greeks themselves from early-19th-century unwelcoming Mediterranean locations to London, these and more examples detailed in previous volumes. Just as no lessons were learnt in 18th-century France, no historical common sense emanated from the Treasury. The City-Westminster alliance that served England/Britain for seven centuries was killed.

Consider the alternatives. From less promising 1945 starts Norwegian, Danish, German and Singaporean tax incentives to own ships were all successful. South Korean shipping turnover targets proved stimulating, although over-encouraged risk. The most successful model was post-war Japan. Its bureaucrats incentivised ship ownership, initially small companies for inter-island ferries, but soon Japanese-built ocean-going ships, chartered long-term to *zaibatsu* shipping companies, with capital gains tax breaks, withdrawn if a ship was sold and the money not reinvested within two years, incentivising continual growth with low risk. Concentrated in Shikoku Island, especially Imabari, home to Japan's largest shipbuilder and Kyushu, especially Kure, there are now <u>hundreds</u> of such companies. The largest three Shoei Kisen, Nisshen and Nissen own over 200 ships each, the fourth Doun Kisen over 140 and many with scores more. Since the 1980s they also long-term chartered to foreign companies. In 2025 Nissen reportedly had about 150 ships on order. All provided local employment and vibrant economic activity and assisted Japanese banks, finance, engineering and insurance companies' expertise and strength. All had cascading revenue implications, competing with legacy British, European and American insurance companies. What a boost similar enlightened schemes might have made to Merseyside, Tyneside and Clydeside, for example. Furthermore, unlike Britain's post-war tax system, Japan's encouraged hard work and capital formation. Japanese workers suggest efficiencies. Britain's unions fight them. Post-war Japan's rational administrative guidance to industry and tax system made it an economic giant, unconcerned with political grandstanding. Had a British-style bureaucracy been created in Japan, Singapore, Taiwan or the UAE they would undoubtedly have continued poor and backward.

Despite government hostility, London's remaining maritime service sector prospered because despite British shipowning almost dying, China-inspired trade growth kept the momentum. In 2007 Clarkson Research calculated world tonnage at <u>one billion dwt</u>, carrying seven billion tons of cargo: bulkers 36%, tankers 35%, containerships 13%, multipurpose and ro-ros 7%, chemical tankers 3%, gas carriers 2%, then car-carriers, reefers and combination carriers. In 2020 it was <u>two billion</u>; double in 13 years! By 2023 bulkers <u>alone</u> were a billion. But most maritime services growth was <u>outside</u> Britain. The Nuclear Energy Maritime Organisation was established in London in 2024 because the IMO was London-based. London's maritime arbitration continues growing, insurance is strong and British shipbroking companies dominate in Singapore and Dubai, the second- and third-largest maritime service hubs. In 2010 Japan's main shipbrokers were Japanese-owned companies. By 2020 the top four were British. But these worthy successes cannot replace hundreds of lost London Greeks, a wholly unnecessary government-inflicted wound. When the author asked a retired senior Treasury official why RBS was ordered to exit ship finance, she claimed it was about tax evasion and promised to send a link with the details. Despite reminders, she did not. No evidence of such activity came to light. It appears they simply didn't understand it, indifferent to its future profit potential. As for forcing-out London-based Greek shipowners, she was casually indifferent and disdainful, denying obvious detrimental revenue effects. Treasury interaction with the Baltic Exchange has tailed-off to an annual breakfast meeting, insufficient to explain the benefits of alternative scenarios to unwilling ears. British shipbuilding was probably doomed by unreformed structure, although its decline was woefully handled by government, but the benefits of ship ownership, encouraged for centuries, was ignored because arrogant bureaucrats refused to learn from history or successful foreign models.

As for British-EU membership, a withdrawal movement gathered momentum when Jacques Delors, European Commission President (1985–1995), promised 'an embryo European government' overriding Thatcher's reforms. Floods of directives were issued, some sinister, others like mandatory condom dimensions, ridiculous. An apparent bulwark against Soviet socialism, after its 1991 demise, threatened Eurocrat socialism. Thatcher feared direction of travel, but Europhiles removed her. Delors' large budget brought so much protest that *Le Monde* thought 'La Grande-Bretagne se mobilise contre les 'eurocrats.'"[20] Unhappiness grew that law was imposed by the undemocratic Council of Ministers behind closed doors without published transcripts, enforced by the politically-driven European Court of Justice, that prescriptive laws were alien to British Common Law, that Britain paid billions to foreign bureaucrats to inflict laws detrimental to it, that EU-imposed protectionist tariffs on manufactured goods hardly produced in Britain, 85% on frozen beef, 65% on fresh beef and lamb, 39% on wines protecting European farms, reminiscent of 1920s-1930s European tariffs and that it regulated businesses whether or not trading with it, and only 8% did, costing 5% of GDP in 2012; £84 billion.[21] All fuelled withdrawal sentiment, vehemently opposed by the establishment with forecasts of doom if Britain left.

However, in 2016 Britain did vote to leave, probably eventually inevitable, but Parliament's vote that withdrawal could only happen with EU agreement, however harmful to Britain, effective surrender to EU-dictated terms, was like the 2008 RBS dictat and 2015 budget, another wound self-inflicted by commercial incompetents. The 1,246-page Brexit deal established a Partnership Council with committees of civil servants, sucking them unnecessarily into EU engagement, its decisions 'binding on the parties', further enhancing their power. Britain's commercially inept establishment joined and left, both on EEC/EU terms, its relationship worse than prior joining; a 47-year aberration, Heath's hubristic mistake.

In 2023, civil service refusal to remove over 4,000 remaining EU laws from Britain's statute books and return to office post-covid drew more criticism. The *Daily Telegraph* (22nd April) called it 'broken', inefficient, run largely for its own benefit with abysmal productivity and (27th April) 'an intellectually bankrupt…elite…overrated for decades, if not generations.' Detaching Northern Ireland meant with the Partnership Council and membership of the ECHR, the EU bear still had its claws into Britain. Despite Northern Ireland-Eire trade being well-under 1% of EU GDP, Northern Ireland was subject to 20% of EU customs checks, 'the price for Brexit,' according to a vengeful senior EU official. Its imperial reach is more effectively resisted by Switzerland, where unlike the EU or Britain, many hundreds of trading and shipping companies operate and where some London Greeks relocated, although with shipowners exempted from Greek income tax from the 1950s, most went there.

Tariff policy as a means of increasing trade dominated 19th and early-20th-century British politics. After Brexit it was hardly mentioned. Many tariffs <u>were</u> reduced but never announced, some still unnecessarily high. Apart from negotiating free trade agreements, British tariff levels slipped below politicians' radar or was beyond their comprehension, so not logically debated until President Trump's 2025 tariff increases concentrated minds.

Risk and success were applauded in 18th-19th-century Britain, militarily by Clive at Arcot and Plassey, Wolff at Quebec or Nelson at Trafalgar, in shipping by Cunard, Holt, et. al, in invention by Harrison, the Darby's, Arkwright, Crompton, Wedgwood Boulton and Watt, Elder, Napier, et. al. Admiral Byng, cautious about risking his ships was executed. In post-1945 Britain as in 18th-century Holland, <u>caution</u>, a respectable word for inertia, and <u>regulation</u> governs <u>official</u> thinking, mirroring President Reagan's negative view of government; 'If it moves tax it. If it keeps moving regulate it. If it stops moving subsidise it.' In 2019 the Centre for Policy Studies of the National Audit Office identified about <u>90</u> regulatory bodies, many overlapping, costing £6.1 billion annually, cascading inefficiencies making that much greater. Engineer/inventor and over-regulation critic James Dyson's 2010 recommendations to Prime Minister Cameron that research and development merited tax relief resulted by 2019 in expenditure doubling, a belated positive development, but moved his headquarters to Singapore and most manufacturing to Malaysia because factory expansion plans were refused. He soon employed double those previously employed in Britain, another effective expulsion of wealth-creation. In Andrew Pears' tradition, his private UK-based Dyson Institute of Engineering and Technology, begun in 2017, aimed to produce engineers which Britain <u>still</u> desperately needs. In 2023 it quit the government's apprenticeship scheme as not academically rigorous enough, with undue interference by regulator Ofsted. In 2024, when he tried giving £6 million to a primary school near his British HQ to expand from 420 to 630 pupils, creating dedicated science, technology, engineering, arts and maths centres, an Education Department's advisory board stalled him, 'a sorry example of how hard it is to get anything done in Britain,' he said. In 2025 Norwegian billionaire shipowner John Fredericton who settled in Britain in 1978, left for Dubai and Lakshmi Mitall, Britain's richest man, owners of Mittal Steel, after 30 years in Britain left for Switzerland and Dubai, joining many more wealth-creators previously attracted to Britain.

Mistakes previously made by Britain's competitors were committed by Britain's post-1945 bureaucrats and politicians, strangling entrepreneurship, hindering capital accumulation, effectively expelling wealth-creators. Shipping and trade are two of many casualties. Hyam thinks the 1902 defeat of Sadler's reforms crucial. Sampson identifies post-1945 expansion especially detrimental. 2020 covid lockdowns were disastrous. All <u>were</u> vital milestones, but technical education recognised as a weakness in the 1840s-1850s, which endless Commons Select Committees and Commissions tried reforming, were all shelved because powerful mandarins, unaffected by elections or consequences, resisted reform and expanded regulations. At the 2024 Core Power Maritime Nuclear Conference, of the dozens of engineer panellists, only one was British. National educational policy <u>still</u> side-lines technology, highlighted by Dyson and BBC's

Panorama (28th March 2024) which revealed that five out of eight software engineers' annual intake at CCS Technology which works with Airbus and Jaguar-Land Rover were immigrants, British ones unavailable. With dependents they constituted 8.2% of the unsustainable 1.44 million Home Office-issued visas it estimated will lead to a 2036 population of 74 million, virtually all by immigration, leading to pressure on public services and housing, uncoordinated civil servant departments staggering from crisis to crisis, without central vision. A problem identified 170 years ago is still unaddressed by any political party, not mentioned in the 2024 General Election, the scale now immense. BBC's *Farming Today* regularly airs farmers' complaints about unnecessary, costly regulations. A 13th April 2024 edition for example highlighted Byzantine-like regulations over flooding compensations, the main point, Whitehall's detachment from farming's needs and 19th December's edition highlighted Treasury figures justifying the October budget's IHT measures as out-of-date and wrong to the extent of affecting 75% not 25% of farms. Britain's maritime community is not the only victim.

Meg Hiller, Labour MP and chair of the accounts committee wrote in the *Financial Times* (30th April 2024) 'the same mistakes are made, the system…incapable of developing institutional learning and memory…money misdirected…squandered… because of groupthink [unwilling] to pivot when necessary.' The Taxpayers' Alliance's Callum McGoldrick in 2024 explained the Treasury's Tax Code, 15,000 pages in 2015, the world's most complex, increased to 23,000 pages, compared to Hong Kong's 300 and most Europeans' 10–15,000, increasing incentives for wealth-creators to emigrate, something Ineos' owner Sir Jim Ratcliffe warned of in 2023 regarding blocking takeovers, over-regulation, over-taxation, banning fracking and high energy costs. Many from all political persuasions acknowledge the problems, but nothing is done. In 2024 it was revealed that the Ministry of Defence had more civil servants, not including its consultants, than trained RAF and Navy personnel. A 2025 proposal for slight civil service reductions prompted Admiral James Burnell-Nugent to recall in a March *Daily Telegraph* letter, his 1996 secondment to the Treasury to reduce government costs, where he found hundreds of useless programmes, concluding sub-departments needed minimum 50% reduction and that was after Derek Rayner's efficiency savings!

In 1900 western Europe's population was about 14% of the world's; in 2000, 6%, yet arrogant European establishments declining in economic importance, continually overrate themselves. Braudel identified 11th-century Baghdad's commercial decline as related to suppressing *falsafa* rationalism. Islam, he said, was convinced 'of being at the centre of the world, of having found all the right answers…not needing to look for any others,' exactly how Europe's and Britain's post-1945 establishments viewed themselves, moralising on world issues from what they called 'western values', incorporating humanitarianism, economic and social liberalism. But these are maritime values, not uniquely western, new and unstable in post-1945 Europe, which gained traction in 1980s maritime Asia, now economic liberalism's heartland. Post-war Britain has not re-examined its failing institutions' fundamental structure.

Economic liberalism also grew in the Persian Gulf. Before the 1970s-1980s, political, social and cultural attitudes there meant there was little commercial vision. Keith Nuttall has convincingly demonstrated the latest successful maritime area, Dubai, put maritime trade and economic liberalism at its policies' heart, favourably influencing the wider region. Briefly backtracking chronologically, the lower Gulf's main post-1819 transhipment port, Lingah, nominally ruled by Persia, marginal in global trade, although increasing due to steamships was formally taken in 1887, imposing high tariffs in 1902. Dubai's emir offered their merchants land, protection and no import tariffs. Like other threatened merchants, they moved almost immediately, doubling Dubai's 1901–1921 population. Nuttall calls it 'the lessons of Lingah…over-regulation and bureaucracy… and the importance of having a stable and welcoming environment,'[22] which included a role in an advisory council. By the 1950s-1960s the Gulf's major commercial air-transport and re-export hub was Bahrain, the Trucial States' headquarters, Sharjah. Gulf maritime trade was small, but ambitious Dubai erected a cargo crane in 1951. Transhipping flourished. Its creek was dredged in 1958–1959 and an airport built in 1960, despite Sharjah's adequately servicing the region.

The Trucial States, independent in 1971 as the United Arab Emirates (UAE) was successful due to increasing economic and social liberalism. Leadership was crucial. Abu Dhabi had 87% of the UAE's seven emirates' land and 96% of its oil reserves. Sheikh Zayed concentrated on oil and gas development, helping poorer emirates and encouraged Dubai's tolerant Indian Ocean trade tradition. It studied Hong Kong's and Singapore's development policies: low taxes, port, airport, business infrastructure and containerisation, which attracted shipowners and shipping services. Sheikh Rashid al Maktoum planned long-term with similar policies. To Port Rashid's 16 berths, developed 1966–1972, more than many thought necessary, 20 more were added from 1974 to 1979 including a container berth. Moreover, Jebel Ali, operational in 1979, was the world's largest man-made port complex, 15 kilometres of quays and 67 berths, leading to its Free Zone without import/re-export duties, the model for other free zones, allowing tax-free foreign company investments. They poured in, triggering a building boom to house them.

Dubai Dry Docks, built 1979–1983, competed with Bahrain's Shipbuilding and Repair Yard. While other Gulf states enlarged ports for imported construction material and consumer goods only, Dubai envisioned a Singapore-like entrepot. Initially assisted by oil revenues, it prepared for a post-oil future with economic liberalism. Many considered its 1970s-1990s expansion foolhardy because the Gulf was insignificant in world trade. But vast purchasing power based on higher oil prices made it increasingly important. Coinciding with containerisation, capitalising on huge Gulf imports, it pro-actively engaged with a globalising world.

Jebel Ali's throughput was 913,363 TEUs in 1990, 1.7 million in 1993, 2.8 million in 1999, 5.2 million in 2003, half local cargoes, half transhipped.[23] A second terminal opened in 2009 with eight berths and 29 cranes, a third in 2014 with 19 more. 2023 throughput reached 14.5 million. As an outward-looking maritime city, appropriately one of the many free zones, Multi-Commodity City, Media City, Internet City for example, is Dubai International Humanitarian City, comprising about 80 members: UN organisations, NGOs, commercial companies, offices and warehouses dispatching aid to world disasters. Dubai's population is 92% foreign. Despite ill-informed criticism, it enabled people from emerging economies to aspire to better lives while sending money

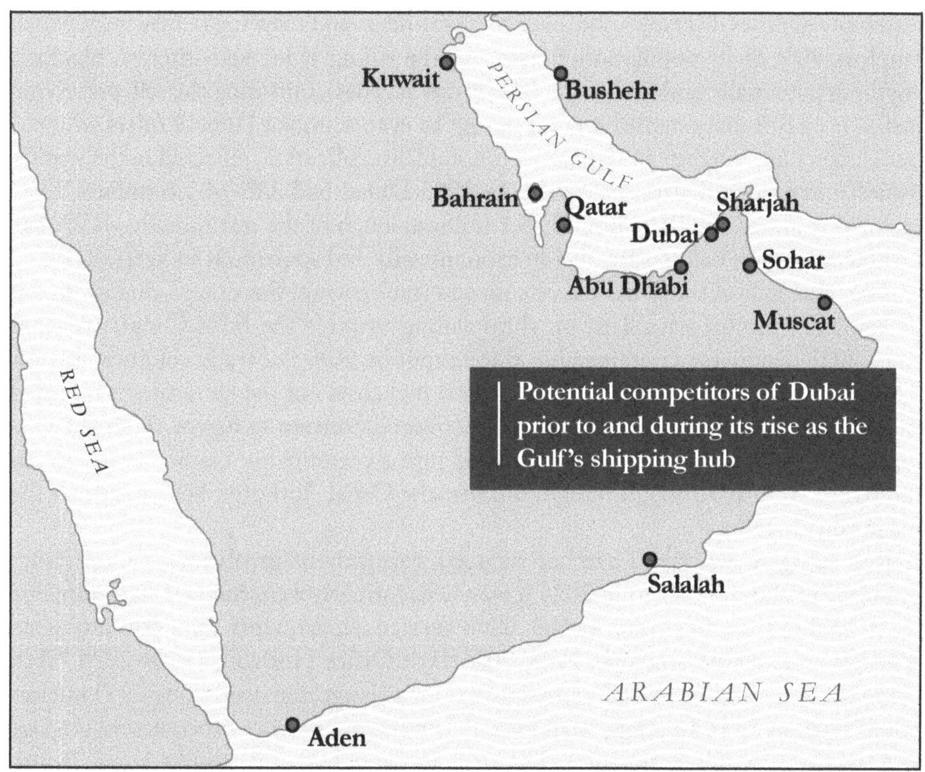

home, making substantial differences to them. Dubai typically extends assistance to new industry, proactive, not reactive, one of the latest, promoting AI development, while Britain increasingly erects barriers.

Dubai's success prompted neighbours to copy its blueprint, helping those economies. Sharjah's east coast Khor Fakkan terminal was inaugurated in 1979 and while efficient, had insufficient hinterland to compete. Fujairah's refinery and bunker terminal built in the 1990s, was by the early-2000s the world's second-largest bunkering port. In 1996 Maersk and Sea-Land developed southern Oman's Salalah, outside the Gulf, targeting Suez traffic. Without an active hinterland, almost all were transhipped, 645,758 TEUs in 1999, 2,466,824 in 2005. In 1999 an Oman-Rotterdam joint-venture took-over Muscat's Mina Qaboos port's cargoes. 2016 throughput was a more efficient 619,000,[24] while a similar joint venture at Sohar also tried competing. Abu Dhabi's Mina Khalifa, built in 2012, berthed the largest containerships and in 2016 handled 1,530,446 TEUs. In 2014 Yemen joined the WTO, boasting that Aden, a former thriving entrepot, would be a potential future hub, pure bravado with illiberal rulers after North Yemen's take-over.

From 2005 Dubai Port World (DPW) began operating container terminals outside the UAE and bought P&O Ports in 2006 for 19-times earnings, considered a good deal for shareholders, having sold well Princess Cruise Lines to Carnival Cruises in 2004. The 2008 Financial Crash made it look inspired. But by 2019, DPW had 78 terminals in 40 countries, fourth-largest in TEUs and continues growing. By contrast, Kuwait's

Assembly opposes diversification, outside investments and reducing bureaucracy, which employs 90% of its population, preserving the ruling elite's self-interest, blocking anything potentially undermining it like private business, mirroring the self-preserving instincts of Britain's establishment, <u>reacting</u> to events, unlike Dubai's rulers who co-opted merchant interests in <u>visionary</u> economic diversification, reflected in the world's busiest international airport in 2014. In 1985 Dubai had 32% of 1.6 million TEU regional volumes, in 2015, 50% of 36.1 million, much of the rest initially via Dubai, its blueprint both helping the region economically and spurring it to keep ahead.

The other side of the Middle East coin was Iran's corrupt theocracy's empowerment of Yemen's Houthis who fired on ships sailing towards the Suez Canal, over 200 since 2023 decreasing containership throughput by 90% and trade volumes by 57%. The alternative route via the Cape increased fuel costs but the extra time supported freight rates. Canal revenue collapsed, an economic concern to Egypt. After the US-brokered Gaza peace deal they were forced into a ceasefire but cautious carriers did not rush to return, although transits did rise, the Canal Authority keen to attract the mega containerships.

Returning to Britain, Thatcher reduced government involvement in Britain's economy to about 37%, but in 2024 it was 47%, formerly a continental state-directed or 1939–1955 war/recovery model. Civil service departments regularly produced scandals and costly cover-ups, 1998–2025 Post Office Horizon, 1970s-2024 NHS blood contamination, HMRC's retrospective loan charge, the continuing 1953 nuclear bomb veterans and Christmas Island scandal, numerous defence procurement wastage and the inability to secure national borders, to name but a few, unlike Japan, Korea, Taiwan, Singapore and the UAE, today's economically liberal economies with secure borders and competent, effective bureaucracies. Britain's civil service from the 19th century's second half gave trade lip service, then indifference and after ballooning in size, finally hostility, not ingredients for successful economies. As with technical education, its necessary radical reform was not politically debated until the end of 2025. The second book in this series ended in the 1650–1700s with England, later Britain's ingredients of success, concentration on shipping and trading, supporting merchants, tolerating useful wealth-creating foreigners and robust championing of those values worldwide. This book ends with the jettosoning of those ingredients for bureaucracy, regulation and wealth destroying ideologies; hence consequential decline.

Britain however, sensibly decided in 2022 to join CPTPP, comprising Japan, Peru, Chile, Canada, Vietnam, Malaysia, Singapore, Mexico, Australia, New Zealand and Brunei, high-growth, economically liberal countries. Membership meant combined GDP leapfrogged the EU. Unlike it, no laws, rules and standards are imposed, no financial contributions demanded. Implemented in 2024, it is too early to determine results. Other dynamic economies have shown interest in joining. EU share of global trade fell to 14.6% in 2023. CPTPP aims to open markets, liberate start-up companies, reduce trading rules of origin, encourage paperless trade, a trade-driven philosophy, as British industry and commerce fights home-grown obstacles or relocates.

Epilogue

Archaeological discoveries have modified some of this series' first book's conclusions. With occupation of the America's now accepted as over 40,000 years ago and that bananas were grown on Rapanui around 1000 BC, previously thought first settled about 900 AD, pre-Flood sea levels 120 metres lower, indicate the Nazca and Salas y Gomes ocean ridges from Rapanui, then an island/atoll chain to Peru, was probably the first conduit to the Americas, the Bering Sea re-entry and Lapita thrust, later post-Ice Age phenomena. This re-interpretation with the similarity of myths, terminology and ideas, Pacific islands' ruins and platforms, relics of what natives call the 'Before People' all described in the first book's chapter 2, reinforces the importance and extent of Ice Age equatorial maritime endeavour and explains why the genetic 'Y' signal is found in populations across the Pacific, Australia and South America, but not in North America or North Asia.

The first book also accepted contemporary wisdom that Roman conquest of Britain did not extend to Devon and Cornwall. It puzzled the author because its *raison d'etre* was mineral exploitation and export, tin especially important. Since publication, archaeologists have found Roman roads and settlements suggesting occupation and tin export. Another update is on Jersey's massive coin horde, demonstrating lucrative cross-Channel trade, buried it was thought, as Caesar defeated Gaul's tribes. A few coins however post-date him. It is now thought it was buried slightly later to hide it from Augustus' tax assessors, an early example of Jersey's later status in offshore financial tax planning!

Following the 2012 discovery of the drowned legendary port of Dvarka in the Gulf of Cambay, since 2019, 25 kilometres off Pumpahar at the then mouth of the River Cauvery, marine archaeologists found an eleven by three kilometre-wide area containing a drowned harbour, dockyards, settlements, walls, staircases and what might even have been a lighthouse, linked by canals up to 250 metres wide, all able to handle 70–80 ships at once which the Bharathidasan University research team think is about 15,000 years old; spectacular evidence of ancient Tamil maritime trade. The deep antiquity of Indian maritime trade seems unquestionable and more archaeeolgy needs to be done near the coast, on ancient rivers or just offshore. As an example the on-shore site of Bhirrana, dated to 7570–6200 BC, 220 kilometres northwest of Delhi is the oldest settlement found on the banks of the then Sarasvati River, which emptied into the Arabian Sea. Its wide streets, planned drainage with water filtration of sand, gravel and charcoal and standard weights and measures mirror later cities after 3000 BC but with advanced metallurgy including bronze, millennia before anywhere else. A potsherd with graffiti replicating the posture of the famous dancing girl of Mohendro-daro dated to 2800 BC implies widespread, long-lasting knowledge networks pre-dating the drowning of Dvarka. With Subash Kak's recent study of the Saka language as Sanskrit-based, it further confirms the Aryan migration/invasion as myth and the Indian subcontinent's northwest and the south, the first two great maritime-oriented civilisations.

The series' first book also postulated that from the third millennium BC or before, India exported timber and food to the Gulf for which gold from Egypt was imported, the reason for Egypt's invasion resulting in Pharaonic domination, gold trading facilitated by Phoenicians. The second book showed Egypt-based Jewish merchants, Phoenician heirs, still trading Indian goods for metals including gold. Calicut's ruler told Vasco de Gama he wanted gold. In the 1950s-1960s gold was a driver of Dubai's economy, exported in dhows at night to avoid Indian tariffs. In 1970 it constituted about 20% of non-communist world gold production.[1] Much continuity in trade patterns exist because of geography, in this case due to the value Indians always placed on gold for dowries and convertible, transportable savings.

One of the first book's main themes, merchant transfer of Indian ideas west, is shown by other examples, not earlier mentioned. In a *Jataka*, a Buddhist disciple walks on water, sinking when he loses faith. In another, Buddha feeds 500 with one piece of bread and another resembles the prodigal son story. This book showed Indian Ocean ideas moved from far earlier in multiple pulses, far further. India continues influencing the world, especially since the 1990s. Its diaspora, 3.1 billion people is the world's largest and most influential with 4.5 million in America, almost half graduates. In India itself, with a more open economy and rising maritime trade, infant mortality has halved in the last 20 years. Its 50 million-strong middle class of 2005 has grown to 550 million. It also began to purposefully rediscover its maritime roots. In 2025 it launched Bharat Container Shipping, a public-private partnership, Cochin Shipyard won an order for six 1,700 TEU LNG-powered new buildings for 2029-2031 delivery from CMA-CGM, the first from a large international operator and its Nicobar project was announced, a plan lifted from the Singapore and Dubai model, container port, airport and tourism resort in Great Nicobar Island, adjacent to the Malacca Strait. Sanjeev Sandal, advisor to the Prime Minister also aims to re-write Indian history text books to reflect its maritime history and entrepreneurship, another lesson Britain needs to copy from liberal Asian countries who recognise the importance of maritime ingredients of success.

*　*　*

This series demonstrates that since antiquity, commercial shipping has been the most important industry and when maritime trade was encouraged, benefits permeated the wider economy, people were enriched, economies stimulated. Dramatic examples are 1649–1913 Britain and post-1945 Japan, Hong Kong, Singapore, Taiwan, South Korea, China and Dubai, whose acceleration gave opportunities to Vietnam, Thailand, Indonesia, India, Bangladesh and Gulf nations. Britain's proud maritime legacy is found in New York, Hong Kong, Mumbai, Calcutta, Singapore, Shanghai, Sydney,

Melbourne, Durban, Dubai and many ports with significant roles in world trade; increasingly ignored by Britain's political/administrative class, which lost its way.

Shipping hugely increased efficiency, mainly due to open registries, containerisation, technological innovation enabling supersizing ships, reduced emissions, increasingly liberal Asian and Gulf economic environments, lowering transport costs in aggressive, competitive and innovative markets where established companies are often overtaken by others offering new ideas. Poor countries have become richer and progressive. Maritime trade is the lynchpin of global trade, transporting 80–90% of goods, 11 billion tons annually, a $14 trillion powerhouse, an important part of which was centred in Britain, which it ignored, then stupidly sent packing. Shipping is high-risk, at the mercy of global economic crises caused by other events. Private shipping companies, mainly multi-generational, originally family-owned, have best adapted.

In the 1960s, docks were lined with general cargo ships, operated by hundreds of companies. Oil companies treated shipping as a core business. The Baltic Exchange's trading floor was packed with brokers dealing face-to-face. Many foreign telephone calls were booked. Communications were the second-highest cost for shipping service companies after wages. Hundreds of liner companies gave-way to a handful of huge containership owners operating with tight margins, making low returns for occasional bonanzas. Massive containerships now take industrial and consumer goods where needed in efficient logistics networks. Manufactured goods' transport costs became an insignificant percentage of their retail price. Huge tankers and bulkers load and discharge quickly, reducing raw material freights. Old docks became marinas and quayside warehouses, apartments. An international regulatory system made shipping the safest form of commercial transport with comfortable seamen's conditions and reduced ship pollution. Compared with other economic sectors, exceptionally maritime trade costs fell, including land-based containers. The pace of technological change from 1700 to 2025 was cumulative, the impact revolutionary, the final 25 years intoxicating in acceleration.

In 2024, 16.4% of world merchant shipping was Greek-owned, 14.4% Chinese, 9.9% Japanese, with substantial Singaporean, German, Norwegian and Taiwanese fleets where governments encourage it, recognising the wider benefits.

The dangers explained in Chapter 1 of this series' first book are continentalist against maritime inspired regions/nations. Russian and Chinese cyberwar interference in peaceful, wealth-creating peripheral powers and occasional invasions, mirroring 13th-14th-century Mongol interference and invasion from this area. China's Xi Jing-ping abandoned Deng Xiaoping's model that delivered 30 years of spectacular growth, reverting to thought-control and threats to Taiwan. War with it would be more insane than the Kaiser's war because China depends on world maritime trade. Attempts to by-pass the sea with a New Silk Road railway increases speed but cannot compete in shipment sizes and volumes. Ending east-west maritime inter-dependence would be economically catastrophic.

After Germany's early World War II's sinking of Norway's *Mira*, its Foreign Minister protested, 'We cannot understand how…German forces…find such a practice in accordance with their honour or humanitarian feelings.' Japanese and

German behaviour shocked maritime-influenced societies. SS units slaughtered Jews, intelligentsia and gypsies initially ad hoc, finally in death camps, copying and intensifying Germany's early-century Southwest African Cleansing Patrols. Millions were killed. The Nuremburg Tribunal estimated 5.85 million Jewish deaths. No responsible estimates are below five million. Japanese regarded Chinese with contempt, living targets for bayonet, flame-thrower and sword practice and 250,000 women were used in military brothels, servicing troops and officials. Unit 731 removed organs without anaesthetic and froze limbs on living victims then shattered them. The 1970s Khmer Rouge taught ignorant peasants to torture and kill imagined enemies. Saudi Arabia's estimated 1950 slaves were 450,000, 20% of the population, Slavery was banned there and Oman in 1963, Mauritania in 1981, criminalising it in 2007. ISIS enslaved prisoners. China reportedly uses Uighur slave labour. Boko Haram captured and sold schoolgirls into slavery. Afghan Taliban deny girls education. Russia's 2022 Ukraine invasion deliberately targeted apartments, schools, nurseries, hospitals and museums. Despite these recent continental examples, humanitarianism is maritime trade's greatest world contribution, which when not government-constrained has always increased global prosperity and enlightenment.

Glossary

Amortise - Repay the purchase price and interest.

Ballast - Heavy material loaded into a ship to increase stability and draft, when **ballasting** or **in ballast** (i.e. empty of cargo) before loading.

Bulk Carrier/Bulker - Single-decker for bulk cargoes.

Bunkers - fuel for ships. **Bunkering** - calling at a bunker port.

Breakbulk cargo - Needs individual handling, unlike bulk.

Capesize - Ships too big to transit the Panama Canal so sail Atlantic-Pacific and vice-versa via the Cape of Good Hope.

Charter Party - Contract between shipowner and charterer for transporting cargo.

Contract of Affreightment (COA) - Multiple voyages of above.

Demurrage - pre-agreed daily payment by the charterer if the ship exceeds the agreed load/discharge time.

Draft - Distance between waterline and keel, fully-loaded.

Dunnage - Temporary cargo separations in ships' holds to prevent sensitive cargo's contact with ship's sides <u>and</u> cargo shifting.

Fixture – Agreement between shipowner and charterer resulting in a **Charter Party**.

Freight rate – Shipowner's payment for shipping and delivering cargo to the receiver, usually paid per ton.

Herring buss - 16–18th-century Dutch fishing/processing vessel.

Hire – Shipowner's payment, payable daily.

Knot – One nautical mile/hour (1.5078 mph).

Packet boats/ships - For mail, passengers and limited freight.

Tonnage - Commercially, ships are measured by **deadweight (dwt)**. It comprises everything onboard including cargo, bunkers, fresh water, crew, stores, equipment and spare parts. All except the cargo should be deleted to give the cargo capacity **(dwcc)**. Plimsoll Lines are seasonally zoned; Tropical, Summer, Winter and Winter North Atlantic. Normally summer dwt is the commercial headline figure. There are complications such as long tons, short tons and metric tons. Because cargo density varies, (e.g. cotton and iron) volume was chosen as the measurement unit by an 1848

Board of Trade-appointed Committee under George Moorsom, setting the basis for **gross registered ton** and **net registered ton (grt/nrt)** at 100 cubic feet/ton, enacted in the 1854 British Tonnage Act, which all nations adopted within 35 years, used to calculate port and canal dues, pilotage, towage, etc. Previously, various methods were used. **GRT** is the measure of the internal volume of enclosed spaces. **NRT** is that for cargo, deducting spaces for crew, navigation and propulsion, now calculated by a formula in the IMO Tonnage Convention. Ton is from tun, a large barrel in medieval wine trades, derived from *tonnerre*, thunder, rumbling noise when rolled. **Lbs** is pounds weight, 112 in one hundredweight. 20 hundredweight/imperial ton (19.6841 metric ton).

Trimming - Balancing ships when loading/discharging.

Tweendeck - Intermediate deck between the weather deck and the hold bottom (tanktop).

VLCC - Very Large Crude Carrier, about 200–270,000 dwt.

ULCC - Ultra Large Crude Carrier, about 300–360,000 dwt.

Select Bibliography

Abulaffia, David; The Great Sea (2011)
—— The Boundless Sea (2019)
Al-Qasimi, Sultan Bin Muhammad; Power Struggles and Trade in the Gulf 1620–1820 (1999)
Atkinson, Robert; The Development of and Decline of British Shipbuilding. Some Thoughts and Comments (1999)
Bakka, Dag; A Century of Shipping. Oslo Shipbrokers Association 1899–1999 (1999)
Barraclough, Martin; Looking for the Silver Lining (2008)
Barty-King, Hugh; The Baltic Exchange. The History of a Unique Market (1977)
—— The Baltic Exchange. Baltick Coffee House to Baltic Exchange (1994)
Belich, James; Replenishing the Earth (2009)
Bowle, John; The English Experience (1971)
Bowring, Philip; Empire of the Winds (2018)
Boxer, C.R; The Portuguese Seaborne Empire 1415–1825 (1969)
—— The Dutch Seaborne Empire 1600–1800 (1965)
Bradshaw, John; Rulers of India. Sir Thomas Munro and the British Settlement of Madras Presidency (1894)
Braudel, Fernand; The Wheels of Commerce (1982)
—— The Perspective of the World (1984)
Brewer, David; The Flame of Freedom. The Greek War of Independence 1821–1833 (2001)
Butel, Paul; The Atlantic (1999)
Cameron, Alan and Farndon, Roy; Lloyds List. 250th Anniversary Special Supplement (1984)
Canny, Nicholas; The Origins of Empire (ed) (1998)
Collins. Nick: How Maritime Trade and the Indian Subcontinent Shaped the World. Ice Age to Mid-Eighth Century (2021)
—— The Millennium Maritime Trade Revolution 700–1700. How Asia Lost Maritime Supremacy (2023)
—— *No More Napoleons* (2025)
Darwin. John; After Tamerlane (2007)
Davis, Ralph; The Rise of the English Shipping Industry in the 17th and 18th Century (1962/1972)
—— A Commercial Revolution (1967)
Davies. Norman: Europe (1996)
Droz, Jacques; Europe Between Revolutions 1815–1848 (1967)
Ebrey, Patricia Buckley; Cambridge Illustrated History of China (1996)
Elliot, J.H; Empires of the Atlantic World. Britain and Spain in America 1492–1830 (2006)
—— Imperial Spain 1469–1716 (1963)
Evans, Chris and Ryden, Goran; Baltic Iron in the Atlantic World in the Eighteenth Century (2007)
Evans, Eric J; The Forging of the Modern State. Early Industrial Britain. 1783–1870 (1983)
Falkus, Malcolm; Britain Transformed (1987)
—— The Blue Funnel Legend (1990)
Findlay, Ronald and O'Rourke, Kenneth; Power and Plenty. The World Economy in the Second Millennium (2007)
Firth, Peter; Mighty Things from Small Beginnings. Clarksons. The First 150 Years (2002)

Fox, Stephen; The Ocean Railway (2004)
Fremont-Barnes, Gregory; The Wars of the Barbary Pirates (2006)
Gelber, Harry G; The Dragon and the Foreign Devils (2007)
Gordon, John Steele; A Thread Across the Ocean (2002)
Goswami Chhaya; Globalisation Before its Time (2016)
Gramp, William; The Manchester School of Economics (1960)
Hague, William; William Wilberforce. The Life of the Great Anti-Slave Trade Campaigner (2007)
Hall, Richard; Empire of the Monsoon. A History of the Indian Ocean and its Invaders (1996)
Harlaftis, Galina; A History of Greek-Owned Shipping (1996)
—— Creating Global Shipping (2019)
Haynes, Douglas E; Rhetoric and Ritual in Colonial India. The Shaping of a Public Culture in Surat City 1825–1928 (1991)
Himmelfarb, Gertrude; The Roads to Modernity. The British, French and American Enlightenments (2008)
Hofstater, Richard; The American Political Tradition and the Men who Made It (1962)
Hoppitt, Julian; A Land of Liberty? England 1689–1727 (2000)
Howarth, David and Howarth, Stephen; The Story of P and O (1986)
Hunt, Tristram; Ten Cities That Made An Empire (2014)
Hyam, Ronald; Britain's Imperial Century (1975/1993)
—— Empire and Sexuality. The British Experience (1990)
—— Understanding the British Empire (2010)
Jamieson, Alan G; Ebb Tide in the British Maritime Industries. Change and Adaptation 1918–1990 (2003)
Jephson, Chris and Morgen, Henning; Creating Global Opportunities in Containerisation 1973–2013 (2014)
Jones, Nicolette; The Plimsoll Sensation. The Great Campaign to Save Lives at Sea (2007)
Jones, Peter M.; Industrial Enlightenment, Science, Technology and Culture in Birmingham and the West Midlands 1760–1820 (2013)
Keay, John; The Honourable Company. A History of the East India Company (1991)
—— India (2000)
Kertzer, David I.; Unholy War (2002)
King, Charles; The Black Sea. A History (2004)
Kulke, Hermand and Rothermund, Dieter; A History of India (6th edition) (2016)
Kurlansky, Mark; Cod (1997)
Lambert, Andrew; Seapower States (2018)
—— No More Napoleons (2025)
Lee, Christopher; Eight Bells and Top Masts (2001)
Levinson, Marc; The Box (2016)
—— Outside the Box (2020)
Livingston, Jon; Moore, Joe; Oldfather, Felicia; The Japan Reader. Imperial Japan 1800–1945 (1973)
Longworth, Philip; Russia's Empires from Prehistory to Putin (2005)
McMullen, Jerry; Star of India. The Log of an Iron Ship (1961)
Mantle, Jonathan; Ship to Shore. J. and J. Denholm 1866–1991 (1991)
Marshall, P.J.; The Eighteenth Century (ed) (1998)
McCord, Norman; The Anti-Corn Law League 1838–1846 (1958)
Nuttall, Keith; Shipping and Development in Dubai (2022)
O'Connell, Sanjida; Sugar. The Grass that Changed the World (2004)
Ogg, David; Europe and the Ancien Regime 1715–1783 (1965)
O'Hara, Glen; Britain and the Sea Since 1600 (2010)
Oppenheimer, Stephen; Eden in the East (1998)
Padfield, Peter; Maritime Supremacy and the Opening of the Western Mind (1999)
—— Maritime Power and the Struggle for Freedom (2003)

—— Maritime Dominion and the Triumph of the Free World (2009)

Parker, Mathew; The Sugar Barons (2012)

Parry, J.H.; Trade and Dominion. The European Overseas Empires of the Eighteenth Century (2000)

Pearson, Michael; The Indian Ocean (2003)

Plumb, J.H.; England in the Eighteenth Century (1950)

Prakash, Om and Lombard, Denys (ed); Commerce and Culture in the Bay of Bengal 1500–1800 (2019)

Pryor, Francis; The Birth of Modern Britain (2012)

Risso, Patricia; Merchants of Faith (1995)

Robinson, Ronald and Gallagher, John; Africa and the Victorians (1961)

Rodger, N.A.M.; The Command of the Ocean (2004)

Roy, Tirthankar; India in the World Economy. From Antiquity to the present (2012)

Rude, George; Revolutionary Europe 1789–1815 (1964)

Sampson, Anthony; The Changing Anatomy of Britain (1982)

Sanyal, Sanjeev; Land of the Seven Rivers. A Brief History of India's Geography (2012)

Sked, Alan; The Intelligent Person's Guide to Post-War Britain (1977)

Schama, Simon; Rough Crossings (2005)

Schonhardt-Bailey, Cheryl; Free Trade. The Repeal of the Corn Laws (1996)

Scott, Jonathan; How the Old World Ended (2019)

Souden, David; The Bank and the Sea (2003)

Stopford, Martin; Maritime Economics 3rd Edition (2009)

Subramanian, Lakshmi; Three Merchants of Bombay (2012)

Thistlethwaite, Frank; The Great Experiment (1955)

Thomson, David; England in the Nineteenth Century (1950)

—— England in the Twentieth Century (1965)

Thornton, Mark and Eklund, Robert B; Tariffs, Blockades and Inflation. The Economics of Civil War (2004)

Tombs, Robert; The English and Their History (2014)

Tracy, James D.; The Rise of Merchant Empires. Long Distance Trade in the Early Modern World 1350–1750 (ed) (1990)

—— The Political Economy of Merchant Empires. State Power and World Trade 1350–1750 (ed) (1991)

Trivellato, Francesca; The Familiarity of Strangers. The Sephardic Diaspora. Livorno and Cross Cultural Trade in the Early modern Period (2009)

Walvin, James; A Short History of Slavery (2007)

Wilson. Charles; England's Apprenticeship 1603–1763 (1965)

Zahedieh. Nuala; The Capital and the Colonies. London and the Atlantic Economy (2010)

Woronoff, Jon; Inside Japan Inc. (1982)

Dampskibsselskabet Norden 1871–1996. 125 Years on the High Seas (1996) (author unacknowledged)

Articles

Allen, Richard B; Slavery and the Slave Trades in the Indian Ocean and Arab Worlds: Global Connections and Disconnections. Yale University (2008)

Andersen, Dan and Voth, Hans-Joachim; The Grapes of War. Neutrality and Mediterranean Shipping Under the Danish Flag 1750–1807 *University of Oxford Discussion Paper in Economic and Social History Number 18 (Sept 1997)*

Cain, P.J. and Hopkins A.G; Gentlemanly Capitalism and British Expansion Overseas II. New Imperialism 1850–1945 *Economic History Review Vol 40 No I Feb 1987*

Clark, Gregory; Review Essay. The Enlightened Economy. An Economic History of Britain 1700–1850 by Joel Mokyr; *Journal of the World Economic Literature 2012. 50:1–85–95*

Chase, Kerry A; Imperial Protection and Strategic Trade Policy in the Inter War Period *Review of International Political Economy 11.1 February 2004*

Davies, Peter N; Japanese Shipping and Shipbuilding. An Introduction to the Motives behind its Early Expansion. *Discussion Paper. The Suntory Centre Nov 1999*

Delis, Apostolos; Mediterranean Wooden Shipbuilding in the Nineteenth Century. Production, Productivity and Ship Types in Comparative Perspective. *Cahiers de la Mediterranee* (2012)

Edwards, Anthony David; International Exhibitions, British Economic Decline and the Technical Education Issue 1851–1910. *Liverpool University 2000*

Eichengreen, Barry; The British Economy Between the Wars. *University of California April 2002*

Ellis, Heather; Efficiency and Counter Revolution: Connecting University and Civil Service Reform in the 1850s. (http//hira.hope.ac.uk/id/eprint/63/1/HeatherEllisCivilService.pdf)

Evans, Chris; How Sweden Went Global and Carolina got its Hoes Common Place. The *Journal of Early American Life Vol 7 No 1 (October 2006)*

Galini, Katerina; The Napoleonic Wars and the Disruption of Mediterranean Shipping and Trade. Greek and American Merchants in Livorno. *The Historical Review Institute for NeoHellenic Research Vol VII pp 179–198 (2010)*

Glaeser, Edward L; Urban Colossus. Why is New York America's Largest City? *Federal Reserve Bank of New York Economic Policy Review (December 2005)*

Grenet, Mathieu; Trade Politics and City Space(s) in Mediterranean Ports (academia.edu 2011)

Gilligan, Jonathan; The Age of Fossil Fuels Part 1. The Middle Ages through 1973. *Nashville Vanderbilt University (2005)*

Griffin, Emma; Review of The British Industrial Revolution in Global Perspective by Robert C. Allen *Reviews in History July 2010*

Harley, C. Knick; Steers Afloat. The North Atlantic Meat Trade. Liner Predominance and Freight Rates 1870–1913 *The Journal of Economic History Volume 68 No 4 2008*

Herson, John; Liverpool as a Diasporic City. Liverpool John Moores University (2008)

Hussin, Nordin; Networks of Malay Merchants and the Rise of Penang as a Regional Trading Centre *Southeast Asian Studies 43 (3) pp 215–237* (2005)

Irwin, Douglas; Political Economy and Peel's Repeal of the Corn Laws *Economics and Politics Volume 1 Spring 1989*

—— Tariffs and Growth in late Nineteenth Century America *The Economic Journal April 2000*

—— Free Trade and Protection in Nineteenth Century Britain and France Revisited: A Comment on Nye. *The Journal of Economic History Vol 33 No I March 1993*

Jacks. David S and Pendakur, Krishna; Global Trade and the Maritime Transport Revolution *National Bureau of Economic Research June 2008*

Jackson, Owen and Ryden, Goran; Baltic Iron and the British Iron Industry in the Eighteenth Century. *Economic History Review LV4 (2002)*

Johansen, Hans Chr.; Scandinavian Shipping in the Late Eighteenth Century in a European Perspective. *Economic History Review XLV3 pp 479–493 (1992)*

Katayama, Kunio; Japanese Economic Development Strategy and the Shipping Industries 1881–1894 *Discussion Paper. The Suntory Centre. Nov 1999*

Keegan, Francis; Shipping and the Development of the Australian Coal Export Trade (Unpublished Thesis for the Institute of Chartered Shipbrokers 1999)

Kert, Faye M; The Fortunes of War. Commercial Warfare and Maritime Risk in the War of 1812 *The Northern Mariner Vlll No 4 Oct 1998 1–16*

Kim, Su Jin and Oldham, James; Insuring Maritime Trade with the Enemy in the Napoleonic Era *Texas International Law Journal Vol 47 Issue 3 (2012)*

Kinealy, Christine; Food Exports from Ireland 1846–7 Eighteenth and Nineteenth Century History *Features Issue 1 Spring 1977 The Famine Volume 5* http://historyireland.com

Kitroeff, Alexander; The Greek Diaspora in the Mediterranean and the Black Sea as Seen Through American Eyes 1851–1861. *www.academia.edu*

Kurinsky, Samuel; The Jews of St Eustatius. Rescuers of the American Revolution *Fact Paper 37 Hebrew History Foundation*

Marks, Sally; Mistakes and Myths. The Allies, Germany and the Versailles Treaty 1918–21 *The Journal of Modern History Vol 85 No 3 Sept 2013*

Marzagalli, Silvia; Port Cities in the French Wars: The Responses of Merchants in Bordeaux, Hamburg and Livorno to Napoleon's Continental Blockade 1806–1813 *The Northern Mariner VI (October 1996)*

Michalatos, Ioannis; The Greek Merchant Marine. The Development of an International Network. *Research Institute for European and American Studies 2006*

Mokyr, Joel; The European Enlightenment, the Industrial Revolution and Modern Economic Growth (2007) *Max Weber Lecture Northwestern University*

Muller, Leos; Swedish Neutrality and Shipping in the Second Half of the Eighteenth Century *EHS Annual Conference (2006)*

—— Swedish Shipping in Southern Europe and Peace Treaties with North African States: An Economic Security Perspective *Historical Social Research Vol 35 pp 190–205 (2010)*

Newman, Aubrey; The Union Castle Line and Emigration from Eastern Europe to South Africa (University of Leicester)

O'Connor, Marion; World Wheat Supplies 1865–1913 (Princeton University 1970)

O'Rourke, Kevin H; The Worldwide Economic Impact of the French Revolutionary and Napoleonic Wars 1793–1815. *Journal of Global History pp 123–149. (2006)*

—— Tariffs and Growth in the Late Nineteenth Century *Economic Journal 110 April 2000*

O'Rourke, Kevin and Williamson, Jeffrey G; Late-Nineteenth Century Anglo-American Price Convergence. *Journal of Economic History 54 (1994)*

Papakonstantinou, Katerina; The Port of Messalonghi. Spatial Allocation and Maritime Expansion in the Eighteenth Century. *The Historical Review. Institute for NeoHellenic Research Vol VI (2010)*

Pelzer, John D; Liverpool and the American Civil War *History Today* Vol 40 Issue 3 (1990)

Perdue, Peter C; The Rise and Fall of the Canton Trade System (Massachusetts Institute of Technology 2009)

Putnis, Peter and Ailwood, Sarah; The Crimean War and Australia's Communications and Media History *Australian Media Traditions* (2007)

Bansal, Usha Rani and Bansal, B.B.; Industries in India during the Eighteenth and Nineteenth Century *Indian Journal of History of Science 1984*

Riello, Giorgio; The Making of a Global Commodity. Indian Cottons and European Trade 1450–1850 *The Proceedings of the First Congress of the Asian Association of World Historians (2010)*

Ryden, Goran; Swedish Economic History and the New Atlantic Economy. Iron Production and Iron Markets in the Eighteenth Century. *Economic History Society Annual Conference 2006*

Sharp, Paul; Pushing Wheat. Why supply mattered for the American grain invasion of Britain in the nineteenth century *Centre of Industrial Economics. Institute of Economics, University of Copenhagen 2008*

Spall, Richard F. Jr; Landlordism and Liberty. Aristocratic Misrule and the Anti-Corn Law League *The Journal of Libertarian Studies Vol VII no 2 1987*

Stopford, Martin; World Sea Trade Outlook. Where China Fits into the Global Picture (Tradewinds Conference 2005)

Thompson, Derek; The Spectacular Rise and Fall of US Whaling. An Innovation Story. *The Atlantic Feb 22, 2012*

Trivellato, Francesca: Discourse and Practice of Trust in Business Correspondence during the Early Modern Period *Yale University)*

Vassals, Carmel; The Maltese Merchant Fleet and the Black Sea Grain Trade in the Nineteenth Century. *International Journal of Maritime History Vol XIII Issue 2 pp 19–36 Dec 2001*

Vink, Markus; The 'World's Oldest Trade' Dutch Slavery and Slave Trade in the Indian Ocean in the Seventeenth Century *Journal of World History (2003)*

Internet

Hubpages; The History of Clyde Shipbuilding 1. The Eighteenth Century and the American Connection

Notes

Introduction
 1. Braudel 1982 p 361
 2. Scott p 250
 3. Collins 2021 pp 39–53, 140–153, 183–201, 286–307
 4. Norwich p 637
 5. Chaudhuri in Tracy 1991 (ed) p 438

Chapter 1
 1. Brady in Tracy 1991 (ed) p 149
 2. Parry p 35
 3. Boxer 1969 p 157
 4. ibid pp 167–169
 5. Elliot 1963 p 361
 6. ibid p 371
 7. Braudel 1984 pp 182, 239
 8. O'Hara p 19
 9. Lambert p 200
10. Collins 2023 p 195
11. Boxer 1965 pp 306–307
12. ibid p 322
13. Braudel 1982 p 396
14. ibid p 442
15. Davis 1962/1972 p 390
16. ibid p 15
17. Zahediah p 287
18. Hoppit pp 319–321
19. ibid p 321
20. Zahedieh pp 131–136
21. Hunt p 86
22. Davis 1967 p 9
23. Zahedieh in Canny (ed) p 399
24. Butel p 203
25. Chaudhuri in Tracy 1991 (ed) pp 428–429
26. Padfield 1999 p 158
27. Rodger pp 171–172
28. ibid p 177
29. Hoppit p 124
30. Padfield 169
31. Parker p 217
32. Hunt p 34
33. ibid pp 35, 48
34. Hoppit pp 124–129
35. Davis 1967
36. Wilson p 283
37. Lambert p 255
38. ibid pp 257–258
39. Hoppit pp 323, 330

Chapter 2
 1. Plumb p 21
 2. Evans and Ryden pp 110–111
 3. ibid p 35
 4. Wier in Canny (ed) p 388
 5. Evans and Ryden p 59
 6. ibid p 6
 7. Wier in Canny (ed) p 388
 8. Evans and Ryden p 6
 9. ibid pp 54–56
10. ibid p 60, Evans 2006
11. Evans and Ryden p 98
12. ibid pp 106–107
13. ibid pp 108–109
14. ibid p 202
15. ibid p 100
16. ibid pp 102–104)
17. Evans 2006
18. Evans and Rydon pp 234–237
19. ibid p 56

Chapter 3
 1. Keay 2000 p 284
 2. ibid pp 321–325
 3. ibid pp 326–32
 4. Darwin p 145
 5. Bernstein p 256
 6. Riello
 7. Findlay and O'Rourke p 266
 8. Chaudhuri p 95
 9. Marshall in Marshall (ed) p 488
10. Chaudhuri p 164
11. Goswami pp 19–26
12. Pearson p 164
13. Mathew in Prakash and Lombard (ed) p 221
14. Kulke and Rothermund p 178

15. ibid
16. Marshall in Marshall (ed) p 488
17. Boxer 1965 pp 226–227
18. Lambert pp 190–191
19. ibid pp 191–200
20. Pearson p 148
21. ibid p 168
22. Neal in Tracy 1990 (ed) p 218
23. Pearson p 168
24. Mathew in Prakash and Lombard pp 223–225
25. Chaudhuri pp 192–193
26. Gungwu in Tracy 1990 (ed) p 419
27. Chaudhuri p 105
28. Pearson p 165
29. Chaudhuri p 104

Chapter 4
1. Davis 1967 p 6
2. Butel p 132
3. Findlay and O'Rourke p 266
4. Prakash in Prakash and Lombard (ed) p 244
5. Braudel 1982 p 398
6. Mathew in Prakash and Lombard pp 227–230
7. Prakash in Prakash and Lombard (ed) p 247
8. Keay 1991 pp 224–226
9. Steensgaard in Tracy 1990 (ed) pp 118–120
10. ibid p 130)
11. ibid pp 130–131
12. Price in Marshall (ed) p 82
13. Chaudhuri pp 193–195
14. Kulke and Rothermund pp 177–178
15. ibid p 135
16. Steensgaard in Tracy 1990 (ed) pp 143–145
17. Boxer 1969 pp 320–321
18. ibid pp 331, 336
19. Braudel 1982 p 212
20. Parry p 60
21. Boxer 1969 p 229
22. Elliot 2006 p 262
23. Kurlansky 1997 p 83
24. Elliot 2006 p 232
25. Parry p 27
26. ibid p 102
27. Hoppit p 169
28. ibid p 7
29. Falkus 1987 p 11
30. Hoppit p 6 footnote 8

31. Sobel pp 37–38
32. ibid p 56
33. ibid p 87
34. ibid p 164
35. Collins 2023 pp 57–60, 69–74
36. Trivellato. Yale
37. Haynes pp 35–39
38. Trivellato 2009
39. ibid
40. Grenet
41. Trivellato 2009
42. Grenet)

Chapter 5
1. Butel in Tracy 1990 (ed) p 169
2. Phillips in Tracy 1990 (ed) p 65
3. ibid p 68
4. Padfield 1999 pp 194–196
5. ibid pp 192–193
6. Parry p 115
7. Butel in Tracy 1990 (ed) p 153
8. Butel in Tracy 1990 (ed) pp 166–167
9. Parry p 115
10. ibid pp 159–160
11. Keay 1991 p 288
12. Parry p 161
13. ibid p 120
14. ibid p 126
15. Rodger pp 301–302
16. ibid p 288
17. McLynn
18. Braudel 1982 pp 584–585
19. Keay 1991 p 378
20. Plumb p 114
21. Ward in Marshall (ed) p 421
22. Butel pp 156–157
23. Butel in Tracy 1990 (ed) p 169
24. Keay 1991 p 375
25. ibid p 349
26. (Prakash in Prakash and Lombard pp 248–251
27. Bhattacharya in Prakash and Lombard (ed) pp 292–293
28. Bowen in Marshall (ed) p 542
29. Al-Qasimi pp 61–62
30. ibid Chapter 3
31. McBrierty and Al Zubair pp 25–26
32. Davis 1962/1972 p 41
33. Rude p 9

Chapter 6
1. O'Hara pp 24–25
2. Wilson p 162

3. Evans and Ryden p 164
4. ibid p 48
5. Klein in Tracy 1990 (ed) p 290
6. Hubpages
7. Davis 1962–1972 pp 92–93
8. ibid p 191
9. Wilson p 227
10. Price in Marshall (ed) p 98, Wilson p 214
11. ibid (ed) p 94
12. Richardson in Marshall (ed) pp 447–450
13. O'Hara p 29
14. Souden pp 50–52
15. Menard in Tracy 1991 (ed) pp 259–262
16. ibid p 260–261
17. ibid pp 266–267
18. Parry p 214
19. ibid p 215
20. Ogg p 75
21. Parry pp 212–213
22. ibid pp 226–228
23. Rude p 9
24. Souden p 48
25. Falkus 1987 p 19
26. Souden p 17

Chapter 7
1. Walvin p 48
2. Parker p 52
3. Collins 2023 pp 9–10
4. Vink
5. ibid
6. ibid
7. ibid
8. Parker pp 49–50
9. Latimer pp 69–70. Parker Chapter 1
10. Walvin p 53
11. Parker p 229
12. Butel pp 181–183
13. Bernstein p 274
14. Parker pp 292–293
15. Hoppit p 56, Parker p 84
16. Hoppit p 474
17. Bernstein p 276, Richardson in Marshall (ed) p 440, Parry p 318
18. Richardson in Marshall (ed) p 441
19. Rude p 23
20. ibid pp 46–47
21. ibid pp 24–25

Chapter 8
1. From Alexander Pope's *Essay on Man* 1733–1734

2. Scott p 44
3. ibid p 123
4. ibid p 269
5. Thomas pp 30, 42
6. ibid pp 44, 48
7. Wilson p 234
8. Himmelfarb p 31
9. Parker pp 197, 201
10. Thomas p 93
11. ibid pp 44, 187
12. Hoppit p 484
13. Thomas p 149
14. ibid p 159, 184
15. Padfield 1999 pp 176–177
16. Parker p 231
17. ibid p 267
18. Collins 2021 p 277
19. Himmelfarb p 32
20. Richardson in Anstey and Hair pp 17, 76
21. Hague p 119
22. Parry pp 318–319
23. Hague p 353
24. Greene in Marshall (ed) p 212
25. Rude pp 32–33
26. Scharma p 47
27. ibid p 73
28. Parker p 339
29. Hyam 2010 Chapter 5
30. Hague p 264
31. ibid p 228
32. Pryor pp 195–196
33. Hague p 156
34. Cameron and Farndon pp 103–105
35. Keay 1991 p 398
36. Allen p 16
37. Chaudhuri in Tracy 1991 (ed) p 433
38. Collins 2021 pp 39–53, 81–87, 140–153, 183–201, 296–307
39. Himmelfarb p 25
40. ibid pp 7, 157
41. Mokyr pp 3–4, 13
42. Darwin p 208
43. ibid p 212
44. Himmelfarb p 151
45. Jones, Peter M pp 143–144
46. Evans and Ryden pp 10–11, 277
47. Padfield 2003 p 27
48. Himmelfarb p 165
49. ibid pp 155–157
50. ibid p 176
51. Davies 1996 pp 577–675
52. ibid p 608

53. ibid pp 699–701
54. Williams in Marshall (ed) pp 558–559
55. Boxer 1965 p 264
56. ibid pp 270–272
57. Jones, Peter M. Chapter 3
58. ibid p 20
59. Padfield 1999 p 280
60. Scott p 293
61. Himmelfarb p 59
62. Parry p 279
63. Padfield 2003 p 24
64. ibid p 26

Chapter 9
 1. Thistlethwaite p 18
 2. Plumb p 126
 3. Hunt p 55
 4. ibid p 92
 5. Kurlansky 1997 p 95
 6. Parker p 320
 7. Butel p 164
 8. Elliot pp 315–317
 9. Parry p 143
10. Riello
11. Hunt p 61
12. Scharma pp 18, 86
13. Elliot 2006 p 351
14. Padfield 1999 p 230
15. Kurinsky
16. ibid
17. Padfield 1999 p 277
18. Kurlansky 1997 pp 100, 283
19. ibid p 407
20. Parry pp 277–278
21. Rude p 54
22. Parry p 286
23. ibid pp 259–260
24. Hunt pp 160–161

Chapter 10
 1. Parry p 237
 2. ibid p 278
 3. Keay 1991 p 431
 4. ibid pp 432–435
 5. Parry p 257
 6. Parry p 264
 7. Gelber p 160
 8. ibid p 165
 9. Lambert p 225

Chapter 11
 1. Elliot 2006 p 404
 2. Butel pp 170–172, 189

 3. ibid pp 153–154
 4. Rude p 9
 5. Braudel 1982 p 207
 6. Collins 2023 pp 312–313
 7. Price in Marshall (ed) pp 84–85, 88
 8. Griffin
 9. Evans pp 24–26
10. Padfield 2003 p 57
11. ibid p 37
12. Butel p 166
13. ibid p 162–164
14. Keay 1991 p 543
15. Hall p 343
16. Risso p 92
17. Marshall in Marshall (ed) p 582
18. Rude p 11
19. Boxer 1965 p 323
20. Jones Peter M. pp 43–46
21. Padfield 2003 p 57
22. ibid p 31
23. ibid p 41

Chapter 12
 1. Stopford p 21
 2. Padfield 2003 p 62
 3. Davies 1996 p 709
 4. Padfield 2003 pp 64–65
 5. Collins 2023 pp 96–97
 6. Parry p 185)
 7. Marzagalli pp 65–67
 8. Padfield 2003 pp 28, 345
 9. O'Rourke p 127
10. Hall pp 345–346
11. Goswami pp 76–85
12. Risso p 86
13. Butel p 211
14. Padfield 2003 p 196
15. ibid p 250
16. ibid p 195
17. Parry p 189
18. Padfield 2003 p 256
19. Kulke and Rothermund p 200
20. Kim and Oldham
21. ibid
22. Rude p 251
23. Kim and Oldham
24. Rodger p 559
25. O'Rourke p 127
26. Marzagalli p 67
27. ibid p 68
28. Rude p 275
29. Collins 2023 pp xiv, 156, 204

30. Padfield 2003 p 277
31. ibid pp 280–283
32. Marzagelli p 69
33. Rodger pp 557–560
34. Marzagalli p 70
35. Padfield 2003 p 291
36. Findlay and O'Rourke p 367
37. Padfield 2003 p 291
38. Parry pp 283–290
39. Darwin p 189
40. Padfield 2003 p 307
41. ibid p 309
42. Stopford pp 108–109
43. O'Rourke p 140
44. ibid p 132
45. O'Rourke p 127
46. ibid p 129
47. ibid pp 129–131
48. ibid pp 132–133
49. bid p 134–135
50. ibid pp 136–138
51. ibid p 140
52. ibid pp 134–149
53. ibid p 149
54. Duffy in Marshall (ed) p 204

Chapter 13
1. Parry p 379
2. Marshall in Marshall (ed) p 579
3. Hague pp 228–229
4. Schama p 355
5. Hunt pp 175–176
6. Abulafia 2011 p 531
7. Hyam 1975/1993 p 80
8. Rude p 235
9. Bowle pp 414–415
10. Oppenheimer p 23
11. Mokyr p 21
12. Clark
13. Fox p 20
14. Falkus 1987 p 114
15. Brewster p 133
16. Ray in Marshall (ed) p 528
17. Padfield 2003 p 384

Chapter 14
1. Muller 2010 pp 191–193
2. Andersen and Voth
3. Muller 2006
4. Fremont-Barnes p 16
5. Muller 2010 p 196
6. ibid

7. Muller 2010 p 199
8. Muller 2006
9. ibid
10. Johansen p 489
11. www.balticconnections.net

Chapter 15
1. Galani p 186
2. Papakonstantinou
3. Harlaftis 1996 p 7
4. King p 156
5. Vassels
6. Papakonstantinou p 293
7. http://www.greece.org/poseidon/work/articles/polemisone.html
8. Galani p 183
9. Grenet
10. Galani p 185
11. Papakonstantinou p 297
12. Galani pp 182–184
13. Brewer p 165
14. Harlaftis 1990 p 29

Chapter 16
1. Abulafia 2011 p 529
2. ibid p 532
3. Fremont-Barnes pp 32–38
4. ibid pp 72–73
5. Lambert p 291
6. Belich p 56, Thislethwaite p 67
7. Marzagalli
8. Fremont-Barnes p 39
9. Galani pp 179–198
10. Kert
11. Rodger p 571
12. ibid
13. Butel p 219

Part Three
1. Hyam 1976/1993 p 22
2. Belich p 107

Chapter 17
1. Keay 1991 pp 345–347
2. Hussin
3. Keay 1991 p 445
4. Arasaratnam in Prakash and Lombard (ed) pp 327–328
5. Bowring pp 203, 229
6. Keay 1991 p 447
7. Hyam 1975/1993 p 15
8. Al-Qasimi p 189

9. Pearson p 198
10. McBriety and Al Zubair p 30
11. Hyam 1976/1993 pp 27, 38

Chapter 18
1. Souden p 63
2. ibid pp 28, 84
3. ibid p 88
4. ibid p 92
5. Butel p 228
6. ibid p 229
7. O'Hara p 28
8. ibid pp 33–34
9. Fox p 28
10. Parry p 213
11. Barty-King 1977 pp 32–33, 55–56
12. ibid p 80

Chapter 19
1. Belich p 109
2. ibid p 281
3. ibid p 226
4. ibid p 281
5. Fox p 171
6. Belich p 174
7. Price in Marshall (ed) p 81
8. Hyam 1976/1993 p 27
9. Butel p 224
10. Padfield 2003 pp 377–378
11. Belich p 112
12. Bernstein p 326
13. Glaeser
14. Fox p 7
15. ibid p 6
16. ibid p 15
17. Padfield 2003 p 375
18. Glaeser
19. Gordon p 19, Belich p 483
20. Belich p 238
21. Glaeser
22. Belich p 484
23. Butel p 226

Chapter 20
1. Howarth and Howarth p 35
2. Fox p 146
3. Pearson p 203
4. Fox p 52
5. ibid pp 88–89
6. ibid p xiv
7. ibid p 94
8. ibid p 105

9. ibid p 176
10. ibid pp 125–131
11. ibid p 138

Chapter 21
1. Haynes p 42
2. Collins 2021 pp 47–50, 68–81
3. Subramanyan p 104
4. Bernstein p 288
5. Prakash in Prakash and Lombard p 258
6. Hague p 162
7. Hyam 1976/1993 pp 28, 113
8. Subramanian p 37
9. ibid pp 100, 116–117
10. Perdue
11. Hunt p 230
12. Padfield 2003 p 372
13. Hyam 1976/1993 p 88
14. ibid p 27
15. Gelber p 188
16. Hyam 1976/1993 p 124
17. Hunt pp 245–246
18. Subramanian pp 119, 121, 123, 125–126
19. ibid pp 137, 142, 201
20. Hyam 1976/1993 p 129
21. Bernstein p 298
22. Hyam 1976/1993 p 119
23. Curtin p 247
24. Livingstone, Moore and Oldfather pp 110–111
25. Hyam 1976/1993 pp 125–126
26. Waley-Cohen p 159
27. Falkus 1990 p 88

Chapter 22
1. Sharp pp 4–5
2. Belich pp 441–446
3. Schonhardt-Bailey p 88
4. Thomson 1950 p 77
5. Evans p 190
6. Barty-King 1977 p 78
7. Evans p 193
8. McCord p 187
9. Gramp p 44
10. ibid p 60
11. Schonhardt-Bailey p 90
12. Spall p 214
13. Gramp p 33
14. Spall p 216
15. Schonhardt-Bailey p 93
16. ibid p 97
17. Barty-King 1977 p 87

18. Kinealy
19. Butel p 245
20. Irwin pp 44–45)
21. ibid pp 48–49
22. ibid p 53
23. Hague p 80
24. Barty-King 1977 p 94
25. ibid p 140
26. Evans p 277
27. Kertzer pp 9–11, 25–59
28. Droz p 189
29. Abulafia 2011 p 559
30. Droz p 161
31. Abulafia p 556
32. Butel p 238
33. Droz p 70

Chapter 23
1. Belich p 115
2. Padfield 2003 pp 356–357
3. ibid p 360
4. Belich p 110
5. ibid p 312
6. ibid pp 264–265
7. Hyam 1976/1993 p 57
8. Roy pp 191–193
9. Bansal and Bansal
10. Belich pp 315–317

Chapter 24
1. Hyam 1976/1993 p 102
2. King p 174
3. Harlaftis 1996 pp 14–25
4. King p 176
5. Harlaftis 2019 p 60
6. Putnis and Ailwood pp 2–11
7. ibid p 17
8. Kitroeff
9. Harlaftis 2019 pp 65–66

Chapter 25
1. Robinson and Gallagher p 2
2. Hague p 392
3. ibid p 434
4. Hall p 377
5. ibid p 381
6. Robinson and Gallagher p 38
7. Hyam 1976/1993 pp 47–48
8. Allen
9. Hall p 446
10. Hyam 1976/1993 p 82
11. Kearney p 134
12. Darwin p 215

13. Goswami pp 208–215
14. ibid pp 159–160, 231
15. Hall p 423
16. Hyam 1976/1993 p 99
17. ibid p 81
18. ibid p 18
19. King p 118
20. Hyam 1976/1993 p 38
21. Hall p 377
22. 600 Allen
23. Hyam 1976/1993 p 27

Chapter 26
1. Souden p 22
2. Cameron and Farndon p 85–93
3. Fox p 200
4. ibid pp 367–368
5. Fox p 230
6. ibid p 130
7. Gordon p 41
8. Fox p 267
9. O'Hara p 35
10. RG Bradshaw A Century of Howard Houlders
11. Firth p 15
12. ibid p 7
13. Mantle pp 12–14
14. Putnis and Ailwood p 3
15. Barty-King pp 140–141
16. Thompson
17. Delis
18. Harlaftis 1996 p 50
19. Michaletos
20. Harlaftis 1996 p 92
21. ibid pp 40–46
22. ibid pp 59–62
23. ibid pp 64–66
24. Harlaftis 2019 p 68
25. Butel p 381
26. Fox p 194
27. Fox p 215, Stopford p 30

Part Four
1. Stopford p 23
2. Souden p 104
3. Jacks and Pendakur
4. Cain and Hopkins p 2
5. Falkus 1987 pp 10, 210
6. Hyam 1976/1993 pp 21–22

Chapter 27
1. ibid p 95
2. Hyam 1990 p 116

3. Hyam 1976/1993 p 93
4. Hall p 378
5. Parry pp 316–317
6. ibid p 310
7. Hyam 1976/1993 p 12
8. ibid p 83
9. ibid p 84
10. ibid pp 89–90
11. ibid p 114
12. ibid pp 116, 76
13. Collins 2021 pp 39–53

Chapter 28
1. Hyam 1976/1993 pp 141–144
2. ibid pp 153–154
3. ibid pp 158–161
4. ibid p 164
5. Sanyal p 235
6. Roy pp 190–191
7. Sanyal pp 232–233
8. Bradshaw p 7

Chapter 29
1. Belich p 244
2. Thornton and Ekelund pp 12–13
3. http://wwwetymonline.com/cw/economics.htm
4. Belich p 264
5. Bernstein pp 320–321
6. Thornton and Ekelund p 22
7. Hofstater pp 111–112
8. Bernstein p 324
9. Belich p 244
10. Butel p 224
11. Hyam 1976/1993 p 28
12. Souden p 117
13. Robinson and Gallagher p 33
14. Subramanian pp 39–40
15. Hunt pp 270–271
16. Padfield 2009 p 44
17. ibid pp 42–44

Chapter 30
1. Kitroeff
2. Fox pp 273–274
3. Falkus 1990 pp 99–103
4. Howarth and Howarth p 105
5. Falkus 1990 p 77
6. Pearson p 211
7. ibid pp 216–220
8. Abulafia 2011 pp 560–561
9. Falkus 1990 p 104

10. Cameron and Farndon p 137
11. Pearson p 211
12. Robinson and Gallagher pp 78–79
13. King pp 193–197
14. Robinson and Gallagher pp 82–83
15. Hyam 1976/1993 p 180
16. Ibid p 28
17. Findlay and O'Rourke p 419
18. Robinson and Gallagher p 13
19. Padfield 2009 p 51
20. R and G p 59

Chapter 31
1. Sharp p 8
2. Vassals p 30
3. King p 167
4. Belich p 448
5. ibid p 318
6. Butel p 245
7. Herson
8. Butel p 247
9. O'Rourke and Williamson
10. Belich pp 345, 449
11. ibid pp 416–417
12. Hyam 1976/1993 p 29
13. Belich pp 366–368
14. ibid p 449
15. ibid p 187
16. Bernstein p 331
17. Belich p 451
18. Falkus 1987 p 210
19. O'Connor
20. Hyam 1976/1993 pp 59–60
21. Bernstein pp 346–347
22. O'Connor

Chapter 32
1. ibid p 314
2. Thomson 1950 p 125
3. Stopford p 24
4. Souden p 142
5. Firth p 18
6. Bakka p 19
7. ibid pp 23–24
8. Hunt p 395
9. Barraclough pp 7–8
10. McMullen p 33
11. Collins 2023 pp 188, 191–192
12. Gilligan
13. *Dampskibsselskabet*
14. Souden p 110
15. Jones pp10–12

16. ibid p 17
17. ibid pp 8–10, 127
18. ibid 143–144, 297
19. ibid pp 147–152, 198–201
20. ibid pp 97, 155–156
21. ibid pp 172, 102, 177, 288
22. ibid pp 195, 116
23. ibid p 241
24. ibid pp 283–284
25. Souden p 139

Chapter 33
1. Robinson and Gallagher p 261
2. ibid p 274
3. ibid pp 302–303
4. ibid p 335
5. ibid p 390

Chapter 34
1. Fox p 235
2. ibid p 260
3. ibid pp 264–265
4. ibid pp 266, 293
5. ibid p 289
6. Belich p 482
7. King p 204
8. Newman
9. Belich p 331
10. Herson
11. Fox p 370
12. ibid pp 371–378
13. ibid pp 378, 388
14. pp 399, 404–405
15. Harley p 1044
16. ibid p 1041
17. ibid p 1048
18. Pearson p 205
19. Falkus pp 124–127
20. Davies, Peter
21. Katayama
22. Davies, Peter
23. Katayama
24. Falkus 1990 pp 136, 34, 140
25. Findlay and O'Rourke p 422
26. Hyam 1976/1993 pp 217–218

Chapter 35
1. Souden p 154
2. ibid p 122
3. ibid p 141–142, 145
4. ibid p 144
5. Harlaftis 1996 pp 85–86, 98, 104
6. ibid p 130

7. Harlaftis 2019 p 131 CHECK
8. Souden p 153
9. ibid p 156
10. Keegan p 7
11. Findlay and O'Rourke p 420
12. Bakka pp 26, 36

Chapter 36
1. Kertzer pp 133–151
2. Falkus 1987 pp 95, 204
3. Hyam 1976/1993 pp 198–202
4. Falkus WHICH p 208
5. Thomson pp 194–215
6. Hyam 1976/1993 p 198
7. Falkus 1987 pp 100–101
8. Hyam 1976/1993 p 210
9. O'Rourke 2000
10. Findlay and O'Rourke p 394
11. Padfield 2009 p 65
12. Belich p 458
13. Robinson and Gallagher pp 395–396
14. ibid p 404
15. Bowring p 232
16. Hyam 1990 pp 118–119, 207–209
17. Hall p 490
18. Hyam 1976/1993 pp 157–159, 303
19. ibid p 304
20. Robinson and Gallagher p 467
21. Belich pp 459–464
22. Falkus 1987 pp 13, 228
23. Jamieson p 4
24. Thomson 1965 p 21
25. Padfield 2009 p 118
26. ibid pp 120–121

Chapter 37
1. Gelber p 248
2. *No More Napoleons*
3. Padfield 2009 p 133
4. Howarth and Howarth p 116
5. Falkus 1990 p 166
6. Howarth and Howarth p 120
7. Butel p 264
8. ibid
9. Falkus 1990 p 159
10. ibid pp 166–167
11. Padfield 2009 pp 185–187
12. Howarth and Howarth p 121
13. Marks
14. Eichchengreen
15. Hyam 1976/1993 p 313
16. Falkus 1990 p 158
17. Souden p 160
18. Falkus 1990 pp 160–161
19. Harlaftis 1996 pp 183–185

Chapter 38
1. Howarth and Howarth pp 124–125
2. Findlay and O'Rourke p 443
3. Bakka p 47
4. Chase p 186
5. ibid p 194
6. Findlay and O'Rourke pp 437–438
7. Eichengreen
8. Howarth and Howarth p 126
9. Souden p 158
10. Stopford pp 115–116
11. Harlaftis 1996 pp 186–187
12. ibid pp 196–197
13. Jamieson p 13
14. ibid p 16
15. Jamieson p 56
16. Falkus 1990 pp 175–176, 194
17. Bakka p 4
18. ibid pp 49–50
19. Stopford p 117
20. Falkus 1990 p 178
21. Butel p 276
22. Falkus 1990 p 209
23. Souden p 162
24. ibid
25. Falkus 1990 p 227
26. ibid p 233
27. ibid p 169
28. Chase p 193
29. Butel p 277
30. Bakka p 48
31. Jamieson pp 15–16
32. Hunt pp 400–401
33. Jamieson p 23
34. Chase p 191)
35. Livingstone, Moore and Oldfather pp 371–372
36. Ebrey p 289
37. Falkus 1990 p 226
38. ibid p 243

Chapter 39
1. Falkus 1990 p 244
2. Padfield 2009 p 225
3. Harlaftis 1996 pp 226–235
4. Lee pp 2–3

Chapter 40
1. Bernstein p 356
2. Howarth and Howarth p 151
3. Falkus 1990 pp 260–262
4. Harlaftis 1996 p 236
5. Cameron and Farndon p 195
6. Harlaftis 1996 pp 241–242
7. Falkus 1990 pp 274–275
8. ibid pp 252–253
9. Cameron and Farndon p 138
10. Stopford p 121
11. Falkus 1990 pp 301–302
12. Keegan pp 11–12
13. ibid p 13
14. Bakka p 82
15. H and H p 162
16. Stopford p 40
17. Souden p 180
18. Falkus 1990 pp 291–305
19. Cameron and Farndon p 75
20. Falkus 1990 pp 327–332
21. Findlay and O'Rourke p 495
22. Hunt p 405
23. Tombs p 717
24. Sked pp 61–64
25. ibid p 64
26. Harlaftis 1996 p 247

Chapter 41
1. Bakka pp 95–98
2. ibid p 103
3. Levinson 2016 pp 43–45
4. Stopford pp 508–509
5. Levinson 2016 p 11
6. ibid p 233
7. Stopford p 510
8. Levinson 2016 pp 245–246
9. Falkus 1990 p 361
10. ibid pp 370–374
11. Levinson 2016 pp 122–129
12. ibid p 35
13. Jephson and Morgen p 31
14. Jamieson p 84
15. Levinson 2016 p 247
16. ibid p 305
17. ibid pp 292–294
18. ibid pp 294–295
19. Jephson and Morgen pp 66–67
20. Levinson 2016 p 309

Chapter 42
1. Bakka p 136
2. ibid p 142
3. Howarth and Howarth p 194
4. Tombs p 800
5. O'Connell p 146
6. Jamieson p 118

7. Hunt p 406
8. ibid p 382
9. O'Connell pp 144–146, 187–197
10. Jamieson pp 139–141
11. Levinson 2016 p 343
12. *Lloyds List* 25th April 2005
13. *The Business Times* June 27th 2005
14. Keegan pp 13–20
15. Stopford pp 127–128
16. ibid p 437
17. Levinson 2020 pp 101–102
18. Cameron and Farndon p 68
19. Keegan pp 22–24
20. Jephson and Morgen pp 174–175
21. Findlay and O'Rourke pp 497–499
22. Woronoff p 139
23. ibid pp 156–157, 228–229
24. Findlay and O'Rourke p 351
25. Levinson 2016 p 318
26. Jephson and Morgen pp 277–279
27. Barty-King 1994 pp 129–130
28. *Lloyds List* 20th Feb 2006
29. Bakka p 162
30. Jephson and Morgen p 214
31. *Baltic Magazine* Winter 2011

Chapter 43
1. Cameron and Farndon p 211
2. ibid p 218
3. Atkinson p 12
4. Stopford p 37
5. Jamieson p 62
6. Falkus 1990 pp 330–332
7. Atkinson pp 28–29
8. ibid pp 6, 9
9. Jamieson p 72
10. Traditions of Excellence, Hyundai Shipyard, Yesterday and Today 1998

Chapter 44
1. Ebrey p 234
2. Levinson 2020 p 126
3. Clarkson Research-CRSL-unless otherwise indicated, most figures in this chapter

4. Coaltrans Conference 2004
5. Levinson 2020 p 173
6. Drewry
7. Levinson 2020 pp 144–145
8. Jephson and Morgen p 311
9. 2008 Metal Bulletin Iron Ore Symposium
10. Jephson and Morgen p 328, 355–357
11. UNCTAD
12. Levinson 2020 p 174
13. Robin King, Consortium Capital Group

Chapter 45
1. CRSL

Chapter 46
1. Collins 2021 pp 229–239, 284–285
2. Collins 2023 pp 56–60, Chapters 15–16, 18 & 22
3. ibid pp 199–200
4. Boxer 1965 p 312
5. ibid pp 327, 321
6. Collins 2023 pp 144–161
7. Ellis
8. Collins 2023 pp 187–188, 257–259
9. Edwards p 28
10. ibid p 31
11. ibid p 147
12. Hyam 1976/1993 pp 273–275
13. Hyam 2010 pp 73–74
14. ibid p 136
15. ibid pp 268–295
16. Sampson pp 164–165
17. ibid p 167
18. Hofstater p 321
19. *Financial Times* 22nd July 2003
20. Davies p 1132
21. John Greenwood *Invesco Perpetual Magazine* April 2017
22. Nuttall pp 21–28
23. ibid pp 120–121
24. ibid pp 128–129

Epilogue
1. ibid p 59

Index

Dear Reader,

We hope you have enjoyed this book, but why not share your views on social media? You can also follow our pages to see more about our other products: facebook.com/penandswordbooks or follow us on X @penswordbooks

You can also view our products at www.pen-and-sword.co.uk (UK and ROW) or www.penandswordbooks.com (North America).

To keep up to date with our latest releases and online catalogues, please sign up to our newsletter at: www.pen-and-sword.co.uk/newsletter

If you would like a printed catalogue with our latest books, then please email: enquiries@pen-and-sword.co.uk or telephone: 01226 734555 (UK and ROW) or email: uspen-and-sword@casematepublishers.com or telephone: (610) 853-9131 (North America).

We respect your privacy and we will only use personal information to send you information about our products.

Thank you!